LIVING WITH THANKS

*With the deepest gratitude to Venerable Daigyōin Reion Takehara,
master of my own late master, Dharma mother Ekai-ni. As a great
admirer, Venerable Takehara encouraged people to receive Rennyo
Shōnin's teaching by listening to The Letters, publishing himself
the Rennyo Shōnin jōgai ofumi shō, The Collection of Rennyo's
Letters Not Compiled in The Five Fascicle Letters.*

The Buddhist Society Trust is a distinguished press
in the United Kingdom which enriches lives around the
world by advancing the study and practice of Buddhism.

Its activities are supported by charitable contributions
from individuals and institutions.

For more information visit: info@thebuddhistsociety.org

First published by The Buddhist Society Trust, 2018
© Kemmyo Taira Sato

The publisher gratefully acknowledges the support for
this book provided by the Shogyoji temple, Chikushino,
Japan and Dr Desmond Biddulph CBE for his generous
support and encouragement.

The Buddhist Society Trust
E: middlewayandpublishing@gmail.com

ISBN: 978–0–901032–53–9 (The Buddhist Society Trust)

A catalogue record for this book is available from the British Library

Edited by Sarah Auld
Designed by Avni Patel

Printed and bound in Wales by Gomer Press Limited

LIVING WITH THANKS

The *Gojō Ofumi*

The Five Fascicle Version of
Rennyo Shōnin's Letters

Translation and Commentary
Kemmyo Taira Sato
Three Wheels, London

THE BUDDHIST SOCIETY TRUST

CONTENTS

Preface

VENERABLE CHIMYO TAKEHARA

Ever since the days of Śākyamuni Buddha it has been said that, if you want to attain Enlightenment, you can only do so by taking refuge in the Three Treasures of Buddha, Dharma and Sangha.

Whether or not you do so, it is said, determines whether or not you are a Buddhist.

Nowadays almost all Japanese Buddhist orders are based on Buddhism for lay followers and in that respect can be said to reveal the ultimate path of Mahāyāna Buddhism. However, despite the existence of a number of such organisations, each boasting over a million followers, it is open to question whether they are really working as true Buddhist 'Sanghas'.

Rennyo Shōnin (1414–1499), the descendant of Shinran Shōnin (1173–1262), the founder of Shin Buddhism, was a high priest who, after the proclamation in 594 by Prince Regent Shōtoku (574–622) of *The Imperial Edict for Promoting the Three Treasures*, created the largest Buddhist order ever to exist in Japan.

In this preface, however, I would like to focus your attention, not on the size of Rennyo's religious order, but on the origin of his *Nenbutsu* Sangha – how exactly it came into being – because I think reading this book with that in mind will accord with the original intention of the author, Reverend Kemmyo Taira Sato.

The Buddha-dharma and the world at large are not two separate entities. Without exception, every difficulty we experience in our daily lives becomes an issue we need to solve on our way to Enlightenment. Such a realisation is the ultimate goal we seek to attain.

First of all, Mahāyāna Buddhism should be understood as a Buddhist movement that functions in a communal society.

In order to explain how it is possible for all human beings to be saved simply by pronouncing the *Nenbutsu*, Hōnen Shōnin (1133–1212), the founder of Pure Land Buddhism in Japan, proclaimed in his main work, the *Senjaku hongan nenbutsu shū,* that the most obvious principle of the *Nenbutsu* was it was 'superior to other practices, as well as the easiest'.

This declaration clearly shows that 'salvation through the *Nenbutsu*' is universally given – to 'anyone', 'any time', 'any place'.

Having received this message, Rennyo Shōnin strongly desired that the Three Treasures and especially the Sangha – so vital for practical Buddhism – should be created in the here and now by virtue of the Buddha's Vow-power.

With considerable energy, he set about writing a stream of letters in simple language that we, his followers both direct and indirect, could understand and that would help us confirm in our own being the working of Amida Buddha's Vow-power. Some time later, eighty of those letters addressed to his followers were published as *The Five Fascicle Letters.*

In the *Commentary on the Śrīmālādevīsiṃhanāda-sūtra* by Prince Shōtoku, mentioned above, we find the golden maxim that was to determine the future direction of Mahāyāna Buddhism in Japan. This commentary forms the essential core of the three *sūtra* commentaries he wrote, which together constitute the oldest Japanese Buddhist documents in existence.

Until Prince Shōtoku's time it had always been thought that the right attitude to adopt towards the Buddha's teaching lay in striving to achieve a proper understanding of his words. But Prince Shōtoku made it clear that the most important point of Mahāyāna Buddhism was not how to grasp the teaching intellectually but how to receive the working of the Buddha, or the absolute good, in one's own being. In Buddhism in general, 'understanding' had been held as the main principle and 'good' merely as the end result, but Prince Shōtoku reversed the relationship between the two. In his seminal re-interpretation of Mahāyāna Buddhism, the 'good', hitherto understood as the 'end result', now became by far the more important element.

How, then, can we receive this good, the working of the Buddha? Prince Shōtoku declared it was only by 'taking refuge in the Buddha himself,' and that 'taking refuge in the Buddha' was the true essence of Mahāyāna Buddhism.

How can this be? Well, if understanding really were the cornerstone of Buddhism, it would follow that only those with sufficient intellectual understanding of Buddhist doctrine could be saved and all those unable to reach such an understanding would be lost. But Prince Shōtoku argued that such an interpretation went entirely against the great working of Mahāyāna Buddhism. In his *Commentary on the Śrīmālādevīsiṃhanāda-sūtra* he declared, "Doing good originates from taking refuge in the Buddha."

In order for sentient beings like ourselves to practise the good, namely the Buddha's teaching, it is enough to say just once with profound sincerity 'I take refuge in the Buddha' and this pure act of taking refuge will bring about all the good based on the Buddha's teaching. It is an action that is freely available to absolutely anyone, hence the message that the original intention of the Buddha's teaching is manifest in this one single, pure act.

In this sense, Prince Shōtoku stated that it was in the one thought-moment, or single instant, that the Dharma, or Truth, became one with the heart of a sentient being. Echoing his words, Rennyo Shōnin in his *Letters* repeated time and again the phrase, "the oneness of *ki*, or the person to be saved, and *Hō*, or the Dharma that saves them, in *Namu Amida-butsu*". It is with this truth of instantaneous awakening constantly uppermost in his mind that Rennyo Shōnin would always teach his followers that we, sentient beings, became one with the working of the Buddha in the 'one thought-moment'.

This point was also central to the teaching of Hōnen Shōnin, Shinran Shōnin's master, who, with his declaration that *Namu Amida-butsu* was the basis of birth in the Pure Land, is seen as the founder of Japanese Pure Land Buddhism.

It should perhaps be explained here that, whereas *Namu Butsu,* or 'I take refuge in the Buddha', is the expression of an individual's 'one thought-moment' act of taking refuge in the Buddha, *Namu Amida-butsu,* or 'I take refuge in Amida Buddha', expresses not only one's own 'one thought-moment' of taking refuge but over and above this also represents the great working of Amida Buddha himself, *Amitâbha Buddha* (Buddha of Infinite Light) or *Amitâyus Buddha* (Buddha of Eternal Life) in Sanskrit.

When trying to create a Sangha, we have to start with a dialogue in our daily lives that is far beyond secular thought, and there has to exist a person who can motivate such a dialogue.

Rennyo's first letter, mentioned by Reverend Sato in the introduction to this book, is known as the *Letter of Kanshō,* having been written in the second year of the Kanshō Era (1461). Rennyo Shōnin composed this letter at the age of forty-seven at the urging of his disciple, Dōsai of Kanegamori, and was then sufficiently motivated to continue writing well over two hundred and fifty more letters to his followers throughout the ensuing forty-seven years.

It so happens that a train of events, ending in an episode not entirely dissimilar to the one that prompted Rennyo Shōnin's first letter, also became the catalyst for the publication of the present book. Let me now tell you about it.

On 2 September 1993, a Japanese Monument was unveiled at University College London to commemorate the very first Japanese students to have come to the U.K. towards the end of the Tokugawa Period back in the nineteenth century.

A special Gagaku music ensemble, known as Chikushi-gakuso, was invited over from Shogyoji Temple in Japan to perform Gagaku music to celebrate this unique occasion. All the members of Shogyoji Temple who attended the ceremony, including Reverend Kemmyo Taira Sato, the translator of *The Letters*, returned home profoundly moved by the event.

On 8 December of the same year, Reverend Sato travelled back to the U.K. and in October 1994, when Three Wheels was first established as a Buddhist Centre in London, he was appointed to be its first Director. Reverend Sato has subsequently remained living in the U.K. for the last twenty-four years.

Initially it was only a small group of people with an interest in Buddhism and Japanese culture that came to attend Dharma talks at Three Wheels, but over the years many people have gathered there, offering help and assistance. In particular, Professor John White, Pro-Provost of UCL at the time of the unveiling ceremony, has given Reverend Sato and his colleagues his unstinting support right from the start. Regarding external matters, too, Three Wheels has consistently benefited from Professor White's excellent advice.

In 2001, eleven years after his initial appointment, Reverend Sato consulted Professor White on which Buddhist document he should next read with the Dharma friends of Three Wheels. Professor White immediately answered that it should be *The Letters* by Rennyo, countering Reverend Sato's "Why?" with the explanation that, because it was the custom for a new letter to be read out in turn every morning and evening, there was no doubt that they constituted a very important piece of Buddhist scripture.

Over the next sixteen years, Reverend Sato and his Dharma friends continued to read *The Letters* by Rennyo, engaging in lively discussions regarding each of the eighty letters. And now the time has come for the book of *The Letters* by Rennyo, in the form of Reverend Sato's English translation with commentaries, to be finally made available to a wider audience.

As between Dōsai of Kanegamori and Rennyo Shōnin, so between Professor John White and Reverend Kemmyo Taira Sato there appeared that one thought-moment, that instant of profound encounter.

Thanks to this encounter, the study of *The Letters* continued without cessation, eventually leading to the creation of the book you now hold in your hands. Grounded in our fervent wish to form a Sangha or ideal Buddhist community, Reverend Sato's commentaries on, and English translation of, Rennyo's *Letters* has finally become a published reality and fitting accompaniment to the actual founding of a Shin Buddhist Sangha in London.

It can be seen that this encounter was born of the deep and unwavering sincerity of Professor White's commitment. At the time of their very first encounter, Reverend Sato confesses to having been extremely moved by the following poem handed to him by Professor White:

You of pure
faith,
I,
who am certain

of nothing,
 travel
 the one
 road.

What should be called the true Dharma is not the verbal transmission of Śākyamuni's deeds and teaching, but rather Śākyamuni's Dharma itself that is constantly being revived in the form of his unfailing response to sentient beings such as ourselves calling out to him.

Śākyamuni's teaching in the *sūtras* is in the form of an endless dialogue, in which one question always leads on to another.

Professor White's *haiku* poem, expressed with such selflessness and purity of mind, must have aroused both joy and considerable surprise on the part of Reverend Sato. And this instantaneous interfusion into oneness of their two selves, through the one thought-moment of encounter, must have been what enabled Reverend Sato down the years to continue reading, translating and commenting on *The Letters* of Rennyo Shōnin.

Their spiritual interaction found sympathy with *Nenbutsu* Dharma friends from various parts of the U.K. Now there exists a true *Nenbutsu* Sangha that includes about fifty fully committed Shin Buddhist members.

As discussed in Reverend Sato's introduction, a number of important phrases in Rennyo Shōnin's first letter, such as 'completing the cause [of birth in the Pure Land] in ordinary life with the awakening of the one thought-moment', crop up again and again in his letters without any kind of alteration, right up until he reached the age of eighty-four, that is to say the year before his death.

Such consistency is truly astonishing, as it runs counter to the usual ideological developments in a person's philosophy, or the customary major turning points in people's lives. It is evidence of Rennyo Shōnin's unshakable grasp of the truth and his consistent adherence to that truth throughout his life.

In one of the letters (the seventh letter of Fascicle Two) there is a passage in which Rennyo Shōnin states that, although those who do succeed in attaining *shinjin* (faith) are few and far between, *anjin* or "peaceful awareness" – the term chosen by the author of this book – which is synonymous with *shinjin*, is actually *yasuki kokoro* – "the mind easy to attain" or, significantly, "great faith".

Most decidedly, the use of the phrase "peaceful awareness" as a translation of *anjin* can only stem from a very real experience of fundamental salvation, of "being embraced in Amida's Light," a light that illumines impartially and without distinction all those who, aware of their own bad karma and despite their involvement in the Sangha, have long been sinking in a world of suffering.

Encompassing the concept of *shinjin*, or 'faith'– the ultimate cause of birth in the Pure Land – the term a*njin*, or 'peaceful awareness', also beautifully conveys the atmosphere at the gatherings of Dharma friends at Three Wheels. There could have been no better choice of word.

Given the fact that even the Hōonkō Ceremony, the most important annual Shin Buddhist event commemorating the death of Shinran Shōnin, has been gradually becoming a mere formality, I feel all the more strongly that this atmosphere of "peaceful awareness," found in a newly born Sangha, can serve as an excellent reminder and lead us back to the true spirituality of the original Buddhist community. I have high hopes of this new Sangha storing up the energy that will allow it to give birth to people of pure faith.

In conclusion, I would like to offer my most sincere prayers that the *Nenbutsu* Sangha of London may continue with its steady development, now and in the future. I am profoundly grateful that this book includes innumerable suggestions on ways to convey the message of Amida Buddha's great love and compassion to those who sincerely seek to find a connection with the Buddha-dharma.

Namu Amida-butsu, Namu Amida-butsu
With palms together.

Chimyo Takehara
Head Priest of Shogyoji Temple

EXPLANATORY NOTES

The document on which this translation is based is *The Five Fascicle Letters* 五帖御文 by Rennyo 蓮如 (1415–1499), the Eighth Head Priest of Honganji, a work annotated by Masamaru Inaba 稲葉昌丸 (1865–1944) in his *Shohan-taikō gojō ofumi teihon* 諸版対校五帖御文定本, originally published in 1933 and republished in 1995, by Hōzōkan, Kyoto. Inaba based his editorial work on *The Letters* written by hand and signed by Jitsunyo 實如 (1458–1525), the Ninth Head Priest of Honganji, who was also Rennyo's fifth son. Inaba completed his editorial work by comparing Jitsunyo's version with the first woodprint version of *The Five Fascicle Letters* published by Shōnyo 證如 (1516–1554), the Tenth Head Priest of Honganji, who was Jitsunyo's grandson.

In this book the English translations of quotations from Buddhist documents are mainly based on Chinese or Japanese texts from *The Taishō (shinshū) daizōkyō* 大正新脩大蔵經, the Taishō Issaikyō Kankō Kwai, *The Shinshū shōgyō zensho* 真宗聖教全書, Shinshū Shōgyō Zensho Hensansho, *The Shinshū shiryō shūsei* 真宗史料集成, Shinshū Shiryō Shūsei Henshū Iinkai, *The Shinshū zensho* 真宗全書, Zōkyō Shoin, *The Jōdoshū zensho* 浄土宗全書, Jōdoshū Shūten Kankōkai, and other important individual works.

Each chapter of the book is allocated to a different letter out of a total of eighty and consists of a translation and a commentary. Each chapter also has two titles, the name of the chapter, chosen by the author, and the traditional name of the relevant letter, chosen originally by Dōon 道隠 (1741–1813), a Shin Buddhist scholar of the Edo Period, in his commentary on *The Letters* by Rennyo, entitled *Ofumi meitō shō* 御文明燈鈔.

Regarding the frequent use of abbreviation to be found in this translation of the letters, Rennyo was addressing himself exclusively to his followers, who would have had no difficulty understanding what he meant, so he often made use of abbreviated expressions such as "Shōnin" or "birth". "Shōnin" stands for "Shinran Shōnin", for example, unless otherwise stated, and "birth" means "birth in the Pure Land". Similarly *The Sūtra*, or *The Larger Sūtra*, refers to *The Larger Sūtra of Eternal Life*, *The Commentary* to Tánluán's *Commentary on the Treatise on the Pure Land*, "rightly assured" to "rightly assured of birth in the Pure Land", "taking refuge" to "taking refuge in Amida Buddha", "entrusting" to "entrusting to Amida Buddha", "Last Age" to "Last Dharma Age", "one thought-moment of awakening" to "one thought-moment of awakening of faith", "coming to meet us" to "Amida's coming to meet us at the moment of death", "Original Vow", or simply "Vow", if there is no special comment, to "Amida's 18th Vow in *The Larger Sūtra of Eternal Life*", "completing the act in daily life" to "the completion in daily life of the act that enables us to attain birth in the Pure Land", and so on. These are just a few of the many examples to be found in the text. It was the translator's express intention to try and keep Rennyo's abbreviations as close as possible to their original form, avoiding additional explanation. The Notes and Glossary are there to help the reader understand these shortened forms.

The Appendices towards the end of the book offer explanations of certain aspects of Shin Buddhism. Though not directly related to the content of *The Letters*, they are important for a clearer understanding of this tradition.

With just two exceptions, the English spellings of Sanskrit, Chinese and Japanese Buddhist terms used in this book are all based on the *Digital Dictionary of Buddhism* edited by A. Charles Muller and established in July, 1995. However the terms 僧伽 and 念佛, from Pali and Japanese respectively, are spelled 'Sangha' and 'Nenbutsu', reflecting popular current English usage.

Introduction

KEMMYO TAIRA SATO

I) "SPEAK UP, SAY SOMETHING!"

It must surely go without saying that, as with all cases of genuine religious transmission, the true essence of Rennyo Shōnin's way of teaching lay in personal encounter with his followers as separate and distinct individuals. According to the many documents chronicling Rennyo's words and deeds still available to us today, Rennyo's teaching was then further characterised by two other notable features: firstly, Dharma talks by Rennyo himself or by his disciples, followed by serious discussions between participants and, secondly, a vast number of letters, both personal and communal, addressed by Rennyo to his followers.

Before embarking upon the presentation of my English translation of the eighty letters compiled into *The Letters* (the five fascicle version)[1] and my commentaries on each of them, which together make up the main body of this book, I would like to bring to the reader's attention a few examples of Rennyo's special way of teaching people. One example is the way he laid such emphasis on universal equality, as epitomised in an account from the *Honganji sahō no shidai,*[2] or *The Details of the Manners of Honganji,* by Jitsugo (1492–1584), the tenth son of Rennyo.

It is recorded in various chronicles that when the [Master's] family used to live in Higashiyama, the then Master would sit on a raised dais. Rennyo Shōnin, however, in his own day decided to do away with the dais and to sit at the same floor level and on equal terms with everyone else. Rennyo said such upper class behaviour would make it impossible to spread the Buddha-dharma and teach others properly. He advised us to encourage everyone by seating ourselves on a level with the lowly. By so doing, indeed, we could make it possible to invite people to come closer and learn more. Thus Rennyo instituted the practice of meeting as equals at the same floor level. It is said that many people appreciated this very much. All the old people talked about it. Jitsunyo Shōnin himself heard the story and there are definitely some people [alive today] who still remember it.[3]

When one considers the hierarchical society of medieval times, it was very bold of Rennyo to defy family convention and, throughout his life whenever he was teaching, to adopt this spiritual stance, known as *hiraza* 平座 or "sitting as equals on the same floor level". A passage illustrative of this pivotal point from the *Daihasso onmonogatari Kūzen kikigaki*,[4] or *Kūzen's Record of the Eighth Patriarch's Words*, reads,

One night Rennyo observed, "I have set aside my own position, by which I mean that, although the former Head Priest was very strict in teaching both ceremonial manners and the right way of chanting, he would never discuss the meaning of a *wasan* (Japanese hymn by Shinran) or chat on equal terms with other residents or people from other districts, whilst seated at the same floor level in the manner known as *hiraza*. In my case, however, no matter whether it's a cold night or a summer evening alive with mosquitoes, I am there to meet and discuss whatever it might be with anyone, sitting as equals on the same floor level, because, regardless of the difficulties, it is my enduring wish that people may ask questions about the Buddha-dharma and be able to attain faith. But nobody seems to realise what I'm doing. They simply hope I'll go to bed soon because of the cold or they just fall asleep themselves in shadowy corners. Furthermore, there is no one who thinks to himself that such efforts are being made for their sake. I don't go to bed early in the evening, nor do I take a nap during the day. It's simply that I happen to think that living the Buddha-dharma is of vital importance."[5]

These two quotations show that holding meetings in the new style of *hiraza* based on the spirit of equality in the sense of "harmonious oneness between different beings" seems to have been his daily practice during his whole life. It became, however, such a long standing routine, and he complained one night according to the *Kūzen kikigaki*, that those around him were not very aware of the meaning of this *hiraza* style, which actually originated from the love and compassion with which he wanted all his followers to attain pure faith and solve their actual problems in this world. Actually, however, Jitsugo says in his *Honganji sahō no shidai*, which is a record made later than the *Kūzen kikigaki,* that many people appreciated this very much.

What Rennyo taught his followers with this spirit of equality, embodied in the *hiraza* style, is profound in its spirituality and includes many intriguing aspects of Shin Buddhist teaching, such as Amida Buddha's unconditional love that knows no discrimination, salvation through faith alone, the instantaneous awakening of faith in Other Power, no attachment to, or pride in, self-power or a self-centred world, living with gratitude for what has been done for us by others and so on. I will be discussing all of these spiritual matters in greater detail later in the chapter-by-chapter commentaries I offer on Rennyo's letters.

In the present context, however, I would just like to bring to the reader's attention one special aspect of Rennyo's way of teaching that might have seemed a little strange or even downright peculiar in the feudal era of Japan, when conformity, obedience and loyalty were considered higher virtues than independence, freedom or equality. It is the way Rennyo would encourage his followers to speak up, talk to one another and express themselves at meetings, in order to attain pure faith in Amida Buddha. With reference to this let me quote some examples from *The Goichidai ki kikigaki.*[6]

Article 87. Rennyo Shōnin said, "Speak up, talk to one another!" and "Anyone who remains silent is a danger." Again he said, "Those who have attained faith and those who have yet to do so should all talk to one another." "If you speak up, then what you have on your mind becomes known to others and can be corrected. Just say something!" Thus spoke Shōnin.[7]

Article 108. He said, "You should prepare yourself mentally as best you can to be corrected by others! Let your hearts be open to your Dharma friends. Some fail to accept advice from others who are of lower status and instead fly into a temper. How deplorable that is! You should maintain a state of mind that allows you to accept the advice of others."[8]

Article 120. After delivering a Dharma talk, the last but one head priest (Rennyo Shōnin) said to four or five of his sons, "Four or five people should get together and discuss the problems. If there is a group of five people, then each of them, without exception, will understand the Dharma differently in their own way. You should discuss the matter deliberately."[9]

Article 121. "Even if what has been said is not right, once someone has said it, you should accept it for the time being. If you immediately respond in a negative way to that person, then that person may never open up to you again. You should be particularly careful when responding to what other people say. There was once a group of people who made a vow to tell one another whatever they felt was wrong with any one of the group. Whilst keeping to this promise, when one of them mentioned what was wrong with another person, the latter responded, 'Although this is the way I think, because other people say it is wrong, I should simply agree with them.' But that is not the right response. Even if you feel that another person's advice is not correct, for the time being you should admit that they may in fact be right."[10]

Article 203. He said, "It is through lack of faith that a person is reluctant to speak out at Buddhist meetings. Such a person feels he should say something he has already carefully worked out and thought about. It is as if he felt he had to cast around and come up with something really special. But happiness should be expressed just as it is. If it is cold, say 'cold' and if it is hot, say 'hot': you should talk about your state of mind exactly as it is. Not speaking at all at Buddhist meetings is a sign of 'no faith'. The problem of lack of awareness is also related to the matter of faith. If fellow devotees gather together and praise [the Buddha], there will be no lack of awareness."[11]

As we can see in Article 120, Rennyo encouraged his followers to meet together in small groups. Such meetings were of course expressly held to discuss matters of faith. After listening to Dharma talks given by priests, Shin Buddhist followers would hold Dharma meetings in order both to discuss their own problems and to thank the Buddha for having enabled them to solve those problems in the light of his teaching. Whenever those whose problems had been solved by the attainment of pure faith expressed their deep gratitude to the Buddha and the Bodhisattvas, those who had not yet attained faith were also encouraged to deepen their involvement in those same meetings and discussions. Under the influence of Rennyo, Shin Buddhist meetings, both monthly meetings and annual assemblies such as Hōonkō[12] and Higane[13], rapidly spread right across the land. This was a highly unusual phenomenon in medieval Japan. Eventually the Shin Buddhist order gained enormous power, even threatening political leaders at times. This was not, however, what Rennyo Shōnin had wanted or intended, for such a situation could unnecessarily endanger the Shin Buddhist Sangha.

The original purpose of Shin Buddhist meetings was solely for priests and lay followers to attain pure faith in Amida Buddha. In these meetings they come together to discuss how to attain faith in Amida Buddha or to express their gratitude to the Buddha after having done so.

When we discuss how to attain faith at such meetings, it is extremely important for us that we express ourselves frankly in front of good friends.

Generally speaking, however, when people express themselves in a discussion, it is to assert themselves by defeating the arguments of others. But that is not the case with Shin Buddhist meetings. Discussions at such meetings are held under the light of the Buddha. In other words, we discuss our problems in order to attain pure faith in Amida Buddha or to be awakened to the truth of life.

Even when trying to carry out our discussions in the light of the Buddhadharma, we are still prone to mistakes because our self-centeredness is deeply rooted in our karmic existence. Not only in respect of worldly matters but even in respect of something as spiritual as the Dharma, and no matter whether or not we have already been awakened to faith, we tend to understand things around us in a selfish and idiosyncratic way that is deeply seated in our human nature and its karmic history. Realising how tenacious our selfish attachments were, Rennyo said, "You should prepare yourself mentally as best you can to be corrected by others! Let your hearts be open to your Dharma friends,"[14] and also "If you speak up, then what you have on your mind becomes known to others and can be corrected. Just say something!"[15] In Dharma meetings other people function as mirrors, reflecting, and even illuminating, our own problems. Expressing ourselves frankly and listening to others with an open mind are exceedingly important but, when we try to do so, we find that neither is easy. Nevertheless, it is through our relationship with others that our problems are illuminated in such a way that, transcending hardships and difficulties, we become aware of how to solve them. Rennyo said that we should accept and take on board the utterances of others' words, even their criticisms, just as they are. Words thrown at you by others can illuminate your position very clearly. Of course, it is not all that easy to accept the observations of others regarding your situation, hence Rennyo Shōnin's admonition in Article 121, "Even if what has been said is not right, once someone has said it, you should accept it for the time being. If you immediately respond in a negative way to that person, then that person may never open up to you again."[16] The point here is that every person has a different opinion and is selfishly attached to his or her own view. Without some understanding of the darkness deeply embedded in our karmic existence, problems of selfishness, pride and discrimination, it would be almost impossible for us to adopt an accepting attitude towards the harmonious oneness of all different individuals that make up our Sangha. Internal awareness of self and harmonious oneness with others will go hand in hand if the pure faith of entrusting ourselves to Amida Buddha is awakened within our being.

All this is taught simply to induce you to become yourself just as you are. If you are too attached to your own world, you will be unable to talk frankly about yourself to others, nor will you be able to listen to them without prejudice or preconceptions. If you have really good friends with whom you can communicate freely on a spiritual level, then they are manifestations of Buddhas or Bodhisattvas. In that way we can all become one and live together on our way to the Pure Land, listening to and understanding one another with love and respect.

II) RENNYO'S LIFE AND LETTERS

TO HIS FOLLOWERS

Rennyo Shōnin (1415–1499) was the eighth Head Priest of the Honganji, the main temple of the Shin Buddhist tradition. Born into the lineage of Shinran Shōnin (1173–1263), the founder of Shin Buddhism, Rennyo was the firstborn son of Zonnyo (1396–1457), the seventh Head Priest of Honganji. It would appear, however, that Rennyo's mother was not actually Zonnyo's legal wife but rather a servant of Zonnyo's mother. When Rennyo was six years old, his father, Zonnyo, married Nyoen who became his stepmother. At that point Rennyo's mother was forced to leave the temple precincts. Taking with her a portrait of her only son,[17] she is said to have slipped away through the back gate and departed westwards, never to return. About her departure, the *Shūjin ki*[18] by Jitsugo states, "On 28 December in the 27th year of Ōei (1420), saying 'I am one from a Western province and shouldn't be here', she slipped away through the side-gate of the house where she used to live, unaccompanied by anyone to serve her. She departed alone and nobody knew where she was."[19]

On reaching the age of fifteen, in accordance with his birth mother's earnest entreaty that he seek to restore in his lifetime the original traditions of Shinran Shōnin, Rennyo made a vow to spread Shinran Shōnin's teaching throughout the land. The *Rennyo Shōnin goichigo ki*,[20] compiled by Jitsugo, referred to this point, "People said it was truly astonishing that when he was still but fifteen years old he should have convinced himself to concentrate exclusively on the study of the teaching, resolving to convey to others the stream of Shinran Shōnin's tradition by every means at his disposal in order that each one of them should attain faith decisively and the teaching should flourish."[21]

In the summer of 1431, at the age of seventeen, Rennyo was ordained as a monk at Shōrenin, a Tendai temple in Kyoto, where Shinran himself had previously been ordained at the age of nine. Rennyo studied Shin Buddhism mainly with his own father, Zonnyo, as his teacher. It is said, too, that at some stage he also studied Buddhism in general with one of his relatives, Kyōkaku (1395–1473), Head Monk of Daijōin in Nara. In the course of his study of

Buddhism in his twenties, thirties and forties, Rennyo would repeatedly copy out all kinds of Shin Buddhist documents such as *The Kyōgyōshinshō*, *Wasan* and *Lamp for the Latter Ages* by Shinran, other important documents by Kakunyo[22] and Zonkaku[23] and present them to followers of the Honganji tradition. This long-standing custom of Rennyo's proved a very good method indeed not only of self-study but also of teaching others and making friends with them. It was a highly effective way of leading people to the awakening of faith, and subsequently evolved into Rennyo's excellent practice of teaching by writing letters to his followers.

When Rennyo married his first wife, Nyoryō, at the age of twenty-seven, Honganji was still very poor and it had not yet been decided who should succeed his father as Head Priest. Under these conditions it is stated in various biographical documents that Rennyo experienced all manner of hardships, extreme poverty, shortage of food and clothes and not nearly enough space for his own growing family. When Rennyo was forty-one years old, Nyoryō passed away leaving behind their seven children. At the age of forty-one or two Rennyo married Nyoryō's younger sister, Renyū, who bore him ten more children. At the age of fifty-six, however, Rennyo lost Renyū as well. Rennyo married five times in all but sad to say was separated from each of his wives by one death after another.

Two years after the death of Nyoryō, his father, Zonnyo, also passed away. At that point a serious dispute arose between Rennyo and his half brother, Ōgen, the eldest son of his stepmother, Nyoen, as to who should succeed Zonnyo at Honganji. With the overwhelming support of kind and influential supporters, however, Rennyo finally managed to become the eighth Head Priest of Honganji Temple. Amongst his supporters Nyojō (1412–1460), Zonnyo's younger brother and thus Rennyo's uncle, played the most important role. After the customary period of mourning, Nyojō came over to Honganji Temple in Kyoto from his own temple, Zuisenji, at Inami in Etchū Province, in order to persuade those involved to agree to Rennyo becoming the new Head Priest at Honganji. Rennyo's cause will have been greatly assisted by the fact that, through his untiring efforts to pass on Shinran's teaching, he had already gathered quite a number of good Dharma friends around him, including his first and foremost disciple, Dōsai (1399–1488) of Kanegamori.[24]

On starting out as Head Priest of Honganji Temple, Rennyo made use of his new confidence and the freedom conferred on him by his position to try and encourage people to attain pure faith in Amida Buddha in the spirit of the original founder, Shinran Shōnin. Rennyo Shōnin's faith movement, epitomised by his insistence on the *hiraza* way of sitting at Dharma meetings and deeply rooted in the pure altruism of Amida Buddha's unconditional love beyond all discrimination, proved highly successful.

With time, just as he had vowed, Rennyo succeeded in dramatically transforming the fortunes of Honganji Temple. For quite some time, as previously mentioned, he had been presenting his followers with various Pure Land documents composed by predecessors of his, such as Shinran, Kakunyo and Zonkaku, copying them himself with sincere and untiring effort. In addition, historical research informs us, along with the development of his faith movement, Rennyo also started giving his Dharma friends various objects of religious significance, such as his own calligraphy of the Buddha-name, images of Amida Buddha, portraits of Shinran or of Shinran and Rennyo himself sitting side by side and illustrated biographies of the founder, Shinran Shōnin. From time to time devout followers, filled with the spiritual joy of faith, would likewise bring donations to Honganji, especially when receiving such special gifts direct from Rennyo. It is not hard to imagine that the spontaneous donations they made to express their gratitude soon became the main financial resource of Honganji.

The temple became much bigger than before and eventually, based on the foundations laid by Rennyo, Shin Buddhism itself developed into the largest religious order in the whole of medieval Japan. A long time before this was to happen, however, and throughout the whole of his own life, Rennyo was compelled to confront and endure a great deal of religious and political conflict. Only eight years after succeeding to the position of Head Priest at Honganji, Rennyo and his temple in Kyoto were twice attacked in both January and March of 1465 by the Tendai School, the biggest Buddhist order of all, situated on Mt. Hiei. On the first occasion advanced warning of the attack leaked out and reached the ears of Rennyo, enabling him and his family to flee, taking with them the image of Shinran Shōnin. But on the occasion of the second attack on the 22nd March, Honganji Temple, located at Ōtani in Yamashiro Province (present day Kyoto Prefecture), caught fire and was completely destroyed. Named after the location, this disastrous incident is known as the "Destruction of Ōtani."

Shortly after the destruction of Honganji at Ōtani, Rennyo managed to escape to Ōmi Province,[25] adjacent to Yamashiro (present day Kyoto). The district there around Lake Biwa has the largest expanse of fresh water in Japan and many of Rennyo's followers, including Hōjū and Dōsai, were scattered in coastal villages around the lake. Rennyo would visit them one after another, staying with them for a time at their place of abode. As Ōmi Province is very close to Mt. Hiei, remaining too long in one place was somewhat dangerous. Indeed, on several occasions the soldier monks of Mt. Hiei attacked Rennyo's followers, using considerable violence and wresting from them at one point a hanging scroll of the name in ten characters of Amida Buddha. Rennyo spent five years living in this district before moving on to Yoshizaki in Echizen Province in 1471. Because Mt. Hiei was still too close, however, he eventually decided to leave the area entirely, in order to avoid conflict with the old religious order on Mt. Hiei. Not only in Kyoto but in Ōmi also, Rennyo did all he could to avoid conflict, moving away from each place in turn.

The story, however, was much the same in Yoshizaki, a small hill township to which people flocked from various provinces in great numbers to receive Rennyo's teaching, and where some two hundred *taya* houses were erected around Rennyo's temple in order to accommodate all the followers. The fact that Rennyo's teaching attracted such vast crowds of people gave rise to a lot of friction, including conflict with several older temples of other schools and involvement in power struggles between local warlords. After remaining at Yoshizaki for five years from 1471 to 1475, Rennyo slipped away to Deguchi in Kawachi Province (part of present day Osaka Prefecture). As already demonstrated, Rennyo himself was never warlike but did his best to avoid conflict. Although there must have been some occasions when Rennyo's followers had no choice but to fight back in defence of their lives, Rennyo is reported to have been seriously displeased on hearing from the leader of a certain Shin Buddhist group that victorious defensive action had been taken in Ōmi Province and a number of soldier monks from Mt. Hiei had been killed. Rennyo told the leader to stop misbehaving and to dismiss the group of fighters immediately.[26]

It would seem that behind each of the conflicts that arose in Kyoto, Ōmi or Yoshizaki there was always some strong financial interest on the part of the attacker, whether that attacker was a religious order or a government authority. Multitudes of people who converted to *Jodo Shinhsū* or Shin Buddhism, started to donate more and more money to Rennyo's Sangha with the joy of faith and gratitude for the teaching, whilst donations to the older Buddhist organisations dwindled rapidly. This, then, was the real reason for the attacks on the Shin Buddhist Sangha's newly emerging power; the older temples were all closely attached to local government and political influence.

The official justification for the attacks on Rennyo's Sangha, advanced by the older temples such as Enryakuji on Mt. Hiei and others in Hokuriku District, was almost identical to that given by the old Buddhist organisations for banning the *Nenbutsu* teaching of Hōnen and his disciples, Seikaku, Ryūkan, Shinran and others. It was alleged that the emphasis laid by Pure Land Buddhism on teaching the sole practice of *Nenbutsu* was in order to eliminate all other practices and could eventually destroy Buddhism as a whole. This criticism, however, was based on a wholly superficial understanding of Pure Land Buddhism. It is certainly true that in the process leading up to the awakening of Other Power faith in the *Nenbutsu*, Shin Buddhists do indeed deny the validity of all other practices, but only in the sense that followers should become aware of the limits of their own self-power practice and entrust themselves instead wholeheartedly to the Other Power of Amida

Buddha, beyond all forms of selfish attachment. Shin Buddhism is actually a peaceful, selfless religion. All the Buddhist values are restored and embraced in the *Nenbutsu*. In the final analysis, Shin Buddhists have considerable respect for other schools. In letters to his followers Rennyo Shōnin repeatedly comes back to this important point, asking them not to belittle other schools but to show them the utmost deference.

Rennyo wrote a great many letters to individual followers and sometimes to particular groups as well. It made no difference to him whether those he addressed were lay followers or ordained priests, whether they were young or old, male or female, already awakened to faith or yet to be so awakened. The number of surviving letters compiled by Osamu Katada into the *Shinshū shiryō shūsei,* Vol. 2, amounts to two hundred and fifty-two – one hundred and eighty-four dated letters and sixty-eight undated ones. Of these, fifty-six have been positively confirmed as being in Rennyo's own handwriting and we have various good reasons to believe the others are authentic copies. Professor Katada carried out his enormous task by extending his own research based on two eminent works, *Rennyo Shōnin ibun* by Masamaru Inaba[27] and *Rennyo Shōnin ofumi zenshū* by Yūsho Tokushi.[28]

After becoming Head Priest of Honganji in 1457 and whilst still in Kyoto, Rennyo began writing his followers a number of letters, the first of which was presented in 1461 to Dōsai, his earliest disciple – this in addition to Rennyo's long-standing practice of presenting followers with copies in his own hand of Shin Buddhist documents, his own beautiful calligraphies of the Buddha-Name or images of Pure Land predecessors.

The single path of faith taught by Shōnin in our tradition is that those who remain at home as lay people have no need to query the gravity of their bad karma, nor to concern themselves within their own existence with the problem of their uncontrollable delusions and attachments, but that they should steadfastly forsake their erroneous attachment to miscellaneous practices and mixed ways of practice and simply take refuge in the Compassionate Vow of Amida Tathāgata. Then, upon the awakening of the one thought-moment that sees them entrust themselves singleheartedly to the Buddha without any doubt, Amida Tathāgata will immediately send forth his light and enfold them in his embrace. This is to say that it is through the Buddha, and through him alone, that we are saved. At the same time it means that our faith is itself a direct gift from the Tathāgata.

From this it can be seen that, when we pronounce the Name, we should not do so for the purpose of beseeching the Buddha to save us. Rather we should realise that our salvation was assured with the one thought-moment of faith, when we entrusted ourselves to Amida, and we should understand that pronouncing the *Nenbutsu* is actually an expression of heartfelt gratitude to Amida Tathāgata for all he has done to save us. Such is the way of understanding of 'one who practises only the *Nenbutsu* with true singleness of mind'. It is also what is meant by 'completing the cause [of birth in the Pure Land] in ordinary life with the awakening of the one thought-moment'.

Most humbly and respectfully
March in the second year of Kanshō (1461)
(Copied by Rennō) [29]

All the essential aspects of Shin Buddhist teaching, that would later appear again and again in Rennyo's many letters, are already present in this initial letter, written at the request of Dōsai. They include:

- His deep appreciation of Shinran Shōnin's profound spirituality.
- The importance of attaining the pure faith of entrusting ourselves entirely to Amida Buddha by forsaking all attachment to our own thoughts and actions.
- Amida's immediate salvation of us through this instantaneous awakening of faith.
- The fact that all this experience is a gift from the Buddha.
- The concept of Other Power.
- The assurance through faith-experience of birth in the Pure Land whilst still living an ordinary life in this world.
- Pronouncing the Buddha's Name (*Nenbutsu*) with gratitude for all that he has done for us.

This is just an introduction to Rennyo's first letter. I will discuss these essential aspects of Shin Buddhism, and particularly Rennyo's own teaching of them, in much greater detail later on when I present my actual commentaries on each of the eighty letters of the five fascicle version of Rennyo's writing, known as *The Letters*.

The fact that Rennyo would so often write letters to his Dharma friends was a natural consequence of close friendship and mutual respect, fuelled by a profound understanding of his followers' needs, both practical and spiritual. He wrote several letters during his stay in Kyoto and Ōmi, but the number of letters increased dramatically after his move to Yoshizaki in Echizen. According to the *Tenshō sannen ki*[30], it would seem that Rennyo once again began writing letters in Yoshizaki at the particular request of Rensō.[31]

After this he practised in a remote country (Yoshizaki). It was at the request of Rensō that, when the Buddha-dharma began to flourish ever more strongly at the temple at Yoshizaki, he started writing letters again. Every recipient felt so grateful for his letters. In order that ignorant people might understand readily and swiftly, he wrote letters choosing a hundred important points out of a thousand, ten out of a hundred, and one out of ten to facilitate comprehension. He wanted to present a quick way for ignorant beings to attain the Buddhist Path. It is due to Rennyo Shōnin's ardent wish that the teaching of the Founder, (Shinran) Shōnin, has now spread all over the world.[32]

Also Kūzen, a constant attendant to Rennyo, quotes the latter's words in his *Daihasso onmonogatari Kūzen kikigaki*:

"Regarding my letters, even though the wording may be odd and the grammar faulty, I have simply been writing them in the hope that others may attain faith, be it no more than a single person. If there are grammatical errors, just tell people to put the blame on me."[33]

Rennyo's way of writing to his followers, summarising the essentials of Shin Buddhist teaching simply and succinctly, reflects the spiritual process of his own intensive study, his clear understanding and internalisation of Shinran Shōnin's religious philosophy. The whole process of writing these letters was so natural and spontaneous, so much an expression of his innermost heart, something that he himself wanted to do despite – and I am simply repeating here in his own self-deprecatory way of speaking – the oddness of his wording and the possible poorness of his grammar. In point of fact, however, the simple way Rennyo expresses himself in the letters is beautiful. The humility so evident in the previous quotation shows the strength of his fervent wish to impart the founder's teaching of Pure Land Buddhism to others, based on the peaceful awareness of faith.

The quintessence of his teaching in the letters is nothing but an expression of his own experience that he directly received Amida Tathāgata's message. This is why we have these following statements by Jitsugo, the tenth son of Rennyo, in the *Jitsugo kyūki*;

The school founded by (Shinran) Shōnin is Amida Tathāgata's message. Thus, Rennyo in his letters used to say, "As said by Amida Tathāgata ...".[34]

It is said that we should receive *The Letters* (by Rennyo) as the Tathāgata's direct message. People say his physical appearance is likened to Hōnen and his words are from Amida's direct message.[35]

The feeling that Rennyo's letters were expressions of Amida Tathāgata's message received directly from the Tathāgata must have been something shared by all of Rennyo's followers. But the important point is that Rennyo himself did not receive the Tathāgata's message as a wise man set apart from the rest, but rather that he did so with a profound sense of being just another ignorant being along with the rest.

In the *Jitsugo kyūki,* Jitsugo includes a further quote, believed to be the words of Jitsunyo, Rennyo's fifth son and the Ninth Head Priest of Honganji Temple:

> *"The Letters* can be seen as a good example of an ignorant person's attainment of birth in the Pure Land. Though there may be some that imagine to themselves the possibility of an even higher teaching than *The Letters*, such people are sorely mistaken." Thus spoke he.[36]

Rennyo was in fact a good example for all his followers of an ignorant person's attainment of faith through which they are absolutely assured of birth in the Pure Land of Amida Buddha. Whilst the above three articles reflect his followers' feeling that his letters are the Tathāgata's message, the following article shows Rennyo's own feeling:

> When Kyōmon was asked by Rennyo Shōnin, confined to bed by his last illness, to read something out loud to him, Kyōmon suggested some of Rennyo's own letters. Encouraged to proceed, Kyōmon read out three of the letters twice each, whereupon Rennyo exclaimed admiringly, "Though written by me, how wonderful they are!"[37]

A similar passage by Kūzen in the *Daihasso onmonogatari Kūzen kikigaki*[38] would appear to record the same event. According to that account, Rennyo had the conversation with Kyōmon on the 9th March 1499, just before his death on the 25th. To express admiration for one's own writing like this would normally appear somewhat odd, but in Rennyo's case he did so listening to his own letters on his death bed, simply because they conveyed to him Amida's message of great love and compassion. Everything Rennyo had received was for him a pure gift from Amida.

In the course of the last five hundred years or so, many of Rennyo's letters may have gone astray. Thus, though the number of letters confirmed by modern academic study as being of his own composition amounts to two hundred and fifty-two, the true figure is probably well in excess of this.

Following the move to Yoshizaki, Rennyo's output increased dramatically, especially in the years 1473 and 1474, and, according to the *Shinshū shiryō shūsei*, eighty-five dated letters, composed during his time at Yoshizaki between 1471 and 1475, are still in existence today. A great deal happened over the course of these five years, starting with the construction of the temple together with a large number of *taya* houses to accommodate the multitudes that flocked to Yoshizaki to receive Rennyo's teaching. Sadly this expansion was then followed by the total destruction of the temple and nine taya houses by fire and Rennyo's own followers' involvement in a number of conflicts amongst local political authorities. Lastly and most serious of all there was the confrontation between Rennyo's rapidly growing Shin Buddhist Sangha and the major political authority of the day, Lord Togashi Masachika. This final clash triggered Rennyo's eventual retreat from Yoshizaki. The five year stay at Yoshizaki had nevertheless been quite successful not only by allowing Rennyo to transmit the proper Shin Buddhist teaching to people of Hokuriku District but also by enabling him to counteract the spread of erroneous interpretations of that teaching, known as *hijibōmon* or 'secret teaching', that had become popular amongst Shin Buddhists in the area.

After relocating to Deguchi in Kawachi Province in 1475, Rennyo built temples at Deguchi, Tonda and Sakai within the present day Osaka area. For the next three years, before moving on again in 1478, this time to Yamashina in Kyoto, Rennyo stayed mainly at Deguchi and from time to time would pay extended visits to the other temples. Amongst the various encounters Rennyo had at Sakai, an international trading port in those days, mention should be made of a spiritual encounter with a Khitan, a member of a nomadic tribe, and his colleagues from China. It is said that the Khitan attained faith through Rennyo's instruction.[39]

In 1478, when he was sixty-four years old, on the recommendation of his oldest disciple, Dōsai, Rennyo decided to move to Yamashina in Yamashiro Province (present day Kyoto) and set about building Honganji Temple there, in order to enshrine the image of Shinran Shōnin that he had so long been protecting following the "Destruction of Ōtani". The Founder's Image Hall and the Amida Hall, modelled exactly after those at Ōtani, were erected in 1480 and 1481 respectively and all these construction works were completed by 1483. Rennyo remained at Yamashina for seventeen years until the beginning of 1495. It was during this long stay there that he lost his third wife, Nyoshō, in 1478 and his fourth wife, Sōnyo, around 1485 and remarried his fifth and last wife, Rennō,[40] a lady forty years his junior, in 1486.

In 1489, at the age of seventy-five, Rennyo asked his fifth son, Jitsunyo, to succeed him as Head Priest of Honganji and in 1496 moved again, this time to Ishiyama in Settsu (present day Osaka), in order to build another temple there. This temple was completed the following year and called Ishiyama-dono, Ishiyama-gobō or Ōsaka-gobō.[41] Rennyo spent the last three years of his life at Ishiyama.

During those final years at Ishiyama, the number of letters written by Rennyo increased again. According to the number of dated letters we still have today, he must have written at the very least thirty-nine letters while there, likely many more. It was probably because he sensed that death was approaching that he felt impelled to write such a great number of letters to his Dharma friends. His one abiding wish throughout the ups and downs of his very stormy life was simply to help others to attain faith. In one of the letters, written towards the very end of his life, he states:

"But I, old ignoramus that I am, have been ill since some time this summer, with no sign of any improvement so far. I am quite sure I will finally fulfill my original desire of attaining birth during the coming season of cold weather. But oh, what I do hope so very much, morning and evening, is that each one of you may attain faith whilst I am yet still alive. Although it so depends on your past good conditions, there is never a moment when I stop longing for each of you to attain faith."[42]

In each and every one of Rennyo's letters, from the very first letter right up until this one, Rennyo's deepest concern was always the awakening in others of true faith. This sincere desire was based on, and accompanied by, feeling of the greatest respect and sincere humility towards Amida Tathāgata and towards Shinran Shōnin as Amida's embodiment. At the very end of his life and facing death, Rennyo wanted to undertake one last trip on a palanquin from Ishiyama-gobō in Osaka to Yamashina Honganji in Kyoto, in order to offer a final greeting to the image of Shinran Shōnin. Jitsugo describes one of these final days in his *Rennyo Shōnin itokuki*[43] as follows:

"Subsequently, on 7th March of the same year, desiring to come before the statue once again, even though he was quite aged and ill, Rennyo Shōnin took off the clothes he had been wearing in his sick bed and donned freshly tailored robes. Borne along on a palanquin, he was taken first to the main Buddha Hall and then, proceeding onwards, before the statue of Shinran Shōnin. Thereupon Rennyo Shōnin reverently addressed the holy image of the former master, saying 'This is the last time I shall see you in this life. Surely I will see you, your true form, in that country.' On hearing Rennyo's words, there were none who did not wring out their sleeves [wet with tears]."[44]

In accordance with his original wish Rennyo Shōnin attained birth in the Pure Land at Yamashina Honganji on the 25th March in 1499.

III) SALVATION OF WOMEN AND

PEOPLE WITH BAD KARMA

The Letters by Rennyo, which I have translated here with commentaries on each letter, is a five fascicle record of Rennyo Shōnin's epistles to his followers, first compiled in its present form by Ennyo (1491–1521), Rennyo's grandson, under the supervision of Ennyo's father, Jitsunyo (1458–1525), Rennyo's fifth son and his successor as Head Priest of Honganji Temple. Fascicle One (*Chapters 1–15*) contains fifteen letters written between 15th July 1471 and 22nd September 1473. Fascicle Two (*Chapters 16–30*) contains fifteen letters written between 8th December 1473 and 9th July 1474. Fascicle Three (*Chapters 31–43*) contains thirteen letters written between 14th July 1474 and 18th July 1476. Fascicle Four (*Chapters 44–58*) contains fifteen letters written between 8th January 1477 and 21st December 1498. The twenty-two letters of Fascicle Five (*Chapters 59–80*) are undated. According to the *Shinshū shiryō shūsei*, in addition to the letters compiled into this formal edition, known as *The Five Fascicle Letters*, there are at least one hundred and seventy-two other letters by Rennyo that were not included.

Our late Master said, "I, Shinran, have no disciples, because, when I expound the Tathāgata's Dharma to sentient beings in the ten directions, I am simply acting as an envoy of the Tathāgata. I, Shinran, do not propagate any new Dharma whatsoever. All I do is simply entrust myself to the Tathāgata's Dharma teaching and teach others to do likewise. Apart from that, I have nothing to teach. How then can I claim to have any disciples?" For this reason, we are in fact all fellow followers and consequently Shinran Shōnin addressed his followers very respectfully as honourable fellow followers and honourable Dharma friends.[45]

The above quotation is from the first letter of Fascicle One. I have quoted it here as it represents so perfectly the essence of the teaching Rennyo Shōnin received from Shinran Shōnin and illustrates the fundamental standpoint of all his letters.

Rennyo's letters are quite unique and totally different from all other Shin Buddhist writings, for they are not commentaries on, or interpretations of Shinran's religious thought, that is Shin Buddhist teaching. The lines above, quoted by Rennyo as being Shinran's words, demonstrate Rennyo's grasp of the true essence of Shinran's teaching, an understanding arrived at as a result of the enormous effort Rennyo put into going through Shinran's writings many times over, even copying passages out himself to give to his followers.

What Shinran actually did is beautifully summarised by Rennyo in the statement, "All I do is simply entrust myself to the Tathāgata's Dharma teaching and teach others to do likewise. Apart from that, I have nothing to teach." It could just as well have been Rennyo's own declaration, given how perfectly in tune he was with Shinran. The quintessence of Shinran's religious thought lies simply in the pure faith of entrusting oneself to Amida Tathāgata and his message of unconditional love, "Come to me just as you are." Rennyo entrusted himself to Amida's call just as Shinran did, and, just as Shinran did, told his followers to do likewise. This is the spiritual source of all Rennyo's letters.

Rennyo's feelings fully accord with Shinran's declaration that he had no disciples. Rennyo says, "For this reason, we are, in fact, all fellow followers." On the way to the Pure Land we are all Dharma friends and equal in potential, in the sense that in Shin Buddhism all beings are able to attain pure faith while living in the world and, ultimately, Buddhahood in the Pure Land. Illumined by the unconditional love of Amida Buddha, we find ourselves much like brothers and sisters. Certainly it was in this spirit that Rennyo, as previously mentioned, insisted on holding meetings with Dharma friends in the form of *hiraza,* with everyone sitting as equals at the same floor level. This spirit of brotherhood is extremely important in the Dharma movement.

Although this attitude is certainly of pivotal importance and almost all modern Shin Buddhist scholars have placed great emphasis on "Shinran's principle of brotherhood or fraternity", there is also another equally important principle, which sadly has all too often been overlooked right up until the present day. To illustrate it I quote Rennyo's own words again, "consequently Shinran Shōnin addressed his followers very respectfully as honourable fellow followers and honourable Dharma friends." Shin Buddhists respect those around them with great humility as bodhisattvas or manifestations of the Tathāgata, whether they are their own relatives or simply Dharma friends. This is because Shin Buddhists feel that those around them actually help them to follow the path to the Pure Land. It is well known, for example, that Shinran respected his own wife as Bodhisattva Avalokitêśvara. Rennyo was deeply aware of this way of thinking, learned from Shinran, and adhered to it throughout his life. His words, *anakashiko anakashiko,* or "most humbly and respectfully", found towards the end of nearly all his letters, are one good demonstration of the respect he felt towards his Dharma friends.

Amongst the eighty letters compiled into the formal five fascicle version of *The Letters* by Rennyo, ten of them are deeply concerned with women's attainment of true faith and subsequent birth in the Pure Land, and most of them are addressed directly to women. A further thirteen letters also refer to the matter of women's salvation through faith alone with no discrimination whatsoever. This fact shows just how seriously Rennyo took this problem. I am reminded here of Ānanda, a constant attendant on Śākyamuni Buddha, and the story of his re-encounter with Śākyamuni Buddha himself, related in *The Larger Sūtra of Eternal Life*. Motivated by a question from Ānanda, Śākyamuni Buddha started speaking about Amida Buddha and his Pure Land. This became, in fact, the origin of Pure Land Buddhism, a Buddhist school that promises salvation through Amida Buddha of all sentient beings without discrimination, based on faith alone.

The story goes that Ānanda suddenly came upon Śākyamuni Buddha shining brilliantly and asked the Buddha why his features were so radiant and wonderful beyond words, infinitely surpassing anything Ānanda had ever previously beheld. "All the Buddhas of the past, future and present are one in thinking of each other", mused Ānanda, "Is it perhaps that you, too, our Buddha, are now thinking of all the other Buddhas? Is that why I am now witnessing your commanding radiance shining forth so resplendently?" Thereupon the Buddha asked Ānanda whether he had been instructed by some *deva* (or heavenly being) to ask such a question. "No *deva* instructed me to ask this question", Ānanda replied. "I am simply asking this question from my own point of view." The Buddha was very pleased with Ānanda's answer and praised his profound wisdom and love and compassion for all beings, saying, "Well done, Ānanda! Your question, eloquently and truthfully expressed, and revealing deep wisdom, pleases me very much. It is out of your loving kindness for all beings that you have asked this question full of wisdom." Then, after indicating that the purport of his appearance with unconditional compassion in this world was in order to illumine the world with the true teaching, through which all beings could be blessed with true and real benefit (understood in Shin Buddhism as Amida Buddha's Original Vow), Śākyamuni Buddha said to Ānanda, "The question you have asked me just now will surely bring immense benefit and enlighten the minds of all human beings and *devas*." Thereupon, spurred by Ānanda's question, he began to relate the account of Amida Buddha for the very first time.[46]

When Shinran wrote his main work, *The Kyōgyōshinshō*, or *The Collection of Passages Expounding the True Teaching, Living, Faith and Realising of the Pure Land*, in the volume *Teaching*, he quoted only this part of *The Larger Sūtra of Eternal Life*, namely the dialogue between Śākyamuni Buddha and Ānanda, which caused the Buddha to begin recounting the story of how Amida Buddha made his vows and created his Pure Land. This fact shows, in Shinran's evaluation of the text, the enormous significance he attributed to this dialogue, Ānanda's question and Śākyamuni's answer.

Ānanda is one of the Ten Great Disciples of Śākyamuni Buddha. He is famous as the narrator of all the sūtras that tell how the Buddha taught his followers. Ānanda was a talented person with an excellent memory and, as a constant attendant to the Buddha, was present at the Buddha's talks at all kinds of meetings. Ānanda is also described in various documents as a monk full of love and compassion towards women too. The Buddha's words, quoted from *The Larger Sūtra of Eternal Life,* refer to him as a monk endowed with profound wisdom and loving kindness for all beings. On the other hand, there are also several documents that describe Ānanda as not yet free of all desires and blind passions by the time his master entered Nirvana. It is said that he only finally achieved enlightenment just before the first Buddhist council when his narrations were formally recorded as sūtras. Before that Ānanda confessed he was a monk who was not yet enlightened, someone still in thrall to worldly desires. Needless to say, embraced in the Buddha's great wisdom and unconditional love, he must have had some awareness of what the experience of Enlightenment was like, even if unconsciously, and would have known how to control himself in the light of the Buddha's teaching. But it was only after the death of the Buddha that Ānanda experienced Enlightenment directly. He was in fact the very last of the ten great disciples to become enlightened.

Closely involved in the problems of others, whether men or women, young or old, ordained or lay people, Ānanda helped others go first to solve their problems, while he himself remained behind, no matter how much he was blamed for his faults in doing so. There are many stories of the assistance he afforded women in sorting out their problems. For example, when Mahāpajāpati, Śākyamuni Buddha's mother's younger sister – later to become Śākyamuni's mother-in-law – wanted to be ordained as a nun following the death of Śākyamuni's father, Śākyamuni was reluctant to allow a woman to be ordained in his Sangha, but at Ānanda's earnest request the Buddha finally allowed her to be ordained, together with five hundred other women. Mahāpajāpati was the first Buddhist nun. Thus Ānanda was responsible for opening the way to the ordination of women in the Buddhist Sangha.

As far as the problem of discrimination against women is concerned, given that the founder of Buddhism allowed women to enter the Sangha, there can be no doubt but that he recognised women as being just as capable of enlightenment as men. In this respect women are equal to men in Buddhism. There are many records in Buddhism of the enlightenment of women.

Fundamentally speaking, therefore, there should not have been any discrimination against women in Buddhism. Unfortunately, however, the history of the tradition tells a different story, but this, I am afraid, I cannot discuss in detail here. In as far as the Buddhist Sangha is a social community, it cannot help but be involved in all kinds of problems, whether stemming from within the Sangha itself or from outside. If women were to join a Sangha where previously there had been only monks, for example, it is not hard to imagine the sort of problems that could arise between two celibate groups of different sexes. This might have been one of the reasons why Śākyamuni Buddha was initially reluctant to invite women to enter the Sangha. The Indian society in which the Buddhist Sangha came into being was extremely androcentric and it would have been highly unusual in those days and in that sort of society to create a community of nuns, essentially homeless women. Indeed, until the appearance of Śākyamuni Buddha, no such community of women had ever existed in India. In that sense the Buddha must have been very cautious about introducing female ordination in India.

Swayed by the fervent and repeated requests of Ānanda, however, and despite the possibility the involvement of women might incur at least as many difficulties as benefits, Śākyamuni Buddha decided to allow women to be ordained and enter the Buddhist Sangha. It is my humble opinion that he probably took the decision because he felt it imperative that the basic ideal of the equality of all sentient beings, whether men or women, be realised in the sense that all should ultimately be able to attain Buddhahood. In the light of the extreme importance he attached to the fulfillment of this sincere desire, all the difficulties to be met along the way paled into insignificance and could be endured.

As already mentioned, when Ānanda questioned Śākyamuni Buddha about the extraordinary radiance of his features, it was because of his surprise at beholding such brilliance of the Buddha for the first time in his life. By way of reply, Śākyamuni Buddha praised Ānanda for his profound wisdom and loving kindness towards others, and then started speaking about Amida Buddha's Vow to save all beings into his Pure Land, as later recorded in *The Larger Sūtra of Eternal Life*. The essence of Amida Buddha's story lies in the salvation of all sentient beings. Without the salvation of those that are the most discriminated against, universal salvation could never come about. Who then are the most discriminated against in society? It has to be women and people perceived to have bad karma. Unfortunately and very sadly, in the androcentric societies typical of ancient and medieval times, women were almost always dependent on men, and people perceived to be heavily burdened with bad karma were treated very harshly. Even in the Buddhist communities of those days they were excluded from the possibility of spiritual liberation, the potentiality of birth in the Pure Land and the ultimate attainment of Buddhahood. That is why eminent Pure Land masters such as Shàndǎo, Hōnen and Shinran were very much taken up with the idea of saving those two categories of people and paid particular attention to Amida Buddha's Thirty-fifth Vow regarding the salvation of women and his Eighteenth Vow regarding the salvation of people with bad karma. Rennyo, too, focused very strongly on this matter when writing letters to his followers.

> Listen, men with bad karma and women in the Last Dharma Age,[47] we should entrust ourselves singleheartedly and deeply with our whole being to Amida Buddha. Otherwise, no matter what teaching we believe in, we will never be saved in the matter of Rebirth.[48]

This is just one example from his letters. The second half of the quotation would suggest that in other Buddhist schools of those days "men with bad karma and women" were indeed excluded from salvation, or birth in the Pure Land.

Although in the realm of morality, or simply of good common sense, it is self-evident that good things should be chosen and bad things forsaken, it is essential to confront the subject at a much deeper, spiritual level and talk about the religious salvation of those who have committed wrongdoing. Although there are many forms of religious teaching that insist on the universal salvation of the whole of humankind as equals, unless such teaching also promises the liberation of those that have previously sinned or committed crimes, it cannot be seen as emanating from a religion of universal salvation or unconditional love that knows no discrimination.

Throughout the entire history of Buddhism, the salvation of the wicked has been a long-standing subject of serious discussion, combined with the problem of whether or not all sentient beings have the potentiality to attain Buddhahood and be saved.

In the Pure Land tradition, predecessors such as Tánluán, Shàndǎo, Hōnen and Shinran treated the matter with the utmost seriousness in their writings. Indeed they had no choice but to do so, given that in *The Larger Sūtra of Eternal Life*, the main text they all depended on, Amida Buddha's Eighteenth Vow (the most important vow that promises the salvation of all sentient beings) contained a passage of exclusion, added at some point to the main text, that read "Excepted from this are those who commit the five grave offenses and those who slander the Right Dharma."[49]

In any discussion of this problem, mention should always be made of the incredibly important role in the history of Pure Land Buddhism played by the Chinese Buddhist master, Shàndǎo. Basing himself on *The Meditation Sūtra*, itself based on *The Larger Sūtra of Eternal Life*, Shàndǎo drew people's attention to the passage that promised salvation through the *Nenbutsu* for the vilest of ignorant beings. In this way he was able to clarify and determine that the very essence of the Eighteenth Vow lay in the universal deliverance of all sentient beings, without any discrimination whatsoever, even of those who had committed the five grave offenses or those who had slandered the Right Dharma. Shàndǎo declared,

> Through the power of the Buddha's Vow, those who have committed the five grave offenses[50] and the ten bad acts[51] are relieved of their unpardonable criminality and are born in the Pure Land, and even those who have slandered the Dharma or who have abandoned the seed of Buddhahood, as soon as their minds turn towards Amida, are also born in the Pure Land.[52]

In the same way as the salvation of people with bad karma, one of the two most important subjects of *The Larger Sūtra of Eternal Life*, was connected to the heavy weight of Ānanda's own awareness of himself as an unenlightened or ignorant person, the other subject, the salvation of women, was also a burden that he continued to carry throughout his life, whether consciously or unconsciously. It must have been because of these problems stored away in his innermost heart that Ānanda found himself impelled to ask the Buddha the incredibly important question that triggered the Buddha's teaching of Amida and his Pure Land for the benefit of all sentient beings now and in the future. Shinran's special appreciation of the spiritual encounter between Ānanda and Śākyamuni Buddha as being the starting point for Pure Land Buddhism is worthy of special attention.

Rennyo Shōnin was very concerned about these problems when writing his letters to his followers. Regarding the letters specifically addressed to women and compiled into this formal version of *The Letters* by Rennyo, I shall discuss their contents in detail in the commentaries that follow. Here in this context, therefore, I would simply like to call to the reader's attention the fact that Rennyo used some special phrases such as "five obstacles"[53] and "three submissions"[54] to describe women's apparent shortcomings.

From a modern perspective, if you say that, because women are heavily burdened with the five obstacles and the three submissions, it will be extremely difficult, if not downright impossible, for them to be born in the Pure Land and attain Buddhahood, then it certainly does sound extraordinarily discriminatory. Why then did Rennyo make use of such expressions? There can be no doubt that, when Rennyo wrote his letters to women, it was to free them from the sad reality of discrimination in a medieval male-dominated society and to encourage them with the assurance that they, too, could attain birth in the Pure Land and ultimately become 'beautiful Buddhas'. In that case, was it not contradictory of him to resort to such discriminatory terms when seeking to liberate women from the androcentric society to the world of pure faith, where, as often mentioned by him in his letters, there is no difference between men and women and both are treated as equals?

Rennyo was not unaware of this contradiction. As a person who entrusted himself absolutely to the Universal Vow of Amida Buddha that promises to save all human beings without discrimination, Rennyo was conscious that discriminatory statements referring to women as being heavily burdened with the "five obstacles and three submissions" might lead to the conclusion that women could never be saved and attain Buddhahood. But that indeed was the general view held by Buddhists in those days, including the old Buddhist orders that had previously attacked Hōnen and Shinran and which, collaborating with the political regime, were now attacking Rennyo. Thus Rennyo, therefore, did not insist directly on the radical viewpoint of

Pure Land Buddhism, namely that all beings were equal and that women as well as men could be saved. It would have been far too dangerous. Under the influence of the androcentric cultures of India and China, discriminatory ideas were by now also deeply embedded in Japanese society also. The social leaders of Japan at that time, both central and local, shared the same discriminatory views as the old Buddhist institutions, with the former being enormously influenced by the latter, culturally, philosophically and socially ever since Buddhism was first introduced to Japan. Discrimination, of course, was also used by the authorities as a way of controlling people and society.

Politically speaking, therefore, Rennyo was in a very delicate position. Every time he was attacked by the powers-that-be, whether religious or political, on account of his putatively radical ideas, he would escape the area of conflict and seek a fresh location. He did not dare to fight back directly. Rather than out and out confrontation with the authorities, whether political or religious, he preferred throughout his life to pursue his ideal of equal salvation by very effectively leading people in their daily lives to the attainment of pure faith and to entrusting themselves to the Universal Vow of Amida Buddha that promises to save all sentient beings with no discrimination at all between young and old, rich and poor, wise and ignorant, men and women, even good and bad.

Although he was fully aware of the discriminatory nature of such phrases as "women heavily burdened with the five obstacles and the three submissions", Rennyo refrained from openly defying those that championed such notions. On the contrary he himself repeatedly employed their own disparaging phraseology in his letters, in order to bring home to his followers, in this case women in particular, the bleakness of their current situation, mired in the sad reality of discrimination, often in ways they barely understood. By so doing Rennyo sought to kindle in them the wish to overcome and liberate themselves from such conditions simply by attaining pure faith and entrusting themselves to Amida's Vow of Universal Deliverance.

Subsequent commentaries will discuss the letters that talk about the salvation of women and people with bad karma.

Taking into account Rennyo Shōnin's relationship to his own mother, we should not underestimate his enormous effort to liberate women from their karmic burdens of discrimination. According to various records of Rennyo Shōnin such as *Shūjin ki, Rennyo Shōnin goichigo ki* and *Daihasso onmonogatari kūzen kikigaki,* he adored his mother throughout his life. As mentioned before, his mother had to leave him behind at Honganji when he was just six years old. His lifelong fervent wish to liberate women from their karmic burdens, loaded with heavy discrimination against them, must have been closely related to this sad experience. His mother left him with the wish that he should restore the tradition of the founder, Shinran Shōnin. The heart of this tradition is nothing but pure faith in Amida's Original Vow of Universal Deliverance that promises to save all beings without any discrimination at all. Although his mother's departure was a tragic experience, as it awakened him to the unconditional love of Amida Tathāgata and at the same time to his great task in life, ultimately he must have been very grateful to his mother.

As already revealed, Rennyo was a man of pure compassion and unconditional love, who continued to practise and promote the teaching of Shinran, the founder of Shin Buddhism, to the very end of his life, fuelled by a burning desire to lead his followers to the attainment of true faith in Amida's Original Vow. To this end he copied a great many Shin Buddhist documents for his followers and wrote a great many letters throughout a life that was all too often beset by misery, disastrous happenings, incredible hardship and miraculous escapes. At the same time, Rennyo was a man of profound wisdom, not only on a spiritual level, dealing with matters of faith and practice, but also in terms of objective knowledge and judgment, whether dealing with interpersonal relationships or difficult political situations. He was very aware of himself, what he represented, what the situation was and how best to act in order to overcome difficulties. With regard to his own personal situation, he was able to make good, often excellent, decisions on how to solve the problems he faced. Eventually he succeeded in building Shin Buddhism into the biggest and most powerful order of those days.

To conclude my introduction, I would like to add one final observation. When writing letters to his followers, Rennyo used certain characteristic expressions that were typical of his own particular style, phrases such as "oneness of *ki* (self) and *ho* (Dharma) in *Namu-Amida-Butsu*", "the Great Matter of Rebirth", "peaceful awareness", "saying the *Nenbutsu* with gratitude for what has been done for us by the Buddha" and so forth. Because the usage of such phrases was special to him, there are some scholars who think that Rennyo's way of understanding the Shin Buddhist faith diverged slightly from tradition, but I myself would not agree. Through my own translation and commentary work I have found Rennyo's knowledge and understanding of the Shin Buddhist tradition to be very accurate and based exactly on Shinran's own faith-experience and philosophical understanding of the quintessence of Pure Land Buddhism. Rennyo's letters greatly helped to summarise Shin Buddhist teaching and to develop the Sangha rapidly, subsequently leading to the emergence of a great number of devout followers known as *myōkōnin*. It is entirely due to the accuracy of his understanding of what Shinran Shōnin wanted to transmit to future generations that we can still receive and enjoy the invaluable fruit of Pure Land thought, a tradition that originated in India, developed and spread through Central Asia, China and Korea and finally achieved its apotheosis in Japan through the advent of Hōnen and Shinran. I am very happy to be able to share Rennyo's *Letters* with you all.

LIVING WITH THANKS

THE FIVE FASCICLE VERSION OF
RENNYO SHŌNIN'S LETTERS

CHAPTER ONE

Interpersonal Relationships in Shin Buddhism

ON FOLLOWERS AND DISCIPLES

FASCICLE I, LETTER ONE

Someone once inquired of me, speaking as follows, "In our tradition should followers necessarily be considered as our own disciples or should we speak of them as disciples of the Tathāgata and of Shinran Shōnin? On this point I have no clear understanding. There are some, too, who have small groups of followers in various places. In fact they even try to conceal this for the time being from the priest of the temple to which they belong. As friends tell me that this is again unjustifiable, I feel very unsure about it, too. I would like to have your kind instruction on these matters."

I replied as follows, "I consider these questions to be of extreme importance. I will tell you what I have duly received.[55] Please listen.

Our late Master said, 'I, Shinran, have no disciples, because, when I expound the Tathāgata's Dharma to sentient beings in the ten directions, I am simply acting as an envoy of the Tathāgata. I, Shinran, do not propagate any new Dharma whatsoever. All I do is simply entrust myself to the Tathāgata's Dharma teaching and teach others to do likewise. Apart from that, I have nothing to teach. How then can I claim to have any disciples?'

For this reason, we are in fact all fellow followers and consequently Shinran Shōnin addressed his followers very respectfully as honourable fellow followers and honourable Dharma friends.

Recently, however, even priests in a high position, ignorant of what is meant in our tradition by 'peaceful awareness (安心 jp. *anjin*)'[56], are heavily castigating certain of their disciples for visiting other places where faith is discussed and trying there to listen to the Dharma. Sometimes the priests have even removed such disciples from their groups. Consequently, as the priests themselves do not clearly understand the single truth of faith and try to hold on to their disciples in this manner, not only the priests but their disciples too fail to attain faith decisively. This means their lives will be lived in vain. It is truly difficult for them to escape blame for harming themselves and others. It is deplorable, quite deplorable. An old poem says,

> Previously
> joy was tucked away in my sleeve.
> But, tonight,
> I am overflowing with happiness!

"Previously joy was tucked away in my sleeve" means that in the past we presumed – without any clear understanding of miscellaneous practices and right practice – that we would attain birth in the Pure Land if only we recited the *Nenbutsu*. "But, tonight, I am overflowing with happiness!" means that the joy of reciting the *Nenbutsu* in grateful response to the Buddha for what he has done for us (*button hōjin*) is especially great now that, having clearly understood the difference between the right practice and the miscellaneous practices, we have decisively attained faith with steadfastness and singlemindedness. Because of this, we are so overjoyed that we feel like dancing – hence "I am overflowing with happiness!"

Most humbly and respectfully[57]
On 15th June, Bunmei 3 [1471].

COMMENTS

This letter begins with questions raised by someone who would appear to have been the leader of a Shin Buddhist group, whether as a priest or a layman. The questions were obviously prompted by the experience of forming a Shin Buddhist community. Shin Buddhist followers are very serious about the questions relating to the relationship between a teacher and his disciples.

In other schools it was very natural at that time for a priest to consider as his disciples those who came to him to be instructed about Buddhism. From the standpoint of Shin Buddhist faith-experience, however, the idea of this sort of relationship was felt to be unnatural or wrong in some way. As Rennyo himself says in the letter, these questions about the relationship between Master and disciple are of the utmost importance in the Shin Buddhist tradition. Shinran Shōnin, the founder of Shin Buddhism, had already clarified this crucial point about the relationship between Master and disciple as recorded in Chapter 6 of Yuien's *The Tanni shō*.

To answer these questions, therefore, Rennyo Shōnin quotes the words of Shinran Shōnin from *The Tanni shō*. He does not do so verbatim, but provides his own interpretation of the text. In addition to a general interpretation of the content of Chapter 6, Rennyo clarifies a new point, something very important that Shinran Shōnin had already touched on in Chapter 6 but only very briefly.

When I discussed the content of the chapter in my translation of *The Tanni shō*[58], I did so by dividing the chapter into four parts, as follows,

I.   "It is completely unreasonable for there to be quarrelling amongst our fellow followers reciting the *Nenbutsu* exclusively, with people saying that such and such are 'my disciples' whilst such and such are not. I, Shinran, have no disciples." Firstly, Shinran Shōnin claims he has no disciples. If one remembers the objective fact that he may have had thousands of followers, what does this statement mean? It means he did not ultimately 'possess' or 'own' any of his disciples. His human relationship with them was not centred on possession. He did not possess anyone and was not possessed by anyone. Possessing and being possessed are two sides of the same coin. He was free from any sort of possessiveness. His followers were basically good friends of his. Usually friendship implies equality of relationship between people. Shinran's friendship was more than that. He respected his followers as also being his protectors on the same true way, just as he revered his wife as a Bodhisattva who would lead him to the Pure Land.

II.   "The reason is this: if a man by his own efforts makes others recite the *Nenbutsu*, then he may call them his disciples. But it is most presumptuous to claim as 'my disciples' those who recite the *Nenbutsu* solely as a result of Amida's working within themselves." Secondly religious experiences such as faith in Amida and saying Amida's Name (*Nenbutsu*) belong absolutely to the individual. Even if one seemed to make another person call Amida's Name, the truth is a person only serves as a motivational condition to another's spiritual development, just like the midwife in the Socratic method of teaching. As to another's spiritual acts, one should not want to go further than the role of midwife. If one did so, one would end up being 'most presumptuous.' Shinran Shōnin's spiritual sternness thus stems from his way of living, in which he constantly returns to the Buddha again and again, day in, day out. Faith in Amida, which causes one to call Amida's Name, is definitely a most private matter reserved for the individual and the Buddha alone.

III. "It is all due to the karmic condition of things that some follow one master while others leave him. This being so, it would be absurd to say that one who turns from one master to another will not attain birth in the Pure Land. Do they mean to take back the faith given to each person by Amida as if it were something of theirs? Such views are most decidedly unreasonable." Thirdly, as faith is awakened through the working of Amida, faith is a gift from Amida; it is not ours to give or take. If one thinks one possesses faith, it is no longer faith. What then in Shinran's teaching is faith exactly? It looks elusive, just like a moment of time, but only if one wants to possess it. Faith is attained instantaneously by coming in touch with the working of Amida. And how does one feel the working of Amida? It is through one's relationship with others. Shinran Shōnin found Hōnen Shōnin to be not only his Master but also an embodiment of Amida Buddha. On encountering Hōnen, Shinran, through the personality of Hōnen, was able to meet and take refuge in Amida Buddha who was what made Hōnen what he was. Since Amida Buddha constantly supports all living beings and their world of interdependent relationships, Amida naturally issues forth through them. Hence, Shinran's conclusion:

IV. "If one follows the truth of reality as it is, one will understand exactly how grateful to be to Amida, and how grateful to be to the master." One who is awakened to faith knows how to thank Amida, how to thank one's Master and consequently how to thank others. The other people in a person's life are the motivational condition for an individual's religious awakening. Consequently they are those who have done a great deal for that individual's spiritual welfare. As a matter of course, one comes to understand just how grateful one should be to others.

When you compare Rennyo's letter with Chapter 6 of *The Tanni shō* you become aware of certain aspects of that text which he specially emphasises. One such aspect is the importance in the Shin Buddhist tradition of respect towards others. In the first letter of Fascicle One, Rennyo says: "For this reason we are in fact all fellow followers and consequently Shinran Shōnin addressed his followers very respectfully as 'honourable' fellow followers and 'honourable' Dharma friends." Such a comment on Shinran Shōnin's attitude to his followers made much clearer than before how important respect towards others is in the context of Shin Buddhist interpersonal relations. Another such important aspect is one's gratitude towards others, something that is closely bound up with the joy or happiness one attains through one's faith-experience. Because we find ourselves extremely happy on the way to the Pure Land, we come to realise that other people are our good friends, companions and protectors.

Another important point Rennyo raises in the letter is the arrogance of certain priests. He deplores such arrogance, showing that he was someone who well knew the reality of this world. The Shin Buddhist notions of respect or gratitude towards others have nothing to do with blind obedience or submission. On the contrary Shin Buddhists appreciate very much their spiritual independence. Whilst well knowing the reality of the world, they can live with pure faith, full of love, respect and gratitude towards others.

There is an absolute standard for the Shin Buddhist moral life: Shin Buddhists live their lives constantly asking themselves whether their actions are 'benefiting the self and others' or 'harming the self and others,' because 'benefiting oneself and others' is the essence of Amida Buddha's Original Vow.

Finally this very special relationship between master and disciple is based on the deepest insight into pure faith-experience. For a Shin Buddhist everything counts as a gift from Amida Buddha that enables him or her to go forward on the way to the Pure Land. It is the same with the people he or she meets. One who understands this will be extremely joyful and happy. According to Rennyo's expression in the last paragraph of the letter, right practice is "saying the *Nenbutsu* in grateful response to the Buddha for what he has done for us" (*button hōjin* 佛恩報尽) and is engendered by the experience of attaining faith. Faith is awakening to the fact that one is embraced in the unconditional love of Amida Buddha. Once faith is attained, the *Nenbutsu* emerges spontaneously from the joy of faith. Right practice is the act of saying the *Nenbutsu* based on pure faith in Amida Buddha, an act of gratitude in return for the Buddha's benevolence. As Shinran Shōnin says, all other practices are to be called miscellaneous practices. In a verse in Japanese he says,

> Although they do not mean exactly the same thing
> Miscellaneous practices and mixed ways of practice are alike.
> Acts that do not lead to the Pure Land
> Are all called miscellaneous practices.[59]

Faith is Attained in the One Thought-Moment

ON BECOMING HOMELESS MONKS

IN ASPIRATION FOR ENLIGHTENMENT

FASCICLE I, LETTER TWO

This school of ours, established by Shinran Shōnin, has as its fundamental principle not that we should become homeless monks in our aspiration for Enlightenment nor that we should renounce family and abandon all worldly desires, but simply that we should attain Other Power faith with the awakening of the one thought-moment of taking refuge in Amida Buddha. Once this faith has been decisively attained there will be no discrimination whatsoever between male and female, old and young. The *Sūtra*[60] describes this state of having attained faith as "immediately attaining birth and dwelling in a stage of nonretrogression"[61] and the commentary[62] states, "With the awakening of the one thought-moment, we enter the company of those who are rightly assured of birth in the Pure Land." This is what is meant by the words "not waiting for Amida to come to meet us at the moment of death" and also by the phrase "completing the cause of birth in the Pure Land in ordinary life."

In a *wasan* (verse in Japanese) Shinran Shōnin says,

Those who aspire to be born in Amida's Land of Enjoyment,
Though their outward forms may vary,
Should receive through faith the Name of the Original Vow,
And, whether awake or asleep, never forget it.[63]

With the words "though their outward forms may vary" Shinran Shōnin means that there are no distinctions to be made between lay persons and priests or between men and women. Next, "should receive through faith the Name of the Original Vow, and whether asleep or awake, never forget it" means that no matter whatever kind of lives we may lead – even if our karmic existences may have involved the ten bad acts and the five grave offences, or even if we are among those who have slandered the Dharma or who lack the seed of Buddhahood – as long as we undergo spiritual reformation, repent and realise through deep faith that Amida Tathāgata's Original Vow is for just such wretched people as ourselves, then if we entrust ourselves without any double-mindedness to the Tathāgata and, whether awake or asleep, always remember to be mindful of Amida, we can indeed be said to be people of faith who have become fully determined to entrust ourselves to the Original Vow.

Beyond this, even if we always recite the Name – whether walking, standing, sitting, or lying down – we should think of it as our grateful response to Amida Tathāgata for what he has done for us. Such a person is called one who has attained true faith and is decisively assured of birth in the Pure Land.

Most humbly and respectfully
On 18th July, Bunmei 3 [1471].

COMMENTS

The subject of this letter is the Shin Buddhist faith to which we are awakened at the one thought-moment when we take refuge in Amida Buddha (ichinen kimyō no shinjin 念帰命の信心). Rennyo Shōnin would often put emphasis on the importance of this concept in letters to his followers. As explained in this letter, what is most important in the Shin Buddhist tradition is not whether one becomes a priest or remains a lay person, but whether one attains faith in this life here and now. True faith is something beyond worldly forms, beyond male or female, old or young, ordained or lay, rich or poor, high or low. Rennyo Shōnin says in the first paragraph, "Once this faith has been decisively attained there will be no discrimination whatsoever between male and female, old and young."

Rennyo's words toward the end of the first paragraph, beginning with a reference to The Larger Sūtra of Eternal Life, are also a beautiful summarisation of the essentials of Shin Buddhism. According to the Sūtra, attaining faith means instantly attaining birth in the Pure Land and reaching a stage of nonretrogression[64] where one becomes assured of attaining Buddhahood in the future. Therefore, according to Tánluán's *Commentary on The Treatise on the Pure Land,* with the awakening of the one thought-moment one "enters the company of those who are rightly assured of birth in the Pure Land." So Shinran Shōnin clearly states that we do not need to wait for Amida to come to meet us at the moment of death. In our tradition we are taught that, at the moment of attaining faith, we complete the cause of birth in the Pure Land in ordinary life.

The Japanese phrase *ichinen hokki* 念発起 translated here as "the awakening of the one thought-moment," stems from the Pure Land tradition and appears repeatedly in Rennyo's writings. Attainment of faith in one thought-moment[65] is the key notion in Shin Buddhism. Faith means taking refuge in Amida Buddha and it is attained in one instant or moment of thought. Just how important this notion of the instantaneous attainment of faith actually is in our tradition can be seen from several examples from *The Goichidai ki kikigaki.*

> Article 1. On the first day of January in the second year of Meiō (1493) a certain Dōtoku, from Kanshūji village, appeared before Rennyo Shōnin. Shōnin addressed him as follows, "How old are you now, Dōtoku? Dōtoku, say the *Nenbutsu!* What is meant by the '*Nenbutsu* of self power (*jiriki*)' is reciting the *Nenbutsu* in the belief that one will be saved by the Buddha through the virtuous act of reciting the *Nenbutsu* many times over, offering to him the virtue acquired through such recitation. That which is called Other Power, on the other hand, saves us immediately with the awakening of the one thought-moment when we utterly entrust ourselves to Amida. To recite the *Nenbutsu* after that is to repeat *Namu Amida-butsu* with great rejoicing, feeling how grateful we are at having been saved. Thus Other Power means 'Power of the Other [Amida Buddha].' By means of this one thought-moment, affecting our lives to the very end, we attain birth."[66]

This 'one thought-moment' is the absolute present, the atom of eternity and the foundation of time. Once experienced, it becomes the spiritual foundation that supports our lives ever after. Thanks to their faith Shin Buddhists live their lives with gratitude and humility. As you may know, birth in the Pure Land has two meanings: Firstly the attainment of faith and secondly the attainment of birth in the Pure Land and subsequent Nirvāṇa.[67] The last sentence of Article 1 refers to the latter.

Article 32. Rennyo Shōnin said: "Because the six characters forming the Name *Namu Amida-butsu* stand for great goodness and great virtue, people in Buddhist schools other than our own tend, when reciting *Namu Amida-butsu*, to offer the virtue of their recitation to all Buddhas, Bodhisattvas and devas, claiming the virtue as their own. In our tradition, however, that is not the case. Only if the Name, with its six characters, were instead our very own, would we be able to offer the virtue of reciting it to Buddhas and Bodhisattvas. All we can really do is proclaim our gratitude for our instantaneous salvation at the one thought-moment when, with utter singleness of mind, we entrust ourselves to Amida Buddha, asking him to help us in the matter of Rebirth."[68]

In Rennyo Shōnin's writings we often come across the Japanese word *goshō* 後生, literally, next life or birth. In the context of his work salvation in the next life means the attainment of rebirth in the Pure Land immediately after death. But it is in our actual lives 'here and now' that we become confident of attaining rebirth in the Pure Land and subsequent Parinirvāṇa, so our ultimate concerns about our next life are something we also have to resolve here and now. When Rennyo Shōnin or other masters of the Shin Buddhist tradition spoke about the "one great matter of one's next birth," they were referring to this ultimate concern about rebirth in the Pure Land.

In order to avoid any serious misinterpretation, I decided to translate the Japanese word *goshō* as 'Rebirth' instead of 'next life', because 'next life' also has connotations of 'afterlife', a Christian term typically meaning the time from death until the last judgment, as well as a sense of 'karmic transmigration through many lives'. The textual origin of the word *goshō* 後生 meaning 'Rebirth in the Pure Land' can be traced back to a phrase found in *The Larger Sūtra of Eternal Life*, "to be born next in the country of the Buddha of Eternal Life" (*goshō muryōju bukkoku* 後生無量壽佛國).[69]

In his Pure Land philosophy Tánluán says that birth or rebirth in the Pure Land is the 'birth of no birth'.[70] It is not birth into another life through transmigration or reincarnation. Through birth in the Pure Land, that is the "birth of no birth," we actually go beyond the world of transmigration involving births and deaths.

Article 38. Rennyo Shōnin said: "With the awakening of the one thought-moment your birth is attained. It depends entirely on Amida Tathāgata whether he saves you after eradicating your bad karma or whether he saves you without doing so. Worrying about your bad karma is of no avail. It is only those who entrust themselves that Amida saves."[71]

That is, faith is something that enables us to go beyond both good and bad.

Article 239. Rennyo Shōnin said: "When you entrust yourself to Amida, you will become the master of *Namu Amida-butsu*. To become the master of *Namu Amida-butsu* is to attain faith." He also said: "The true treasure in our tradition is *Namu Amida-butsu*, that is the attainment of faith in one thought-moment."[72]

This article is quite special. Entrusting yourself to Amida Buddha you become one with *Namu Amida-butsu* and work as *Namu Amida-butsu*. *Namu Amida-butsu* in this sense is the expression of faith attained at this absolute present moment.

In order to clarify the Shin Buddhist experience of instantaneous attainment of Other Power faith, I would like to refer briefly to Shinran Shōnin's own special method of classifying all the Mahāyāna Buddhist schools into two "ways," each with two "approaches" (*nisōshijū* 二雙四重).[73]

Firstly, all the Mahāyāna teachings are classified into two approaches: either crosswise or lengthwise. "Crosswise" stands for the teaching of Other Power, meaning "approach by Other Power," whilst "lengthwise" stands for the teaching of self power, meaning "approach by self power." In other words, "lengthwise" implies following our own way of thinking and practising with self power, and "crosswise" indicates the working of Other Power that takes us beyond such self-centred consciousness.

Each of the two approaches also has two ways: either transcending or departing. "Transcending" means leaping over to the world of Enlightenment or the Pure Land or an immediate, sudden attainment of the objective – the tradition of sudden awakening. By contrast "departing" means walking out into the world of Enlightenment or a gradual, slow approach to the objective – the tradition of gradual awakening.

Thus all the Mahāyāna teachings can be classified into four groups:

1. Transcending lengthwise (*juchō* 竪超): The Mahāyāna teachings that are true and real, including the Kegon, Tendai, Zen, and Shingon sects.

2. Departing lengthwise (*jushutsu* 竪出): The Mahāyāna teachings that resort to provisional means, including the Hossō and Sanron sects.

3. Transcending crosswise (*ōchō* 横超): The true Pure Land teaching as the fulfilment of the Original Vow, expounded in *The Larger Sūtra of Eternal Life* and Shinran Shōnin's own Pure Land teaching of the *Nenbutsu* of true faith.

4. Departing crosswise (*ōshutsu* 横出): The Pure Land teachings that resort to provisional means, mainly expounded in *The Meditation Sūtra*. Regarding the teachings of the meditative and nonmeditative ways, the nine grades and the three classes, although the teachings

come from Other Power, followers are still attached to their own self power. Hence, this is called "self power in Other Power."

The first and second are the Holy Path teachings of Mahāyāna Buddhism and the third and fourth are the Pure Land teachings of Mahāyāna Buddhism. According to the *Gutoku shō*,[74] Shinran Shōnin does not apply this way of classification to the Theravada teachings, which were called Hīnayāna in those days and categorised into a different group of teachings. It is therefore apparent that the Shin Buddhist tradition that teaches the instantaneous attainment of true faith is the only school that belongs to the third category of "transcending crosswise."

CHAPTER THREE

No Discrimination Amongst People No Matter What Their Occupation

ON HUNTING AND FISHING

FASCICLE I, LETTER THREE

First of all what we call 'peaceful awareness (*anjin*)' in our tradition does not require us to push out the bad thoughts, delusions and attachments that arise in our minds. We can simply make our living, whether in trade or domestic service, in hunting or fishing. For if we deeply believe in Amida Tathāgata's Original Vow that vows to save such useless beings as ourselves, deludedly engaged as we are morning and evening in these wretched jobs of bad karma, and furthermore if we also singlemindedly entrust ourselves to the compassionate Vow of the one Buddha, Amida, and finally since true faith is awakened in the one thought-moment we entreat Amida Buddha to save us, then without fail we will find ourselves embraced in the Tathāgata's salvation.

Furthermore, if you ask me with what understanding we should say the *Nenbutsu*, my answer is that we should say it with deep gratitude for as long as we live, grounded on the realisation that through the recitation of the *Nenbutsu* we thank Amida Buddha for all that he has kindly done for us in order to give us the power of faith right here and now that has just assured us of birth in the Pure Land.

Those who realise this are to be called followers of faith who have decisively attained the peaceful awareness of our tradition.

Most humbly and respectfully
On 18th December, Bunmei 3 (1471).

COMMENTS

Generally speaking, in Buddhism all beings are expected to become Buddhas. In so far as everyone has the potential to become a Buddha because of their Buddha-nature,[75] everyone is acknowledged as being of equal value. This is the most important point in Buddhism in general, not only in Early Buddhism but also in Mahāyāna Buddhism.

Unfortunately, it cannot be said that over the long course of Buddhist history Buddhists have always been fully aware of this point. Although Buddhists have always considered impartial love for all beings as being one of the essential components of their faith, Buddhism has not been free of various forms of discrimination, influenced to a great extent by historical circumstance. Even within Buddhist orders, just as in Buddhist teachings, discrimination could be found on the basis of sex, race, religion, class or occupation.

Pure Land Buddhists, especially Shin Buddhists, are very concerned about this problem, because the teaching of Amida Buddha is based on his Original Vow of Universal Deliverance in *The Larger Sūtra of Eternal Life* in which Amida Buddha vows to save all beings with no discrimination whatsoever.

The first half of *The Letter on Hunting and Fishing* is reminiscent of Chapter 3 of *The Tanni shō,* which contains the paradoxical statement referring to Amida's Original Vow of Universal Deliverance: "Even a good man can attain birth, how much more readily, then, the person with bad karma!" What is called the peaceful awareness or true faith in Shin Buddhism is simply the act of entrusting oneself to Amida Buddha now, at this very moment, with one's whole being just as it is. It does not require one to wait until one has first ceased thinking bad thoughts and become a good person. Pure faith is spiritual freedom beyond the duality of good and bad.

Rennyo Shōnin declares, "We can simply make our living, whether in trade or domestic service, in hunting or fishing." Coming from a Buddhist leader, such a statement sounds very bold, because *ahiṃsa* – not to kill living beings – is one of the basic precepts of Buddhism. Killing is prohibited in Buddhism. Then what about the salvation of those who do make their living by hunting or fishing? Is there no way for them to become enlightened? Are they unable to attain birth in the Pure Land or to become Buddhas? If this were the case, it would contradict Amida's Original Vow of Universal Deliverance that preaches no discrimination at all, and is the very essence of Buddhism. Rennyo, the advocate of the teaching of Amida Buddha, would have been faced with this very serious problem. Amongst his followers there must have been both hunters and fishermen. Observing the reality of the society in which he lived with great insight whilst at the same time admitting that hunting and fishing were jobs of sinful karma, Rennyo Shōnin taught how those hunters and fishermen could still be saved. The only way to be saved from our own karma is to be awakened to the reality of our existence and at the same time to entrust ourselves to Amida Buddha.

The latter part of the letter discusses the meaning of the *Nenbutsu* after the attainment of Faith. The *Nenbutsu* is not a means to reach some goal, but an expression of gratitude for Amida's salvation. The *Nenbutsu* wells up from pure Faith. We express our thanks through the *Nenbutsu*. It is not an act performed in order to obtain something, but, as Rennyo says in the second paragraph, an expression of gratitude made purely for its own sake.

"*Nenbutsu* and Daily Living," one of the letters Hōnen gave his disciples, is also about how to live in this world and reads as follows,

Again Hōnen said, "As to how to lead your life, you should do so in a way that allows you to keep reciting the *Nenbutsu*. You must give up and turn your back on anything that might interfere with your life of the *Nenbutsu*. If you cannot live life reciting the *Nenbutsu* as a *hijiri,* or wandering holy person, then say the *Nenbutsu* as a married person. If you cannot live life saying the *Nenbutsu* as a married person, recite the Nenbutsu as a *hijiri*. If you cannot live life saying the *Nenbutsu* whilst staying in one place, then recite the *Nenbutsu* whilst on the move undertaking a religious pilgrimage. If you cannot live life reciting the *Nenbutsu* whilst undertaking a religious pilgrimage, then say the *Nenbutsu* whilst remaining at home. If you cannot live life reciting the *Nenbutsu* whilst feeding and clothing yourself by your own endeavours, then recite the *Nenbutsu* whilst others help you look after yourself. If you cannot live life saying the *Nenbutsu* whilst being helped by others, then say the *Nenbutsu* clothing and feeding yourself by your own endeavours. If you cannot live life reciting the *Nenbutsu* alone as an individual, then say the *Nenbutsu* together with your friends. If you cannot live life saying the *Nenbutsu* in the company of others, then say the *Nenbutsu* in seclusion all on your own. Three things – clothing, food and shelter – all help you live life saying the *Nenbutsu*. That is to say that, for the purpose of attaining birth peacefully and quietly through the *Nenbutsu*, everything works to help you say the *Nenbutsu*. Even if you are the sort of person whose wrongdoings lead to the three evil realms, you still nurture yourself with great care because you cannot abandon yourself. How much more, therefore, should you nurture and help yourself as the sort of person who recites the *Nenbutsu* to attain the great matter of birth? If you simply follow your desire without thinking of it as an activity to allow you to recite the *Nenbutsu*, it can become a karma that leads you to the three evil realms. But if you pursue your own desire in order to help you live life saying the *Nenbutsu* for birth in the Land of Bliss, then doing so can become an act that enables you to say the *Nenbutsu*. Everything is like this."[76]

I like this letter by Hōnen Shōnin. The *Nenbutsu* in this context is something coming forth from within, something profound welling up from the world beyond all duality. Hōnen declares that if there is any obstacle that prevents you from saying the *Nenbutsu*, you should just avoid it. According to my own interpretation, he is saying that you should live your life in a way that allows the *Nenbutsu* to come forth naturally.

The disciple asked Hōnen, "If only we put our trust in Amida's Original Vow, there is no doubt whatsoever about our future destiny, but what are we to do with the present world?" His understanding of Pure Land Buddhism was not deep enough. His words reveal that his trust or faith in Amida Buddha was only about his future destiny. Hōnen answered that we should live in this present world in a way that does not prevent us from saying the *Nenbutsu*.

The *Nenbutsu* often seems to be understood as a means whereby one attains birth in the Pure Land. People tend to believe that the *Nenbutsu* is a means to attain a certain goal. This is, however, different from the Shin Buddhist notion of the *Nenbutsu*. In Shin Buddhism it is already clear that through the attainment of faith in this present life we are assured of birth in the Pure Land. For Shinran Shōnin and Rennyo Shōnin, the *Nenbutsu* was entirely an expression of one's gratitude for Amida's gracious benevolence. In this context the *Nenbutsu* is not a means of obtaining that goal but a manifestation of the goal itself. The *Nenbutsu* is a spontaneous act that springs forth from pure faith.

Hōnen Shōnin's religious conversion was the very start of Japanese Pure Land Buddhism as an independent school. However this new way still retained many old religious concepts and traditions that were not compatible with Hōnen's own core philosophy. The most important point of this philosophy was that the Nenbutsu should be pronounced through one's encounter with the Original Vow of Amida Buddha. Hōnen Shōnin himself had attained pure faith in the Original Vow and started practising the *Nenbutsu* having felt the great compassion of Amida Buddha. For him the *Nenbutsu* was not a practice for attaining birth in the Pure Land but a manifestation of faith in Amida's Great Compassion expressed in the Original Vow. Furthermore, the *Nenbutsu* as the very manifestation of Amida's Great Compassion is both fundamental and beyond all duality. It is present prior to our choice of whether to pronounce it or not, or believe in it or not. Hōnen Shōnin continued to encounter the Original Vow throughout his life after the attainment of faith. In this sense it goes without saying that he recited the *Nenbutsu* with gratitude. Shinran follows him saying,

> As I reverently reflect on the outgoing ekō,[77] I find therein the great living and the great faith. The great living is to pronounce the Name of the Nyorai of Unimpeded Light.[78] In this living are embraced all good things and all the roots of virtue. They are instantly perfected [as soon as the Name is pronounced]. The Name is the treasure-ocean of virtues accruing from the absolute reality of Suchness. Therefore, it is called the Great Living.[79]

In Shinran Shōnin's case, it is apparent that to him the *Nenbutsu* is something beyond our self power. It is the great working of the Buddha coming out through our finite existence. Hence, the expression "the Great Living." Our act of saying the *Nenbutsu* is a manifestation of the great compassion of Amida Buddha. It is an expression of our gratitude for Amida's impartial love.

CHAPTER FOUR

Living with Thanks
without Any Thought
of Expectation

QUESTIONS AND ANSWERS

FASCICLE I, LETTER FOUR

QUESTION: I have learned that in Shinran Shōnin's tradition we are expected "to complete the act in daily life"[80] and not to adhere to Amida's "coming to meet us"[81] at the moment of death. What do you mean by this? I know very little about "completing the act in daily life" or about "not coming to meet us." I would like to listen to your teaching in greater detail.

ANSWER: Your questions do, indeed, touch on matters of vital importance in our tradition. As a basic principle our school teaches that "with the one thought-moment of awakening" "the act is completed in daily life." Once we have understood that it is due to the unfolding of the past good conditions that we come to be aware, through listening in our daily lives, of the way Amida Tathāgata's Original Vow saves us, then we can also understand that it is not by our own power but by the help of Other Power from the Buddha's Wisdom that we become aware of the way Amida's Original Vow works upon us. This is the meaning of "completing the act in daily life." Therefore "completing the act in daily life" refers to the state of mind of those who by listening have realised the above-mentioned principle and are confident that birth is assured. It is what is meant by such phrases as "with the one thought-moment of awakening, joining the company of those who are rightly assured,"[82] "completing the act in daily life" and "immediately attaining birth and dwelling at the stage of nonretrogression."[83]

QUESTION: I have fully understood the notion of "birth in the Pure Land with the one thought-moment of awakening." However, I still do not understand the meaning of "not coming to meet us." Could you kindly explain it for me?

ANSWER: Regarding the meaning of "not coming to meet us," once we comprehend that "with the one thought-moment of awakening, we join the company of those who are rightly assured of birth," then we do not need to wait for "Amida's coming to meet us." It is the people who perform various other practices that "wait for Amida to come to meet us." For those who practise true faith there is no longer any need to wait for "Amida's coming to meet us," because we realise that at the one thought-moment of instantaneous awakening we immediately receive "the benefit of the light that embraces all beings and never abandons them."[84]

Shinran Shōnin teaches, therefore, "Amida's coming to meet us is related to the notion of birth through various other practices. Because followers of true faith are embraced and never abandoned, they live in the company of those who are rightly assured. Because they dwell in the company of those who are rightly assured, they will attain Nirvāṇa without fail. Therefore, there is no need to wait for the moment of death and no need to expect Amida to come to meet us."[85] I hope these words have made things clearer for you.

QUESTION: Should we understand "being rightly assured" and "attaining Nirvāṇa" as being one benefit, or two?

ANSWER: With the one thought-moment of awakening of faith we join the company of those who are rightly assured of birth. This is the benefit we receive in this world of defilement. Following that, we should understand that it is in the Pure Land that we attain Nirvāṇa. We should therefore see them as two benefits.

QUESTION: I see now that birth is assured once we understand matters in the way you have explained. When we are still told, however, that we should go to the trouble of attaining faith, how should we understand that?

ANSWER: This question is indeed of great importance. If you understand matters in the way I have explained above, such understanding is exactly what we mean by "to have attained faith decisively."

QUESTION: I have clearly understood through listening that "having attained faith decisively" refers to "having completed the act in daily life," "Amida's not coming to meet us" and "dwelling in the company of those who are rightly assured." However, what I do not yet understand is whether, after attaining faith decisively, we should say the *Nenbutsu* for the sake of attaining birth in the Land of Utmost Bliss or as a way of expressing our gratitude to the Buddha for all he has done for us.

ANSWER: I think this question, too, is of vital importance for the good reason that we should not think of the *Nenbutsu* pronounced after the one thought-moment of awakening of faith as an act carried out for the sake of attaining birth. It should be understood solely as a grateful response to the Buddha for what he has done for us. This is why Shàndǎo made the following comment about the *Nenbutsu*, "spending one's whole life at the upper limit, one thought-moment at the lower."[86] I understand "one thought-moment at the lower" to refer to "attaining faith decisively" and "spending one's whole life" to mean the *Nenbutsu* pronounced as a grateful response to the Buddha for all he has done for us. Hence, it is extremely important that you really grasp this point.

Most humbly and respectfully
On 27th November, Bunmei 4 [1472].

COMMENTS

As can be seen from the last line, this letter was written during the Hōonkō, the most important ceremony of the year in Shin Buddhism, held to commemorate the death of Shinran Shōnin (1173–1262). Over two centuries later, at the time of the memorial service for the founder, Rennyo must have had some very special thoughts and feelings as he wrote the letter.

The points Rennyo refers to are very important in Shin Buddhism and help clarify some essentials of Shin Buddhist thought that distinguishes the school sharply from other Pure Land schools. Amongst those points two are of vital importance: firstly *heizei gōjō* 平生業成 – to complete the act in daily life, and secondly *furaikō* 不来迎 – Amida's not coming to meet us. It is particularly noteworthy that these two points are closely related to the content of a letter written by Shinran Shōnin at the age of seventy-nine, which Rennyo Shōnin succinctly summarises here in his own letter. Another point, namely that we should say the *Nenbutsu* as a way of expressing our gratitude to the Buddha for what he has done for us, is also typically Shin Buddhist and is closely connected to the point that we should not practise the *Nenbutsu* in the expectation that it will make us attain birth in the Pure Land. The *Nenbutsu* is a pure act free of all expectations. It is "doing for the doing," or, if you like, it is the art of living a life full of thanks.

Considering the emphasis of other Pure Land schools on the deathbed ceremony during that period, the first two points Rennyo Shōnin refers to in his letter are extremely important. As I mentioned in my book *Great Living: In the Pure Encounter between Master and Disciple*[87], Genshin (源信 942–1017) and his friends organised Pure Land meetings, known as the *Nijūgo sanmai kō* 二十五三昧講, where much emphasis was laid on the importance of the *Nenbutsu* at the moment of death:

"Through his main work the *Ōjō yōshū* (*The Essentials for Rebirth in the Pure Land*) Genshin demystified the practice of *Nenbutsu*, making it much more accessible to ordinary people. Although this is not the place to go into details about his doctrine, the crucial point is that he laid particular emphasis on reciting the *Nenbutsu* at the very end of one's life. If one pronounced Amida's Name singlemindedly at that point, he declared that one would surely be born into the Pure Land, even if one had not been able to practice the *Nenbutsu* during one's lifetime as often as the priests might have done. In his opinion the power of a single pure thought at the very end of one's life would far outweigh the karma accumulated over an entire lifetime.

"Based on this conclusion of the *Ōjō yōshū*, Genshin organised the *Nijūgosanmaikō*, meetings for groups of twenty-five people to practise the *Nenbutsu-samādhi*. In these religious groups, twenty-five members formed one unit and would help each other practise the *Nenbutsu*, especially in the last moments of life. When one of them lay on his death-bed, all the others would gather around and, as his good friends, encourage him to pronounce Amida's Name.

"In the *Ōjō yōshū* we read: 'It may be asked, "All good practices are virtuous, and each enables one to attain birth in the Pure Land. Why is it then that the teaching of the *Nenbutsu* alone is encouraged?" In answer, I would say "When I now encourage everyone to practise the *Nenbutsu* I do not mean to set aside the various other good practices. What I mean to say is that the *Nenbutsu* is not difficult to perform for either man or woman, whether high-born or low-born, whether walking or staying, sitting or lying, and no matter when, where and under what kind of karmic condition. Moreover, when anyone is on his death-bed and desires to be born in the Pure Land, no practice is more accessible than the *Nenbutsu*.'[88]

"Once Genshin had introduced the idea of the *Nijūgo sanmai kō* the number of these religious groups multiplied rapidly. One group had their own special house for funerals. When one of them lay dying, he was brought to the house, and a special ritual was held for his birth in the Pure Land. This was available not only to priests but also to ordinary people, women as well as men. In this way Genshin made the practice of *Nenbutsu* much more popular and widespread than before."[89]

As Genshin exercised enormous influence over his contemporaries, the emphasis on pronouncing the *Nenbutsu* at the moment of death was deeply embedded in Japanese Pure Land Buddhism. Whilst on the one hand the stress laid on the deathbed ceremony popularised the practice of *Nenbutsu* among people by making it more accessible and practicable, on the other hand it caused the psychological postponement of a decision that needed to be made straight away. If they are to be solved at all, we should solve our problems here and now. If we postpone such an important decision to the future, we will never find the solution. In Shin Buddhism what is most important is the instantaneous awakening of faith and it comes about here and now in daily life. Thus Rennyo Shōnin explains that our school teaches as a basic principle that the act that enables us to attain birth is completed in daily life through the one thought-moment of awakening of faith. For this reason we do not need to wait for Amida Buddha to come to meet us at the actual moment of death.

These two original features of Shinran's religious thought were repeatedly clarified by Rennyo in his own way, not only in this letter but also in several other letters as well. As mentioned before, these two points covered in this letter seem to be deeply related to the contents of Shinran's letter addressed to one of his disciples at the age of seventy-nine.

The textual origin of such an interpretation by Shinran Shōnin and his followers can be traced back to a passage in *The Larger Sūtra of Eternal Life*: "When they desire to be born in the Pure Land, they will immediately attain birth and dwell at a stage of nonretrogression." This passage, too, is quoted in this letter as "immediately attaining birth and dwelling at a stage of nonretrogression." In this context the one thought-moment of awakening of faith is referred to as "birth in the Pure Land."

In Shin Buddhism it is clear that birth in the Pure Land has two meanings: firstly awakening of faith and secondly ultimately attaining Nirvāṇa in the Pure Land. These two meanings pertain respectively to "the two benefits" mentioned in the letter. With the instantaneous awakening of faith we are immediately born in the Pure Land.

However, as long as we live in this world, we cannot get rid of the bifurcation of consciousness. Immediately after the awakening of faith, our everyday consciousness comes flooding back and we are not completely free of dualistic consciousness. So Rennyo Shōnin says that those who have attained true faith are called those who have completed the act in daily life. They are said "to dwell in the company of those who are rightly assured of birth," and also "to dwell at a stage of nonretrogression." And they are absolutely confident of ultimately attaining Nirvāṇa.[90]

A Seeker after Truth

ON PILGRIMAGE IN THE SNOW

FASCICLE I, LETTER FIVE

To begin with, although a large number of pilgrims, priests and lay people, both men and women, especially from the three provinces of Kashū, Noto and Etchū[91], have flocked to this hill at Yoshizaki this year, I am not quite certain of what sort of understanding each of these visitors actually has.

The reason for this is that in our tradition, most importantly, assurance of birth in the Land of Utmost Bliss is something given through the attainment of Other Power faith. Within our school, however, there seems to be no one who has attained firm faith. How can people like this readily attain birth in the Land of Enjoyment? This is a matter of great importance. What is the state of mind of those people who have come to visit the temple under this fall of snow, having been fortunate enough to withstand a long journey of some twenty to forty kilometres? This is something that worries me greatly. Whatever has been their understanding in the past, I would like to tell them in detail what they should bear in mind from now on. I ask you to open your ears and listen very carefully.

The point is to embrace with your mind Other Power faith very firmly and, basing yourself on that, to pronounce the *Nenbutsu*, whether walking, standing, sitting or lying down, in grateful response to the Buddha for all he has done for you.

If you understand this point your birth to come is absolutely assured. If you are filled with joy like this you should go to the temples of the priests whom you respect as teachers and give a donation to express your gratitude. Such a follower could be called a person of faith, one who has fully understood the teaching of our tradition.

Most humbly and respectfully
On 8th February, Bunmei 5 [1473].

COMMENTS

The letter was written on 8th February 1473, two years after Rennyo Shōnin had established a temple at Yoshizaki in Echizen Province within Hokuriku District. He had moved from Kyoto to Ōmi and again from Ōmi to Yoshizaki in order to escape the repeated attacks of militant soldier monks on Mount Hiei. Within a few years of moving to Yoshizaki, he had become so popular and his teaching had spread so rapidly, that huge numbers of people would come flocking to Yoshizaki not only from Echizen but also from Kashū, Noto and Etchū to attend the meetings he held there.

February is the coldest month in Japan and Hokuriku District is famous for its heavy snowfalls. In winter the snow lies several metres deep and in some areas people go in and out through doors at an upper floor level. Observing the multitudes who had gathered at the temple in order to listen to his teaching, Rennyo wrote this letter.

Whenever I read out *On Pilgrimage in the Snow*, it reminds me of Dōshū (d. 1516), one of Rennyo's disciples, who is also known as a Myōkōnin. Amongst Shin Buddhist followers those particularly rich in faith and goodness are called Myōkōnin. Their faith is extremely pure.

Although it is by no means certain whether Dōshū was already present amongst those followers who had gathered at Yoshizaki on the day the letter was written, Dōshū was actually brought up in that same district and became a devout Pure Land Buddhist through his encounter with Rennyo Shōnin. He is also said to have served as an escort-guard to Rennyo for a certain length of time. There is no doubt that, as a seeker after truth, possessed of extremely strong mental fortitude, he worked for Rennyo with utmost spiritual devotion. Dōshū's relation to Rennyo is a very good example of the relationship between master and disciple in Shin Buddhism.

Of Dōshū's life we know very little except through a number of historical documents: *The Rennyo Shōnin Goichidai ki kikigaki*, Articles 45, 130, 131, 192 and 281, and *The Resolutions Made on 24th December, First Year of Bunki*. These records that are believed to have been made by his contemporaries are very important for finding out about Dōshū. In particular the last document, usually known as *Dōshū's Twenty-one Resolutions*, is invaluable because it was written by him. It gives us a glimpse of his spiritual life.

Firstly I would like to introduce you to Articles 45, 130, 131, and 192 of *The Goichidai ki kikigaki*.

> Article 45. Dōshū of Akao said, "As a matter of daily concern, you should never neglect the morning service at the family altar, you should make monthly visits to the nearest temple to worship the Founder of our tradition; and each year you should make a pilgrimage to the Head Temple." On hearing what he had said, Reverend Ennyo declared, "How remarkable for him to have spoken like that!"[92]

Dōshū died in 1516 but the date of his birth is unknown. He was born in Etchū Province now called Toyama prefecture in a small village named Akao near the upper reaches of the Shō River. Akao is now part of the World Heritage site, Shirogamisanchi, comprising several villages with traditional thatched houses. To reach Akao one must travel a distance of over twenty miles after leaving Jōgahana, a perilous journey through deep valleys and high mountains. Nowadays we can go there by car. In those days, however, the mountain path was so dangerous that the slightest misstep would have meant a lethal fall. There was at least one particularly dangerous gully one had to negotiate using a box and ropes. In winter the region lies under more than 20 feet of snow. A trip between Akao, where Dōshū lived, and the Honganji Branch Temple at Jōgahana must have been made at the risk of his life.

According to *The Shūjin ki* Dōshū would travel from time to time to the Head Temple in Kyoto or to the other temples in his country, usually spending very little time at home. He would go to see Rennyo two or three times a year. Whenever he visited him, he stayed with him for a few months, enjoying discussions about faith with him and also attending to him as an escort-guard. When he went back to his own country, he often visited his friends at various temples.

One evening Dōshū arrived in Kyoto to see Rennyo, and found him sitting in a room without any light. Whilst seated outside the room, Dōshū received a very warm greeting from the Master. Rennyo Shōnin was actually delighted to have Dōshū visit his place and declared, "You are most welcome to Kyoto." As soon as Dōshū heard these words, the room shone with light. Dōshū thought at first it was moonlight entering the room but then found that the light was issuing from his Master's body. In a while the light was gone. Then he gazed at the features of Rennyo. If nothing else this story from *The*

Shūjin ki indicates how much Dōshū revered Rennyo, who was to him an embodiment of Amida Buddha.

According to the legend of Gyōtokuji Temple[93], whilst Rennyo was staying in the Branch Temple at Jōgahana, Dōshū would visit him every day travelling twenty miles from Akao. One day, however, apparently due to a heavy snowstorm Dōshū had difficulty in arriving in time for the service. Rennyo turned to the people around him, saying "Please, wait for him to arrive. He will definitely appear." After a while Dōshū did arrive, frozen and covered in snow. Then they rang the bell to start the service. What a beautiful story it is of the relationship between these two! It defies description.

> Article 131. Dōshū said, "Even though I have been hearing one particular word repeatedly, I always feel as grateful as if I were hearing it for the very first time."[94]

What Rennyo states in Article 130 seems to be related to this.

> Article 130. Rennyo Shōnin said, "After attaining faith you should feel each thing as new and fresh, even though you might have heard the same thing many times before. Usually people wish for something completely new and different. However, no matter how many times you hear something, it should be heard in a way that is as fresh and as new as if it were being heard for the very first time."[95]

These two items illustrate something important about spiritual life, showing how with the Myōkōnin spirituality is always fresh and new. A man of pure faith is not attached to anything from the self-centred world, but is always open to what is happening to him. Because he knows how to free himself from attachment, in his spiritual life each thing is always experienced as if for the very first time. No matter how many times he encounters something, it is always fresh and new.

> Article 192. It would be very shameful to think that an order given by our Master might be impossible to achieve. You should consider anything possible if it is Master's order. If it is feasible for an ordinary person to become a Buddha, how can anything else remain impossible? Therefore Dōshū once said he would fill Lake Biwa up with mud with his own hands if ordered to do so by his Master.[96]

Let me quote some other beautiful stories recorded in D. T. Suzuki's *Japanese Spirituality*:

"[Dōshū] took great pains to collect the *Ofumi* (*Gobunshō,* 'Honorable Letters'),[97] letters written by Rennyo to his followers. This was not merely because he wished them for his own sake, to help him attain faith. He wanted them to show to the villagers of Akao as well, to help instruct them in the Way. Number 281 in Rennyo's *Goichidai ki kikigaki* states: 'Dōshū, begging Rennyo to give him some written instruction, was told: 'You may lose a letter, but faith kept in the heart can never be lost.' Nevertheless, the following year [Rennyo] acceded to Dōshū's request.'[98]

The next story tells how once, while Dōshū was setting out for Kyoto, his wife asked that he obtain from Rennyo some instruction for her concerning the acquiring of faith. After a long and arduous return trip from Kyoto, before even stopping to take off his straw sandals, he produced a piece of paper on which was written the six letters, *Namu Amidabutsu.* This brought a look of some disappointment from his wife, who had obviously expected something more detailed. Seeing her reaction, and still without having taken off his footwear, he said, 'All right,' and set off for Kyoto once again, many miles, days, and hardships distant. Though he had that very moment returned from a more than ten day trip through the mountains, he began the same journey once more. I think this story – even if only legendary – enables us to understand the extent of Dōshū's purity and honesty, such that hardship and privation could make no inroad."[99]

Dōshū's *Twenty-One Resolutions* is a marvellous piece of writing that will surely give you an insight into the essence of his religious experience.

The Resolutions Made on 24th December, 1st Year of Bunki

1. As long as you live, never be negligent of the One Great Matter of Rebirth.
2. If anything other than the Buddha-dharma enters deeply into your heart, consider it shameful and renounce it immediately.
3. When you find yourself reluctant to proceed positively and self-indulgent, you should resolutely break free of such a selfish mind and move forward.
4. If you are hoping for some unfair, selfish gain from your relation to the Buddha-dharma, you should consider it shameful and immediately and without any hesitation withdraw your hands and relinquish all connection with it.
5. Hold no favouritism in your heart. Do no harm to others out of favouritism.
6. Being aware that you are always being watched [by the Buddha],

you should give up all your wrong thoughts even when no one is watching you.

7. You must deeply believe and highly respect the Buddha-dharma. Be thoroughly humble yourself and behave with care.

8. It is deeply shameful to consider trying to get others to give you an important position on the strength of the Buddha-dharma. Should such an intention ever cross your mind, remember that the only reason for having faith in the Buddha-dharma is to help you attain the One Great Matter of Rebirth on this occasion, and relinquish all such thoughts.

9. If you find yourself in some quarter where wrongdoing is being committed, leave without arguing whether it is right or wrong.

10. The very thought that You are watching how wretched I am brings me the deepest sadness and pain. Though I am well aware You have forgiven me for all my former actions, the fact that You know my inner state of mind is cause for utter shame, making me realise my extreme wretchedness and sadness. When I consider that my heart was anchored in such wretchedness in the previous world and that as a result it still is so even now, I am at a loss for words to express how utterly wretched I am. Even if I chanced to meet You in the end, I would still feel what a wretched heart is mine! Oh, how humbly I receive your compassion! I have lived up until today solely begging Your forgiveness for my prior bad acts. I am coming to You entrusting myself to Your teaching.

11. If you are still alive today or tomorrow and you become lazy with regard to the Dharma, you must consider it shameful. Break free of your laziness of mind and behave yourself.

12. If your heart does not fill with a sense of wonderment you should consider it shameful and irreverent. Resolve that, though you starve or freeze to death in this present life, you will now attain the One Great Matter of Rebirth, considering that this will be the fulfilment of your desire from beginningless time. Do investigate yourself resolutely, with a critical mind, in order to recover your sense of wonderment as soon as possible. If even then the sense of wonderment is missing, consider that you are probably being punished. Break free of your laziness of mind and praise the Dharma in the presence of fellow devotees, because these acts will lead you at least to a sense of wonderment.

13. You must not fall into the worst mistake of being self-indulgent. Do not sleep away your life in vain, failing to consider the One Great Matter.

14. Do not use the fact that you do not have any good friends as an excuse. When you meet members of your family, though they themselves

may not be conscious of the Dharma, behave towards them as well as possible, and ask them first of all what they think about the One Great Matter. Preserving a sense of wonderment in your heart, behave yourself.

15. Bear in mind fully that the matters of the *dōjō*[100] are of great importance.

16. You must not harbour thoughts of hate or revenge toward those who hate you.

17. You must simply cherish the One Great Matter deep in your heart. Do not be negligent of it. You should immediately follow the corrections proffered by your fellow-followers.

18. Do not become attached to anything! Oh, my mind! Just hold deep in your heart this One Great Matter!

19. The reason why I am writing like this is because I am shallow-minded and full of shame. If I talk about my mind in this way, therefore, and make resolutions, I hope something will be forthcoming. I will not fail over and over again to follow the corrections of others.

20. I do hope You will pour Your special compassion over me, to keep me from going astray and to correct what is in my heart. Nothing else.

21. Oh, this wretched heart! If I am able to attain the One Great Matter I will not count my life as of any importance. Wherever I am ordered to go, I will go. I will even resolve to journey to China or India in search of the Dharma. As long as I hold to this resolve, it is easy, isn't it, to obey Your order and follow Your teaching unreservedly? Again, my heart! Life only lasts but a moment. You will not be here long. Do not mind starving or freezing to death. Never be neglectful of the One Great Matter. My heart! Do not go against these resolutions. Investigate yourself with a critical mind, and behave yourself to the very end. Never breach the laws and rules of society. Also, inwardly be mindful of the great virtue of the one thought-moment and be grateful for it, and outwardly behave yourself with deep humility. I entreat you, my heart!

Dōshū[101]

The most important point we should bear in mind when reading Dōshū's *Resolutions* is that we should not interpret this kind of religious document from a so-called objective viewpoint. If you depend on objective observation, the document will lose its integrity and become fragmented. The speaker, Dōshū, is talking to himself from beginning to end. Almost all of his words are addressed to himself using the word "you." Being always illumined by Rennyo's teaching of Amida Buddha, he looks into himself, the sad reality of his karmic existence. In doing so, he calls himself "you", which shows his humble and sincere confrontation with his own existence. This strict self-examination, however, naturally leads to his re-encounter with Amida Buddha, for, in accordance with Rennyo's teaching, Dōshū himself, one of the *Nenbutsu* followers, and Amida Buddha are originally one in *Namu Amida-butsu.*

To conclude Dōshū is always facing Rennyo, hence Amida Buddha, because Rennyo Shōnin *is* an embodiment of Amida Buddha to Dōshū. Especially in the context of Resolution 10 and the first half of Resolution 21, the one who is addressed as "You" can be Amida and also Rennyo Shōnin at the same time. If you read the text with this point in mind, the whole document will sound much more profound and lively. The date of *The Twenty-One Resolutions* shows that it was written two years and nine months after the death of his Master, Rennyo Shōnin, on the eve of the monthly memorial service to him.

CHAPTER SIX

Drowsiness and Living by Faith

ON DROWSINESS

FASCICLE I, LETTER SIX

Recently, since the beginning of summer in fact, I have been feeling unusually drowsy. When I ask myself why I am so sleepy, it appears obvious to me that the moment of death leading to birth is now fast approaching. This thought makes me feel really miserable and I am very conscious of the sorrow of parting. Right up until this very moment, however, I have always prepared myself diligently, mindful that the time of birth might be at hand. It reminds me that all I continuously pray for day and night is that, after my death also, those who have been decisively awakened to faith at this temple may suffer no retrogression. As long as things continue as they are, there should be no immediate difficulties if I die. This having been said, however, I must also say that I find you all very negligent. As long as we live, this is the general tendency. I am altogether dissatisfied with your present state of mind. As regards our lives, even tomorrow is uncertain and, no matter what we say, nothing will be of any avail when our lives come to an end. If our doubts are not entirely dispelled during this life, we will surely end up with regrets. This point is something you really must understand.

Most humbly and respectfully

This is addressed to those on the other side of the sliding doors. In future years, please take it out and read it.

Written on 25th April, Bunmei 5 [1473].

COMMENTS

At first glance there appears to be nothing of special note in this letter. In his usual way Rennyo Shōnin is simply encouraging people to be awakened to faith (*shinjin*) and to continue to keep their faith alive and active. The important point, however, is that he does this especially by cautioning them against "drowsiness."

In Buddhism, as you may know, sleeping is recognised as something that makes our minds sluggish. Whilst asleep, our intellect and five senses do not work effectively. Desire for sleep, therefore, is counted as one of the blind passions.

We know, however, that adequate sleep will give us rest and refresh our bodies and minds, particularly when we are too tired to work any longer. Medically speaking it is also known that some measure of peaceful sleep is necessary to maintain health, both mental and physical. The problem is how far to control our desire for sleep, given that we are also aware that sleep makes the body and mind inactive. Too much sleep or indulgence in sleep is definitely considered an obstacle to mental activity.

When we face serious problems, sometimes we cannot sleep because of the tension caused by those problems. This state of mind is not too bad, because we are still aware of the problems. What is worse is our mental attempts, whether conscious or unconscious, to avoid confronting those problems. One such attempt is to adopt the psychological attitude whereby our minds become inactive and we refuse to see the reality of the world. If we take this to extremes, we could suffer from insanity. This may sound very peculiar, but if we look at the people around us we will find such mental phenomena are not peculiar but rather general and commonly found in the daily consciousness of those who are still sleeping in illusion. In this sense we are all sleeping, not yet awakened or enlightened. More or less everyone has such psychological problems, but people are usually unaware of them.

When we find Rennyo referring to drowsiness or sleepiness in his letter, it goes without saying that we have to understand the words in the context of Buddhism, for Rennyo understands our daily drowsiness from a deeper level, where sleeping is illusion, the opposite of Enlightenment or awakening.

In addition to gaining some philosophical or psychological insight into the matter, it would also seem to be very important for us to know something of the historical background to this letter. Although there are very few relevant historical documents, fortunately two other letters exist which seem closely related to this one. I would like to try and clarify the purport of Rennyo's letter by referring to them. Rennyo wrote those letters in the same year, 1473. One of them, entitled *The Family Members from Kyoto*, was written in May and the other, entitled *Kengyoku-ni's Birth*,[102] was written on 22nd August. Both are included in *The Other Letters Not Compiled in The Five Fascicle Letters.*[103]

In this context the postscript at the end of Rennyo Shōnin's letter *On Drowsiness* is very important, mentioning as it does those to whom the letter is addressed. "This is addressed to those on the other side of the sliding doors. In future years, please take it out and read it."

Amongst several opinions concerning the genesis of this letter, the most reliable holds that the letter was written when Kengyoku-ni, Rennyo Shōnin's second daughter, was seriously ill in bed and that "those on the other side of the sliding doors," therefore, meant those who attended her at that time. Because her attendants were exclusively taken up with nursing her at that time, Rennyo said, "In future years, please take it out and read it." The sickness finally led to Kengyoku-ni's death.

According to the letter *Kengyoku-ni's Birth*, Kengyoku-ni died on 14th August after having been confined to bed for over three months. When she was young, because of the poverty of her family at the time, Kengyoku-ni was sent to a Zen temple to work as a *kasshiki*, a young attendant in a Zen temple, whose duties included such things as saying when meals were ready, and then went to Jōke-in, a temple belonging to the Pure Land School (浄土宗 Jōdoshū). Rennyo says in the letter *Kengyoku-ni's Birth*:

Whilst confined to bed by illness, Kengyoku-ni said that she was extremely happy to have attained peaceful awareness (*anjin*) according to our traditions, having forsaken the traditions of Jōke-in. In particular, just one day before her death, she said that her peaceful awareness had been decisively settled, at a far deeper level than before, and expressed her gratitude to the people around her for taking the trouble of being with her over the past days. Moreover, she talked about every thought that she had held in her daily life. Finally she attained birth around the end of the time of dragon (10:00 a.m.) on 14th August, with her head to the north and her face to the west.[104]

Rennyo talks about his own dream in the same letter,

> There is a person who had a wondrous vision at dawn after the cremation
> on 15th August. In this dream three blue lotus flowers appeared from
> the white bones burnt into smoke at the garden of cremation. A golden
> Buddha one inch in height and shining with light was observed emerging
> from those same lotus flowers. Then the Buddha appeared to turn into
> a butterfly and was gone and the person came out from the dream. This
> was a manifestation of the Jewel called Tathatā or Dharmatā, known as
> Kengyoku-ni. The reason why it seemed to have become a butterfly and
> gone is because her soul, having become a butterfly, flew into the Sky
> of Dharmatā, the Land of Extreme Bliss, the Castle of Nirvāṇa. This is
> known for a certainty.[105]

When he himself is involved in a story he is relating, Rennyo sometimes refers
to himself in the third person.

These two quotations come from the beautiful, long letter, *Kengyoku-ni*,
written eight days after Rennyo Shōnin's daughter's death. From the paragraphs quoted above you can see how happy Rennyo was to be able to confirm
his daughter's attainment of faith just before her death at the age of twenty
five. The narration of his own dream, in which his daughter flew into the Sky
of Dharmatā as a butterfly, is extremely beautiful.

His fourth child, Kengyoku-ni, was an unfortunate girl in a worldly sense.
When Rennyo Shōnin wrote the letter, *On Drowsiness*, she was ill in bed,
having returned home to him after some bitter experience in life. He addressed
the letter to Kengyoku-ni and those around her who were taking care of
her. According to his letter, *Kengyoku-ni's Birth*, it seems that his daughter
attained faith in her final days after coming back to her father. Judging from
the first part of the letter, *On Drowsiness*, Rennyo himself was not very well.
He must have felt great love and tenderness towards his unfortunate daughter
as he watched her ill in bed, attaining pure faith towards the end of her life.

Whilst the first half of the letter sounds as if Rennyo was talking to
his daughter, the latter part is quite severe and strict. This part was really
addressed to those who were taking care of her, including several members
of his family who were not very serious about the attainment of faith, the One
Great Matter of Rebirth in the Pure Land.

The other letter closely related to this one is entitled, *The Family Members
from Kyoto*.[106] The content of the letter is Rennyo Shōnin's strict admonition
of his own family members, mainly his children, against their indulgence in
sleep. Some of them must have been amongst "those on the other side of the
sliding doors." They may have been unaware of the problem of drowsiness.
Rennyo says in the letter that, although 'a person', namely Rennyo himself,

talked about his own drowsiness as something shameful, a young man from Kyoto, actually one of Shōnin's children, responded badly, saying they would not mind even if such drowsiness came about, because they knew about faith, reciting the *Nenbutsu* frequently and doing no miscellaneous practice. This is just one example of the conversation between Rennyo and his sons that he refers to in the letter.

This letter, *The Family Members from Kyoto*, was written in May 1473. Because the letter, *On Drowsiness*, had been written on 25th April of the same year, the conversation mentioned in *The Family Members from Kyoto* could have occurred after reading the latter. Rennyo strongly criticises his children because of their attitude towards drowsiness and also because of their laziness and arrogance.

As I said at the beginning of this chapter, we need to understand why Buddhists are rather negative in their attitude to drowsiness or sleepiness.

The situation with Kengyoku-ni was really serious. If those attending her were not fully awakened and did not know what to do or how to behave towards her, however, they could have indulged in sleeping to avoid the problem.

Rennyo says to such people, "As regards our lives, even tomorrow is uncertain and no matter what we say, nothing will be of any avail when our lives come to an end. If our doubts are not entirely dispelled during this life, we will surely end up with regrets." We should never be negligent of the One Great Matter of Rebirth in the Pure Land, always aware of Amida Buddha's Original Vow, at the same time keeping insight into the reality of our own world. Drowsiness and indulgence in sleep are apt to make our consciousness dull and inactive, sometimes leading to the destruction of life. With alert awareness of the problem of drowsiness and desire for sleep, we should go forward step by step in the direction of love and respect for all the lives under the light of Amida Buddha's Original Vow. The essence of vigilant attentiveness against drowsiness or sleepiness lies in loving life with the deepest respect. When we find ourselves continuously drowsy and our minds do not work actively, we should be very careful about such mental conditions. For such drowsiness is often embedded in self-centredness and leads us to harm others by making our minds inactive. Rennyo Shōnin's vigilant attentiveness against sleepiness is based on his love and respect for others.

CHAPTER SEVEN

On Women's Attainment of Birth in the Pure Land

HALFWAY THROUGH MARCH

FASCICLE I, LETTER SEVEN

As I remember, halfway through March of last year, the fourth year of Bunmei (1472), a few women of obvious good upbringing, accompanied by their male attendants, were talking about this hill. "A temple has recently been built on the hill known as Yoshizaki," they said. "What a wonderful place it is, it quite defies description! It is widely known that a multitude of followers—priests and lay people, men and women—flock to the hill, particularly from the seven provinces of Kaga, Etchū, Noto, Echigo, Shinano, Dewa, and Ōshū.[107] How marvellous it is that this should be happening in this Last Dharma age. It seems no trivial matter. We would like to know in detail how all these followers are encouraged to practise the *Nenbutsu* teaching and, in particular, what it means when people say that faith is taught as being the most important thing of all. As we are wretched women, weighed down by bad karma, we too would like to attain birth [in the Pure Land] simply by listening humbly and learning to understand what is called faith."

When they sought to question a priest living on the mountain, he answered, "Without doing anything special but simply realising that we are wretched beings burdened with the ten bad acts, the five grave offences, the five obstacles and the three submissions, we must understand at a very deep level that Amida Tathāgata is a manifested form appearing to save such wretched persons as ourselves. When the one thought-moment arises in which we entreat Amida Tathāgata to help us by entrusting ourselves to him without double-mindedness, the Tathāgata sends forth eighty-four thousand rays of light in order to enfold us with loving grace. This is what is meant by the phrase[108] that Amida Tathāgata embraces those who practise the *Nenbutsu*. 'To embrace and never to abandon' means 'to welcome and not to forsake.' People who understand this point are called those who have attained faith. In addition to this, we should understand that the *Nenbutsu*, "*Namu Amida-butsu*," which we say all the time, whether sleeping or waking, standing or sitting, is exactly the same *Nenbutsu*, "*Namu Amida-butsu*" that, after having been saved by Amida, we pronounce as an expression of our gratitude to Amida for all that he has done for us."

When he had kindly explained all this, the women and those accompanying them replied, "We cannot tell you how ashamed we feel at not having entrusted ourselves until now to Amida Tathāgata's Original Vow which so perfectly suits those like ourselves of limited capacity. From now on we will entrust ourselves wholeheartedly to Amida; and, believing at this one thought-moment without any double-mindedness that our birth has already been assured by the saving work of the Tathāgata, we will bear in mind that the *Nenbutsu* is henceforward the pronouncing of the Name to express our gratitude to the Buddha for what he has done for us. There is no way to express how grateful and reverential we feel towards the incomparable Dharma we have chanced to encounter through inconceivable conditions from the distant past. Now it is time for us to depart." At that, with tears in their eyes, they took their leave.

Most humbly and respectfully
On 12th August, Bunmei 5 [1473].

COMMENTS

This letter is one of a number of letters in the five fascicle collection that refer specifically to women's attainment of birth in the Pure Land, which is one of the most important teachings emphasised in Shin Buddhism.

Historically it was Śākyamuni Buddha himself who allowed women to enter the Sangha. The ultimate purpose of living in a Sangha is to attain

Enlightenment, so it follows that the Buddha thought that not only men but women also were able to attain Enlightenment. In Buddhism all human beings are of equal value in their spiritual quality. Mahāyāna Buddhism saw the development of the notion of Buddha-nature. Everyone, it is believed, has Buddha-nature, the possibility of themselves becoming a Buddha. It is a matter of principle that there should be no petty discriminations in Buddhism.

In actual fact, however, in the long history of its transmission Buddhism underwent a great many changes. Not only in India, where it first originated, but also in the other countries to which it spread, Buddhism was much influenced by the different societies, cultures, philosophies and religions with which it came into contact. Furthermore, because those countries to which Buddhism spread were already androcentric societies, where men were believed to be superior to women, Buddhism itself was considerably affected by androcentric influences. In the course of adapting to different times and societies, Buddhism deviated from the original idea of perfect equality and absence of discrimination. Regretfully a number of examples of discrimination against women can be found in Buddhist documents. For example, we find in the early stages of Buddhism in ancient India that the idea of discriminating against women was deeply connected with the concept of karma.

In Pure Land Buddhism and particularly in Shin Buddhism the birth of women in the Pure Land was vigorously proclaimed by Shinran Shōnin and Rennyo Shōnin and any kind of unpleasant discrimination was strongly repudiated. To accomplish his purpose Rennyo adopted with great care the course of discrediting the discriminatory ideas which can be found in Buddhist texts.

This letter by Rennyo, relaying a conversation between "a few women of obvious good upbringing" and a priest living at Yoshizaki, reminds me of a group of ladies I once came across at Shogyoji Temple when I was young. They were all disciples of Daigyōin-sama, the Venerable Reion Takehara. There was an aura of spiritual nobility about them. They cooperated in the creation of the Shogyoji Sangha with pure faith in their hearts. One of the ladies was Ekai-sama, my first spiritual leader and master, who enabled me to change the course of my life and choose the path that led to my becoming a Buddhist priest. After the death of her own master, Daigyōin-sama, Ekai-sama became the effective leader of Shogyoji Temple for some forty years. She brought numerous people to the Shin Buddhist faith and was instrumental in making young people such as my present master, the head priest of Shogyoji, and me become Shin Buddhist priests. She really was the spiritual leader of the temple. The reason why I am talking about Ekai-sama in this context is because I think Ekai-sama provides a very good example of a woman's attainment of pure faith, way beyond the reaches of social discrimination against women. Indeed Ekai-sama provides the very best model of this kind of woman in the whole history of Pure Land Buddhism. Acutely aware of the reality of this world, she gave spiritual advice and suggestions not only to those who lived alongside her in the temple but also to those who visited the temple, seeking to solve problems in their own lives. Everything she did was a natural manifestation of her own pure faith. Needless to say there were many problems in daily life even in the temple. But with pure faith in her heart Ekai-sama would help people solve their own problems in the light of the teaching of Shinran Shōnin, the founder of Shin Buddhism.

The name of Yoshizaki, where Rennyo Shōnin had so successfully built a temple in Hokuriku District, is connected in my memory somehow to the development of Shogyoji Temple. When first I visited Shogyoji Temple it was still a little temple. Small as it was, however, the temple had an atmosphere of absolute purity, complete peace and utter tranquility. It seemed almost like a Zen temple. Under the leadership of Ekai-sama the temple steadily developed. Now over two hundred people, both priests and lay followers, live together harmoniously in the temple with my present master, Venerable Chimyo Takehara, as their leader.

Coming back now to the phrase, "a few women of obvious good upbringing," there are several different opinions as to who these women may have been. The most trustworthy opinion found in the *Ofumi kiji shu* by Erin[109] would have us believe that one of those women was the wife of Asakura Tsunekage, younger brother of Asakura Toshikage, the then Lord of Echizen Province. She visited the temple at Yoshizaki accompanied by some people for the purpose of inquiring about the Shin Buddhist faith. The "priest living on the mountain" who replies to them in the second paragraph of the letter is believed to have been Kūzen,[110] one of Rennyo Shōnin's disciples and the author of *The Daihasso onmonogatari kūzen kikigaki*, an important part of *The Rennyo Shōnin goichidai ki kikigaki*.

In order to explain how heavily we are burdened with karma, Kūzen refers to "the ten bad acts, the five grave offences, the five obstacles, and the three submissions." Whilst the first two classifications stand for human beings in general, the last two refer to women's karma. The notion of "the five obstacles" is something believed to be introduced to Buddhism under the overwhelming influence of the Hindu tradition. The idea of "the three submissions" is said to be found not only in the Hindu tradition but also in Confucianism.

In androcentric societies women were deemed to be inferior to men and such discrimination was one of the elements that sustained those social orders. Sexual discrimination was thus so closely related to political power that Buddhist documents compiled in androcentric societies were politically obliged to exhibit such discriminative tendencies.

Taking into consideration such social conditions, the advent of Amida's Original Vow for universal deliverance against all sorts of discrimination must have been an epoch-making event. According to *The Larger Sūtra of*

Eternal Life Amida Buddha vowed to save all sentient beings without any discrimination through the Eighteenth Vow and in addition he is also said to have made a further vow to deliver all women through the Thirty-fifth Vow. The Thirty-fifth Vow says:

> If, upon my obtaining Buddhahood, women in all the innumerable and inconceivable Buddha-worlds throughout the ten quarters should not be filled with joy, faith and aspiration upon hearing my name and, abhorring their femininity, not awaken their thoughts to Enlightenment, and if after death they should yet again assume female form, may I not attain the Highest Enlightenment.[111]

The compiler of the sūtra when drawing up his account of Amida Buddha some time in the first century, appears to have been influenced by the attitudes of the androcentric society from which he came. Such expressions as "abhorring their femininity" or "after death they should not assume the female body again" bear testimony to this, whilst the vow to save women from their miserable conditions is added as an extension of Amida's fundamental Original Vow of universal deliverance of all beings.

Viewed from the deepest level of Buddhist thought, however, the sūtra-master who compiled *The Sūtra of Eternal Life* did so based on the fundamental Buddhist ideal of universal deliverance of all sentient beings, as is shown by the Eighteenth Vow. To accomplish this ideal, women had to be saved. In order to save women from their miserable situation the sūtra-master tried to give expression to a special vow for women, the Thirty-fifth Vow. Unfortunately, however, in trying to accomplish this ultimate purpose, he was unable to transcend the language and thought processes of his time, leaving us with the paradox of a vow to save women from the discriminations of an androcentric society that is itself couched in discriminatory terms.

Nevertheless, we should not forget that the Thirty-fifth Vow was originally intended to save women. Viewed from the fundamental level of Buddhist thought, salvation is to be attained through Enlightenment. In this sense Shinran called this vow the "Vow to Make Women Attain Buddhahood." Shin Buddhism follows this fundamental view that men and women are equal in the sense that all sentient beings have Buddha-Nature, the potential to become a Buddha. In Shin Buddhism this view comes from Amida Buddha as his gift to all sentient beings.

In Buddhism salvation means the attainment of Buddhahood which goes beyond all forms of discrimination. Not only women but also men should be aware of the karmic bondage of sexual discrimination and seek to overcome it in their own way, for without the salvation of women, men could not be saved and vice versa. Therefore Rennyo states that not only women but also men "must understand at a very deep level that Amida Tathāgata is the manifested form of *Dharma-kāya* for saving such wretched persons as ourselves."

The suppression of the female sex in the medieval period was, however, unspeakably dreadful which is why Rennyo Shōnin himself made every effort to focus on the salvation of women.

Another important term in this letter is "to embrace and never to abandon,"[112] as taken from *The Meditation Sūtra*. In Japanese the word used is *sesshufusha* 摂取不捨. To illustrate the meaning of this phrase which requires some explanation, let me quote an interesting story of Shōma, a devout Shin Buddhist follower, from my book *Great Living: In the Pure Encounter between Master and Disciple*.

When Shōma (1800–1872), [an illiterate Shin Buddhist devotee], was staying in a certain temple, the Head priest asked him, "What is the meaning of the phrase, '[Amida's Light] embraces all beings forsaking none (*sesshu fusha*)'?"

At that Shōma suddenly jumped up in front of him, with arms flung wide, shouting loudly. The priest, fearing the fellow had become too worked up by the difficult question, took flight.

But Shōma ran after him. The priest fled from the front of the Buddha Hall to the back. But Shōma went into the back after him. Escaping from the back to the front and again from the front to the back, the priest finally fled into the innermost recesses of the temple and hid himself in the storage cupboard for lampstands.[113] Pulling the doors closed from inside, the priest thought to himself; "Dear dear! I should never have put such a difficult question to Shōma. He may not be able to find me."

On the contrary, Shōma quickly arrived and threw open the cupboard doors shouting, "My dear Head-priest! I Am Here!" Then he stretched his arms out to their fullest extent, and declared, "This is the meaning of the words 'embracing all beings and forsaking none.'"

Brimming with joy, the priest declared, "Now I understand. That which never lets me go after all the desperate attempts to escape I have been making for so long – that is the meaning of 'embracing all beings and forsaking none'."[114]

There is another interesting story on the subject of *sesshu fusha* in the *Rennyo Shōnin goichidai ki kikigaki,*

Article 205 "A certain person, Yuiren-bō by name, prayed to Amida Tathāgata at Ungoji Temple, in order to know the meaning of *sesshu fusha*, 'embracing all beings and forsaking none'. In a dream Amida Buddha appeared and grasped him by the sleeve. Although he tried to flee, Amida held on to him firmly. Through this dream he understood that 'embracing (*sesshu*)' means catching and not releasing one who may want to run away. Rennyo taught by quoting this story." [115]

At the end of the letter Rennyo describes how these women took their leave of Yoshizaki after receiving very kind guidance from Kūzen about how to attain faith. Their parting words are so moving, overflowing with joy and gratitude due to their attainment of faith and at the same time inevitably mixed with a sorrowful feeling of parting from their teacher. This is a good example from Rennyo Shōnin's followers of a direct expression of their own faith-experience.

If you go back to the last paragraph of the letter, their words of joy and gratitude indicate that they had been listening to the teaching of Amida Buddha somewhere else and that on the day they finally attained faith for the first time through their meeting with Kūzen on the hill of Yoshizaki. In actual fact, even before Rennyo's arrival, people in Hokuriku District were able to hear the Pure Land teaching, if they wanted, because there were already several Shin Buddhist temples, related to the Honganji tradition, such as Zuisenji 瑞泉寺 at Inami, in Etchū Province, Kōgyōji 興行寺 at Arakawa and Chōshōji 超勝寺 at Fujishima in Echizen Province and Honrenji 本蓮寺 at Komatsu and Honsenji 本泉寺 at Futamata in Kaga Province and furthermore the *Nenbutsu* activities of the Jishū school[116] were becoming popular in this area. Not satisfied with the teachings they had received previously and on hearing the good reputation of Rennyo Shōnin, those women visited Yoshizaki, received the true teaching of the Pure Land from Kūzen and, with tears in their eyes, took their leave.

CHAPTER EIGHT

The Ultimate Concern
of Our Sangha

ON THE CREATION OF A TEMPLE

AT YOSHIZAKI

FASCICLE I, LETTER EIGHT

Around the beginning of 'Early Summer' (April) of the third year of Bunmei (1471), without any fixed plan in mind, I stole away from a place just outside Miidera's southern branch temple at Ōtsu in Shiga County in Ōmi Province, and travelled through various parts of the provinces of Echizen and Kaga. Eventually, finding the site known as Yoshizaki in Hosorogi County of this province exceedingly attractive, we cleared the land on the hill that had long been the domain of wild beasts. Since the twentyseventh of July when the temple was duly built, night has followed day and one season has followed another, on and on, until a good three years have passed.

Although a multitude of priests and lay people, men and women, have been gathering here in recent years, they seem to do so with no real purpose in mind and as of this year I have prohibited their coming and going like this. What is the fundamental reason for our being in this place? If we consider the matter, we will see how shameful it would be if it were all in vain and we tumbled into hell despite having received the gift of life in the human realm and having actually met with the Buddha-dharma that is so very difficult to meet. Thus I have reached the decision that all those whose concern is not the decisive awakening of *Nenbutsu* faith and the attainment of birth in the Land of Utmost Bliss should not gather here at this place. This is purely because our ultimate concern is not the attainment of fame and wealth but solely the attainment of Enlightenment through Rebirth. Therefore, let there be no misunderstanding by those who see this or hear about it.

Most humbly and respectfully
In September, Bunmei 5 [1473].

COMMENTS

This letter was written in September 1473, about two years after a new temple had been built on a hill they call Yoshizaki. Its main theme is Rennyo's admonition of people for visiting the temple merely in order to satisfy their worldly desires.

Rennyo Shōnin's Sangha expanded very rapidly in Hokuriku District. Before he came to the area, there had already been a number of Pure Land priests living there, including some from the Honganji tradition, but after Rennyo Shōnin's arrival at Yoshizaki the expansion of the Shin Buddhist Sangha in Hokuriku District became extremely rapid and wide-ranging. According to a letter written by Rennyo on 2nd August 1473, one or two hundred *taya* houses[117] had already sprung up around the main temple at Yoshizaki. This means that at any one time there were always several hundred followers living in the vicinity and on special occasions thousands more would flock there. The steep hill provided a very good natural stronghold, surrounded as it was by the sea in three directions.

Rennyo had purposefully chosen such a site for the new temple because of the bitter experience that he and his followers had had of being attacked by warrior priests from Mount Hiei, both at Ōtani in Kyoto in 1465 and at Katada in Ōmi Province in 1468. His move to Yoshizaki was actually a good way of escaping the aggression from Mount Hiei.

When he moved to Hokuriku District he was accompanied by a number of followers. The Sangha was already quite big and powerful at that time. His disciples helped him promote the Shin Buddhist faith in the area. When he wanted to build a temple on Yoshizaki he had to negotiate with the then Shōgun, Ashikaga Yoshimasa, through the office of Lord Asakura Toshikage in order to be allowed to acquire the site for his new temple.

It is said that the rapid expansion of Rennyo's Sangha was largely attributable to the fluid social situation at the time—the decline of the aristocracy hitherto sustained by manorialism, the rise of the warrior class that was still waging wars for the new hegemony, the improvement of agricultural tools due to an increased use of iron, making the farmers more powerful than before, and so on. In short, farmers, though they had so much more power, could find no one they could trust or rely on. The sudden appearance of Rennyo Shōnin, the great figure of the Shin Buddhist tradition accompanied by trustworthy disciples, strongly appealed to their spiritual needs.

As you can imagine, this Sangha that had expanded so fast was very much a mixture of pure spirituality and worldly desires. Rennyo had to pick his way forward with the burden of such a Sangha on his shoulders, always mindful of pure faith deep in his heart. To hold on to pure faith and still live in the real world one needs to be constantly remoulding one's attitude and way of thinking, eschewing the mind's tendency to become self-centred, seeking instead always to go back to Amida's Original Vow to benefit others and oneself simultaneously.

In August, one month before Rennyo wrote this letter, there was a battle in Hosorogi County between two opposing factions, the Kai and the Asakura. The Asakura who had helped Rennyo establish the temple on Yoshizaki asked him to fight and support their army with his followers. He himself retreated to Yamanaka spa for his health in order to avoid being involved in the conflict. Such a maneuver was quite successful on this occasion. Perhaps he knew that his followers would not be seriously involved. He was a peace-lover on principle, always trying to distance himself as much as possible from any conflict. In his formal letters he always asked his followers not to oppose the government. It seems, however, that on one or two occasions in his life he did have to make up his mind to fight in order to protect the lives of his followers against some threatening political power. Also at times his disciples had actually helped him escape from danger at the risk of their lives. When he wrote the letter, Rennyo must have had in mind not only the political forces but also the religious powers surrounding his Sangha.

A famous Japanese writer, Nobuhiko Matsugi[118], was of the opinion that, because Rennyo actually prepared for his journey very carefully, he was not speaking the truth when in the first paragraph of his letter he declared that he had slipped away "without any fixed plan in mind." Certainly it may appear as an untruth if you are not clear about its deeper spiritual dimension. It is true that he prepared everything meticulously but the way I understand it, however, is that Rennyo simply slipped away from his temple at Ōtsu, forgetting everything—"without any fixed plan in mind"—simply entrusting his whole being to Amida Buddha's great compassion despite the hardships and difficulties he was facing at that time. The writer did not appreciate the innermost dimension of Rennyo Shōnin's spirituality. Desiring to benefit both himself and others in the light of the teaching of Amida Buddha, Rennyo in advance prepared everything very carefully and then "stole away" from the temple where he had been living for several years. From this point of view his quiet escape from Ōmi Province was in fact very dramatic.

In this letter Rennyo asks people not to come to the temple if they have no particular purpose in mind. The letter seems to have been addressed to the public in general, not to any special persons or groups of persons. It must have been quite a harsh request to his followers.

Whilst on one hand the rapid expansion of his religious order was something to celebrate, on the other hand it brought him a host of difficult problems to solve. As mentioned above, the actual Sangha was very much a mixture of pure spirituality and worldly desires and the resultant problems were the focus of much criticism and attack from political forces within Hokuriku District as well as from other indigenous religious orders. The political forces wished to capitalise on the obvious power of the Sangha but, if that were to prove impossible, they feared the huge energy of the religious order. The old religious systems also attacked Rennyo Shōnin's Sangha out of envy and hate on account of its popularity.

At this stage it was absolutely necessary for him to clarify his own standpoint, not only to his followers but also to the public. He asks himself in this letter, "What is the fundamental reason for our being in this place?" Obviously it was solely in order to attain faith here and now and to then live in gratitude throughout the rest of one's life and attain Enlightenment in the Pure Land. Therefore, Rennyo declares, "Thus I have reached the decision that all those whose concern is not the decisive awakening of *Nenbutsu* faith and the attainment of birth in the Land of Utmost Bliss should not gather here at this place. This is purely because our ultimate concern is not the attainment of fame and wealth but solely the attainment of Enlightenment through Rebirth."

Rennyo's ultimate concern was the attainment of faith by each and every one of his followers. He followed the path of *Nenbutsu* together with his followers, desiring to benefit both himself and others at one and the same time.

In Article 122 of *The Goichidai ki kikigaki* Rennyo Shōnin says, "The prosperity of the tradition does not lie in the number of those who meet together, nor indeed in the strength of their power. Only if people attain faith, even if it is only just one person, that is what constitutes the prosperity of the tradition."[119]

When he was young Rennyo vowed to restore the Shin Buddhist tradition. With this vow in mind he made enormous efforts throughout his long life to promote the Shin Buddhist teaching. Regarding the restoration of the tradition this statement represents his fundamental standpoint and I do feel it comes from the bottom of his heart full of love and respect for his followers, each and every one of them.

CHAPTER NINE

To Be Free
of Superstitions

ON AVOIDING INAUSPICIOUS THINGS

FASCICLE I, LETTER NINE

For some time now people have been unanimous in condemning our school as being ridiculous and unclean. Nor indeed is this an unreasonable criticism, for there are some people in our school who openly proclaim the teaching of our tradition without regard for the presence of those from other schools or other traditions. This is a grave mistake. "Observing the rules of conduct of our tradition" means cherishing the teaching of our tradition deep within ourselves without betraying any sign of it to the outside. Those who do so may justly be called people of discretion. These days, however, some of us speak carelessly and heedlessly about our tradition in the presence of others from different traditions and different schools. As a result, our tradition is considered shallow. Because there are some of us who are mistaken in their understanding of our tradition, people from other traditions come to see our school as unclean and an abomination. We should understand that this is not because others are mistaken in their views, but because our own people have got things wrong.

Next, regarding the matter of avoiding inauspicious things, it is confirmed in our tradition that within the Buddha-dharma we do not try to avoid something because it seems inauspicious. When we meet with other schools, however, or with the civil authorities, are there not certain things that should be avoided? Of course, when in the presence of those of other traditions and other schools, we should recognise that there are things to be avoided from their perspective. Nor should we criticise others when they avoid things they consider inauspicious.

It is clearly stated, however, in many passages in the sūtras that people who practise the Buddha-dharma, and not just those who practise the *Nenbutsu*, should not go too far out of their way to avoid things that seem inauspicious. Firstly, a passage in *The Nirvāṇa Sūtra* says, 'Within the Tathāgata's Dharma, there is no choosing of auspicious days and good stars.'"[120] Also a passage from *The Sūtra of the Samādhi of All Buddhas' Presence* states: "Lay women who hear of this *samādhi* and want to practice it! ... Take refuge in the Buddha; take refuge in the Dharma; take refuge in the Sangha. Do not follow other paths; do not worship heavenly beings; do not enshrine ghosts and spirits; do not seek to find auspicious days."[121]

Although other passages similar to these are to be found in the sūtras, I have selected just these two. The documents seem to be saying in particular that followers of the *Nenbutsu* should not serve those beings. Let this be thoroughly understood.

Most humbly and respectfully
In September, Bunmei 5 [1473].

COMMENTS

The main subject of this letter is about "avoiding inauspicious things". "Avoiding inauspicious things" stands for a religious act known as *bukki* or *monoimi* in Japanese. *Monoimi* means that, in order to serve a deity or Buddha and thus to lead a better life, one avoids defilements and inauspicious things whilst seeking to achieve purification of body and mind. It includes various acts such as fasting, observing votive abstinence, staying at home on unlucky days and avoiding travelling in an ill-omened direction. This practice is closely connected with the Japanese notion of purification found in Shintoism, with the Chinese divination based on the philosophy of Yin and Yang (*Onmyōdō* in Japanese) and also with the ceremonies of purification or exorcism found in Esoteric Buddhism. The custom of *monoimi* was deeply embedded in the Japanese way of life at that time. Even today various forms of *monoimi* are widely found in Japanese culture.

According to a commentary on *The Letters*, known as *Ofumi kōyō*,[122] there is an interesting story behind the ninth letter of Fascicle One. In Kaga

Province there lived a follower of Rennyo Shōnin called Horiuchi Jūbe. Even after attaining faith he still lacked discretion and was in the habit of mocking other schools because of their *monoimi* ritual of avoiding things as impure or inauspicious. When he proclaimed the Shin Buddhist view on *monoimi* to a Shingon priest whom he happened to meet one day in Echigo Province, the Shingon priest laughed at him, saying how shallow was the teaching of the Shin Buddhist tradition. When another follower recounted the story to Rennyo, he warned Jūbe not to repeat the same error and gave this letter to followers in Echigo Province.

According to my understanding, Shin Buddhism is a religion completely free of any kind of superstition. There is no *monoimi* at all in it, because it is based on pure faith and that alone. Shin Buddhism has no selfish prayers, no exorcism, no astrology, no divination by lot, no *onomancy*[123] and no divination by palm or facial features.

Monoimi seems to be based on mankind's dualistic way of thinking— distinction between good and evil, purity and impurity, fortune and disaster. Those who practise *monoimi* try to obtain good, purity and fortune by avoiding evil, impurity and disaster. The notion of *monoimi* is religious in so far as it involves seeking to avoid suffering, but it is an attitude not yet mature enough to go beyond duality. When Buddhists talk about the Pure Land, the purity they refer to is an absolute purity beyond the opposition between purity and impurity. The true essence of Buddhism lies beyond duality.

In Shin Buddhism, when we attain true faith we go beyond our dualistic way of thinking. In order to attain true faith we have to abandon self power in its entirety. If we are attached to our self-centred dualistic way of thinking and remain unable to entrust ourselves to Amida Buddha, it is called self power, not Other Power. Other Power that we find actually working within us is the absolute Other Power beyond the division between 'self' and 'other.'

Horiuchi Jūbe, the Shin Buddhist devotee in the account mentioned above, had already attained faith and was proud of it. So he boasted of the teaching of Shin Buddhism to a Shingon priest. The Shingon priest must have been a person who practised *monoimi*. According to the thinking behind *monoimi*, however, those who do not practise the *monoimi* purification remain impure or defiled. Whilst Shin Buddhists think their faith-experience is beyond the duality of *monoimi*, those attached to *monoimi* consider Shin Buddhists as still being impure.

Although Rennyo does not specifically refer to *monoimi* in the first paragraph, I feel it is *monoimi* that is on his mind in this letter right from the start. Nor is this just my own impression but amply borne out by the *Ofumi kōjutsu*, or "The Lectures on the Letters," by Professor Kakuju Yoshitani[124]. Professor Yoshitani states in the book, "This whole letter seems to be based on the *Haja kenshō shō*, or 'Passages to Destroy the False and Expound the

Correct' by Zonkaku."[125] Zonkaku Shōnin, in fact, had discussed the problem of *monoimi* in detail in the *Haja kenshō shō*,[126] referring to a passage in *The Nirvāṇa Sūtra*, "Within the Tathāgata's dharma, there is no choosing of good days and auspicious stars."[127] This line is actually quoted by Rennyo in the third paragraph of his letter.

Shin Buddhists, with their complete disregard of *monoimi*, appear 'ridiculous' to those who think the *monoimi* purification is the only way to rid oneself of defilement. From their viewpoint Shin Buddhism seems 'unclean and an abomination.'

The religious philosophy of Shin Buddhism is both profound and radical, based as it is on faith-experience that transcends duality in a unique way. Because those from other schools cannot see this, however, Shin Buddhist followers should be very careful when they speak to people from other traditions, or our school will be considered "shallow." Therefore, "We should understand that this is not because others are mistaken in their views, but because our own people have got things wrong."

In the second paragraph of this letter, Rennyo confirms that Shin Buddhists should not be involved in *monoimi* purification in any way at all. "It is confirmed in our tradition that within the Buddha-dharma we do not try to avoid something because it seems inauspicious." In the latter part of the second paragraph he states that we should try to understand other traditions just as they are and that we should not criticise them because of their *monoimi*.

In the last two paragraphs of the letter Rennyo gives textual evidence to further corroborate his teaching on *monoimi*. One of them is a passage from *The Nirvāṇa Sūtra*, one of the most famous Mahāyāna Sūtras, and the other is *The Sūtra of the Samādhi of All Buddhas' Presence*, a Pure Land sūtra, less popular but of vital importance, from the earliest stage of the Mahāyāna movement. The latter sūtra was translated into Chinese by Lokarakśa 支婁迦讖, a priest who came to China from Yuèzhī 月支 Tokhara, a country west of India, in a.d. 147 and translated a number of Mahāyāna sūtras, including this one. The Sūtra consists of sixteen chapters and expounds the method of viewing Amida Buddha and all Buddhas through the practice of constantly pronouncing the Buddha Name. The passage quoted from this Sūtra can be said to be evidence that Pure Land Buddhism was free of *monoimi*, or of superstitions in general, from its earliest stage. Rennyo concludes after giving these quotations that those who live the *Nenbutsu* should not serve other beings such as heavenly beings, ghosts and spirits.

CHAPTER TEN

The Meaning
of *Taya*

THE WIVES OF THE PRIESTS

WHO ARE IN CHARGE OF TAYA HOUSES

AT THIS TEMPLE

FASCICLE I, LETTER TEN

Women who become the wives of priests in charge of *taya* houses at this temple at Yoshizaki should realise that they only do so because of the karmic conditions of their previous lives being closely related to the Buddha Dharma. This, however, cannot be understood by them until they have realised that Rebirth is their One Great Matter of Concern and until they themselves have attained faith decisively. Therefore, those who become the wives of priests should by all manner of means attain faith.

First of all you should understand that, because what is called a peaceful awareness (*anjin*) in our tradition is something very special and sets us apart from all other Pure Land schools, it is known as the great Other Power faith.

You should understand, therefore, that those who have attained this faith are all of them – ten out of every ten, one hundred out of every hundred – absolutely assured of birth in the Pure Land that is to come.

QUESTION: How should we understand this peaceful awareness? We do not know about it in any detail.

ANSWER: This question is indeed a matter of great importance. I will tell you how to attain the faith of our tradition. To begin with, you should understand that, because you are women and therefore wretched beings of very bad karma, burdened with the five obstacles and the three submissions,[128] you have already been abandoned by the Tathāgatas of the ten directions and also by all the Buddhas of the three periods. Amida Tathāgata alone, however, graciously vowed to save such wretched beings and fashioned long ago the Forty-eight Vows. Among these Vows, in addition to the Eighteenth Vow to save all bad persons and women, Amida also composed a further Vow, the Thirty-fifth, to save women because of the depth of their bad karma and doubts. You should have a deep sense of gratitude to Amida Tathāgata for what he has done for you in undertaking such painstaking work.

QUESTION: When we have come to realise how much we owe Amida Tathāgata for composing the Vows again and again in this way to save people like us, then with what sort of self-understanding should we entrust ourselves to Amida? We would like to have this explained in detail.

ANSWER: If you would like to attain faith and to entrust yourselves to Amida, first of all you must realise that human life lasts no longer than a dream or a vision and that Rebirth is indeed the blissful fruit of eternal life; that human life is no more than the enjoyment of fifty to a hundred years and that Rebirth should be our One Great Matter of Concern. Then, abandoning any inclination toward miscellaneous practices and discarding any tendency to avoid inauspicious things, you should entrust yourselves singlemindedly and steadfastly to Amida Buddha and, without concerning yourselves with any other Buddhas, Bodhisattvas or various gods (*kami*),[129] you should take refuge solely in Amida and realise this birth to come is absolutely assured. And so, pronouncing the *Nenbutsu* with an outpouring of feelings of thankfulness, you should respond in gratitude to Amida Tathāgata for all the work he has done in order to save you. This is the way that the *taya* priests' wives who have attained faith should be.

Most humbly and respectfully
On 11th September, Bunmei 5 [1473].

COMMENTS

Taya is a typically Shin Buddhist form of accommodation in which Shin Buddhist priests and lay followers live together with pure faith in the light of the Buddha's teaching. As a brief introduction to this letter let me quote from my essay, entitled *The Meaning of Taya*:

> The origin of the word *Taya* can be traced back to the time of Rennyo Shōnin (1415–1499), the Restorer of Shin Buddhism in the medieval period. According to *The Dictionary of Shin Buddhism* (*Shinshū Jiten*) *taya* is written as 多屋 or 他屋 in Japanese, meaning 'many houses' (多屋) built within the temple or perhaps, originally, 'houses built in other areas' (他屋) than within the temple. When Rennyo Shōnin established a temple at Yoshizaki in Hokuriku District as the centre of his mission, many people gathered there to listen to his sermons. Subsequently a lot of houses were built in the area to accommodate his followers who had come from various other provinces. I would guess that these houses must originally have been built outside the temple. Later on, as the temple's land was enlarged at the request of Rennyo Shōnin's followers, more and more houses were built inside the temple instead. A *taya* was run by a priest (坊主 *bōzu*) and his wife (内方 *naihō*) and they took care of visitors from far off countries. In one of *The Letters* by Rennyo, the first letter of Fascicle Two, he says, 'It has come to my ears that, in the course of the seven days of this year's Hōonkō Assembly, almost all the wives of the priests in charge of the *taya* houses, along with a number of other people staying in them, have attained faith decisively. This is a matter for great congratulation. We could not have hoped for anything better. If we just let things drift as we please, even the faith thus attained will disappear. It is taught somewhere, I have heard, that "again and again we should clean out the channels of faith and let the waters of Amida's Dharma flow freely".'[130] This short quotation suggests the main purpose of running a *taya* was to enable those who lived in it, not only priests and their wives but also visitors from outside, to attain faith and live their lives with pure faith.[131]

Taya houses are found both in and around a Shin Buddhist temple. When *taya* as a form of accommodation first appeared at Yoshizaki, they were built not only inside the temple and but also in its vicinity. A letter written by Rennyo on 2nd August 1473[132] states that there were already one or two hundred *taya* houses at Yoshizaki. According to another letter, entitled *Fire at Yoshizaki* and written by him in September in 1474, the Buddha Hall and nine *taya* houses inside the main temple were destroyed by fire on 28th March in 1474. All the other houses apart from these ten buildings might have been outside the main temple.

This, the tenth letter of Fascicle One was written on 11th September 1473 a little earlier than those other letters mentioned above. This means the letter was written by Rennyo to provide instructions at the early stage of forming *taya* houses around him at Yoshizaki.

The letter is addressed to women and, in particular, to the wives of the priests in charge of *taya* houses at Yoshizaki. A document known as *Gōshōji ki* says that it was given to the wife of Kyōnen-bō, one of Rennyo's disciples.[133] Having such a person live close by could well have been his motivation for writing this letter. But even so the problem was not limited to her alone but was more universal, applying to all the wives of the priests living in *taya* houses. My translation of the letter is based on just such an interpretation.

The fifth year of Bunmei [1473], when Rennyo Shōnin actually wrote this letter, was just two years after he and his small band of followers first arrived at Yoshizaki. Those followers gathered there were doubtless an active and lively group with Rennyo as their leader. At the same time, however, their mental attitudes must have been chaotic. Some of them like Dōsai (1399–1488) had been Shōnin's followers for decades whilst others had only just become involved in this faith movement. There will have been a great deal of variety in their understanding of Shin Buddhist teaching. Obviously the priests at Yoshizaki concentrated on the most important matter of all, namely attaining and living with faith in their daily lives. But how about their wives? They differed a great deal in their concern. Some of them just followed their husbands and remained very much involved in worldly things. Some must have already been awakened to how important it is to solve one's problems in the light of the Buddha's teaching. There were probably some wives even who understood the One Great Matter of Concern actually better than their husbands and who themselves guided their husbands on the way to the Pure Land.

We should try to appreciate the important role that the priests and their wives performed in their *taya* houses. Rennyo's personality and teaching attracted a vast number of people from various provinces. Visitors to the temple at Yoshizaki differed a great deal in age, occupation, education and interest. The wives of priests were of course well placed to take care of those visitors, cleaning houses, cooking meals, making beds and so forth. If they had only been interested in and concerned with worldly things such as fame or wealth, the result of their influence on visitors would have been disastrous. This special letter, addressing for the first time the priests' actual wives, was extremely important to bring order into the chaotic situation of the temple at that time.

All Rennyo asked the wives of priests to do was to simply live their lives based on the attainment of faith. In this context, let me again quote from *The Meaning of Taya*.

Taya is the Shin Buddhist form of accommodation in which people, priests as well as lay followers, live together with pure faith in the light of the Buddha's teaching. It is simply a result of faith-movement. People solve their own problems by attaining faith and then, having attained faith, continue to live with pure faith, helping others to solve their problems. For those who have already attained faith, the act of helping others with their problems is no different from the act of dealing with their own problems, because they feel others' problems are their own. In Buddhism, one particular person and other people or, if you like, you and I are "not one and yet not two" (*fuitsu-funi* 不一不二) in greater oneness. The ultimate goal is to benefit oneself and others by achieving the highest spiritual development (Enlightenment) of each individual. To accomplish this faith-movement we need a place where we can be together to discuss, read and think. This is the function of the *taya*.

Then what is faith? I have been talking about the notion of faith as the reality of encounter – encounter accompanied by spiritual awakening. In Buddhism, faith is awakening, awakening of the mind as a result of its purification. When we talk about faith, we usually imagine that I am here and something holy, whether God or Buddha, is over there, and that I believe in the object though it is beyond my understanding. This interpretation of faith or belief in a holy object is dependent on the bifurcation of our minds into subject and object. I think that faith is originally the pure experience of awakening, or, if you like, of encounter. In Shin Buddhism, faith is said to have two essential aspects: 1) awakening to oneself or the reality of the individual and 2) awakening to the Dharma or Amida Buddha's Great Compassion. If I use the word encounter, one sense is encounter with oneself, the other, encounter with the Buddha. They are two aspects of the one reality – pure faith. This awakening of faith can also be called self-realisation of the Dharma through the individual.[134]

In the context of the salvation of women Rennyo describes one of the two aspects of faith – "awakening to oneself" or awareness of one's bad karma. If you carefully observe the questions and answers in the letter, you will find an interesting aspect of the Shin Buddhist consciousness of one's bad karma closely related as it is to the notion of impermanence.

As he clearly describes in this letter, those who are aware of their bad karma entrust themselves absolutely to Amida Buddha through their deep contemplation on impermanence. Contemplation on impermanence of worldly life leads them to the instantaneous attainment of faith. Deep awareness of impermanence helps them abandon their worldly attachment instantaneously and entrust their whole existence to Amida Buddha in the here and now. The relationship between the consciousness of one's 'sin' or bad karma and the Buddhist philosophy of impermanence will be a good subject to discuss in the study of Shin Buddhist religious consciousness.

"Women's birth in the Pure Land" is a subject which appears in *The Letters* repeatedly. Women are said to have the five obstacles and the three submissions for their attainment of Buddhahood.

The three submissions found in Buddhist documents such as *The Chōnichimyō zanmai kyō* and *The Gyokuya kyō* are: firstly that women have to obey their parents when they are young; secondly that they have to obey their husband when they are married; and thirdly they have to obey their children when they become old.

It is because of their dependence on their parents, their husband and their children, that women are supposed to have to obey them. Objectively speaking, however, everything is interdependently related. There is nothing absolutely independent. It is true with people as well. Through not being aware of their dependency on others, however, people become attached to the outward form of their relationships. The problem is their mental dependency on others. Blind dependency causes one's attachment to the object.

In the spiritual dimension we should become independent by going beyond our mental dependency on others. Too much blind dependency will make people mentally ill, even insane. Only if women depend on their husbands too much, do they have to stick to their husbands.

Our blind dependency on others will destroy our spiritual independency and freedom. If we try to keep our self-centred world with no awareness of its limitation, we will find ourselves forced to obey those we depend on. The problem is our selfish attachment to them. This will lead us to harm not only ourselves but also people around them.

The only way to escape from this is to become aware of the problem itself. If you try to run away from the problem, there will be no solution at all. To know the way they are dependent on others, to become aware of how much they are attached to those they depend on, and also to realise how their selfish and tenacious attachments have been hurting themselves and others is vital. Quite often such attachment comes about unconsciously. It happens that despite their conscious effort to love and help others they have to hurt others unconsciously. All this is their own karma for which they are absolutely responsible.

Of course, when they become aware of their bad karma, they look for the way to become free from it. Having failed to liberate themselves in terms of self power they come to entrust themselves absolutely to Other Power. When the stronghold of their selfish consciousness collapses by entrusting themselves to Amida Buddha, their whole existence will be purified through the awakening of true faith in Other Power and they will come to realise how much they have been receiving from others. This experience of the awakening of faith is followed by endless feelings of gratitude.

If the true problem of the three submissions is blind dependency and selfish attachment, it is apparent that in modern times such mental conditions are indeed prevailing amongst men as well. Nowadays men are quite dependent on others, whilst women are much more independent of men than they were in the past. The Thirty-fifth Original Vow was composed in ancient times in order to save women from their karma. In those days discrimination against women was more predominant in androcentric society. The true purport of the Thirty-fifth Vow must have laid in the spiritual liberation of women from discrimination against them and resultant karmic dependency on others, typified by the discriminatory notion of "three submissions."

As was discussed in *Chapter 7*, despite the fundamental idea of universal deliverance underlying *The Larger Sūtra of Eternal Life*, the composer of the sūtra, when writing the Thirty-fifth Vow, seems to have failed to express such an important notion of universal, impartial and equal salvation. For, in order to bring about equality between men and women, he used the discriminatory notion deeply imbued with the colour of the androcentric society in which he lived. In other words, he employed the discriminatory concept that to be equal to men women have to become men. As a result, from a modern way of thinking, the Thirty-fifth Vow is by no means free from discrimination against women. If we take into account the sūtra's original purport based on the deepest level of Buddhist awakening, however, there will be no doubt that the Thirty-fifth Vow was made for the salvation of women, for their attainment of Buddhahood.

It was the unconditional love of Amida Buddha that Rennyo received from the tradition and wanted to transmit to followers, the unconditional love with no discrimination that would lead us all without exception to birth in the Pure Land and the resultant attainment of Buddhahood.

CHAPTER ELEVEN

The Impermanence
of Life

LIGHTNING AND MORNING DEW

FASCICLE I, LETTER ELEVEN

Upon quiet contemplation we realise that life is but a dream or an illusion and that the pleasures of human life vanish as swiftly as a flash of lightning or as the morning dew.[135] Even if one lives in splendour and glory and is able to enjoy one's life as one wishes, it will only last some fifty to a hundred years. If the winds of impermanence were to blow quickly at this very moment and summon us, would we not suffer illness of whatever kind and die? And indeed, as we face death, nothing of all that we have depended on for so long, nothing from our lives, whether wife, child or wealth, can accompany us. It is therefore entirely alone that we cross the great river of three bad paths[136] at the end of the mountain path that one takes after death.[137] We ought to realise therefore that what we should aspire to more deeply than all else is Rebirth in the Pure Land, that the Buddha we should entrust ourselves to is Amida Tathāgata, and that the place to which we should go, once awakened decisively to faith, is the Pure Land of Peace and Rest.

Regarding this important point, however, the priests who of late have been practising the *Nenbutsu* in this area are seriously at variance with the Buddha-dharma. That is they are calling 'good disciples' those who are best able to gather donations from their followers and they are speaking of them as 'people of faith.' This is a serious error. Moreover, followers believe that only if they contribute an abundance of things to the priests, will they be saved by the spiritual power of those priests, even when the power of the followers themselves is insufficient. This is also an error. Thus, between the priests and their followers, there is no sign of a proper understanding of the faith of our tradition. This is indeed most shameful. Without a doubt, neither priests nor disciples will be born in the Land of Utmost Bliss. Their efforts will have been in vain and they will fall into hell. Even though we lament this, we cannot lament deeply enough. Though we grieve, we should grieve even more deeply. From now on, therefore, priests should ask someone who is fully awakened for details of the great Other Power faith and should attain their own faith decisively, and then teach the essentials of that faith to their disciples. Then both priests and their disciples will surely attain birth in the Pure Land, which is what is most important.

Most humbly and respectfully
In mid-September, Bunmei 5 [1473].

COMMENTS

Beginning with an observation regarding the impermanence of human life, Rennyo describes how life passes away as swiftly as a flash of lightning or as the morning dew. The philosophy of impermanence is one of the main pillars of Buddhism. According to the Buddha's teaching everything in this world is in a constant state of flux and human life cannot be an exception to this rule.

This letter consists of only two paragraphs. In the first paragraph Rennyo points to the importance of attaining faith in Amida Buddha based on the Buddhist philosophy of impermanence. In the second he deals with more practical problems to be found amongst his followers of those days. Rennyo Shōnin insists that Shin Buddhist followers, both priests and lay people, should cope with their financial problems – donations from followers and the expenses of the Sanghas – firmly on the basis of their faith. In other words, Buddhists should solve their economic problems based on their own pure faith, not separated from it.

In this world practical problems and spiritual problems appear to be different from one another. Certainly they have their own different spheres or dimensions. In this respect we should not be confused between the two. According to Buddhist philosophy, however, they are "not one and not two," in other words they are at once different and the same. What is important is our attitude towards coping with and solving those problems. It is we humans who actually solve the problems. Our fundamental spiritual attitude when solving those problems as human beings should be a consistent one and when seeking a solution we should always be aware of our absolute responsibility towards everything. Faith, in Shin Buddhism, is something that includes this fundamental spiritual attitude.

In order to clarify the situation that he refers to in his letter, I would like to quote from another letter by Rennyo, which is found in the *Rennyo Shōnin ibun.* This is a letter written on 1st February of the same year and seems to have a close connection with the 11th Letter of Fascicle One.

"What I'm about to talk to you about is for my own repentance. I would like to ask you to listen to me. Amongst my followers there is a virtuous layman. Wishing to teach him as much as possible I said to him, 'You have no pure faith at all.' At that he reacted harshly towards me, his eyes wide with anger, 'Our parents were always faithful to their priest. They contributed some money to the temple and also helped the priest build a house. We, too, have been helping you in daily life. Besides we always make donations when seasonal greetings are expected. We have been faithful to the practice of donating things to priests. In addition we have also been pronouncing the *Nenbutsu* to attain Rebirth in the Pure Land. Why do we have to listen to you telling us that we have no faith? If you insist on saying such nonsense we will simply leave your group.' Because that person was the most powerful of all followers, I thought that should he leave us and join another group of Shin Buddhists, then our group would be severely weakened. I said to him, therefore, 'You are right. Because I had heard other people say so, I gave you that advice. I will never say such a thing again. Please do not join another group.' I was wrong to have behaved in such a way, however, and because of this I now repent again in front of you."[138]

This whole paragraph quoted in one of Rennyo's letters represents a certain priest's words of repentance spoken at a meeting of Shin Buddhist followers. If a group of spiritual people come together and form a religious community, one of their chief concerns will be how to run their community. There will be a need for money. Those responsible for the community will have to think about running costs. It is no easy matter for a religious community. How can we produce money for this purpose? As Rennyo wrote in the fifth letter of Fascicle One,

"If you understand this point your birth to come is absolutely assured. If you are filled with joy like this you should go to the temples of the priests whom you respect as teachers and give a donation to express your gratitude. Such a follower could be called a person of faith, one who has fully understood the teaching of our tradition."

The joy engendered by faith is the sole source of finance of a Shin Buddhist Sangha. If you are filled with the joy of faith and are happy with your own life, you can go to your Sangha and make a donation to express your gratitude. This kind of faith-movement is the only source of energy whereby a Shin Buddhist Sangha can develop altruistically. Both priests and followers should be pure in faith. Let's go back to the letter of 1st February in 1473.

With regard to the priest's conversation with one of his followers as recorded in the letter, the priest would seem to have eventually recovered his pure faith through serious repentance. At the beginning of their conversation the priest said to his follower, "You have no pure faith (*shinjin*) at all." He probably spoke like this as a way of encouraging his follower towards the true attainment of faith. He does seem, however, to have been a little bit injudicious in his choice of words!

Concerning the follower's reaction, every line of the man's response betrays that there was indeed something seriously wrong with his understanding of the Shin Buddhist faith. At that time the priest, encountering this strong reaction on the part of his follower, simply gave in to him. As the priest admitted afterwards, however, he was wrong to have done so. He must have thought and worried about the financial difficulties that his Sangha would face if that follower left. It was not simply a personal problem but something that would involve all his fellow believers. Despite his concerns about the Sangha's welfare, however, he was wrong to give in to the follower because his capitulation was motivated by purely material considerations and not based on faith at all. When this story was taken up by Rennyo in his letter dated 1st February in 1473, though, the priest must have returned to pure faith through repentance of his previous action.

This is just one example of the problems that numerous groups of followers around Rennyo Shōnin confronted in those days. The fundamental problem is that we tend to try and solve problems of the Sangha based on a worldly viewpoint, not through spiritual introspection and faith. This is an eternal problem for us. Because of the lack of living faith in today's world, temples and Sanghas face many hardships. This is a result of the separation of the practical from the spiritual. We should be aware that those difficulties can be solved through pure faith.

As I said at the beginning of this chapter, the first paragraph of the letter beautifully describes that insight into the impermanence of all things that leads us to concentrate on the attainment of faith. Following this concentration on faith-experience Rennyo then goes on to the main subject of this letter, namely that salvation cannot be attained through the giving of financial contributions. It is through faith alone that we attain birth in the Pure Land. We should not entrust ourselves to outward forms such as money, property and people, but to the Buddha within.

Because people make donations out of gratitude to the Buddha, their gifts are pure. The Sangha naturally becomes richer through their faith-movement.

When people see only the superficial results, however, they can seriously misunderstand the cause of Sangha's wealth. We must be very careful about our own donations, because they are not always pure, being motivated by selfish desires such as fame, profit and competitiveness. The essential thing is to keep returning to living in pure faith throughout our everyday life.

CHAPTER TWELVE

The Purpose of
Our Meeting Together

ON CHŌSHŌJI TEMPLE'S PAST TEACHING

FASCICLE I, LETTER TWELVE

This was written at Chōshōji Temple.[139]
The followers at Chōshōji Temple[140] have for many years been seriously mistaken in their way of understanding the Buddha-dharma. The reason I say this has primarily to do with the leaders of the assembly. They think that what is really the most important thing in the Buddha-dharma is to occupy the place of honour, to be permitted to have sake and the like before anyone else and to win the respect of those seated around them, as well as of others outside the assembly. But actually none of this is of any use at all for attaining birth in the Land of Utmost Bliss. Worldly fame is all it is good for, that and nothing else.

This being so, what is the purpose of holding monthly meetings in our tradition? Although we are ignorant lay people who spend our days and nights in vain and end our lives meaninglessly, falling at last into the three bad paths[139], nevertheless our monthly meetings are occasions when, even if it is only once a month, those who practise the *Nenbutsu* should gather in their meeting house and at very least discuss what they mean by their own faith and what others mean by theirs. These days, however, because there has never been any discussion as to whether one's faith is right or wrong, the situation really is unspeakably awful.

In conclusion, therefore, there must from now on definitely be discussions of faith among those at the meetings, for this is the true way of attaining birth in the Land of Utmost Bliss.

Most humbly and respectfully
In late September, Bunmei 5 [1473].

COMMENTS

When Rennyo Shōnin visited a Shin Buddhist temple known as Chōshōji at Fujishima in Echizen Province in September in 1473, he found that the followers of the temple were holding their meetings in an undesirable way.

According to *The Hogo no uragaki*,[142] a historical record of the Shin Buddhist tradition, written by Kensei (Rennyo's grandson) in 1568, the first Head Priest of Chōshōji, Rangei, was one of the younger brothers of Rennyo Shōnin's grandfather, Gyōnyo Shōnin. When Rennyo Shōnin visited the temple, however, he found that Head Priest Gyōjun, incumbent at that point, was not the sort of priest to be able to maintain the temple properly. Feeling very much responsible for the situation, Rennyo Shōnin asked Gyōjun to retire as Head Priest and to allow his young son, Renchō, to take over the position. This was the serious state of affairs that existed at the temple at the time the letter was written.

The content of this letter is not difficult to understand, as Rennyo Shōnin's intention is clearly expressed. The letter was actually addressed directly to the Shin Buddhist followers at the temple.

The first paragraph of the letter constitutes Rennyo Shōnin's very severe criticism of the meetings at Chōshōji, the temple he visited in September, and is especially damning about the way in which the leaders of the assembly were accustomed to hold those meetings. Although they may have thought that they were conducting the meetings for the Buddha-dharma, Rennyo discovered that their actual concern was mere worldly fame, something far removed from the Buddha-dharma. Those false values of theirs were vividly described at the beginning of the letter. So shocked was Rennyo he resorted to drastic measures to try and reform the temple, and made the Head Priest retire from his position.

All that Rennyo Shōnin really wanted to do was to return Shin Buddhist meetings there to how they were originally supposed to be. In the second paragraph Rennyo Shōnin refers to "the purpose of holding meetings in our tradition." That purpose is simply for all those involved in the meetings to attain pure faith through discussions, through listening and speaking to one another with sincerity. Thus he ends his letter, "In conclusion, therefore, there must from now on definitely be discussions of faith among those at the meetings. For this is the true way of attaining birth in the Land of Utmost Bliss."

Why should we hold meetings to help us live our lives with faith? It is simply because it is not easy for us to have pure faith, heavily burdened as we are with blind passions and always creating our own little worlds self-centredly through our five sense organs and intellect. Our attachment to such a self-centred world causes us to harm not only ourselves but others too. This is the cause of all kinds of suffering.

Becoming aware of this sad reality of ours and at the same time recognising the unconditional love of Amida Buddha that embraces all without any discrimination, we entrust ourselves to Amida Buddha without reservation. This is the Shin Buddhist faith. Through the awakening of faith we are entirely freed of our karmic burden of blind passions and tenacious attachment. This faith-experience is attained instantaneously but it does not last long. In the sense that, through this absolute moment of attaining faith, we come into touch with eternity, i.e. the Buddha of Eternal Life, this spiritual experience, known as the 'one thought-moment of faith,' has about it something eternal. And yet it does not last for ever. Nevertheless, because we come to realise, through the attainment of faith, how to be freed from our karmic world, this faith-experience becomes something very important that leads us on, after our attainment of faith, to solve all the problems we meet in daily life.

In his letter Rennyo Shōnin points out that the leaders of the assembly at Chōshōji temple were very much concerned with their "worldly fame." Desire for fame is one of the three dangerous desires[143] that go on working away energetically in our minds, consciously or unconsciously, even after our attainment of faith. These three desires are referred to as "three kinds of topknot" a Buddhist monk still kept in mind after his ordination and attainment of faith in one of the twenty-one accounts related in *The Kuden shō*[144] by Kakunyo Shōnin (1270–1351).

When one of his disciples went to Hōnen Shōnin to take his leave, Hōnen Shōnin murmured, as he watched him depart, "Why ever is this monk leaving without cutting off his topknot (hair)!" On hearing Hōnen Shōnin say this, the monk came back and asked him, "It was a long time ago that I was first ordained as a Buddhist monk, yet I have just heard you remonstrate about my leaving without cutting off my topknot. I wonder why you said so. With your words echoing in my mind I could not proceed further. I have returned in order to ask why you spoke like this so I can understand your meaning." Then Hōnen Shōnin answered, "Dharma Master, you still have three kinds of topknot: desire for domination, desire for wealth and desire for fame. For the last three years you have been recording my teachings, which you are now taking with you. Returning to your native country with those teachings you will look down on people and make them become your followers. Is this not your desire for domination? Doing so you will wish to be known as a good scholar. Is this not your desire for fame? Furthermore you will probably wish to have wealthy donors. Is this not your desire for wealth? Except you shave off these three kinds of topknot, it will be impossible to call you Dharma Master. This is the reason I made my comment." The monk expressed his repentance, burnt all the documents in his baggage and once again took leave of his Master.[145]

This famous story of the "three kinds of topknot" is a good example to illustrate the most serious problems we all meet after attaining faith or entering the priesthood. When we come to experience the religious world, we tend to think we have overcome the karmic world of blind passions and attachment. What is important is for us Shin Buddhists to be aware, under the light of Amida Buddha, that we are still burdened with various kinds of blind passion, even after the attainment of faith. Amongst all the blind passions those three, the desire for fame, for wealth and for domination, are the most insidious, invading our religious consciousness. If it were not for the light of the Buddha, we would be unable to be awakened to the fact that those desires exist within ourselves. The only way to solve this problem is to entrust ourselves to the unconditional love of Amida Buddha, or, in short, faith.

It is in order to make this point clear that we hold meetings and discuss our personal problems by listening and speaking to others. Other people are mirrors that illumine our own personal reality.

In this letter Rennyo Shōnin refers only to "worldly fame." As seen in his letter of criticism, however, desire for fame is closely connected with the other two desires. They are all included in the discussion. The phrase "desire for fame" represents all three.

The intention of this letter is to show how we can live our lives with pure faith and the letter emphasises the importance of discussion in our meetings. It is through discussion that we come to face the reality of our karma and to entrust our whole being to Amida Buddha. In actual fact, Rennyo is himself 'discussing' in this letter the karmic reality of those three desires, treating the matter as one of the most important subjects. Awareness of our karma is part of true faith. Without awakening to our bad karma we would not be awakened to the unconditional love of the Buddha. In the Shin Buddhist tradition, faith is the foundation of our lives, no matter whether one is a priest or a lay person.

CHAPTER THIRTEEN

The Meaning of Faith

ON THE FALSE TEACHING

IN THIS AREA OF AMIDA'S

ENLIGHTENMENT TEN KALPAS AGO

FASCICLE I, LETTER THIRTEEN

This was also written at Chōshōji Temple.[146]

Recently some of the *Nenbutsu* followers here in Echizen Province have been expressing themselves in strange language, insisting that they have already attained faith. What is worse, they assume that they know everything there is to know about the faith of our tradition. They insist that faith is simply a matter of not forgetting what has been done for us by Amida Buddha, who arranged everything necessary for our birth in the Pure Land when he attained Supreme Enlightenment ten kalpas ago. This is a great mistake. For even if we knew how Amida Tathāgata attained Supreme Enlightenment, such knowledge would be useless if we did not know for ourselves how to attain the Other Power faith through which we are to be born in the Pure Land.

From now on, therefore, above all else we should have a clear grasp of the true faith of our tradition. In *The Larger Sūtra of Eternal Life* this faith is taught as the "triple mind," in *The Meditation Sūtra* it is called "three minds," and in *The Amida Sūtra* it is expressed as "one mind." Although the terms used to express our faith differ in each of the three sūtras, they are simply meant to express the one mind of Other Power.

What, then, is the meaning of faith?

First of all we should set aside all miscellaneous practices and entrust ourselves steadfastly to Amida Tathāgata. If we give no thought to any other gods (*kami*) or Buddhas and singlemindedly take refuge in Amida alone, then the Tathāgata will embrace us in his light and never forsake us. This is the way the one thought-moment of awakening of faith has been attained decisively.

Once we realise this, we should understand that the reason we say the *Nenbutsu* is in order to express our gratitude to Amida Tathāgata for what he has done to help us acquire Other Power faith. Because of this we are called *Nenbutsu* followers who have attained faith decisively.

Most humbly and respectfully
Written in late September, Bunmei 5 [1473].

COMMENTS

The 12th, 13th and 14th letters of Fascicle One are all closely connected having been written at Chōshōji temple, all around the same time in late September 1473. If you read the three letters carefully, you will find they are closely related as to their real meaning, despite the apparent difference of subject matter.

We saw in the previous chapter that the 12th letter of Fascicle One was written by Rennyo Shōnin for the purpose of criticising the *Nenbutsu* followers of Chōshōji temple for their blind involvement in the three desires: the desire for fame, the desire for wealth and the desire for domination. Ultimately Rennyo was also seeking to encourage the followers to try and attain faith through awakening to the reality of the karmic conditions of their temple.

What then was the main intention of his other letter, the 13th letter of Fascicle One subtitled "Also at Chōshōji Temple" and likewise written during his stay at the temple? Well, of course, Rennyo wrote all these letters primarily in order to encourage people to attain true faith so that they could be freed of their own karma. In this respect the three letters are full of love and compassion. The ultimate intention is the same in each case, namely to encourage his followers to attain true faith whereby they will be able to live their lives with the *Nenbutsu* of gratitude. It goes without saying, however, that each letter was also written in response to a particular situation and with some special purpose in mind.

Whilst the main problem Rennyo referred to in the 12th letter was the karmic attachment of those *Nenbutsu* followers to their desires for fame, wealth and domination, he pointed out in this letter that at Chōshōji they were also involved in some serious problems regarding dogma.

Generally speaking, when people have some serious problems deep within, whatever problems these problems may be, whether psychological or practical, domestic or social, such people are inclined to seek to escape from their problems and then to try and hide them, consciously or unconsciously. In order to cover up this act of concealment, they will resort to some persuasive teaching or dogma so that, being engaged in such concealment, they forget their real problems. The more serious their problems, the more tenacious their dogmatic attachment. They close their minds to others and are afraid of the possibility that their problems may be revealed to others. They try to justify themselves and insist on their own dogmatic opinion, declaring that they have already got the point and that they know everything.

The dogmatic attachment I have talked about above appears in the letter as the followers' insistence that "faith is simply a matter of not forgetting what has been done for us by Amida Buddha, who arranged everything necessary for our birth in the Pure Land when he attained Supreme Enlightenment ten kalpas ago." Rennyo Shōnin says that this is a great mistake. Based on this misinterpretation the *Nenbutsu* followers of Chōshōji claim that they know everything about "faith." Indeed, if the Shin Buddhist faith were merely a matter of knowledge or philosophy, it might sound reasonable to state that what is most important is to understand and not forget the work of Amida, undertaken on our behalf many aeons ago. In reality, however, faith is not knowledge or understanding. In order to attain faith you have to transcend the realms of intellectual understanding.

Faith is not to know what Amida Buddha is, but to take refuge in the Buddha singlemindedly, going beyond all attachment to one's own knowledge or understanding. Unless we entrust ourselves to Amida Buddha absolutely, the instantaneous attainment of faith can never come about.

The Shin Buddhist faith is to "entrust ourselves steadfastly to Amida Tathāgata." In other words, it is called "the faith of taking refuge in Amida Buddha singlemindedly." Unless we become aware of the limits of our knowledge, we can never take refuge in Amida Buddha singlemindedly. Faith is not a matter of knowledge. In the case of the followers of Chōshōji at that time, as long as they remained attached to their dogmatic knowledge – their misconception that faith was simply a matter of not forgetting what Amida had done for us – they were unable to take refuge in Amida Buddha, for they were still basing themselves on their own power of understanding. Therefore, in order to lead them to attain true faith, Rennyo Shōnin wrote this letter in an attempt to make them aware of the terrible misunderstanding they had attached themselves to. Their misunderstanding of the notion of faith was not separate from their desire for fame, wealth and domination, deeply embedded in their karmic existence. "Taking refuge in Amida Buddha singlemindedly," true faith in other words, must have been the only way for those followers to rid themselves of such selfish karmic conditions.

In Shin Buddhism this singlemindedness of faith is expressed as "one mind," something absolute that comes from Amida Buddha. In other words "one mind" in this sense is Amida's true mind that operates freely and unrestrictedly to save all beings in the world of birth-and-death. To explain this "one mind" at work when we attain "the faith of taking refuge in Amida Buddha singlemindedly," Rennyo Shōnin refers to "triple mind" in *The Larger Sūtra of Eternal Life*, "three minds" in *The Meditation Sūtra* and "one mind" in *The Amida Sūtra.*

These three terms for "faith" from the three different sūtras need some explanation. According to Shinran's religious philosophy, the most important of the three sūtras is *The Larger Sūtra of Eternal Life,* for it is in this sūtra that the true significance of Amida's vow to save all beings is fully expounded. The other two sūtras are said to possess "apparent" and "hidden" meanings with their different roles respectively. Regarding "three minds" in *The Meditation Sūtra* and "one mind" in *The Amida Sūtra*, their "apparent" or literal meaning that urges *Nenbutsu* followers to attain to true faith by their own effort functions as a skillful means by which to lead them to understanding the true nature of "One Mind of Other Power faith." Ultimately the role of their "hidden" meaning, identical to the singlemindedness of Other Power faith of *The Larger Sūtra*, is just to effect the salvation itself.

The "triple mind" in *The Larger Sūtra of Eternal Life* is understood to be composed of "sincerity," "faith" and "aspiration for birth in the Pure Land." These three are considered to be the three aspects of the "One Mind of Other Power faith." Thus they are called the "three minds of Other Power." In contrast to this are "the three minds" in *The Meditation Sūtra*, "the mind that is true and sincere," "the deep mind" and "the mind desiring to be born in the Pure Land." These three states of mind are considered as something to be achieved as a result of effort by *Nenbutsu* followers who have yet to attain the pure Other Power faith. Therefore they are called the "three minds of self power," which is their "apparent meaning." As with "the three minds" of *The Meditation Sūtra*, the "one mind" of *The Amida Sūtra* is also supposed to come as a result of the *Nenbutsu* followers' effort and is called the "one mind of self power." After the attainment of pure faith, known as the "triple mind" in *The Larger Sūtra of Eternal Life* or the "one mind of Other Power" in *The Treatise on the Pure Land* by Vasubandhu,[147] *Nenbutsu* followers come to realise the "hidden" meaning of both the "three minds" of *The Meditation Sūtra* and the "one mind" of *The Amida Sūtra* and discover that they are originally from Amida Buddha. Rennyo states, therefore, that, although the three terms used to express our faith differ in the case of each of the sūtras, they are all simply meant to express "the one mind of Other Power."

CHAPTER FOURTEEN

Faith and Inner Peace

ADMONITION AGAINST SLANDERING

FASCICLE I, LETTER FOURTEEN

This was written again at Chōshōji Temple.[148]

Now *Nenbutsu* followers in our tradition should not slander any other teachings. In the provinces of Etchū and Kaga, before anywhere else this applies to Tateyama, Shirayama and the other mountain temples and, in Echizen Province, to temples such as Heisenji and Toyoharaji. This is why we can already find an admonition against slander in *The Larger Sūtra of Eternal Life*: "Excluded are those who commit the five grave offences and slander the Right Dharma." Based on this, *Nenbutsu* followers in particular should not slander other schools and it seems only fair that scholars from the various schools of the Path of Sages should not slander *Nenbutsu* followers either. To support this there are many passages in the sūtras and the commentaries admonishing those that slander others, but by far the strictest warning is to be found in the *Commentary on the Mahāprajñāpāramitā Sūtra*[149] by Bodhisattva Nāgârjuna, the founder of the Eight Schools. The passage states, "If, because of his attachment to the teaching he follows, a person speaks ill of other teachings, he will not escape the sufferings of hell, even if he is one who observes the precepts."

There are clear proofs, such as this text, that all schools depend on the Buddha's teachings and so we should not slander them mistakenly. Each school has its own texts. The point is that we ourselves do not need to make use of them. It would be highly irreverent for followers of our tradition, who have no understanding of these matters, to criticise other schools. Those who are head priests in the various areas should make quite sure this does not happen.

Most humbly and respectfully
In late September, Bunmei 5 [1473].

COMMENTS

Rennyo Shōnin's intention when writing this letter was to admonish those same *Nenbutsu* followers of Chōshōji Temple for slandering other schools. The content of this letter seems to be fairly self-explanatory so I would simply like to give a short commentary on it from my own personal viewpoint. What emerges, it seems to me, is that it is absolutely essential for us to attain inner peace in order to bring about world peace.

Amongst the *Nenbutsu* followers of Chōshōji Temple there was a close connection between the problem of their threefold desire for fame, wealth and domination, pointed out by Rennyo in the 12th letter of Fascicle One, and the problem mentioned in 13th letter Fascicle One, those same followers' tenacious attachment to a dogmatic opinion that faith is simply a matter of not forgetting what Amida Buddha did for us ten kalpas ago. The problem of slandering others, taken up by Rennyo in the 14th letter, can be said to be an aggressive outward manifestation of a dogmatic attachment within our minds, already discussed in the 13th letter of Fascicle One.

When with narrow-minded dogmatic attachment one sets oneself up in opposition to others, those dogmatic attachments can become a means by which to go on the attack. As such people's minds are not directed inwardly so as to solve their inner problems, they tend to reach outwardly and conflict with others. In order to hide or avoid their own real problems they simply fight with enemies on the outside. Seeking to bolster their identity, they attack and slander others. To lack inner peace results in having conflicts with others on the outside. What is most important is to maintain inner peace whilst seeking to solve one's own problems in the light of the Buddha's teaching.

The realisation of inner peace is crucial in the modern world, especially in the mutual relationship between religions. Without each individual attaining inner peace, we can never hope to realise harmony between different religions, nor world peace between different nations. Although there may seem to be many advocates of peace in the world, there are all too few able to introspect and attain that level of inner peace necessary to bring about any lasting accord with others.

CHAPTER FIFTEEN

The True
Teaching of the
Pure Land

ON THE NAMING OF OUR TRADITION

FASCICLE I, LETTER FIFTEEN

QUESTION: There is a widespread tendency to refer to our tradition as the "Ikkōshū" (literally, Steadfast School). I wonder how this custom came about amongst the people of this world and I would like to ask you about it.

ANSWER: It was not our founder's decision to refer to our tradition specifically as the "Ikkōshū." Generally speaking, the reason people use this designation is because we "steadfastly" (ikkō) entrust ourselves to Amida Buddha. In fact, however, given that a passage from the *Sūtra* teaches us to "think of the Buddha of Eternal Life steadfastly and exclusively,"[150] the naming of our tradition as the "Ikkōshū" presents no problem in as much as the implication of the word *ikkō* is "to think steadfastly of the Buddha of Eternal Life." What our founder did call our school, however, was the "Jōdo Shinshū (the True Teaching of the Pure Land)." We should be aware, therefore, that followers of the tradition do not themselves actually use the term "Ikkōshū." In reality, whilst followers in all the other Pure Land schools are allowed to use miscellaneous practices, our own master decided to abandon such miscellaneous practices. It is on this basis that we attain birth in the True Land of Enjoyment. For this reason, our founder specifically added the character 真 (jp. *shin*, meaning "true") to the name of our tradition.

ANOTHER QUESTION: I now understand clearly that our tradition was actually designated the "Jōdo Shinshū." In our tradition, however, we are taught that even those lay people who are heavily burdened with bad karma and grave offences can still readily attain birth in the Land of Utmost Bliss by entrusting themselves to the Power of Amida's Vow. I would like to hear in detail how birth can be attained.

ANSWER: What we teach in our tradition is that when we attain faith decisively we will be born without fail in the True Land of Enjoyment. If now you ask what this faith is, then the answer is that it is simply the entrusting of oneself to Amida Tathāgata singlemindedly and without worry. On entrusting ourselves steadfastly and without any doublemindedness to Amida, we do not give any thought to other Buddhas or Bodhisattvas. This is what we mean by "attaining faith decisively." The two Chinese characters *shinjin* 信心 (ch. *xìnxīn*), meaning 'faith,' can be understood as "true mind." We say that faith is the "true mind" because those who practise the *Nenbutsu* are not saved by their wrong mind of self power (*waroki jiriki no kokoro*), but by the good mind of Tathāgata's Other Power. Further, we are not saved simply by repeating the Name without any understanding of it. Therefore, *The Larger Sūtra* teaches that we "hear that Name and rejoice in the awakening of faith." "Hearing that Name" is not simply hearing the six-character Name (*Namu Amida-butsu* 南无阿彌陀佛) pointlessly and fruitlessly. "Hearing that Name" actually means that when we meet a good teacher, receive his teaching and entrust ourselves to the Name, *Namu Amida-butsu*, then Amida Buddha saves us without fail. This attainment of faith is described in *The Larger Sūtra of Eternal Life* as "rejoicing in the awakening of faith."[151] We should understand therefore that *Namu Amida-butsu* shows how Amida saves us.

After having come to this realisation we must understand that the Name we recite walking, standing, sitting and lying down is simply an expression of gratitude for all that Amida Tathāgata has done to save us. It follows that we may be permitted to call ourselves Other Power *Nenbutsu* followers who have attained faith decisively and will be born in the Land of Utmost Bliss.

Most humbly and respectfully

I have completed writing this letter between nine and eleven in the morning of the second day of the latter part of September, in the year Bunmei 5 [1473], at the hot springs at Yamanaka in Kaga Province.

COMMENTS

In this the last letter of Fascicle One, Rennyo Shōnin discusses the proper naming of the Shin Buddhist tradition. Broadly speaking there were at that time two names for this tradition: the Jōdo Shinshū 浄土真宗 and the Ikkōshū 一向宗. Jōdo Shinshū means 'True Teaching of the Pure Land,' and is the name for the Pure Land tradition which Shinran Shōnin, the founder of Shin Buddhism, luckily became involved in. In his writings Shinran Shōnin quite often used the name with a feeling of gratitude for his encounter with this true Pure Land Teaching. Of the instances where this name appears in his writings, the most important place is the very beginning of the first chapter entitled "The Collection of Passages Expounding the True Teaching of the Pure Land" of his main work, *The Kyōgyōshinshō,* Shinran Shōnin starts the chapter with these words:

> As I respectfully reflect on the true doctrine of the Pure Land, there are two forms of *ekō* (virtue-transference): the outgoing *ekō* and the returning *ekō*. It is in the outgoing *ekō* that we have the true teaching, true living, true faith and true realisation.[152]

On looking at the way he uses this name, it can easily be seen that he had no intention at all of establishing a new school. This use of the name was in fact just an expression of his gratitude and joy at having been able to encounter this true teaching of the Pure Land Tradition. And what is then the meaning of Sangha or community in Shin Buddhism? Those who shared the same feeling as Shinran Shōnin began to gather and live together in order to continue to proceed along the same path to the Pure Land. As a result the first Shin Buddhist group or Sangha was formed. We should never forget this as being the original starting point. If you ever fail to find the joy of true faith in your Sangha, you should not remain attached to this feeling. The problem is not your Sangha but your own attachment. Taking upon yourself responsibility for the Sangha, you should return to that original starting point.

In complete contrast to the name "Jōdo Shinshū" that emerged actually from within the Shin Buddhist group itself, the other name "Ikkōshū" seems to have been bestowed on it by people from outside the Shin Buddhist Sangha. Rennyo suspected that this usage of the name "Ikkōshū" became commonplace when Shin Buddhist followers were confused with members of a branch of the Jishū School with that name.[153]

From the perspective of religious philosophy there are three important points in this letter. Firstly, the naming of this Pure Land tradition as Jōdo Shinshū, literally "True Teaching of the Pure Land," is deeply connected with the Shin Buddhist way whereby we set aside all miscellaneous practices and simply perform the *Nenbutsu* alone as being the right practice that rightly assures our birth in the Pure Land. To bear this out, let me quote again from *The Kyōgyōshinshō*. Referring to the main writing of his own master, Hōnen Shōnin, Shinran Shōnin states,

> *The Senjaku hongan Nenbutsu shū* (compiled by Genkū) begins: "*Namu Amida-butsu*, the work for rebirth is based in the *Nenbutsu*." It says further:
> "If one wishes speedily to be free from birth-and-death, there are two excellent ways, of which the teaching of the 'way for holy men' may be disregarded for a while. Let us rather specifically choose the teaching of the Pure Land. There are, again, two ways to enter into the Pure Land teaching: the right way and the mixed way. Of the two, let us give up the mixed way and specifically choose the right way. Of the right practice and the supportive practices, the latter is to be set aside. Let us specifically choose the right practice and concentrate our efforts upon the right practice that rightly assures [our birth in the Pure Land]. The right practice that rightly assures [our birth in the Pure Land] is to pronounce the Buddha Name. When this is done, one shall assuredly be born [in the Pure Land], on the strength of the Buddha's Original Vow."
> Thus, it is evident that the *Nenbutsu* is not an act of self power performed by ordinary beings or even by the wise. So it is known as the practice which does not originate from our side, but which originates from the other side [that is, from Amida]. Major [Mahāyāna] as well as minor [Hīnayāna] sages and light as well as heavy sinners are all uniformly to take refuge in the great-ocean of specific selection, and attain Buddhahood by the strength of the *Nenbutsu*.[154]

It was Shinran Shōnin's master, Hōnen Shōnin, who clarified the importance of absolute reliance on the *Nenbutsu*. This teaching of *Nenbutsu* became the foundation of Japanese Pure Land Buddhism. However, to rely on the *Nenbutsu* alone is not so easy, because our attachment to various practices is deeply embedded in the consciousness of self power. In fact it is impossible for us to entrust ourselves absolutely to the *Nenbutsu* alone until such a time we come to be awakened to the fact that it is based on the Buddha's Original Vow.

The *Nenbutsu* is in reality the working of Amida Buddha's Original Vow. What is called true faith in Shin Buddhism is this experience of awakening to the Original Vow through which we entrust ourselves just as we are to Amida Buddha, becoming at the same time aware of the limitation of our self power. We absolutely rely on the *Nenbutsu* as the act that enables us to attain birth in the Pure Land, because it is entirely based on the Original Vow of Amida Buddha.

The second important point about this letter is that faith (*shinjin*) is referred to as the "true mind." Rennyo Shōnin says in his letter, "We say that faith is the "true mind" because those who practise the *Nenbutsu* are not saved by their wrong mind of self power (*waroki jiriki no kokoro*), but by the good mind of Tathāgata's Other Power." Faith is the "true mind" because it is the pure mind of the Buddha, the mind that the Buddha has already given us.

The third and most crucial point about the letter is found in the middle of the fourth paragraph, beginning with the statement, "Further, we are not saved simply by repeating the Name without any understanding of it." In this paragraph Rennyo Shōnin clarifies the fundamental reality of the Shin Buddhist faith. As you know there is a passage in *The Larger Sūtra of Eternal Life* that describes how people attain faith – the passage relating to the fulfilment of the Original Vow. It reads as follows,

> As all beings hear his Name, faith is awakened in them and they are gladdened down to one thought. This comes to them from having been turned-over from Amida's sincere mind. When they desire to be born in the Pure Land, they are born there at that moment and abide in the stage of nonretrogression.[155]

When Rennyo states, "Therefore *The Larger Sūtra* teaches that we 'hear that Name and rejoice in the awakening of faith'," he is actually referring to the first part of the quotation. The phrase of eight characters, 聞其名號 信心 歡喜, is the original for the English version "to hear that name and rejoice in the awakening of faith." In the above quotation, the phrase "that Name 其名 號" is translated as "his Name." I cannot say this translation is wrong, because it is after all Amida's Name and in this respect the translation is correct. But the phrase "that Name" actually implies something more, not simply Amida's Name but Amida's Name as pronounced by all the Buddhas. The phrase "that Name" refers to the Name that all Buddhas pronounce in praise.

The above quotation relates to the fulfilment of the Eighteenth Original Vow. It is actually preceded in the same sūtra by the following lines, "All the Buddha-Tathāgatas in the ten quarters, who are as numberless as the sands of the river Ganga, unanimously praise the awe-inspiring dignity and the inconceivable virtues of the Buddha of Eternal Life."[156]

This passage from *The Larger Sūtra* is known as the one that relates to the fulfilment of the Seventeenth Original Vow: "If, upon my attaining Buddhahood, all the innumerable Buddhas in the ten quarters were not approvingly to pronounce my Name, may I not attain the Supreme Enlightenment".[157]

To support my argument here I have quoted these documents to you, showing as they do the interrelationship between the Seventeenth and Eighteenth Original Vow. It is clear from traditional Shin Buddhist studies that the phrase "that Name" referred to in the passage on the fulfilment of the Eighteenth Original Vow is indeed Amida's Name that all the innumerable Buddhas pronounce in praise.

In this context, moreover, the phrase "all Buddhas" stands for a good teacher. Unfortunately, nowadays scholars do not pay much attention to this central notion of Shin Buddhist faith-experience. Rennyo Shōnin, the Restorer of Shin Buddhism, emphasised this crucial point, however, because he well understood the dynamics of faith in daily life. Our relationship to our master or teacher is therefore of critical importance as we proceed together on our way to the Pure Land.

The essential starting point of every religion lies in the spiritual encounter between individuals. If it wanders too far from this point, no religion could survive. Each stage of our spiritual journey should be accompanied by this living relationship between master and disciple.

Life after the Attainment of Faith

ON CLEANING OUT

THE CHANNELS OF FAITH

FASCICLE II, LETTER ONE

It has come to my attention that, in the course of the seven days of this year's Hōonkō Assembly, almost all the wives of the priests in charge of the *taya* houses, along with a number of other people staying in them, have attained faith decisively. This is a matter for great congratulation. We could not have hoped for anything better. If we just let things drift as we please, even the faith thus attained will disappear. It is taught somewhere, I have heard, that "again and again we should clean out the channels of faith and let the waters of Amida's Dharma flow freely."

Regarding this point, it should be understood that it is only Amida Tathāgata who graciously saves women, whereas all the other Buddhas of the ten directions and the three periods have abandoned trying to save them. This is because, however true women's minds may become, their doubt is deep-seated and their inclination to avoid inauspicious things is also very difficult to eradicate. Lay people in particular, taken up by worldly affairs and their concern for their children and grandchildren, give themselves only to this life. Whilst already evidently aware that the human world is impermanent, being 'a realm of uncertainty for young and old alike', they spend nights and days in idleness, giving no thought at all to the fact that they are fated soon to fall into the three bad paths and the eight difficulties.[158] This is the way ordinary people live their lives. It is indescribably sad.

You should take refuge, therefore, singleheartedly and steadfastly in the Compassionate Vow of 'the One Buddha', Amida Buddha, and entrust yourselves entirely to him. Discarding all attachment to miscellaneous practices, you should also cast off all subservient thoughts of gods (*kami*) and other Buddhas. Then, in the realisation that Amida Tathāgata's Original Vow, created by him for the sake of miserable women such as yourselves, is indeed the product of the Buddha's inconceivable wisdom, and admitting yourselves to be bad and wretched beings, you should hold on to the deep mind to entrust yourselves to the Tathāgata. At this point you should realise that your faith of entrusting yourselves to the Buddha and your thought of being mindful of the Buddha are both awakened by virtue of Amida Tathāgata's Skillful Means.

Those who get to the heart of the teaching in this way are called those who have attained Other Power faith. People at this stage are also described as "dwelling in the company of those rightly assured," "being sure to reach Nirvāṇa," "reaching the stage proximate to Supreme Enlightenment," and "being equal to Maitreya." We also call them "those whose birth has been assured with the awakening of the one thought-moment of faith." You should realise that, on the basis of this understanding, the *Nenbutsu* in the way of pronouncing the Name is the *Nenbutsu* of joy, expressing our gratitude for all that Amida Tathāgata has done for us in order to enable us to attain birth in the Pure Land.

Most humbly and respectfully

Concerning the matters mentioned above, you should first of all observe the regulations of our tradition very carefully. The reason for this is that, if you understand the way to attain faith detailed here, you should be very careful to store it deep within yourselves and not give away any sign of it in the presence of strangers or members of other sects. You should not talk about faith either. As for gods (*kami*) and the like, it is simply that we do not trust in them; we should not be disrespectful towards them. Shōnin referred to one who is genuine both in faith and conduct as being 'a devout follower who fully understands the teaching.' Quite simply we are to preserve the Buddha-dharma deep in our hearts.

Most humbly and respectfully

I have written this letter on the eighth day of December in the fifth year of Bunmei [1473] and am giving it to the wives of the priests who are in charge of the *taya* houses on this hill. If there are other matters still to be discussed, you should inquire again.

Seeing off the old year, both hot and cold, at the age of fifty-eight. [Seal]

> May these Dharma words,
> I have written down as a landmark for later generations,
> Be my memento.

COMMENTS

Towards the end of his letter Rennyo states that it was written on 8th December in 1473 (Bunmei 5), soon after the close of the Hōonkō Ceremony which would have been held for seven days from the Evening Service on 21st November to the Day Service of 28th. He also writes in his postscript that he is now "at the age of fifty-eight." If both statements refer to the date he wrote the letter, however, they apparently contradict one another, because in the fifth year of Bunmei he would have already been fifty-nine years old. Probably in the fifth year of Bunmei he simply copied the letter he had written in the preceding year.

This letter is read out at the morning service immediately after the close of the Hōonkō Ceremony, the most important ceremony of the year, at all Shin Buddhist temples belonging to the Honganji tradition. The ritual of reading out the letter has been pursued for some five hundred and forty years, which goes to show how important it is to Shin Buddhists.

The letter was actually addressed to the wives of the priests who were in charge of the *taya* houses at Yoshizaki. The fact that this letter was, and still is, held in such high regard shows us how important women have always been in the Shin Buddhist tradition. Rennyo Shōnin wrote this letter to these ladies because he so appreciated all their hard work during the ceremony.

Earlier in *Chapter 8* I referred to the rapid expansion of Rennyo Shōnin's Sangha in Hokuriku District, immediately after his arrival at Yoshizaki in 1471. According to a letter written by Rennyo on 2nd August 1473, about four months before he copied the first letter of Fascicle Two, no less than one or two hundred *taya* houses had already been built around the main temple at Yoshizaki. This means that at that time there would have been several hundred followers living in and around the temple constantly, while on special occasions their ranks would have been swollen by thousands more. Innumerable people must have gathered at the temple for the Hōonkō Assembly of 1473 as well.

As one can easily imagine, welcoming so many people all at once to Yoshizaki would have been a huge problem. Before the construction of the main temple, the area had been completely wild, as described in the eighth letter of Fascicle One, where Rennyo Shōnin writes, "Eventually, finding the site known as Yoshizaki in Hosorogi County of this province exceedingly attractive, we cleared the land on the hill that had long been the domain of wild beasts."[159] There were no inns in the area, so it was the women folk who prepared the accommodation and meals for those who gathered at Yoshizaki, an enormous undertaking that must have cost a huge amount of effort. There were a large number of *taya* houses on the hill, where priests along with their wives and Dharma friends enjoyed their spiritual way of life, spending their days and nights seeking after truth under the instruction of Rennyo Shōnin. On special occasions such as the Hōonkō Ceremony, these *taya* houses suddenly became lodgings for a great many visitors from far away places.

The amount of work women are faced with during these special occasions at Shin Buddhist temples is tremendous. Not only priests but also their wives and their helpers have to work very hard to prepare for the events and then welcome people warm-heartedly. What is most important is not so much the practical chores the women have to perform, such as cooking, washing, bed-making and cleaning, but the spiritual development they undergo in the course of all this work. Without the attainment of true faith, the goal of their spiritual training, all this hard work would remain meaningless. The same is true for the priests. Without attaining faith, all their efforts to decorate the Buddha shrine, clean the precincts, chant sūtras and give Dharma talks would end completely in vain. Thus, whilst working very hard, the wives of the priests also aim to attain true faith. However little time they may have, they try to find opportunities to attend Dharma meetings or to listen and speak to their Dharma friends.

In a Shin Buddhist temple it would be almost impossible to hold a big event like the Hōonkō Assembly without the help of the women. The role they play on such occasions is fundamental. Despite their extremely heavy workload, such occasions provide the greatest opportunity for them to attain faith, because a great number of Dharma friends, men and women, young and old, priests and lay people gather there with one and the same purpose. The mutual influence of good friends is vital in guiding the women to the awakening of true faith.

You can imagine how extremely difficult it must be to attain faith whilst at the same time being deeply immersed in practical matters such as kitchen duties and cleaning. Carrying out such chores with a lot of other people can also cause many problems because of the diversity of different people's opinions. This is why Rennyo was so grateful to the women for their hard work as well as so happy to hear about their attainment of faith. "This is a matter for great congratulation," he wrote, "We could not have hoped for anything better." Wishing for their happiness from the bottom of his heart, however, Rennyo Shōnin also asked them to take a further step, which I would like to examine in greater detail.

The quotation in the first paragraph is said to be based on a text from another Pure Land tradition, so Rennyo says very cautiously, "It is taught somewhere, I have heard, that 'again and again we should clean out the channels of faith and let the waters of Amida's Dharma flow freely.'" The actual source of this quotation is the *Ōjō raisan shō* by Gyōe (*d.* 1395) of the Seizan sect of Japanese Pure Land Buddhism, which reads,

> As we find blind passions arising, we repent. Regarding how to interpret the phrase 'Every time one commits a wrongdoing, one repents,' it is said to mean that, although we do not lose the White Path, we repent and remove the clouds caused by the blind passions that actually arise. It is like wiping away dust on a mirror or cleaning dirt out of a channel. The faith of taking refuge in Other Power that is the right cause [for birth in the Pure Land] is clearing out the channels to let the waters of Other Power virtue flow freely. We always, each moment of thought, continue to clean away the dirt of blind passions accumulated [in our minds].[160]

The main purpose of this letter is, firstly, to encourage women, the wives of priests in this case, to attain true faith and, secondly, to encourage those women who have already attained faith to keep their faith pure by "clearing out the channels of faith and letting the waters of Amida's Dharma flow freely." The first point can be found in a great number of Rennyo Shōnin's letters but, as the second point is unique to this letter, I would like to focus on it in more detail in this part of my commentary.

Rennyo says that the reason we should try to clean out the channels of faith is that, "If we just let things drift as we please, even the faith thus attained will disappear." He also says in the second paragraph, "This is because, however true women's minds may become, their doubt is deep-seated and their inclination to avoid inauspicious things is also very difficult to eradicate."

For those who study Shin Buddhism as an academic subject and do not live this faith in their daily life, this observation by Rennyo about women's minds may sound odd, to say the least. It is taught in Shin Buddhism that once faith is attained it is indestructible because it is a gift from Amida Buddha. Rennyo refers to this point when he says, "Those who get to the heart of the teaching in this way are called those who have attained Other Power faith. People at this stage are also described as 'dwelling in the company of those rightly assured,' 'being sure to reach Nirvāṇa,' 'reaching the stage proximate to Supreme Enlightenment,' and 'being equal to Maitreya.' We also call them 'those whose birth has been assured with the awakening of the one thought-moment of faith.'" It is absolutely true that faith is indestructible. Facing the reality of this world, however, our awareness of this faith is actually obscured and sometimes looks as if it has vanished. We can see such cases amongst people around us, myself included sometimes. To remain aware of the truth that faith is as indestructible as a diamond, we have to examine our consciousness in the light of the Buddha. Illuminated by the Buddha's light we become aware of the clouds that cover our true faith. The clouds sometimes seem like immovable obstacles. When they do, we become severely depressed. What is important is for us to be awakened to the obstacles that surround us through the light of the Buddha. This reminds me of Shinran Shōnin's words found in *The Shōshinge*,

> The mind-light that embraces us always illumines and protects us.
> Though the darkness of ignorance is already broken through,
> The clouds and mists of tenacious greed and repulsive hatred
> Still continue to cover the sky of true and real faith.
> It is as if, though the sun-light is veiled by clouds and mists,
> Below the clouds and mists brightness reigns and there is no darkness.[161]

Just like the wives of priests in charge of the *taya* houses at Yoshizaki, when we are involved in practical matters and face serious problems, we feel as if the channels of faith are being blocked by obstacles of some sort. These hindrances are not external, however, but internal. As Shinran Shōnin says in the above quotation, the reality of the obstructions is our blind passions, tenacious greed and repulsive hatred. When, through the light of the Buddha, we become aware of these dense clouds and mists that shroud the sky of true faith, in other words, when we realise that the real problems are caused by ourselves, what we can do is simply say "I am sorry." Along with this repentance comes a welling up of the *Nenbutsu*. This *Nenbutsu* of repentance is at the same time the *Nenbutsu* of joy, because Amida Buddha vowed to save the wretched beings that we are. Rennyo Shōnin says, "You should realise that, on the basis of this understanding, the *Nenbutsu* is the *Nenbutsu* of joy, expressing our gratitude for all that Amida Tathāgata has done for us in order to enable us to attain birth in the Pure Land." If this is realised, we are filled with happiness knowing that Amida's mind-light always shines upon us piercing the thick clouds and mists of our consciousness. "It is as if, though the sun-light is veiled by clouds and mists, below the clouds and mists brightness reigns and there is no darkness." What a wonderful inner-world full of light this is!

By way of conclusion I would like to emphasise how deeply Rennyo Shōnin appreciated the role of women in Shin Buddhism. Because of his heartfelt love and compassion towards women, he left many letters addressed to them. Amongst these letters this is probably the most important and moving. Since Rennyo emphasised the spiritual importance of women, their roles in the Shin Buddhist tradition have become more diverse over the centuries and nowadays there are more and more women who choose to become priests.

CHAPTER SEVENTEEN

The Two Truths

ON THE POINT OF DEPARTURE

FOR THE PURE LAND

FASCICLE II, LETTER TWO

In the tradition of Shinran Shōnin, the founder of our school, priority is given first and foremost to faith. What then is the purpose of faith? It is the very starting point that enables us, wretched beings that do no good and commit only wrongdoing, to travel readily to Amida's Pure Land. If we do not attain faith, we can never be born into the Land of Utmost Bliss but will fall instead into the Hell of Incessant Pain.

How then can we attain this faith? We should entrust ourselves absolutely to the "One Buddha," Amida Tathāgata, giving no thought to other good deeds and myriad practices, abandoning our inclination to petition various gods and Bodhisattvas just for the sake of our earthly lives and forsaking all our wrong, erroneous thoughts of self power attachment. If we entrust ourselves joyfully to Amida Buddha not with double-mindedness but with single-heartedness and steadfastness, then Amida will embrace us in his all-encompassing light and never abandon a single one of us. Once we have attained this faith, we should understand that the *Nenbutsu* we pronounce at all times, whether sleeping or waking, is an expression of our gratitude for all that Amida has done to save us.

People who understand in this way are rightly called true examples of those who have attained faith in accordance with our tradition. If there are people who say that there is anything other than this that can be called "faith," they are gravely mistaken. We should not accept any such opinion.

Most humbly and respectfully

What I have set down in this letter is the true meaning of faith, taught by Shinran Shōnin, of our tradition. Those who fully understand this point must never talk about matters of faith to people from other traditions or persons they do not know. The simple matter is we do not rely on any of the other Buddhas and Bodhisattvas or on any of the gods. Yet we must never make light of them. We should realise that all the gods are contained within the virtue of Amida, the One Buddha. Without exception you must never blaspheme against any of the Dharma teachings. If you understand this, you will be called a person who faithfully follows the rules of conduct of our tradition. Hence Shōnin urged, "Even if you are called a 'cattle thief,' do not act in such a way that you are seen as an aspirant for birth in the Pure Land, or as a good person, or as a follower of the Buddha-dharma." We should be careful to understand this point whilst practising the *Nenbutsu*.

Written on the evening of 12th December, Bunmei 5 [1473].

COMMENTS

As the last line shows, this letter was written on 12th of December in 1473. According to *The Ofumi raii shō* 御文来意鈔,[162] a commentary on *The Letters*, it was composed when Jōyū, a believer from Ōshū with erroneous views, visited Rennyo Shōnin at Yoshizaki. When he learned that Jōyū had been teaching people not to respect the gods and not to pronounce the *Nenbutsu* because it is self power, Rennyo reprimanded him severely. After that, Rennyo wrote this letter and gave it to Dōshū,[163] saying that if followers from Ōshū, perhaps affected by Jōyū's wrong teaching, or Jōyū himself, came to Yoshizaki, he should show the letter to them.

Traditionally, the main letter and its postscript are said to refer respectively to *shintai* 真諦, the ultimate aspect of truth or absolute truth (skt. *paramārtha-satya*) and *zokutai* 俗諦, the secular aspect of truth or relative truths (skt. *saṃvṛti-satya*). These two aspects are indispensable to one another. In Buddhism they are each considered to support the other.

In Shin Buddhism *shintai*, or ultimate truth, means the way in which one should attain Buddhahood, whilst *zokutai*, or secular truth, means the way one should behave as a member of the Shin Buddhist society.

After talking in the first paragraph about the vitally important role faith plays in Shin Buddhism, Rennyo Shōnin in the second paragraph expounds on *shintai*, the way of attaining Buddhahood within this tradition. According to the religious philosophy of Shinran Shōnin, the only possible way to become a Buddha is through the attainment of faith, after which life on the way to the Pure Land is lived with the deepest gratitude to the Buddha, he who saves absolutely everyone without any sort of discrimination. Rennyo Shōnin actually reveals two aspects of *shintai* in this second paragraph: firstly how to attain faith by entrusting oneself entirely to Amida Buddha and secondly how to live life with pure faith once faith has been attained. In the Shin Buddhist tradition these two aspects of *shintai* are all-important on the way to attaining Buddhahood in the Pure Land.

Rennyo Shōnin goes on in this paragraph to describe in detail how to attain the Shin Buddhist faith and concludes, "the *Nenbutsu* we pronounce at all times, whether sleeping or waking, is an expression of our gratitude for all that Amida has done to save us." Faith is explained as "entrusting oneself to Amida Buddha." When we attain this faith, we do so "giving no thought to other good deeds and myriad practices" because it is only to Amida Buddha that we entrust ourselves and to nobody and nothing else. If we take pride in what we have done, however faintly, then the faith engendered by entrusting ourselves to the Buddha cannot be pure. If we say we entrust ourselves to the Buddha, then we have no "inclination to petition various gods and Bodhisattvas just for our earthly lives," because Amida Buddha is not an object of petition or prayer with regard to our earthly lives. Shin Buddhists should make no petitions to gods or superior beings for worldly gain. Rennyo Shōnin also says that when we attain faith we "forsake all our wrong, erroneous thoughts of self power attachment." The Japanese word *jiriki* is usually translated as "self power." If one takes "self power" as simply meaning one's power to feel, think and do things, then there is nothing really wrong with it. Divorced from good and bad, right and wrong, holy and secular, "self power" is more of a neutral notion.

In the Pure Land tradition, however, the word "self power" is used in a negative way, because we are usually very much attached to "self power," taking a great deal of pride in it. What is wrong, false and erroneous is this attachment to self power. Attachment to "self power" precludes the pure action of "doing for the doing." When the Japanese word *jiriki* is used in a negative sense, what it actually refers to is this attachment of ours to "self power."

In the context of this letter, therefore, I have translated *jiriki* as "self power attachment." I thought about the problem for quite some time. Every time I came across the word, I tried to work out whether it really included the meaning "attachment" or not. I am now confident that it does. If there remains any attachment to "self power," the faith by which we entrust ourselves to the Buddha cannot be pure, precisely because we still partly depend on the self power of feeling, thinking and acting.

When we truly attain faith, we entrust our whole existence to the Buddha just as we are, no matter whether we still retain an attachment to self power. To describe this pure faith Rennyo uses the terms "no double-mindedness," "single-heartedness," and "steadfastness." These are important features of true faith for Shin Buddhists. Psychologically speaking, when we find ourselves exposed to Other Power, or the unconditional love of Amida Buddha, and entrust ourselves to it, our self-consciousness attached to self power is breached and we pass through to a pure world of no discrimination, a world filled with light. Rennyo Shōnin says, "Then Amida will embrace them in his all-encompassing light and never abandon a single one of them."

To conclude his description of *shintai,* or the way to become a Buddha in the Shin Buddhist tradition, Rennyo states that, "once we have attained this faith, we should understand that the *Nenbutsu* we pronounce at all times, whether sleeping or waking, is an expression of our gratitude for all that Amida has done to save us." This is another very important aspect of *shintai,* namely the Shin Buddhist way of living after the attainment of faith. Being filled with gratitude to Amida Buddha, Shin Buddhist followers really enjoy their journey to the Pure Land.

When I was younger I did have rather less of a sense than I do now of being on my way to the Pure Land. These days, as I get closer and closer to the end of my life, the feeling is getting very much stronger. I am not sad but rather happy really to be allowed to go on living in this world, surrounded and supported by good Dharma friends. At the same time I feel a strong sense of responsibility and concern as to how I can best impart this joyful feeling of faith to younger generations. Reciting the *Nenbutsu* at all times, performing the morning and evening service, writing essays every day like this, I do find myself on the way to the Pure Land, getting nearer to the end certainly, while all I really wish to do is to help young people realise how important it is for them to attain faith here and now. I was very impressed by Rennyo Shōnin's words, "Faith is the very starting point that enables us, wretched beings that do no good and commit only wrongdoing, to travel readily to Amida's Pure Land."

As mentioned before, the postscript to the letter refers to the teaching of *zokutai,* the way in which one should behave as a member of the Shin Buddhist community in society. In this letter *Zokutai* is expounded by means of three rules of conduct: firstly one should not talk about matters of faith carelessly to unfamiliar people, secondly one should not make light of other Buddhas, Bodhisattvas or gods and thirdly one should not blaspheme against any of the Dharma teachings. I will be discussing the last two regulations in the next chapter as they feature again in the third letter of Fascicle Two. In relation to the first regulation, I would like to mention only the words that Rennyo Shōnin quotes Shinran Shōnin as saying, namely, "Even if you are called a 'cattle thief,' do not act in such a way that you are seen as an aspirant for birth in the Pure Land, or as a good person, or as a follower of the Buddha-dharma." These words are not easy to understand without some knowledge of the historical background. The passage, which appears repeatedly in the second letter and thirteenth letters of Fascicle Two and the eleventh letter of Fascicle Three, is being quoted from *The Gaija shō* by Kakunyo (1270–1351),[164] great grandson of Shinran Shōnin. Concerning the source of Shinran Shōnin's allusion, there is an interesting story in a sūtra known as *The Zōho zō kyō*[165] in Japanese. An *arhat* called Revata was mistaken for a cattle thief and thrown into prison. After spending twelve years mucking out stables, he was finally discovered by one of his disciples and liberated. Despite what had happened to him he did not argue with the authorities who punished him.

Why Shinran Shōnin and Rennyo Shōnin talked about the importance of this kind of attitude is another problem. There must have been several reasons for it and they are interrelated to one another. Rennyo Shōnin might have thought that we should not talk about matters of faith carelessly to unfamiliar people, firstly because we should avoid others' criticism against our tradition as much as possible, secondly because we should warn ourselves not to be proud of our thought and school, thirdly because we should always cherish inner peace, not directing our minds outwardly only, and fourthly because we should follow the rules of this world as much as possible. I think Rennyo Shōnin's deep consideration was focused on how happily his followers could fulfil their journey to the Pure Land. From the modern way of thinking, however, there must be different opinions about how to deal with this problem based on our contemporary situations.

CHAPTER EIGHTEEN

Three Articles
of Instruction

CONCERNING THREE ARTICLES

INCLUDING ONE ON SHINMEI[166]

FASCICLE II, LETTER THREE

Within this tradition of ours, disseminated by our founder Shōnin, everyone's way of teaching appears to differ. Henceforth, therefore, all priests, from those in charge of the *taya* houses down to those who will read one volume after another from the sacred scriptures, and all the lay followers who assemble here, including even those who have enrolled just in name only as followers of our school, absolutely everyone in fact, should understand these three articles and from now on deal with problems in accordance with them.

The first article is that we should not slander other teachings or other schools.

The second is that we should never belittle any gods (*kami*), nor belittle Buddhas and Bodhisattvas.

The third is that we should attain faith to attain birth in the Land of Enjoyment.

Those followers who fail to observe the above three articles, do not store them deep in their hearts, nor take them as fundamental principles, are not permitted to enter this temple.

I left beautiful Kyoto in May of the third year of Bunmei (1471) and constructed a hut on this hill, a wild place constantly lashed by wind and waves, in the latter part of July of the same year. My ultimate purpose in remaining here for over four years has simply been to lead equally, in terms of these three articles, all those dwelling throughout the provinces of Hokuriku District, who have not yet awakened faith decisively according to our tradition, to attain the same peaceful awareness as ourselves. For this reason I have endured [every hardship] up until today, up until this very moment. Therefore, if you understand and treasure what is meant by these articles, you will accord with my original purpose in staying in this country all these months and years.

Regarding the second article, gods called *shinmei* are all provisional manifestations of Amida Buddha. He has appeared as *kami* in order to save sentient beings in whatever way possible, lamenting that those who lack faith in the Buddha-dharma will fall helplessly down into hell. Wishing to make use of even the most tenuous of connections, he employs skillful means to appear provisionally as *kami* in order to lead [all sentient beings] at last to the Buddha-dharma. Thus, if sentient beings of the present time have attained faith decisively by entrusting themselves to Amida Buddha and if they pronounce the *Nenbutsu* and come to be assured of birth in the Land of Utmost Bliss, then all the gods, recognising this as the fulfilment of their original desire, will rejoice and protect those who practise the *Nenbutsu*. Therefore, although we do not make a particular practice of worshipping gods, all is already included in the faith in which we entrust ourselves solely to the One Buddha, Amida Buddha. Consequently, even though we do not take refuge in any particular god, faith in Amida naturally encompasses trust in gods. That is the reason why.[167]

Regarding the first article that in our tradition we should not slander other teachings and other schools, because the teachings are all based on the sermons Śākyamuni delivered during his lifetime, they should be fruitful if they are practised according to his instructions. In this Last Dharma Age, however, lay people such as ourselves are unable to follow the teachings of the various schools of the Path for the Holy, so we simply do not rely on them or entrust ourselves to them.

Regarding the second article, because Buddhas and Bodhisattvas are manifestations of Amida Tathāgata, Amida Buddha is the original teacher and the original Buddha for all the other Buddhas of the ten directions. For this reason, when we take refuge in the One Buddha, Amida Buddha, this immediately means that we take refuge in all the Buddhas and all the

Bodhisattvas; the Buddhas and Bodhisattvas are all encompassed within the One Body of Amida Buddha.

Regarding the third article, the essence of the true Other Power faith in Amida Tathāgata, taught by our founder Shinran Shōnin, lies in entrusting ourselves to the Original Vow, whereby we discard all miscellaneous practices and steadfastly and singleheartedly take refuge in Amida, exclusively pronouncing the *Nenbutsu* with absolute concentration. Thus, in accordance with what we have often learned from our predecessors, we should understand that our true faith in Amida Tathāgata is in itself the inconceivable working of the Buddha's wisdom, imparted through Other Power, and we should fully understand that the one thought-moment is the time when birth is assured. If we continue to live on after realising all this, this will naturally lead us to utter the *Nenbutsu* many times. We should now understand that, after birth in the Pure Land is assured in ordinary life with the awakening of the one thought-moment of faith, many utterances of the *Nenbutsu*, many thought-moments of pronouncing the Name, are simply a grateful response to the Buddha for all that the Buddha has done for us.

Therefore, the essence of our tradition as transmitted by our founder Shōnin is just this one thing, faith alone. Those who do not know this point are from other schools; those who know it are distinguished as belonging to the Jōdo Shinshū tradition. Furthermore, in the presence of others, you should never disclose outwardly your way of living as a follower of the *Nenbutsu* within this tradition. This is the basic principle for the conduct of those who have attained faith in Jōdo Shinshū. [You should follow the instructions] as stated above.

Written on 11th January, Bunmei 6 [1474].

COMMENTS

As this letter by Rennyo is not only lengthy but full of terms that are difficult to render in English, it has been no easy task to translate. One of the problems I was faced with is the meaning of the Japanese phrase, *kudan no gotoshi* 件 の如し. This is actually a special phrase used in public notices. If the translation is just "as stated previously," its meaning would still remain ambiguous.

This letter is believed to have been an official notice to the public, posted up on a board in front of the temple at Yoshizaki. Such a speculation is supported by Venerable Kōgon-in Enen (1749–1817), one of the most famous of the Shin Buddhist scholars of the Edo Period, in his *Short Commentaries on The Letters*.[168] This would explain the use of a legal expression, *kudan no gotoshi*, to conclude the letter. This would also explain why this letter does not have the special phrase *"Anakashiko anakashiko"* (Most humbly and respectfully) at the end despite the fact that all the other letters in this collection end with this expression.

The fact that Rennyo actually posted the letter up on a board in front of the temple just goes to show how serious he was about his followers' attitude towards other religious orders and their teachings. Around that time Rennyo had to defend his Sangha against the criticism and aggression received from outside society.

As can be seen from the fact that this letter is traditionally entitled *"Concerning Three Articles including one on shinmei,"* special emphasis is placed on the second article and particularly on the point that we should never belittle any gods.

When seeking to explain these three articles of instruction, Rennyo divides the second of them into two distinct parts, pointedly referring to the first part, with its strict warning against belittling any gods, before going on to comment on the other articles. In *The Letters* this warning is repeated seven times, in the first, second, third, sixth, and tenth letters of Fascicle Two, the tenth and thirteenth letter of Fascicle Three.

According to traditional teaching our relationship to gods is such that we do not entrust ourselves to gods or have faith in them but we do respect them. As mentioned before, Rennyo says in this letter, "All is already included in the faith in which we entrust ourselves solely to the One Buddha, Amida Buddha. Consequently, even though we do not take refuge in any particular god, faith in Amida naturally encompasses trust in gods. This is why." In this case what is meant by the words "trust in gods" is having trust and respect for the part they play in the working of Amida's Compassionate Vow, but not entrusting ourselves to them in the sense of *shinjin* or faith.

Why must we not belittle gods but instead respect and trust them? There are said to be three reasons. Firstly, according to traditional Shin Buddhist teaching, the gods are all manifestations of Amida Buddha. Secondly, as manifestations of the Buddha, the gods have long been leading sentient beings to the Buddha-dharma through their religious connection to those that worship them. Lastly, precisely because they are manifestations of Amida, the gods are believed to protect the followers of the *Nenbutsu*. As you can see, the common theme here is that the gods are all manifestations of Amida Buddha. This Shin Buddhist thought is based on Mahāyāna philosophy regarding the three kinds of *Buddha-kāya*, a Sanskrit term meaning 'Buddha-body': *Dharma-kāya, Saṃbhoga-kāya,* and *Nirmāṇa-kāya*.[169] I would like now to examine in a little more detail the background to this way of thinking.

Dharma-kāya is the content of Enlightenment, that is, Dharma-in-itself. When *Dharma-kāya* starts to move with unconditional love, it is recognised as being two: *Dharma-kāya* as Dharma-in-itself, which is formless,

∴ Shakyamuni is not manifestation of Sambhogakaya Amida "pure land".

and *Dharma-kāya* in its manifested form, or *Saṃbhoga-kāya*. In Tánluán's Pure Land philosophy found in his *Commentary on The Treatise on the Pure Land*, the latter refers to Amida Buddha as *Saṃbhoga-kāya* or Enjoyment Body, originally coming from formless truth, Dharma-in-itself. *Nirmāṇa-kāya* stands for Śākyamuni Buddha, a Buddha who appears as a human being in this world. The very foundation of *Nirmāṇa-kāya* is again *Dharma-kāya* as Dharma-in-itself. *Dharma-kāya* is also believed to appear as "various body-forms," including Bodhisattvas and gods. According to the philosophy of Mahāyāna Buddhism, all the phenomena of the universe are viewed as manifestations of *Dharma-kāya*, formless truth or Emptiness.

Returning to the third letter of Fascicle Two, gods (*kami* or *shinmei*) are "various body-forms" that appear with great compassion as manifestations of *Dharma-kāya*. Because Amida Buddha as *Dharma-kāya* in its manifested form, *Saṃbhoga-kāya*, originally comes from *Dharma-kāya* as Dharma-in-itself, it can be said that not only Buddhas and Bodhisattvas but also gods are manifestations of Amida Buddha, originally *Dharma-kāya* as Dharma-in-itself.

Taking all this into consideration, we can see now that Rennyo's warning against slandering other teachings or belittling the gods is not in itself separate from his emphasis on "peaceful awareness" – the third article of instruction, enjoining us to attain pure faith in Amida Buddha.

But the same could therefore be said of any Buddha or god. ie as it is originates in the Dharma kaya, all other Buddhas and gods are it manifestation.

The Original Vow Beyond The World

ON SEVERING CROSSWISE

THE FIVE BAD PATHS

FASCICLE II, LETTER FOUR

QUESTION: In the first place, the reason Amida Tathāgata's Original Vow is described as being entirely beyond this world[170] is because it is the Incomparable Vow that was especially composed to save ignorant beings like us who, in this defiled world of the Last Age, remain woefully lacking in goodness and merely go around committing wrongdoings. Even now we still have not understood how we should embrace the teaching or entrust ourselves to Amida Buddha in order to attain birth in the Pure Land. Teach us, please, about all this in great detail.

ANSWER: Sentient beings today in this Last Age should entrust themselves to Amida Tathāgata with absolute singlemindedness; there is no need for them to entrust themselves to other Buddhas and Bodhisattvas as well. For, based on his vow to save with great love and compassion all those, no matter how burdened they are with bad karma, who nevertheless take refuge in him as the One Buddha, Amida Tathāgata sends forth his Great Light and embraces them all within it. Consequently *The Meditation Sūtra* states, "Light illuminates all the worlds in the ten directions and embraces all who say the *Nenbutsu* never to abandon them."[171] In this way, through the inconceivable power of his Vow, Amida Tathāgata closes off all the bad paths, whether you count them as the "five paths" or the "six paths," which otherwise we would most certainly have been doomed to travel. *The Sūtra* also makes reference to this as follows: "Then you will sever crosswise the five bad paths and those bad paths will naturally cease to be."[172]

Thus, even if it were our desire to descend into hell, once we have entrusted ourselves without doubt to the Tathāgata's Vow, those of us already received by Amida Tathāgata's all-embracing light can never fall into hell by our own design but must surely attain birth in the Land of Utmost Bliss. Now that this truth has been clarified and seeing that we ourselves have been receiving the infinite benevolence of the Tathāgata's great compassion, as copious as rainfall and as towering as a mountain, morning till evening, night and day, all we ourselves can do is say the *Nenbutsu*, or pronounce the Buddha Name, over and over again in gratitude for all the Buddha has done for us. This is how every follower of true faith should behave.

Most humbly and respectfully

Evening of the 15th February in the 6th year of Bunmei [1474], mindful of the day, long ago, when the Great Sage, the World-Honoured One, entered Nirvāṇa. Beneath the lamplight, rubbing my weakened eyes, I have just completed the last brushstroke.

At the age of sixty. [Seal]

COMMENTS

As you can see from the postscript, Rennyo wrote this letter on the 15th February 1474 when he was sixty years old. According to a description found in the Chinese version of *The Mahaparinirvāṇa-sutra*,[173] in China and Japan Gautama Buddha was believed to have entered Nirvāṇa on the 15th February. In the East Asian countries such as China, Korea and Japan, therefore, an annual ceremony, known as "The Nirvāṇa Assembly" (jp. *Nehan-e*), to commemorate the death of Gautama Buddha, has long been held in every Buddhist temple on 15th February. They celebrate this special occasion by chanting sūtras, often *The Last Teaching Sūtra* (jp. *Yuikyō gyō*),[174] in front of a picture or statue of the Buddha entering Nirvāṇa. In our Shin Buddhist tradition it is said that a formal ceremony of this nature used to be held at the Honganji Temple right up until the days of Rennyo Shōnin. Even today some Shin Buddhist temples are still happy to hold this kind of formal celebration.

On the evening of 15th February, after performing the *Nehan-e* Ceremony, Rennyo Shōnin composed this letter. Finally left alone by a great multitude of followers, he must have still been pondering over the life of Śākyamuni Buddha. In this letter Rennyo noted down what seemed to him to be essential in the Buddha's life.

Reflecting upon the Buddha, whilst far removed in time from when Gautama, or Śākyamuni Buddha as he is often called, actually lived, we constantly find ourselves asking all sorts of questions about him: Where did Śākyamuni Buddha come from? Where did he go to? What was he like? What sort of truth was he awakened to? What was it he taught his followers? What was the reality of his life? What does he mean to us personally? and so forth. Rennyo, welcoming followers to the *Nehan-e* ceremony on this particular day, must have had ample opportunity to reflect at length on the founder of Buddhism and his teaching.

Rennyo Shōnin himself was a direct descendant of Shinran Shōnin, the founder of Shin Buddhism, and was now the person most responsible for this school and its teaching, the essence of which lay in the message of Amida's salvation through faith alone. For Rennyo, therefore, Śākyamuni Buddha was the most important teacher of all, the first person in the world to have related the story of Amida Buddha.

In Shin Buddhism the essential meaning of Śākyamuni Buddha's life can be said to lie in his teaching about Amida Buddha and his Pure Land. Why, you may wonder. At the beginning of his letter Rennyo refers to a phrase from Amida's *Gāthā of Three Vows* in *The Larger Sūtra of Eternal Life*: "I have made a vow that is entirely beyond this world."

According to Rennyo's view, the Original Vow is said to be entirely beyond this world because Amida Buddha vowed to save all beings without discrimination, even the most wretched of people. Because of his unconditional universal love, the teaching of Amida Buddha is unequalled. His teaching is particularly meaningful and true for those who have come to be awakened to how ignorant they are and how heavily burdened with bad karma.

Basing himself on the Original Vow for universal deliverance, Rennyo encourages his followers to entrust themselves absolutely to Amida Buddha. For this purpose he quotes two extracts from the Pure Land sūtras, one from *The Meditation Sūtra* and the other from *The Larger Sūtra of Eternal Life*. These two phrases are of extreme importance because they constitute the foundation of Pure Land teaching.

The quotation from *The Meditation Sūtra* runs "Light illuminates all the worlds in the ten directions and embraces all who say the *Nenbutsu* never to abandon them."[175] This describes the way Amida Buddha's far reaching light saves us, ignorant beings. Rennyo actually states in his letter, "For, based on his vow to save with great love and compassion all those, no matter how burdened they are with bad karma, who nevertheless take refuge in him as the One Buddha, Amida Tathāgata sends forth his Great Light and embraces them all within it." Once awakened to how heavily we are burdened with blind passions and bad karma, all we need do is simply entrust ourselves to Amida Buddha.

Amida's light in *The Meditation Sūtra* is described as coming from every pore of his body. In the Shin Buddhist tradition it is called *shikkō* 色光, literally form-light, meaning the physical or bodily light of the Buddha. In contrast to this kind of light there is another kind known as *shinkō* 心光, literally mind-light, to which Shinran refers in *The Shōshinge*. Here in this context, however, it should be noted that it is not that there are two different kinds of light. Whereas *shikkō* describe a function of Amida's light that illuminates all over the world reaching its furthest end, *shinkō* is another function of his light that embraces all those who pronounce his Name. Tracing them back to their origin there is no difference between them. Apart from *shikkō* there could be no *shinkō*. It is only at the moment of attaining faith in saying *Namu Amida-butsu*, however, that we become aware of *shinkō* or mind-light, the unimpeded light of Amida's love that embraces all of us unconditionally. This 'mind-light' is the very source of our peaceful awareness. At all times it illumines and embraces every one of us. However, only those who pronounce the *Nenbutsu* through the attainment of faith can see Amida's 'mind-light' embracing all of us, penetrating to the deepest recesses of our minds.

The other quotation in the letter, a phrase from *The Larger Sūtra of Eternal Life*, reads, "Then you will sever crosswise the five bad paths and those bad paths will naturally cease to be."[176] This describes the way Amida's 'mind-light' works at the moment of our awakening of faith. What makes all this possible is the inconceivable power of Amida Buddha's Original Vow, described in the *Gāthā of Three Vows* as being entirely beyond this world. In his letter Rennyo says, "In this way, through the inconceivable power of his Vow, Amida Tathāgata closes off all the bad paths, whether you count them as the 'five paths' or the 'six paths,' which otherwise we would most certainly have been doomed to travel." Based on his Original Vow Amida Buddha built his Pure Land, the Land of Enlightenment, where every dweller can be equally enlightened. Amida's Buddha-land is 'pure' because it is entirely beyond this world. When Vasubandhu in his *Treatise on the Pure Land* refers to the 'purity' of the Pure Land as its general feature, he writes "As regards 'the virtue of Purity perfected, which is the constituent part of the Land', the gāthā has this: 'As we observe the nature of that Land, they surpass the ways of the triple world.'"[177] Thus, when you are born in the Pure Land which is the fulfilment of Amida's Original Vow, its purifying power enables you "to sever crosswise the five bad paths."

Coming now to whether we should think of there being five or six bad paths, there is a certain amount of speculation. Whilst one school, for instance, holds that as *asura* or fighting spirits can be included as part of hell generally, there are just five bad paths: the paths of hell, of hungry ghosts, of animals, of human beings and of heavenly gods. Another school says that if you separate the *asura* group from the realms of hellish beings, hungry ghosts, animals, humans and heavenly gods then you have six bad paths. From my point of view this kind of research is unnecessarily complicated. I would like to finish my reference to the bad paths by this short explanation.

In the third paragraph of the letter Rennyo states, as he usually does in conclusion, that we should pronounce the *Nenbutsu* in gratitude for what the Buddha has done for us. I would like you now to pay special attention to the following words, "Thus, even if it were our desire to descend into hell, once we have entrusted ourselves without doubt to the Tathāgata's Vow, those of us already embraced by Amida Tathāgata's all encompassing light can never fall into hell by our own design but must surely attain birth in the Land of Utmost Bliss." Rennyo Shōnin makes the point very clearly here that the purifying power of the Pure Land enables each one of us to sever crosswise all the bad paths because it is completely beyond this world of ours, known as the triple world, including even the worst realm of all, hell. Based on this, Rennyo dares to add, "even if it were our desire to descend into hell." Now it is crystal clear that the Pure Land into which we are born through faith is totally beyond the six paths. Hell is the worst place we can go to and needless to say we do not usually desire to go there, though sometimes we may wish it in the agony of extreme suffering.

As you know, once we meet Buddhism our agony can be even greater because we are now in contact with truth or Dharma far more closely than before. Once we become aware of ourselves as wrong, false or evil our suffering is incredible. For as long as we remain in this state and do not entrust ourselves to the Buddha-dharma, we may desire to escape somewhere else. In fact even hell may seem less terrible by comparison. This kind of demoniac state of mind accompanied by uncertainty is truly horrible and can only be overcome by faith. Thus Rennyo states, "once we have entrusted ourselves without doubt to the Tathāgata's Vow, those of us already embraced by Amida Tathāgata's all encompassing light can never fall into hell by our own design but must surely attain birth in the Land of Utmost Bliss." This is entirely due to the power of Amida's Pure Land as the fulfilment of his Original Vow. Hence Rennyo concludes the letter by emphasising how important it is for us to pronounce the *Nenbutsu* in grateful response.

We can see then that, though Rennyo's exegetical way of writing letters may at first appear very academic, it is actually based on his own faith-experience. The precise and detailed style of *The Letters* is actually a reflection of Rennyo Shōnin's compassionate concern for his Dharma friends.

CHAPTER TWENTY

The Buddhist Rosary

ON A BUDDHIST ROSARY

FASCICLE II, LETTER FIVE

Having been a close observer of the demeanour of the *Nenbutsu* followers of this temple over the last three to four years, I can find no sign whatsoever that they have attained decisively that peaceful awareness (*anjin*) of Other Power. I say this because no one carries so much as even a rosary (*juzu*) around with them. Their manner is such that they appear to be grasping the Buddha with their bare hands. Shōnin never said that we should revere the Buddha by forsaking our rosaries. Nevertheless, even if we do not have rosaries, the only thing absolutely necessary in order for us to attain birth in the Pure Land is Other Power faith, and that alone. Not carrying a rosary can never be an obstacle to birth in the Pure Land.

In the first place, if major priests should wear robes or carry rosaries, there will be no problem. Next, those who have already attained true faith should voice their faith unfailingly; it should also be manifest in their way of being.

As already observed, it would seem that those who have correctly attained true faith are very few and far between. But why should this be? It is because people fail to realise how invaluable the Original Vow of Amida Tathāgata is and how suitable it is for them personally; they always assume that they understand everything there is to know about faith and pride themselves on already knowing whatever it is they are hearing. And yet they do not really listen to others but merely copy them superficially. As long as this is the way they think, even their own birth in the Land of Utmost Bliss is open to doubt, and it goes without saying that it will never be possible for them actually to teach their fellow followers and Dharma friends. With such an attitude of mind they will find it impossible to attain birth in the Land of Enjoyment.

Alas, what a sorry state of affairs! We must concentrate our minds and reflect deeply on this problem. Human life is impermanent indeed, ending at any instant when breathing out fails to wait upon breathing in. We should be constantly vigilant, carefully receive the Buddha-dharma into our hearts and attain faith decisively.

Most humbly and respectfully
Written in haste, early on the morning of 16th February, Bunmei 6 [1474].

COMMENTS

It is not so easy to understand what Rennyo is endeavouring to teach us in this, the fifth letter of Fascicle Two, entitled *On a Buddhist Rosary*, because the message he wishes to impart in the letter is closely bound up with the subtleties of the Shin Buddhist faith.

As you already know, in the Shin Buddhist tradition the absolute prerequisite for birth in the Pure Land, in other words for salvation, is faith alone. Yet in this letter Rennyo is saying that followers should carry Buddhist rosaries. What then does it mean to carry a rosary?

The way a Buddhist rosary is used is very similar to the way people use a Catholic rosary. In the Catholic tradition believers hold a bead and pass it through their fingers, each time uttering a prayer such as Ave Maria, Gloria and Paternoster. In the Buddhist tradition followers recite Buddha Names or *dhāraṇī* whilst counting the beads in their hands. Such devotional recitation stands for mindfulness, praise, gratitude, prayer for goodness, penitence and elimination of bad karma.

In the Buddhist tradition a formal rosary is made up of several large beads and 108 smaller ones. The 108 smaller beads stand for 108 types of blind passion, whilst the larger beads symbolise Buddhas, Bodhisattvas and guardian deities.

Whilst the number of small beads remains the same, the number of the larger beads varies with the different traditions. The Buddhist rosary is not believed to have a particularly long history, but dates back perhaps to some time around the Suí and Táng Dynasties. There exist several Chinese sūtras expounding the meaning of a 'Buddhist rosary'. According to one of those sūtras, the Buddha says that if you fashion a rosary by threading 108 beads together and recite the Triple Treasure of 'Buddha, Dharma and Sangha' as many times as possible whilst passing the rosary between your fingers, one bead after another, it will eventually lead you to Enlightenment. What seems important to me is the fact that those 108 beads standing for blind passions are pierced and held together by a string that symbolises the Buddha's great compassion. Through their connection to the Buddha all the blind passions are eventually made virtuous.

In Pure Land Buddhism in general *Nenbutsu* followers try to pronounce the name of Amida Buddha as many times as possible in order to accumulate good deeds or lessen the burden of past wrongdoings. In Shin Buddhism, however, followers do not need to make such efforts to ensure their salvation, because their salvation is the work of Amida Buddha. All that they need to do is simply attain pure faith. The Shin Buddhist faith-experience is accompanied by one-mindedness or mindfulness, penitence for one's bad karma, gratitude to the Buddha, humility and respectfulness.

In Shin Buddhism, as mentioned above, the usage of a rosary does not lie in making numerous recitations. So what then does a rosary represent? As Rennyo says immediately after the above statement, "Not carrying a rosary can never be an obstacle to birth in the Pure Land." A rosary is not a device for attaining faith and birth in the Pure Land but the means through which those who have attained faith can express their humility and respect. The phrase "grasping the Buddha with their bare hands" indicates the arrogance of those temple followers and their disrespect towards the Buddha. A rosary reminds us that we are fully burdened with blind passions and that all the blind passions are pierced and held together by Amida Buddha's great compassion. The function of a Buddhist rosary, in other words, is to make us aware of our own karmic existence, heavily burdened with blind passions, but at the same time to remind us of Amida Buddha' great compassion penetrating our whole being. Thus the habit of carrying a rosary helps us, Shin Buddhist followers, to continue to be humble and respectful. This is what Rennyo had in mind when he wrote in his letter, "In the first place if major priests should wear robes or carry rosaries, there will be no problem. Next, those who have already attained true faith should voice their faith unfailingly; it should also be manifest in their way of being."

According to his understanding expressed in the second paragraph, the improper attitude of followers, such as arrogance and disrespect, stems from the lack of true faith. Those who have attained true faith remain humble and respectful. Their true faith is naturally expressed in their way of being. The incorrect understanding and wrong attitude of the temple followers as described in the last quotation are to be attributed to their lack of faith. Thus Rennyo concludes this second paragraph with the warning, "With such an attitude of mind they will find it impossible to attain birth in the Land of Enjoyment."

Lastly Rennyo encourages his followers to attain faith, with the sorrowful words, "Alas, what a sorry state of affairs! We must concentrate our minds and reflect deeply on this problem. Human life is impermanent indeed, ending at any instant when breathing out fails to wait upon breathing in. We should be constantly vigilant, carefully receive the Buddha-dharma into our hearts and attain faith decisively." Very strict as his advice sounds, Rennyo's intention is solely to see his followers' attainment of faith and resultant birth in the Land of Peace and Happiness, by going beyond the fact of impermanence and their own karmic attachments.

CHAPTER TWENTY-ONE

Faith and Society

ON RULES OF CONDUCT

FASCICLE II, LETTER SIX

If you are amongst those who have learned through careful listening what is meant in our tradition by Other Power faith and if you have attained faith decisively, you should store your understanding of faith in the deepest recesses of your hearts and not talk about it with strangers or people from other traditions. Additionally you should not praise it openly, without careful consideration of your audience, in alleyways and main roads or in the places where you live. Furthermore do not be so proud of your attainment of faith that you neglect the feudal lords or lords of the manor and do not fail to perform your legal duties (*kuji*) to the full. Likewise do not belittle the *kami* and the Buddhas and Bodhisattvas, any of them, for they are all encompassed within the six characters (*Na-mu-a-mi-da-butsu* 南无阿彌陀佛). Lastly and very importantly, let your attitude to the outside world be to observe the laws of the state, store Other Power faith deep within your hearts and hold the principles of love and justice (仁義 jp. *jingi*) in society as absolutely essential. Never forget that these are the rules of conduct established within our tradition.

Most humbly and respectfully
Written on 17th February, Bunmei 6 [1474].

COMMENTS

Rennyo wrote a number of letters about the attitude *Nenbutsu* followers should adopt towards the world once they attained faith. Amongst them is this beautiful summary.

The first point had already been discussed by Rennyo in several previous letters such as the ninth letter of Fascicle One, and the first, second and third letters of Fascicle Two. Similarly the third instruction had also already featured in the first, second and third letters of Fascicle Two. The second and fourth instructions, on the other hand, appear now for the first time in this particular letter. Rennyo's reference to the second item indicates that his Sangha was embroiled in a very serious dispute involving a number of its followers failing to pay tax to the local government because they were too proud of their faith. It would seem he issued the fourth instruction after deep consideration of the problem from the standpoint of his faith. Indeed it is actually a general summarisation of the attitude *Nenbutsu* followers should take towards the outside world. It may appear to outsiders as a sort of secularisation of the Sangha, but we should not forget that, whenever Rennyo gave this sort of instruction, he never failed to state that we should at the same time maintain true faith deep in our hearts. He means that, whilst holding onto our faith in our hearts, we should still observe the laws of the state. In this letter he actually states, "Lastly and very importantly, let your attitude to the outside world be to observe the laws of the state, store Other Power faith deep within your hearts and hold the principles of love and justice (仁義 *jingi*) in society as absolutely essential."

Rennyo's ultimate concern was always how to preserve true faith. Thus, in his eyes, the attitude of *Nenbutsu* followers towards the outside world should follow on naturally from their own inner faith, a faith that should at all times play a vital part in their daily activities. Whenever he asked his followers to observe the laws of the state, Rennyo never forgot to refer to the importance of inner faith.

Shin Buddhists have a duty to respect secular authority and appreciate the laws of the land, devised to establish and maintain social balance. Ultimately, however, the emphasis must be on faith. Where these two principles come into opposition, Shin Buddhists should base their actions on listening to the Buddha's teaching in their current situation.

I would like to briefly mention a few events in the history of Shogyoji Temple that illustrate very clearly how Shin Buddhists' attitude to society is not simply blind obedience to secular authority.

In 1961, when I was a student at Kyoto University, the Soviet Union restarted a series of nuclear tests, which as said at that time would soon be followed by similar tests carried out by the United States. I took what was happening so seriously and was so worried about the threat such tests posed to the future of mankind, that I wrote a very long letter to my master, Dharma-mother Ekai. She then took me by surprise writing back and saying, 'Stand up! Collect signatures and petition the Soviet Union and the United States to stop any future tests.' Our Dharma friends went out onto the streets and gathered over one hundred thousand signatures for a petition addressed to both countries. This they submitted, together with all the signatures, to the embassies of both parties in Tokyo. At that time, the American ambassador was Edwin O. Reishauer and we had a pleasant conversation, referring, too, to his father's translation of Genshin's *Ōjō yōshū* or *The Essentials for Rebirth in the Pure Land*.[178]

Another illustration is Reverend Reion Takehara's[179] involvement, together with that of Reverend Jōkan Chikazumi,[180] in a social movement aimed at preventing the proposed introduction of the Law of Religious Groups that was designed to protect and improve conditions in Japan for three major religions: Shintō, Buddhism and Christianity. One of the main reasons for this petition was the feeling that, if these religions came under state protection, they would be legally controlled by the political authorities and their integrity thus compromised. The Shin Buddhist leaders of this widespread movement, including Reverends Chikazumi and Takehara, felt very strongly that religious choice should be left entirely to the individual and were particularly anxious to secure freedom of thought and expression. Thanks to their valiant efforts and those of their followers, the bill was withdrawn and never became law. This experience gave rise to the authorship of a wonderful article by Reverend Reion Takehara, entitled *Shakaimondai kaiketsu*[181] or *How to Solve Social Problems*.

The third example occurred in wartime. During World War II the Japanese government ordered Buddhist temples and Shintō shrines to hand over any religious artefacts made of metal, so that they could be turned into weapons. Reverend Reion Takehara, former Head Priest of Shōgyōji, strongly objected to an order that would cause tokens of peace to be turned into instruments of war. When, in 1943, a band of some thirty vigilantes arrived to collect the temple bell, his foremost disciple, Mrs Miyo Nonaka, later to be known as Dharma-mother Ekai, rushed out in her bare feet and scolded them fiercely, saying "You men, have you ever heard of the teaching of Prince Shōtoku? He tells us that a premium should be placed on harmony, and that it is absolutely crucial you revere the Three Treasures!" The vigilantes left empty-handed. On hearing of this incident Reverend R. Takehara was very pleased but thought of the danger to her life. In the end he decided to hand over the bell, saying "The temple bell can go, because I now have you as a living temple bell." Following a farewell service in the Buddha Hall, it was finally borne away. That is not quite the end of the story, however. Thanks to the efforts of some Dharma friends, the top of the bell was eventually cut off before the rest of the bell was melted down at the Saganoseki refinery. This portion of the old bell, known as "Dragon Head", is still preserved at the temple to this day.[182]

We should be mindful, however, that our ultimate concern must always be how to maintain inner peace, however difficult the situation.

CHAPTER TWENTY-TWO

On Birth in
the Pure Land

GOING TO THE PURE LAND

IS EASY BUT NO ONE IS THERE

FASCICLE II, LETTER SEVEN

Upon quiet reflection we see that it is indeed by virtue of our observance of the five precepts that we receive life in the human realm. Being born as a human is an extremely rare occurrence and human life itself is nought but a bubble of brief duration. Rebirth is the blissful fruit of eternity. Even if we boast of prosperity and live in splendour, still we cannot maintain such affluence for long, for it is in the nature of things that "those who prosper are sure to decline, and those who meet are certain to part." Human life lasts but fifty to a hundred years and when we hear, too, how uncertain life is for old and young alike, we realise there is indeed very little on which we can rely. Sentient beings of the present time, therefore, should attain Other Power faith and aspire for birth in the Pure Land.

For the attainment of faith there is no need of wisdom or learning, nor does it matter one iota whether one is rich or poor, good or bad, male or female. What is essential is just to forsake all miscellaneous practices and take refuge in the right practice. Taking refuge in the right practice simply means entrusting oneself to Amida Tathāgata singlemindedly and steadfastly without any difficulty at all. All the sentient beings who entrust themselves in this way are embraced within Amida's light. Amida never abandons them, but sends them when their lives end without fail to the Pure Land. It is alone through this one thought-moment of 'peaceful awareness' that we are born in the Pure Land. How easily we attain this peaceful awareness with no effort on our part! Thus, when the two Chinese characters *anjin* 安心 (ch. *ānxīn*) are read as *yasuki kokoro* or 'the mind easy to attain' in Japanese, they have indeed this meaning.

Singlemindedly and steadfastly entrusting ourselves to the Tathāgata through this faith alone, we will be born with no difficulty at all in the Land of Utmost Bliss. How easy it is to attain this peaceful awareness! How easy it is to go to the Pure Land! Accordingly *The Larger Sūtra* states, 'Going is easy but no one is there.' This passage from the sūtra means that if we attain this peaceful awareness and entrust ourselves to Amida steadfastly, it is easy to go to the Pure Land; but, because those who attain faith (*shinjin*) are rare, though it is easy to journey to the Pure Land, no one is there.

Once we have realised this, the Buddha Name we pronounce day and night, morning and evening, is entirely an expression of our gratitude [to Amida Buddha] for all that he has done for us through the Universal Vow of Great Compassion. Becoming deeply mindful of the Buddha-dharma and aware of the meaning of faith that is so easy to obtain, we should unfailingly attain birth in the Land of Enjoyment, the 'One Great Matter of Concern'.

Most humbly and respectfully
I made a fair copy [of this letter] on 3rd May, Bunmei 6 [1474].

COMMENTS

It is apparent from the last line that this is a clean copy of a letter already written to some particular person or group. Though opinions vary, it is not possible to ascertain with any certainty whom Rennyo was actually addressing in his letter.

The very beginning of this letter describes what a rare event it is for us to receive life in the human realm, because "it is indeed by virtue of our observance of the five precepts" that we do so. This idea is traditionally believed to be based on sūtras such as the *Judaika kyō* 樹提伽經 (ch. *Shùtíjiā jīng*)[183] and the *Makebiku kyō* 魔化比丘經 (ch. *Móhuàbǐqiū jīng*).[184] Concerning the famous lines, expressing the impermanence of this world, "Those who prosper are sure to decline, and those who meet are certain to part," the first half is to be found in the *Heike Monogatari* 平家物語 and the latter in the *Taiheiki* 太平記.[185] The main point made in this first paragraph is that, although human life is such an extremely rare event, it only lasts for a very short time; therefore we should attain birth in the Pure Land, the realm of eternity. As clearly observed with a number of other letters of his, such as the 11th letter of Fascicle One, the fourth letter of Fascicle Three, the fourth letter of Fascicle Four and the 16th letter of Fascicle Five, Rennyo Shōnin's teaching in this letter is deeply rooted in the Buddhist philosophy of impermanence.

Regarding my translation, "Human life itself is nought but a bubble of brief duration. Rebirth is the blissful fruit of eternity," some explanation of the word "Rebirth" is necessary. The original word I translated as "Rebirth" is *goshō* 後生 in Japanese. This Shin Buddhist term *goshō* is usually translated as "afterlife," but this has too much of a Christian connotation. In Pure Land Buddhism the compound 後生 *goshō* is found in the first part of the phrase *goshō* muryōju bukkoku 後生無量壽佛國[186] from *The Larger Sūtra of Eternal Life*, one of the principal Pure Land sūtras, meaning "You will next be born in the country of the Buddha of Eternal Life." Taken in this context it is without doubt that the term *goshō* 後生 refers to "next birth in the Pure Land." Therefore, "rebirth or next birth in the Pure Land" will be a better way of translating this special Shin Buddhist term. According to my understanding, the word *goshō* is also closely related to the well-known phrase by Shàndǎo 善導 (613–681), "In one thought-moment life ends, in the next you are immediately born" (前念命終 *zennen myōju*, 後念即生 *gonen sokushō*).[187] In this case, too, the term *goshō*, taken from the last part of the phrase, means "birth or rebirth in the Pure Land in the next moment," not "afterlife." In Buddhist terminology the character *shō* 生 often refers to birth, rather than life. This is why I am uncomfortable about the constant translation of the word *goshō* as "afterlife," and chose to translate it as "Rebirth."

The subject of the second paragraph is the attainment of faith. Rennyo clarifies the subject in regard to the right practice by saying "What is essential is just to forsake all miscellaneous practices and take refuge in the right practice. Taking refuge in the right practice simply means entrusting oneself to Amida Tathāgata singlemindedly and steadfastly without any difficulty at all." Why can 'taking refuge in the right practice' mean 'entrusting oneself to Amida Tathāgata'? It is because the right practice is what Amida Tathāgata in his Original Vow wanted all sentient beings to take refuge in. Thus the attainment of pure faith – 'entrusting oneself to Amida Buddha' – is always accompanied by the act of 'taking refuge in the right practice.' Rennyo states that all those who entrust themselves to Amida are embraced in his light. Here in this context Rennyo refers to 'faith' (*shinjin*) as 'peaceful awareness' (*anjin*). In Shin Buddhism the two expressions are used synonymously, because the original meaning of *anjin* 安心 (ch. *ānxīn*) was 'to quiet or settle the mind' (jp. *kokoro o yasunzuru*). Taking into consideration this original meaning, the word *anjin* is often translated as 'settled mind.' Frankly speaking, this translation sounds a little too technical, being confined simply to consideration of the original Chinese. In actual usage the term *anjin,* when read as *yasurakana kokoro* (literally, peaceful mind) in Japanese, also means absolute peacefulness or imperturbability of mind, attained through pure faith. In this respect it can be rendered as 'peaceful mind,' 'inner peace of mind,' or 'peaceful awareness.' The second character of the compound 安心 *anjin* is actually very wide-ranging in meaning but in this case the character 心 can be best rendered as 'awareness.' According to my interpretation, the original Japanese for *shinjin* that we translate into English as 'faith' also has the meaning of 'awakening' or 'awareness.' Having considered the various possible renderings of the term 安心 *anjin* which I proposed, I have chosen 'peaceful awareness' as being the most fitting in this special context.

Towards the end of the second paragraph, Rennyo refers to the term *anjin* when it is read as *yasuki kokoro* in Japanese. *Yasuki kokoro* means 'mind easy to attain' or 'easily attained mind.' In this way of reading the key notion is 'easy' or 'easily.' To attain *anjin* or *shinjin* is 'easy' because faith is given by Amida Buddha. Rennyo emphasises this aspect of *anjin* in this letter. Because *anjin* is a gift from Amida Buddha, it is the peaceful mind or awareness that is easily attained.

In the third paragraph Rennyo talks about how easy it is to be born in the Pure Land through the attainment of faith. Here in this letter he also mentions how easy faith is to attain. Customarily the teaching of the *Nenbutsu* is said to be easy to practise but difficult to attain faith in. Why does Rennyo say then that it is so easy to attain faith? As mentioned before it is because faith is given by the Buddha. It is from the standpoint of self power that faith is difficult to attain. If you entrust yourself to Other Power, you realise faith comes to you from Amida Buddha. Therefore he admires how easy it is to attain faith, and hence how easy to be born in the Pure Land. Quoting from *The Larger Sūtra of Eternal Life,* "Going is easy and yet no one is there,"[188] Rennyo Shōnin states, "This passage from the sūtra means that if we attain this peaceful awareness and entrust ourselves to Amida steadfastly, it is easy to go to the Pure Land. At the same time, because those who attain faith are so rare, though it is easy to journey to the Pure Land, no one is there." In *The Annotated Inscriptions on Sacred Scrolls,* Shinran Shōnin comments on the same passage as follows;

> Regarding the statement, *'Going is easy and yet no one is there,'* the words *'going is easy'* means that when we leave everything up to the working of the Original Vow we will surely arrive in the True Land of Enjoyment without fail. That is why it is so easy to go there. As to the words, *'and yet no one is there,'* the reason why no one is there is because it is very difficult to attain true faith. Accordingly it is rare for people to be born

in the True Land of Enjoyment. That is why Genshin Kashō says that there are not many who are born in the Land of Enjoyment, but there are quite a few who are born in the Land of Transformation.[189]

In this commentary by Shinran Shōnin the meaning of the passage is clearly explained. Whilst those born in the Land of Enjoyment means *Nenbutsu* followers of Other Power, "those born in the Land of Transformation" means *Nenbutsu* followers of self power.

Regarding the last paragraph of this letter, I really do not think there is anything I need to add. Rennyo is simply teaching his *Nenbutsu* followers how to live after their attainment of faith. To encourage us *Nenbutsu* followers, he repeats his fervent conviction that our *Nenbutsu* practice is entirely an expression of our gratitude to Amida Buddha for all that he has done for us and that, by living our *Nenbutsu* life with gratitude, we should certainly attain birth in the Pure Land without fail.'

CHAPTER TWENTY-THREE

An Ancient Buddha
from the Timeless Past

ON THE ORIGINAL TEACHER
AND THE ORIGINAL BUDDHA

FASCICLE II, LETTER EIGHT

First of all, what is meant by "people of wrongdoing who have committed the ten bad acts and the five grave offences" and "women burdened with the five obstacles and the three submissions" is in fact ourselves, ignorant beings, each of us helplessly passed over and forsaken by the compassionate vows of all the Buddhas of the ten directions and the three periods. But Amida Tathāgata is the original teacher and the original Buddha of all the Buddhas of the three periods and the ten directions, and it is thus Amida alone who, as an ancient Buddha who attained Buddhahood in the timeless past, has made the great Vow that is entirely beyond this world, vowing that he himself will save all of us sentient beings without any discrimination at all – all those, as mentioned above, who have been abandoned by all the Buddhas, whether such people be women burdened with the five obstacles and the three submissions or ignorant beings who are not free from wrongdoings in this Last Age. Thus, by making this supreme vow, he became Amida Buddha. Apart from entrusting themselves solely to this Tathāgata, there is no way at all for sentient beings of the Last Age to be born in the Land of Utmost Bliss. Accordingly, those who have fully understood Other Power faith as taught by Shinran Shōnin will without fail all of them be born in the Pure Land, ten people out of every ten.

QUESTION: When we desire to attain faith and proceed to Amida's Land of Enjoyment, how should we see ourselves, and how should we seek to attain that which is called faith? I would like to be told about this in detail.

ANSWER: The main point of Other Power faith, as taught in our tradition by Shinran Shōnin, is that when we realise quite simply that we are wretched beings heavily burdened with bad karma and entrust ourselves singleheartedly and steadfastly to Amida Tathāgata, discarding all the miscellaneous practices and devoting ourselves to the sole practice with singlemindedness, then we will without fail be embraced within Amida Buddha's all-encompassing light. This indeed is the way we attain birth decisively.

Furthermore what should also be clearly understood is that, once birth is assured through the one thought-moment of awakening of faith when we singleheartedly and steadfastly take refuge in Amida, then our pronouncing the Name, whether walking, standing, sitting or lying down, is the *Nenbutsu* through which we show our gratitude to Amida Tathāgata for the great compassion he has shown in helping us attain birth easily. One who thus understands is called a follower of our tradition who has attained faith decisively.

Most humbly and respectfully
In mid-March, Bunmei 6 [1474].

COMMENTS

This letter has long been known under the title *On the Original Teacher and the Original Buddha*. Understanding Amida in this way is not a new idea of Rennyo's, but can be traced back to the founder of this tradition, Shinran Shōnin. The notion is in fact deeply related to the Shin Buddhist teaching of Amida's universal deliverance of all sentient beings, seen as devoid of all discrimination even against the most wretched beings, otherwise passed over by every other Buddha.

As seen in the last line, this letter was written in the middle of March 1474. The expression "the original teacher and the original Buddha" is also to be found in the third letter of Fascicle Two, written on 11th of January 1474, in this the eighth letter of Fascicle Two some two months later and again in the ninth letter of Fascicle Two, written on 17th of March 1474.

What then is meant by the phrase "the original teacher and the original Buddha"? 'The original teacher' means that Amida Buddha is a teacher for all the Buddhas of the ten directions and the three periods and that it is through his teaching that they attain Supreme Enlightenment. 'The original Buddha' means that Amida Buddha is the origin of all the Buddhas and that they are his manifestations. In short, Amida Buddha is both teacher to all the other Buddhas and also their origin. Regarding the relationship between Amida Buddha and all the other Buddhas, I gave a brief comment in *Chapter 18*.

All this seems to be firmly based on the Pure Land Buddhist view that Amida Buddha is "an ancient Buddha who attained Buddhahood in the timeless past." Shinran Shōnin himself understood it this way. The idea of "Amida Buddha who attained Buddhahood in the timeless past" is expressed in the following two verses in Japanese (*wasan*) composed by Shinran Shōnin,

> Although it is taught that ten kalpas have now passed
> Since Amida's attainment of Buddhahood,
> He appears to be a Buddha older
> than countless kalpas as many as particles of dust.[190]

> Amida Buddha, having attained Buddhahood in the timeless past,
> Taking pity on ignorant beings of the five defilements,
> Now appears in Gayā castle,
> Assuming the form of Śākyamuni Buddha.[191]

On the other hand, according to the account of Amida Buddha given in *The Larger Sūtra of Eternal Life*, Amida is a Buddha who attained Buddhahood ten kalpas ago. Based on this sūtra, Shinran Shōnin composed another,

> Ten kalpas have now passed
> Since Amida's attainment of Buddhahood.
> There is nowhere the Dharma-body's wheel of light does not reach,
> As it shines its light on the ignorant and unenlightened of this world.[192]

Although it might seem to be something of a contradiction here between these two concepts of Amida Buddha – Amida who attained Buddhahood ten kalpas ago and Amida who attained Buddhahood in the timeless past, they should be understood as the two aspects that co-exist in one and the same Buddha. Viewed from our modern way of calculation, the number 'ten kalpas' stands for 43.2 billion years, which is more than three times the age of the universe. This figure already belongs to the concept of infinity, or timeless time in this context. This helps us understand more easily that they are two aspects of one and the same Buddha.

In order to understand the matter properly, we should have a look at the development in Mahāyāna of the notion of Dharma-kāya or Dharma-body.[193] In fact the two different concepts of Amida Buddha stand for the two distinct modes of the *Dharma-kāya*. Let me quote here from *The Commentary on The Treatise on the Pure Land* by Tánluán (476–542),

> Two modes are distinguishable in the *Dharma-kāya*, whose manifestations are Buddhas and Bodhisattvas. One mode is *Dharma-kāya* as Dharma-in-itself, and the other is *Dharma-kāya* in its manifested form. The manifested form exists depending on the Dharma-in-itself, and the Dharma-in-itself is known by expressing itself in its manifestations. These two modes are distinguishable but are not to be regarded as two independent existences. They are one and yet not to be identified. Therefore, they are to be understood as the interfusion of the general and the particular under the one word, Dharma. If the Bodhisattva fails to understand this interfusion, he may not be able to work out the self-benefiting and the others-benefiting.[194]

The interdependent nature of the paradoxical relationship that exists between *Dharma-kāya* as Dharma-in-itself and *Dharma-kāya* in its manifested form is beautifully set out in the above quotation. Amida Buddha's *Dharma-kāya* as Dharma-in-itself is formless and timeless or, if you like, eternal beyond history. "Amida Buddha who attained Buddhahood in the timeless past" refers to this aspect of Amida Buddha, the *Dharma-kāya* as Dharma-in-itself. As explained in the quotation, "the Dharma-in-itself is known by expressing itself in its manifestations" or, in other words, "Amida Buddha who attained Buddhahood in the timeless past" comes to be known only through its manifested form – "Amida who attained Buddhahood ten kalpas ago," the Amida Buddha described in the account of *The Larger Sūtra of Eternal Life*. Similarly the phrase "the manifested form exists depending on the Dharma-in-itself," signifies that Amida Buddha as related in *The Larger Sūtra* is firmly based on the Dharma-in-itself or formless truth, in other words on "Amida Buddha who attained Buddhahood in the timeless past."

Dharma-kāya is the content of Enlightenment that is Dharma itself. When *Dharma-kāya* starts to move with unconditional love, it is recognised as being two: *Dharma-kāya* as Dharma-in-itself, which is formless, and *Dharma-kāya* in its manifested form. To my way of thinking, the account of Amida Buddha given in *The Larger Sūtra of Eternal Life* amounts to the most concrete expression we have of the dynamics between *Dharma-kāya* as Dharma-in-itself and *Dharma-kāya* in its manifested form.[195]

Some textual proof to support the Shin Buddhist view that Amida is the original teacher and the original Buddha can be found in the *Kuden shō*, or *What Shinran Taught*, by Kakunyo (1270–1351).[196]

As clearly stated in the first paragraph of the eighth letter of Fascicle Two, the important point this letter makes is that Amida Buddha, as the most ancient Buddha who attained Buddhahood in the timeless past, is both the original teacher and the original Buddha and that as such he composed the incomparable Vow, entirely beyond our world, by which he sought to save all sentient beings with no discrimination at all.

CHAPTER TWENTY-FOUR

Discarding
Miscellaneous
Practices

THE LOYAL RETAINER

AND THE FAITHFUL WIFE

FASCICLE II, LETTER NINE

To begin with, as you are already aware, in entrusting ourselves to Amida Tathāgata we are discarding all other myriad good deeds and practices, referring to them all as miscellaneous practices. Why should this be? It is because of Amida Buddha's Great Vow, wherein he vowed to save all sentient beings who entrusted themselves to him steadfastly and singleheartedly, no matter how grave their wrongdoings. "Singleheartedly and steadfastly" thus means that, when taking refuge in Amida Buddha, we see no other Buddha as his equal. Similarly in human society we also follow just the one master for the same reason. Indeed there exists a non-Buddhist text where are to be found the words: "A loyal retainer does not serve two lords. A faithful wife does not have two husbands."[197] Since Amida Tathāgata is the original master and teacher of all the Buddhas of the three periods, how can all the Buddhas, themselves the disciples of Amida Buddha, fail to rejoice when we entrust ourselves to the Buddha who is their master? It is very important, therefore, that you fully understand this point. Since the substance of practice known as *Namu Amida-butsu* encompasses within itself all the gods, the Buddhas and the Bodhisattvas, and likewise all the myriad good deeds and practices, what need have we to continue with the various practices and good deeds whilst feeling that something is missing? As the Name *Namu Amida-butsu* is the substance that embodies all the myriad good deeds and practices, it is felt to be far more reliable.

How then should we entrust ourselves to Amida Tathāgata? With what faith should we attain birth in the Land of Utmost Bliss? It can be very easily done; once we become deeply aware that Amida Tathāgata alone graciously vowed to save us, wretched beings that we are, heavily burdened with transgressions and thus destined only for hell, then in that one thought-moment of taking refuge our faith will be awakened. Set in motion by the unfolding of past good conditions, Other Power faith is imparted to us from the Wisdom of the Buddha, with the consequence that the heart of the Buddha and the heart of an ignorant being become one. Followers who have realised this are called those who have attained faith. Furthermore, we should understand that, simply by saying the *Nenbutsu*, no matter whether sleeping or waking, we should express our gratitude for what has been done for us by Amida Buddha, his Great Compassion, the Original Vow of Universal Deliverance.

Most humbly and respectfully
Written on 17th March, Bunmei 6 [1474].

COMMENTS

According to the last line of this letter, Rennyo wrote it on the 17th March 1474, soon after writing the previous, eighth letter of Fascicle Two. Broadly speaking, the main thrust of this letter is to encourage people to attain faith by explaining to them in detail why they should discard all miscellaneous practices unrelated to Amida Buddha. The letter is divided into two: the first paragraph explaining why in our tradition we are expected to forsake all the other myriad practices, and the second paragraph encouraging us to attain faith in the one thought-moment when we take refuge in Amida Buddha.

In the first paragraph Rennyo raises the question why we should discard all other miscellaneous practices, and then goes on to answer it by way of the following three reasons.

Firstly we should do so because of Amida Buddha's vow to save all those who entrust themselves to Amida "steadfastly and singleheartedly." There exists a non-Buddhist text where are to be found the words: 'A loyal retainer does not serve two lords. A faithful wife does not have two husbands.' The last part of the quotation is a slight variation on the original version, "A loyal retainer does not serve two lords and a faithful wife does not take a second husband," which in fact comes from Chapter 82 of *Shiji* 史記, or the *Historical Records*, written by Sīmǎ Qiān 司馬遷 (B.C. 145?-86?). Another variation of the original text is also to be found in a famous Japanese book, the *Genpei suisei ki* 源平盛衰記, written in the late Kamakura Period. It is not clear whether Rennyo Shōnin is quoting directly from the *Shiji* or indirectly from the *Genpei suisei ki*.

'All other miscellaneous practices (jp. *zōgyō* 雑行)' refers to all good deeds related not to Amida Buddha but to the other Buddhas or Bodhisattvas. All practices other than 'the right practices' related to faith in Amida Buddha are called miscellaneous practices. There are, according to the Pure Land tradition since the time of Shàndǎo 善導 (jp. Zendō), 'five right practices' connected to Amida Buddha,

- Reciting the Pure Land Sūtras,
- Contemplating Amida Buddha and his Pure Land,
- Bowing to Amida Buddha, Pronouncing Amida's Name,
- Praising and making offerings to Amida.

These five right practices are further subdivided: 'Pronouncing Amida's Name' is called 'the practice that rightly assures birth in the Pure Land' and the other four are called 'supportive practices.' What is known as *Nenbutsu* refers to 'pronouncing Amida's Name,' that is 'the practice that rightly assures birth in the Pure Land.'

To come back to the letter, the main point is the discarding of all miscellaneous practices, namely all practices other than the five right practices, as they are all connected with other Buddhas.

The second reason given for discarding all miscellaneous practices is that Amida Buddha, who Rennyo Shōnin emphasises is the only Buddha who vowed to save all sentient beings no matter how grave their wrongdoings, is the original master of all the Buddhas of the three periods – past, present and future. For a more theoretical explanation of the relationship between Amida and other Buddhas, please refer to my commentaries on the third and eighth letters of Fascicle Two.

However we choose to describe these other practices, whether as sundry or miscellaneous, we do appear to be investing them with somewhat negative connotations. What is important for us to understand, however, is that this teaching is meant for those involved in the Pure Land tradition. Because they are aspirants for birth in the Pure Land, if they undertake practices unrelated to Amida Buddha, then such practices are necessarily thought of as "miscellaneous practices." There is no intention to denigrate practices that belong to other traditions. All too often we fail to grasp this crucial point. Unless we do fully understand it, however, there can be no respect for other traditions and hence no mutual understanding between different religions. What Pure Land followers would like to see is not egoistic conflicts but unselfish harmony within diversity. If such followers will but entrust themselves to Amida Buddha with all sincerity, says Rennyo Shōnin, all the Buddhas will be pleased, because Amida is the original teacher of all the other Buddhas. According to the Buddhist philosophy of interdependence, each and every Buddha is recognised as abiding at the centre of their world.[198]

If we gain a proper understanding of the true meaning of the notion 'miscellaneous practices,' we will not be in danger of failing to respect practices belonging to other traditions.

The third reason for discarding all miscellaneous practices when taking refuge in Amida Buddha is because such practices are already included in Amida's Name *Namu Amida-butsu*. Rennyo says in his letter, "Since the substance of practice known as *Namu Amida-butsu* encompasses within itself all the gods, the Buddhas and the Bodhisattvas and likewise all the myriad good deeds and practices, what need have we to continue with the various practices and good deeds whilst feeling that something is missing?" This part of the letter reminds me of the following passage from *The Kyōgyōshinshō* by Shinran Shōnin, "In this living (practice) are embraced all good things and all the roots of merit. They are instantly perfected [as soon as the Name is pronounced]. The Name is the treasure-ocean of the merits accruing from the absolute reality of Suchness."[199] Our pronouncing the Name is the working of the Name *Namu Amida-butsu* as the substance of practice. As such it is a gift to us. A mother's milk is a gift to her child and yet still has its origin in the mother. Likewise the Name is a gift to sentient beings even as it remains something that has its origin in Amida.

The second paragraph of the letter is concerned with our attainment of faith. The Shin Buddhist notion of true faith incorporates two kinds of awareness: firstly awareness of oneself or the reality of our existence and, secondly, awareness of Amida Buddha and his unconditional love. At the selfsame moment that we are awakened to the reality of our existence, heavily burdened with transgressions and thus destined only for hell, we are also awakened to the unconditional love of Amida Buddha, a love that saves us, wretched beings, without any discrimination. At this point we immediately entrust ourselves to Amida Buddha with our whole being. It's apparent that Rennyo Shōnin was fully conscious of how essential these two aspects of awareness are to the Shin Buddhist faith.

Rennyo states in the second paragraph of the letter, "Set in motion by the unfolding of past good conditions, Other Power faith is imparted to us from the Wisdom of the Buddha, with the consequence that the heart of the Buddha and the heart of an ignorant being become one." The point here is that at the precise moment when faith is attained, the heart of the Buddha "becomes" one with the heart of an ignorant being, though they are recognised as being two and separate at the start. Then the heart of an ignorant being is embraced by and merged into the heart of the Buddha. In the case of the teaching of "the oneness of *ki* (機) or oneself and *Hō* (法) or the Dharma," this oneness is understood to have originally been created in *Namu Amida-butsu*, the fruit of Amida's Original Vow. The latter notion of oneness is the foundation for the realisation of the former.

CHAPTER TWENTY-FIVE

The Great Working
of the Buddha-dharma

THE ONENESS OF THE HEART

OF THE BUDDHA

AND THAT OF AN IGNORANT BEING

FASCICLE II, LETTER TEN

The essence of the teaching of our tradition expounded by Shinran Shōnin is, first of all, that Other Power faith is of the highest importance. It is clearly stated in the sūtras and commentaries that, if we do not fully understand this Other Power faith, it will never be possible for us after this life to attain birth in the Land of Utmost Bliss – the One Great Matter. Therefore, once we understand what Other Power faith is and desire to attain birth in the True Land of Enjoyment, how should we prepare ourselves and how should we maintain ourselves in order to attain birth in the Land of Utmost Bliss? I do not have sufficient knowledge about all this. Could you kindly instruct me? By listening to your teaching I would surely like to attain firm faith.

To answer the question, what is meant in our tradition by Other Power faith is that, without worrying in any way about how heavily burdened we are with bad karma, we simply entrust ourselves singleheartedly and steadfastly to Amida Tathāgata, deeply aware that it is the inconceivable power of the Vow that saves everyone – even wrongdoers like ourselves who have committed the ten bad acts and the five grave offences, even women, burdened with the five obstacles and the three submissions. When there is not a moment's doubt in the Original Vow, the Tathāgata with great kindness, fully knowing every follower's heart, makes the bad heart of the follower become exactly the same as the good heart of the Tathāgata. This is what is meant when we say that "the heart of the Buddha and the heart of an ignorant being become one." We should realise, therefore, that we have been received within the all-encompassing light of Amida Tathāgata and that we will dwell within this light for the rest of our lives. Then, when life is exhausted, Amida Buddha will immediately take us to the True Land of Enjoyment.

What a gracious and priceless gift he has made us! How, then, can we respond gratefully to all the Buddha has done for us out of his Great Compassion?

It is simply by saying the *Nenbutsu* alone – pronouncing the Name – day and night, morning and evening that we respond to Amida Tathāgata with gratitude for what he has done for us. You should understand that this is what is meant in our tradition by the teaching of "completing the cause of birth in the Pure Land in ordinary life with the awakening of the one thought-moment." Therefore, when we entrust ourselves singleheartedly to Amida in this way, there is no need of any special effort on our part. As it is so easy to attain faith, it is easier still to become a Buddha by being born in the Land of Utmost Bliss. How precious Amida's Original Vow is! How precious Other Power faith is! There is no doubt at all about our birth.

In addition to this, however, there is another point that should be clearly understood to do with the way we conduct ourselves. The point is that all the gods and Buddhas have been made manifest in their various forms by virtue of skillful means to enable us to attain this singular gift of Other Power faith we have now received. Thus, as all the Buddhas and Bodhisattvas are originally manifestations of Amida Tathāgata, they are all of them also included in the one thought-moment when we take refuge in Amida Buddha by saying '*Namu Amida-butsu.*' For this reason we should never allow ourselves to belittle them.

Furthermore there is yet another point that needs to be understood. You must never be discourteous to the provincial military governors or local land stewards on the grounds that you are a person who reveres the Buddha-dharma and has attained faith. Rather should you accomplish your public duties all the more assiduously because of it.

People who have acquired such understanding can rightly be looked upon as those who exemplify the conduct of *Nenbutsu* followers in whom faith has been awakened and who aspire to Rebirth in the Pure Land. They are, in other words, those who faithfully follow both the Buddha-dharma and the laws of the state.

Most humbly and respectfully
Written on 13th May, Bunmei 6 [1474].

COMMENTS

This letter was composed on 13th May 1474, nearly two months after the previous one, the ninth letter of Fascicle Two, with no other letters in between.
It would seem no letters were written during this two month period because
the temple at Yoshizaki, where Rennyo was living at that time, was burnt
down on 28th March.

   The main subject of this letter is Other Power faith. It is of vital importance in Shin Buddhism for us to become aware of the reality of our karmic
existence and to entrust ourselves to Amida Buddha with the whole of our
being. As described previously, the Shin Buddhist faith includes two kinds of
awareness; firstly the awareness of the reality of one's karmic existence and
secondly the awareness of the unconditional love of Amida Buddha. These are
two aspects of one and the same faith-experience. Concerning this point, of
particular significance is the line: "without worrying in any way how heavily
burdened we are with bad karma, we simply entrust ourselves singleheartedly and steadfastly to Amida Tathāgata." This comment by Rennyo in this
particular letter clarifies that once we are awakened to the reality of our
karmic burden we should immediately entrust ourselves to Amida Buddha
singleheartedly and steadfastly and no longer remain tied down by our consciousness of bad karma.

   If you make a careful observation of those around you in your daily life,
you will find there are some who remain too conscious of their weak points or
negative aspects, tending even to display a certain pride in such awareness as
a result of paying it so much attention. Our Shin Buddhist awareness of bad
karma should not be that sort of consciousness. Although it is very important
for us to become aware of how heavily we are burdened with wrongdoings,
nevertheless, as soon as we are awakened to this sad reality of our existence,
we should immediately entrust ourselves to Amida Buddha with our whole
being, going beyond all sorts of attachment to self-power, including such over-
awareness of the negative aspects of our karma. When we entrust ourselves
to Amida Tathāgata, we do not need to worry how heavily burdened with
bad karma we may be.

   To explain this dramatic alteration of our consciousness through the
experience of Other Power faith, Rennyo refers to "the oneness of the heart
of the Buddha and the heart of an ignorant being." The good heart of the
Buddha swiftly flows into the bad heart of an ignorant being and the latter
becomes exactly the same as the good heart of the Tathāgata. The notion of

"the oneness of the heart of the Buddha and the heart of an ignorant being" points to the actual alteration of our consciousness that takes place by virtue of the good heart of the Buddha.

Regarding the notion of "the oneness of the heart of the Buddha and the heart of an ignorant being," *The Goichidai ki kikigaki* states, [see note N° 6] Remyos

Article 64. "The Buddha kindly amends (*shitsurau*) [the hearts of] sentient beings. What here is meant by '*shitsurau*' is that, whilst allowing the hearts of sentient beings to remain as they are, Amida Buddha adds his heart to theirs to make their hearts good. It is not that Amida Buddha completely replaces the hearts of sentient beings with hearts remade by his Wisdom alone."[200] —[Honey in Tea]

In Shin Buddhism this passage is often quoted as an important statement expressing "the oneness of the heart of the Buddha and the heart of an ignorant being." It is by virtue of the Buddha's heart that the heart of an ordinary man becomes one with the heart of the Buddha. Regarding this point Shinran Shōnin in his main writing, *The Kyōgyōshinshō*, quotes from *The Commentary on The Treatise on the Pure Land* by Tánluán (476-542):

[para 16 in contemplation sutra]

This heart becomes Buddha[201] means that the heart itself can become Buddha. *This heart is Buddha*[202] means that there is no Buddha outside this heart. It is like fire coming out of the wood. Fire cannot be produced outside the wood. As fire cannot separate itself from the wood, fire burns the wood and the wood is burned by fire to become the fire itself.[203]

These two statements from *The Meditation Sūtra*, "*This heart becomes Buddha*" and "*This heart is Buddha*," are known as the original textual source upon which the Shin Buddhist thought of "the oneness of the heart of the Buddha and the heart of an ignorant being" is based. Tánluán's metaphorical explanation of the relationship between the two different hearts helps us understand how effective the virtue of the Buddha's heart is. Needless to say, 'wood' refers to the heart of an ignorant being and 'fire,' to the heart of the Buddha.

If you view this relationship between the heart of the Buddha and the heart of an ignorant being as being the great working of the Buddha-dharma, these two will appear as one and the same. If, on the other hand, in the course of your own way to the attainment of oneness, you look at the relationship from the viewpoint of understanding yourself as an ordinary ignorant human being, they will appear as two. The oneness of the two is produced through the great working of the Buddha-dharma.

Another metaphorical example may help explain this oneness more clearly. Suppose that a big rock is being carried on a boat. The rock stands for an ignorant being and the boat for the Buddha. Of course the rock does not change in weight when it is carried on board but, due to the dynamic function of the boat and not any intrinsic power of the rock, it does not sink into the water as long as it remains on board. The direction the rock then proceeds in is the same as that of the boat. The gravity of the rock is always sustained by the buoyancy of the vessel. The duality is turned into oneness through the power of the boat itself, just as if we ourselves are carried to the Pure Land through the power of Amida's Original Vow. The more aware we are of the karmic gravity of our existence, the more aware we are of the buoyancy of the ship of Amida Buddha.

A verse in Japanese (*wasan*) composed by Shinran Shōnin says,

> Lacking even a modicum of love and compassion,
> How could I hope to benefit others?
> Were it not for the ship of Amida's Vow
> How could I myself cross the sea of suffering?[204]

After his description in this letter of the oneness of the Buddha and an ordinary human being, Rennyo goes on to talk about the benefit of Amida Buddha's all-encompassing light: "We should realise, therefore, that we have been received within Amida Tathāgata's all-encompassing light and that we will dwell within this light for the rest of our lives. Then, when life is exhausted, Amida Buddha will immediately take us to the True Land of Enjoyment."

The latter half of the letter is concerned with the way we should live our *Nenbutsu* lives after the attainment of Other Power faith. Rennyo Shōnin makes the following three points regarding this. Firstly he writes that the only way for us to respond to all that Amida Buddha has done for us is to pronounce the *Nenbutsu* with gratitude, morning and evening, day and night. Secondly, Shin Buddhist followers should always respect gods, Bodhisattvas and Buddhas as they are all manifestations of Amida Buddha, which he made in order to enable us to attain Other Power faith. The final point he makes is that, by virtue of our having attained faith in Amida Buddha, we should continue to respect the laws of the state by not being discourteous to those in positions of authority.

CHAPTER TWENTY-SIX

The Fivefold Meaning
of True Faith

ON THE FIVEFOLD MEANING

FASCICLE II, LETTER ELEVENTH

In recent years the purport of Shinran Shōnin's teaching of our tradition has been interpreted differently in different provinces, resulting in a lack of consistency. This is utterly deplorable, firstly because, despite the primal importance in our tradition of Other Power faith, through which ignorant beings are believed to attain birth in the Pure Land, there are those who ignore the matter of faith and fail to take it into consideration. They persuade others to believe that "the essence of faith lies in not forgetting that Amida Tathāgata already secured our birth in the Pure Land when he attained Supreme Enlightenment ten kalpas ago." What is completely missing in such a declaration is the experience of attaining Other Power faith through taking refuge in Amida Buddha. This being so, even if such people know their birth has been secured since the time Amida attained Supreme Enlightenment ten kalpas ago, unless they understand what is meant by Other Power faith, through which we attain birth, they will not attain birth in the Land of Utmost Bliss.

There are also those who declare, "Even if we take refuge in Amida, this will be of no avail without a good teacher. Therefore, all we have to do is entrust ourselves to a good teacher." To judge from their words, these people do not appear to be the kind to have truly attained faith according to our tradition. The function of a good teacher is simply to encourage people to take refuge singleheartedly and steadfastly in Amida.

Therefore, a doctrine has been established consisting of five elements: firstly, past good conditions; secondly, a good teacher; thirdly, light; fourthly, faith; and, fifthly, the Name. Without the fulfilment of all five of these elements it is definitely not possible for us to attain birth in the Pure Land. Thus a good teacher is a messenger who tells us to take refuge in Amida Buddha and unless we meet a good teacher, through the unfolding of past good conditions, it is not possible to attain birth in the Pure Land. Nevertheless it should be clearly understood that to abandon Amida, in whom we should take refuge, and to regard a good teacher as the only essential requisite is a most grievous error.

Most humbly and respectfully
On 20th May, Bunmei 6 [1474].

COMMENTS

This particular letter is known under the title *On the Fivefold Meaning*, a reference to the five separate aspects of Shin Buddhist faith-experience. According to Rennyo Shōnin, Shin Buddhist faith is always accompanied by all five of these aspects. Should any one of them be missing, true faith will not be attained.

Rennyo would appear to have written the whole letter expressly in order to tell his followers how essential it was in this tradition for them to attain true faith. It must have been extremely disheartening for him to see the way a number of Nenbutsu followers ignored the matter of faith and completely failed to take it into consideration. The beginning of the letter shows how serious Rennyo was about the attainment of true faith.

Then, Rennyo goes on to refer to a sort of heterodoxy known as 'Ten Kalpas Faith.'[205] People imbued with this wrong view insist that faith is a matter of knowing that birth in the Pure Land has been ensured for them ever since Amida Buddha attained Supreme Enlightenment ten kalpas ago. Because Amida's attainment of Supreme Enlightenment means the fulfilment of his Original Vow to save all sentient beings without any discrimination, they assume that it is enough for their salvation simply to know that birth in the Pure Land has been secured since the time of Amida's Supreme Enlightenment ten kalpas ago.

According to Rennyo's explanation what is wrong with those followers of 'the Ten Kalpas Faith' is that they mistake faith for a form of knowledge. Consequently they think that if they know and do not forget that their birth has been secured since the time Amida attained Supreme Enlightenment ten kalpas ago, that in itself is enough to ensure their birth in the Pure Land. In Shin Buddhism faith is not a matter of knowledge or intellectual understanding but something far beyond them. What is of crucial importance in the Shin Buddhist tradition is the instantaneous awakening of faith attained through taking refuge in Amida Buddha. Taking refuge in Amida Buddha is the pivotal point in attaining faith. Taking refuge in Amida Tathāgata in the true sense or, in other words, entrusting one's whole being to the Buddha in the here and now, brings about the instantaneous awakening of faith. Entrusting ourselves to Amida Buddha enables us to abandon all that attachment to knowledge with which we imprison ourselves. Entrusting ourselves to the Buddha is a big leap of faith, going beyond the self-centred world of knowledge. The sharp contrast described here in this letter by Rennyo puts me in mind of Chapter Two of *The Tanni shō*. The relevant part from my translation of the text says that

> "Having crossed the borders of ten provinces or more, each of you has come to see me at the risk of your life. Your purpose is solely to hear from me how to be born in the Pure Land. If, however, assuming that I know other ways of being born in the Pure Land apart from pronouncing the *Nenbutsu* or thinking that I may be acquainted with some Buddhist texts that teach those special ways, you are concerned to know some hidden truth, I am afraid you are making a big mistake. If that is indeed your concern, there are many eminent scholars in the Southern Capital (Nara), or on the Northern Mountain (Mount Hiei), whom you would be better off visiting in order to inquire to your hearts' content about the essentials for birth in the Pure Land.
> "As for myself, Shinran, there is nothing else involved apart from simple faith in the *Nenbutsu,* according to the instruction of my good teacher, 'Just say the *Nenbutsu* so as to be saved by Amida.'"[206]

In Shinran Shōnin's immediate response to his disciples who wanted to know how to be born in the Pure Land there was a sharp contrast drawn between intellectual concern and pure faith. He told the disciples that they were making a great mistake if their concern was simply to understand by intellect alone and if they assumed that he knew any other ways of solution apart from simple faith in the *Nenbutsu*. The essential point is that the *Nenbutsu* is not an object of knowledge one may try to comprehend logically but something transcendental that emanates naturally from within. Faced with his disciples' very intellectual concern, therefore, Shinran Shōnin's answer was simply to reaffirm his own simple faith in Hōnen's teaching of the *Nenbutsu*: "As far as I, Shinran, am concerned, there is nothing else involved apart from simple faith in the *Nenbutsu,* according to the instruction of my good teacher, 'Just say the

Nenbutsu so as to be saved by Amida','" declaring that if their concern was only intellectual, then it would be better for them to consult eminent scholars in Nara or on Mount Hiei. Faith is not simply a matter of information or even belief if such belief amounts to no more than intellectual assent. Faith-experience definitely includes a phase of transcendence that enables one to go beyond objective knowledge or the intellectual approach.

Now I would like to move on to the second of the two false teachings, commonly known as 'Entrusting Only to a Good Teacher,' the erroneous claim that all we need do is entrust ourselves to a good teacher, nothing more.

Although 'a good teacher' is encompassed in the Fivefold Meaning of True Faith, in other words, represents one of the five requisites for birth in the Pure Land, if you simply think that "all we have to do is entrust ourselves to a good teacher," you are greatly mistaken. As Rennyo Shōnin says, "The function of a good teacher is simply to encourage people to take refuge singleheartedly and steadfastly in Amida." The danger lies in absolutising a relative existence, in other words, in relating to a relative finite being as if that being were something absolute and infinite. The true significance of a good teacher is that he points his followers in the direction of truth. You should not mistake your master for truth itself. Your master's individual existence (skt. *rūpa-kāya*, 色身) is absolutely finite within this world. On the other hand, it is also true that formless truth manifests itself through form or finite individual existence. In this respect every form is a manifestation of formless truth or Emptiness. The *rūpa-kāya* or form-body of a good teacher can be seen as a manifestation of the *Dharma-kāya* or Dharma-body, that is, formless truth. You should understand the mutual relationship between form and formlessness or Emptiness but you should be careful not to confuse one with the other. They are different and at the same time one and the same. Rennyo's statement, "The function of a good teacher is simply to encourage people to take refuge singleheartedly and steadfastly in Amida Buddha," is very important and crystal clear. We should not overlook that the main purport of his teaching is to encourage people to take refuge in Amida Tathāgata, in other words to attain faith.

It goes without saying that the central idea of these five requisites for birth in the Pure Land outlined in the letter is the attainment of true faith. Regarding their composition or nature it would seem a good idea to describe each one in order. You could, for example, explain them as follows: firstly, your past good conditions become mature enough to encounter the Buddha-dharma. Secondly, when your past good conditions become mature, you will be able to encounter a good teacher. Thirdly, when you encounter a good teacher, through the maturity of your past good conditions, you will find yourself embraced in the Infinite Light of Amida. Fourthly, on finding yourself embraced by the Light of the Buddha, you will attain faith by entrusting yourself to the Buddha, and finally, after attaining faith, you will pronounce the Name of the Buddha with joy and gratitude.

Let me now give a brief explanation of each of the five. Firstly, the maturity of past good conditions means not only the maturity of your consciousness but also all the external conditions related to it that have led you to meet the Buddha-dharma. The present is the result of the whole of the past. Your present in which you meet the Buddha-dharma can be seen as the result of all your past good conditions. Rennyo says in his letters that, when we guide people to attain faith, we should be careful as to whether their past good conditions are mature enough to receive the teaching or not. Needless to say we should try to guide them as much as possible to attain true faith, but we should also exercise considerable caution because it is unsafe to presume that everyone is ready to attain true faith straight away. If we hasten to expend enormous efforts on encouraging everyone around us to attain faith as soon as possible without taking into account their mature ability to do so, such efforts on our part may become a source of considerable aggravation to them.

Secondly, the original Japanese word for 'a good teacher' is *zenchishiki* 善知識 (skt. *kalyāṇamitra*). Roughly speaking this term has three meanings; firstly 'good friend,' secondly 'good protector' and thirdly 'good teacher.' In Shin Buddhism it mainly means a good teacher who guides people to attain faith for birth in the Pure Land. For example, Hōnen Shōnin was a good teacher for Shinran Shōnin. In the Shin Buddhist tradition a good teacher represents all Buddhas and his *Nenbutsu* represents all Buddhas pronouncing the Name. All Buddhas pronouncing the Name is the great working of the Tathāgata's Love and Compassion prior to our own pronouncing of the Name. Through the maturity of his past good conditions, Shinran Shōnin was able to encounter a good teacher, Hōnen Shōnin, and the *Nenbutsu* that Hōnen Shōnin was reciting. The nature of Shinran Shōnin's encounter with Hōnen Shōnin is also described in *The Tanni shō* Chapter Two:

"I do not profess to know whether the *Nenbutsu* will really work as the seed that allows me to be born in the Pure Land or whether it may prove the karmic act for which I am condemned to hell. If, however, by pronouncing the *Nenbutsu*, I were ultimately to find myself misled by my Master Hōnen and cast into hell, even then I would have no regrets. The reason is this: if I were actually capable of attaining Buddhahood by my own endeavours while following other practices but nevertheless simply pronounced the *Nenbutsu* and so fell into hell, then indeed I would feel regret at having been deceived. But I am quite incapable of any other practice, so hell would have to be my abode in any case."[207]

Through this awareness that "hell would have to be my abode in any case" Shinran Shōnin found himself embraced by the Original Vow of Amida Buddha or, in other words, by Amida's Infinite Light of Unconditional Love. Therefore he continues to state with confidence,

> "If the Original Vow of Amida is true, the teaching of Śākyamuni cannot be untrue; if the teaching of Śākyamuni is true, the commentaries by Shàndǎo cannot be untrue; if Shàndǎo's commentaries are true, the teaching of Hōnen Shōnin cannot be untrue; if the teaching of Hōnen Shōnin is true, how can it be possible for me, Shinran, to utter untruth? This being so, it is up to you to choose whether to believe in the *Nenbutsu* or to reject it."[208]

Thirdly, 'light' is Amida's Infinite Light that "embraces all and abandons none." Through his encounter with Hōnen Shōnin Shinran Shōnin found himself embraced in this Light. On meeting a good teacher, our existence is illumined by the Light that radiates through the teacher's pronouncing of the Name. Under this light we become aware how wretched we are, and all the attachments and hindrances of our self-centered consciousness melt away. The Light penetrates our consciousness through and through and embraces our whole existence just as it is.

Fourthly, on meeting Amida's Light we find ourselves embraced in the Light of Unconditional Love. Awakened to the Light, we entrust ourselves to Amida Buddha singleheartedly and steadfastly. This is Other Power faith. On attaining this faith we are assured of being born in the Pure Land.

Fifthly and finally, by attaining faith and joy, we pronounce the Name of Amida Buddha with immense gratitude. The Name as the fifth element is the Name of the Buddha, pronounced by us with gratitude after the attainment of faith. When Shinran Shōnin states in *The Kyōgyōshinshō*, "True faith is surely provided with the Name," the Name refers to the Name we pronounce with gratitude after the attainment of faith. Our own pronouncing of the Name with gratitude is different from all Buddhas' pronouncing the Name, or a good teacher's *Nenbutsu*, because the latter is the great working of the Tathāgata that embraces us all prior to our pronouncing the Name. From the perspective of another person who comes later, however, one's pronouncing the Name after the attainment of faith can be seen as the *Nenbutsu* of a good teacher.

Rennyo Shōnin's teaching on "the Fivefold Meaning" in this letter was not entirely new but was based on traditional texts such as *The Kuden shō* 口伝鈔 by Venerable Kakunyo,[209] and *The Jōdo kenmon shū* 浄土見聞集 by Venerable Zonkaku.[210] According to my interpretation, Rennyo's real intention when writing this letter is clearly expressed in the phrase, "Thus a good teacher is a messenger who tells us to take refuge in Amida Buddha and unless we meet a good teacher, through the unfolding of past good conditions, it is not possible to attain birth in the Pure Land." Rennyo criticised the erroneous teaching known as 'Entrusting Only to a Good Teacher' in order to establish the true meaning of 'a good teacher.' Our view of a good teacher should not be confined to his *rūpa-kāya* or individual existence. Absolutising the *rūpa-kāya* is extremely dangerous. It is important for us to have a clear insight into the *Dharma-kāya* behind the *rupa-kāya*. Thus Rennyo Shōnin carefully concludes in his letter, "Nevertheless it should be clearly understood that to abandon Amida, in whom we should take refuge, and to regard a good teacher as the only essential requisite is a most grievous error."

CHAPTER TWENTY-SEVEN

The Notion of Hell in Shin Buddhism

ON THE FIFTY YEARS OF HUMAN LIFE

FASCICLE II, LETTER TWELVE

Consider the fifty years of human life and you will find they correspond to a day and night in the Four-King Heaven. Furthermore, fifty years in the Four-King Heaven (jp. *shiōden*) is but a day and night in the Hell of Repetition of Painful Life (jp. *tōkatsu jigoku*). From this view-point all of you will be found making light of falling into hell and receiving suffering therein, giving no thought to going to the Pure Land and receiving unsurpassed bliss. Thus you live in idleness and, passing days and months in vain, have never experienced the decisive attainment of the One Mind by yourselves. You do not read even a single volume of the sacred scriptures, nor do you teach followers by citing a single phrase of the Buddha-dharma. From morning till evening, you simply watch for spare time and stretch out to sleep with your pillows. How deplorable it is! Quietly reflect upon this fact!

From now on, therefore, those who have been negligent of following the Dharma should seek to attain faith definitely even more than before, wishing to be born in the Land of Enjoyment; this will indeed bring virtues to you. It should be realised that this also accords with the principle of benefiting oneself and benefiting others.

Most humbly and respectfully

This is written on the twelfth day of June, the sixth year of Bunmei [1474]. In the midst of this extreme heat I have just finished writing this as though the brush flowed of itself.

COMMENTS

It is generally believed in the tradition that this letter was addressed by Rennyo Shōnin to priests around him including his own sons. As they appeared to be living in idleness, Rennyo gave this letter to them.

According to the postscript of the letter it was an extremely hot day. This unusual heat of the day seems to have reminded Rennyo of the notion of the Eight Hot Hells.[211] The name of this particular hell referred to in his letter is *saṃjīva* (jp. *tōkatsu*), meaning the hell of repetition of painful life. The suffering of this hell is said to be the lightest among the Eight Hot Hells. According to Rennyo, a day and night in this hell corresponds to fifty years in the Four-King Heaven, *cātru-mahārāja-kāyikāḥ* (jp. *shiōden*) and one day and night in this heaven, fifty years of human life. Rennyo Shōnin's way of counting is believed to be based on the detailed description of the Buddhist hells found in *The Shōbōnen sho kyō* 正法念處經.[212]

According to my understanding, hell in Buddhism is not an actual place outside our consciousness. We should not substantialise it as something apart from our mind. Basically it is a manifestation of our mind or consciousness, closely related to our experience of suffering in the present. The depth and severity of our suffering is represented as images of hell. In other words various kinds of hell are projections of the deep sufferings of our mind. Separated from our experience of suffering, hell images would be meaningless. Despite the fact that hell is the reality of our mind, we are unaware of it in daily life. Hell images are described as the means to help awaken us to the reality of our suffering.

The case is the same with the notion of heaven. Various heavens in the Buddhist view of the world are also manifestations of our mind. According to the Buddhist view the world of illusion consists of the Six Paths or Forms of Existence (jp. *rokushu*, skt. *sadgati*): 1) hell (skt. *naraka*), 2) hungry ghosts (skt. *preta*), 3) animals (skt. *tiryagyoni*), 4) fighting demons (skt. *asura*), 5) human beings (skt. *manuśya*) and 6) gods or heavens (skt. *deva*). Regarding heaven there are twenty-eight heavens: the first six heavens belong to the World of Desire (skt. *kāma-dhātu*), the next eighteen heavens to the World of Form (skt. *rūpa-dhātu*) and the last four to the World of Formlessness (skt. *ārūpya-dhātu*). The Four-King heaven referred to in the letter is the lowest heaven, the first one of the six belonging to the World of Desire.

In the letter, each realm described in the Buddhist world view seems to have its own time. In Buddhism the concept of time is not absolute but relative: time in the Four-king Heaven shifts much more slowly than that in the world of human beings and time in the Hell of Repetition of Painful Life (jp. *tōkatsu jigoku*) runs more slowly than that in the Four-king Heaven.

The latter part of the first paragraph of the letter contains a very strong admonition addressed to his followers, especially to those priests around him. The true purpose of this admonition lies in his encouragement of those followers, as fully expressed in the last paragraph. With his great love and compassion, Rennyo wanted for them to attain faith definitely.

He concluded the letter by saying that their attainment of faith would lead those priests to accomplish their principle of benefiting oneself and benefiting others.

CHAPTER TWENTY-EIGHT

Holding on to the Sleeve
of Amida Buddha

ON THE REPUTATION OF OUR SCHOOL

FASCICLE II, LETTER THIRTEEN

We should correctly observe the regulations established in our tradition and their very essence lies in behaving toward other schools as well as toward society carefully enough not to draw public attention by exposing our way of living to the world. Recently, however, there have been some among the *Nenbutsu* people in our tradition who have intentionally told others what our school is all about. They assumed that this would enhance the reputation of our school and in doing this they particularly sought to condemn and belittle other schools. There is nothing more absurd than this. Furthermore it deeply contradicts Shinran Shōnin's intention. For Shōnin once stated, "Even if you are called a 'cattle thief,' do not show yourself off as a participant in our tradition." We should thoroughly understand the matter through these words.

Next, those who would like to know correctly what 'peaceful awareness' in our tradition means need no wisdom or learning at all. It does not matter either whether they are male or female, noble or humble. All we need is simply to realise that we are wretched beings heavily weighed down by bad karma and understand that it is Amida Tathāgata alone who saves even such persons. When, without any effort of contriving on our part, but simply with only the

181

thought of holding fast to the sleeve of this Buddha Amida, we entrust ourselves to the Buddha, saying "Help me attain Rebirth," then Amida Tathāgata
rejoices profoundly and, emitting from himself eighty-four thousand great
rays of Light, embraces us within that Light. This is clearly expounded in the
Sūtra:[213] "The Light shines throughout the worlds of the ten directions, and
embraces all those pronouncing the *Nenbutsu* and abandons none of them."
This you should understand.

This being so, there is no worry about our becoming Buddhas. How
incomparable is the Original Vow beyond the World! And how gracious is
Amida Tathāgata's Light! Without being conditioned to see this Light, there can
be no cure at all for the dreadful sickness of ignorance and karma-hindrance,
with which we have been burdened from the beginningless past. Thanks to
the condition of this Light, however, those who have their past good conditions matured have already attained Other Power faith. The case being so, it is
immediately clear that this is faith granted by Amida Tathāgata. Therefore we
now understand clearly that this is not faith generated by the actual devotee
but Amida Tathāgata's great Other Power faith. Consequently we, all those
who have ever gratefully received Other Power faith, should reflect deeply on
the extent of Amida Tathāgata's gracious benevolence and always recite the
Nenbutsu, that is pronounce the Name, in order to respond to the Buddha
with gratitude for what he has done for us.

Most humbly and respectfully
Written on 3rd July, Bunmei 6 [1474].

COMMENTS

In the Higashi Honganji tradition this letter is entitled "Holding on to the
Sleeves," whereas it is known in the Nishi Honganji tradition under the title
"The Reputation of Our School." These titles each refer to one of the two main
subjects of the letter discussed in the first two paragraphs. The first is that
we should not seek after the fame of our tradition by talking about matters
of faith carelessly to unfamiliar people. The second is that we should attain
true faith or peaceful awareness by making the thought of holding fast to the
sleeves of Amida Buddha. The first subject was discussed in detail in *Chapter
17* in the commentary on the 'Two Truths'. In this chapter I will be focusing
my attention on the subject of the second paragraph of the letter.

The original Japanese word that I rendered as 'peaceful awareness' is
anjin 安心. Usually this special term is translated as 'settled mind,' because,
when the same compound was used in Shàndǎo's main writing known as the
Kangyō sho 觀經疏 (ch. *Guānjīng shū*), or *The Exposition of The Meditation*

Sūtra, the first character 安 of *anjin* 安心 meant 'to settle' and the second character 心 meant 'mind.' During the development of Pure Land Buddhism the meaning of *anjin* was given a deeper dimension and the term came to be used synonymously with faith or *shinjin* 信心. According to my view the word *anjin* 安心 conveys two aspects of faith: inner peace and awareness. Hence, my translation of the word as 'peaceful awareness.'[214]

For us to attain faith or 'peaceful awareness,' Rennyo Shōnin says, there is no discrimination such as wise and ignorant, male and female, noble and humble. All we need to attain faith is two kinds of awakening: firstly awakening to oneself or the reality of one's existence and secondly awakening to the unconditional love of the Buddha. They are two aspects of true faith. Rennyo states, "All we need is simply realise that we are wretched beings heavily weighed down by bad karma and understand that the only Buddha who saves even such persons is Amida Tathāgata." This awakening of faith is accompanied by a leap experience of entrusting ourselves to the Buddha beyond understanding. The next passage in the letter beautifully describes how we entrust ourselves to Amida Buddha: "When, without any effort of contriving on our part, but simply with the only thought of holding fast to the sleeve of this Buddha Amida, we entrust ourselves to the Buddha, saying 'Help me attain Rebirth!', then Amida Tathāgata rejoices profoundly and, emitting from himself eighty-four thousand great rays of Light, embraces us within that Light." This part of the letter reminds me of my father. Whenever he read out this passage of the letter, he came to tears, tears of joy and gratitude. The beautiful and concrete phrase, "simply with the only thought of holding fast to the sleeve of this Buddha Amida," must have been associated with some memory of his faith-experience, perhaps with his good teacher.

According to the traditional interpretation, "the sleeve of Amida Buddha" symbolises the Original Vow of Great Compassion. "With the only thought of holding fast to the sleeve of Amida Buddha" can be said to be a beautiful poetic expression given to the faith-experience of absolute entrusting to the Original Vow. This phrase is followed by the words "Help me attain Rebirth!"[215] This is characteristic of Rennyo Shōnin.

This expression of entreaty, "Help me attain Rebirth!" is actually the awakening to and acceptance of Amida's absolute command "Entrust yourself to me to attain Rebirth in the Pure Land."

Amida Buddha with his unconditional love wants to save all sentient beings. To help all beings to attain Rebirth is Amida's will coming from his great love and compassion. Hence, Amida's absolute command "Come to me immediately! I will welcome you just as you are!" The sincere entreaty "Help me attain Rebirth" is an immediate response to Amida's command that calls us from within and a heartfelt expression of our absolute entrusting to Amida's unconditional love.

As Rennyo states in the concluding part of the letter, on attaining true faith in this way, we come to understand that everything is a gift from Amida Buddha, including our act of entreating Amida Buddha to help us attain Rebirth in his Pure Land.

CHAPTER TWENTY-NINE

Admonition Against Secret Teachings

ON SECRET TEACHINGS

FASCICLE II, LETTER FOURTEEN

The 'secret teachings (*hijibōmon*),'[216] so popular in Echizen Province, are in no way the true Buddha-dharma. They are contemptible, non-buddhist teachings. Relying on them is useless, for to do so merely creates karma through which one will sink for a long time into the Hell of Incessant Pain. You must never ever follow those who are still attached to these secret teachings and who, by assuming them to be of vital importance, flatter and deceive other people. Part immediately from those who teach these secret teachings, confess the teachings just as you have received them, and reveal to others what sort of teachings they are.

Those who desire to realise fully the meaning of the teaching in our tradition and wish to be born in the Land of Utmost Bliss should first and foremost learn about Other Power faith. What is the main purpose of attaining Other Power faith?

It grants us, wretched ignorant beings, the provision by which we readily travel to the Pure Land.

What is Other Power faith like?

It is the kind of faith that moves us to entrust ourselves exclusively, singleheartedly and steadfastly to Amida Tathāgata with no contrivance on our own. When the one thought-moment in which we entreat Amida to save us is awakened, Amida Tathāgata unfailingly emits his all-encompassing light and continues to embrace us within this light for as long as we live in this world. It is in this way that our birth is assured.

Namu Amida-butsu is thus by its very nature the expression of our attainment of Other Power faith. We should understand that this faith is a realisation of the original purport of *Namu Amida-butsu*. It is because we attain this Other Power faith that there is no doubt at all that we will be born readily into the Land of Utmost Bliss.

How magnificent is the Original Vow of Amida Tathāgata! And how should we respond to Amida Buddha's gracious benevolence? Whether sleeping or waking, we should respond to Amida Tathāgata for what he has done for us simply by pronouncing *Namu Amida-butsu, Namu Amida-butsu*. With what sort of understanding, then, should we pronounce *Namu Amida-butsu*? We should understand that we pronounce *Namu Amida-butsu* with a joyful mind, feeling very grateful and respectful to Amida Buddha for that great work of his through which we have been saved.

Most humbly and respectfully
On 5th July, Bunmei 6 [1474].

COMMENTS

In *The Letters* by Rennyo Shōnin there are two letters which refer to 'secret teachings': this, the fourteenth Letter of Fascicle Two and the third letter of Fascicle Three. In addition to them there are several letters on this subject by Rennyo that were not compiled into *The Letters* by Venerable Ennyo (1491–1521), the third son of Venerable Jitsunyo (1458–1525).

Concerning the actual contents of 'the secret teachings,' however, Rennyo himself only left two short remarks in his letters. One of them is a statement in the third letter of Fascicle Three of *The Letters*, "In addition you should be aware that those who subscribe to complicated secret teachings and fail to revere the Buddha are nothing but troublemakers."[217] This is known as the secret teaching of 'No Worship.' The other appears in a paragraph from one of those letters that were not compiled into *The Letters*,

> I have heard all those people in that area say that, once one attains faith, then one will already be a Buddha having attained Enlightenment. This is unspeakably wrong. It is really contemptible. In the tradition of [Shinran] Shōnin there is a distinction between 'the benefit of being rightly assured' and 'the benefit of attaining Nirvāṇa.' When we take refuge in Amida

Buddha forsaking all the miscellaneous practices, we receive 'the benefit that embraces all beings and never abandons them' and enter the stage of those rightly assured of birth. This is called 'completing the act in daily life.' When our conditions for living in this life are exhausted and we die, we will attain Enlightenment.[218]

The erroneous doctrine mentioned here is known as 'the teaching of One Benefit.'

Why did not Rennyo talk much about the contents of the secret teachings? Perhaps he did not need to explain them because people at that time were familiar with religious groups based on those secret teachings and knew quite well what the teachings were like. It is not easy, however, for us today to know them in detail from his writings.

The Account of Rennyo Shōnin, written by Senkei in 1759,[219] refers to the secret teachings in Echizen Province as follows,

During Shōnin's stay in Echizen Province for five summers and winters, many of those who were attached to the secret teachings prevalent in that province confessed their faults with penitence. Those secret teachings were diverse. For instance, there was a group, known as the 'No Worship' school in Echizen, which teaches that Amida is merely a piece of wood or paper and that your own mind is the Buddha. Even if you happen to put your palms together, those people make you direct your hands to yourself and worship your mind. Or they teach that, unless you recite the *Nenbutsu* very loudly, it is useless and that it is only by reciting the *Nenbutsu* very loudly that you can destroy all your illusion and attain birth in the Pure Land. Or they teach that, because our birth has already been settled since ten kalpas ago, when Amida attained Buddhahood, simply knowing this is what is called faith. Or they teach that what is called Buddha is none other than your good teacher. As they were making these teachings spread there, Shōnin lamented this fact and taught people with a variety of skillful means. As a result many of them mended their ways and took refuge in the right Dharma.[220]

From this document we can roughly know what the secret teachings were like, at least what people meant by the words in the Edo Period. It is apparent that they can be found amongst the distorted teachings that the Shin Buddhist writings such as *The Tanni shō* (*A Record of Lament over Divergence*) by Yuien and *The Gaija shō* (*Setting the Claims Straight*) by Kakunyo had been trying to criticise and refute in order to keep the Shin Buddhist faith pure. For example, Rennyo's criticism of the 'No Worship' school, the most popular secret teaching in Echizen, is likely to be related to Chapter 15 of *The Tanni shō*[221] that criticises the misconception that one can become a Buddha in one's own earthly body (即身成佛章). Another case is an erroneous teaching that tells followers to worship their good teacher as Amida Buddha. Chapter 18 of *The Gaija shō*[222] criticises this wrong teaching, saying that it is unreasonable that, amongst those who regard themselves as disciples of the Honganji Shōnin (Shinran), there are those who worship their good teacher as if he were Amida Tathāgata himself. This particular secret teaching was also widespread and usually criticised as 'Entrusting Only to a Good Teacher.'

The secret teachings seem to be closely interrelated and together make a set of erroneous doctrines. Roughly speaking what they claim can be summarised as follows. They make a distinction between what they call superficial recitations of the *Nenbutsu* and the *Nenbutsu* based on the most profound doctrine. The latter is to be secretly transmitted from person to person and not to be made open to the public. In this particular religious order one who has received this secret transmission is to be called a true teacher. Those who believe this conception of *Nenbutsu* think that they themselves are originally enlightened and one and the same with Amida's *Dharma-kāya*. They presume they are Amida Buddha. According to their opinion, ignorant beings filled with blind passions are simultaneously identical with the Buddha, the Enlightened. Thus they believe the Buddha is not far from here in a very peculiar way. They think that not only their master who teaches this is Amida Buddha but also they themselves, who have received it, are the Buddha. Therefore, they insist that they do not need to worship the Buddha images made of wood or paper, because they are dead objects and taking refuge in them is useless. They maintain that they should take refuge in their master and worship themselves. Their self-centred way of thinking makes them consider that, because they are already Buddhas, they can do anything no matter what it is, good or evil. All of this is only to be transmitted secretly at night.

Rennyo mentions in this letter the secret teachings are widespread in Echizen Province. Besides this, according to some other letters, not compiled into *The Letters*, these teachings were popular in some areas such as Kaga Province and Mikawa Province. Some scholars say, based on *The Hogo no uragaki* by Kensei,[223] that the origin of secret teachings can be traced back to Nyodō 如道 (1253–1340), who is the founder of one of the Shin Buddhist schools known as Sanmonto-ha 三門徒派 and is said in a Shin Buddhist document[224] to have married Zenran's daughter. Regarding the lineage of the secret teachings, however, there are many different opinions amongst scholars and it is not clear whether Nyodō was actually the founder of this tradition of secret teachings or not.

One day, when I was studying Buddhism under D. T. Suzuki, he said to me that, whilst his father was a Confucian, his mother was a Shin Buddhist, somehow connected with the tradition of secret teachings. He described the followers of the tradition as holding a ritual in which one is put into a dark box and, when reciting the *Nenbutsu*, suddenly given light through a tiny window. I am not sure how long his mother was involved in the tradition of secret teachings. D. T. Suzuki is originally from Kanazawa in Kaga Province. This interesting story proves at least that in the Meiji period this tradition was still remaining in Kanazawa.

Although I am not absolutely sure, the secret teachings mentioned above seem to have been connected with some religious rituals to be kept hidden from others. It is noticeable that secret rituals called "storehouse secrets (*dozo-hiji* 土蔵秘事)" or "duvet-covering (*futon-kaburi* 布団被り)" have long been practised in various provinces in Japan.

Pride or arrogance, self-centredness, blind dependence, over-emphasis on rituals and knowledge, strong secretiveness and subjection or exposure to evil, these negative aspects of the human mind are found in the tradition of secret teachings. If followers are strongly attached to these negative aspects, all of them will be found within their minds, overlapping and strengthening each other. They are dreadful, indeed. Rennyo Shōnin says in the letter that "they are contemptible, non-buddhist teachings." In short, their followers ignore the Buddha and respect themselves, claiming that the self filled with illusion is immediately the Buddha. This is definitely not Shin Buddhism. Such an erroneous thought can never be called Buddhism.

Rennyo felt very sad to see followers who were so greatly mistaken despite their relatedness to the Pure Land tradition. Taking pity on them he tried to awaken them to how wrong they were. His effort to awaken them to the misery of their karma was quite successful. As stated in *The Account of Rennyo Shōnin*, "As a result many of them mended their ways and took refuge in the right Dharma."

After describing to his followers the nature of these mistaken teachings, Rennyo's sole aim, as clearly stated in the letter, was to encourage them to attain true faith. In Shin Buddhism the notion of true faith is simply entrusting oneself to Amida Buddha singleheartedly and steadfastly. However, it is not easy at all for us to attain, for we have to go beyond all our selfish attachments in order to entrust ourselves to Amida Buddha without any reservation. Entrusting ourselves to Amida Buddha or Other Power means forsaking all our attachments to self power. Feeling Other Power working within ourselves inspires and enables us to entrust ourselves to Amida Buddha by going beyond all selfish attachments. Once true faith is attained, all the negative aspects of our minds vanish and they are replaced by the positive aspects – humble awakening, fullness of light, inner peace, joy of pure faith, unselfish altruistic love, absolute relief in daily life, endless feeling of gratitude and the positive attitude to live our lives to the fullest extent towards the future.

The literal meaning of the phrase 'Namu Amida-butsu' is that I take refuge in Amida Buddha. This is nothing but the fulfilment of Amida's Original Vow, in which he desired all of us to attain pure faith by entrusting ourselves to the Name, Namu Amida-butsu. At the very moment of attaining faith Namu Amida-butsu wells up with joy from within. In this respect Namu Amida-butsu is also the natural expression of our gratitude to the Buddha. For our salvation through faith alone was originally promised in his Original Vow.

In the concluding part of the letter Rennyo praises Amida Buddha's Original Vow by expressing his immense gratitude to Amida Buddha for all that he has done for us. We can imagine his heart brimming over with joy and thankfulness as he pronounces the Nenbutsu "in response for that great work of his through which we have been saved." This is not only the teaching that he gave those around him but also the humble expression of his own gratitude to Amida Buddha.

The Original Teaching of Other Power Faith

ON KUBON AND CHŌRAKUJI

FASCICLE II, LETTER FIFTEEN

The Pure Land School of Buddhism established in Japan has become divided into a number of different branches – Seizan, Chinzei, Kubon, Chōrakuji and many more besides. Although Hōnen Shōnin's teaching followed a single thread, when those who had been following the Path of Sages came to Shōnin and listened to the teaching of the Pure Land, they did not grasp the heart of his teaching correctly. Because they themselves were not yet free of the ideas of their original schools, they tried to incorporate those thoughts into the Pure Land School with the result that a number of discrepancies exist in their teachings. We should never thoughtlessly slander them, however.

What is important is simply to cherish our tradition's 'peaceful awareness'; we ourselves should attain faith decisively and at the same time encourage others to do so likewise.

What is the meaning within our tradition of 'peaceful awareness'?

First of all we should really take to heart the fact that we are worthless beings burdened with the ten bad acts and the five grave offences, the five obstacles and the three submissions. Next we should become aware that it is the inconceivable working of Amida Tathāgata's Original Vow that saves such wretched beings as ourselves by making them its main object of salvation. When we entrust ourselves wholeheartedly and do not entertain the slightest doubt, Amida will embrace us without fail. It is precisely this awareness that constitutes the true Other Power faith that we have already attained. In order to gain this faith in one thought-moment there is no need of effort on our part.

How easy it is to realise this Other Power faith! How easy it is to practise the Name of Amida Buddha! Thus, the attainment of faith is nothing other than understanding the six characters 南无阿彌陀佛 (*Na-mu-a-mi-da-butsu*); this is the essence of Other Power faith.

What is the meaning of *Namu Amida-butsu*?

The two characters *Namu* 南无 mean that, aspiring for birth in the Land of Utmost Bliss, we entrust ourselves wholeheartedly to Amida Buddha and the characters *Amida-butsu* 阿彌陀佛 mean that Amida Buddha takes pity on all of us who entrust ourselves in this way. Although we have been heavily burdened with horrible transgressions for myriads of kalpas from the beginningless past, because we are fortunately conditioned to encounter Amida Tathāgata's Light, all the deep transgressions that we have committed through our ignorance and karmic hindrances are immediately extinguished and thus we already find ourselves in the company of those who are rightly assured of birth in the Pure Land. Therefore, leaving our 'ignorant being's body' we will realise the 'Buddha-body'.[225] This is what 'Amida Tathāgata' means. It is on these grounds that the three characters 'Amida 阿彌陀' have been interpreted as meaning 'to embrace, impart, and save.'

If, once faith has been decisively attained in this way, we simply recite the *Nenbutsu* of "pronouncing the Name," mindful always of how much has been done for us by Amida Tathāgata, then that will truly accord with the principle of responding with gratitude to Amida Tathāgata for all that he has done for us.

Most humbly and respectfully
Written on 9th July, Bunmei 6 [1474].

COMMENTS

Pure Land Buddhism, which originated in India around the first century, already had a long history before Hōnen Shōnin (1133–1212) first established in Japan an independent Pure Land school known as 'Jōdo-shū.' This was a great spiritual movement that spread across the country involving countless numbers of people of all classes. Up until then the Pure Land tradition had been a sort of 'dependent school' (*gūshū* 寓宗), practised in conjunction with other traditions. At Chinese and Korean temples, for example, Zen and Pure Land Buddhism were practised together. The advent of Hōnen Shōnin turned the Pure Land tradition into an independent school.

The most conspicuous feature of the Pure Land school founded by Hōnen Shōnin is the overriding emphasis on "Other Power," namely the power of the Original Vow of Amida Buddha. On awakening to the working of Other Power within themselves, Pure Land followers entrust themselves wholeheartedly to this Power. This is their faith and this faith is held to be a gift from Amida Buddha, given that Amida's Great Love embodied as Other Power is found already working in all sentient beings, causing them to awaken, entrust themselves and take the leap, in other words to gain faith. This is why it is called 'Other Power faith.' To clarify this point, there is an interesting story from *The Life of Shinran Shōnin*, who was formerly called Zenshin, written by Shinran's great grandson, Kakunyo Shōnin (1270–1351).

[Shinran] Shōnin said, "A long time ago, when a large number of people, including Shōshin-bō, Seikan-bō and *Nenbutsu*-bō, were gathered together in the presence of the Great Master Venerable Genkū (Hōnen Shōnin), we found ourselves engaged in an unexpectedly heated discussion, triggered by a remark I myself had made: 'The Master's faith and Zenshin's faith do not differ at all. They are one and the same.' The others were all arguing against me declaring, 'We can see no grounds for you to say the Master's faith and yours are one and the same. How could they be so?' But I replied, 'Why am I not allowed to say they are so? It would indeed be presumptuous of me to claim that I am equal to the Master in depth of wisdom or breadth of learning. In as far as the faith that enables us to be born in the Pure Land is concerned, however, ever since I learned the teaching of Other Power faith I have never added to it any kind of selfish thought. Thus the Master's faith is a gift from Other Power and Zenshin's faith is also Other Power. For this reason I declare that they are one and the same'. On hearing this the Great Master just observed, 'If one's faith differs from that of other people it is because their faith is based on self-power. Since each person possesses their own differing intellectual capacities, faith based upon such capacities cannot be identical. Other Power faith is a gift from the Buddha to ignorant beings, whether they be good or bad. For this reason, Genkū's faith and Zenshin's faith are not different, but one and the same. It is not because we are wise that we entrust ourselves to Amida Buddha. If your faith is different from mine, you may not be born in the same Pure Land that I am bound for.' With this, those present all held their tongues and uttered no further word."[226]

If Other Power faith forms your true basis, your faith will be identical to that of Hōnen Shōnin, Shinran Shōnin or Rennyo Shōnin. Thus Hōnen Shōnin was able to go on and say, "For this reason, Genkū's faith and Zenshin's faith are not different, but one and the same." Can you imagine how happy Shinran Shōnin must have been to hear these words from his Master? Since the whole conversation centered on Shinran's ultimate concern, namely the great matter of faith, Shinran Shōnin's happiness must have known no bounds. The entire story is based on what Kakunyo Shōnin heard about the core of true faith from some direct disciples of his grandfather, Shinran Shōnin, who had already learned it from his Master, Hōnen Shōnin, through their initial encounter.

In so far as they realise that what is known as Other Power faith is a gift from Amida Buddha, every follower knows their faith to be the same as everyone else's. As Hōnen Shōnin clearly states, "If one's faith differs from that of other people it is because their faith is based on self-power; since each person has their own differing intellectual capacities, faith based upon such capacities cannot be identical." Pure faith is not a matter of intellectual understanding or knowledge. When people entrust themselves to Other Power, they forsake all attachment to self-power, becoming fully aware of the problems caused by their tenacious attachment. As long as their faith remains based on self-power, their faith will not be the same. If they become teachers still based on their own faith, their teachings will become quite diverse and differ from the original notion of Other Power faith taught by Hōnen Shōnin.

In the first paragraph of this letter Rennyo explains briefly how a number of different Pure Land schools deviated from Hōnen Shōnin's original teaching of Other Power faith. Brief as it is Rennyo's clarification of the historical conditions governing the appearance of so many diverse schools of Pure Land Buddhism sounds realistic, with his viewpoint well grounded in the original notion of Other Power faith, the core of Shin Buddhist philosophy. Simply because the founders of those different Pure Land schools were still not free of their attachment to their previous sects, their teaching of Pure Land Buddhism includes a number of divergencies from the original teaching of Hōnen Shōnin.

Concerning the four branches referred to by Rennyo Shōnin in the letter, I would like to give you a very short commentary on each.

The Seizan Branch of the Jōdo-shū or Pure Land School: a Pure Land school founded by Venerable Zen'e-bō Shōkū (1177–1247), who followed Hōnen Shōnin for twenty-three years. After the death of Hōnen, while living at Seizan Sangoji Temple in Kyoto, Venerable Shōkū taught the Pure Land doctrine. This branch was named after the place where he lived. The teaching of this branch is very close to Shin Buddhism, or the Jōdo Shinshū, because they recognise only the *Nenbutsu* and nothing else as the practice that enables us to attain birth in the Pure Land. But Shin Buddhism puts more emphasis on the teaching about salvation through faith alone, realising the *Nenbutsu* as an expression of gratitude welling up after the awakening of faith.

The Chinzei Branch: a Pure Land school founded by Venerable Shōkō-bō Benchō (1162–1238), one of Hōnen Shōnin's disciples, so called because he taught at Kōmyōji Temple in Chinzei (Kyūshū). The teaching of this branch accepts not only the *Nenbutsu* but a number of other practices also as helping us attain birth in the Pure Land.

The Kubonji Branch: a Pure Land school founded by Kakumyō-bō Chōsai (1184–1266), one of Hōnen Shōnin's disciples, so called because he taught at Kubonji Temple in Kyoto. This branch no longer exists. It emphasised the importance of reciting the *Nenbutsu* as many times as possible.

The Chōrakuji Branch: a Pure Land school founded by Precept Master Ryūkan (1148–1227), one of Hōnen Shōnin's disciples, is named after Chōrakuji Temple in Kyoto where he practised the *Nenbutsu*. It is said that this branch adopted the teaching that advocates reciting the *Nenbutsu* as many times as possible. We cannot find, however, any tendency for "many recitations" in Ryukan's own writings such as *Gose monogatari*, *Ichinen tanen funbetsu ji* and *Jiriki tariki ji*.[227] This branch must have adopted a policy of 'many recitations' after the death of the founder. It no longer exists today.

Towards the end of the first paragraph, Rennyo warns us, "We should not slander them in a self-centred way, however," before drawing our attention to what we ought to be doing in the here and now, "What is important is simply to cherish our tradition's 'peaceful awareness'; we ourselves should attain faith decisively and at the same time encourage others to do so likewise."

The original Japanese word for 'peaceful awareness' is *anjin* 安心, which is understood as synonymous with faith (*shin* 信 or *shinjin* 信心) in the context of Shin Buddhist teaching. The original meaning of the compound 安心 is 'to settle the mind.' In Shàndǎo's lineage of Pure Land Buddhism, including the teachings of Hōnen and Shinran, the only way truly to settle the mind is to entrust oneself to Amida Buddha wholeheartedly, in other words to attain faith. The Japanese term *anjin* is also often translated as 'settled mind.' If you settle your mind in the embrace of Amida Buddha, your mind can be said to have been 'settled.' In this sense faith is a 'settled mind.'

When *anjin* means 'settling the mind,' it pertains to 'attaining faith.' After the attainment of faith *anjin* means the 'settled mind,' the state of mind when faith has been attained. Nowadays the word *anjin* is more frequently used in the latter sense, referring to the state of mind after the attainment of faith. In this sense some people translate the word as 'peaceful mind,' which well conveys the sense of 'inner peace' contained in the word. Another important meaning attached to the word *anjin* in Shin Buddhism is 'awareness,' awareness of *ki* 機, or the self, and at the same time awareness of *Hō* 法, or the Dharma. In as far as it is true that the essence of Shin Buddhist faith lies in awakening to the reality of one's wretched existence and simultaneously to the great compassion of the Buddha, *anjin* can be said to include the element of awareness. When taking this interpretation I understand the Chinese character 心 of a*njin* 安心 as the word that can convey the sense of awareness. This is the reason that I would like to render the word *anjin* as 'peaceful awareness.'

Rennyo Shōnin's *anjin*, or 'peaceful awareness,' entirely accords with the traditional Shin Buddhist teaching that the notion of "true faith" includes two kinds of awareness, *nishu jinshin* 二種深信: Firstly awareness of *ki* or the self and secondly awareness of *Hō* or the Dharma. Underlying Rennyo's kind teaching of the real meaning of *anjin* or peaceful awareness is this fundamental realisation of the awareness of *ki* and *Hō*.

Almost all of those Pure Land schools talk about the merit, or virtue, of practising the *Nenbutsu* or other good deeds and thus many of them are very much concerned about the number of *Nenbutsu* recitations or the amount of good deeds. Through introspection a sort of blind belief in the accumulation of merits may be found to secretly lie behind our attachment to self-power. Shin Buddhist teaching, however, has nothing whatsoever to do with the idea of accumulating merits by practising virtuous deeds, because the Shin Buddhist faith is not based on self-power but simply on Other Power. It is not in order to accumulate merits or virtues that Shin Buddhist followers pronounce the Name of Amida Buddha, '*Namu Amida-butsu*,' so singlemindedly.

What then does '*Namu Amida-butsu*' mean? *Namu Amida-butsu* represents the essence of the Shin Buddhist faith in which the oneness of *ki* (self) and *Hō* (Dharma) is realised. Rennyo Shōnin says, "The two characters *Namu* 南无 mean that, aspiring for birth in the Land of Utmost Bliss, we entrust ourselves wholeheartedly to Amida Buddha and the four characters *A-mi-da-butsu* 阿彌陀佛 mean that Amida Buddha takes pity on all of us who entrust ourselves in this way." *Namu* stands for the expression of our 'entrusting' or 'taking refuge' and *Amida-butsu* stands for the working of Amida's great compassion or his embrace. Those two elements, *ki* and *Hō*, are one in *Namu Amida-butsu*.

Once true faith, or the oneness of *ki* and *Hō*, is attained, *Namu Amida-butsu* is our spontaneous expression of gratitude to the Buddha. Rennyo always concludes his letters with words of gratitude: "If, once faith has been decisively attained in this way, we simply recite the *Nenbutsu* of 'pronouncing the Name,' mindful always of how much Amida Tathāgata has done for us, that will truly fulfil the principle of responding with gratitude to Amida Tathāgata's benevolence."

CHAPTER THIRTY-ONE

Embraced within the Light of Amida Buddha

SOMEONE WHOSE NAME HAS JUST BEEN ADDED TO THE LIST OF FOLLOWERS

FASCICLE III, LETTER ONE

No matter whether you are a long time member of our tradition or whether you are someone whose name has only just been added to our list of followers, if you do not fully grasp what is meant by 'peaceful awareness,' you should most definitely, from this day forwards, make careful enquiry amongst Dharma friends regarding their great Other Power faith, in order that you too may become completely assured of birth in the Land of Enjoyment.

All you need do to attain the 'peaceful awareness' of our tradition is entrust yourself deeply and singlemindedly to Amida Buddha without any contriving on your part.

So what sort of Buddha is this Amida Buddha and what sort of people does he save?

It is the Buddha who made the Great Vow whereby he alone would save us, wretched ignorant beings and women too, already abandoned by all the Buddhas of the three periods. Vowing to save all sentient beings, even those who committed wrongdoings such as the ten bad acts and the five grave offences, those who slandered the Dharma and those known as *icchantika*,[228] Amida Buddha first meditated for five kalpas and then underwent further discipline for countless more kalpas.

Surpassing all the compassionate vows of other Buddhas, he fulfilled this Vow and became Amida Tathāgata, whom we also call Amida Buddha.

How then should we entrust ourselves to this Buddha, and what should be our state of mind in order that we be saved?

Forget the depth of your bad karma and simply entrust yourselves to Amida Buddha, steadfastly and without doublemindedness, and when you thus become completely free of doubt, Amida will surely save you.

It is by means of these two principles, 'embracing' and 'light,' that Amida Tathāgata liberates all sentient beings. Firstly, as concerns 'light,' when those with good past karma are illumined by this 'light,' the bad karma that has accumulated as their karmic hindrances is completely extinguished. And what is meant by "embracing"? Simply that, since all the karmic hindrances of such people are extinguished when they encounter the condition of this light, they now find themselves immediately 'embraced within this light.' Thus it is said that these two principles, 'embracing' and 'light,' are both of them essential for Amida Buddha's work. Accordingly, when we say that faith is awakened with the one thought-moment of taking refuge in Amida Buddha, what we mean is that it is at the very moment we encounter Amida's all embracing light that faith is awakened within us. It should now be clear that the essence of *Namu Amida-butsu*, the working of Amida Buddha, lies in the expression through these six characters of precisely how it is that we are to be born in the Pure Land. Having become aware of this, we feel more and more grateful and reverential.

So, once faith has been decisively attained, what we should do, whether asleep or awake, is simply recite the *Nenbutsu* out of gratitude, joyfully remembering all we have received from Amida Buddha, as copious as rainfall, as massive as a mountain. That is indeed the way we should respond to the Buddha in gratitude for all he has done for us.

Most humbly and respectfully
Written on 14th July, Bunmei 6 [1474]

COMMENTS

What exactly is meant at the very beginning of the first paragraph is not entirely clear. There are several opinions as to the nature of the difference between "someone whose name has only just been added to our list of followers" and "a long time member of our tradition." Whilst some scholars say the difference referred to is that between lay people and priests, others say that it is the difference between old, traditional followers and new followers who have only recently shown interest in Shin Buddhism. Frankly speaking, it is almost impossible to determine what the difference was at that time because there exists no other example of the expression "someone whose name has only just been added to our list of followers." Nor does it really matter, for either way it is all his followers that Rennyo is encouraging here to attain 'peaceful awareness.' The original Japanese word which I have chosen to render here as 'peaceful awareness' is the term *anjin*.

In the first paragraph there is another word which I have likewise translated in my own way. That word is *hōdo* 報土 in Japanese. It is usually translated as "Reward Land," "Land of Recompense," "Land of Fulfilment," "Land of the Fulfilled Vow" or "Fulfilled Land." I previously used translations such as "Land of Recompense" or "Land of Fulfilment" but I am afraid none of these translations work very well. During his stay at Three Wheels in 2006 I discussed the problem with Professor Masahiro Shimoda, a renowned scholar in the study of early Mahāyāna Buddhism.

Towards the end of our discussion Professor Shimoda observed that, in accordance with the Mahayanist theory of the "Three Bodies (*tri-kāya*) of the Buddha,"[229] *saṃbhoga-kāya* or *hojin* in Japanese can be translated as the reward-body or Enjoyment Body. This is because the original Sanskrit for *hōjin* 報身, usually translated as the Body of Reward or Recompense, is the same as the word for *juyūshin* 受用身, or Enjoyment Body, meaning the Buddha enjoying himself tasting the fruit of Awakening (*jijuyū* 自受用) and at the same time enjoying others receiving the fruit of Awakening (*tajuyū* 他受用). When a Bodhisattva attains Buddhahood through long term effort and self-discipline, he not only enjoys savouring the experience of Awakening but at the same time enjoys others receiving the fruit of Awakening. Because his attainment of Buddhahood is a result of his long time discipline as a Bodhisattva, he is called the Buddha of Reward or Recompense Body. In the case of Amida Buddha his Pure Land, completed as a result of his long time Bodhisattvaship, is a place where everyone who is born there can enjoy the fruit of Awakening. Hence I translated *hōdo* 報土 not as the Land of Recompense or Reward but as the Land of Enjoyment as this more directly conveys the sense of enjoyment of the Pure Land, a land where Amida Buddha and all the visitors share and enjoy the fruit of Awakening or Enlightenment.

Thus the Pure Land is the Land of Enjoyment, where you can enjoy yourself receiving the fruit of Awakening and also enjoy others receiving the fruit of Awakening. Once you attain 'peaceful awareness,' it will surely lead you to the Land of Enjoyment, even though your life may be heavily burdened with karmic hindrances.

'Peaceful awareness'[230] means awareness of the sad reality of one's existence, filled with blind passions and karmic hindrances and at the same time
awareness of the Buddha's unconditional love that saves all beings just as they
are without any discrimination at all. Such peaceful awareness of salvation
through the Buddha is gained through the experience of having the pure faith
to entrust oneself absolutely to the Buddha just as one is.

After describing Amida Buddha as the Buddha who vows to save all
sentient beings, even those who commit evil karma such as the ten bad acts
and the five grave offences, those who slander the Dharma and those called
icchantika, Rennyo Shōnin goes on to tell us how we should entrust ourselves
to Amida Buddha, "Forget the depth of your bad karma and simply entrust
yourselves to Amida Buddha, steadfastly and without doublemindedness."
It is amazing to find such a statement within a tradition that appreciates
introspection as being of pivotal importance. What is most important of all,
however, is to entrust oneself to Amida Buddha going beyond any kind of
selfish attachment. If we take into consideration the fact that our consciousness of bad karma or wrongdoing often tends unknowingly to be a sort of
negative pride, or if you like, narcissism, we must say Rennyo's remarks are
extremely important in leading us to attain pure faith.

As the title "Embraced within the Light of Amida Buddha" shows, the
main subject of this letter is Amida Buddha's 'embracing and light.' In this
letter 'light' refers to the working of the light whereby Amida Buddha illumines
and helps all beings develop inwardly and eventually break through the darkness of their minds. At the very moment we attain faith, when the darkness
of our minds is breached, we find ourselves 'embraced within this light.'

Ever since his attainment of Buddhahood, Amida's light illumines all
sentient beings, establishing various connections with them, drawing their
interest towards the Buddha. What is called their 'good past karma' is actually
the relations established with them by Amida Buddha through the working
of his light. At the moment of attaining faith sentient beings become aware
of being embraced within the light of Amida Buddha.

There is another important point in this letter. This is related to
Rennyo's words, "when those with good past karma are illumined by this
'light,' the bad karma that has accumulated as their karmic hindrances is
completely extinguished."

If it is true that we are filled with blind passions and are burdened with
karmic hindrances for as long as we live in this world, what does Rennyo mean
by this? Does he mean that after the attainment of faith we have no blind
passions or karmic hindrances? Concerning this problem, *The Goichidai ki
kikigaki* states,

Article 34. Junsei[231] asked Rennyo Shōnin: "In one of *The Letters* you taught that as soon as the one moment's thought of faith is awakened in an individual, all his bad karma is extinguished and that person joins the stage of nonretrogression of those rightly assured of birth in the Pure Land. On the other hand you have also stated that our bad karma exists as long as we live, which seems to contradict your statement in *The Letters*." Rennyo Shōnin replied: "The extinction of all bad karma at the one thought-moment of attaining faith means that all past bad karma no longer becomes a hindrance, when our birth into the Pure Land becomes assured with the power of the instantaneous awakening of faith. Therefore, bad karma is as if it were extinguished. However, as long as we dwell in this world, we commit wrongdoings. Have you, Junsei, by any chance attained Enlightenment and become free from all bad karma already? The Sacred Scriptures state that all bad karma is extinguished as soon as the one moment's thought of faith is awakened. Rather than debating the existence or nonexistence of our bad karma, it is better for us to repeatedly consider whether we have truly attained faith or not. It is completely within Amida's discretion to save us with or without our bad karma. We should not discriminate. Simply faith is all important," so Rennyo Shōnin reiterated thoughtfully.[232]

Viewed from our standpoint, our bad karma still exists but from the standpoint of the Buddha-Dharma it is as if it no longer does, because it is entirely embraced in the light of the Buddha. As the attainment of faith takes place through the power of the Buddha-Dharma, bad karma cannot be any hindrance to it. Although the heavy weight of our bad karma remains the same even after the attainment of faith, it is carried to the Pure Land by the power of Amida's Original Vow. As described in an earlier chapter, it is as if a weighty stone were being born away easily to the other shore through the buoyancy of a boat.

CHAPTER THIRTY-TWO

Living in
This Last
Dharma Age

ON PRACTISING EXACTLY AS TAUGHT

FASCICLE III, LETTER TWO

Although schools differ in their teachings, they were all given by Śākyamuni Buddha during his lifetime, and, consequently, any one of them is actually the superlative Dharma. It can rightly be said there is not a grain of doubt but that those who practise his teaching, just as he taught it, will definitely attain Enlightenment and themselves become Buddhas. All beings of this present time, known as 'the Last Age,' are of the lowest capacity to practise, however. Ours is an age where those who practise the teaching just as it was taught are very rare indeed.

This being so, it was precisely to save all sentient beings in times like this present age that Amida Tathāgata's Original Vow of Other Power was especially composed. With this purpose in mind, Amida meditated for five kalpas and practised self-discipline for measureless kalpas more, vowing he would not attain Perfect Enlightenment unless he could enable sentient beings, who had not been good but had committed wrongdoings, to attain

Buddhahood also. Having fulfilled that Vow, he became the Buddha known as Amida. Sentient beings of 'the Last Dharma Age' will never be able to become Buddhas unless they hold steadfastly on to Amida's Original Vow and deeply entrust themselves to this Buddha.

How, then, can we entrust ourselves to Other Power, the power of Amida Tathāgata's Original Vow, and what sort of self-awareness should we have in order to be saved?

As to how to entrust ourselves to Amida, there is no difficulty at all. Quite simply those who truly understand the nature of Other Power will all of them, ten out of every ten, be born in the Land of Utmost Bliss.

So what exactly is this Other Power faith? It is simply *Namu Amida-butsu* 南无阿彌陀佛. If you fully understand those six characters (*na-mu-a-mi-da-butsu* 南无阿彌陀佛), this is the reality of Other Power faith. You should thoroughly realise, therefore, the essence of those six characters.

To begin with, what do the two characters *Namu* mean?

Namu means simply to entrust ourselves singleheartedly and steadfastly to Amida, without any double-mindedness, but through pure faith alone, entreating him to save us in the matter of attaining Rebirth.

The four characters *A-mi-da-butsu* (阿彌陀佛) signify the Buddha whose light, emanating continuously from his body, illumines all sentient beings who, as described above, entrust themselves to him singleheartedly and without harbouring the slightest doubt, the Buddha who holds all those beings within the embrace of that light and, when their lifespan is at an end, leads them assuredly to the Pure Land of Utmost Bliss. That is the meaning of *Amida-butsu*.

According to what is taught in this world about the *Nenbutsu*, people think they will be saved merely by repeating *Namu Amida-butsu* with their lips. That is too uncertain to rely upon. There are nevertheless those within the Pure Land tradition who do teach exactly that. It is not for me to argue whether such a view is right or wrong. I simply seek to explain our tradition's peaceful awareness, as taught by the founder of our school. If those endowed with good karmic conditions hear this, they will swiftly be born in the Land of Utmost Bliss at the end of their lives in this world. Those who understand this recite the Name of the Buddha. Given all Amida Tathāgata has done for us so that we might be saved without difficulty, his benevolence being as abundant as rainfall and as weighty as a mountain, we should repeat in gratitude the *Nenbutsu* of pronouncing the Name.

Most humbly and respectfully
On 5th August, Bunmei 6 [1474]

COMMENTS

Rennyo makes two points in the first paragraph by way of introduction to the letter as a whole. The first point he raises is that, because the different Buddhist teachings are all based on the Buddha-dharma taught by Śākyamuni Buddha during his lifetime, those who practise the teaching just as they have been instructed will without doubt attain Perfect Enlightenment. Buddhism speaks about "84,000 paths" to Perfect Enlightenment. Śākyamuni Buddha is said to have guided people in accordance with their individual capabilities. There are in fact countless different kinds of people in this world, all with infinitely varying capacities and all karmically conditioned by feelings and thoughts they have formed self-centredly based on past experiences. In short, people have their own, very different, illusions. The phrase "84,000 paths" symbolises the innumerable ways that can lead sentient beings through their illusions to peaceful awareness, ultimately to the spiritual world of Perfect Enlightenment. According to Rennyo Shōnin, there is no doubt that, if people practise any of these teachings properly, they will be able to become Buddhas.

Sadly, however, we live in a world where it is extremely difficult to practise the teachings in the way the Buddha intended. Thus Rennyo goes on to lament, "All beings of this present time, known as 'the Last Age,' are of the lowest capacity to practise, however. Ours is an age where those who practise the teaching just as it was taught are very rare indeed." This is the second point he makes in the first paragraph. Although Pure Land Buddhism is one of 84,000 paths, it is a teaching revealed especially to help those of the present age. The notion of "the Last Age," is a sort of eschatological or end of the world view that evolved in the course of Buddhist history.

There is a Buddhist doctrine that talks about the three periods of the Dharma following the death of Śākyamuni Buddha. The three periods described are the age of 'the right Dharma,' the age of 'the Semblance Dharma' and the age of 'the Last Dharma.' As to how long these periods were thought to last, there are a number of different opinions. According to one view, popular at the time of Shinran Shōnin, the first period was believed to have lasted for 1,000 years following the death of the Buddha. It is called the time of 'the Right Dharma,' when Buddhist teaching, practice and realisation or Enlightenment all co-existed. The second period, again of 1,000 years, was a time of 'the Semblance Dharma,' in which teaching and practice both existed but without realisation. This means that, although there were both those who taught and those who practised, there was no one who had attained true realisation or was really enlightened. The third period, this time lasting 10,000 years, is the age of 'the Last Dharma', in which only teaching remains. This means that in this period of 'the Last Dharma' there exist neither those who practise properly nor those who are really enlightened or awakened.

In his main writing, *The Kyōgyōshinshō*, however, Shinran Shōnin states that, according to sūtras such as *The Gengō kyō, The Ninnō kyō and The Nehan gyō* (*Nirvāṇa Sūtra*),[233] the first year of Gennin (1224) in the Kamakura Period was already 673 years into the period of 'the Last Dharma'. This would indicate that Shinran Shōnin had adopted a different view and thought of the period of the right Dharma as having lasted for 500, rather than the conventional 1,000 years.

According to the doctrine of the three periods of the Dharma, Buddhism itself is destined to disappear after the age of 'the Last Dharma.' This means that the doctrine itself is firmly rooted in the Buddhist philosophy of impermanence. Faced with the serious problem of the eventual demise of Buddhist teaching, Hōnen Shōnin, Shinran Shōnin and other Buddhist leaders of the time were deeply concerned with the urgent question of how to attain Awakening or Enlightenment in the age of 'the Last Dharma.' Pure Land leaders such as Shinran Shōnin and Hōnen Shōnin taught that people in the period of 'the Last Dharma' are unable to attain Enlightenment through their own efforts and that their only hope of doing so lies in entrusting themselves unreservedly to the unconditional love of Amida Buddha, for the Buddha, they explained, had vowed to save all sentient beings without any discrimination whatsoever and would welcome everyone into his Pure Land to enjoy with him the fruit of Perfect Enlightenment.

This relationship between people of the period of 'the Last Dharma' and Amida Buddha's Original Vow is beautifully portrayed by Rennyo in the second paragraph of this letter. "Sentient beings of 'this Last Dharma Age'," he declares, "will never be able to become Buddhas unless they hold steadfastly on to Amida's Original Vow and deeply entrust themselves to this Buddha."

To quote some verses in Japanese composed by Shinran Shōnin from *The Shōzōmatsu wasan*,

Concerning the age of the Last Dharma he laments,

> Since Śākyamuni Tathāgata passed away,
> Some two thousand years have elapsed.
> Now that the Right and Semblance Dharma ages have ended,
> Weep bitterly, Disciples of the Tathāgata![234]

> Sentient beings in the world of the five defilements of the Last Dharma age
> Are incapable of meeting the demands of practice and realisation.
> The teachings that Śākyamuni left to posterity
> Have all been hidden away in the Nāga Palace.[235]

Talking about people of the lowest capabilities who live in the Last Dharma age, he says,

> As ignorance and blind passions increase,
> They pervade everywhere like innumerable particles of dust.
> The way love and hatred repeat assent and objection is
> Like high peaks and mountain ridges competing against one another.[236]

> As the wrong views of sentient beings grows up furiously
> They are like a thick forest filled with thorns and brambles.
> Heaping suspicion and slander on the *Nenbutsu* believers
> The destructive poison of their anger spreads out wildly.[237]

Regarding sentient beings entrusting themselves to the unconditional love of Amida Tathāgata, he has this to say,

> In the fifth five hundred year period[238] in the Last Dharma age
> There will not be a single sentient being left in the entire world
> Who will ever have a chance of gaining liberation
> Unless they entrust themselves to the Tathāgata's Compassionate Vow.[239]

> Those who have truly received the joyous faith
> Transferred to them through Amida's Vow of Wisdom,
> Out of the benefit of being embraced and never abandoned,
> Arrive at the stage proximate to Supreme Enlightenment.[240]

> Those who have entered the stage of the definitely assured
> At the very moment of receiving true faith,
> Being equal to Maitreya, the Bodhisattva ready to be the next Buddha,
> Will awaken Perfect Enlightenment.[241]

After the first two paragraphs, the rest of the letter is mainly concerned with the meaning of *Namu Amida-butsu*. Rennyo declares that the essence of *Namu* lies in taking refuge absolutely in Amida Buddha, by entrusting oneself to Amida Buddha with single-heartedness, without any double-mindedness. In other words, it is an expression of pure faith. As you know, in the Shin Buddhist tradition faith is seen as being quite simply a gift from Amida Buddha. It does not involve any sort of request or demand on our part but is entirely the virtue-transference coming to us directly from Amida. In that case, though, how are we to interpret Rennyo's use of the word "entreating"? Does it not imply the addition of self power to Other Power? Certainly the word "entreating" signifies a desperate call to Amida Buddha from the core of our existence. Prior to this use of the word "entreating," *Namu* is said to be the absolute command of Amida Buddha which says, "come to me immediately just as you are." "Entreating," that desperate call of ours to Amida, is actually our response to this absolute command, a command that comes to us from Amida far beyond the confines of our existence. It is one that is always bidding us to come to Amida Buddha prior to our own "entreating" of him. When we are awakened to Amida's absolute command as an expression of his unconditional love, then our "entreating" arises spontaneously, breaking through our whole existence. Our "entreating" can be seen as a manifestation of Amida's great compassion.

Concerning Amida-butsu, Rennyo explains, "The four characters *A-mi-da-butsu* (阿彌陀佛) signify the Buddha whose light, emanating continuously from his body, illumines all sentient beings who, as described above, entrust themselves to him singleheartedly and without harbouring the slightest doubt, the Buddha who holds all those beings within the embrace of that light, and who, when their lifespan is at an end, leads them assuredly to the Pure Land of Utmost Bliss. That is the meaning of *Amida-butsu*."

Towards the end of this letter, there is an interesting observation made about the *Nenbutsu*. Rennyo points out the difference between the *Nenbutsu* in Shin Buddhism and the *Nenbutsu* found in many other Pure Land schools. "According to what is taught in this world about the *Nenbutsu*," he writes, "people think they will be saved merely by repeating *Namu Amida-butsu* with their lips. That is too uncertain to rely upon." Those who think they can attain birth in the Pure Land merely by repeating the *Nenbutsu* tend to be proud of the act of reciting the *Nenbutsu*, considering it to be somehow meritorious in itself. This is far removed from pure faith, and is suggestive of the conceit of self power.

What is most important in Shin Buddhism is the attainment of true faith that brings about peaceful awareness in our daily life. If you attain true faith, the *Nenbutsu* will arise spontaneously from within you. The *Nenbutsu* is a natural expression of gratitude that wells up from the experience of *shinjin* or *anjin*.

CHAPTER THIRTY-THREE

Diversion from the *Nenbutsu* of Other Power Faith

FOLLOWERS OF SHŌKŌ AT KAWAJIRI

FASCICLE III, LETTER THREE

When I ask myself how each of you in this area, followers of Shōkō at Kawajiri, understand faith in the Buddha-dharma, I feel very unsure of your views. However, I would like to discuss in detail for you now what the essential teaching of our tradition really is. You should each of you listen to this attentively, take it as being very important, and become assured of your birth to come in the Land of Utmost Bliss.

If you ask what is meant by Amida Tathāgata's Original Vow of Birth through the *Nenbutsu*, the answer is that, if they decisively attain Other Power faith alone, lay people lacking wisdom and even those who have committed the ten bad acts and the five grave offences will all be born in the Land of Utmost Bliss.

How difficult is it then to attain faith? Not difficult at all if you simply entrust yourselves steadfastly to Amida Tathāgata, without hint of double-mindedness, and if you refrain from allowing your thoughts to err in other directions. Ten out of ten of you will then all become Buddhas. It is easy to maintain this simple awareness of faith. Followers who merely try to recite the *Nenbutsu* out loud have but a superficial understanding of the teaching. They will not be born in the Land of Utmost Bliss. It is only those who fully understand the meaning of the *Nenbutsu* who will become Buddhas. If you can just establish and maintain a singlemindedness that allows you to entrust yourselves fully to Amida, then you will proceed easily to the Pure Land.

In addition you should be aware that those who subscribe to complicated secret teachings and fail to revere the Buddha are nothing but troublemakers.

Accordingly, as Amida Tathāgata's Original Vow of Other Power is especially meant to save people now at this Last Age who find themselves heavily burdened with bad karma, it is this same Original Vow of Other Power that is suitable for lay people like ourselves. How grateful I am for Amida Tathāgata's Vow! And how grateful I am for Śākyamuni Tathāgata's golden words! Venerate them! Entrust yourselves to them! Thus it is those whose understanding is as I have set out above who truly exemplify the *Nenbutsu* follower who has decisively attained the faith of our tradition.

Over and above all this you should also remember that the *Nenbutsu* we recite throughout our lives expresses our gratitude to Amida Tathāgata for all he has done so readily to save us, his benevolence being as copious as rainfall and as mighty as a mountain.

Most humbly and respectfully
Written on 6th August, Bunmei 6 [1474].

COMMENTS

Shōkō was one of Rennyo Shōnin's disciples, said to have originally been a Zen monk who converted to Shin Buddhism. Kawajiri is the name of a place not far from Yoshizaki, where Rennyo Shōnin himself lived. It seems that Shōkō invited Rennyo Shōnin to deliver Dharma talks at his *dōjō* at Kawajiri. According to a commentary on The Letters, known as *Ofumi Ryakuge*,[242] Rennyo Shōnin stayed at the *dōjō* for three days in 1474 from 4th to 6th of August, this letter having been written on the 6th, as stated in the last line. I rather suspect that the true purpose of Shōkō's invitation of his master, Rennyo, must have been to enlist his aid in resolving certain problems regarding 'secret teachings' (*hijibōmon* 秘事法門) prevalent amongst Shōkō's followers at that time. Maybe Rennyo left a summary of his teachings given at Shōkō's *dōjō* in the form of a letter to Dharma friends.

These brief background facts should make the meaning of the first paragraph of the letter much clearer. What Rennyo wanted to see was simply that all the followers should become assured of their birth in the Pure Land by attaining true faith themselves. So, towards the end of the opening paragraph, Rennyo Shōnin says, "You should each of you listen to this attentively, take it as being very important, and become assured of your birth to come in the Land of Utmost Bliss."

Because the essence of Shin Buddhist faith lies in entrusting oneself absolutely to "the Original Vow of Birth through the *Nenbutsu*," Rennyo refers to this crucial point straightaway in the second paragraph. The title "the Original Vow of Birth through the *Nenbutsu*" is a name for the Eighteenth Original Vow of Amida Buddha. This name is popular and used in all the Pure Land schools. What is meant by it, however, varies according to their interpretations of the word "*Nenbutsu*." In the Shin Buddhist tradition the act of *Nenbutsu* is understood as a manifestation of the great working of the Buddha through the individual. When you pronounce the *Nenbutsu* it is simply the working of the Buddha manifesting itself through your individual existence. The *Nenbutsu* is the pronouncing of the Buddha Name of the Eighteenth Original Vow in which Amida Buddha vowed to welcome into his Pure Land without discrimination all sentient beings who pronounce his Name. When you attain pure faith by entrusting yourself simply to "the Original Vow of Birth through the *Nenbutsu*," all of you, ten out of ten, even those most heavily burdened with bad karma, will absolutely become assured of birth in the Pure Land.

Thus it is said in the Shin Buddhist tradition that there is no virtue-transference from our side, from the side of those who practise the *Nenbutsu*. Virtue-transference occurs only from the side of Amida Buddha. When I returned to Shōgyōji Temple in Japan recently, I was both surprised and delighted to hear my master declare in a talk he was giving that the teaching of "no virtue-transference," originated by Hōnen Shōnin and confirmed by Shinran Shōnin, is something that reveals the wonderful working of the Buddha which is beyond words. The *Nenbutsu* comes to us as the great virtue of Amida Buddha. When we attain pure faith, the *Nenbutsu* that wells up from within us is entirely the working of the Buddha. Shin Buddhists should not expect that the *Nenbutsu*, or pronouncing the Name, will become their virtue or merit. Therefore, it is not their intention to accumulate merits to ensure their own birth in the Pure Land or for the birth of others. They simply do not believe in such a practice. Nor should they set any store by so-called self power achievements. They are aware that all virtues belong to the Buddha.

Accordingly, what is important is for us to attain pure faith by entrusting ourselves absolutely to Amida Buddha. The attainment of true faith is naturally followed by the *Nenbutsu*. If, on the other hand, without actually attaining true faith we merely endeavour to pronounce the *Nenbutsu* as a way of gaining birth in the Pure Land, then that is called "*Nenbutsu* by self power." A popular teaching within Pure Land Buddhism, that we should try to say the *Nenbutsu* aloud as many times as possible, is quite misleading and wrong. Attaining pure faith is of vital importance and is really not that difficult, as Rennyo Shōnin makes clear in the third paragraph. He then goes on, however, to utter a note of caution regarding the erroneous belief discussed above, saying, "Followers who merely try to recite the *Nenbutsu* out loud have but a superficial understanding of the teaching. They will not be born in the Land of Utmost Bliss." This last quotation concerns the first of the two wrong teachings Rennyo criticises in his letter which was written for the express purpose of guiding Shōkō's followers to move forward to the Pure Land. Shōkō-bo must have been highly annoyed that such an erroneous view should have been so widespread amongst his followers at that time. It is said in our Shin Buddhist tradition, however, that the meaning of the *Nenbutsu* can be summarised in a short phrase "Entrust yourself and it will save you."

The other wrong view Rennyo criticised in this letter is widely known as one of 'the secret teachings' (*hijibōmon*). His criticism is contained in two lines found in the fourth paragraph: "In addition you should be aware that those who subscribe to complicated secret teachings and fail to revere the Buddha are nothing but troublemakers." This distorted belief is known as the secret teaching of "non-worship."

The two distorted beliefs, "pronouncing [the Name] without faith" and "non-worship," may well be interconnected but it is very difficult to discuss any putative relationship between the two because of the lack of any detailed description. Out of the secret teachings Senkei talked about in *The Account of Rennyo Shōnin*,[243] the two beliefs that he criticised in this letter, must have been the two most prevalent amongst Shōkō-bo's followers.

Concerning the secret teaching of "pronouncing the Name without faith," *The Account of Rennyo Shōnin* explains "they teach that, unless you recite the *Nenbutsu* very loudly, it is useless and that it is only by reciting the *Nenbutsu* at full volume that you can destroy all your illusions and attain birth in the Pure Land."[244] Can you imagine how people try to recite the *Nenbutsu* out loud, without having attained faith, in order to eliminate their blind passions and bad karma? Without the attainment of true faith, the essence of which, in the context of Buddhism, lies in becoming awakened, people can easily be drawn to extremes and become mentally unbalanced, sometimes fanatical even. In Shin Buddhism the attainment of faith means instantaneously entrusting oneself to Amida Buddha at the one thought-moment one is awakened to both the reality of one's existence and to the unconditional love of the Buddha. Because faith is simultaneously an awakening, it causes gratitude to arise, as Rennyo is careful enough to point out in every letter he writes including this one.

The unbalanced extremities of blind faith are serious symptoms of the sickness of religions. To follow the Middle Way is one of the most important teachings of Buddhism. According to my understanding it does not mean walking along the middle line of the path. Indeed, if you become attached to the idea of a middle line which is simply an intellectual compromise between opposing dualities, you will be far from what is meant by the Middle Way. The Middle Way is rather a well-balanced way of living that is completely free from any attachment, and fully aware of the dangers of extremism, in whatever circumstances you find yourself. Where this Middle Way is lost, as the sickness of our mind becomes deeper and deeper, various kinds of mental extremes gather together in its darkness and become ever more closely interwoven to one another. A number of distorted views, which had to be kept as "secret teachings," must have been combined together in inexplicable ways. The secret teaching of "non-worship" is one of the worst examples. The author of *The Account of Rennyo Shōnin* declares, "There was a group in Echizen, for instance, known as the school of 'non-worship', which taught that Amida was merely a piece of wood or paper and that your own mind was the Buddha. Even if you happened to put your palms together, those people would have you direct your hands to yourself and worship your own mind."[245] Lack of humility and respect is another serious aspect of the sickness of religions. Followers are proud of their extreme views and ways of living. They fail to see the reality of others. They are not humble but arrogant. Because they insist on their own extreme ways of living, there is no end to the conflicts or quarrels they engender. "Do not worship the Buddha but only your own mind" is one of the worst instances of extremism to be found amongst the secret teachings.

My Master in Japan, Venerable Chimyo Takehara, has been teaching over and over again how important it is to respect others just as they are. When we lose respect for others, it immediately signifies our own lack of humility. Lack of humility towards others eventually causes us to be arrogant towards the triple treasure – Buddha, Dharma and Sangha. I think an awareness of this problem is of vital importance, for it is not only other people but ourselves also who have to face the threat of "secret teachings." If we live our lives carelessly, without humility and respect, the problems of "secret teachings" sneak up on us. Because the structure of our consciousness is self-centred, we are always faced with the danger of becoming selfish and arrogant and going to extremes. It is our karma.

With all of this in his mind, Rennyo gives us his kind instruction:

"Over and above all this you should also remember that the *Nenbutsu* we recite throughout our lives expresses our gratitude to Amida Tathāgata for all he has done so readily to save us, his benevolence being as copious as rainfall and as mighty as a mountain."

A sense of gratitude is, indeed, here as so often, a prime indicator of a healthy mind.

CHAPTER THIRTY-FOUR

Impermanence and Other Power Faith

ON THE GREAT SAGE,

THE WORLD HONOURED ONE

FASCICLE III, LETTER FOUR

When we reflect deeply on the transient nature of human life, we see that all who live are born to die and all who prosper are destined to decline. Consequently all we are really doing is just living out our days and nights, our months and years, to no purpose. This is indeed unutterably sad. So then, what is impossible to escape is impermanence – impossible for every being from the Great Sage, the World Honoured One, right down to Devadatta,[246] that perpetrator of bad acts and grave offences.

Taking all this into consideration, what is rare and difficult for us to receive is human life and what is difficult to meet is the Buddha-dharma. Even though we may happen on the Buddha-dharma, the path of self power practice is so difficult for us to achieve in this Last Age that it is almost impossible at the present time for us to free ourselves from birth-and-death. This means that, unless we encounter the Original Vow of Amida Tathāgata, our lives will pass by in vain.

But indeed we have now encountered the one-dharma of the Original Vow. Thus the only place we can desire to go to is the Pure Land of Utmost Bliss, and the only one we can entrust ourselves to is Amida Tathāgata. We should pronounce the *Nenbutsu* therefore, with faith decisively attained.

What is generally understood in the world, however, is that, only if we recite '*Namu Amida-butsu*' loudly, will we be able to be born in the Land of Utmost Bliss. That is not at all to be relied upon.

What we should realise when we ask the real meaning of the six characters *Namu Amida-butsu* 南无阿彌陀佛 is that, when we entrust ourselves steadfastly to Amida Tathāgata, the Buddha saves all of us sentient beings, fully knowing us for what we are. This is what is expressed by the six characters *Namu Amida-butsu*.

How, then, should we entrust ourselves to Amida Tathāgata in order to be saved in the One Great Matter of Rebirth?

When we entrust ourselves to Amida Tathāgata without any misgivings or doublemindedness, forsaking all miscellaneous practices and miscellaneous good acts[247] and placing our full confidence in the Tathāgata singleheartedly and steadfastly, the Tathāgata beams forth his light, embracing within it all those sentient beings that entrust themselves to him. This is called "receiving the benefit of Amida Tathāgata's all embracing light." It is also called "receiving the benefit of his promise that never abandons us." Once we have been embraced within Amida Tathāgata's light like this, we will be born into the true Land of Enjoyment as soon as our own lives are exhausted. Let there be no doubt about this.

In as much as this is so, there is really no point in relying on other Buddhas or performing other virtues or roots of good. How sublime and how kind is Amida Tathāgata! How can we express our gratitude for what he has done for us, for his benevolence as copious as rainfall and as mighty as a mountain?

You should understand that it is simply by reciting out loud '*Namu Amida-butsu, Namu Amida-butsu*' that we are responding to the Buddha in deepest gratitude for all he has done for us.

Most humbly and respectfully
On 18th August, Bunmei 6 [1474].

COMMENTS

In this letter Rennyo firstly talks about the impermanence of life. As you know, impermanence, or the transience of things, is one of the three laws that traditionally distinguish Buddhism from other teachings. They are called the "three Dharma seals": impermanence, selflessness and Nirvāṇa. Everything, whether on a mental or physical plane, is subject to the flux of change. Things in this world arise, mutate and perish. Nothing remains constant, not even for a moment. There is nothing that escapes the truth of transience and our lives are no exception. Rennyo begins his letter concentrating on the impermanency of human life. The original Japanese text of the first passage is one of the most famous in all Shin Buddhist literature as it describes so beautifully the transient nature of our lives. The epithet "the Great Sage" refers to Śākyamuni Buddha, the founder of Buddhism and one of the greatest spiritual leaders mankind has ever known. Even the Buddha could not escape impermanence, the impermanence of his physical body or *rūpa-kāya*. Devadatta was a cousin of the Buddha and the elder brother of Ānanda, who in turn was the Buddha's closest attendant throughout the Great Sage's life. To begin with Devadatta was himself a follower of the Buddha, but at a later stage set out to oppose him and eventually even tried to kill him. During his life he committed all kinds of wrongdoings, persecuting the Buddha, slandering the Dharma and attempting to destroy the Sangha. His incorrigible behaviour was considered to have deprived him of the possibility of salvation. He is generally considered as being an *icchantika*, one who is utterly devoid of any vestige of virtue. Nevertheless, in some of the Pure Land traditions it is also said that, just as he was falling into the lowest depths of Buddhist hell, his thoughts turned to the Buddha and with his last breath he cried out "*Namu-butsu!*" whereupon he immediately found himself caught up in the Buddha's all-embracing compassion.

In the second paragraph Rennyo talks to his followers in his usual way about the importance of their encounter with the Original Vow of Amida Tathāgata. Because self power practice is utterly ineffectual now that we are in the period of Last Dharma, he stresses how vitally important it is for us to encounter Amida's Original Vow, or Other Power.

Once we encounter the Original Vow it is of supreme urgency for us to take refuge in it. Thus, in the third paragraph, Rennyo Shōnin encourages us to entrust ourselves to Amida Tathāgata. How to understand the notion of *Nenbutsu*, which Rennyo refers to towards the end of this paragraph, is the main subject of the latter part of this letter.

Roughly speaking in the Pure Land tradition the term *Nenbutsu* has two meanings: firstly contemplating on Amida Buddha and his Pure Land and, secondly, pronouncing the Name of the Buddha. In mainstream Pure Land Buddhism, ever since the time of Tánluán (476–542), the concept of *Nenbutsu* has been understood to mean pronouncing the Buddha Name. It is well known that Shàndǎo (613–681) laid particular emphasis on this aspect of the *Nenbutsu*. Indeed, according to Shàndǎo, the real purpose of

The Meditation Sūtra lies in teaching about pronouncing the Name to those too heavily burdened with karmic transgressions to be in any sort of position to contemplate Amida Buddha and his Pure Land. The only alternative they have is to invoke his Name. After the transmission of Pure Land Buddhism to Japan, Hōnen Shōnin and his disciples, including Shinran Shōnin, continued along this course. Thus, when Rennyo Shōnin talks about the *Nenbutsu* within the Shin Buddhist tradition, what he refers to is not contemplating Amida and his Pure Land but pronouncing his Name or, more precisely, pronouncing the Name after the attainment of pure faith.

As you may have already noticed, within the confines of this short letter, the act of pronouncing the Name is in fact mentioned in two different lights, first negative and then positive.

Negatively speaking, "What is generally understood in the world, however, is that, only if we recite '*Namu Amida-butsu*' loudly, will we be able to be born in the Land of Utmost Bliss. That is not at all to be relied upon."

Positively speaking, "You should understand that it is simply by reciting out loud '*Namu Amida-butsu*' that we are responding to the Buddha in deepest gratitude for all he has done for us."

In the first case '*Namu Amida-butsu*' is recited loudly in order for the person invoking the Name to be born in the Pure Land. It is still part of self power practice and not yet freed from selfish attachment to good acts or their attendant virtue or merit. It is in short the *Nenbutsu* of self power practice.

The second quotation, by contrast, refers to that other *Nenbutsu*, uttered not to attain some special goal, but as an expression of gratitude to the Buddha for all he has done for us. It is a spontaneous outflow of our gratitude towards the Buddha. It wells up spontaneously from within our being. The *Nenbutsu* is a manifestation of the working of Other Power. The *Nenbutsu* in this sense is really spiritual. This expression of gratitude is an invocation of the Name, *Namu Amida-butsu*.

These two kinds of *Nenbutsu* – the *Nenbutsu* of self power and the *Nenbutsu* of Other Power – are identical in form but different in quality. In the case of the *Nenbutsu* of Other Power, there is no virtue-transference on our part. The reason for this is that all virtue-transference stems solely from Amida.

Article 1 of *The Goichidai ki kikigaki* says:

"What is meant by the '*Nenbutsu* of self power (*jiriki*)' is reciting the *Nenbutsu* in the belief that one will be saved by the Buddha through the virtuous act of reciting the *Nenbutsu* many times over, offering to him the virtue acquired through such recitation. That which is called Other Power, on the other hand, saves us immediately with the awakening of the one thought-moment when we utterly entrust ourselves to Amida.

To recite the *Nenbutsu* after that is to repeat *Namu Amida-butsu* with great rejoicing, feeling how grateful we are at having been saved."[248]

The difference between the *Nenbutsu* of self power and the *Nenbutsu* of Other Power is clearly expressed in this quotation. Both at and after that special moment of entrusting ourselves to Amida Buddha the *Nenbutsu* of Other Power streams out of the ocean of faith as an expression of gratitude to the Buddha for his unconditional, all-embracing love. If we focus our attention at the moment of attaining faith, the *Nenbutsu* – forsaking all self power practice and pronouncing *Namu Amida-butsu* – is one with the faith of entrusting ourselves to Amida Tathāgata. In this respect the *Nenbutsu* is faith and faith is the *Nenbutsu*.

In Shin Buddhism, faith (信心 *shinjin*) is said to be synonymous with *anjin* 'peaceful awareness.' This is closely related to the notion of the *Nenbutsu* of Other Power as a natural expression of our gratitude. There is no need for us to exert ourselves in devotional practices, but still we practice devotion because our joy and gratitude wishes to express itself in form. It is said in Shin Buddhism that there is no virtue-transference through self power. Extreme dogmatism or fanaticism is incompatible with the notion of *anjin* or 'peaceful awareness.' Everything is effortless and a simple letting go. The *Nenbutsu* of Other Power is absolutely free and a natural outflow from the ocean of faith in great 'peaceful awareness.'

CHAPTER THIRTY-FIVE

The Relationship between Amida and All Other Buddhas

ON THE COMPASSIONATE VOWS

OF ALL OTHER BUDDHAS

FASCICLE III, LETTER FIVE

If you are moved to ask in detail why it should be that the Original Vow of Amida surpasses the compassionate vows of all other Buddhas, the answer must be that it does not lie within the power of those other Buddhas of the ten directions to save sentient beings heavily weighed down by the worst karma, or indeed women burdened with the five obstacles and three submissions. Thus it is said that Amida Buddha's Original Vow is superior to the vows of other Buddhas.

This Great Vow of Amida Tathāgata, which comes to us from far beyond this world of ours, what type of sentient beings does it save? Well without exception it is all wrongdoers who have committed the ten bad acts and the five grave offenses, and women, too, burdened with the five obstacles and the three submissions. Thus it is through the power of Amida's Great Vow, known as Other Power, that Amida promises to lead without fail to the Land of

Utmost Bliss all sentient beings, ten out of every ten, who entrust themselves to him singleheartedly and steadfastly.

How then should I, wretched ignorant person that I am, entrust myself to the Original Vow of Amida Buddha, and with what kind of self-awareness should I do so? Please inform me in detail. I would like to attain faith according to your instructions, entrusting myself to Amida, aspiring to birth in the Land of Utmost Bliss and pronouncing the *Nenbutsu*.

To answer: First of all, the *Nenbutsu* teaching so prevalent in the world today advises people that they will all be saved merely by repeating *Namu Amida-butsu*, no matter whether or not they understand the meaning behind the words. That, however, is in no way to be relied upon. Not only in the capital but in the provinces as well the traditions of Pure Land Buddhism have splintered into any number of different schools. It is not that I wish to discuss which are right or wrong, however. Simply I would like to explain our founder's teaching as transmitted within our own tradition.

Now, listen carefully to this teaching, straining your ears to achieve emancipation and lowering your heads in reverence, and you will be able to rejoice in the awakening of faith. Those of you who have remained lay followers and even those who have committed wrongdoings throughout your lives, you should simply pay no heed to the depth of your bad karma but entrust yourselves sincerely to Amida Tathāgata's Original Vow, seeing it as the inconceivable Vow-power, the quintessence of which lies in saving such wretched beings as yourselves. By entrusting yourselves singleheartedly and steadfastly to Amida, try to understand just one thing: Other Power faith.

What, then, is Other Power faith? The essence of the six-character Name *Namu Amida-butsu* 南无阿彌陀佛 is the expression of the way Amida Buddha saves us. A person who has understood this in detail is called one who has attained Other Power faith. The two characters *Namu* 南无 signify sentient beings entrusting themselves to Amida Buddha singleheartedly and steadfastly, with no other thought but that of asking him to save them; this is called 'taking refuge.' The next four characters *Amida-butsu* 阿彌陀佛 signify that Amida Buddha saves, without exception, all those who entrust themselves to him by saying 'Namu.' This means, in other words, that he 'embraces and never abandons us.' 'Embracing all abandoning none' means that Amida Tathāgata receives all those who practise the *Nenbutsu* within his light and will never abandon those that practise the *Nenbutsu*. Accordingly in essence *Namu Amida-butsu* can be understood as a six-character Name chosen by Amida Buddha to be an expression of himself as evidence of his vow to save us. Once we are able to grasp this we are assured of birth in the Land of Utmost Bliss. Overflowing with gratitude and respect towards Amida for having saved us once and for all, we recite the *Nenbutsu* as an expression of our joy at having been saved. Hence we describe the *Nenbutsu* as "pronouncing the

Name with gratitude to the Buddha for what he has done for us" and also as "pronouncing the Name after the attainment of faith."

Most humbly and respectfully
Written on 6th September, Bunmei 6 [1474].

COMMENTS

This letter speaks principally of the special vow made by Amida Buddha that surpasses all those of other Buddhas. In previous letters such as the third, eighth, and ninth letters of Fascicle Two and the first letter of Fascicle Three we have already listened to his observations on the relationship between Amida Buddha and all the other Buddhas.

Two main points regarding the relationship between Amida Buddha and all the other Buddhas come up again and again in those letters. Firstly, it is Amida Buddha, the original Buddha, who attained Buddhahood in the timeless past, who is the teacher of all Buddhas. Secondly, Amida Buddha surpasses all the other Buddhas because he saves through his great Vow each and every sentient being without any discrimination, even those heavily burdened with bad karma who cannot be liberated by any of the other Buddhas.

I would like to expand a little on the previous discussion in my commentary on the eighth letter of Fascicle Two. Firstly let me introduce you to Shinran Shōnin's own comment on the subject found in his main writing, *The Kyōgyōshinshō*. In Chapter 4 of the book entitled *The Collection of Passages Expounding the True Realizing of the Pure Land*, he says, "Being so, Amida Nyorai (skt. *tathā+āgata*), coming (*āgata*) from Suchness (*tathā*), reveals himself in various bodies, such as the Body of Recompense, the Body of Response and the Body of Transformation."[249]

"Bodies" in this passage means the various forms that the Buddha's Dharma-body (*Dharma-kāya*) takes in response to the different needs of human beings. The Dharma-body in itself being formless, it has to take on various forms in order for human beings to understand it. According to the doctrine of *tri-kāya* or "three bodies," the Dharma-body (*Dharma-kāya*) manifests itself in the following two ways.

The first is *Saṃbhoga-kāya* (*hōjin* 報身 ch. *bàoshēn*), the Enjoyment Body. As a result of the self-discipline undertaken by a Bodhisattva through his vows, he becomes a Buddha of Enjoyment Body in which he enjoys the fruit of his own Awakening or Enlightenment and also the pleasure of the Awakening of others. Amida Buddha is a good example.

The second is *Nirmāna-kāya* (*ōge-shin* 應化身 ch. *yìnghuà-shēn*), the Body of Response and Transformation, the Sanskrit word *nirmāṇa* meaning "magical creation or transformation." When this is translated as the Body of Response (ōjin 應身 ch. *yìngshēn*), it means the Buddha in human form, as Śākyamuni Buddha for example, adopted for the benefit of unenlightened sentient beings. When it is translated as the Body of Transformation (*keshin* 化身 ch. *huàshēn*), it means manifestations of the Buddha in every kind of form imaginable—as rock, insect, animal, human being, demon, Bodhisattva and so on. In fact the Buddha can be understood as being manifest in anything or anyone around you in as far as they are for you part of the working of the Buddha and lead you to the world of Awakening or the Pure Land. Shinran Shōnin's statement that "Amida Nyorai, coming from Suchness, reveals himself in various bodies, such as the Enjoyment Body, the Body of Response and the Body of Transformation" is of vital importance, revealing his profound spiritual interpretation of the working of Amida Tathāgata. This is related to the second of the two main points emphasised by Rennyo Shōnin concerning the relationship between Amida and all the other Buddhas. It is in order to be able to save all sentient beings without any discrimination, even those weighed down with bad karma, that Amida Tathāgata reveals himself in all kinds of forms. If, through pure faith, you are truly awakened, then for you all of those around you, whether they are your wife or husband, mother or father, brother or sister, friend or foe, demon and god, trees in your garden or animals by your hearth, all of them will be manifestations of Amida Buddha, leading you forward in daily life along the path to the Pure Land.

Thus Rennyo's view of the relationship between Amida and all the other Buddhas is firmly based on the religious philosophy of the founder of Shin Buddhism, Shinran Shōnin himself, and it is extremely important for Shin Buddhists to understand this relationship both through their faith-experience and in their daily lives after the attainment of faith.

Regarding the relationship between Amida Buddha and all other Buddhas, Rennyo Shōnin states in the 27th letter of *The Jōgai gobunshō*,[250]

Furthermore all the reflections of the moon are mirrored images of one and the same moon. The light of the same moon reflects itself everywhere. With this in mind, understand. Therefore, relying on One Buddha, Amida Buddha, implies simultaneously relying on all Buddhas and all gods. Accordingly, if you entrust yourself to One Buddha, Amida Buddha, all gods as well as all Buddhas will be pleased and will protect you.[251]

And the 45th letter of *The Jōgai gobunshō* reads,

Because everything is included in the virtue of One Buddha, Amida Buddha, if you take refuge in the Original Vow of Amida Tathāgata and entrust yourself to Other Power, the compassionate Vow that is way beyond this world, all the gods will be pleased and will protect you. For this reason there is found in sūtras the teaching that 'one Buddha is in all Buddhas and all Buddhas are in one Buddha.' The meaning of this, you will understand, is that taking refuge in One Buddha, Amida Buddha, means simultaneously relying on and thinking of all Buddhas and Bodhisattvas.[252]

According to these quotations it is clear that Rennyo's view of the relationship between Amida and other Buddhas is firmly based on the philosophy that one Buddha is in all Buddhas and all Buddhas are in one Buddha. As has already been demonstrated, this philosophical view found in our tradition is based on the teaching of Shinran Shōnin in *The Kyōgyōshinshō* or that of Kakunyo Shōnin in *The Kuden shō.*

Rennyo Shōnin's words, "you should simply give no heed to the depth of your bad karma but entrust yourselves sincerely to Amida Tathāgata's Original Vow," encapsulates perfectly what is important for our attainment of faith in the here and now.

After the attainment of faith we recite the *Nenbutsu* with gratitude to the Buddha for all that he has done for us. The *Namu Amida-butsu* we pronounce with such gratitude is the actual working of Amida Buddha appearing in daily life through the medium of our own individual existence. In other words *Namu Amida-butsu* is the expression of Amida Buddha himself or the manifestation of his innermost desire known as the Original Vow. In this letter Rennyo gives his own interpretation of *Namu Amida-butsu*: "Accordingly in essence *Namu Amida-butsu* can be understood as a six-character name chosen by Amida Buddha to be an expression of himself as evidence of his vow to save us." Rennyo Shōnin also states in the eighth letter of Fascicle Four, "You should understand that Amida Buddha's attainment of Supreme Awakening is working as *Namu Amida-butsu* you recite just now. This is evidence that our birth in the Pure Land is truly assured."

Article 174 of *The Goichidai ki kikigaki* says,

> As people gathered at the Southern Hall were speaking to each other about their state of mind, Rennyo Shōnin appeared and asked, "What are you talking about? If you will only entrust yourselves to Amida singlemindedly and with no doubt, forsaking all your own ways of dealing with things, your birth [in the Pure Land] will be settled by the Buddha. Evidence of this is *Namu Amida-butsu*. What else have you got to worry about?"[253]

From these words we can discern Rennyo's absolute reliance on the Buddha Name, *Namu Amida-butsu*, that he recites with heartfelt gratitude.

He enjoys entrusting himself to *Namu Amida-butsu* as the working of Amida's Original Vow. The *Nenbutsu* he is now saying is the actual evidence of Amida's Original Vow to save all sentient beings without any form of discrimination. Thus Rennyo concludes: "Hence we describe the *Nenbutsu* as 'pronouncing the Name with gratitude to the Buddha for what he has done for us' and also as 'pronouncing the Name after the attainment of faith.'"

CHAPTER THIRTY-SIX

The Meaning of
Namu Amida-Butsu

SOLELY BY ALWAYS

PRONOUNCING THE NAME

FASCICLE III, LETTER SIX

When we are asked to explain the meaning of '*Namu Amida-butsu*,' we should first of all point out that its two-character-long element *Namu* 南无 signifies both *kimyō* (歸命 taking refuge) and *hotsugan ekō* (発願廻向 vow-making and virtue-transference).

At the same time, '*Namu*' is his Vow and '*Amida-butsu*' is his Practice. When you cast aside miscellaneous practices and miscellaneous good acts and entrust yourselves to Amida Tathāgata by practising the *Nenbutsu* alone with singlemindedness, thereby awakening the one thought-moment of taking refuge wherein you entreat Amida to save you, Amida then graciously radiates forth his all-encompassing light and embraces within it all those who practise. This is exactly the meaning of the four characters *Amida-butsu* 阿彌陀佛 and also of 'vow-making and virtue-transference (*hotsugan ekō*)'. Thus we realise that the six-character Name, *Namu Amida-butsu* 南无阿彌陀佛, fully expresses the meaning of the Other Power faith through which we come to be born in the Pure Land.

For this reason, the passage on the fulfilment of the Vow[254] reveals that we 'hear that Name and rejoice in the awakening of faith.' The meaning of this passage is that, on hearing that Name, we rejoice in the awakening of faith. 'Hearing that Name' does not just mean hearing the Name bluntly; when, through our encounter with a good teacher, we both hear and fully understand the meaning of the Name of the six characters, then that is Other Power faith, through which we are born in the Land of Enjoyment. Thus 'to rejoice in the awakening of faith' means that, when faith is attained, we rejoice in its awakening, knowing that our birth in the Pure Land is fully assured.

Accordingly, as we reflect on Amida Tathāgata's five kalpas of hard work and infinite immeasurable kalpas more of further labour and thus become aware of how sincerely we should thank and revere him for saving us so readily, we realise there are simply no words to express all we feel. Shinran Shōnin thus states in one of his *wasan*,

> What we receive through the virtue-transference of *Namu Amida-butsu*
> Is vast and inconceivable.
> Through the benefit of the virtue-transference that enables us to go there,
> We enter the virtue-transference that enables us to return here.[255]

Also, in *The Shōshinge* (*The Gāthā of True Faith in Nenbutsu*), there is the following passage,

> Solely by always pronouncing the Name of the Tathāgata,
> We respond with gratitude to his Great Compassion, to the Vow of Universal Deliverance.[256]

All the more for this reason, irrespective of time, place, or other circumstance, whether walking, standing, sitting, or lying down, we should simply repeat the *Nenbutsu*, pronouncing the Name of the Buddha with gratitude for what he has so kindly done for us.

Most humbly and respectfully
Written on 20th October, Bunmei 6 [1474].

COMMENTS

In this letter Rennyo Shōnin discusses the Shin Buddhist teaching of the Buddha Name, *Namu Amida-butsu*. Before examining this interpretation, I would like to look briefly at the background to the first explanation of the Name, *Namu Amida-butsu*, by Shàndǎo 善導 (613–681).

Concomitant with the development of the flourishing Pure Land teaching in China at the time of Dàochuò 道綽 (562–645) and Shàndǎo, there also emerged a strong current of criticism against those who would teach people to recite the *Nenbutsu* or *Namu Amida-butsu* if they wished to attain birth in the Pure Land of Amida Buddha. The source of this criticism was a representative body of Buddhist monastics, who based their arguments on the Shèlùn School (摂論宗) founded on The Mahāyānasaṃgraha (Shōdaijō ron 摂大乘論 ch. Shèdàchéng lùn) by Asaṅga 無着 (310–390).[257] The bitter criticism of *Nenbutsu* teaching can be summarised as follows: "*Namu Amida-butsu* or the *Nenbutsu* is pronounced with the desire to be born in the Pure Land, but that is not the true practice that leads to Enlightenment. In *The Meditation Sūtra* Śākyamuni Buddha taught pronouncing the Name as an expedient means to save those who have no capacity for performing other Mahāyāna practices. There is only one's desire to be born in the Pure Land but no proper practice relating to it. According to the idea of Mahāyāna Bodhisattvaship, one who vows to attain Enlightenment or birth in the Pure Land should seek to accomplish the proper practices. *Namu Amida-butsu*, or the pronouncing of the Buddha Name, is merely an expression of one's desire to attain birth in the Pure Land and not a true practice at all."

In order to respond to these criticisms Shàndǎo confirmed in his *Exposition of The Meditation Sūtra* that *Namu Amida-butsu* already encompassed within itself a desire for, or vow to attain, Enlightenment, as well as all the necessary practices to accomplish that aim. According to Shàndǎo's interpretation of *Namu Amida-butsu*, the term '*Namu*' means 'to take refuge (歸命 ch. *guīmìng*, jp. *kimyō*)' and also 'to make a vow and transfer virtue for birth (発願廻向 ch. *fāyuàn huíxiàng*, jp. *hotsugan ekō*),' while the term '*Amida-butsu*' means 'practice' (行 ch. *xíng*, jp. *gyō*). Practice in this context refers to all the practices already carried out by Amida Buddha in order to enable us sentient beings to attain birth in the Pure Land. This is to say in effect that Amida Buddha, by virtue of all the practices performed by him to attain Supreme Enlightenment, himself brings about our birth in the Pure Land and our attainment therein of Enlightenment.

In the context of the teaching of Other Power these three elements of *Namu Amida-butsu*, 'refuge,' 'vow' and 'practice,' can all be seen as manifesting the working of Amida Buddha and they are clearly understood as such by every follower through their own experience of pure faith.

As Shinran Shōnin says at the start of his unique interpretation of the term *Namu* in his main writing, *The Kyōgyōshinshō*, "This being so, *Namu* 南无 (skt. *namas*) is *kimyō* 歸命 (taking refuge in Amida Buddha)."[258] He then concludes his argument with the famous passage, "Thus, *kimyō* is the solemn command of the Original Vow."[259] On encountering the solemn command for us to do so, contained in the Original Vow of Great Love and Compassion, we simply accept and obey Amida Buddha's call by taking refuge in him. On hearing his call we are impelled from within to entrust ourselves to Amida Buddha. In this way our taking refuge in Amida Buddha is set in motion by his calling to us and our responding to that call.

The second element 'vow' (*gan*) stands for the words 'vow-making and virtue-transference (*hotsugan ekō*).' Almost all other Pure Land schools understand this phrase differently. To them *hotsugan ekō* means that they themselves make a vow and, earnestly desiring to be born in the Pure Land, cultivate virtue for their birth, but this is not the case in Shin Buddhism where it is basically Amida Buddha who is understood to be making the vow and transferring virtue. Shinran Shōnin states in *The Kyōgyōshinshō*: "*Hotsugan ekō* 'vow-making and virtue-transference' means that Amida Tathāgata is the one who has already made the vow and transferred to all sentient beings the practice (*Nenbutsu*)."[260] Thus traditional Shin Buddhist teaching holds that our desiring birth in the Pure Land is made possible only through Amida's Original Vow and virtue-transference for our birth comes solely from Amida Buddha. In other words our own aspiration for birth in the Pure Land is firmly founded on what has been done for us by Amida Buddha through his Original Vow. It is not particularly unusual, therefore, for us to come across a few Shin Buddhist texts in which the phrase *hotsugan* is explained as meaning our aspiration for birth in the Pure Land.

In Shinran Shōnin's own comment on Shàndǎo's interpretation of *Namu Amida-butsu* as recorded in his *Annotated Inscriptions on Sacred Scrolls*, Shinran Shōnin refers to *hotsugan ekō* as meaning "our aspiration to be born in the Land of Peace and Happiness in response to the call of the two Honoured Ones."[261] In the case of Rennyo Shōnin a phrase found in the 15th letter of Fascicle Two, "The two characters '*Namu* 南无' mean that, aspiring for birth in the Land of Utmost Bliss, we entrust ourselves wholeheartedly to Amida Buddha" can be seen as the only example of such an interpretation in *The Five Fascicle Letters*. Concerning the phrase *hotsugan ekō*, almost all of the Shin Buddhist documents are consistent in understanding it as Amida's Original Vow and virtue-transference. Why should this be? The reason is that if those who have never attained Other Power faith should happen upon a document that explains *hotsugan ekō* as being the aspiration initiated from our side for birth in the Pure Land, there is a danger they may concentrate on their own self-power efforts to attain birth without understanding this cannot be accomplished without the help and support afforded by Amida's Original Vow. Thus we have to say that Rennyo Shōnin sees *hotsugan ekō* almost exclusively as the work initiated from the side of Amida Buddha. It goes without saying that in the current letter, too, Rennyo interprets *hotsugan ekō* as Amida's Original Vow and virtue-transference. Hence, my translation of the first paragraph of the letter: "When we are asked to explain the meaning of 'Namu Amida-butsu,' we should first of all point out that its two-character-long element 'Namu (南无)' signifies both kimyō (歸命 taking refuge) and hotsugan ekō (発願廻向 vow-making and virtue transference)."[262]

The third paragraph refers to the passage on the fulfilment of the eighteenth Vow, in particular the phrase "to hear that Name and rejoice in the awakening of faith." In the seventeenth Vow Amida insists that unless all Buddhas pronounce his Name in praise he would refrain from attaining Supreme Enlightenment for himself. In the account of Amida Buddha related in *The Larger Sūtra of Eternal Life*, however, this seventeenth Vow has already been fulfilled and there then appears the passage on the fulfilment of the eighteenth Vow. Thus the words 'that Name' means the Name all Buddhas say in praise. A good teacher then stands for "all Buddhas" of the seventeenth Vow. What is important, then, is to meet a good teacher. It is through such an encounter with an individual who teaches us truth that we awaken to the faith that lies within.

The third element 'practice (行 gyō)' stands for all the many good practices carried out for our sake by Amida Buddha. These good practices have all been brought together for us in the one simple practice of saying the Name 'Namu Amida-butsu' or the *Nenbutsu* that we now see welling up in front of us in the person of an individual who is our good teacher. This pronouncing of the Name is called daigyō (大行 'great practice') in Shin Buddhism. In this context I recall again the fact that D. T. Suzuki translated the word 大行 'great practice' as 'great living.' It is when we awaken to faith that our life attains to the plane of the truly greater way of living embraced in the infinite light of Amida Buddha.

Hence, Rennyo Shōnin's quotation of the following *wasan*,

What we receive through the virtue-transference of *Namu Amida-butsu*
Is vast and inconceivable.
Through the benefit of the virtue-transference that enables us to go there,
We enter the virtue-transference that enables us to return here.[263]

In accordance with the ideal of every Mahāyāna Bodhisattva, every Pure Land follower wants to save not only themselves but also others. Our return to this world after birth in the Pure Land is simply in order to do just that: save others.

Our going to the Pure Land to be saved and our return to this world to save others are both the great working of Amida's virtue-transference. We owe both these spiritual activities entirely to Amida.

To end his letter Rennyo focuses on the vital importance of living our lives with gratitude based on true faith and quotes a few highly relevant lines from *The Shōshinge*,

Solely by always pronouncing the Name of the Tathāgata,
We respond with gratitude to his Great Compassion, to the Vow
of Universal Deliverance.[264]

CHAPTER THIRTY-SEVEN

The Oneness of *Namu* and *Amida-Butsu*

ON THE THREE ACTS OF THE BUDDHA AND THOSE OF SENTIENT BEINGS

FASCICLE III, LETTER SEVEN

The essential teaching that Shinran Shōnin encourages us to embrace is the single path of Other Power faith, through which ignorant lay followers in the defiled world of the Last Age are able to be born in the Pure Land swiftly and instantaneously and without the slightest difficulty. Thus everyone is fully aware that Amida Tathāgata saves all sentient beings, even those ignorant beings who have already committed the ten bad acts and the five grave offences, even womankind burdened with the five obstacles and the three submissions.

But if you now ask, "In order to be born in the Land of Utmost Bliss, what sort of faith should we ignorant beings embrace and how should we entrust ourselves to Amida Buddha?," then the answer is that we should simply entrust ourselves to Amida Tathāgata alone; discarding all other beliefs, we should take refuge steadfastly in Amida. When we singleheartedly entrust ourselves to the Original Vow and entertain no doublemindedness towards Amida Tathāgata, then we will surely be born in the Land of Utmost Bliss. This truth is called the attainment of Other Power faith.

Originally faith means taking refuge singlemindedly in Amida Buddha through fully understanding the meaning of Amida Buddha's Original Vow; this is termed the decisive attainment of the peaceful awareness of Other Power. Therefore, the full realisation of the meaning of the six characters *Namu Amida-butsu* 南无阿彌陀佛 is the essence of the decisive attainment of faith. In this phrase the two characters *Namu* 南无 refer to *ki* 機, the momentum through which the Dharma works, or the sentient beings who entrust themselves to Amida Buddha. The next four characters *Amida-butsu* 阿彌陀佛 signify Hō 法, the Dharma through which Amida Tathāgata saves all sentient beings. This is expressed as 'the oneness in *Namu Amida-butsu* of *ki* [the person to be saved] and *Hō* [the Dharma that saves].' Thus the three acts of sentient beings and the three acts of Amida become one. It is this point that Master Shàndǎo is referring to in *The Exposition of The Meditation Sūtra*, when he writes "The three acts of the Buddha and those of sentient beings are not separate from each other."[265]

For this reason there should be no doubt at all that those who have attained faith decisively with the one thought-moment of taking refuge will all be born without fail in the Land of Enjoyment. Those who resolutely cast off their own bad attachment to themselves, their tenacious attachment to self power, and entrust themselves singleheartedly to Amida with the deep awareness that this is entirely the inconceivable working of the Vow, will all unfailingly attain birth in the true Land of Enjoyment, ten people out of each ten. After realising this we should recite the *Nenbutsu* in gratitude at all times, mindful solely of the depth of what Amida Tathāgata has done for us.

Most humbly and respectfully
On 23rd February, Bunmei 7 [1475].

COMMENTS

Each letter in *The Letters* by Rennyo in the Five Fascicle version has its own distinctive title. When he originally wrote those letters to his followers, none of them had a name, but Shin Buddhist scholars, for their own personal convenience, started identifying the letters by using some characteristic catchphrase from each. The letter under discussion is usually called the letter of *hishisangō*. The literal translation of the Japanese term is "three kinds of karma on this side and on that side," *hishi* meaning "on that side and on this side" and *sangō*, "three kinds of karma." As you may already be aware, the Sanskrit term that stands for the Japanese word *gō* is karma and the basic meaning of this is simply 'act,' 'working' or 'deed.' In the case of the title of this letter, *gō* means 'act.' In Buddhism in general human actions are organised into three categories: physical, oral and mental. Thus, the title *hishisangō*, "three kinds of karma on that side and on this side," actually means the three acts of the Buddha on the other shore and the three acts of sentient beings on this shore. The main subject of the letter as a whole is how the three acts of the Buddha and the three acts of sentient beings all become one.

When Rennyo refers in his letters to the oneness of sentient beings and Buddha, he uses the Japanese phrase *kihō ittai no Namu Amida-butsu* 機法 一体の南无阿彌陀佛. This special expression is found not only in the seventh letter of Fascicle Three, but also in the eighth, eleventh, and fourteenth letters of Fascicle Four. In Pure Land Buddhism the term *ki* is used synonymously with the self, sentient beings or aspirants for Amida's Pure Land, whilst Hō stands for the Dharma, Amida Buddha or Amida's Original Vow. The word *ittai* 一体 means oneness. Thus the expression *kihō ittai* indicates the oneness of *ki*, the person to be saved, and Hō, the Dharma that saves.

It is well known that the phrase *kihō ittai no Namu Amida-butsu* appears in *The Anjin ketsujō shō* 安心決定鈔,[266] a work that, from his sayings in *The Goichidai ki kikigaki*, Rennyo Shōnin is believed to have read over and over again. Thus we find him declaring, "Although I have been reading *The Anjin ketsujō shō* for over forty years, I have never tired of reading it", and also saying, "It is a sacred document from which one can excavate gold."[267] Strongly influenced by this book, believed originally to belong to the Seizan School, Rennyo uses the phrase *kihō ittai no Namu Amida-butsu* in his own special way, firmly based on the Shin Buddhist tradition.

In the Shin Buddhist tradition, there are two kinds of *ki*: the self that remains attached to self-power and the self that entrusts itself to Other Power. When Rennyo speaks of the oneness in *Namu Amida-butsu* of *ki and Hō*, it is this latter *ki* he is referring to, namely the *ki* that has attained the Other Power faith. *Hō* in this context means Amida Buddha, the Dharma that has been received by the *ki* through the absolute entrusting.

The oldest Shin Buddhist text in which the phrase *kihō ittai*, "the oneness of *ki* and Hō, " appears is *The Gangan shō* 願々鈔, *Commentary on Vows*, by Venerable Kakunyo (1270–1351),[268] the third Head Priest of the Honganji. Referring to how this oneness comes about, Kakunyo says in this book,

> It is because [Amida Buddha], as a result of his Vow of Immeasurable Light, embraces the *ki* who rejoices in the awakening of faith at least for one thought-moment. As this *ki* rejoices in the awakening of faith in the embrace of the all-encompassing Light, the *ki* attains oneness with *Hō*. And in this oneness of *ki and Hō*, though they may appear as two, what illumines and what is illumined are no longer two but one.[269]

When Rennyo says that '*Namu*' pertains to *ki*, this *ki* is not one who depends on self power, but one who has entrusted him or herself unreservedly to Amida Buddha. As long as we remain attached to self-power, we cannot entrust ourselves entirely to Amida Buddha. However small our attachment to self power may be, if there remains the slightest vestige of such attachment still within us, then our entrusting ourselves to the Buddha can never be perfect. Those who depend on self power can never entrust themselves to Other Power.

Amida Buddha calls to us, saying "Come to me immediately." Usually, however, we respond to the Buddha saying "Please, wait a while. After solving the problems I now face, I will come to you. Let me think, let me struggle on a bit more by myself so that I can come to you without any problems!" As you can see, there remains in such an attitude a certain degree of attachment to self power, to our ability to try and solve our problems through our own thoughts and actions. It is one thing for us to try and solve worldly problems by worldly means. But the real problem underlying all worldly problems is our attachment to self power, our attachment to our own ways of thinking and acting, basically our attachment to the notion of self. Our tenacious attachment to our own ways of living is the root cause of so much suffering. Once we are freed from this attachment, we will become aware of how self-centred we have been and of how much such attachment has narrowed our world. Shin Buddhism teaches us how to liberate ourselves from this selfish attachment to self power that underlies so many of the different forms of suffering we face.

The moment of attaining faith by entrusting ourselves to Amida Buddha is none other than the moment we are awakened to the reality of the Buddha's unconditional love. However miserable we may be, the instant we recognise that we are already embraced in the great love and compassion of the Buddha is also the instant we entrust ourselves entirely to him, without retaining the smallest remnant of self-attachment. As soon as we awaken to the unconditional love of Amida Buddha we are impelled to entrust ourselves to him. In itself, then, this very entrusting is a gift from the Buddha. Through this faith of entrusting ourselves to the Buddha, the citadel of our tenacious attachment to self power crumbles away very naturally and we find ourselves in the world of Emptiness, or of interdependent origination. In other words we become one with the Buddha in *Namu Amida-butsu*.

Our faith is expressed through our three actions: the physical action of bowing to the Buddha, the oral action of pronouncing the Name of the Buddha and the mental action of becoming mindful of the Buddha. These three acts are three aspects of *Namu Amida-butsu*. The oneness in *Namu Amida-butsu* of *ki* and *Hō* appears in the way that the virtues of the Buddha become manifest in these three actions of ours. Shàndǎo's words quoted above refer to this point.

What we should never forget is that all this is a gift or virtue-transference from Amida Buddha. If we ourselves try to attain oneness with the Buddha by virtue of these three acts, such conscious effort on our part will cause confusion among us as to the true nature of the oneness of self and Buddha. Such confusion, known as the *Sangō Wakuran* 三業惑乱 or "The Three Acts Confusion", occurred amongst members of the order of Nishi Honganji during the Edo Period, from the mid-eighteenth century to 1806.

Related to this problem, however, there is one thing to consider. In the Higashi Honganji tradition they hold that '*Namu*' has the meaning of entreaty or earnest request. This is a very delicate problem, for if you understand this entreaty as self-effort, then such a doctrine could lead to attachment to self power. Looking into ourselves, however, we do have to admit to the existence of just such a cry or call to the Buddha, "Help me, please help me!" Such an entreaty from the very bottom of our hearts is again evidence of the absolute compassion of the Buddha. As I see it, even this entreaty is a gift that appears through our contact with the unconditional love of the Buddha. In this context I recollect D. T. Suzuki's statement that "The very fact of *kleśa's* activity makes us long for a something beyond ourselves, which is however really in us. This longing is the work of the Primary Body, which fact is given us in the form of myth, in the story of Dharmākara."[270] "The longing" in this quotation is that deep-seated cry for help and is actually the working of the Primary Body, by which D. T. Suzuki means the Dharma-body of the Buddha.

CHAPTER THIRTY-EIGHT

Everything is the Working of Amida's Great Compassion

ON THE FALSE TEACHING IN THIS PROVINCE AND OTHERS OF AMIDA'S ENLIGHTENMENT TEN KALPAS AGO

FASCICLE III, LETTER EIGHT

At the time of writing there are a great many followers in this and other provinces whose views deviate widely from our tradition's teaching of 'peaceful awareness.' Each of them is convinced of the correctness of their own personal understanding and there are few that show any inclination to attain true faith by talking to others about their views, though they be quite possibly at variance with the Dharma teaching. This is indeed a wretched attachment. Unless they make haste to confess their views with proper repentance, unless they come to abide in the true faith of our tradition and get to be decisively assured of their birth in the Land of Enjoyment, it is indeed just as though they had returned empty-handed from a mountain of treasures. The belief of theirs, so at variance with our faith, goes as follows: "Faith is never forgetting or doubting that Amida Tathāgata already secured for us our birth when he attained Supreme Enlightenment ten kalpas ago." By simply embracing this belief instead of attaining faith decisively through taking refuge in Amida, such people cannot be born in the Land of Enjoyment. This is thus a deviant and erroneous belief.

To clarify, then, what we mean by 'peaceful awareness' in our tradition, it can be said that fully understanding the essence of 'Namu Amida-butsu' is to attain Other Power faith. Hence the assertion by Shàndǎo, when explaining the six characters 南无阿彌陀佛 'Namu Amida-butsu,' that "'Namu' means 'to take refuge.' It also signifies 'vow-making and virtue-transference'."

What does this mean?

When Amida Tathāgata, in his causal stage,[271] chose the practice whereby we ignorant beings might attain birth, he worked very hard on our behalf because the virtue-transference of ignorant beings is based on self power and is therefore difficult to bring to fruition. In order to impart to us his own virtue, he completed the practice of virtue-transference, whereby the virtue of Amida is transferred onto ourselves. When the one thought-moment of taking refuge by saying 'Namu' is awakened within us, Amida's own virtue is transferred by him onto us ignorant beings. Thus this virtue-transference comes not from the side of us ignorant beings but from the side of the Tathāgata. Consequently this virtue-transference from the Tathāgata is called by his followers "no virtue-transference from self." Thus the two characters Namu mean 'to take refuge'; they also mean '[Amida's] vow-making and virtue-transference.' For these reasons, he unfailingly embraces and never abandons those beings who take refuge in Amida by saying 'Namu.' Thus it is we say 'Namu Amida-butsu.'

You should realise that this is exactly what is meant by the phrase "Nenbutsu followers who have attained Other Power faith through the one thought-moment of taking refuge and who have completed the cause in ordinary life." Those who understand in this way should recite the Nenbutsu, pronouncing the Name of the Buddha, no matter whether walking, standing, sitting, or lying down, their awareness of how much has been done by Amida Tathāgata deepened and widened by virtue of their faith. This is what is meant by the following lines,

> He taught that, at the very moment we become mindful of Amida's
>   Original Vow,
> We naturally enter the stage of the definitely assured,
> And that, solely by always pronouncing the Name of the Tathāgata,
> We respond with gratitude to his Great Compassion, to the Vow
>   of Universal Deliverance.[272]

Most humbly and respectfully
On 25th February, Bunmei 7 [1475]

COMMENTS

According to the date found in the last line, this letter was written two days
after the seventh letter of Fascicle Three, at a time when Rennyo Shōnin was
teaching in Echizen Province. Around that time various 'secret teachings'
(*hijibōmon* 秘事法門) were highly prevalent in Echizen Province.[273] In this
the eighth letter of Fascicle Three, the wrong belief that Rennyo Shōnin is
criticising, known as the 'Ten Kalpas Secret' (*jikkō-hiji* 十劫秘事), is one
of these secret teachings.[274]

Although at a first glance the Ten Kalpas Secret might seem a perfectly
viable philosophical observation, it is actually a highly superficial view restricted
by the confines of human knowledge and intellectual understanding. Having
brought up the subject of the 'Ten Kalpas Secret' in the 13th letter of Fascicle
One, Rennyo Shōnin goes on to make the criticism, "This is a great mistake.
For even if we knew how Amida Tathāgata attained Supreme Enlightenment,
such knowledge would be useless if we did not know for ourselves how to attain
the Other Power faith through which we are to be born in the Pure Land." The
criticism that Rennyo Shōnin then levels at this erroneous view is very sharp and
to the point: "What is completely missing in such a declaration is the experience
of attaining Other Power faith through taking refuge in Amida Buddha."[275] The
experience of entrusting ourselves absolutely to Amida Buddha is certainly a
great leap of faith, a leap that takes us way beyond the horizons of intellectual
knowledge or human understanding. Only those who have experienced this
leap of faith for themselves can fully appreciate the sharpness of the contrast
between faith-experience and intellectual concern.

If those people who are unable to distinguish between faith and knowledge become seriously concerned about the religious realm, they will try to
understand the religious world, something beyond intellectual understanding,
by means of their own circumscribed intellect. Unaware of the limits of the
intellect, they are often rather proud of their intellectual ability and cling fast
to their own ways of understanding. The greater their pride, the stronger their
attachment, for both are closely related. Followers of the Ten Kalpas Secret
are certainly just such people. They "insist that they have already attained
faith" and "assume that they know everything there is to know about the faith
of our tradition."

Because of their tenacious attachment to intellect, such followers cannot
take refuge in Amida Buddha by means of absolute entrusting. Hence Rennyo
Shōnin's saying, "What is completely missing in such a declaration is the

experience of attaining Other Power faith through taking refuge in Amida Buddha." In this context what is of vital importance is not intellectual understanding but the actual attainment of faith through taking refuge in Amida Buddha. As I wrote in my commentary on *The Shōshinge*,

> To summarise, our 'taking refuge' is the Solemn Command of the Original Vow. It is we ourselves who take refuge in Amida Buddha and yet we are moved to do so through his command. 'Taking refuge in the Buddha' is our faith and at the same time it is a gift from Amida Buddha, the result of his virtue-transference. We realise that our 'taking refuge' is actually embraced in the 'Command of the Original Vow.' As you know, the essence of the Original Vow lies in Amida's compassionate wish to save all beings without any discrimination at all. Thus the Command of the Original Vow is the ultimate expression of Amida's Love and Compassion.[276]

Amida Buddha, still at his Bodhisattva stage, vowed to save all sentient beings without any form of discrimination. In order to fulfil this Original Vow, Amida is said to transfer to sentient beings all the virtues he accumulates so that they can attain birth in his Pure Land on the strength of these virtues. Amida's act of virtue-transference is a pure gift that comes from his unconditional love for all sentient beings.

In Shinran Shōnin's religious philosophy virtue-transference comes only from Amida Buddha. This means that there is no virtue-transference from our side, from the side of sentient beings. In the teaching of Shin Buddhism we are not expected to be capable of transferring virtue, because our actions are not free from selfishness but are always contaminated by impurities such as ignorance, greed, anger, tenacious attachment and undue pride. Fully awakened to the limits of our own thoughts and actions, we come to entrust ourselves absolutely to Amida Buddha. It is through the faith of entrusting ourselves to Amida that we become selfless and can humbly receive Amida's pure act of virtue-transference.

The original Japanese word that I translated as virtue-transference is 廻向 *ekō*. The Sanskrit term that stands for *ekō* is *pariṇāma*, meaning 'to transfer one's own virtue to others to help them attain Buddhahood.' The concept of this Mahayanist term is altruistic in essence. Although it also means 'directing one's virtue for one's own attainment of Buddhahood,' it should be noted that, in the context of Mahāyāna Buddhism, a Bodhisattva's attainment of Buddhahood cannot be separated from his work of helping others attain Buddhahood. In Mahāyāna Buddhism benefiting oneself and benefiting others are not separate from one another. The notion of virtue-transference is thus an altruistic one. Why then does Shinran Shōnin say 'no virtue-transference from our side'?

Does it mean the negation of altruism? No. It is through our altruistic endeavour to love others that we become aware how difficult it is for us to love them just as they are. Without this altruistic inclination underlying our way of living, we would not become aware of the near impossibility of doing so. This awareness of the difficulty of loving others is the key notion that leads us to turn from self power to Other Power. Reaching this awareness or, in other words, through this existentialistic despair, we take refuge in Amida Buddha. The one thought-moment of taking refuge in Amida Buddha is also the very moment we encounter the unconditional love of Amida.

When, on entrusting ourselves absolutely to Amida Buddha, we forsake our attachment to all kinds of form, Amida's unconditional love, formless in itself, manifests itself through all manner of forms. In Shin Buddhism we talk about how difficult it is for us to love others, but not about the difficulties or limitations of other people's love. Once we receive the unconditional love of Amida Buddha through true faith, this opens up further possibilities for us to encounter the love of others, a love that is in itself a further manifestation of Amida's own love. In this respect the unconditional love can be defined as 'absolute altruism.' It is formless and manifests itself through many forms. It underlies all forms of life. As D. T. Suzuki discussed in one of his lectures compiled in *Buddha of Infinite Light,*

> Some people go so far as to say that we are devoid of altruistic impulses, but I cannot agree with such views. We do have altruistic impulses and we often show evidence that we do. We forget ourselves and risk our lives for others, and in pursuing that course of conduct we do not think about anything. We do it impulsively, indicating that our actions arise from our fundamental nature.
>
> Amida is shown to represent this altruistic impulse that is deeply rooted in human nature, perhaps rooted in the cosmos itself. This is why I speak of the Original Vow as being an expression of original will. To achieve altruism, according to the Indian way of thinking, one must be purified of all defiled sentiments, feelings or emotions. Otherwise, one cannot expect to save others. So Amida sought such a perfection.[277]

CHAPTER THIRTY-NINE

Faith and Our Expression of Gratitude

THE DATE OF SHINRAN SHŌNIN'S DEATH REMEMBERED EACH MONTH

FASCICLE III, LETTER NINE

Today being the day on which every month we remember Shinran Shōnin's death, there are few who would not wish to come and make some expression of their gratitude to Shinran Shōnin for all that he has done for us. What followers must understand, however, is how nigh on impossible it will be for them to find themselves in accordance with the true intention of our master,[278] if they make a perfunctory visit, for this day only, on the assumption that all that really matters is to fill the meeting hall, and do not first acquire peaceful awareness by attaining true faith through entrusting themselves to the Other Power of the Original Vow. All the same, it is probably better for those who would otherwise remain at their home village with no thought of expressing their gratitude to attend the meeting, even if they do so reluctantly.

Fellow-followers, therefore, who are firmly committed to coming on the twenty-eighth day of every month, including those who have not yet reached peaceful awareness through the decisive attainment of faith in daily life, should quickly seek to attain Other Power faith, based on the truth of the Original Vow, and become assured of their next birth in the Land of Enjoyment. It is this that will fulfil our personal resolve to express our gratitude to Shōnin for all that he has done for us. At the same time it assures us of our own way of attaining birth in the Land of Utmost Bliss. It is entirely in accordance with the message of the commentary,

> To attain faith ourselves and to guide others to attain faith
> is the most difficult of all difficulties;
> To transmit the great compassion and awaken all beings universally
> is truly to respond in gratitude to what the Buddha has done for us.[279]

Although over a hundred years have already passed since the death of Shōnin, we revere the image before our eyes with deepest gratitude. Although the voice of the virtuous one is far away, separated from us by the wind of impermanence, his words of true teaching have been personally transmitted from master to disciple and still reverberate clearly deep in our ears. Thus it is that the true faith of our tradition grounded on Other Power still lives on to this day without sign of cessation.

Therefore, given so much occasion to do otherwise, if still we fail to attain true faith based on the Original Vow, we must conclude that we are amongst those whose past good conditions have not yet come to maturity. And if we are indeed such people whose past good conditions have not yet unfolded, then all is in vain and we remain unsecured of our future birth. It is this one thing that we should lament above all else. However, despite the great difficulty of meeting the single path of the Original Vow, we have, on rare occasions, encountered this supreme Original Vow. This is indeed the joy of all joys – what can be compared with it? It should be revered; we should entrust ourselves to it.

People who have overturned the bad delusions lingering in their minds, month after month and year after year, and have grounded themselves in Other Power faith, based on the ultimate truth of the Original Vow, will truly accord with the intention of Shōnin. This in itself is something that fulfils our resolve to express our gratitude to Shōnin for all that he has done for us.

Most humbly and respectfully
Written on 28th May, Bunmei 7 [1475].

COMMENTS

This letter, written on the 28th May 1475, is about the significance of attending a meeting regularly held on the 28th of every month to remember the teaching of Shinran Shōnin. He himself passed away on the 28th of November 1262, hence the choice of day by Shin Buddhist followers. Shinran Shōnin's lifelong teaching was directed solely at leading people to attain true faith by entrusting themselves to Amida Buddha. Thus the true meaning of such a monthly meeting lies in the attainment of true faith. Without attaining faith, participants in such meetings cannot be in accordance with the true intention of Shinran Shōnin. Towards the end of the first paragraph of this letter, however, Rennyo states, "All the same, it is probably better for those who would otherwise remain at their home village with no thought of expressing their gratitude to attend the meeting, even if they do so reluctantly." It is typical of Rennyo's loving kindness towards his followers that he still encourages those who have not yet reached peaceful awareness to attend those meetings and finally attain inner peace, even if they are somewhat reluctant.

An important point that he wanted to make clear in this particular letter was that it is through the attainment of faith that we can truly respond in gratitude to all that has been done for us by Shinran Shōnin. The heart of Shinran's work was his exhortation to us to attain true faith. Unless we do so, therefore, we will remain unable to respond with gratitude to what has been done for us by Shinran Shōnin.

What, then, is Rennyo actually referring to when he talks about the attainment of faith as an expression of gratitude? The Shin Buddhist faith-experience is the entrance to a realm in which the *Nenbutsu* practice can be seen as a spontaneous expression of joyous faith. This faith-experience in itself is an act of grateful repayment for what has been done for us by Shinran Shōnin. The crucial point Rennyo makes in this letter is that the attainment of faith is the most fundamental experience by which we can respond gratefully to all that has been done for us by Shinran Shōnin. Hence, Rennyo's words "It is this that will fulfil our own resolve to express our gratitude to Shōnin for all that he has done for us." This is indeed a spiritual experience that opens up the dimension in which we can say our heartfelt thanks to Amida Tathāgata and all the Buddhas, Shinran Shōnin and all the patriarchs, for the many preparatory stages through which they have led us to the attainment of faith.

Rennyo's own journey to the Pure Land, whilst encouraging his followers to attain faith themselves, is indeed a joyous voyage home, filled with deepest gratitude to Amida Buddha and all the predecessors. In this context these lines from Shàndǎo's *Liturgy for Birth* (往生禮讚 *Ōjō raisan*) cited in his letter perfectly express his feeling,

> To attain faith ourselves and to guide others to attain faith
> is the most difficult of all difficulties;
> To transmit the great compassion and awaken all beings universally
> is truly to respond in gratitude to what the Buddha has done for us.

These lines are said in our tradition to represent the quintessence of Shin Buddhist teaching.

The paragraph that follows, a beautifully poetic piece, then goes on to praise Rennyo Shōnin's own fortunate encounter with the true teaching of Shinran Shōnin whose words still reverberate in his mind as though spoken only yesterday. Most of the moving expressions in this paragraph originate from *The Hōonkō Shiki*,[280] a eulogy dedicated to Shinran Shōnin by Venerable Kakunyo. Being imported direct from the eulogy, however, Rennyo's statement at the beginning of the following paragraph, "over a hundred years have already passed since the death of Shōnin," is not actually correct. *The Hōonkō Shiki* was written by Venerable Kakunyo at the age of twenty-five, thirty-three years after the death of Shinran Shōnin, but it is believed that Kakunyo's son, Venerable Zonkaku, added the relevant passage about one hundred years after the death of Shinran Shōnin. Rennyo Shōnin then incorporated the passage just as it was, out of respect for the text perhaps, though in actual fact when he himself actually wrote this letter Shinran Shōnin had already been dead for two hundred and thirteen years.

By introducing the notion of past good conditions in the second to last paragraph of this letter, Rennyo talks about how happy he is to be able to attain Other Power faith. In order to understand in greater detail what is meant by the notion of past good conditions, Rennyo Shōnin talks about the unfolding of past good conditions with the happiest and most grateful feeling of attaining faith: "This is indeed the joy of all joys – what can be compared with it?" Certainly Rennyo distinguishes between those whose past good conditions have already unfolded and those for whom past good conditions have yet to unfold. Yet it is not a petty discrimination but one based on love and compassion. His attitude towards those whose past good conditions have not yet matured is simply to encourage them to grasp every opportunity to meet the Buddha-dharma in the meantime. The attainment of faith is the most joyful experience in the world. Since he has this joy of faith, he invites others to share the same experience by going beyond all their tenacious attachments. This is simply a manifestation of his love and compassion towards those around him.

At the moment of attaining faith we find everything in the past has helped guide us to that point. Nothing has been in vain and our whole past becomes meaningful, as long as we achieve this awakening in the here and now. The awakening of faith that takes place instantaneously or, to use the more traditional expression, in the one thought-moment, is such a fundamental experience that it immediately changes one's view of life, bringing about an affirmation of one's entire past karma. This present moment of awakening allows us to accept all the past experience as gifts that have helped guide us to this spiritual experience.

The Relationship between *Kami* and Amida Buddha

CONCERNING SIX ARTICLES

INCLUDING ONE ON SHINMEI

FASCICLE III, LETTER TEN

Followers of our tradition should understand the meaning implicit in the following six articles. They should entrust themselves in their innermost hearts entirely to the Buddha-dharma but make no sign of this in their outward behaviour. For this reason the way *Nenbutsu* followers of our tradition deliberately set out these days to show people of other schools how we live our faith is a grievous error. From now on, therefore, we should learn and follow the Buddha-dharma, observing what is meant by each one of these articles. Those who flout these rules can no longer be counted as fellow followers of our tradition.

First: We should not belittle Shintō shrines.
Second: We should not belittle Buddhas and Bodhisattvas, nor temples.
Third: We should not slander other schools or teachings.

Fourth: We should not slight the provincial military governors or local land stewards.

Fifth: With the wrong interpretation of the Buddha-dharma so prevalent in this province, we should make sure we turn to the right teaching.

Sixth: As established in our tradition, we should attain Other Power faith decisively, deep down in our hearts and minds.

1 First of all, as regards *shinmei,* they in their original state were all Buddhas and Bodhisattvas. When they looked at the sentient beings of this world, they realised how difficult it must be for such beings to approach them. Thus Buddhas and Bodhisattvas appear provisionally in the form of *kami*, this being a skillful way of forming closer ties with sentient beings and of encouraging them, through the strength of those relationships, to enter at last into the Buddha-dharma. This is the meaning of the saying "'Softening the light and conforming to the dust' is the first step in forming relationships [with sentient beings]; 'Attaining Enlightenment by going through the eight stages' is the completion of the act of benefiting sentient beings." Thus sentient beings of the present world should realise that the *shinmei* will surely recognise those who entrust themselves to the Buddha-dharma and pronounce the *Nenbutsu* as satisfying the *shinmei*'s own original intention. For this reason, though we do not specifically worship *kami* nor entrust ourselves to them, nevertheless, when we take refuge in the compassionate Vow of the one Buddha Amida, the process also includes our trust.

2 Secondly, as regards "Buddhas and Bodhisattvas," since they are the origin of *shinmei* and they all rely on their original teacher, Amida Tathāgata, when sentient beings of the present time entrust themselves to Amida Tathāgata and say the *Nenbutsu*, all the other Buddhas and Bodhisattvas feel this to be a fulfilment of their own original intentions. For this reason, though we do not rely specifically on other Buddhas but entrust ourselves to the one Buddha, Amida Buddha, this also includes all the Buddhas and Bodhisattvas, each and every one of them. You should realise, therefore, that, if we just take refuge in Amida Tathāgata singleheartedly and steadfastly, all the other Buddhas, together with their wisdom and their virtue, come to be encompassed within that one body, the body of Amida Buddha.

3 Thirdly, it is a great mistake for us to slander other schools and other teachings. The reason for this has already been made clear in the Three Pure Land Sūtras. Similarly scholars of different schools should not in their turn slander *Nenbutsu* followers either. In light of the truth of karmic law, it is clear that neither our school nor other schools can hope to escape responsibility for any such violations.

4 Fourthly, with regard to provincial military governors and local land stewards, you should be careful in your dealings, providing the fixed yearly

tributes and payments to officials. In addition human love and justice should be seen as essential norms.

5, Fifthly, since the interpretation of the Buddha-dharma that prevails in this province is not based on the true teaching of our tradition, it would appear to be an erroneous view. In plain words, therefore, we should listen from now on to the correct teaching of our own tradition, a teaching that is true and real, and overturn our old bad attachment to the acquisition of a good mind.

6, Sixthly, in our tradition, genuine *Nenbutsu* followers with a thorough grasp of the true teaching, as set out by our founder, should understand that it is the fundamental intention of our tradition that, despite their lack of goodness or the weight of their wrongdoings, they should nevertheless succeed in attaining birth in the Land of Utmost Bliss.

In our tradition the true meaning of peaceful awareness is that although we are wretched beings, heavily burdened with bad karma and blind passions, on becoming aware of how inconceivable it is that the Power of Amida's Vow – the efficient cause [of birth in the Pure Land] – is directed toward saving us such worthless beings, we entrust ourselves singleheartedly and steadfastly to Amida Tathāgata without any contriving on our part. When we thus become completely free of doubt and firm in mindfulness, Amida's unimpeded light shines forth and embraces us. People who have attained faith decisively in this way will, each and every one of them, be born in the Land of Enjoyment – ten out of every ten. People who understand in this way are called people who have attained Other Power faith decisively.

What we should understand after this is that, whether sleeping or waking, all we should do is pronounce "*Namu Amida-butsu*" out of gratitude to Amida Tathāgata for all he has done for us and out of appreciation for the vastness of the Buddha's loving kindness. What else, then, do we need besides this for Rebirth? Is it not truly deplorable that there are some who confuse others by propagating false teachings that have not been transmitted properly and about which they themselves are by no means certain, and that by doing so they furthermore contaminate the stream of the Dharma? This matter calls for a great deal of careful thought.

Most humbly and respectfully
On 15th July, Bunmei 7 [1475].

COMMENTS

This is the last of the ninety-one dated letters written by Rennyo Shōnin during his five-year stay (1471–1475) at Yoshizaki in Echizen Province.[281] After writing this letter on 15th July 1475, Rennyo Shōnin was forced to leave Yoshizaki toward the end of August of that year, despite the fact that as a result of his teaching the number of Shin followers was still rapidly expanding. According to one letter written on 2nd August in 1473,[282] there were by then already over one hundred *taya* houses in existence at Yoshizaki.

Not only in Yoshizaki, where Rennyo lived, but also in many other villages of Hokuriku District, strong communal ties between Shin Buddhist followers sprang up. On the other hand such very rapid growth on the part of such communities in Hokuriku led to a certain amount of involvement in the political conflicts of local government. In July 1474 Rennyo Shōnin's Honganji Sangha helped Togashi Masachika in his fight against his own younger brother, Togashi Yukichiyo, himself allied with another Shin Buddhist tradition, the Senjuji Sangha. Having emerged victorious against his brother, Togashi Masachika became the provincial lord of Kaga Province, but was later vanquished in the Shin Buddhist uprising of 1488, after which Kaga Province was governed for ninety years by farmers belonging to the Shin Buddhist community. During the long years of the Japanese feudal period Kaga Province was the only one to be governed by farmers.

Reading the fourth article set out in this letter "We should not slight the provincial military governors or local land stewards," it is safe to assume there must have been some conflicts with local government. At least one instance of disagreement went on historical record when in 1475 Honganji followers in Kaga Province refused to pay their taxes. Rennyo, however, based on an inner conviction, often repeated in his letters, that one should entrust oneself entirely to the Buddha-dharma in the inner world and at the same time respect and observe the regulations of society in the outer world, expressly warned his followers against violating the rules of this world. His words in the first paragraph, "They should entrust themselves in their innermost hearts entirely to the Buddha-dharma but make no sign of this in their outward behaviour," are related to this inner conviction. He must have come to cherish this principle as a natural result of his experiences following the Shin Buddhist teaching as a leader of the Honganji Sangha.

Since people and society are forever changing, any generalisation such as saying that it is always right to obey the rules of society can at times be dangerous. We have to be alert to the change of our society and from time to time steer our course in a better direction. When doing so, however, we should always be careful to maintain a sense of inner peace and make sure we constantly return to the Buddha-dharma. Unless we are careful to do this, social activities, even those undertaken in pursuit of world peace, will only create further conflicts. In Buddhism the principle of returning to inner peace should always be seen as our ultimate concern, regardless of what we may be doing in the world. Social activities and regulations are relative and limited. If they become our ultimate concern, this can lead to discord in human relationships and as well as to mental distortion. Taking refuge in Amida Buddha allows us to keep our ultimate concern ultimate, and secondary concerns secondary. Through the attainment of pure faith Amida's light shines through our consciousness transparently. We are better able to live peacefully in the world if we maintain this inner relation with the Buddha-dharma.

Another important concern of this letter is, as highlighted in article number one, "We should not belittle Shintō shrines," is the Shin Buddhist relationship to *kami* or *shinmei*.

The descriptions Rennyo gave to the notion of *kami* or *shinmei* in his letters, including the third letter of Fascicle Two and the tenth letter of Fascicle Three are all based on the Buddhist theory known as *honji suijaku setsu*,[283] in which Japanese gods are explained as being manifestations of Buddhas or Bodhisattvas. As regards this term, *honji* means the original state, *suijaku*, manifestation and *setsu*, theory. According to both the Tendai and Shingon systems of Esoteric Buddhism, which were introduced to Japan by Saichō and Kūkai and developed in the Kamakura period, Japanese gods in their original state are held to have been Buddhas and Bodhisattvas.

Generally speaking Japanese Buddhism as a whole adopted this syncretic system, based on the teaching of *tri-kāya* or three-fold Buddha-body, and it was through the doctrine of *honji suijaku* that the notion of *kami*, deeply rooted in the Japanese tradition, was assimilated into Buddhism. An illustration of this philosophy can be found in the following phrase quoted by Rennyo Shōnin in his letter: "'Softening the light and conforming to the dust' is the first step in forming relationships [with sentient beings]; 'Attaining Enlightenment by going through the eight stages' is the completion of the act of benefiting sentient beings." This quotation is based on a passage from the *Makashikan* 摩訶止觀 (ch. *Móhēzhǐguān*) by Zhìyǐ 智顗 (538–597)[284] and the specific phrase "softening the light and conforming to the dust" originates from Lǎozǐ's *Dàodéjīng*.[285] It is a famous poetic expression of the manifestation of the Buddhas and Bodhisattvas as *kami*.

In the history of Shin Buddhism the *Shojin hongai shū*[286] or *Collection of Passages on the Original Intention of Gods* by Zonkaku Shōnin (1290–1373) is important as a systematic description of the Shin Buddhist attitude to *kami*. According to Zonkaku, there are two groups of *kami*: benevolent gods as manifestations of Buddhas and Bodhisattvas who protect and lead people to entrust themselves to Amida Buddha and malevolent spirits – departed or living – that often threaten people with curses or punishments. Zonkaku states that we should respect gods of the first group but refrain from worshiping those of the second. It is not to any kind of god but to Amida Buddha that we should entrust ourselves with our whole being. It is said that the references to gods made by Rennyo in his letters are based on the *Shojin hongai shū*.

It may be difficult for us, however, to draw a distinct line between the two different groups of *kami*, because how they appear to us depends on our state of mind. If we have serious problems and seek the help of some external entity to provide a solution, that is not the Buddhist way. The cause of our problems in life lies definitely within our own existence, not outside it. If we follow the Buddha-dharma, we should look into ourselves for the solution of our difficulties in life. If we conjure up the image of outside help for the solution of our problems, we will be fettered by the image of some external being, god or demon, standing outside of ourselves. Looking for external aids like this gives rise to the concepts of demons, malevolent deities which are in themselves but reflections of our own minds. To put it more simply, if we seek a solution outside our own selves, we will find that our lives appear to be at the mercy of invisible and unpredictable forces.

Through the process of deep introspection, we become aware of the reality of our limited human consciousness and simultaneously of the working of the Dharma which is the unconditional love of Amida Buddha. At the very moment of this awakening we entrust ourselves to Amida Buddha and the illusory horizon of our former self, within which we were painfully attached to our world and existence, becomes transparent and permeable. Then, as we are freed from all attachments to our own world, Buddhas, Bodhisattvas and gods all appear to us as manifestations of the hidden truth or *Dharma-kāya*; indeed everything and everybody around us radiate the Light of Amida Buddha. The profound implication of this is that although we take refuge in Amida Buddha alone, and never in other Buddhas, gods or spirits, we find that those beings, too, support and protect us on our way to the Pure Land.

In summary, therefore, our experience of attaining pure faith leads us to encounter the true nature of *all* gods and spirits as protectors of the Dharma, and the distinction between benevolent and malevolent deities simply disappears. As Shinran Shōnin's *Verses on Benefits in the Present Life*[287] in the *The Jōdo Wasan* states,

> All the deities of heaven and earth
> Are called good gods,
> They all work together
> To protect *Nenbutsu* followers.[288]

> In the light of the Buddha of Unimpeded Light
> There reside innumerable Amida Buddhas.
> These Transformed Buddhas, all without exception,
> Protect followers of true faith.[289]

Being aware of this fact Shinran Shōnin teaches us that we need no longer be afraid of evil beings and their curses,

> Faith received from the inconceivable Power of the Vow
> Is none other than the Great Mind of Enlightenment,
> The bad deities that abound in heaven and earth
> All stand in awe of those who have ever attained it.[290]

The Meaning of the Annual Memorial Service for Shinran Shōnin

ON THE ANNUAL SERVICE HELD

EVERY YEAR WITHOUT FAIL

FASCICLE III, LETTER ELEVEN

To begin with, the twenty-eighth of this month is the day we commemorate the death of our Founder, Shōnin. We have been holding this Buddhist ceremony every year without fail in order to appreciate everything he has done for us and to respond in gratitude. Amongst all the Dharma friends from the various provinces and districts, including those of lower status, anyone failing to recognise all they have received from Shinran Shōnin is no different from wood or stone.

Old ignoramus that I am, for the past four or five years I have been living in a remote country spot in Hokuriku District, without really knowing why, surrounded by mountains and sea. And yet, against all expectations, here I am still alive and well, able to come to this province and attending this year, for the first time, the Hōonkō ceremony held here to honour Shōnin's anniversary.

All this is indeed the inconceivable result of past karmic conditions. It is certainly something to rejoice over time and time again.

Therefore, those who gather together from this and other provinces should first of all fully comprehend the meaning of the precepts laid down by our Founder, Shōnin. He told us, "Even if someone brands you a 'cattle thief,' do not react in such a way as to let them know you are a follower of the Buddha-dharma or as an aspirant for birth in the Pure Land." In addition to this, Shinran was kind enough to lay down that we should practise human love, justice, politeness, wisdom and fidelity, that we should honour the laws of the state, and that, deep within our hearts, we should take as our bedrock Other Power faith in the Original Vow.

Speaking from my own observation of the way people of today go about pretending they know the Buddha-dharma, such individuals may give the outward appearance of relying on the Buddha-dharma, but in reality they show no sign of decisive attainment of 'peaceful awareness', the one single path in our tradition. In addition, relying on their own literary abilities, they interpret sacred texts in idiosyncratic ways never learned from the tradition, and propagate false teachings about which they themselves are by no means certain. Strolling around among the followers of our own and other schools, they make up lie after lie and eventually, ostensibly under "orders from the head temple," they succeed in deceiving people, taking things from them and debasing the essential teaching of our tradition. Is this not truly despicable?

Therefore, unless in the course of the seven-day Hōonkō ceremony that commemorates the anniversary of the death of the Founder on the twenty-eighth of this month, such individuals repent and confess their bad thoughts, and turn each one to the right teaching, their visit to the temple will be entirely pointless; and if they attend this seven-day Hōonkō ceremony merely in order to imitate others, though they may profess to do so in response to all Shinran Shōnin has done for them and as an expression of their gratitude for his loving kindness, their coming will be of no avail whatsoever. Thus, it is only those who have attained faith through the working of Amida's Vow that can thank the Buddha from the bottom of their heart for all that he has done for them or respond gratefully to their teachers for all that they have done for them. Only those who thoroughly understand this and come to pay respect to Shōnin are truly in accord with Amida's intention. In particular they are possessed of a deep resolve to give thanks for what he has done for them and express in the course of the seven days of this month's anniversary their overriding sense of gratitude for his loving kindness.

Most humbly and respectfully
Written on 21st November, Bunmei 7 [1475].

COMMENTS

Buddhist memorial or anniversary services, currently somewhat popular in Japan, are a mixture of Confucian, Shintō and Buddhist ideas. For the most part, such ceremonies are held in order to placate or pacify the spirits or ghosts of the departed, or to guide the dead, supposedly still lingering in the dark world of illusion, more truly in the direction of the Pure Land or the world of Enlightenment. The living can do this, it is believed, by transferring to the deceased their own virtue, accrued from good deeds such as chanting sūtras, making offerings, building temples and stupas, producing Buddhist images and holding Dharma events. Generally speaking, behind such Buddhist services lies the Mahayanist philosophy that we are able to guide and save others by transferring to them a stock of virtues, accumulated by us as the result of our own good deeds.

In Shin Buddhism, however, the meaning of all these ceremonies is very different from that in other traditions. We, as Shin Buddhist followers, whether priests or lay people, hold memorial services simply in order to express our gratitude to the deceased for leading us to the teaching of salvation through faith alone. This teaching is of huge importance in our lives; it leads us to the most joyous experience, the ultimate solution of all life's problems, and it solves, too, problems involved in our relationships with those that have died. The purpose of conducting Shin Buddhist ceremonies, it must be stressed, is not to assist the dead on their journey to the Pure Land. It has nothing to do with virtue-transference.

Shinran Shōnin, Founder of Shin Buddhism, firmly rejected the idea of transferring virtues or merits from ourselves to others, regardless of whether those others are alive or dead. As a result of his own awakening of faith, arising from a deep introspection into his personal karmic existence, he contradicted the traditional notion of virtue-transference on the part of sentient beings, even the idea of transferring the virtue of our own *Nenbutsu* practice to others to assist in their birth in the Pure Land. To Shinran Shōnin there was something basically impure in the consciousness of transferring the virtue of any *Nenbutsu* practice onto others. According to his religious philosophy firmly based on his own pure faith-experience, not only the Buddha Name itself but also the *Nenbutsu* practice of pronouncing the Name has to be ascribed to Amida Buddha, since it is he who brought both about through his Original Prayer. Despite this basic truth, Shinran Shōnin declares, we still maintain a tenacious inclination to view the Name, or the *Nenbutsu*, as virtues on our part. Let me quote his own explanation from his main writing, *The Kyōgyōshinshō*: "Generally all the sages of Mahāyāna and Hinayāna and all good people take the auspicious Name of the Original Prayer for their own root of good. Therefore, they cannot give rise to faith and do not realise the Buddha's wisdom."[291]

Even if we are entirely engaged in a pure act, or in doing for the doing, if we still retain a conscious sense that we are doing something good and remain proud of our good deed, our minds cannot be called pure. The fundamental problem here is our tenacious attachment to the dualistic notion of good, or the opposition between good and bad. Usually we think we are good, practise what is believed to be good and are attached to the thought that we have been doing good as good people. The only way for us to solve this problem is, Shinran Shōnin declares, attaining pure faith by entrusting ourselves entirely to Amida's Original Vow or to his Name given to us through the Original Vow. In our world of duality there appears that which is good and that which is bad, but under the light of the Buddha's teaching, there can in fact be no discrimination between good and bad or even evil. Actually there is no goodness on our part, no goodness that we can be proud of.

The highest good in Pure Land Buddhism is the act of pronouncing the Name, something that originates in the Buddha's Original Vow and belongs to the Buddha. The words cited above from *The Kyōgyōshinshō* refer to this point and criticise the impurity of our minds that takes the Auspicious Name or the act of reciting the Name for "our own root of good." It was one of Shinran Shōnin's greatest achievements to clarify this fundamental problem of our lives, namely our tenacious attachment to the notion of good or self-power achievement of good, and to open up a path to salvation or the ultimate awakening through faith alone, the faith of entrusting ourselves absolutely to the Name of the Original Vow. Shin Buddhist followers are confident that this is the only gateway that leads them unfailingly to solve all their life problems in the here and now, freely and spontaneously. Hence their boundless sense of gratitude to Shinran Shōnin for all that he has done for them. They hold this Hōonkō ceremony every year, saying that their spiritual calendar stretches from the very end of Hōonkō right up until the next Hōonkō celebration to be held in one year's time.

Towards the end of the first paragraph of this letter, you will notice a rather strange phrase, "no different from wood and stone." The comparison, in fact, is based on a line from the *Shōbōnen sho kyō* 正法念處經: "If people witness aging and death and feel no fear, they are called 'thoughtless,' they remain 'like wood and stone.' Although they are born as human beings, they are like animals."[292] The phrase "no different from wood and stone" implies an insensitivity to matters that should be of the utmost importance to us as human beings.

The second paragraph of the letter is about Rennyo's own happiness at being able to attend the Hōonkō ceremony in this particular province after four or five years spent at Yoshizaki in Hokuriku District. He stayed at Yoshizaki, in fact, from 1471 to 1475. What is referred to here as "this province" is actually Kawachi Province, part of modern day Ōsaka.

The third paragraph refers to Shinran Shōnin's caution to his followers: "Even if someone brands you a 'cattle thief,' do not react in such a way as to let them know you are a follower of the Buddha-dharma or as an aspirant for birth in the Pure Land." According to a reliable source, the *Nihon kokugo daijiten* 日本國語大辞典 *The Great Dictionary of the Japanese Language*, this Japanese term of reproach, *ushinusubito* 牛盗人, a cattle thief or stealer of cows, has two meanings: either those who really do steal cows or secondly taciturn, sluggish individuals. The second meaning, already prevalent in the time, may well have stemmed from the first, as most of those caught stealing cows remained silent. Shinran Shōnin and Rennyo Shōnin would have been using the term in this secondary meaning.[293]

In the latter part of the third paragraph Rennyo states: "In addition to this, Shinran was kind enough to lay down that we should practise human love, justice, politeness, wisdom and fidelity, that we should honour the laws of the state, and that deep within our hearts we should take as our bedrock Other Power faith in the Original Vow." Of the three regulations that we are asked to observe as Shin Buddhists, the first two, concerning morality and law, relate to the way we should conduct our lives in the actual world. The third relates to the way we should live out our faith in the spiritual world. In Shin Buddhism the third is always the foundation of the first and second. Without attaining pure faith we are unable to lead our lives peacefully in this world.

The next paragraph of the letter is about the erroneous way of living observed in those who have never attained peaceful awareness, despite their outward appearance of relying on the Buddha-dharma. It concerns those who try and teach people without having first attained true faith themselves. This is a very serious problem within the Sangha.

Thus what is of vital importance for those who would like to be true followers of the Shin Buddhist Sangha is the attainment of faith by entrusting themselves entirely to Amida Buddha. It is said in the Shin Buddhist tradition that once we attain true faith we are brought to the stage of nonretrogression and we find ourselves numbered amongst those who are assured of birth in the Pure Land. In the concluding paragraph, however, Rennyo refers furthermore to "repentance." Why do we need to repent even after the attainment of faith? It is because, even if we have reached the stage of nonretrogression, as long as we continue living in this world, we will frequently find ourselves in conflict with others, entangled as we are with blind passions and tenacious attachments. Amida Buddha made his Original Vow in order to save just such wretched beings like us. Becoming aware of the sad reality of our existence enables us to be awakened to the unconditional love of Amida Buddha, the working of his Original Vow, itself the foundation that sustains the stage of nonretrogression. Repentance and joy are two aspects of faith-experience, being inextricably mingled with each other.

When you feel dismayed at finding yourself enmeshed in your tenacious attachments, selfishly hurting others, there is no need to hesitate before you shed tears and repent. Let your tears flow as much as you like under the light of the Buddha. You will immediately find yourself in the embrace of Amida's great compassion. To put it another way, because you are full of blind passions and unpleasant attachments, your birth in the Pure Land is even more assured by virtue of the Original Vow.

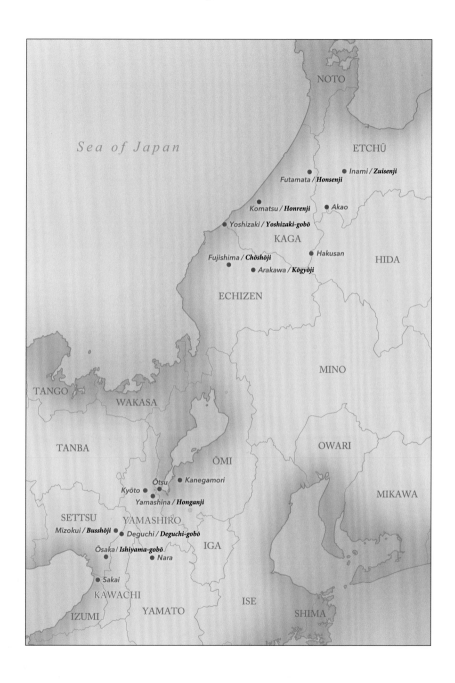

FIG.1 A map showing places in the Medieval Period
related to Rennyo's life, produced by Emmyo Sato.

FIG. 2 Rennyo's self-portrait in the possession of Gantokuji, Osaka.

FIG.3 Statue of Rennyo owned by Shogyoji, Fukuoka. Carved by Kōkei Eri modelled after the statue of Rennyo in the possession of Gantokuji, Osaka.

FIG. 4 Rennyo's calligraphy of the Name in six
characters of *kaisho* style, at Kōshūji, Fukui.

FIG.5 Rennyo's calligraphy of the Name in nine
characters of *gyōsho* style, at Gantokuji, Osaka.

FIG.6 Rennyo's calligraphy of the Name in six
characters of *sōsho* style, at Hōrenji, Ōita.

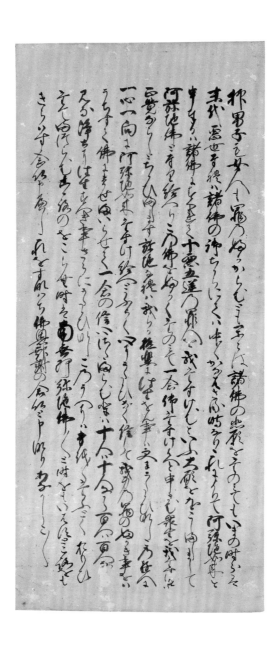

FIG.7 The fourth Letter of Fascicle Five, Rennyo's handwriting,
in the possession of Otani University Library, Kyoto.

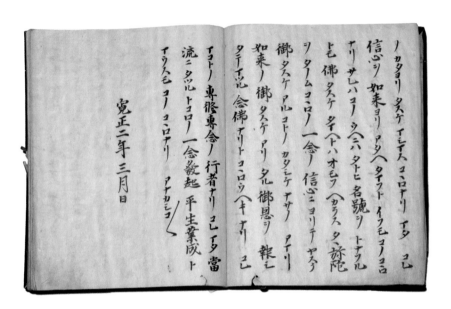

ノ カタヨリ タスケ イモアヌ ココロアリ イタ ゝム

信心ヲ 如来ヨリ アタヘ タイフト イフモ コノ ココ

ナリ サレハ ヨリ ゝ ハ タトヒ 名號ヲ トナフル

ヒモ 佛 タスケ タイ〈トハオモフ〈カラス タ弥陀

シ タ〆ム コヽロノ 信心ニヨリテ ヤスウ

御 タスケ アルコトノ カタシケ ナサ〈 アイ〈

如来ノ 御 タスケ アリ 名 御恩ヲ 報シ

タシテイ况 念佛 ナリトココロウ〈〜…

イコトノ 専脩 専念ノ 行者ナリ コレタ 當

流ニ タツル トコロノ 一念 發起 平生業成 ト

イフスモ ヨノ ココロナリ アナカシコ

寛正二年三月日

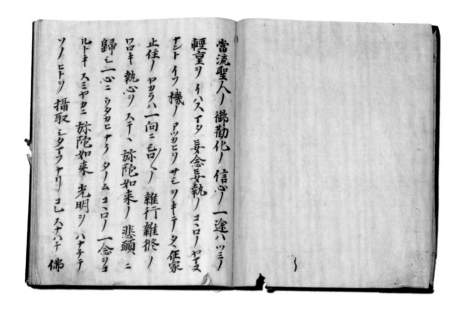

當流聖人ノ御勸化ノ信心ノ一途ハ、ツラ
ツラ愚案ヲメクラスイタ妄念妄執ノ、ココロ、ヤマヌ
モトイワ機ノアツカヒヲサミシキテタ征家
止住ノヤカラハ一向ニ吾レ／ノ雜行難終ノ
ワロキ執心ヲ、ステ、彌陀如来ノ悲願ニ
歸シ一心ニ、ウタカヒナク、タノム、ココロノ一念シ
ルトキ、スミヤカニ、彌陀如来、光明シ、ハナチテ
ソノ、ヒトヲ、攝取シタマフナリ、コレスナハチ佛

FIG. 8A & 8B Rennyo's first letter copied by Rennō,
his last wife, in the possession of Gantokuji, Osaka.

265

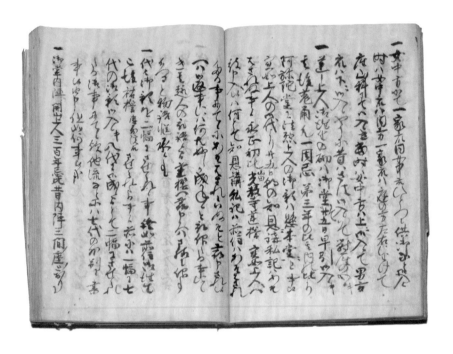

FIG.9 Article 45 of *Honganji sahō no shidai* by Jitsugo in his
own handwriting, in the possession of Gantokuji, Osaka.

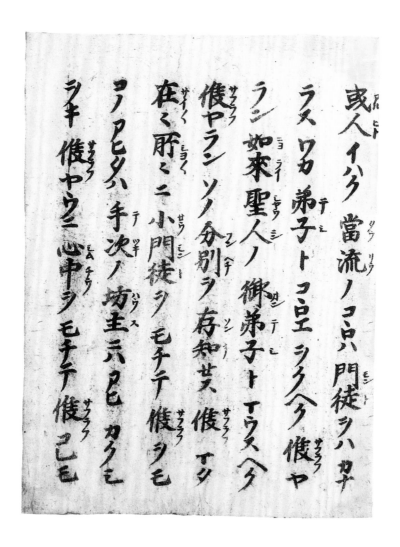

FIG.10 First page of the woodblock print version of *The Letters* published
by Shōnyo, in the possession of Otani University Library, Kyoto.

FIG.11 Pictures of the first scroll of *The Illustrated Biography of Rennyo Shōnin* at Hōtakuji, Shiga.

Chronologically from the bottom to the top

6) Escapes to Ōmi with Shinran's statue and leaves for Hokuriku.

5) Destruction of Honganji by warrior monks from Mt. Hiei.

4) Succession as Head Priest and attacks by warrior monks.

3) His ordination at Shōrenin.

2) Ishiyamadera Temple, where the portrait was later found.

1) Mother leaving Honganji with his portrait.

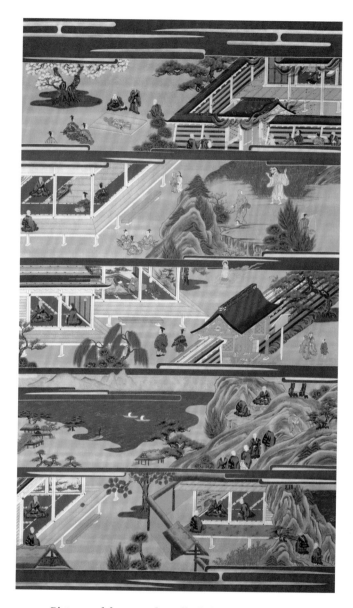

FIG.12 Pictures of the second scroll of *The Illustrated Biography of Rennyo Shōnin* at Hōtakuji, Shiga.

Chronologically from the bottom to the top

11) Fire at Yoshizaki-gobō and a priest dies saving a text.
10) The story of the flesh-adhering mask and Lord Asakura's homage.
9) His second daughter's death and teaching women.
8) Selection of Yoshizaki for a new temple.
7) Teaching at Echizen Province.

FIG.13 Pictures of the third scroll of *The Illustrated Biography of Rennyo Shōnin* at Hōtakuji, Shiga.

Chronologically from the bottom to the top

16) A Khitan and his family from China ask him to teach at Sakai.

15) Rennyo's radiance seen by Dōshū. A dream of Shinran and Hōnen.

14) Teaching at a temple at Deguchi in Kawachi Province.

13) Teaching at Wakasa Province on his way to Kawachi.

12) Departure from Yoshizaki due to a conflict in Kaga Province.

FIG.14 Pictures of the fourth scroll of *The Illustrated Biography of Rennyo Shōnin* at Hōtakuji, Shiga.

Chronologically from the bottom to the top

21) Cremation.

20) His death.

19) Building Ōsaka-gobō based on a vision and teaching Kyōkō.

18) Shinran's statue returns to Honganji at Yamashina.

17) Reconstruction of Honganji at Yamashina in Yamashiro.

FIG.15 *Kanoko no miei*, Rennyo's portrait wearing
a dapple-dyed cloth at the age of six owned by Hōrenji, Ōita.
A copy of the original portrait in the possession of Honsenji, Osaka.

CHAPTER FORTY-TWO

The Notion of Past Good Conditions in Shin Buddhism

ON THE PRESENCE OR ABSENCE

OF PAST GOOD CONDITIONS

FASCICLE III, LETTER TWELVE

In olden times and still to this day, many followers, calling themselves Buddhists, praise the Buddha-dharma and seek to impart its message at different places throughout the provinces, without, it would appear, having their hearts truly grounded in the right teaching of our tradition.

How can this be?

The reason first of all is that these people, despite never having received instruction from an authentic teacher, still believe they fully understand the fundamental principles of the Buddha-dharma. Their attitude to the Dharma is that of an outsider who, with no serious involvement, approaches and listens to the Dharma, from the edge of a veranda, as it were, or from outside a sliding door. Although their aspirations towards the Buddha-dharma remain in fact very shallow, such people nevertheless consider that no one knows better than they what the Buddha-dharma is all about. Consequently, on coming across others who joyfully extol the right teaching of our school in the traditional manner, such people remain tenaciously attached to their own particular views. Is it not in the first place arrogance on the part of these people that leads them to assume that they alone understand the teaching very well?

It is with this attitude of mind that they travel amongst followers of our tradition and read the sacred texts. In addition they flatter people, tell untruths, and take from others, declaring themselves to be messengers from the head temple whilst all the while merely going about doing their own private business. How can they be called good followers of the Buddha-dharma or readers of the sacred texts? This is utterly deplorable. There is nothing that we should lament more bitterly. Those wishing to speak about the teaching of our tradition and instruct others, therefore, should realise first and foremost that there are certain essential steps for them to follow.

When thinking about how to teach the Other Power faith of our tradition, we should first of all distinguish between those with past good conditions and those with no past good conditions. This is because, however long ago it may be that a person added his name to the list of participants in our tradition, it will still be difficult for someone with no past good conditions to attain faith. In the case of those whose past good conditions have unfolded, however, faith will come about decisively, indeed, of its own accord. Thus, when we discuss the two kinds of practice – right practice and miscellaneous practice – in the presence of people with no past good conditions, it may provide cause for slander quite contrary to our expectations. It is entirely against the rules of conduct of our tradition for us to extensively teach worldly people without ourselves understanding this principle of the presence or absence of past good conditions.

Thus *The Larger Sūtra* states, "If a person is bereft of roots of good, he will be unable to hear this sūtra" and, "To hear this sūtra and to maintain joyful faith *(shingyō)* are the most difficult of all difficulties, with nothing surpassing these difficulties."[294] In addition Shàndǎo states, "If those who already practised this Dharma at one time in the past are able to hear it again now, they will immediately give birth to joy."[295] According to the sūtra as well as the commentary, it is clear that everything depends on past good conditions. Thus we now understand that we should watch over those with past good conditions and transmit to them the dharma of our tradition. In order to instruct others we must be fully aware ourselves of what this teaching is all about.

In particular, first of all, the laws of State are to be respected as fundamental. While according priority to the principles of human love and justice, follow the generally accepted customs of society, deep within yourself embrace the peaceful awareness of our tradition and, outwardly, conduct yourself in such a way that the transmission of the dharma you have received will not be evident to those of other schools and other traditions. A person with this kind of understanding is seen as someone who has fully realised the right meaning of the true teaching of our tradition.

Most humbly and respectfully
On 27th January, Bunmei 8 [1476]

COMMENTS

After withdrawing from Yoshizaki for political reasons, Rennyo Shōnin moved to Kawachi Province, part of modern day Ōsaka, in the summer of 1475. This letter was written at Deguchi in Kawachi Province on 27th January 1476 when he was sixty-two years old.

This letter is all about how to teach people Shin Buddhism. The first half represents Rennyo's admonition of those who try and teach the Buddha-dharma without first attaining true faith themselves. And the second half is about the importance of distinguishing between the audience who have past good conditions and those who have not.

The problem referred to in the first paragraph is in no way confined to Rennyo Shōnin's Sangha but is generally to be found in all kinds of religious orders, be they Buddhist, Christian or Muslim. To me what seems of significance is the fact that Rennyo pointed out the problem so exactly and chastised his followers so vigorously right in the process of establishing his own religious order. Sadly, however, there is something about our intellectual nature as human beings that makes us want to teach others about fundamental aspects of religion, be it Faith or Enlightenment, when we ourselves have not experienced them. "Without having our hearts truly grounded in the right teaching of our tradition," as Rennyo says in his letter, we still try to instruct others in matters beyond the scope of words, beyond the reach of intellectual, logical understanding.

"How can this be?" Rennyo Shōnin answers his own question: "The reason first of all is that these people, despite never having received instruction from an authentic teacher, still believe they fully understand the fundamental principles of the Buddha-dharma."

This answer brings to the surface the problem underlying the attitude of all those who would teach others without first experiencing the Buddha-dharma themselves. As you know, it is through the interpersonal relationship between master and disciple that the Buddha-dharma is handed down to succeeding generations. It is transmitted from person to person through each individual's experience of true encounter. These would-be religious instructors described by Rennyo as "never having received instruction from an authentic teacher," however, appear to enjoy no such interpersonal involvement.

Reluctant to face the real problems with their lives that they would be forced to confront in an encounter with a real teacher, they choose to remain outsiders. Rennyo says, "Their attitude to the Dharma is that of an outsider who, with no serious involvement, approaches and listens to the Dharma, from the edge of a veranda, as it were, or from outside a sliding door." Do you not love this beautiful description by Rennyo of these people's attitude to the Dharma, an attitude that may be ours, too, from time to time as we try and avoid facing up to our lives? Because they have no insight into the true problems underlying their lives, their understanding of Buddhism, despite what they think, has no depths whatsoever. In his letter Rennyo says "Although their aspirations towards the Buddha-dharma remain in fact very shallow, such people nevertheless consider that no one knows better than they what the Buddha-dharma is all about." As described in the last lines of the second paragraph, such lack of depth is the reason not only for these people's tenacious attachment to their own views but also for their arrogant assumption that they alone are fully conversant with the Dharma.

In the second half of the letter, Rennyo goes on to speak of the vital importance of awareness of 'past good conditions' (宿善 shukuzen).

What does he mean exactly when he refers to distinguishing between those with past good conditions and those without?

When considering this question, I would first of all like to reflect briefly on the Shin Buddhist definition of true faith discussed in previous chapters. The essence of Shin Buddhist faith lies in simultaneous awakening, firstly to oneself (機 ki), or the irredeemable reality of one's karmic existence, and secondly to the Dharma (法 Hō), or Amida Buddha's unconditional love that saves all beings with no discrimination. These are two aspects of one and the same experience.

As concerns awakening to the Dharma (ho), it is absolutely clear that there exists no discrimination whatsoever. True faith is an awareness of the Dharma, or Amida's unconditional love, that vows to save all sentient beings without discrimination. At the same time, true faith is also an awareness of self, or the sad reality of one's karmic existence. Each individual has his or her own unique karmic existence. Illumined by the light of Amida Buddha's unconditional love for us, we awaken to the sad reality of our whole existence and entrust ourselves to that unconditional love that never discriminates.

What, then, does the distinction between those with past good conditions and those without signify in the context of the Sangha? If we think of the multitudes of people who must have come flocking to Rennyo Shōnin's temple from far and near, some would have already awoken to pure faith, whilst others would not. Whilst some would have been very serious about the Great

Matter of Rebirth in the Pure Land, others might simply have been there out of curiosity. People's motives for visiting the temple would have been varied to say the least. Given this situation, Rennyo would have wanted to be very careful when issuing instructions to his followers about the direction they should take. Within the context of the Sangha, the right way to lead people to peaceful awareness would have been extremely difficult for Rennyo to manage and closely connected with the emphasis he laid on the distinction between those with past good conditions and those without. If, for instance, we fail to take into consideration the maturity or otherwise of people's spiritual condition when encouraging them to understand Shin Buddhism, it may be too much for those who are not yet ready to listen and will merely invite slander or opposition to our tradition. Rennyo's deep consideration of the notion of 'past good conditions' may have been closely related to such practical problems within the Sangha.

CHAPTER FORTY-THREE

Ultimate and Relative Truth

FOLLOWERS OF OUR TRADITION

FASCICLE III, LETTER THIRTEEN

Followers of our tradition, both those who have already attained peaceful awareness and those who have yet to do so, should bear in mind the following points:

First and foremost, as concerns the outward world, look upon the laws of the state as fundamental, never belittle any of the gods, Buddhas, or Bodhisattvas and never slander other schools or other teachings. Regarding your relationship to local authorities such as provincial military governors and local land owners, do not treat them disrespectfully and be sure to meet in full all fixed yearly tributes and payments to officials. In addition, respect as absolutely fundamental the principles of human love and justice.

In your inner world, in order to attain Rebirth, entrust yourself single-heartedly and steadfastly to Amida Tathāgata without attachment to any of the miscellaneous practices and miscellaneous good acts. When you entrust yourself with not a single doubting thought, you will be born without fail in the true and real Pure Land of Utmost Bliss. Once you have realised this you are to be called a *Nenbutsu* follower who has attained Amida Tathāgata's Other Power faith.

When you attain faith in the *Nenbutsu* in this way, you should also realise that, although we are wretched beings deeply burdened with bad karma and committing wrongdoing throughout our lives, once we awaken to faith with the one thought-moment of taking refuge, we are readily saved by the working of the Buddha's Vow-power. Thus, with deep appreciation of Amida Tathāgata's inconceivable Original Vow, that entirely surpasses this world, as being the strongest condition for our awakening of faith, we should simply recite the *Nenbutsu*, sleeping or waking, responding with gratitude to Amida Tathāgata for all he has done for us.

Whatever else you may know beyond this truth, it will be of no use for Rebirth in the Pure Land. Nevertheless, there are many people nowadays who speak incorrectly – I wonder what impels them to do so – about strange, distorted teachings that have been transmitted improperly, thereby not only confusing others but also polluting the unsurpassed flow of the Dharma water. What a deplorable situation this is! We must think about it very carefully.

Most humbly and respectfully
On 18th July, Bunmei 8 [1476]

COMMENTS

As you see from the last line, Rennyo wrote this letter on 18th July, 1476, a year after his departure from Yoshizaki.

Looking back at the various experiences he underwent in his Sangha, especially at Yoshizaki, he carefully gives his followers instructions about the direction they should take in their lives, regardless of whether they have already attained faith or are yet to attain it. The letter is addressed to those who are aware of the vital importance faith plays in Shin Buddhism.

This letter discusses the way of life Shin Buddhists should adopt in order to attain birth in the Pure Land, focusing particularly on *shintai* 真諦, the ultimate aspect of truth or absolute truth (skt. *paramārtha-satya*) and on *zokutai* 俗諦, the secular aspect of truth or relative truths (skt. *saṃvṛti-satya*). In Buddhism these two aspects are considered to be indispensable to one another. Generally speaking they are closely interrelated and support one another.

In Shin Buddhism *shintai*, or ultimate truth, means the way in which one should attain Buddhahood, whilst *zokutai*, or secular truth, means the way one should behave in this world as a member of the Shin Buddhist society.

In the second paragraph of the letter Rennyo asks his followers, who are very much taken up with *shintai*, or the attainment of true faith, to be mindful also of *zokutai* and the need to respect others. Those who are not involved in *shintai* or the absolute truth will not be very serious about the problem of their relationship to *zokutai* or relative truths. Based on the true faith of entrusting themselves to Amida Buddha, Shin Buddhists lead their worldly lives harmoniously with others, always aware of Amida's unconditional love that embraces all and forsakes none.

In the third paragraph Rennyo talks about *shintai*, the way of becoming a Buddha within this tradition in words that are solely concerned with how we are to attain pure faith. According to the religious philosophy of Shinran Shōnin, the only possible way for us ignorant beings to become Buddhas is through the attainment of faith, after which life on the way to the Pure Land is lived with deepest gratitude to the Buddha who saves absolutely everyone without any sort of discrimination.

In Shin Buddhism, entrusting oneself absolutely to Amida Buddha is accompanied both by an instantaneous awakening to oneself, or to the unredeemable reality of one's karmic existence and at the same time by an awakening to the Dharma, or to the unconditional love of Amida Buddha. After entrusting oneself to Amida Buddha at the moment of this awakening, faith continues as a peaceful awareness of oneself and of the Buddha by virtue of the infinite light of Amida Buddha that protects all those of pure faith throughout their lives, embracing all and abandoning none. The fourth paragraph of the letter beautifully describes this aspect of Shin Buddhist life.

It then continues as a twofold form of awareness: awareness of the unredeemable reality of one's existence and awareness of the unconditional love of Amida Buddha. This is known in Japanese as *nishu jinshin,* literally "two aspects of deep faith." Shin Buddhism holds that 'true faith' always has these two aspects. True faith is dynamic in this respect, but it is at the same time peaceful as followers are aware of it as the working of Amida Buddha. After the attainment of this peaceful awareness their practice of *Nenbutsu* is actually the expression of "gratitude to Amida Tathāgata for all he has done for us." What underlies and supports their way of living *zokutai,* or the secular aspect of truth, in this world is this peaceful awareness of Amida's unconditional love that embraces all and forsakes none.

It goes without saying that respect to *zokutai* is not some kind of blind submission to the worldly authority. A Shin Buddhist with true faith who is really aware of him or herself keeps their sense organs and intellect free and open. Let us think about interpersonal relationships, for example, that of husband and wife. Respect for one another is absolutely essential, but their relationship should not be that of blind obedience. Otherwise their love would all too easily falter. We should be aware of the reality of this world as it is and should not be afraid of facing that reality. It is through this confrontation with reality that we are awakened to ourselves and to Amida Buddha.

The last paragraph of the letter shows just how widespread various mis-construed teachings were at that time. Rennyo Shōnin frequently admonishes his followers for deviating from true teaching. See particularly the fourteenth letter of Fascicle Two and the eighth letter of Fascicle Three. Misconstrued teaching is actually caused by failure to attain Other Power faith, or, in other words, by dependence on self power. If you remain attached to divergent wrong teachings, it will damage not only yourself but also those around you. The only way we can avoid this perversion of Buddhist teaching is to return to true faith by taking refuge in Amida Tathāgata.

CHAPTER FORTY-FOUR

Attaining Faith and Teaching Others

ON SHINSHŪ *NENBUTSU* FOLLOWERS

FASCICLE IV, LETTER ONE

Amongst the Shinshū Nenbutsu followers there are all too many who have simply failed to grasp the heart of the teaching. For this reason I set down almost all the salient points and from now on, therefore, followers of the same faith should regard those points as being fundamental.

Two matters in particular need emphasising. Firstly, before all else, you must attain peaceful awareness (*anjin*) through which you become assured of your own birth [in the Pure Land]. Secondly, when teaching others, you should be aware of whether or not they have past good conditions (*shukuzen*). It is vital for you to keep these two principles in mind.

With regard to your own birth, therefore, take care to preserve in the depths of your innermost mind the faith that was awakened in the one thought-moment. Take pleasure, too, in pronouncing the Buddha Name in gratitude to him for all that he has done for us through Other Power. In addition be sure to prioritise the laws of the state and look upon human love and human justice as of fundamental importance. Furthermore, do not slight other Buddhas or other Bodhisattvas or belittle other teachings or other schools. Simply pursue a normal way of life as practised in this world. In dealing with the outside, do not show to those who belong to other schools and other teachings the way we teach the Dharma in our tradition. Those who behave correctly in this way can be rightly declared Shinshū *Nenbutsu* followers who observe the regulations of our tradition, the tradition of Shōnin. Since nowadays we live in an age when people with their biased way of thinking are determinedly listening out for things to criticise and spread in a slanderous way, you should be very careful when choosing what to do.

The 'threefold faith of Other Power,' as taught in our tradition, is described in the Eighteenth Vow as 'sincerity, joyous faith and aspiration for birth in my land.' Although we call this 'threefold faith,' it is simply the One Mind with which followers take refuge in, and entrust themselves to, Amida. For it is with the awakening of the one thought-moment, in which those followers whose past good conditions have been unfolded take refuge in Amida Buddha, that the Buddha with his mind-light embraces those who have thus taken refuge. Referring to this moment, we speak of 'threefold faith – sincerity, joyous faith and aspiration for birth.' The passage on the fulfilment of the Vow further explains this faith as 'immediately being born and abiding in nonretrogression.' A person in this stage is also called 'a follower of true faith,' 'a follower deeply endowed with past causes [for birth in the Pure Land],' or 'one who has completed the cause in ordinary life.'

Thus, whether we call it taking refuge in Amida or attaining faith, there is nothing that is not related to one's 'past good conditions.' We realise in this way that if those who seek birth through the *Nenbutsu* are not endowed with past causes that impel them to attain faith, then it is impossible for them to attain birth in the Land of Enjoyment. With regard to this point Shōnin stated, "If you happen to realise this practice and faith, rejoice over your karmic conditions accumulated since the distant past."[296] Consequently people in our tradition hold that our efforts to teach others will be completely futile if we fail to be aware of whether or not they have past good conditions. For this reason you should teach others in a way that takes into consideration the presence or absence of their past good conditions.

Recently followers of the Buddha-dharma from within our tradition have been talking indiscreetly about the teaching, with no clear understanding of what is right and what is wrong. We realise that it is for this reason that the true meaning of Shinshū has been utterly lost. Before you can proclaim the teaching of our tradition you must first comprehend the details discussed above.

Most humbly and respectfully
On 8th January, Bunmei 9 [1477]

COMMENTS

This letter, the first of Fascicle Four, was written on 8th January 1477, as you see in the last line. The first paragraph refers to the reason Rennyo Shōnin has been writing quite so many letters to his followers since handing the very first one to Dōsai in 1461, a letter that was itself, in fact, not included in *The Letters*.

In the second paragraph Rennyo states the two main points he wishes to make clear in this letter. The first is about 'how to practise the Buddha-dharma by oneself (*jigyō* 自行)' and the second about 'how to teach it to others (*keta* 化他).' Needless to say, it is absolutely essential for Buddhists to fulfil these two requirements properly, both *jigyō* and *keta*. It is said in Buddhism in general that either one of these is indispensable for the completion of the Buddhist way. In the context of Shin Buddhism, *jigyō* corresponds to how to attain the peaceful awareness in the here and now and continue to live the faith for the rest of one's life and *keta* stands for how to lead others to the attainment of pure faith.

The third paragraph of the letter is all about the Shin Buddhist concept of *jigyō*, or how to attain pure faith and live it to the very end of one's life. Concerning the awakening of faith, Rennyo asks his followers to take care to preserve in the depths of their innermost mind "the faith that was awakened in the one thought-moment." Regarding the third paragraph, however, it seems that the most important request Rennyo Shōnin wants to make of his followers is contained in the last sentence, "Since nowadays we live in an age when people with their biased way of thinking are determinedly listening out for things to criticise and spread in a slanderous way, you should be very careful when choosing what to do."

In the fourth paragraph of the letter Rennyo concentrates on clarifying the notion of faith, the most important part of the *jigyō* aspect in the Shin Buddhist teaching and one that is firmly based on Pure Land texts such as *The Larger Sūtra of Eternal Life*, Vasubandhu's *Treatise on the Pure Land* and Shinran Shōnin's main work *Kyōgyōshinshō*. First of all, he talks about 'threefold faith of Other Power': "The 'threefold faith of Other Power,' as taught in our tradition, is described in the Eighteenth Vow as 'sincerity, joyous faith and aspiration for birth in my land.'" The Eighteenth Vow from *The Larger Sūtra of Eternal Life* states:

"If, upon my attaining Buddhahood, all beings in the ten quarters, in all sincerity and joyous faith, aspiring to be born in my country and pronouncing my Name up to ten times, were not to be born there, then may I not attain the Supreme Enlightenment."[297]

Shinran Shōnin, in his interpretation of the Eighteenth Vow,[298] had pointed out in *The Kyōgyōshinshō* that the true faith, as expounded in *The Larger Sūtra of Eternal Life*, consists of three elements, 'sincerity, joyous faith and aspiration for birth in the Pure Land,' and called it the triple mind of the Original Vow and, sometimes, the threefold faith. He then went on to argue in *The Kyōgyōshinshō* that the triple mind of the Original Vow – sincerity, joyous faith and aspiration for birth – amounted to three aspects of the One Mind, referred to in the *gāthā* portion of *The Treatise on the Pure Land* by Bodhisattva Vasubandhu: "O World-honoured One, *with one mind*, I take refuge in the Tathāgata of Unimpeded Light entirely pervading the ten quarters."[299]

The special term mind-light (心光 *shinkō*) needs some explanation. According to Shinran Shōnin's usage of the word 'mind-light,' it is understood as standing in contrast to 'form-light (色光 *shikikō* or *shikkō*).' As such it refers to Amida's Great Compassion that embraces all who entrust themselves to him and abandons no one. 'Form-light,' or the physical light that issues from Amida's body, on the other hand, though it illumines all sentient beings all over the world, is said to work simply as a form of "one-way light," so to speak, invisible to us actual beings. Only when we entrust ourselves to Amida Buddha at the moment of awakening to Amida's light, it reveals itself to us as the mind-light that embraces all and abandons none. When we talk about Amida's light, we ourselves differentiate between 'mind-light' and 'form-light,' but actually there is no difference between the two other than that occasioned by our own state of mind.

The fourth paragraph, written to clarify the content of the Shin Buddhist faith in greater detail, ends with the suggestion that 'a follower of true faith' is a person "deeply endowed with past causes for birth in the Pure Land." Thus it leads seamlessly to the fifth paragraph that deals with the *keta* aspect of faith.

In the fifth paragraph Rennyo states that, because the attainment of true faith is inevitably related to the maturity of one's past good conditions, when we teach others how to attain faith, we must be aware of whether or not their past good conditions are sufficiently mature for the attainment of faith.

If, as a Shin Buddhist devotee, you urge someone to embrace the Shin Buddhist teaching at a time when their past good conditions are not yet sufficiently mature to allow the attainment of faith, then it will certainly lead to many serious problems, both on a personal and social level. Whether or not to embrace a religion is strictly a matter of personal decision and trying to impose religious faith on others will only serve to stir up trouble, if they are not yet mentally ready for such a step. If, on the other hand, you simply ignore those around you who need your help and whose mental state is ripe for the attainment of faith, then you will be demonstrating a lack of true friendship and concern for others. Thus, Rennyo says, "For this reason you should teach others in a way that takes into consideration the presence or absence of their past good conditions."

What does the word *shukuzen* really mean? Literally it can be translated as 'past good conditions,' so does *shukuzen* refer to the accumulation
of one's own past good deeds? If so, might it not imply the need to try and
accumulate good deeds simply in order to attain true faith and, in that case,
indicate a reliance on doing good by self-power? But then would it not be
totally at variance with the notion of Other Power faith? In Buddhism, in
fact, *shukuzen* does not mean reliance on doing good by self-power. Rather
it represents the notion of faith in Other Power, the faith of entrusting
oneself absolutely to Amida Buddha. It is said in *The Tanni shō*, Chapter 3,
"Even a good person can attain birth [in the Pure Land], how much more
readily, then, a person with bad karma. Normally, however, people of the
world would say: 'Even a person with bad karma can attain birth, how much
more readily, then, a good person.' Although at first sight this latter view
appears perfectly reasonable, actually it runs counter to the purport of the
Original Vow, Other Power faith. This is because people who rely on doing
good through their own self-power fail to entrust themselves to Other Power
and are not, therefore, in accord with Amida's Original Vow. If, on the other
hand, they discard their reliance on self-power and entrust themselves to
Other Power, they will attain birth in the True Land of Enjoyment."[300]

According to my understanding, *shukuzen,* or 'past good conditions,'
stands for the individual relationship we each of us have to the Buddha-
dharma, a relationship gifted to us by the outside world, no matter whether
we are conscious of it or not. In this respect, *shukuzen* is essentially that
which has been given to us. Roughly speaking *shukuzen* comprises:

1. All our connections with formless truth or the Dharma in itself since
   the beginningless past, of which we ourselves are usually totally
   unconscious.
2. All our connections with manifested forms of truth or the Dharma
   in its manifested forms, including Buddhist teachers and their
   teachings.
3. All our connections with people in this world as they help us attain
   the awakening of faith.
4. And, ultimately, all our connections with everything and everyone
   that work to help us reach true faith.

At the moment of attaining faith, all that is around us is seen and accepted
as 'good' beyond all forms of discrimination, even the distinction between
good and bad in this world. In other words, through the attainment of faith,
everything that we have ever been through or come across in the past is
seen and accepted as unequivocally 'good,' because they have cooperated
to help us reach the very moment of attaining faith, an instant when the

ultimate solution is to be given to all the problems of our lives. In short, *shukuzen* is at once both something good that has been given to us and our own involvement in it.

CHAPTER FORTY-FIVE

Pronouncing the *Nenbutsu* throughout Our Lives

ON THE LIFESPAN OF HUMAN BEINGS

FASCICLE IV, LETTER TWO

Listen, if we calculate the length of human life, the lifespan allotted to us in this period is fifty-six years. Thus, if we live to be fifty-six these days, that is really something special in itself. Taking into consideration the fact that I have now reached the grand old age of sixty-three years, therefore, I have already lived seven extra years. As everything is an effect of past karma, I cannot help wondering what kind of illness it will be that will eventually lay me low and lead to my death. But this is something that simply cannot be predicted.

As we observe the confusion of the world around us, especially because now is a time of utter instability, very sadly human suffering is totally out of control. If this world were a place where we could die on the spot whenever we wanted to, why would we have gone on living until now? The only place where we aspire to be born quickly is the Pure Land of Utmost Bliss, and the only thing that we desire to attain is the Buddha-body of no defilement. Those who, thanks to the wisdom of the Buddha, have obtained peaceful awareness of Other Power, through the one thought-moment of taking refuge, should respond with gratitude to the Buddha for all he has done for them by pronouncing the Name right up to the very end of their lives. Once they have realised this, why should their time of death, determined as it is by their past lives, be cut short prematurely? I cannot help wondering if they might be foolishly deluded. Such are the reflections I have concerning my own person, old ignoramus that I am. Others, too, should abide in this state of mind.

In particular our way of living in this world shows how oblivious we are to the uncertainty of life for young and old alike. Unaware that our existence is as ephemeral as a flash of lightning or the morning dew, we live our lives without realising that the wind of impermanence may blow at any moment. We go on, firmly believing that our lives will continue indefinitely, never aspiring at all for Rebirth into the Pure Land. This is an absolutely pitiful state of affairs.

From now on we should make haste to entrust ourselves to the Other Power of Amida Tathāgata's Original Vow. Steadfastly taking refuge in the Buddha of Eternal Life, we should aspire to birth in the true Land of Enjoyment and recite the *Nenbutsu*, that is, the pronouncing of the Name.

Most humbly and respectfully

When all of a sudden these thoughts entered my mind, I wrote them down in great haste, finishing before seven in the morning, on 17th September, Bunmei 9 [1477].

Shinshōin [Rennyo]
At the age of sixty-three.

> Although I wrote this
> it is simply a letter that
> flowed from my brush.
> Some of my wording, therefore,
> may indeed sound very odd.

COMMENTS

As seen from the last part of the letter, Rennyo wrote this letter quite suddenly and with considerable sense of inner urgency on 17th September 1477 when he was staying at Deguchi, now in modern day Ōsaka. The poem added at the very end of the letter further demonstrates how spontaneously his innermost feeling of compassion came out in the course of his writing to his followers. What it was actually that persuaded him to write this letter will be discussed later.

Rennyo starts with the subject of human lifespan. This notion of "the lifespan allotted to us in this period" calls for some explanation. In medieval Japan there were a number of different ways of calculating human lifespan based on Buddhist commentaries such as *Abhidharmakośa-bhāṣya* (阿毘達磨俱舎論 jp. *Abidatsuma kusha ron*). An explanation given by Minor L. Rogers and Ann T. Rogers in their book *Rennyo* says that "During Rennyo's time, there were various explanations in regard to the period in which Śākyamuni Buddha appeared in the world, but it was widely held to be the ninth period of the kalpa of existence (*jūkō* 住劫), during which the human lifespan decreased from 84,000 to 10 years at the rate of one year every hundred years. In *Kyōgyōshinshō* Shinran states that, as of Gennin 1 (1224), it has been 2,173 years since the Buddha's death. Therefore, when Rennyo wrote this letter in Bunmei 6 [1474], 2423 years after the Buddha's death, understood to have occurred when he was eighty, the life-span would have decreased from eighty by twenty-four years, to fifty-six."[301] This dogmatic explanation generally accepted by Buddhists at that time is what lies behind the first sentence of the first paragraph: "Listen, if we calculate the length of human life, the lifespan allotted to us in this period is fifty-six years."

Having attained 'the grand old age of sixty-three,' Rennyo, thinking about his approaching death, expresses his serious concern about the state of mind of his followers in the Sangha and states, "Those who, thanks to the wisdom of the Buddha, have obtained peaceful awareness of Other Power, through the one thought-moment of taking refuge, should respond with gratitude to the Buddha for all he has done for them by pronouncing the Name right up to the very end of their lives." For Rennyo his own death is not merely a matter of personal concern but also a reason to worry about the future of the whole Sangha. This statement is a strong message to his followers, encouraging them to overcome all negative thoughts and feelings in the here and now and to continue to live their lives to the full extent with gratitude to the Buddha to the very end.

He wishes to share this special concern with his followers and says, "Once they have realised this, why should their time of death, determined as it is by their past lives, be cut short prematurely? I cannot help wondering if they might be foolishly deluded. Such are the reflections I have concerning my own person, old ignoramus that I am. Others, too, should abide in this state of mind." He is seeking here to communicate to all those around him his innermost desire that they may go on living the *Nenbutsu* throughout the rest of their lives, never escaping from but shouldering all the problems they will meet in the Sangha. According to his teaching we should not have our time of death cut short prematurely but should live out our karmic lives in the embrace of Amida's unconditional love.

Rennyo's message in this letter reminds us of the sad occurrences we sometimes read about in the history of religions. After the death of a great spiritual leader, for example, followers from the same religious order may, for a number of reasons, try and kill themselves. Sometimes this is because their blind adoration for and dependence on the leader have been such that they are now unable to find any hope in this world without him. Sometimes failing to find a way to solve their problems themselves, both individual and communal, they feel there is no other course but to destroy everything around them left behind after their leader's death, or, having lost their leader as their spiritual centre, they simply become too attached to their own self-centred concerns, whether at a practical or spiritual level. These negative inclinations are inextricably interrelated to one another. Usually one of the three is accompanied by the other two. For example, the more dependent on others these followers are, the stronger their desire for destruction and the more selfish attachment they show. If these inclinations become extreme, they tend to lead to insanity. If instead these followers achieve better self-awareness and greater spiritual independence, if they cultivate a love for life and acquire more altruistic qualities, then they will become saner and come closer to the truth of life. In short, what is important is to love life by overcoming the desire for destruction or death. In Buddhist terms, the path towards love for life is expressed as the Mahayanist vow of benefiting oneself and at the same time benefiting others. In other words, in essence, loving one's true self and loving others just as they are do not contradict each other but actually bring about great spiritual benefits in the deepest dimension.

If we look into ourselves, however, we find ourselves heavily burdened with those negative, karmic inclinations. Although it is very sad to see this reality of our existence, the only way to the Pure Land, the great land of infinite light and unconditional love, is firstly to become aware of this sad reality in the light of Amida Buddha and then to entrust our whole being to him without any reservation. In this respect it is said in Shin Buddhism that salvation is realised through faith alone.

I am absolutely sure that he did not want his followers to commit suicide after his death as happened with the followers of Ippen Shōnin (1239–1289). Although it is not clear if Rennyo was conscious of this problem or not when he wrote this letter, his love and compassion towards his followers never altered throughout his life. And here in this letter his love for others again wells up spontaneously with his humble awareness of himself as an 'old ignoramus'.

Although his admonition to his followers against committing suicide, in the second paragraph of the letter, may seem quite strict, it actually reflects his humble awareness, his deep compassion for others and his pure faith in Amida Buddha. Rennyo was undoubtedly a wonderful spiritual leader, full of love for his followers.

In the third paragraph of the letter he draws our attention to how oblivious we are to the fact of impermanence of this world, with this phrase of immortal beauty, "Unaware that our existence is as ephemeral as a flash of lightning or the morning dew, we live our lives without realising that the wind of impermanence may blow at any moment." This leads on to the concluding lines of the letter that urges us with great compassion to attain faith in the *Nenbutsu* without delay.

I have been translating the Chinese word *bàotǔ* 報土 (jp. *hōdo*) as "the Land of Enjoyment," as appears in my translation. Usually this special term has been translated into English as "the Land of Recompense," "the Land of Reward" or "the Land of Fulfilment." I was not very happy with any of these translations. The Chinese compound 報土 in question refers to the Land of Amida Buddha. Amida Buddha is a *Saṃbhoga-kāya* Buddha,[302] translated as *bàoshēnfó* 報身佛 (jp. *hōjinbutsu*) or *bàofó* 報佛 (jp. *hōbutsu*) in Chinese and the Buddha of Recompense in English. It seems simply for this reason that Amida's land came to be called *bàotǔ* 報土 (jp. *hōdo*), literally, Land of Recompense or Reward.

Whilst I was thinking about how to translate this compound *bàotǔ* 報土 *hōdo*, I found that, although there is a Sanskrit original, *Saṃbhoga-kāya Buddha* for the Chinese term *bàoshēnfó* 報身佛 (jp. *hōjinbutsu*) or *bàofó* 報佛 (jp. *hōbutsu*), there is no Sanskrit original for *bàotǔ* 報土 (jp. *hōdo*). This means that influenced by the Chinese translation of *Saṃbhoga-kāya Buddha* as *bàofó* 報佛, Amida's land was called *bàotǔ* 報土, "Land of Recompense." This special use of the word "reward" or "recompense" refers to the fulfilment of the Original Vow of Bodhisattva Dharmākara.

There is another important point I have to refer to in this special context. While making research for this purpose, I found that the Sanskrit word *Saṃbhoga-kāya* could be translated as "Enjoyment Body," or "Body of Enjoyment," as well, meaning the Buddha himself enjoying not only tasting the fruit of his Supreme Enlightenment but also freely sharing it with others in his Pure Land. Hence, my idea of translating the Chinese word *bàotǔ* 報土 (jp. *hōdo*) as "the Land of Enjoyment."

Having said this, I will finish with that beautiful poem added to the end of the letter by Rennyo Shōnin himself.

> Although I wrote this
> it is simply a letter that
> flowed from my brush.
> Some of my wording, therefore,
> may indeed sound very odd.

CHAPTER FORTY-SIX

The Lotus Sūtra and the *Nenbutsu* Teaching

THE CURRENT CONDITION OF THE WORLD

FASCICLE IV, LETTER THREE

The current condition of the world is so chaotic, no one can tell if or when all the conflicts will be brought to an end. Accordingly, as this is a period when it is not even safe to travel on the roads from one province to another, it is an age of utter vexation not only for the Buddha-dharma but also for worldly affairs. As a result, less and less people are visiting holy sites such as temples and shrines.

Regarding this point, when we hear that we human beings, both young and old, are filled with uncertainty, we should make haste to practise noble acts of virtue and aspire to Enlightenment or Nirvāṇa, whatever we may mean by them. At the present time, in fact, even though our era is called 'the Last Dharma age of defilement and confusion,' Amida Tathāgata's Original Vow, working as Other Power, is flourishing as never before in an utterly unbelievable way. Therefore, unless lay followers hold fast to this boundless, compassionate Vow, awaken to the one thought-moment of faith, and attain birth in the Pure Land that is the *Dharmatā*[303] of eternal bliss, it is indeed as if they travel to a mountain of treasure and return empty-handed. Quieten your minds and contemplate this thought thoroughly.

Now, when we look closely at the vows of all the Buddhas, we come to see that their vows are insufficient to save women, burdened as their sex is with the five obstacles, or wrongdoers who have committed the five grave offenses. It is Amida Tathāgata, and he alone, who made the incomparably virtuous Vow – the Great Vow whereby he promised to save ignorant beings heavily burdened with bad karma and grave offenses and women burdened with the five obstacles. Even if we try and express our gratitude, words are totally inadequate.

This promise was made and so, a long time ago, Śākyamuni, though busy at the time on Vulture Peak expounding the *Lotus Sūtra*, the sublime teaching of the One Vehicle, nevertheless also undertook to teach Vaidehī[304] to aspire for the Land of Peace and Rest, after Devadatta[305] had goaded Ajātaśatru[306] into committing grave unfilial acts. Ever since the day that Śākyamuni graciously withdrew from the assembly on Vulture Peak, where he was teaching the *Lotus Sūtra*, and descended to the royal palace to expound the Pure Land teaching to Vaidehī, Amida's Original Vow has continued to flourish right up to the present day. This is why the *Lotus Sūtra* and the *Nenbutsu* teaching are called the 'sermons given at the same time.'

In other words, Śākyamuni gave an account of how Vaidehī, Devadatta and Ajātaśatru all attained birth in the Pure Land despite their involvement in the five grave offenses, as a compassionate way to lead women and those who have committed the five grave offenses in the age of the Last Dharma to aspire for birth in the Land of Peace and Rest. In short, Śākyamuni teaches us that even such as they will unfailingly attain birth in the Land of Peace and Rest if they take refuge in the inconceivable Original Vow. This you should know.

Most humbly and respectfully
Written on 27th September, Bunmei 9 [1477].

COMMENTS

It is obvious from the last line that the third letter of Fascicle Four was written on 27 September 1477, when Rennyo was staying at Deguchi in Kawachi Province (modern Ōsaka prefecture) after his withdrawal from Yoshizaki.

As regards the historical background of this special letter, scholars differ, but I would like to introduce you to the following account that is particularly intriguing.

According to *The Ofumi raii shō* by Enin, published in 1759, Rennyo had, from April of 1476, been a frequent visitor to Sakai, the most prosperous commercial town in Japan at that time. At Rennyo's request, Katagiya Dōken, one of the master's disciples, had donated a piece of land on which to build a temple. In September 1477 construction had not yet started, when a Khitan Tiāntāi follower,[307] accompanied by a few of his fellow countrymen, travelled to Japan aboard a foreign ship in order to receive the Buddha-dharma from Rennyo Shōnin.

Having witnessed the attainment of pure faith by this foreigner, Dharma friends in Sakai decided to build a temple straight away, arguing that it would be a great pity for them not to create a place where they themselves could listen to Rennyo Shōnin's teaching, the Buddha-dharma that even foreigners had come looking for. Rennyo accepted their offer and the new temple was quickly erected.

This account summarised above from *The Ofumi raii shō* of a Khitan traveler coming to Japan and following Rennyo Shōnin's teaching is also supported by the details of a brief account recorded in an earlier historical document, *The Rennyo Shōnin ōse no jōjō* (*The Itemised Record of Rennyo Shōnin's Sayings*) edited in 1574 by Jitsugo (1492–1584), Rennyo's tenth son. I have translated this document, Article 199 of *The Rennyo Shōnin ōse no jōjō* as follows,

> Four or five Khitans came over to Japan to visit Rennyo Shōnin. This took place during Rennyo Shōnin's stay at a temple in Sakai. One of the Khitans had lost a child and, grieving over the child's sudden death, prayed to Bodhisattva Avalokiteśvara to find out his child's condition after death and make this child attain the fruition of Buddhahood. Responding to the father's prayer, the Bodhisattva had manifested himself in person to him and said, "You should travel to Japan to realise where you are going after death." As advised by the Bodhisattva, the Khitan journeyed to Japan and arrived in Sakai harbour. In accordance with the Bodhisattva's message, he went round looking for a connection [with a master teaching the truth of life] until he finally encountered Rennyo Shōnin. The Khitan declared himself extremely grateful to Rennyo Shōnin for his teaching. When he visited the temple wearing the costume of his native country, it was so voluminous it occupied an entire square *ken* (1.8 square metres). I imagine his descendants must still live in this country.[308]

The Ofumi raii shō states that it was this special event that motivated Rennyo Shōnin to write this letter and that it was also the reason why he referred to the Lotus Sūtra, on which the Tiāntāi school is based, and the *Nenbutsu* teaching, Rennyo Shōnin's Buddha-dharma, as "the sermons given at the same time."

Compared to this description by Jitsugo, Enin's account in *The Ofumi raii shō* of the same story appears considerably embellished. Although I am not sure whether the embellishments are due to Enin's own fertile imagination or to some extra other documents, what I am certain about is that there was indeed a historical Khitan who followed Rennyo Shōnin. Thinking about the international quality of Shin Buddhist teaching and the very spontaneous and natural genesis of Three Wheels, the Shin Buddhist centre we established in London, I was particularly struck by this spiritual encounter between Rennyo Shōnin and the Khitan. What is so intriguing is that it took place in Japan about some six hundred years ago.

Another subject of this letter is the doctrinal assertion that the teaching of the *Lotus Sūtra* and that of the *Nenbutsu* are in fact the "sermons given at the same time." The *Lotus Sūtra* tradition, represented by the Tiāntāi school in China and the Nichiren school in Japan, maintains that it is the only teaching in which the ultimate truth was revealed and all the other teachings before it are but provisional ways of leading sentient beings to the truth.

The Indian tragedy in a royal setting referred to by Rennyo is an extremely sad story and can be compared to the ancient Greek story of Oedipus. Whilst "Oedipus," the name of the Greek king, meant "swollen leg," Ajātaśatru used to be called "Prince Broken Finger." In both cases there is a strong correlation between what occurred and predictions made by soothsayers involved with the respective royal families. In both cases it was foretold that the child in question would kill his father, the king. Fearful of this grave prophecy of patricide, the royal parents in both cases sought to dispose of their son and heir. Whilst the Greek royal family abandoned the baby on the mountain side with a skewer through his legs, Ajātaśatru's parents, King Bimbisāra and Queen Vaidehī, threw the baby prince down from a high tower of the palace. Even so each baby survived. On learning the truth about the origin of their names, both princes and their relatives collapsed into these dreadful tragedies.[309]

Whilst all the members of the Greek royal family fell victim to their circumstances, the Indian family members, and Devadatta too, were saved through their encounter with Śākyamuni Buddha. The *Meditation Sūtra*, Śākyamuni's teaching at Rājagṛha, opened up for all sentient beings, heavily burdened with bad karma, the way of salvation through faith in the *Nenbutsu*.

The *Kuden shō* by Kakunyo (1270–1351) states,

> The Pure Land teaching has the same taste as the *Lotus Sūtra* teaching that all the Buddhist schools recognise as the original purport of the Buddha's appearance in this world. The reason is that, one day during the eight years that the Buddha taught the *Lotus Sūtra*, when he saw the incident of the five grave offenses of the royal family appearing in the palace, he withdrew from the assembly on Vulture Peak, descended to the royal palace and gave the sermon on Other Power. The general principle is that the original purpose of each and every Buddha's appearance in

this world, from Kaitoku down to Śākyamuni, solely lies in revealing the teaching of Amida Buddha.[310]

In this context what is important is to recognise the fact that the truth of the Buddha's great compassion was received by ignorant beings, such as Vaidehī and Ajātaśatru, through awakening to the reality of their karmic existence. The Shin Buddhist faith can be separated neither from the supreme truth of the Buddha-dharma nor from the down-to-earth reality of our karmic existence. Both aspects are united in the Shin Buddhist experience of pure faith, which is thus seen as "true and real (真實 jp. *shinjitsu*)." At the very moment we are awakened to the supreme truth of the Buddha-dharma or the unconditional love of Amida Buddha, we are also awakened to ourselves, or the irredeemable reality of our karmic existence, and vice versa. There can be no awakening to the one without an awakening to the other.

It was at the request of Queen Vaidehī, who was deeply involved in the tragedy of the royal family, that Śākyamuni Buddha immediately descended from Vulture Peak to Rājagṛha in order to deliver the queen and the members of her family from their dreadful karmic sufferings. To accomplish this he instructed her in the teaching of the *Nenbutsu*, or *Namu Amida-butsu*, known as *The Meditation Sūtra*. The supreme truth of the Buddha-dharma that Śākyamuni Buddha preached at the royal palace was received by Vaidehī and all the others involved in the tragic karmic reality at the moment of their awakening of faith.

Thus, we Pure Land followers maintain that the real purport of the Buddha's appearance in this world was to impart the message of universal deliverance for all sentient beings through faith in the *Nenbutsu*. Hence, Rennyo's words: "This is why the *Lotus Sūtra* and the *Nenbutsu* teaching are called the 'sermons given at the same time.'"

As described in *The Ofumi raii shō* by Enin, the reason why Rennyo referred to a connection between *The Lotus Sūtra* and *The Meditation Sūtra* may have had to do with the Khitan's awakening of faith through his visit. When we read the letter with the Khitan disciple in mind, Rennyo's teaching appears very powerful and full of love towards the foreign seeker after truth.

When we read this letter and think of all the great love and compassion Rennyo bestowed on the Khitan, it is absolutely clear that anyone who is involved in the work of promoting mutual understanding and spiritual exchange between international Dharma friends, or even at a local level building relationships with the wider community, should not be negligent, even for one instant, in performing this task given to us in the light of Amida's Original Vow.

CHAPTER FORTY-SEVEN

The Two Types
of Birth into
the Pure Land

ON MAKING THREE VERSES OF *WAKA*

FASCICLE IV, LETTER FOUR

Spring and autumn have now passed. As the months and years slip away, yesterday is already gone and today, too, all but over. I have reached old age unaware of the way the years were accumulating. At times I must have enjoyed the birds and the flowers, the wind and the moon, I must have met with joy and sorrow, pleasure and pain. But there is nothing in particular I remember now of all those things. Idly passing my mornings and evenings, I feel very sad to have grown old and grey. And yet, when I deeply reflect on my own existence as it is, still surviving and not yet carried away by the violent wind of impermanence, it is like a dream or a fleeting illusion. In the present moment there is nothing to aspire to but the single path that emancipates us from birth-and-death. Thus, when in this situation we learn of the existence of Amida Tathāgata's Original Vow that readily saves us sentient beings in this bad present age, we embrace it gratefully as that which is truly reliable.

Since we simply take refuge in this Original Vow with absolute sincerity and without doubt in one thought-moment, at that very moment we die to ourselves and are assured of attaining birth without any difficulty. Throughout the rest of our lives and as long as we continue to live in this world we should recite the *Nenbutsu* up until the very end of our lives in grateful recognition of all that the Buddha has done for us.

Through profound listening I have come to realise that this is precisely what is meant by 'the completion of the cause [of birth] in daily life.' Thus the faith-experience I once attained has never retrogressed but still reverberates deep in my ears. Even if I say thank you, words can never adequately express the depth of gratitude I feel.

Be this as it may, out of the whole-hearted respect and gratitude I feel to Amida Tathāgata for his Original Vow of Other Power, I would like to express the above as *waka*,[311] just letting go what rises to my lips,

> It is through the mind
> of entrusting yourself
> even only once
> that you will accord with
> the truth of the Dharma.

> Becoming aware
> of your own deep, bad karma
> entrust yourself to the Tathāgata
> and you will go to the West
> by virtue of the Dharma-power.

> When the mind is determined
> to go on this path
> of listening to the Dharma,
> then you will be pronouncing
> *Namu Amida-butsu.*

Despite my poor abilities, I dared to write these poems simply as a way of responding to the incomparability of this single Dharma of the Original Vow. The meaning of the three verses is as follows:

The first poem refers to the way we attain faith through the one thought-moment of taking refuge. The second expounds the benefit of 'entering the company of those who are truly assured [of birth in the Pure Land]'[312] and the meaning of 'attaining Nirvāṇa without fail'.[313] The third and last poem is to explain that, once we have rejoiced in diamond-like faith, we come to know what has been done by Amida for us and respond with gratitude.

I thought that even such poor compositions as these, since they welled up out of the awakening of Other Power faith, might at least serve as an act of grateful response in the face of all that has been done for us by Amida Buddha. I also hoped that those who heard [the poems], if they were sufficiently karmically conditioned to receive them, might come to share the same mind. As someone already in his seventh decade, however, and particularly as someone who is both ignorant and untalented, I find it rather ridiculous for me to be speaking of the Dharma in this idiosyncratic, ungrounded way. But at the same time, heedless of the criticisms of others and filled purely with respect and gratitude for the single path of the Original Vow, I have set down these halting words, letting them emerge from the brush as they do. Those who view them in the future, please, do not disparage them. Indeed, they may serve as a condition leading to the praising of the Buddha Vehicle and as a cause leading to the turning of the Dharma Wheel. There should never be any slandering of them.

Most humbly and respectfully

I have written this down in a short space of time by the fireplace, in the middle of December, the ninth year of Bunmei (1477). Thus said he.

This writing was picked up on the road and brought back to this temple by [the head priest of] Busshōji who was out on an errand and walking from Harinokihara to Kukenzaike.

On 2nd December Bunmei 9 (1477)

COMMENTS

As seen above, two brief postscripts are attached to this, the fourth letter of Fascicle Four. Because the two postscripts have different dates, there are various opinions about the time this letter was written.

If we consider the two words, "this" (之 *kore* in Japanese) found in the first postscript and "this writing" (この書 *konosho* in Japanese) in the second, as referring to the same letter, the two different dates – the middle of December 1477 in the first and 2nd December 1477 in the second – contradict each other and are impossible to explain.

Although there are a number of views claiming to solve this contradiction, my own conclusion is that, whereas the first date refers to the time this letter was written, the second date refers to the time of the composition of the three poems, the main subject of the letter. Namely, "this" in the first postscript indicates this letter as a whole and "this writing" in the second, the three poems.

To understand this better, let me introduce you to the background account of the letter which we can find in commentaries on the *Letters* by Rennyo such as *Ofumi meitō shō* and *Ofumi kijishu*.[314]

At the time of Rennyo Shōnin there was a big Shin Buddhist temple known as Busshōji 佛照寺 at Mizokui in Settsu Province. The founder of this Shin Buddhist temple was Shōkō-bō, one of Shinran Shōnin's disciples. Being born a grandson of Sasaki Shirō Takatsuna, a famous warrior in Kamakura period, Shōkō-bō became a Shingon monk. Through his encounter with Shinran Shōnin, however, he became a Shin Buddhist priest and founded this temple, Busshōji. Later the temple became very big and owned some one thousand branch temples. Kyōkō, Head Priest of Busshōji in the days of Rennyo Shōnin, was not very keen on studying the Buddha-dharma but deeply involved in his hobby of composing Japanese poems known as *waka*. Feeling very sorry to hear about Kyōkō's mental condition, which was causing a gradual deterioration of the temple's activities at that time, Rennyo wanted to lead him to the Buddha-dharma. For this purpose he made those three poems and dropped them in the road Kyōkō used to take quite often for his coming and going. Luckily Kyōkō picked up the poems, enjoyed reciting them and eventually visited the composer of the verses at his temple in Deguchi in order to ask about the true meaning of those religious poems. After teaching him with great compassion he wrote this particular letter on the poems.

This story accords perfectly with the existence of the two postscripts appended to the letter. Although some scholars consider that the latter postscript, found also in another letter, was wrongly attached to this letter by Ennyo Shōnin, the compiler of the Five Fascicle version of the *Letters*, I myself would like to trust the careful editorial work of *The Letters* carried out by Ennyo Shōnin. The first postscript is accompanied by the editor's special words, "Thus said he." Ennyo Shōnin must have inserted the first postscript, which is found in several other copies of the same letter, between the main body of the letter and the original postscript of the letter he edited (the second one in this version).

It is therefore evident from this background that this letter on the three poems was given by Rennyo to Kyōkō, Head Priest of Busshōji, so as to help him attain the Shin Buddhist faith. As a letter addressed to a priest who was versed in poetry, this is filled with beautiful literary expressions such as the poetic phrases of the starting paragraph, the three poems on Pure Land faith and a quotation from Bái Jūyì 白居易 (772–846), a famous Chinese poet of the Táng Dynasty. It also conveys Rennyo's humble and respectful attitude towards the literary world, in which Kyōkō was deeply engaged at that time. This is a good example of Rennyo's skillful means that comes directly from his great compassion towards others. It seems that, as a result of the composition of those three verses and the letter regarding them, not only did Kyōkō attain true faith, but Rennyo himself also very much enjoyed his own journey to the Pure Land simply pronouncing the Name of Amida Buddha.

Now let us examine the meaning of these three verses which so beautifully express the Shin Buddhist faith. They are all traditional Japanese poems called *waka*, being made of five lines with 5, 7, 5, 7, 7 syllables, whereas a *haiku* consists of three lines of 5, 7, 5 syllables.

According to Rennyo's own commentary found in the letter, the phrase "entrusting yourself even only once" in the first *waka* stands for 'the one thought-moment of taking refuge', "you will go to the West by virtue of the Dharma-power" in the second *waka* speaks of the meaning of the quoted phrases, 'entering the company of those who are truly assured' and 'attaining Nirvāṇa without fail,' while "you will be pronouncing *Namu Amida-butsu*" in the third *waka* actually indicates the way 'we come to know what has been done by Amida for us and respond with gratitude'.

Although he says in his postscript, "I have written this down in a short space of time by the fireplace, in the middle of December, the ninth year of Bunmei (1477)," it seems that he humbly put great care and consideration into preparing this letter for Kyōkō. We can see the evidence of this in his inclusion of the paragraph preceding the three *waka* which is an excellent summation of the Shin Buddhist teaching.

According to the *Ofumi kōjutsu* by Kakuju Yoshitani,[315] "Since we simply take refuge in this Original Vow with absolute sincerity and without doubt in one thought-moment," corresponds to the first *waka*, the second part of the quotation, "at that moment we die to ourselves and are assured to attain birth without any difficulty," to the second *waka* and the third and last part, "Throughout the rest of our lives and as long as we continue to live we should recite the *Nenbutsu* up until the very end of our lives in grateful recognition of all that the Buddha has done for us," to the third *waka*.

It is also pointed out in traditional commentaries such as the *Gobunshō kōwa* by Shirō Sugi and the *Ofumi kōjutsu* by Kakuju Yoshitani that these three poems are based on the following lines on Nāgârjuna's Pure Land thought found in *The Shōshinge*.[316]

> He taught that, at the very moment we become mindful of Amida's
>> Original Vow,
> We naturally enter the stage of the definitely assured,
> And that, solely by always pronouncing the Name of the Tathāgata,
> We respond with gratitude to his Great Compassion, to the Vow of
>> Universal Deliverance.[317]

The first *waka* reminds us of the first line of the quotation from *The Shōshinge*, the second *waka*, of the second line and the third *waka*, of the last two lines. Regarding the last point, it is vital for us to recognise that Nāgârjuna, the first patriarch of our Pure Land tradition, was already aware of the important notion of "what has been done by the Buddha for us" (佛恩) and that pronouncing the Name of Amida Buddha is the only way we respond with gratitude for it.

Going back to the paragraph preceding the three poems I wish to explain why I translated a special Japanese passage in it – *sonotoki rinjūseba* そのとき 臨終せば – as "at that moment we die to ourselves." Minor Rogers translated it as "if we die at that time."[318] The difference of the two translations comes from the different interpretations of the Japanese word *rinjū*.

Usually the term *rinjū* means death or the end of our life. In the Shin Buddhist tradition the same word has two different implications: either physical death or the ending of our physical life or death in the spiritual sense or the ending of our illusion of self power. What is meant by my translation "at that moment we die to ourselves" refers to the latter, the word "at that moment" meaning when "we simply take refuge in this Original Vow with absolute sincerity and without doubt in one thought-moment." In this case *rinjū* does not mean the end of the physical life (身命) but the end of the mental life of illusion (心命). Shin Buddhists call this the death of our self-power attachment or self-power illusion.

In the Shin Buddhist tradition we talk about two different kinds of birth in the Pure Land: birth in the Pure Land to be realised at the moment of attaining faith and birth in the Pure Land at the moment of our physical death. The death of our mental illusion or self-power attachment mentioned above refers to the first kind of birth in the Pure Land. This notion of birth in the Pure Land to be attained at the moment of rejoicing in the awakening of faith is described in the passage that relates to the fulfilment of the Eighteenth Original Vow in *The Larger Sūtra of Eternal Life*,

> All beings, on hearing that Name, rejoice in the awakening of faith at least for one thought-moment. It is indeed from Amida's sincere mind that all this has been transferred to them. Desiring to be born in that land, they are immediately born there at that moment and abide in the stage of nonretrogression.[319]

In short this means that at the moment of awakening of faith we immediately attain birth in the Pure Land and reach the stage of nonretrogression. This is the meaning of the Shin Buddhist teaching known as 'the completion of the cause of birth in daily life.' As Rennyo says, "Through profound listening I have come to realise that this is precisely what is meant by 'the completion of the cause in daily life.' Thus the faith-experience I once attained has never retrogressed but still reverberates deep in my ears. Even if I say thank you, words can never adequately express the depth of gratitude I feel."

What I understand about the Japanese phrase *sonotoki rinjūseba* is the first kind of birth in the Pure Land to be completed at the moment of attaining of faith in daily life. This is an important point of the letter that represents the essential part of the Shin Buddhist teaching. I am very happy to be able to confirm this crucial point in Kakuju Yoshitani's understanding of the same phrase in his *Ofumi kōjutsu*.

Towards the end of the letter Rennyo Shōnin states, "Indeed, they may serve as a condition leading to the praising of the Buddha Vehicle and as a cause leading to the turning of the Dharma Wheel." The original source of this special passage is an adaptation of the words by Bái Jūyì, who has long been highly appreciated in the world of Japanese literature. Bái Jūyì himself was a devout Buddhist and stated in one of his verses, "I pray that my literary work in this world and its errors of making mad statements and flattering words may turn into a cause leading to the praising of the Buddha Vehicle and a condition for the turning of the Dharma Wheel."[320] This highly literary way of ending the letter could be seen as Rennyo's humble but strong prayer that Kyōkō may attain true faith by turning his worldly karma into an efficient cause for his birth in the Pure Land.

CHAPTER FORTY-EIGHT

On Teaching Others

EVER SINCE THE MIDDLE PERIOD

FASCICLE IV, LETTER FIVE

Ever since the middle period and up to the present day, there have been preachers of our tradition whose teaching has failed to take account of whether or not their audience have past good conditions. Put succinctly, it is vitally important that from now on you yourselves should be aware of the difference whenever you are teaching. Whether reading out the sacred texts or expounding the teaching at your usual meetings, you should always bear the distinction in mind as you teach the Dharma of our tradition. At large gatherings, too, where people come together to listen to the Buddha-dharma, you should not discuss the true teaching of our tradition without first considering whether there could be anyone present who has no past good conditions. In recent times, however, I have noted from the way priests go about their teaching that they lack any such insight. They simply say to themselves, "It does not matter what the individual is like. As long as I preach well enough, why should anyone not be able to ground themselves in the peaceful awareness of our tradition?" You must understand that this is entirely false. You should carry out the teaching of our tradition with a full understanding of what I have just mentioned above. Ever since the middle period and right up to the present day, there has been not a single individual who has realised this point clearly enough to preach without errors. Fully aware of the problem, you should propound the teaching in the formal way adopted by our tradition.

The twenty-eighth of this month marks the date of the annual ceremony for Shinran Shōnin, the founder of our tradition, and a great many people are diligently planning to practise the *Nenbutsu* and join in the service on the day in order to express their gratitude to him for all he has done for us. This is because they understand the truth of the words "to receive from the stream and trace its flow back to its source." This is entirely due to the universal nature of Shōnin's teaching.

In recent years, however, a number of individuals have been found to be confusing others by creating distorted teachings (*higa bōmon*), never voiced in our tradition. They have also been reprimanded by local land stewards and feudal lords. They abide in erroneous views and are far from being in accord with the peaceful awareness of our tradition. Is this not lamentable? It is indeed very sad, disgraceful, in fact.

In conclusion, I wish to say that it is incumbent upon each and every one of us this month to show deep remorse during the seven days and nights of Hōonkō. Purging our innermost hearts of all erroneous thoughts, we should go before the temple's Image of the Founder and turn our minds in penitence, putting into words night and day what it is we are doing so that others may learn about it. This accords with [Shàndǎo's] commentary: "It is with this turning of the mind that slanderers of the dharma and *icchantika* will all be born," and it also corresponds to the meaning "One should attain faith oneself and help others do so." In this way honest people, when they hear of others turning their minds around and repenting, will think that the same holds true for themselves, and some will overturn their bad mind in ordinary life and return to the good mind. This will truly accord with the original purpose of Shōnin's anniversary this month. In other words, this will be an offering that will allow us to respond in gratitude for what has been done for us [by Shinran Shōnin].

Most humbly and respectfully
On 21st November, Bunmei 14 [1482]

COMMENTS

This letter was written at Yamashina Honganji on 21st November 1482, the first day of the week long Hōonkō Ceremony. According to the *Rennyo Shōnin itoku ki* by Rengo,[321] acting on the advice of Dōsai-bō Zenjū (1399–1488), Rennyo Shōnin's first and oldest disciple, Rennyo left his temple at Deguchi in Kawachi Province and started building his headquarters at Yamashina in Yamashiro Province in 1478, completing the work in 1480. He was extremely happy to be able at last to carry the original image of Shinran Shōnin out from a thatched hut at Chikamatsu in Ōtsu in Ōmi Province and welcome it into this formal setting of a main temple.

The opening phrase of the letter, "Ever since the middle period," is difficult to understand without some knowledge of Shin Buddhist history. "The middle period" is actually the middle period of the history of our faith, referring to the time of Kakunyo Shōnin (1270–1351), the third Head Priest of Honganji Temple. Thus, the opening sentence means that, ever since his death and right up until the days of Rennyo Shōnin, there were Shin Buddhist preachers who had failed to take account of whether or not their audience had past good conditions and this had caused the gradual decline of the Shin Buddhist order.

One of the main subjects of this letter is a person's past good conditions or *shukuzen* 宿善. The notion of *shukuzen* has already been discussed several times in the course of the previous commentaries on the eleventh letter of Fascicle Two, the ninth and twelfth letters of Fascicle Three, and the first letter of Fascicle Four, where the special meaning of *shukuzen* in Shin Buddhism is explained.

Returning to Rennyo's point that, when attempting to teach people, we should be aware of whether or not they have past good conditions. The original Japanese for this phrase is *shukuzen no umu*, literally "the presence or absence of one's past good conditions." This is not to say that there exists some insurmountable barrier between the two, as is made clear in the two lines from Shàndǎo that Rennyo quotes in this letter: "It is with this turning of the mind that slanderers of the dharma and [those called] *icchantika* will all be born [in the Pure Land]," and "One should attain faith oneself and help others do so." The first quotation assures us that even the vilest people in the world can be saved through faith alone, and the second indicates that, with Amida's unconditional love firmly in mind, we should continue our journey forward to the attainment of birth in the Pure Land. In this letter Rennyo is telling Shin Buddhist teachers that they should be aware of the maturity or immaturity of people's past good conditions and, if necessary, wait for their past good conditions to mature. If such teachers try and force their congregations to attain faith when their minds are still immature, this may cause a lot of problems not only for the congregation of followers but also for all those around them. This could result in a very serious problem indeed for the Sangha. We should bear in mind that in his letter Rennyo was cautioning those preachers and also those who felt they had already attained faith and were able to teach others.

In Shin Buddhism it is said that true faith consists of two inseparable aspects: firstly awakening to the irredeemable reality of one's karmic existence and secondly awakening to the unconditional love of Amida Buddha. At the very moment we are awakened to the irredeemable reality of our karmic existence, we are simultaneously awakened to Amida's great love and compassion.

In other words, when we come to grasp the existential reality of having no past good conditions, then at that very moment we entrust ourselves absolutely to Other Power, the unconditional love of Amida Buddha. Once we find ourselves in the embrace of Amida's great compassion, we see our whole past, everything and everyone, as "good." At the moment we realise we have no past good, we find our whole past is good. This is the beautiful paradox of the Shin Buddhist faith.

In the immediacy of the instantaneous faith-experience, our awareness of the absence of past good conditions becomes our awareness of the presence of past good conditions, or, in other words, nonbeing is being. At the very moment we find ourselves as having no past good conditions, paradoxically enough, we simply find ourselves as being good within the absolute affirmation of Amida's embrace since the beginningless past.

The subject of the second half of the letter is how to overcome *higa bōmon* or "distorted teachings." The meaning of the Japanese term *higa bōmon* in this paragraph is the same as that of *ese bōmon*, or "false teachings," in the eleventh letter of Fascicle Three, or of *kuse bōmon*, "strange, distorted teachings," in the thirteenth letter of Fascicle Three. A similar term known as *hiji bōmon* or "secret teachings" relates to more organised forms of erroneous teaching that were quite influential amongst followers of those days.

When we look deeply into our minds, however, we have to admit that there is no one who knows right from the start what the true teaching is. Each and every one of us has their own view of the self and the world. It is the same with people's approach to the teaching. When they start to access the teaching, their understanding is necessarily quite limited and self-centred. Thus *higa bōmon* is a serious problem not only for preachers but also for their congregations.

This Hōonkō Ceremony was the first one that Rennyo Shōnin held after installing the image of the Founder in this newly constructed headquarters in Yamashina. Taking into consideration this special occasion it must have been so moving for him to see his followers, not only priests but also lay people, returning to true faith by repenting in front of the wooden statue of Shinran Shōnin after the evening service. The way followers performed their confessions in those days is described in detail in the *Honganji sahō no shidai* by Jitsugo.[322]

Nowadays the Hōonkō Ceremony at our Shin Buddhist headquarters includes a beautiful ceremony called *gaike-hihan*, literally "examination of repentance," in which a priest who plays the role of *gaike-sō*, "repenting priest," reads out a passage known as *The Gaikemon* 改悔文 or *Passage of Repentance,* and then another priest who plays the role of *shisō*, "master priest," examines this confession of faith according to the traditional teaching. The ceremony takes place in front of the image of the Founder Shinran Shōnin and its origins are believed to lie in a ceremony of confession as described in this letter by Rennyo Shōnin where he urges his followers to show their repentance.

CHAPTER FORTY-NINE

Inappropriate Ways of Behaviour

ON THREE ARTICLES

FASCICLE IV, LETTER SIX

The Hōonkō Ceremony to be held this month is a longstanding service that takes place every year to commemorate the death of Shōnin. Given the importance of the occasion, followers of our tradition from provinces far and wide desire to visit to express their sincerest gratitude for all that he has done for them. And so every year, for seven days and nights, these followers devote themselves with great concentration to the *Nenbutsu* and the chanting of sacred texts. This is because followers of true faith are really flourishing. Indeed, we might even say the time has finally come when people can abide firmly in the *Nenbutsu*.

Given this situation, however, it is no surprise that among those who attend during the seven-day period there are some for whom coming and doing the service before the Image is no more than a gesture, a mere imitation of others. These people should straightaway bow down their heads before the Image and, having their minds turned with repentance, return to the truth of the Original Vow so that they may cherish the true faith with the awakening of the one thought-moment.

You should realise that *Namu Amida-butsu* is the essence of the peaceful awareness of *Nenbutsu* followers. This is because *Namu* means 'to take refuge.'

You should know too that, for ignorant beings like ourselves who do no good but only bad, 'taking refuge' means entrusting ourselves to Amida Buddha. This entrusting mind is nothing other than the mind of Amida Buddha, who embraces sentient beings in his great light of eighty-four thousand rays and who grants them the two forms of virtue-transference, outgoing and returning.[323] Thus faith has no other meaning than this. It is all encompassed in *Namu Amida-butsu*. Recently, however, there are some who think otherwise.

Regarding this point, there are many amongst worshippers of our tradition from all the various provinces, who obfuscate the teaching by presenting distorted, false teachings that differ from the doctrines in the sacred documents authorised by our Founder. This is indeed a disgraceful state of affairs and, to be brief, what people like this should do in this seven-day period of the Hōonkō Ceremony is to have the determination of mind to forsake their erroneous beliefs and ground themselves instead in the right teaching.

First: It is said of some who promote the Buddha-dharma and formally occupy the position of priest that they are instructing others in strange and false teachings that have never been formally handed down to us. Recently there has been an upsurge here, there and everywhere in the popularity of these kinds of priests whose only concern is their own reputation for knowledge. This is inexcusable!

Second: It is a great mistake for followers to announce that they are on the way to visit and pay respects to the Image at Honganji Temple in Kyoto, or, irrespective of the company they find themselves in, to speak unreservedly to others about the Buddha-dharma, whether on highways or byways, at checking stations or on ferryboats.

Third: Should someone ask you what sort of Buddha-dharma you believe in, you should not just respond carelessly that you are a *Nenbutsu* follower of our tradition. You should merely answer that you are not much concerned about sects and that you simply respect the *Nenbutsu* as something of great value. In other words, the way of our tradition, as taught by Shōnin, is not revealing yourself to be a follower of the Buddha-dharma.

So then, you should keep in mind that the right teaching of our tradition is to make sure you understand these points thoroughly and also that you give no outward sign of them. Furthermore, none of the instructions during the Hōonkō Ceremony over the past two or three years for fellow followers to observe should be altered in any way. Any fellow-followers who fail to be in accord can no longer be seen as followers of the Founder Shōnin.

Most humbly and respectfully
November, Bunmei 15 [1483]

COMMENTS

Although the title of this, the sixth letter of Fascicle Four, is similar to the title of the third letter of Fascicle Two, namely *"Concerning Three Articles including one on shinmei,"* a distinction needs to be made as the titles refer to two different letters.

For a five year period (1481–1485), consequent to moving to Yamashina Honganji in 1480, Rennyo issued his followers with a number of similar sounding letters of instruction during the Hōonkō Ceremony. Four of them, the fifth, sixth, seventh and eighth letters of Fascicle Four, are found in *The Letters* (the Five Fascicle version) compiled by Ennyo Shōnin. One further letter, written on 24th November 1481, is not included in this collection. In each case what prompted him to write these letters was his concern that his followers should behave in the way prescribed by these instructions, always with pure faith in their minds no matter whatever circumstances they might find themselves in.

All of Rennyo Shōnin's letters in Ennyo Shōnin's compilation are read out at different times morning and evening towards the end of daily service, with the exception of the seven Hōonkō letters – namely, the eleventh letter of Fascicle Three, the fifth, sixth, seventh, eighth and fifteenth letters of Fascicle Four and the eleventh letter of Fascicle Five   which are read out only during the Hōonkō Ceremony.[324] The current letter, then, is one of those seven, all of which are fairly long and all of which were written by him to his followers at the time of the Hōonkō Ceremonies. Each of them is filled with the great love and compassion that he constantly showed to his followers, teaching them not only how to attain faith but also how to go on living with pure faith in this world.

In the first paragraph, on welcoming the advent of the third Hōonkō Ceremony three years after his move to Yamashina Honganji, Rennyo expresses his great joy and appreciation at seeing his followers participate in the *Nenbutsu* service of the Hōonkō Ceremony. Concerning the phrase "the death of Shōnin," there are a few words I need to say about my translation of the original Japanese word *senge* 遷化, which has no exact English equivalent. Generally speaking, *senge* stands for 'death' or 'passing away,' hence my choice of the word 'death' in this context. In Buddhism, however, there are a number of different ways of referring to death. According to the *Shakushi yōran* 釋氏要覽 (ch. Shìshì yàolǎn),[325] or *Short Lexicon of Buddhist Terms*, there are seven different Buddhist expressions that mean death: Nirvāṇa 涅槃 *nehan*; perfect extinction 円寂 *enjaku*; return to truth 歸真 *kishin*; return to tranquillity 歸寂 *kijaku*; to die and cross over to the other shore 滅度 *metsudo*; to proceed to further spiritual instruction 遷化 *senge*; and to follow the way of the world 順世 *junsei*. The first five expressions will not be difficult for Buddhists to understand. The last and seventh one, *u*, is used by Zen monks, meaning that, although there is no birth or death for the enlightened, they follow the way of ordinary people. *Senge*, the term in question, is used in Buddhism only for the death of Bodhisattvas, eminent monks or priests, whose death is considered as a transition to another life to continue teaching. Thus Rennyo Shōnin's use of the word *senge* 遷化 for the death of Shinran Shōnin shows his respect for him as a Bodhisattva or an embodiment of the ultimate truth.

The last sentence of the first paragraph, "Indeed, we might even say the time has finally come when people can abide firmly in the *Nenbutsu*," is based on a passage in *The Anraku shū* 安楽集 (ch. *Ānlè jí*),[326] which Dàochuò (jp. Dōshaku), the author of the book, slightly adapted for his writing from the closing part of the *Daijikkyō* 大集經 (ch. *Dàjí jīng*, skt. *Mahasamnipata Sūtra*).[327] The message of the sūtra is a doctrinal explanation of the Buddhist eschatology that sees a decline in the quality of Buddhist spirituality with the passage of time from the first five hundred years following the death of the Buddha to the fifth five hundred years. Regarding this fifth and last age, the one in which Rennyo Shōnin found himself, the passage in *The Ānlè jí* states, "People can firmly abide in a good Dharma that scarcely still remains."[328] What is meant by "a good Dharma" is the teaching of *Nenbutsu*. Although the ages decline as time passes, paradoxically enough even those living in this age of deterioration are said to be able to abide in the firmness of the Buddha-dharma through the practice of the *Nenbutsu* alone. Rennyo must have been very happy to see those who attained faith gathering for the ceremony and pronouncing the Name.

In the second paragraph, he encourages those who have gathered at the temple but not reached true faith to take refuge in the truth of the Original Vow, repenting of their attachment to worldly fame and gain.

The third paragraph is a doctrinal examination of *Namu Amida-butsu* that clarifies the way to attain faith. Concerning the interpretation of *Namu Amida-butsu*, I have already discussed the subject in detail when dealing with the fifteenth letter of Fascicle Two and the second, sixth and seventh letters of Fascicle Three, which contain a detailed doctrinal explanation of *Namu Amida-butsu*. In brief, *Namu*, namely, "taking refuge in Amida Buddha" by entrusting ourselves absolutely to him, is nothing other than the mind of Amida Buddha. This is because Amida Buddha embraces us all in his great light of compassion, desiring us to take refuge in him, so that we may receive the two forms of virtue-transference, going to the Pure Land and returning to this world. In other words, "*Namu*" is *Namu Amida-butsu* and "*Amida-butsu*" is *Namu Amida-butsu*, and thus "*Namu*" and "*Amida-butsu*" are one in *Namu Amida-butsu*. Rennyo's reference to the two forms of virtue-transference is extremely important in this context. The virtue-transference for going to the Pure Land is for the fulfilment of benefiting oneself and the virtue-transference for return is for the fulfilment of benefiting others. If the oneness of self and others is the ultimate truth of Buddhism, one's own salvation cannot be realised without saving others, and vice versa. Rennyo Shōnin's reference to the two forms of virtue-transference is of vital importance in this respect. Amida Buddha embraces not a part of our existence but our whole existence that desires "to benefit both the self and others." Amida's virtue-transference, both outgoing and returning, is for the fulfilment of our own salvation in its truest sense. All this is included in the Name, *Namu Amida-butsu*. To summarise, *Namu Amida-butsu* in itself is the virtue-transference from Amida Buddha, or the working of Amida's Original Vow, that helps us to attain birth in the Pure Land to benefit ourselves and to return freely to this world to benefit others. With the awakening of pure faith we entrust ourselves absolutely to this virtue-transference of Amida Buddha. Our pronouncing the Name, "*Namu Amida-butsu,*" is a manifestation of the Mahayanist ideal of "benefiting oneself and benefiting others" through our existence.

In the fourth paragraph Rennyo laments the spread of the false, distorted teachings amongst his followers. It was out of the compassion he felt for them that Rennyo gave his disciples such strict instructions to repent their erroneous beliefs and return to true faith. According to *The Lectures on the Letters* by Kakuju Yoshitani, those whom he was seeking to admonish in this context were actually the priests themselves. It was they who were being asked "to forsake their attachment to erroneous beliefs and ground themselves instead in the right teaching." Rennyo Shōnin could not ignore the influence the priests had over their followers.

Next he imparts three important articles of instruction to his followers. The first one is again aimed at priests, whilst the latter two are meant not only for priests but for followers in general. Honganji Temple in Kyoto, which Rennyo refers to in the second article of instruction, does not mean the present Honganji but refers to its predecessor temple situated at that time in Yamashina.

Rennyo issued this kind of instruction quite often in his letters. For example, in the ninth letter of Fascicle One, written in September 1473,

> 'Observing the rules of conduct of our tradition' means cherishing the teaching of our tradition deep within ourselves without betraying any sign of it to the outside. Those who do so may justly be called people of discretion. These days, however, some of us speak carelessly and heedlessly about our tradition in the presence of others from different traditions and different schools. As a result, our tradition is considered shallow.[329]

Similarly, in the thirteenth letter of Fascicle Two, written on the 3rd July, 1474,

We should correctly observe the regulations of our tradition, which essentially means behaving carefully toward other schools as well as toward society in general in such a way as not to draw public attention by exposing our way of living to the world at large. Recently, however, there have been some among the *Nenbutsu* people of our tradition who have intentionally told others what our school is all about. They assumed that this would enhance the fame of our school and in doing this they particularly sought to condemn and belittle other schools. There is nothing more absurd than this.[330]

As seen from these examples, Rennyo was very serious about this kind of problem. It is not easy to talk about Shin Buddhism properly, for the faith-experience that lies at the core of its teaching is not only somewhat radical, but very profound and full of paradoxes. Even after having experienced the attainment of faith, if you try to understand and explain it to others with too much reliance on intellect, you will certainly miss the point. Unless we return to the Buddha with pure faith, any approach that is restricted to the intellect will simply serve to distort the traditional teaching taught by Shinran Shōnin.

Speaking without due care about Shin Buddhism can be confusing, dangerous even, not only for the speaker but for the listeners as well. To put it simply, there are two problems: one is social and the other psychological.

In point of fact, admonishments such as those issued by Rennyo would appear to have been closely connected to the then social situation which saw the Shin Buddhist community confronting enormous difficulties. Some Shin Buddhist priests preaching without pure faith and certainly without due care must have caused any number of problems in the community, as well as the society as a whole.

In many cases there will have been an invisible connection between the actions of the priests and their inner state of mind. Priests are supposed to have experienced their own wonderful awakening to faith. But if they allow themselves to take any pride in this, then self-centred distortion caused by pride will damage the notion of true faith and harm the teaching of Shin Buddhism itself. This kind of undue pride may even cause such priests to seek fame through their preaching not only for themselves but also for their school, as Rennyo observes in this letter.

CHAPTER FIFTY

Behave Carefully with Peaceful Awareness

ON SIX ARTICLES

FASCICLE IV, LETTER SEVEN

The first thing to be said is that this month's annual seven-day Hōonkō Ceremony has been faithfully celebrated by us every year without fail right up to the present day. So it is that on this special occasion fellow-followers from various different provinces come to express their sincerest gratitude for all that has been done for them and to devote themselves to the *Nenbutsu* of pronouncing the Name as the fundamental practice. This is indeed the virtue of the sole practice carried out with singlemindedness, making us assured of birth in the Pure Land.

Amongst those fellow-followers from various provinces, however, it would seem that only a few dwell in one and the same 'peaceful awareness'. This is because, rather than truly aiming for the attainment of the Buddha-dharma, so many followers are merely mimicking others or, at best, following the conventions of human morality. This is indeed utterly deplorable. Why does it happen? If those who have yet to attain peaceful awareness remain without asking questions, they are betraying a complete lack of faith. This being the case, even though they undertake a long journey of countless *ri*[331] and undergo a great deal of hardship in coming to the capital, their journey will be of no avail whatsoever. This is terribly, terribly sad. But if they are those who have no past good conditions, then we have to concede that there is absolutely no point in discussing the matter.

First: These days, although the Buddha-dharma appears to be thriving, we hear that it is, indeed, only those who hold the position of priest who have never been concerned about their own faith. This is utterly deplorable.

Second: Although amongst fellow-followers there are many who have heard the truth of Other Power faith, it is said that some priests have been angry about it. This is so bad I am at a loss for words!

Third: Followers travelling in from the countryside, no matter whether they are on highways or byways, at checking stations or on ferry boats, should bear in mind that it is presumptuous for them to praise the Buddha-dharma unreservedly, without due regard to the company in which they find themselves. This must definitely be stopped.

Fourth: Even if a *Nenbutsu* follower of our tradition is asked what school he belongs to, he should never answer outright that he is a *Nenbutsu* follower of our school. He should simply reply that he is a *Nenbutsu* follower of no special school. This, then, is the way our master would have us conduct ourselves, careful not to betray the fact that we are followers of the Buddha-dharma. Be fully aware of this point and give no outward appearance. This is, indeed, the correct mode of conduct to be demonstrated by *Nenbutsu* followers of our tradition.

Fifth: Even if you feel, listening through sliding doors or over a hedge, that you have understood the Buddha-dharma and say to yourself "That's it," you should carefully question others again and again about your own understanding and attain faith decisively. If you simply allow yourself to understand the matter in whatever way pleases you, you will always make mistakes. It has recently been said that there are many such cases these days.

Sixth: You should question others again and again about the manner in which you attained faith, until peaceful awareness of Other Power becomes firmly established within you. If your listening to the Dharma is left untended, there will surely be mistakes.

It is important that the above six articles be fully understood. Although everyone listens to the Buddha-dharma these days, because of their superficial understanding of the teaching, there is no one who has truly attained faith. Thus, they remain unfamiliar with peaceful awareness itself.

Most humbly and respectfully
On 21st November, Bunmei 16 [1484].

COMMENTS

This is again one of the four letters concerning Hōonkō found in Fascicle Four that I referred to in commenting on the sixth letter of Fascicle Four. This particular letter was written at Yamashina Honganji on 21st November 1484, the first day of the seven-day annual ceremony, at a time when Rennyo was seventy years old.

In the first paragraph he refers to the spiritual importance of the Hōonkō ceremony for Shin Buddhist followers and to the fact that so many people come from provinces near and far to attend the ceremony. What is important here in this context is how to understand the last passage of this first paragraph: "This is indeed the virtue of the sole practice carried out with singlemindedness, making us assured of birth in the Pure Land." In Shin Buddhism the *Nenbutsu* is "the right practice that rightly assures us of birth in the Pure Land" and should be practiced exclusively, that is to say not in conjunction with other practices. Even if you just practice the *Nenbutsu* and that alone, however, if your mind does not have a single focus, that is to say is not pure, then you cannot attain true faith. Shinran Shōnin states in his main work, *The Kyōgyōshinshō* Vol. VI, "Truly we know that those who solely practice [the *Nenbutsu*] and yet whose minds remain adulterated do not attain great joy."[332] This means that those who solely practise the *Nenbutsu* should also be completely singleminded. If their mind is divided or bifurcated in any way, then theirs is not pure faith. The word "singlemindedness" in Rennyo's letter actually refers to true faith, out of which the singleminded practice of the *Nenbutsu* wells up with joy and gratitude. Hence my rendering of the first sentence of the last passage in this first paragraph: "This is indeed the virtue of the sole practice carried out with singlemindedness." The latter part of the sentence refers to the working of singlemindedness or pure faith, the impetus for the sole, or singleminded, practice of the *Nenbutsu*.

In the second paragraph he points out that, of those visitors to the Honganji Temple who come to attend the Hōonkō ceremony, despite all the efforts they have made, braving the not inconsiderable hardships of travel in those days, many remain without 'peaceful awareness.' This notion of 'peaceful awareness' appears along with the concept of 'past good conditions' in all the Hōonkō letters, and is synonymous with true faith, that is Other Power faith, based on the Eighteenth Vow. According to Shinran Shōnin's philosophical self-examination of the faith-experience, known as 'The Awakening of Faith through the Three Vows' (*Sangantennyū*),[333] true faith is not faith as depicted in the nineteenth or twentieth Vows, but Other Power faith as conceived in the eighteenth Vow. In other words, true faith comprises two types of simultaneous awareness, peaceful awareness of oneself, or the irredeemable reality of one's karmic existence, on the one hand, and an awareness of the Dharma, or the great compassion of the Buddha, on the other. The *Nenbutsu* of gratitude springs from this peaceful awareness, in which one finds oneself in the embrace of Amida's boundless compassion. Whenever Rennyo Shōnin talks about *anjin* or 'peaceful awareness', what he means is true faith based on the eighteenth Vow. Any other form of faith, deviating from 'peaceful awareness', is called *i-anjin*, if we take it as our ultimate foundation.

Closely related to this notion of *anjin*, is *shukuzen* or 'past good conditions,' that appears repeatedly in the Hōonkō letters. Quite paradoxically, the notion of *shukuzen* (past good conditions) is fully understood only through our awakening to the irredeemable reality of our karmic existence as *mushukuzen* (no past good conditions). At the moment of awakening to ourselves we realise that our whole existence is already embraced within Amida's great compassion. In other words our present existence as the accumulation of the whole of our past karma is rediscovered as "good" through our encounter with the Buddha-dharma. It is worthwhile noting that these two notions, *anjin* and *shukuzen*, so important to Rennyo's thinking, feature most prominently in his more serious letters, such as those dealing with the Hōonkō Ceremony.

Of the six articles listed in this letter the first two are criticisms of priests, who are concerned not for their own faith but merely for their authority over their followers. These two articles bring to mind two important Shin Buddhist documents: the first letter of Fascicle One of *The Letters* by Rennyo and Chapter 6 of *The Tanni shō*.[334]

If the ultimate concern of priests, who are supposed to be leaders of the Sangha, lies somewhere else than in their own faith, it will endanger the whole Sangha, which is in its essence a community of followers with pure faith. If followers of the Sangha are guided in wrong directions by priests who are mainly concerned with how to collect more donations, how to organise their groups, how to draw up regulations governing the order or how to teach their followers without reflecting on their own faith, their Sangha will eventually collapse.

When the present Buddha Hall at Shogyoji Temple was built in 1956, one of the Responsible Trustees of the Religious Corporation of Shogyoji Temple suggested that consideration should be given to introducing new rules and regulations governing its use and upkeep. To this request my master, Dharma-Mother Ekai-ni, immediately responded with the words "No, those things are not important. I would like to concentrate on educating young people, for Shogyoji is a temple of followers of pure faith. It is faith alone that is the foundation of Shogyoji Temple."

The other articles in the letter, the third and fourth, are cautions addressed to visitors travelling in from further afield. Those articles, in fact, are almost the same as the second and third articles of the sixth letter of Fascicle Four, entitled *On Three Articles*. I shall not, therefore, repeat the discussion here.

Whilst the fifth article addresses those who have yet to attain faith, the sixth is aimed directly at those who have already done so. What is emphasised in both these articles is that followers should ask others over and over again how to proceed along their chosen path. Regardless of whether we are yet to attain faith or have already done so, we should humbly keep on questioning our other Dharma friends. Asking questions comes from facing up to our problems and not avoiding them. In the case of those who have not yet attained faith, they should humbly ask others how to achieve peaceful awareness, and in the case of those who have already attained faith, they should proceed on the path to the Pure Land through this finite world of ours, constantly confirming and returning to their original point of awakening. Peaceful awareness is the start to a new spiritual life but also, for those who have already attained faith, the absolute bedrock of their journey to the Pure Land.

CHAPTER FIFTY-ONE

Preserving the Peaceful Awareness of Our Tradition

ON EIGHT ARTICLES

FASCICLE IV, LETTER EIGHT

First and foremost, the Hōonkō Ceremony to be held on the twenty-eighth of this month is a traditional service that has been repeated every year ever since the olden days. Accordingly, followers from provinces far and near gather together to show their sincere gratitude for all that has been done for them. From distant times right up to the present day we have continuously and unfailingly been saying the *Nenbutsu*, that is, pronouncing the Name. For this we have to thank our Founder's peerless transmission of the Dharma extended to all beings under One Heaven and across the Four Seas.

During this ceremony of seven days and seven nights, therefore, those without Dharma or faith should attain the faith that leads them to birth in the Pure Land. What more fitting expression of gratitude for all that Shinran Shōnin has done for us could there be at this month's annual memorial! Those who fail to attain faith are indeed similar to those who have no intention of responding with gratitude for all that has been done for them. Thus, these days, amongst those who call themselves *Nenbutsu* followers of the Shin Buddhist tradition, there are some who fail to attain decisively the peaceful awareness of our tradition right through to the very bottom of their hearts. As a result it is said that some of them, just for the sake of their reputation, or merely to imitate others, simply put on a pretence of gratitude. They really should not behave like this. It is quite unutterably sad that the followers who come to the capital, after enduring untold hardships in the course of long journeys of countless *ri*, should still be vain enough to be so concerned about their reputation that they resort to imitating others. Such conduct betrays an extreme lack of thought on their part. In the case of those whose past good is immature, however, there is nothing that we can do to help. Yet, if only they would repent with all their hearts and turn to the right thought with singlemindedness, why should they too not be able to achieve what Shōnin truly wants them to attain?

First: Followers travelling in from various provinces, no matter whether they are on highways or main streets, at checking stations or on ferry boats, should never talk openly and unreservedly to others about the Buddha-dharma.

Second: In different places, here and there, not a few people relate strange teachings unknown in our tradition or discourse on curious subjects entirely foreign to our school. These teachings are completely erroneous. Henceforth this should no longer be allowed to happen.

Third: In the course of the seven days of Hōonkō, each and every one whose faith has not yet been awakened should, without exception, take it upon themselves to make an unreserved confession with sincere repentance in order that they may attain true faith.

Fourth: There are some who have not attained the state of peaceful awareness. For this very reason they should be full of questions to ask, and yet they do not speak out about their state of mind just as it is, preferring to keep it hidden. Although we question them and press them for a reply, still they try and avoid confronting the matter and refuse to speak openly about their state of mind. But this is too precious an opportunity to miss. They should speak about their own state of mind unreservedly and ground themselves in the true faith.

Fifth: It would seem that nowadays, although traditional followers and Dharma friends have been experiencing the decisive attainment of faith, priests who ought to be pillars of the Buddha-dharma have been neglecting the matter of faith in a serious way. Priests under these circumstances, whenever mention is made of their lack of faith, tend to fly into a furious temper. This is an absurd situation. From now on, both priests and disciples should abide in the one same faith.

Sixth: There are rumours nowadays that priests have got into the habit of drinking very heavily. This is utterly disgraceful; they should not be behaving like this. I do not necessarily mean that they should give up the consumption of *sake* altogether. But if they drink as heavily as this, there are bound to be occasions when intoxication throws into confusion their relationship with the Buddha-dharma and with Dharma friends. This is totally unacceptable. If priests in such cases are stopped from drinking, it will definitely contribute to the promotion of the Buddha-dharma. If such priests find it impossible to give up drink altogether, then just one cup might be acceptable. It is seriously worth considering, however, whether the reason they find it so difficult to give up drinking is perhaps because their aspiration for the Buddha-dharma is too shallow.

Seventh: At meetings with fellow Dharma friends even those who have already attained faith should talk about it repeatedly to one another. This will provide the foundation for Shin Buddhism to prosper.

Eighth: It should be realised that the essence of the decisive attainment of faith in our tradition is expressed in the form of the six characters 南无阿彌陀佛 *Namu Amida-butsu*. Shàndǎo already stated in his commentary: "*Namu* means 'to take refuge.' It also means the 'vow-making and virtue-transference [of Amida Buddha].' *Amida-butsu* means 'his practice'."[335] When sentient beings take refuge in Amida by saying *Namu*, Amida Buddha, well aware that they are doing so, graciously bestows on them the virtues of a myriad good deeds and practices, innumerable as the grains of sand in the river Ganges. This is what is meant by the statement "*Amida-butsu* means his practice." Those who take refuge by saying *Namu* are, therefore, one with *Amida-butsu*, Amida Buddha's Dharma that saves them. Referring to this unity, we call it "the oneness in *Namu Amida-butsu* of *ki* and *Hō*."[336] We should realise, therefore, that *Namu Amida-butsu* attained in the here and now expresses the fulfilment of the Supreme Enlightenment of Amida Buddha who, as Bhikṣu Dharmākara, vowed a long time ago that, unless sentient beings attained Buddhahood, he too would not attain Supreme Enlightenment. This, in other words, is the evidence that our birth has been secured. Thus, it should be concluded that our attainment of Other Power faith is quite simply the heart of these six characters.

Briefly put, the meaning of these eight items is as stated above.

Meanwhile, nine years have passed by already since the construction of this temple. Although it is reported that at the Hōonkō Ceremony every year each individual participant feels that they have fully undergone the decisive attainment of faith, in so far as what is meant by faith appears to differ from person to person even up until yesterday and today, it may amount to nothing at all. But if those who lack faith fail to attain true faith quickly in the course of the Hōonkō Ceremony to be held this month – especially during this year's Hōonkō Ceremony – it appears likely that things will remain the same, however many years go by.

In the meantime, I, a foolish old man, have already completed my seventh decade and can no longer look forward with any confidence to being present at next year's Hōonkō Ceremony. For this reason, if there are some amongst you who really do undergo the decisive attainment of faith, it will be seen first as our expression of gratitude this month to Shōnin, and then as the fulfillment of a heartfelt desire this old fool has cherished over the last seven or eight years.

Most humbly and respectfully
On 23rd November, Bunmei 17 [1485]

COMMENTS

This letter, written on 23rd November 1485, is again one of the seven Hōonkō letters I made detailed reference to in my commentary on the sixth letter of Fascicle Four. Those comparatively long letters – the eleventh letter of Fascicle Three, the fifth, sixth, seventh, eighth and fifteenth letters of Fascicle Four and the eleventh letter of Fascicle Five – were all written by Rennyo Shōnin in the course of conducting the Hōonkō Ceremony and for this reason, perhaps, it became a convention in this tradition to read them out only on the occasion of the Hōonkō Ceremony.

This is a very long letter, actually the longest of all eighty letters in Rennyo's Letters, and it goes without saying that the Hōonkō Ceremony is the most important event of the year for Shin Buddhists to express their deepest gratitude to Shinran Shōnin, Founder of the tradition, for all that he has done for us. When he wrote the letter, he seems to have been very much concerned about the transmission to fellow Dharma friends, both priests and lay people, of Shinran Shōnin's original teaching. In other words, he was concerned about how his contemporaries could best be helped to receive true faith and convey it to future generations. Thus this lenghty letter is full of deep affection towards his fellow followers and each of the eight articles can be seen as an expression of his love and compassion. Because the love he bore his fellow Dharma friends was so profound, the concern he felt was all the more serious. Accordingly his teaching may appear very strict, particularly to the ears of those who are yet to attain faith, as they will be unable to recognise the love and compassion underlying his instructions.

As the first paragraph of this letter resembles that of the sixth and seventh letters, I will merely seek to clarify one or two phrases. The first is the phrase, "since the olden days." It is believed amongst traditional Shin Buddhists that "the olden days" in this particular context refers to the time of Nyoshin Shōnin (1235–1300), Shinran Shōnin's grandson, who formally succeeded the founder, Shinran Shōnin, as the second Head Priest of Honganji Temple. Another difficult phrase, "all beings under One Heaven and across the Four Seas" means all sentient beings all over the world, with both "under One Heaven" and "across the Four Seas" referring to the whole world. According to the Buddhist world view, Mount Sumeru is believed to be surrounded by the Four Seas.

The second paragraph is deeply imbued with the sympathy and compassion Rennyo feels for those who travel from distant provinces to Kyoto to attend the Hōonkō Ceremony at Honganji Temple. What he wants so much to see is their own attainment of peaceful awareness. Listening to his lamentation over the followers' lack of faith in this paragraph, I rather get the feeling that he is actually speaking to us, too, the ignorant beings of today, merely concerned with fame, gain and predominance.

He then proceeds to give his followers important instructions known as 'eight articles.' As some of these are repetitions of the 'three articles' in the sixth letter of Fascicle Four or of the 'six articles' in the seventh letter of Fascicle Four, I will simply show you which corresponds to which. It is very important for us to remember, however, that it was because he was so concerned about the followers' state of mind that Rennyo spoke to them repeatedly about these matters.

The first article in this letter is very similar to the second of 'the three articles' in the sixth letter of Fascicle Four and the third of 'the six articles' in the seventh letter of the same fascicle. It is a warning from Rennyo Shōnin to his followers to be prudent and refrain from talk that could unnecessarily arouse the general public, or followers of other schools, and trigger serious social problems.

The second article reminds us of the statement in the thirteenth letter of Fascicle One and is a serious warning to those who misunderstand the Shin Buddhist teaching and lead people to false beliefs.

The third article reminds us of a passage in the sixth letter of Fascicle Four: "These people should straightaway bow down their heads before the Image and, having their minds turned with repentance, return to the truth of the Original Vow so that they may cherish the true faith with the awakening of the one thought-moment." What Rennyo Shōnin wants to see is every individual follower's attainment of true faith.

The fourth article is important in terms of the human relationships between Dharma friends. Rennyo often suggested to those around him that they should not hide the problems they had with their faith but should speak about it to others at group meetings and listen to what they had to say. There are a number of examples of such suggestions made by him such as Articles 87, 108, 120, 121 and 203 from *The Goichidai ki kikigaki*.

Article 87. Rennyo Shōnin said, "Speak up, talk to one another" and "It is dangerous for anyone to remain silent." Again he said, "Those who have attained faith and those who have yet to do so, they should all talk to one another," and also "If you speak up, then what you have on your mind becomes known to others and can be corrected. Just say something!"337

Article 108. He said, "You should prepare yourself mentally as best you can to be corrected by others! Let your heart be open to your Dharma friends. People fail to trust and accept advice from others who are younger or of lower status and fly into a temper. How deplorable that is! You should maintain a state of mind that allows you to accept the advice of others."338

Everyone has difficulties. If you want to solve your problems and become happier by being freed from karmic ties, it is of vital importance that you face the reality of your existence in the light of the Buddha's teaching and do not run away from your problems or hide them from others. If you are awakened to yourself or the sad reality of your karmic existence, the solution will be there. All you need do is entrust yourself to the unconditional love of Amida Buddha. What is most important on our part is a truthful dialogue between fellow Dharma friends, speaking to and listening to one another in the light of the Buddha's teaching of impermanence, selflessness and inner peace.

The fifth article overlaps with the first and second of "the six articles" in the seventh letter of Fascicle Four.

And the sixth article is about priests' bad habit of excessive drinking. Priests are absolutely responsible for the Sangha. They should never allow confusion in the form of quarreling, confrontation and the like to be introduced into the Sangha as a result of their intoxication. Although Rennyo shows great sympathy for those struggling to abstain from drinking to excess, he encourages them to recognise that their attachment to this worldly habit reflects a lack of sincerity towards the Buddha-dharma.

The seventh article clarifies his intentions in writing each of the preceding ones. Whilst superficially sounding like moral precepts, all the articles reflect his sincere wish that every Dharma friend involved in the Sangha attain pure faith.

In the eighth article he goes on to discuss the essential aspects of faith-experience through an analysis of Shàndǎo's interpretation of *Namu Amida-butsu*. Regarding the Shin Buddhist faith-experience, Rennyo's explanation of its relationship to *Namu Amida-butsu* in this article is very clear and particularly his teaching of "the oneness in *Namu Amida-butsu* of *ki*, or the person to be saved, and *Hō*, the Dharma that saves that person" (*kihō ittai no Namu Amida-butsu* in Japanese) is of vital importance.

There are many poems on the notion of *kihō ittai no Namu Amida-butsu,* the oneness in *Namu Amida-butsu* of *ki and Hō*, composed by the Shin Buddhist *myōkōnin* poet, Asahara Saichi,[339] who loved reading *The Letters* by Rennyo Shōnin. One of them says,

> How wretched this being is!
> Indescribably wretched.
> How benevolent the Dharma is!
> Indescribably benevolent.
> My being is taken into the Dharma,
> The Dharma, into me.
> This taste is the oneness of *ki and Hō.*
> How happy I am with the favour, *Namu Amida-butsu.*"[340]

In his daily service both mornings and evenings Saichi would carefully trace each line with his index finger, saying "This is all about me." His understanding was truly incredible.

According to the *Rennyo Shōnin itoku ki,*[341] "over the last seven or eight years" in the concluding passage of the letter refers to the time Rennyo spent at Yamashina Honganji, the construction of which he had started planning at the request of his first disciple, Dōsai (1399–1488), in 1477, eight years before. Based on this fact we can truly sense his compassionate concern for the future of the faith movement he had nurtured for so long in this area.

CHAPTER FIFTY-TWO

The Shin Buddhist Attitude towards Death

ON AN EPIDEMIC

FASCICLE IV, LETTER NINE

People have been falling sick and dying in large numbers in the recent epidemic. However, it is not that they are simply dying because of an epidemic. Death is the karmic termination for which our whole life is destined from the first moment of birth. We should never be too frightened by this. When people die these days, however, everyone feels that it must be as a result of the epidemic. This is perfectly understandable.

Because of this, Amida Tathāgata has vowed he will save without fail all those sentient beings who entrust themselves singleheartedly to him, even ignorant beings of the Last Age such as ourselves, heavily burdened with bad karma, no matter how heavy their karmic transgressions might be. At such a time as this, we should trust in Amida Buddha all the more deeply. Realising that we will be born in the Land of Utmost Bliss, we should never entertain the slightest speck or droplet of doubt towards Amida Buddha, but revere him steadfastly and singleheartedly. Once we have realised this, saying '*Namu*

Amida-butsu, Namu Amida-butsu,' whether sleeping or waking, becomes a joyful expression of our gratitude to Amida Buddha for saving us so easily in this way. This, in other words, is the *Nenbutsu* of grateful response to the Buddha for all that he has done for us.

Most humbly and respectfully
In June, Entoku 4 [1492].

COMMENTS

The *Kūzen nikki,* or *Kūzen's Diary,*[342] confirms that there was a serious epidemic in which many people perished and that Rennyo composed this letter and gave it to Junsei (Hōkyō-bō), one of his disciples. The original letter in his own handwriting still exists and bears the date of 10th June of that year when the epidemic was at its height.

Broadly speaking there are two parts to the letter: The first paragraph that refers to the epidemic and talks about human death in general and the second paragraph that speaks about the Shin Buddhist faith, or more precisely, about the way we should entrust ourselves to Amida Buddha and continue living our lives with gratitude to him for all that he has done for us.

No human being, not even Śākyamuni Buddha, can escape from death. According to Buddhist philosophy, death is just one phase of impermanency. The unique combination of various karmic conditions that allows each individual to live for a while in this world will eventually be exhausted and so we are destined to die. Rennyo says, "Death is the karmic termination for which our whole life is destined from the first moment of birth." Even modern science acknowledges that each individual human being will eventually die. This Buddhist philosophy of impermanence is absolutely free of any superstition.

An epidemic can be a factor in our death, but not the sole cause. Some die and others do not. Needless to say, death is closely related to each person's karmic conditions as well. It is the dissolution of various causative conditions that combine to constitute each person's life, including basic karmic factors. Therefore, as Rennyo says, "We should never be too frightened by this." The really important point Rennyo makes in the first paragraph of this letter resides in those kindly words of advice to followers fearful of dying in the epidemic. In order to understand the letter properly, we should not forget that in those days people were very superstitious and an epidemic, or *ekirei* in Japanese, was thought to be the work of an evil spirit or to be brought about by an overwhelming flow of bad air. Such superstitious beliefs caused a lot of unnecessary anxiety. It was even rumored amongst *Nenbutsu* followers at that time that, as death in the epidemic represented an unnatural exhaustion of people's karma, victims would be unable to attain Buddhahood after death. By expounding the basic Buddhist notion of death in this letter, Rennyo is kindly advising his followers, intimidated by such a superstitious belief, not to be overly frightened by the epidemic. Thus his basic intention in writing this letter was to dispel his followers' misconceptions about the epidemic and to get them to ground themselves in the true faith in Amida Buddha.

Although the meaning of the opening phrase of the second paragraph, "Because of this," is not very clear, if we take into consideration the general flow of thought in this letter, it could signify "Amida Buddha knowing all this in advance." The first sentence of the second paragraph is traditionally interpreted as referring to Amida's call to us, sentient beings, as portrayed in Shàndǎo's main work, *Exposition of The Meditation Sūtra*, by the parable of "The White Path between the River of Fire and River of Water." According to the traditional interpretation by Shin Buddhist scholars such as Kakuju Yoshitani and Shirō Sugi, "Amida Tathāgata has vowed that he will save without fail all those sentient beings" corresponds to "Then someone calls him from the western shore, saying, 'You there! Concentrate singlemind-edly and come immediately. I will protect you fully! Do not be afraid of the misfortune of falling into the fire or water'," and the phrase "even ignorant beings of the Last Age such as ourselves, heavily burdened with bad karma, no matter how heavy their karmic transgressions might be" corresponds to "You there!" in the parable. Similarly the words in the letter "no matter how heavy their karmic transgressions might be" correspond to "Do not be afraid of the misfortune of falling into the fire or water" in the parable and "all those sentient beings who entrust themselves singleheartedly to him" corresponds to "Concentrate singlemindedly and come immediately!" Finally "he will save without fail" in the letter recalls "I will protect you fully!" in the parable.[343] This kind of traditional interpretation is both intriguing and helpful because it shows us, modern followers of the path, exactly what direction to take when reading the text.

CHAPTER FIFTY-THREE

Encouraging Women to Attain Faith

ON [WOMEN IN] THE PRESENT AGE

FASCICLE IV, LETTER TEN

All you women living in the present age, you should entrust yourselves absolutely to Amida Tathāgata with singlemindedness. You should realise that, whatever other teaching you may believe, you will never be saved in Rebirth through any teaching apart from this.

How, then, should one entrust oneself to Amida, and how should one aspire to Rebirth?

You should have no doubt at all, not even as much as a single droplet of dew, but that there will unfailingly be salvation for those who, without any worry, simply entrust themselves singleheartedly to Amida and sincerely beseech him to help them attain Rebirth. Once you have realised this, you should simply recite the *Nenbutsu* in thanks for all that the Buddha has done for you, feeling how grateful you are to have already been assured of deliverance.

Most humbly and respectfully
At the age of eighty-three [Seal]

COMMENTS

The *Rennyo Shōnin Itoku ki* by Rengo states: "In the autumn of the fifth year of the Meiō period (1496), at the age of eighty-two, the former master (Rennyo Shōnin) purchased the perfect piece of land on which to build a temple as his retreat at Ōsaka in Ikutama no sho, the county of Higashinari, Sesshū Province."[344] So, it was after moving to Ōsaka that he wrote this letter at the age of eighty-three. Not only this letter but also the following five letters of Fascicle Four were all written in Ōsaka during the last three years that preceded his death at the age of eighty-five.

Opinions differ as to whom the letter may have been addressed to. The *Ofumi Ryakuge*[345] maintains that the letter was written for the wife of Katagiya Yūshin, a devout disciple of Rennyo Shōnin in Sakai, whilst *The Ofumi raii shō*[346] maintains that it was given to the mother of Hōkyō-bō,[347] another devout follower. Neither of these suppositions, however, seems particularly well grounded. Although there are no historical documents to support or gainsay their conclusions, it is interesting that the authors of both books feel that the letter must have been addressed to one particular woman. I have to say I agree with them. Nearly all of Rennyo's letters appear to have been addressed to particular individuals or groups with the aim of helping them attain pure faith and entrust themselves absolutely to Amida Buddha. What is important with regard to all those who receive or read Rennyo's letters is that they feel he is addressing them personally, that they become aware of their own karmic problems in the light of his teaching and that they entrust themselves to Amida Buddha.

The *Ofumi kōjutsu* maintains[348] that the first paragraph of the letter is essentially based on a passage in the *Anraku shū* 安楽集 (ch. Ānlè jí), which Dōshaku 道綽 (ch. Dàochuò), the author of the book, produced based on the *Daijikkyō* 大集經 (ch. Dàjíjīng, skt. *Mahasamnipata sūtra*). The passage reads, "In this, the Last Dharma Age, though billions of sentient beings decide to undertake practice and discipline themselves to attain Enlightenment, none in fact attains it. In the current age of the Last Dharma, the bad world polluted with the five defilements, the teaching of the Pure Land alone is the only access to Enlightenment."[349] Shinran Shōnin in *The Shōshinge* summarises Dàochuò's view, presented in the *Anraku shū*, as follows: "It is Dàochuò who has made indisputably clear the difficulty of the Path of Sages in attaining Awakening. Our only access to it is via the teaching of the Pure Land."[350] One of Shinran Shōnin's own verses in Japanese (*wasan*), praising Dàochuò's clarification of the Pure Land way, also makes this point,

Our patriarch, Dhyāna Master Dàochuò,
Putting aside the myriad practices of the Path of Sages,

Taught that only the gate of the Pure Land
Is open for us to access.[351]

The rest of the letter is entirely concerned with how to attain pure faith and how to express our gratitude to Amida Buddha. Each and every word of the passage is in itself the sincere and powerful expression of Rennyo's innermost desire at the age of eighty-three that his fellow followers may attain this faith.

CHAPTER FIFTY-FOUR

Oneness with Amida in *Namu Amida-Butsu*

ON ONENESS OF 'KI' AND 'HO'

FASCICLE IV, LETTER ELEVEN

What is the meaning of Namu Amida-butsu? In other words, how should we entrust ourselves to Amida and attain birth in the Land of Enjoyment?

In order to understand it, first of all we should realise exactly what is meant by the six characters '*Namu Amida-butsu*' 南无阿彌陀佛 and entrust ourselves to Amida. *Namu Amida-butsu* is essentially nothing other than the mind of sentient beings, such as ourselves, entreating Amida Tathāgata to help them attain Rebirth. In other words, Amida Tathāgata, fully knowing the sentient beings who entrust themselves to him, has already bestowed on them the unsurpassed virtue of great benefit. This is what is meant by 'virtue-transference to sentient beings.' Thus it is Amida Buddha's Dharma (*Hō*) that saves those (*ki*) who entrust themselves to Amida Buddha. Therefore, we speak of this as 'the oneness in *Namu Amida-butsu* of *ki*, or the person, and *Hō*, or the Dharma.' We must realise that this is Other Power faith, through which our birth is assured.

Most humbly and respectfully

I finished writing this on 25th May in the sixth year of the Meio period [1497]. At the age of eighty-three.

COMMENTS

This letter, too, was written in Ōsaka in 1497, the same year as the tenth letter of Fascicle Four. *The Ofumi raii shō* explains the background to the letter.[352] In the autumn of 1496, apparently, a disciple of Rennyo's in Komatsu, Ryōchin by name, asked the master for an explanation of the meaning of *Namu Amida-butsu* and in May 1497, when he returned to Ōsaka to receive Rennyo Shōnin's teaching, he asked Rennyo to write down the meaning of *Namu Amida-butsu* in the form of a letter.

This story, however, differs somewhat from what appear to have been the facts. There exists a letter, entitled *An enquiry about the meaning of the six characters, Namu Amida-butsu,*[353] that was not compiled into the Five Fascicle version of *The Letters*. This letter is very similar in content to the eleventh letter of Fascicle Four above, though it does not refer to the teaching of *kihō ittai no Namu Amida-butsu* or 'the oneness in *Namu Amida-butsu* of *ki*, or the person, and *Hō*, or the Dharma.' The notion of *kihō ittai* must have been added to it subsequently when the eleventh letter of Fascicle Four was written down in May 1497. According to Rennyo's own note in the uncompiled letter, this was the letter he gave to Ryōchin in 1493. Although one cannot be absolutely sure whether or not he did in fact hand Ryōchin this other letter, the author of *The Ofumi raii shō* would appear to have been seriously misinformed.

As I have already discussed the notion of the oneness in *Namu Amida-butsu* of *ki*, or the person to be saved, and *Hō*, or the Dharma that saves, in relation to the seventh letter of Fascicle Four, I will not go into detail again here.

Rennyo expounds the notion of the oneness of *ki and Hō* in the letter, "In other words, Amida Tathāgata, fully knowing the sentient beings who entrust themselves to him, has already bestowed on them the unsurpassed virtue of great benefit. This is what is meant by 'virtue-transference to sentient beings.' Thus it is Amida Buddha's Dharma (*Hō*) that saves those (*ki*) who entrust themselves to Amida Buddha."

When we talk about *kihō ittai no Namu Amida-butsu*, *ki* in this context does not mean the person who is still attached to his or her self power but the person who entrusts himself or herself absolutely to Amida Buddha, Other Power. This is the *ki* of Other Power faith based on the Eighteenth Vow, not the *ki* of self power based on the 19th or 20th Vow. Without entrusting ourselves absolutely to Amida Buddha's Original Vow (Eighteenth Vow), our person or self cannot be the *ki* of pure Other Power faith that is entirely one with *Hō*, Amida Buddha.

CHAPTER FIFTY-FIVE

The Meaning
of Our Monthly
Dharma Meetings

ON OUR TWO MONTHLY MEETINGS

FASCICLE IV, LETTER TWELVE

We come together twice a month for the sole purpose of attaining faith for our birth in the Land of Utmost Bliss. And yet, despite these two monthly meetings being regularly held everywhere since the olden days, they never seem to include any proper discussions about faith. In recent years in particular, whenever and wherever such meetings are held, everyone just ends up dispersing after simply enjoying *sake*, rice, tea, etc. But this is entirely contrary to the original intent of the Buddha-dharma. Although anyone who is without faith should, of course, raise their own questions and talk about the issue of whether faith has been attained or not, people just disperse without finding any meaning. I feel this is not at all as it should be. This is a matter you should consider carefully.

In summary, it is essential that from now on all of you without faith should openly have discussions on faith with others.

The meaning of peaceful awareness in our tradition is that, despite our deep karmic hindrances, we should have no doubt whatsoever that Amida will save all sentient beings who simply forsake their inclination for miscellaneous practices, singleheartedly take refuge in Amida Tathāgata, and sincerely entreat Amida to help them in the Great Matter of Rebirth to come. Those who truly understand the heart of this matter will indeed be born, one hundred out of every hundred.

So, if you understand that we hold meetings every month to respond with gratitude for all that has been done for us, you may indeed be called followers endowed with true faith.

Most humbly and respectfully

Written on 25th February, Meiō period 7 [1498].
To all those who attend the two monthly meetings.
At the age of eighty-four

COMMENTS

The last four letters of Fascicle Four from this one to the fifteenth were all written by Rennyo Shōnin in Ōsaka at the age of eighty-four, just one year before his death in 1499. According to *The Rennyo Shōnin Ibun* or *Writings by Rennyo Shōnin* compiled by Professor Masamaru Inaba, the number of the dated letters written by Rennyo in 1498 amounts to nineteen, including the last four of Fascicle Four. If we add undated letters to the dated ones, it seems that he wrote more than thirty letters during this one year, despite the fact that he became ill in April. With the exception of this year, it was only in 1473 and 1474 during his stay at Yoshizaki that he produced more than twenty dated letters per year. What does it mean that he created such a great number of letters during the one year just before his death? According to the next letter, the thirteenth letter of Fascicle Four, apparently he knew that he was already terminally ill when he was writing those letters. It was nothing but his love and compassion for his Dharma friends around him that urged him to write those letters energetically in spite of his serious illness. As you can see from the letter, what Rennyo hoped for from the bottom of his heart was his Dharma friends' attainment of faith through their serious discussions on the matter of faith at regular meetings.

What is said in the opening paragraph is not difficult at all to understand. He just confirms that those "two monthly meetings" (*maigatsu ryodo no yoriai* 毎月両度の寄合) should be held solely for the attainment of faith.

We should discuss there the difficult problems we face in attaining pure faith. Sadly, however, what we usually do in Buddhist meetings is quite contrary to the original meaning of the Buddha-dharma, just attending Dharma talks and dispersing meaninglessly after simply having meals and drinks at those gatherings.

Thus, Rennyo emphasised the vital importance of these two monthly meetings in this special letter he wrote thirteen months before his death. Then, what was it that he intended in holding those two monthly meetings?

Nowadays, in Shin Buddhism in general, the expression 'two monthly memorial days' (*maigatsu ryōdo no gomeinichi* 毎月両度の御命日) refers to the memorial day of Shinran Shōnin and that of the last Head Priest of the tradition. According to Articles 45, 49, and 53 of the *Honganji sahō no shidai* and Article 7 of the *Yamashina gobō no koto narabini sono jidai no koto* by Jitsugo,[354] which are now compiled in the *Rennyo Shōnin zenshū, Vol. 4* by Chōjun Ōtani, however, what was meant by the expression 'two monthly memorial days' since the early stage of the Shin Buddhist history until the days of Rennyo Shōnin was very different from our present understanding of the phrase. It actually meant the memorial day of Hōnen Shōnin and that of Shinran Shōnin for more than two hundred years.

The historical document, *Honganji sahō no shidai*, states that until the time of Rennyo Shin Buddhist followers had been holding the memorial service for Hōnen Shōnin, in which they used to listen to a brief biography of Hōnen Shōnin, *The Chionkō shiki*,[355] being read out by the Head Priest of Honganji Temple.

Likewise, on the other monthly memorial day, *The Hōonkō shiki,* which had been written by Kakunyo Shōnin (1270–1351), the third Head Priest of Honganji, on the day of 33rd annual memorial service for Shinran Shōnin, would be read out by the Head Priest of Honganji. Although this document, together with *The Tandoku mon*,[356] is nowadays only read out once a year at the Hōonkō Ceremony, the fact that *The Hōonkō shiki* had been read out every month at the memorial service for Shinran Shōnin in the olden times is confirmed by the historical document known as *The Boki eshi*, as it states "The whole three sections [of *The Hōonkō shiki* by Kakunyo Shōnin] are to be read out every month at our meetings to commemorate the death of Shinran Shōnin."[357]

The Chionkō shiki had long been believed to be a writing by Venerable Zonkaku in 1357, until the time its oldest copy, made by Shin Amidabutsu in 1228, was found at Hōbodaiin, Tōji Temple in Kyoto, in 1964. It is now recognised that *The Chionkō shiki* was composed by Ryūkan (1148–1227) around ten years after the death of Hōnen Shōnin (1133–1212).

As you know, Venerable Ryūkan was one of the best Dharma friends of Shinran Shōnin and the latter gave his followers copies of the former's essays such as *Ichinen tanen funbetsu ji*[358] or *Jiriki tariki ji*.[359] In addition to this fact, in his *Annotated Inscriptions on Sacred Scrolls,* he has a detailed phrase by phrase commentary on the verses Venerable Ryūkan composed in praise of his master, Hōnen Shōnin. Every time Shinran Shōnin conducted a monthly memorial service for Hōnen Shōnin, he must have been using that scroll on which both the image of Hōnen Shōnin and those verses by Ryūkan were drawn. More importantly in this context, Shinran Shōnin must have been reading out *The Chionkō shiki* by Ryūkan during the monthly ceremony in order to keep in mind and respond for all that had been done for him by Hōnen Shōnin.

Shinran Shōnin's way of conducting the memorial service for his master Hōnen Shōnin with utmost gratitude was transmitted to later generations after his death. Furthermore, his disciples adopted this way in their memorial service for Hōnen Shōnin. Needless to say, they knew how crucial Shinran Shōnin's encounter with his master was in his own faith-experience and hence in their Shin Buddhist tradition. It was in this sincere effort to create their own way of holding a memorial service for Shinran Shōnin that Kakunyo Shōnin, the third Head Priest of Honganji, composed *The Hōonkō shiki*, a ceremonial document very similar to *The Chionkō shiki*. Although they are very similar not only in form but also in content, it is not that *The Chionkō shiki* was made after the model of *The Hōonkō shiki* since it is in actual fact the older of the two texts. Professor Zenshin Mita states in his main work, *A Study of the Various Biographies of Hōnen Shōnin*,[360] that amongst the various biographies of Hōnen Shōnin *The Chionkō shiki* is one of the earliest.

The Chionkō shiki consists of five sections: Firstly, "Praising his virtue of being thoroughly versed in all traditions." In this section the author described Hōnen Shōnin as "the first and foremost in Wisdom" for the first time in the history of the biographies of Hōnen Shōnin. Secondly, "Praising his virtue of promoting the Original Vow." In this section the author refers to the vital importance of taking refuge in Amida's Original Vow, describing Hōnen Shōnin as an embodiment of Amida Buddha. Thirdly, "Praising his virtue of solely following the right practice." The author emphasises it matches the original intent of the Buddha that we solely follow the right practice that is in accordance with the Original Vow. Fourthly, "Clarifying his virtue of definitely attaining birth." In this section Ryūkan describes Hōnen Shōnin's way of reciting the *Nenbutsu* loudly on facing his own death. It is quite intriguing to know that, although several disciples tried to help him in reciting the *Nenbutsu*, in actual fact, they were overwhelmed by Hōnen Shōnin's consistent and loud recitation and became quite tired. Fifthly, "Describing his virtue of saving all beings after death." There is an interesting description of multitudes of people performing the memorial service for him in front of the scroll of his image.

The special Shin Buddhist custom of holding a monthly meeting on the 25th to commemorate the death of Hōnen Shōnin and conducting a memorial service for him by reading out *The Chionkō shiki* continued to the days of Rennyo Shōnin. As already mentioned above, therefore, when he talked about two monthly meetings in this letter, one of them was to remember Hōnen Shōnin and the other, to remember Shinran Shōnin. After the death of Rennyo, Jitsunyo Shōnin, his fifth son and successor of Honganji, stopped holding this particular meeting in which *The Chionkō shiki* was read out.

Article 45 of *The Honganji sahō no shidai* by Jitsugo explains his reason for doing so as follows,

Around the beginning of the Eishō period (1504), Rensei[361] from Kyōkōji Temple asked Jitsunyo Shōnin, "Despite the fact that the former Head Priest, Rennyo Shōnin, used to read out *The Chionkō shiki* on the morning of 25th, why do you not do so?" It is said that Jitsunyo Shōnin replied to this question, saying "Somehow I cannot read it out with a proper intonation." When, having heard of this conversation between them from someone else, I (Jitsugo) asked Rensei about their conversation, Rensei answered to me, "Yes, he has replied so." Certainly I can confirm this story.[362]

Even apart from Jitsunyo Shōnin's personal feeling of difficulty in reading it out, it must have been quite hard for him to conduct two heavy memorial services on the 25th every month not only for Hōnen Shōnin but also for Rennyo Shōnin, who had actually passed away on the 25th March in 1499. After this, "two monthly meetings" came to mean two memorial days of Shinran Shōnin and the former Head Priest of Honganji Temple. Although Shin Buddhist followers stopped reading out *The Chionkō shiki* in a heavily ceremonial way, they continued to hold their monthly memorial service for Hōnen Shōnin in a simpler way. They do so even today.

Although the ceremony of reading out *The Chionkō shiki* faded away in the other Pure Land schools at the early times of their history, my quite reasonable speculation that it must have been started by Shinran Shōnin himself, as suggested by Rennyo's words "since the olden days" in the first paragraph of this letter, will be followed by a possible conclusion that it might have continued in the Shin Buddhist tradition for about two hundred and seventy years. Professor Zenshin Mita from the Jōdo School states in his book, *A Study of the Various Biographies of Hōnen Shōnin*, that it is a great pleasure for him to see *The Chionkō shiki* had been transmitted in the Shin Buddhist tradition.[363]

All this means that Shinran Shōnin and his followers understood the vital importance of his encounter with Hōnen Shōnin for their awakening of pure faith. In a *wasan* in praise of Hōnen Shōnin Shinran writes,

Even though we had gone through many births for long kalpas,
We were still unaware of the powerful condition for our emancipation.
If our master, Genkū, had not appeared,
This round of life, too, might well have passed in vain.[364]

The fundamental purpose of holding those monthly meetings is just to attain pure faith through mutual encounters and serious conversations amongst Dharma friends. Rennyo Shōnin quite often asks his followers to say something to one another without hiding themselves from others. In order to be awakened to yourself, it is very important for you not to run away from your own problems but to become aware of them. In the matter of attaining faith it is extremely important for us to speak to and listen to one another amongst Dharma friends at such meetings.

Regarding this subject there are a number of sayings by Rennyo in *The Goichidai ki kikigaki*, as already mentioned in the *Introduction*. Our Dharma meetings should not end up with drinking, eating or chatting like worldly meetings, because they are solely for our own awakening of faith.

Regarding the latter half of the letter, the special expression "They will be born, one hundred out of every hundred" (百即百生 jp. *hyakusoku hyakushō*) is originally from *The Ōjō raisan* 往生禮讚 by Shàndǎo 善導,

> If, as mentioned above, you continue to practice the *Nenbutsu* every moment to the very end of life, you will be born ten out of every ten and one hundred out of every hundred. It is because your practice is the right practice and not mixed with any other practices, and because it is in accordance with the Original Vow of the Buddha, because it is not against the teaching and because it is based on the words of the Buddha.[365]

The essential thought of this passage is summarised in the following sentence from Shàndǎo's main work, *The Exposition of The Meditation Sūtra*:

> This is called the right practice which truly assures one to be born in the Pure Land, as it is in accordance with Amida's Original Vow.[366]

In Japanese Pure Land Buddhism this is recognised as the famous passage that led Hōnen Shōnin to convert to Pure Land Buddhism. What underlies this passage is the absolute awakening of faith through which Shàndǎo entrusted himself to Amida Buddha's Original Vow. On coming across this passage after going through the whole *Tripitaka*[367] several times, Hōnen Shōnin must have seen in this particular sentence Shàndǎo's absolute reliance or faith in Amida Buddha. At that very moment Hōnen Shōnin entrusted himself entirely to Amida's Original Vow. What Shinran Shōnin was awakened to after visiting Hōnen Shōnin at Yoshimizu for a hundred days at the age of twenty-nine was this pure faith in Amida of Hōnen Shōnin. Through this encounter Shinran Shōnin immediately "abandoned the miscellaneous acts and took refuge in the Original Vow."[368]

Rennyo wanted all the participants in the two monthly meetings to attain pure faith of the same quality and be born in the Pure Land "one hundred out of every hundred."

Concerning Vinaya Master Ryūkan, the author of *The Chionkō shiki*, taking into account Shinran Shōnin's reliance on him, I feel we need a more detailed study of his life and thought. Although he is said to have been the founder of the Chōrakuji School 長楽寺派, which is classified as the sect of "Many Recitations," as far as I am able to learn from his essay *On the Difference between One Recitation and Many Recitations*, what he wanted to clarify in the essay is that the first recitation that issues from the joy of pure faith naturally develops as many further recitations and that we should not be attached to the notion of 'one recitation' nor to that of 'many recitations.' The point of his well-balanced thought is "One Recitation is Many Recitations and Many Recitations is One Recitation."[369] Although we do not know in detail why the Chōrakuji School disappeared so soon, all that I can guess is that Ryūkan's disciples emphasised the aspect of 'Many Recitations' too much, unable to understand the true intention of his religious thought. Ryūkan's religious philosophy might have been too profound for them to understand and sustain properly in that particular historical situation.

CHAPTER FIFTY-SIX

The Importance
of the Instantaneous
Awakening of Faith
amidst the Uncertainty
of This World

IN THE MIDDLE OF 'EARLY SUMMER'

FASCICLE IV, LETTER THIRTEEN

Autumn and spring having flown away, it is already in the middle of 'early summer' (孟夏 *mōka*) of this seventh year of the Meiō period. Accumulating year after year my age has now reached eighty-four. This particular year, however, being unusually beset by illness, the conditions of my whole body – ears, eyes, hands and feet – are not very comfortable. As a result I have come to realise that this illness is the outcome of my past karma and also the harbinger of birth in the Land of Utmost Bliss. Related to this there is a saying by Hōnen Shōnin, "Followers who aspire for the Pure Land, when they suffer from illness, entirely enjoy it." Despite this, the feeling of enjoyment over illness never occurs to me. How wretched I am! How shameful this is! How sad I feel! Nevertheless, now entirely settled in this single path of 'peaceful awareness' of the essential teaching of our school that "the act is completed in daily life with the one thought-moment of awakening," I never forget pronouncing the Name to respond to the Buddha with gratitude for all that he has done for us, whether walking, standing, sitting, or lying down.

Regarding this point, here are some thoughts that I myself, an old ignoramus, would like to express.

Generally speaking, having seen the mental attitude of followers of our school in the various places where we reside, I feel there is no one who is truly serious in attaining faith decisively. This is a matter of great sadness to me. For, if, as a result of this old man having already lived over eight decades, there were a thriving group of followers who have decisively attained faith, this could be considered to be evidence of my long life. However, I see no definite sign at all of the decisive attainment of faith.

What is the reason for my saying this? Taking into account the uncertainty of the human world for young and old alike, why shall we not die suffering from any kind of illness? Everyone should understand that, given such conditions living in this world, it is essential for us to attain faith as soon as possible, even one day or one moment earlier, so that we can become absolutely assured of our birth in the Land of Utmost Bliss. After this it is also important for us to live out our lives just as they are in accordance with the ordinary circumstances of the human world. Accepting what is said above in our innermost mind, we should deep within give rise to the awakening of faith in one thought-moment whereby we entrust ourselves to Amida.

Most humbly and respectfully

Written on the first of the middle ten days of early summer (初夏 shoka) in the seventh year of the Meiō period [1498]. Written by this old priest at the age of eighty-four.

> If ever you are able to hear
> the Name of Amida,
> entrust yourselves to it, all of you,
> saying '*Namu Amida-butsu*'.

COMMENTS

Amongst the dated letters of the *Letters* by Rennyo (Five Fascicle version), this is the third from the last.

The Japanese word *mōka* 孟夏, meaning "early summer," found in the opening paragraph of this letter, means the fourth month, April, of the lunar calendar. Another similar Japanese expression *shoka* 初夏, appearing in the dating of the letter towards the ending, also means April of the lunar calendar. The Japanese expression *chūjun daiichinichi* 中旬第一日 in the dating means the first day of the middle ten days of a month. Accordingly, the letter was written on the 11th of April in 1498.

In *The Kūzen kikigaki*, Kūzen (dates unknown), one of the disciples who served Rennyo towards the end of his life, states in Article 117,

> Around the beginning of April he became ill again like last year and went to see the medical doctor Keidō. On the 17th [Doctor] Nakarai came to visit him and on the 19th [Doctor] Itasaka came. The only thing he ate was rice broth.[370]

Before and after the eleventh of April, the date Rennyo composed the letter, he met with physicians at least three times to ask them about the condition of his health. Actually his illness was getting worse and worse. Coming to realise that the illness would terminate his life, he desired to travel to Kyoto in order to see once again the image of the Founder, Shinran Shōnin, enshrined in the main hall of Yamashina Honganji.

> Article 118 of *The Kūzen kikigaki* states,
> On the 25th May he attended the service at the Main Hall. Since all those around requested him resolutely not to attend the morning service on the 28th, he did not do so. He attended, however, the daytime service and read out the first section of *The Hōonkō shiki* only and the Head Priest (Jitsunyo Shōnin), read out from the second. From 7th May to 1st June there were six days in which he did not attend the service.[371]

This document indicates that Rennyo visited Yamashina Honganji in Kyoto on 7th May and stayed there until his return to Ōsaka Gobō on 1st June. Despite his serious illness he attended the service at the Founder's Image Hall as many times as possible, probably thinking that this would be the last chance during his lifetime to express his heartfelt gratitude to Shinran Shōnin directly facing his statue at Yamashina Honganji. On the 28th of May, the monthly memorial day of Shinran Shōnin, he even tried to read out *The Hōonkō shiki*, engaging himself in the performance of this heavy ceremony as he did in the past. It must have been, however, too difficult for him to recite this sacred document at that time. After managing to read aloud only the first section of *The Hōonkō shiki*, a eulogy dedicated to Shinran Shōnin, he asked Jitsunyo Shōnin to read out its remaining two sections. Terminally ill as he was at that time, his adoration for Shinran Shōnin was so profound and immeasurable that he wanted by using all means possible to continue to express his sincerest gratitude to the founder of the tradition.

Towards the very end of his life, Rennyo decided again to return to Yamashina Honganji. In actual fact he wanted to spend his last days at the temple where the statue of Shinran Shōnin was enshrined. Article 130 of *The Kūzen kikigaki* reads as follows:

> In February of the eighth year of the Meiō period (1499), Rennyo Shōnin declared at a meeting that he was now certain to die soon and the venue for his funeral was prepared. Suddenly, however, he changed his mind. Saying he would like to return to Yamashina Honganji in Kyoto and attain birth there, Rennyo Shōnin immediately decided that the date of his departure for Kyoto should be the 18th. As Rennyo Shōnin suggested that under this condition Kūzen should go to Kyoto for his funeral, I, Kūzen, went to see him respectfully on the 16th. I prepared this journey together with those who came to move him. Thus, he started his journey on 18th and spent three days travelling on a palanquin. Taking a very quiet trip to Kyoto, he arrived at Nomura-dono (Yamashina Honganji) on the 20th.[372]

The Rennyo Shōnin itoku ki edited by Rengo and Jitsugo describes this journey as follows:

> At the beginning of summer of the 7th year of the Meiō period (1498), when the former master was eighty-four years old, he was beset by some illness. In September he said from time to time that, his health condition being like this, surely he would close his eyes in March next year. After winter passing away quickly, spring of the 8th of the Meiō period arrived. In the middle of February Kōken Sōzu (Jitsunyo Shōnin) sent those who would help move Rennyo Shōnin. Thus, Rennyo Shōnin entered Kyoto on 20th February. The talks that he gave during this illness were all 'golden sayings' without exception.[373]

The same biography also describes his last days:

> In March of the same year (1499), when the former master was eighty-five years old, being caught by a long illness that continued day after day,

he became infirm and unable to eat and his physical condition was not like in the past. More than at ordinary times, however, he appeared resolute and dauntless in spirit and free from greed and anger. It was when he was in this condition, that one warm day with the spring sunlight calmly shining on this world, whilst gazing at flowers in the surroundings, he composed these poems:

Whenever I enjoy viewing flowers in full bloom,
it is the other shore in the West that I aspire for all the more.

How long should I, a man of very old age, suffer from an illness like this?
Please, welcome me into your Pure Land, Amida Buddha!

Now that I have reached eighty and five years old,
Please, know that I cannot live any longer!

Subsequently, on 7th March of the same year, wanting to come before the statue once again, although he was quite aged and suffering from illness, Rennyo Shōnin took off the clothes he wore when ill in bed and put on newly made robes. Carried on a palanquin he first moved to the main Buddha Hall and then proceeded before the statue of Shinran Shōnin. Rennyo Shōnin then reverently spoke to the holy image of the former master, saying 'This is the last time I see you in this life. Surely I will see you, your true form, in that country.' On listening to his words there were none who did not wring their sleeves [that had become wet with tears].[374]

As seen from the documents I quoted above regarding Rennyo's stay at Yamashina Honganji both from 7th May to 1st June 1498 and from 20th February to 25th March 1499, his spiritual adoration for Shinran Shōnin was absolutely pure and unfathomably profound. In this respect nobody can separate them. They are one in faith just as they are. Being independent of each other, they are united in the truth of their own faith-experience. The Shin Buddhist faith can be said to be 'true' in this respect because it is entirely a gift from Amida Buddha.

Towards the very end of his life Rennyo just wanted to return to Shinran Shōnin, to be with him and to speak to him. Despite his sickness leading him to death, he wanted to attend the daily services as many times as possible. I myself was very much moved to discover the very fact that he tried to conduct the heavy ceremony of reading out *The Hōonkō shiki* even with such a serious health condition.

Towards the end of his life, another great concern that occupied his mind, along with his devotional adoration for Shinran Shōnin, was whether his fellow followers had attained faith or not. Needless to say, Rennyo had been carrying these two kinds of spiritual concern throughout his life. However, those two thoughts, both essential in Shin Buddhism, seem to have become more urgent and outstanding towards the end of his life. Rennyo always wanted his fellow followers to attain *anjin* or the peaceful awareness in which they find themselves, the irredeemable reality of their karmic existence, in the embrace of Amida Buddha's unconditional love. He related to Kūzen an account that showed how deeply he was concerned about their attainment of faith. According to *The Kūzen kikigaki*, he said to Kūzen at some time between July in 1497 and April in 1498:

> "First of all, attain faith yourself and help others do so. When I visited Ōshū (Mutsu Province) last time, I asked whether I could meet a certain person whom I had met on my previous visit to Ōshū, for he had been overjoyed at listening to the teaching. On hearing that not only this person but also his wife were enjoying their attainment of faith, I went to see them taking a two day trip. The husband expressed his sadness, however, asking me, 'Although I feel extremely grateful to you for visiting us, what could I offer you?' On hearing these words, I asked them, 'What do you normally eat?' When they answered, 'We only eat millet grains,' I said, 'I would like to eat what you eat.' Receiving the millet gruel, I talked to them one night so that they could appreciate the teaching." Thus he spoke. Therefore, on realising that Rennyo Shōnin had been teaching by abandoning himself and undergoing all kinds of hardships, I recorded this story.[375]

What underlies all the letters by Rennyo is this sincerest desire that all those he meets may become happy by attaining true faith. You can find it in any one of his letters. In the case of this special letter that he wrote when confronting a serious illness, his pure desire to help others attain faith is expressed here accompanied by a feeling of great sadness that he could see no definite sign at all of their decisive attainment of faith.

Not only in this particular letter but also in some of his letters written before, this kind of lamentation is expressed together with this feeling of sadness. Desiring those who lack faith to attain faith, Rennyo wrote his letters. He addressed them mainly to those without faith. If there had been some with pure faith amongst the audience, they would not have been upset to listen to his words. For, although those of pure faith are absolutely confident in it, they are never proud of their faith. In Shin Buddhism faith is entirely a gift from Amida Buddha. His great desire to save others that underlies his lamentations is more clearly expressed in the last paragraph of this letter.

There is one delicate point about which we, Shin Buddhists today, should be very careful as to how to understand it. That is a seemingly strong contrast between Hōnen Shōnin's words about illness and Rennyo's statement: "Related to this there is a saying by Hōnen Shōnin, 'Followers who aspire for the Pure Land, when they suffer from illness, entirely enjoy it'. Despite this, the feeling of enjoyment over illness never occurs to me. How wretched I am! How shameful this is! How sad I feel!"

Hōnen Shōnin's statement, which is almost the same as the above quotation, is found in *The Kanmuryōjukyō shijōsho dentsūki nyūshō*[376] by Shōgei (1341–1420): "Whereas merchants are surprised and even pleased to hear the crowing of a rooster, followers who aspire for the Pure Land, when they suffer from illness, entirely enjoy it."

How can one understand Rennyo's words? If one thinks that, whereas Hōnen Shōnin's attitude is that of Jodoshū followers, Rennyo's attitude is that of Shinshū followers and discriminate the former against the latter, one is greatly mistaken. As discussed previously, Rennyo's respect for Hōnen Shōnin is indescribably profound. He was in fact regularly conducting the ceremony of reading out *The Chionkō shiki* at the monthly memorial service. There is no sign of criticism of him in this letter. On the contrary, reflecting deeply upon Hōnen Shōnin's statement, Rennyo repents and expresses his feeling of shame in the context of this letter. His faith does not differ from Hōnen Shōnin's at all. Their faith is one and the same. Certainly, however, there is a difference of emphasis in their way of expression.

In Pure Land Buddhism true faith has two essential aspects: firstly deep awareness of *ki* or the irredeemable reality of one's own karmic existence and secondly deep awareness of *Hō* or the unconditional love of Amida Buddha that saves all beings without any discrimination. Whereas, in the case of Rennyo Shōnin's repentance, an emphasis is placed on the awareness of *ki* accompanied by a feeling of extreme sadness, Hōnen Shōnin simply expresses his joy of attaining birth in the Pure Land abiding in the peaceful awareness of Amida's great love and compassion.

From careful reading of the letter, it is clear that the passage that follows the above quotation expresses Rennyo's awareness of *Hō* and joyous faith, reminiscent of the ending part of the first letter of Fascicle One, where he expresses his overflowing joy of attaining faith: "'Previously joy was tucked away in my sleeve' means that in the past we presumed – without any clear understanding of miscellaneous practices and right practice – that we would attain birth in the Pure Land if only we recited the *Nenbutsu*. 'But, tonight, I am overflowing with happiness!' means that the joy of reciting the *Nenbutsu* in grateful response to the Buddha for what he has done for us (*button hōjin*) is especially great now that, having clearly understood the difference between the right practice and the miscellaneous practices, we have decisively attained faith with steadfastness and singlemindedness. Because of this, we are so overjoyed that we feel like dancing – hence 'I am overflowing with happiness!'"

A further illustration of Rennyo Shōnin's awareness of *ki* and serious repentance is a similar expression by Shinran Shōnin in Chapter 9 of *The Tanni shō*,

> Furthermore, not being desirous of hastening to the Pure Land, we feel very much dejected when we become ill, however mild the illness, at the thought of our possible death. This is likewise caused by the effect of blind passions. We feel reluctant to abandon this old home of pain and suffering, where we have been transmigrating from time immemorial right down to the present day, and we feel no longing for the Land of Peace and Happiness, where we have yet to be born. This is again due to our blind passions, so fierce and powerful. But when our karma in this *sahā* world expires, we will nevertheless proceed to the Pure Land. Amida especially pities those who are not desirous of hastening to the Pure Land. When you consider all this, you may realise all the more clearly how trustworthy the Great Compassionate Vow is and how firmly your birth in the Pure Land is assured.[377]

In that particular passage of this letter, Hōnen Shōnin's expression of joy in the awareness of *Hō* and Rennyo Shōnin's expression of sadness in the awareness of *ki* are found to be two sides of the same coin.

CHAPTER FIFTY-SEVEN

Peaceful Awareness in *Namu Amida-Butsu*

THE PEACEFUL AWARENESS

OF OUR SCHOOL

FASCICLE IV, LETTER FOURTEEN

You should know that the ultimate reality of peaceful awareness in our tradition is expressed in the form of six characters *Namu Amida-butsu* 南无阿彌陀佛. Great Master Shàndǎo explains these six characters as follows, "*Namu* means to take refuge. It also means vow-making and virtue-transference. *Amida-butsu* means his practice. It is because of this that we will unfailingly attain birth."

First of all, the two characters *Namu* 南无 mean 'to take refuge.' 'To take refuge' signifies sentient beings' entrusting themselves to Amida Buddha and asking for his help in the matter of Rebirth. Then 'vow-making and virtue-transference' expresses the mind that embraces and saves all the sentient beings who entrust themselves. This is then the meaning of the four characters '*Amida-butsu*' 阿彌陀佛.

How should we then, ignorant beings that we are, understand ourselves and how should we entrust ourselves to Amida? When we forsake all the other miscellaneous practices, entrust ourselves steadfastly and singleheartedly to Amida and entreat his help in the matter of Rebirth, there is no doubt at all but that we will without fail attain birth in the Land of Utmost Bliss. Thus the two characters *Namu* refer to one side, the side of sentient beings, those who entrust themselves to Amida, whilst the four characters *Amida-butsu* refer to the other side, the side of the Dharma, one who saves those sentient beings who entrust. This, then, is precisely what is meant by 'the oneness in *Namu Amida-butsu* of *ki* (the person) and *Hō* (the Dharma)'. For this reason, we realise that the ultimate reality that carries all of us sentient beings to birth is *Namu Amida-butsu*.

Most humbly and respectfully
In April, Meiō 7 [1498].

COMMENTS

There are a few other very similar versions of this letter in existence but with different dates.[378] It would seem that Rennyo provided his followers with such slightly varying versions of the same letter on several different occasions. Indeed amongst the two hundred and fifty-two letters there are a number of cases of duplication of content with marginally different wording.

Of those dated letters which are similar in content to the fourteenth letter of Fascicle Four, the one in *The Compilation of Copies by Dōshū* has the earliest date: "10th April 1498." As mentioned before, according to *The Kūzen kikigaki*, Rennyo became seriously ill at the beginning of the same month. Even so he wrote at least a further sixteen letters, three of them edited by Ennyo Shōnin and compiled into the formal Five Fascicle version of *The Letters*. This letter will have been included in the formal version certainly on account of its dogmatic importance.

In the first paragraph of the letter we find the notion "peaceful awareness," a term which Rennyo referred to quite often in his letters. Usually *anjin*, or "peaceful awareness," is used synonymously with *shinjin* or faith, denoting accompanying inner peace or such a peaceful state of mind. Just as the essence of faith, or *shinjin*, in Shin Buddhism lies in awakening, the notion of *anjin* is always accompanied by the sense of inner awareness of *ki*, the person to be saved, and *Hō*, the Dharma that saves. Because of "the oneness in *Namu Amida-butsu* of the person to be saved and the Dharma that saves," to which Rennyo refers towards the end of the letter, this awareness in *anjin* is absolutely peaceful. Here in this context, several poems by Asahara Saichi

(1850–1932), a Shin Buddhist poet who loved reading the *Letters* by Rennyo morning and evening, are extremely touching. I found this poem, written on a little piece of wood, some fifty years ago, when I traveled to Yunotsu, a small village where Saichi had lived.

> Worried over this, worried over that—
> That heavy burden has been taken away from me.
> Ever since the burden was taken away,
> How perfectly at peace I am!"[379]

The sense of inner peace expressed by Saichi in the above poem comes from the profound awareness of the absolute oneness of *ki and Hō*, which is beyond any kind of conceptual duality,

> The Name of the Parent cuts too well,
> Too sharp to feel is the Parent's Name.
> Not conscious of the borderline between *Namu* and *Amida Butsu*—
> Such is the sharpness of the six-character Name.
> *Ki* is *Hō*,
> Through the kindness of the Parent, true Love and Compassion.
> To this does Saichi surrender.[380]

Abiding in this peaceful awareness of *ki and Hō*, Saichi simply enjoys his *Nenbutsu* life like a child just playing with a ball no matter whether happy or unhappy,

> O Saichi, are you happy, are you counting your blessings?
> When it is a day to count my blessings, I count my blessings,
> When there is nothing special, there is nothing special.
> O Saichi, when there is nothing special, what do you do with yourself?
> Then, there is nothing I can do:
> All the same it is *Namu Amida-butsu* up and down and all around.
> Today, tomorrow, every day that dawns, it is hello! and hello again![381]

Stating in the first paragraph of the letter that the essence of this peaceful awareness lies in the six-character Name, Rennyo quotes from Shàndǎo's *The Exposition of The Meditation Sūtra*, "*Namu* means to take refuge. It also means vow-making and virtue-transference. *Amida-butsu* means his practice. It is because of this that we will unfailingly attain birth."[382] This is a very famous and extremely important passage in the history of Pure Land Buddhism, because this interpretation of *Namu Amida-butsu* was Shàndǎo's response to the criticism from the *Shōron shū* school (攝論宗 ch. *Shèlùn zōng*) that Pure Land Buddhists only aspire to be born in the Pure Land whilst failing to observe any of the necessary practices. The essential point Shàndǎo made in order to refute this criticism was that the Name *Namu Amida-butsu* already includes the practice Amida Buddha accomplished to fulfil his vows to save all sentient beings. This crucial point is referred to in the simple statement, "*Amida-butsu* means his practice." Shàndǎo's interpretation of *Namu Amida-butsu* can be understood as his declaration that Pure Land Buddhism is the teaching of absolute Other Power.

Of the eighty letters in the Five Fascicle version of *The Letters* by Rennyo, there are seventeen in which Rennyo Shōnin tries to explain to his followers the meaning of the six-character Name, *Namu Amida-butsu*, and six of those letters are explanations of the Name based on Shàndǎo's interpretation of *Namu Amida-butsu* quoted above.

Many Pure Land schools other than Shin Buddhism take the view that the "vow-making and virtue-transference," to which Shàndǎo refers, is on the part of the devotee. It indicates the devotee's faith to aspire to be born in the Pure Land through his or her own acquisition of virtue. This is the view of those who are yet to awaken to the absolute working of Other Power, still remaining attached to their self power.

From the Shin Buddhist point of view, however, the "vow-making and virtue-transference," to which he refers, is on the part of Amida Buddha and means Amida Buddha's own great compassionate vow and his pure act of virtue-transference that saves all sentient beings without any discrimination. This is the view of those who are awakened to the Other Power of Amida's Original Vow. Shin Buddhists should follow this path.

Regarding Shàndǎo's statement, Shinran Shōnin's own explanation from his main work, *The Kyōgyōshinshō*, is that, "Therefore, the word *Namu* means *kimyō* or 'to take refuge' . . . Thus, *kimyō* is the solemn command of the Original Vow to come. The phrase *hotsugan ekō*, 'vow-making and virtue-transference', indicates the mind of the Tathāgata who, having already made his Vow, transfers to all beings the practice. The phrase 'Amida Buddha is the practice' indicates the practice selected in his Original Vow."[383]

As indicated by this passage, in Shin Buddhism, our taking refuge in Amida Buddha originates in the Buddha's sincere wish that we, sentient beings, may come to him to be liberated from our own karmic bondage. In short, our taking refuge in Amida Buddha is entirely due to the working of *Namu Amida-butsu*, the *Nenbutsu* of the Original Vow.

All of Rennyo Shōnin's explanations in his letters of the meaning of *Namu Amida-butsu* are seen as "vow-making and virtue-transference" on the part of Amida Buddha.

According to those explanations, the devotee's fervent aspiration for the Pure Land originates from Amida's Original Vow. In other words it is a gift from Amida. Shinran Shōnin himself clearly shows this aspect in his *Annotated Inscriptions on Sacred Scrolls*,

> Shàndǎo states that *what is meant by 'namu' is 'to take refuge'*. 'To take refuge' is to follow the holy call of the two honoured ones, Śākyamuni and Amida, and meet their wishes. Thus, Shàndǎo says *Namu is to take refuge*. *It also means 'vow-making and virtue-transference'*: this means the aspiration to be born in the Pure Land of Peace and Happiness following the call of the two honoured ones.
>
> *What is meant by Amida Buddha is the practice*: this means that the practice is that of the Original Vow selected by Bodhisattva Dharmākara. It is the causal act that truly secures birth in the Land of Peace and Happiness.[384]

The last paragraph of the letter is such a beautiful address, full of dynamic energy, despite the fact that Rennyo wrote it towards the end of his life after being overtaken by serious illness. Expressed here is the quintessence of the Shin Buddhist thought, "the oneness in *Namu Amida-butsu* of *ki* and *Hō*."

If we re-examine the meaning of *hotsugan ekō* (vow-making and virtue-transference) in the light of "the oneness in *Namu Amida-butsu* of *ki* and *Hō*," it can be said that when *hotsugan ekō* is seen as the expression of pure faith or *shinjin* it forms part of *ki* and when it is taken as the working of Amida Buddha that saves us it is certainly part of *Hō*. In this religious philosophy, "the oneness in *Namu Amida-butsu* of *ki* and *Hō*," even our own faith-experience of *Namu* or taking refuge in Amida Buddha is recognised as part of the working of Amida Buddha. In this respect Shin Buddhism is the teaching of absolute Other Power.

One of Saichi's poems reads as follows,

> In Other Power
> There is no self-power, no Other Power.
> All around is Other Power.
> *Namu Amida-butsu, Namu Amida-butsu.*[385]

The very heart of this poem is expressed in the last line, "*Namu Amida-butsu, Namu Amida-butsu.*" In forsaking all his conceptual understanding, even this wonderful realisation, "All around is Other Power," he just returns to *Namu Amida-butsu*, becoming *Namu Amida-butsu* itself. His becoming *Namu Amida-butsu* is in itself the working of *Namu Amida-butsu* that carries him to the Pure Land.

The last line of the letter reminds us of the fact that, even as he was writing this letter, Rennyo was actually facing his own death which was not very far away from him. With his pure faith of entrusting himself to *Namu*

Amida-butsu, we can imagine him advancing on his way to the Pure Land, always saying "*Namu Amida-butsu, Namu Amida-butsu.*" Rennyo Shōnin is *Namu Amida-butsu* itself.

CHAPTER FIFTY-EIGHT

The Main Reason for Living in a Shin Buddhist Temple

ON BUILDING [A TEMPLE] IN ŌSAKA

FASCICLE IV, LETTER FIFTEEN

Ever since the olden days the area of Ōsaka in Ikutama estate, Higashinari County, Settsu Province, appears to have been blessed with a truly excellent connection.

Seeing the place for the first time at some point during the last ten days of September in the fifth year of the Meiō period, I took it upon myself to have a single temple built there in the traditional style. Now three whole years have flown by and I feel this to be entirely due to the deep connection ever since the early days.

With reference to the above, my main reason for residing here has never been to live out my life in tranquillity, nor yet to live in splendour and glory, nor even to enjoy the beauty of flowers and birds, the bright moon and cool breezes. Rather it is for the Supreme Enlightenment and my one and only desire whilst living here is for the decisive attainment of faith by more and more followers and the pronouncing by them of the *Nenbutsu*. If any fellows appeared here in this world who harboured strong prejudices or if any serious problems came about that proved difficult to solve, we would give up our attachment to this place and immediately withdraw. So, then, if you finally come to attain faith decisively, as firm as a diamond, no matter at all whether you are of noble or humble birth, whether you are a priest or a lay person, this will truly be in accord with the Original Vow of Amida Tathāgata and will specifically correspond to the original wishes of Shōnin.

Regarding this point, I have to confess that it is inconceivable that this year, old ignoramus that I am, I have already reached the age of eighty-four! And what greater satisfaction can I have than to think that maybe my whole life has been truly in accord with the meaning of the teaching in our tradition? But I, old ignoramus that I am, have been ill since some time this summer, with no sign of any improvement so far. I am quite sure I will finally fulfil my original desire of attaining birth during the coming season of cold weather. But oh, what I do hope so very much, morning and evening, is that each one of you may attain faith whilst I am yet still alive. Although it so depends on your past good conditions, there is never a moment when I stop longing for each of you to attain faith. That will be what makes my having spent three years in this place really worthwhile. By all means, you should attain faith decisively during this seven-day period of the Hōonkō Ceremony so that every single one of us, ourselves and others, may fulfil our original desire of attaining birth in the Land of Utmost Bliss.

Most humbly and respectfully

This letter is to be read out starting from the 21st November, Meiō 7 [1498], so that everyone may attain faith [during the Hōonkō Ceremony].

COMMENTS

Of the eighty letters constituting the formal version of *The Letters* by Rennyo, the fifty-eight compiled in Fascicle One to Four bear definite dates, whilst the twenty-two in Fascicle Five are undated. The present letter, the fifteenth letter of Fascicle Four, was written by Rennyo Shōnin towards the end of his life, about four months before his death, and is the last of the dated letters in the formal Five Fascicle version. At that time Rennyo was already well aware that he was terminally ill. Although there exist two further dated letters that postdate the fifteenth letter of Fascicle Four, they were not compiled in the formal version, probably because they are more private in nature and not really addressed to a wider public.

The fifteenth letter of Fascicle Four is also included as one of the seven Hōonkō letters. These letters were originally written for the Hōonkō visitors of the day and even now are still only read out at Hōonkō Ceremonies. Needless to say, this letter is the last of this special set of Hōonkō letters. In the last paragraph Rennyo describing himself as an 'old ignoramus' and realising that his attainment of birth in the Pure Land is near, addresses himself specifically to the participants of that particular year's Hōonkō Ceremony.

The subject of this special letter is all about how Rennyo Shōnin came to build "the temple in Ōsaka." In his day, the temple had not yet come to be "the Honganji" or the headquarters of the Shin Buddhist tradition, and so it would have been called "Ōsaka-dono" or "Ōsaka-gobō."[386]

The ninth and tenth Head Priests[387] of the Shin Buddhist tradition resided in Yamashina Honganji until August of 1532, when Yamashina Honganji was burnt down by Rokkaku Sadayori[388] and followers of the Nichiren tradition. At that point Shōnyo Shōnin moved into the temple in Ōsaka and started calling it "Honganji." The hill on which the Honganji was located came to be called by people Ishiyama or "rocky hill" because it was a huge outcrop of rock, covered with boulders. The temple in Ōsaka was thus called "Ishiyama Honganji."

In May 1533 Nichiren followers, along with a number of warriors, again attacked Ishiyama Honganji, but this time Shōnyo Shōnin and followers of the Honganji Temple managed to protect themselves with the help of Honganji Temple followers from the warrior class. In fact Ishiyama Honganji proved a very good natural fortress. Later on, in the days of Kennyo Shōnin (1543–1592), Ishiyama Honganji was again attacked, this time by the warrior lord Oda Nobunaga, who conquered almost all the provinces of Japan in 1582. Ishiyama Honganji's resistance against Nobunaga continued for eleven years from 1570 to 1580. After these years of fighting, known as the Ishiyama Conflict, Kennyo Shōnin accepted a settlement negotiated by the Imperial Court between Honganji and Nobunaga and withdrew from Ishiyama Honganji to Saginomori in the Kii Province in 1580.

Although this took place eighty-five years after Rennyo Shōnin built the temple in Ōsaka, it is generally believed in the Shin Buddhist tradition that Kennyo Shōnin withdrew from Ishiyama Honganji in accordance with the predictive advice found in this letter, "If any fellows appeared here in this world who harboured strong prejudices or if any serious problems came about that proved difficult to solve, we would give up our attachment to this place and immediately withdraw." Incidentally, Toyotomi Hideyoshi (1536–1598), successor to Oda Nobunaga as ruler of the whole country, converted the site of Ishiyama Honganji to Ōsaka Castle and made it his own residential headquarters.

Concerning the initial construction of the temple in Ōsaka referred to in the first paragraph of the letter, a similar description is found in the

Rennyo Shōnin Itoku ki compiled by Rengo (1468–1543), the seventh son
of Rennyo Shōnin:

> In the course of the last ten days of September in the 5th year of the Meiō
> period (1496), the former Head Priest purchased, at the age of eighty-
> two, an area of land in Ōsaka in Ikutama estate, Higashinari County,
> Settsu Province, on behalf of the Buddha-dharma, and built a temple
> as a place of retirement.[389]

According to the *Shūjin ki* by Jitsugo (1492–1584), his tenth son, Rennyo
Shōnin viewed the site for the first time on 24th September in 1496, arranged
for carpenters to start construction work on 29th of the same month and
saw the completion of this temple on 4th October of the same year. It would
appear that, as the period of construction lasted a mere seven days, his place
of retirement must have been but a very small temple. Why did he talk about
a possible withdrawal from this small Ōsaka temple in this letter written
in 1498? Realistically speaking, there were at least three reasons: Firstly
wherever he went his teaching became very popular and as a result he was
often forced to leave places such as Kyoto, Shiga, Yoshizaki and so forth.
Secondly the area of Ōsaka he chose for the temple was a very good natural
fortress, protecting his followers against outside attack, and thirdly there
was a possibility that it could become the target of attack by warlords, who
might want to convert it into a stronghold for themselves. The fundamental
reason, however was that, because the temple should be a place of mutual
encounter of Dharma friends where they could attain peaceful awareness,
they must not become attached to it.

Another historical document, *The Hogo no uragaki* by Kensei (1499–
1570), one of the grandsons of Rennyo, offers an interesting account of the
building of the temple in Ōsaka;

> Regarding the creation of the invaluable temple at Ōsaka in Ikutama
> estate, Higashinari County, Settsu Province, Rennyo Shōnin saw the site
> for the first time on his way to the harbour of Sakai in the course of the
> last ten days of September, the 5th year of the Meiō period, and then built
> a temple there. It is said that there were various auspicious auguries and
> mysteries. First of all, stones for the foundation of the main hall were
> already in place as if they had been collected for this purpose. Although
> it was an area where there was no water, when they bored into the ground
> according to Rennyo Shōnin's instruction, there sprang forth a plenti-
> ful supply of pure water. At the beginning there was only one well, but
> now we can get water as we wish. It is said to have been foretold in *The
> Tennōji Shōtoku Taishi miraiki*[390] that a Buddhist Temple will be built

in the direction of northeast of this temple (Tennōji Temple) in the latter days. Certainly it goes without saying that this place has been blessed with its deep connection to the Buddha-dharma.[391]

As *The Tennōji Shōtoku Taishi miraiki* is said to exist in the temple as a secret document, there is no way of confirming whether or not the manuscript does actually include the passage above. It would seem that Venerable Kensei, the author of *The Hogo no uragaki*, wished to produce tangible evidence of the place's deep connection to the Buddha-dharma. I am not sure if Venerable Kensei himself saw the document. Practically speaking, however, it can be said that evidence enough of this special connection is provided by the fact that, after surveying the site, Rennyo Shōnin immediately decided to build a temple there.

In Article 123 of *The Kūzen kikigaki*, Kūzen records the words that he heard directly from Rennyo Shōnin concerning the construction of this temple in Ōsaka,

He said, "When I built Ōsaka-dono, I did so in the hope of encouraging people to attain faith. Incidentally, when Miidera Temple burnt down, it really flourished after its reconstruction. At that time the Dharma Master of the temple had a vision in which he was told 'Through this it is of vital importance that you be freed from birth-and-death. As a result of the temple burning down there will be many people aspiring to attain birth after death. You should build a new temple, not just in the hope that the new construction will be a success, but so that everyone may attain birth after death.' As indicated in the dream, even if the temple itself proves prosperous, there will be no point in it unless it leads to the emergence of people attaining faith."[392]

"The building of a temple in Ōsaka" was the last project for Rennyo Shōnin. His real intention, however, was not simply to construct another temple. His sincere desire, underlying all the construction work, was that his followers should be helped to attain pure faith or inner peace, that is to say "peaceful awareness" of oneself and Amida Buddha. Rennyo's words to Kūzen, his constant attendant, begin with the explanation, "When I built Ōsaka-dono, I did so in the hope of encouraging people to attain faith." He then mentions the uplifting story of the reconstruction of Miidera Temple and ends by saying, "As indicated in the dream, even if the temple itself proves prosperous, there will be no point in it unless it leads to the emergence of people attaining faith."

Shin Buddhist followers have the tradition of reading out one after another of *The Letters* by Rennyo Shōnin in the course of daily services, morning and evening. This is because his teaching is still alive within us. His words of pure faith, full of loving kindness, and the essentials of his teaching, expressed clearly and concisely, still exert a strong appeal to the hearts of modern followers. They reverberate beautifully among us even five hundred years after his death.

Shinran Shōnin's special mission in the history of Pure Land Buddhism was to transmit the teaching of "salvation of all beings through faith alone without any discrimination." On this path to the Pure Land he was followed by Rennyo Shōnin who received the teaching, just as it was, unfettered by the confines of time and space. Rennyo spent his whole life in entrusting himself to the teaching and at the same time helping others do so. In this letter, written towards the end of his life, he expresses his utmost happiness, looking back over a life that enabled him to entrust himself absolutely to Amida Buddha and to help others do so too.

In order that we may better understand the supreme happiness felt by Rennyo Shōnin, let us take a look at another very moving account, found in *The Goichidai ki kikigaki*, Article 266,

> When Hōkyō-bō (1421–1510) visited the last but one former Head Priest at Ōsaka-dono, Rennyo Shōnin said to Hōkyō-bō, "Even if I myself attain birth, you should go on living for another ten years". Although Hōkyō-bō queried this, Rennyo Shōnin reiterated, "You should live on." One year after the death of Rennyo Shōnin, when someone remarked to Hōkyō-bō, "What Rennyo Shōnin said accorded with reality, your life that has continued for a year is actually a gift from Rennyo Shōnin," Hōkyō-bō said with palms together, "Indeed, that is right. How grateful I am!" Hōkyō-bō, in fact, lived on for a further ten years just as Rennyo Shōnin had wished. Hōkyō-bō was someone completely in accord with the invisible aid of the Buddha. A man of mystery![393]

Hōkyō-bō was one of Rennyo Shōnin's disciples, six years of age younger than his master. When Hōkyō-bō uttered these words, I feel he must have realised that his entire life was not only a gift from Rennyo Shōnin, but also from Shinran Shōnin and, ultimately, from the Tathāgata.

Rennyo's exclamation in the letter, "And what greater satisfaction can I have than to think that maybe my whole life has been truly in accord with the meaning of the teaching in our tradition?" comes from an awareness that one's life is a gift from the Tathāgata. Expressing this sense of infinite gratitude for having been able to dedicate his whole life to the transmission of the teaching of Shinran Shōnin, Rennyo Shōnin is now proceeding on his way to the Pure Land.

The Essential Message of the Original Vow of Amida Buddha

IGNORANT LAY PEOPLE

OF THE LATTER DAYS

FASCICLE V, LETTER ONE

Dear fellow men and women, ignorant lay people of the latter days, it is vital we entrust ourselves singlemindedly and wholeheartedly to Amida Buddha. If, steadfastly and singleheartedly, we entreat the Buddha to save us and do not turn our thoughts in any other direction, then, no matter how much we may be weighed down by bad karma, Amida Tathāgata will surely save us. This is the message of the Eighteenth Vow that promises birth in the Pure Land through the *Nenbutsu*. Once faith has been decisively attained in this way, we should repeat the *Nenbutsu*, that is, pronounce the Buddha Name, whether asleep or awake, for as long as we may live.

Most humbly and respectfully

COMMENTS

Short as it is, this letter would appear of vital importance, having been selected as the first of twenty-two undated letters to be compiled into Fascicle Five. In itself it is a brief and beautiful summarisation of Shin Buddhist faith. The essence of the Shin Buddhist faith lies in awakening and entrusting oneself to the Fulfilment of the Eighteenth Original Vow of Amida Buddha to welcome and save all beings without any kind of discrimination, as described in *The Larger Sūtra of Eternal Life*. The passage referring to the Fulfilment of the Eighteenth Original Vow reads as follows,

> All beings, on hearing that Name, rejoice in the awakening of faith at least for one thought-moment. It is indeed from Amida's sincere mind that all this has been transferred to them. Desiring to be born in that land, they are immediately born there at that moment and abide in the stage of nonretrogression.[394]

"All beings" in this extract means all those who hear the Name being pronounced by all Buddhas. They are addressed in the opening letter of Fascicle Five as "Dear fellow men and women, ignorant lay people of the latter days." The reference in the extract to "the awakening of faith" is expanded in the letter to "we should entrust ourselves singlemindedly and wholeheartedly to Amida Buddha." Where the extract reads, "It is indeed from Amida's sincere mind that all this has been transferred to them" – a reference to how Amida awakens faith in us – this is expressed in the letter as "If steadfastly and singleheartedly we entreat the Buddha to save us and do not turn our thoughts in any other direction, then, no matter how much we may be weighed down by bad karma, Amida Tathāgata will surely save us."

Everything thus comes from Amida Buddha. All the virtue-transference that issues from Amida and helps us attain birth in the Pure Land is the working of his unconditional love embodied in the Eighteenth Original Vow. In fact, according to traditional Shin Buddhist understanding, even our "entreating the Buddha to save us" is something already prepared for us by the Buddha and simply a response to the Buddha's call for us to come to him.

Finally, the last sentence in the Fulfilment of the Eighteenth Vow, "Desiring to be born in that land, they are immediately born there at that moment and abide in the stage of nonretrogression" is also briefly referred to in the letter where it says, "This is the message of the Eighteenth Vow that promises birth in the Pure Land through the *Nenbutsu*."

Thus it can be seen that the whole letter is closely related to the passage on the Fulfilment of the Eighteenth Original Vow and very naturally expresses the essence of the Shin Buddhist faith.

Incidentally, on reading the *Ofumi kōjutsu* (*Lectures on The Letters*) by Kakuju Yoshitani, I came across an important comment on a Japanese word frequently found in Shin Buddhist texts, particularly in *The Letters* by Rennyo. This is the Japanese verb, *mōsu* 申す. Professor Kakuju Yoshitani's lecture on this particular point is actually based on a lecture Venerable Kōgatsuin Jinrei (1749–1817) gave on the first letter of Fascicle Five, in which the latter argued that the word *mōsu* in this particular context meant "to entreat," "to implore," "to beg" or " to ask." According to Venerable Kogatsuin Jinrei, *mōsu* used to be used in this sense in the days of Rennyo Shōnin.[395]

In modern Japanese, however, this usage of the word has almost completely disappeared, which explains why relevant parts of the text containing the word *mōsu* are not clearly expressed in modern interpretations or English translations. Not only in this letter but also in the following three letters of Fascicle Five, the proper translation of the Japanese *mōsu* is the English word "entreat." Concerning our actual interpretation of the word *mōsu* or "entreat," however, we should be very careful not to misunderstand what is meant: in this particular context it is not a demand for Supreme Enlightenment or the fruit of the Pure Land whilst living in this world, but an aspect of the attainment of "faith" or "peaceful awareness" and as such it is the humble and grateful response to Amida's call or command that we should come to him.

It goes without saying that the phrases found in the last passage of the letter, "reciting the *Nenbutsu*" and "pronouncing the Buddha Name," simply wells up from within on our attainment of faith and are an expression of our gratitude to the Buddha for his great compassion in saving us all.

CHAPTER SIXTY

Knowledge and Faith

ON THE EIGHTY THOUSAND

BUDDHIST SCRIPTURES

FASCICLE V, LETTER TWO

Even though they may understand the eighty thousand Buddhist scriptures, those who do not know the afterworld are said to be ignorant. Though they be but illiterate priests and women priests pursuing a lay life with shaven heads, others who know the afterworld, are said to be wise.

You should understand, therefore, that in the teaching of our tradition, for those who have never realised what the one thought-moment of faith really is, though they may have read a great many scriptures and be widely informed, all is in vain. Thus it is that Shōnin says, "Unless they entrust themselves to Amida's Original Vow, none of them, whether male or female, will ever be saved."

Hence, as far as women are concerned, whatever kind of women they may be, there should be no doubt but that, if they forsake the miscellane-ous practices and at this one thought-moment entrust themselves to Amida Tathāgata deeply with their whole being and entreat him to save them in the matter of Rebirth to come, they will all be born in Amida's Land of Enjoyment, whether ten persons or one hundred.

Most humbly and respectfully

COMMENTS

There is a belief amongst some Shin Buddhist scholars that the first paragraph of this second letter of Fascicle Five is based on a divine message from a great *kami* or Japanese god known as "Amaterasu-ōmikami." This divine message, found in *Ruizō shū* vol. 5,[396] reads, "Even though they know the eighty thousand scriptures, those who do not know about the afterworld are ignorant. Even though they are illiterate, those who stand in fear of the afterworld are wise."

There is a story about how this particular letter came to be written by Rennyo. A Shintō priest from Mount Hakusan[397] was in the habit of visiting Shijimamura village where he would voice his criticism of the teachings of the Shin Buddhist tradition. When a Shin Buddhist follower from the village mentioned the matter to Rennyo, he wrote this follower a special letter quoting from the divine message. The Shin Buddhist follower placed the letter in his Buddha shrine where it came to the notice of the aforementioned Shintō priest. After a period of complete silence the priest embraced the Shin Buddhist teaching with great repentance. Through Rennyo's teaching and his way of quoting from a Shintō-related scripture, that Shintō priest was persuaded to take refuge in the Shin Buddhist teaching.

Regarding the phrase "the eighty thousand scriptures," this is not quite accurate but represents a rounding down because, in the Buddhist tradition, it is said that there are eighty-four thousand Dharma paths corresponding to our eighty-four thousand blind passions.

The second paragraph of this letter is reminiscent of a rather more important matter in our tradition, namely, the sharp divide between knowledge and faith, a subject clearly addressed by Shinran Shōnin himself in Chapter 2 of *The Tanni shō,*

"Each of you has come to see me, crossing the borders of more than ten provinces at the risk of your lives. Your purpose is solely to hear from me how to be born in the Pure Land. However, if your concern is to learn from me something hidden, on the assumption that I know other ways of being born in the Pure Land apart from pronouncing the *Nenbutsu,* or if you think that I may be acquainted with some Buddhist texts that teach those special ways, then I am afraid you are making a very grave mistake. If that is indeed your concern, there are many eminent scholars in the Southern Capital, or on the Northern Mountain,[398] whom you would be better off visiting in order to enquire to your hearts' content about the essentials for birth in the Pure Land.

As for myself, Shinran, there is nothing else involved apart from simple faith in the *Nenbutsu,* according to the instruction of my good teacher, 'Just say the *Nenbutsu* so as to be saved by Amida."[399]

This is a message that Venerable Yuien, author of *The Tanni shō*, heard directly from Shinran Shōnin himself and I reflected in my own Commentary on that work, emphasising the vital importance of faith and the contrast between the experience of pure faith and intellectual understanding.

> Firstly there is a sharp contrast drawn between knowledge and pure faith in Shinran Shōnin's immediate response to the disciples who want to know how to be born in the Pure Land. He tells them they are making a great mistake if their concern is simply to understand by intellect alone and if they imagine that he, Shinran Shōnin, knows any other ways of salvation apart from the *Nenbutsu*. The essential point is that the *Nenbutsu* is not something one may try to comprehend logically but something that emanates naturally from within. Faced with his disciples' very intellectual concern, therefore, Shinran Shōnin's answer is simply to reaffirm his own simple faith in Hōnen's teaching of the *Nenbutsu*, "As far as I, Shinran, am concerned, there is nothing else involved apart from simple faith in the *Nenbutsu,* according to the instruction of my good teacher, 'Just say the *Nenbutsu* so as to be saved by Amida'." He goes on to declare that if their concern is only intellectual, then it would be better for them to consult eminent scholars in Nara or on Mount Hiei. Faith is not simply a matter of information or even belief if such belief amounts to no more than intellectual assent. Faith-experience definitely includes a phase of transcendence that enables one to go beyond objective knowledge or the intellectual approach. In the Western tradition, for example, having in mind the aphorism *credo quia absurdum est* (I believe because it is absurd), which is usually attributed to Tertullian, Kierkegaard states "I believe in God against my understanding." These statements epitomise well the transcendental phase of faith-experience.[400]

As I see it, the first letter of Fascicle Five corresponds to Chapter 1 of *The Tanni shō*. Both of them refer to the salvation of all human beings through pure faith in the Eighteenth Original Vow. At the same time the second letter of Fascicle Five has some important kinship to Chapter 2 of *The Tanni shō* in that both have as their common subject the vital importance of faith-experience in contrast to the standpoint of reason and intellectual understanding. I am unsure, however, whether Venerable Ennyo, the editor of *The Letters* by Rennyo, was himself aware of these close correlations. No matter whether he was conscious of *The Tanni shō* or not, it is somewhat intriguing to note a certain similarity between Venerable Yuien's editorial attitude and that of Venerable Ennyo when organising the compilation of their material, especially in the early part of their respective editions. Placed first are those texts that emphasise the faith of entrusting oneself to the Eighteenth Original Vow, followed by texts that highlight the contrast between faith-experience and intellectual interest, emphasising faith as the ultimate concern. In this respect the understanding emphasised in the second paragraph of the letter on the contrast between scriptural knowledge and faith is of vital importance.

CHAPTER SIXTY-ONE

Women as the Object of Amida Buddha's Salvation

CONCERNING BOTH WOMEN PRIESTS WHO PURSUE A LAY LIFE WITH SHAVEN HEADS AND ORDINARY WIVES

FASCICLE V, LETTER THREE

Women priests who pursue a lay life with shaven heads and ordinary wives, too, should realise that, if they simply entrust themselves with steadfastness and single-heartedness to Amida Buddha deeply with their whole being and entreat the Buddha to save them in the matter of Rebirth, they will all be saved. There should be no doubt about this whatsoever. This is the Original Vow of Other Power, the Vow of Amida Tathāgata. Once awakened and filled with gratitude and joy regarding their salvation in the matter of Rebirth, they should simply recite "*Namu Amida-butsu, Namu Amida-butsu.*"

Most humbly and respectfully

COMMENTS

The content of the letter is very similar to the first letter of Fascicle Five, concentrating on the importance in the Shin Buddhist faith of entrusting oneself absolutely to Amida's Original Vow. However, whereas the first letter addresses a wide audience with the words "Dear fellow men and women, ignorant lay people of the latter days," this other letter is one of five particularly aimed at women.

Although I am not entirely sure how justified the comparison is between the third letter of Fascicle Five and Chapter 3 of *The Tanni shō*, it is nevertheless interesting to note the way both texts are particularly concerned with the audience or the object of salvation. Whereas in Chapter 3 of *The Tanni shō* the object of salvation is whoever is aware of themselves as "a person with bad karma," in the third letter of Fascicle Three it is women who are being addressed. If Venerable Ennyo had indeed been conscious of the existence of *The Tanni shō*, I would have to say this transference of emphasis on the object of salvation is especially intriguing. Rennyo Shōnin of course was particularly concerned about the salvation of women because they were so severely discriminated against in those days.

CHAPTER SIXTY-TWO

The Original Vow is beyond All Discrimination

THE EIGHTEENTH VOW AND THE MEDITATION SŪTRA

BOTH MEN AND WOMEN

FASCICLE V, LETTER FOUR

Even if they entrust themselves to the compassionate vows of all the Buddhas, it will be extremely difficult for both men and women, weighed down by karmic transgressions, to be saved through the power of those Buddhas, given that the time of the wicked world of the Last Age is now upon us. So the Buddha known as Amida Tathāgata, surpassing all other Buddhas, made a great Vow to save even wrongdoers who have committed the ten bad acts and the five grave offences. Thus it was that he became Amida Buddha. Since Amida is the Buddha who vowed that he would not attain Supreme Enlightenment if he failed to save those beings who entrusted themselves to him deeply with their whole being and at this one thought-moment entreated him to save them, there can be no doubt at all but that such people will attain birth in the Land of Utmost Bliss.

Thus those who entrust themselves to Amida Tathāgata singleheartedly and steadfastly and, without any doubt at all, entreat him with their whole being to save them and leave everything to him, even their heavy burden of bad karma, and attain the awakening of the one thought-moment of faith, such people, beyond any shadow of doubt, will all be born in the Pure Land, ten out of every ten of them, one hundred out of every one hundred. Furthermore, whenever more and more feelings of respect well up in their hearts, they should say the *Nenbutsu,* "*Namu Amida-butsu, Namu Amida-butsu,*" no matter what time it is or where they may be. This is called the *Nenbutsu* of gratitude for all that has been done for us by the Buddha.

Most humbly and respectfully

COMMENTS

In my commentary on the third letter of Fascicle Five, I referred to the fact that the letter was addressed to women, and that it focused on people to whom the Original Vow offered the promise of salvation. I also noted that in this respect the letter bore some similarity to the viewpoint expressed in Chapter Three of *The Tanni shō,* as edited by Venerable Yuien, though it is debatable whether Venerable Ennyo, the compiler of the Five Fascicle version of *The Letters,* was aware of this or not.

The subject of this letter is again those whom Amida would save through the power of his Original Vow, but in this case the emphasis, rather than being on women alone, is on "both men and women, weighed down by karmic transgressions," also described as "wrongdoers who have committed the ten bad acts and the five grave offences."

The principle of Amida's Original Vow is that all sentient beings shall be saved, without trace of discrimination, through the power of unconditional love. Thus there can be no discrimination against women or wrongdoers as Amida's salvation is for all sentient beings. There will be no Shin Buddhists who do not agree that this is a fundamental principle of the Shin Buddhist teaching.

From the doctrinal point of view, however, there is a serious problem with the text of Amida's Eighteenth Vow, as it includes an exclusion clause that directly contradicts the content of the first half of the Eighteenth Vow. The Eighteenth Vow states,

If, upon my attaining Buddhahood, all beings in the ten quarters, in all sincerity and joyous faith, aspiring to be born in my country and pronouncing my Name up to ten times, were not to be born there, then may I not attain the Supreme Enlightenment. *Excepted from this are those who commit the five grave offenses and those who slander the Right Dharma.*[401]

Generally speaking Shin Buddhist scholars think that this exclusion clause must have been added to the main body of the vow at a later date in order to admonish followers against wrongdoing. Others simply view the exclusion clause as Śākyamuni Buddha's admonition and the first half of the vow as Amida's true intention. If you leave such doctrinal explanations aside, however, and simply view the Eighteenth Vow of *The Larger Sūtra of Eternal Life* as the textual evidence of Amida's universal deliverance, there does remain a very serious problem as the exclusion clause directly contradicts the message of equal salvation within the same text.

Fortunately there exists another Pure Land sūtra, written at a later date and known as *The Meditation Sūtra,* that plays an important role in solving the problem. This sūtra refers to the salvation of "those sentient beings at the lowest grade of the lowest rank who have committed the five grave offences, the ten bad acts and all kinds of immorality,"[402] meaning that we can be confident that the ultimate intent of the Original Vow is indeed the universal salvation of all beings without any discrimination whatsoever. Because the passage from *The Meditation Sūtra* concerning the salvation of the very worst kinds of ignorant being can be conflated with the apparently contradictory Eighteenth Vow of *The Larger Sūtra of Eternal Life*, it is easy to confirm the true intention of the Eighteenth Vow.

It was Shàndǎo who discovered the huge importance of *The Meditaion Sūtra* in this respect. He wrote *The Exposition of The Meditation Sūtra* to clarify that Pure Land Buddhism is a teaching in which all sentient beings, even the vilest, can be saved solely by saying *Namu Amida-butsu*. He thinks the essence of the *Meditation Sūtra* lies in the salvation of the vilest wrong-doers. The *Sūtra* states,

Due to such bad karma, an ignorant person like this will sink into bad realms and spend many kalpas suffering endless pain. When he comes to the end of his life, he will meet a good teacher, one who will comfort him in various ways. This person expounds to him the wonderful Dharma, encouraging him to be mindful of the Buddha. But he is too tormented by suffering to do so. Then this good friend says to him, 'If you cannot be mindful of the Buddha, then you should call to the Buddha of Eternal Life instead.' In this way he comes to sincerely and continuously pronounce *Namu Amida-butsu*[403] ten times. Because he calls the Buddha's Name, with each invocation, the transgressions which he has committed in births and deaths for eighty billion kalpas are extinguished.[404]

In connection with the exclusion clause in the Eighteenth Vow, there is one further important point that has long been the subject of serious concern in the history of Pure Land Buddhism. The problem is that, although *The Meditation Sūtra* talks about the salvation of "those who commit the five grave offenses," it does not mention the salvation of "those who slander the right Dharma." Does Amida's Vow exclude "those who slander the right Dharma"? How can we find out?

To this serious question Shàndǎo delivers the following answer in his *Exposition of The Meditation Sūtra*,

It is taught, concerning the lowest grade of the lowest rank, that those who commit the five grave offences are taken up but those who slander the Dharma are excluded; this is because beings of the lowest grade have already committed the five grave offenses, but must not be abandoned to endless transmigration. Thus Amida, awakening great compassion, grasps them and brings them to birth. Since they have yet to commit the karmic evil of slandering the Dharma, however, and in order to prevent them from doing so, it is stated that if one slanders the Dharma one will not attain birth. This is to be understood as relevant to those who have not committed this evil. Even if one has committed it, one will never-theless be grasped and brought to attainment of birth. Although one will attain birth in the Pure Land, however, one must pass many kalpas enclosed in a lotus bud.[405]

Further he states in *The Hōji san*,

Through the power of the Buddha's Vows, the karmic evil of the five grave offences and the ten transgressions is eradicated and all are brought to attainment of birth. When those who slander the Dharma or who abandon the seed of Buddhahood turn about at heart, they all reach the Pure Land.[406]

According to Shàndǎo, therefore, ultimately all beings are to be saved without any discrimination. Important figures in the mainstream of Japanese Pure Land Buddhism, such as Hōnen, Shinran, and Rennyo, follow this line.

All religious traditions, however, reflect in their teaching some influences from the societies in which they flourish, which often include examples of discriminatory practices. Very sadly, discrimination against women, even in developed countries, is still widespread to this day, and almost all the religions of this world have found it perfectly natural to discriminate against wrongdoers by denying that they can be saved. If you are born a woman, does that mean you cannot be liberated? If you commit a transgression, does that exclude you from those who may be freed from karmic bondage? Even in the Buddhist faith there have been many schools which, because of social influences prevalent at the time, have refused to allow that women or wrongdoers can be saved.

The essence of Amida's Original Vow, however, lies in its message of universal deliverance for all sentient beings beyond all discrimination. As one of those entrusting themselves to the Original Vow of universal deliverance, Rennyo is very much concerned with the liberation of women as well as with the salvation of those heavily burdened with karmic hindrances. As he states in this letter, "So the Buddha known as Amida Tathāgata, surpassing all other Buddhas, made a great Vow to save even wrongdoers who have committed the ten bad acts and the five grave offences. Thus it was that he became Amida Buddha."

Rennyo Shōnin's reference to the salvation of wrongdoers is something that makes absolutely clear to us sentient beings heavily burdened with karmic hindrances, how universal and lacking in any form of discrimination is the promise of deliverance of the Original Vow. The *Tanni shō* is notable for its clarification of this subject. As is said in my own translation of Chapter 3 of *The Tanni shō,*

> It is impossible for us, fully burdened with blind passions, to free ourselves from birth-and-death through the pursuance of any religious practices whatsoever. Full of sadness at this, Amida brought forth his Vow, the essential purport of which is the person with bad karma's attainment of Buddhahood. Hence those who are aware of their bad karma and so entrust themselves to Other Power are precisely the ones who possess the true key to birth.[407]

When the unconditional love of Amida Buddha enables us to become aware of the misery of our karmic existence, we entrust ourselves absolutely to Amida Buddha and pronounce his name as an expression of the feelings of gratitude welling up within us, as described in detail in the latter part of the letter.

CHAPTER SIXTY-THREE

Amida Buddha's Great Working of Virtue-transference

ON THE ATTAINMENT OF FAITH

FASCICLE V, LETTER FIVE

Attaining faith means realising the Eighteenth Vow. Realising this Vow means understanding what *Namu Amida-butsu* really is. Thus the true meaning of 'vow-making' and 'virtue-transference' manifests itself at the one thought-moment we take refuge by saying "*Namu.*" In other words, this is Amida Tathāgata's transferring his virtue to all sentient beings. In *The Larger Sūtra*, it is described as "enabling all sentient beings to reach the fulfilment of virtue." As this means that the bad karma and blind passions, accumulated from the beginningless past, are all extinguished without trace by the inconceivable working of the Vow, they are said to dwell in the company of those who are rightly assured, of those, in other words, who have reached the stage of nonretrogression. This, then, is what we mean by "attaining Nirvāṇa without destroying blind passions." This teaching, however, is exclusive to our tradition. The point should not be insisted upon when dealing with those who belong to other traditions. Bear this carefully in mind.

Most humbly and respectfully

COMMENTS

Like all the other letters of Fascicle Five, this, the fifth letter, bears no date but it is said that Rennyo Shōnin wrote it at the age of seventy-two whilst on a journey to Kii Province.

Short as it is, the letter is of vital importance, being a brief summarisation of the crucial points of Shin Buddhist teaching. Two matters in particular stand out: firstly the Shin Buddhist interpretation of *Namu Amida-butsu* and secondly the Shin Buddhist understanding of the phrase "attaining Nirvāṇa without destroying blind passions."

How to interpret Amida's Name, *Namu Amida-butsu*, has been the greatest conundrum of all in Pure Land Buddhism. *Namu Amida-butsu* literally means "I take refuge in Amida Buddha," *Namu* meaning "to take refuge" and *Amida-butsu* meaning "Amida Buddha."

Of particular importance in the history of Pure Land Buddhism is the very famous pronouncement concerning *Namu Amida-butsu* made by Shàndǎo, "*Namu* means 'to take refuge'. It also means 'vow-making and virtue-transference'. *Amida-butsu* means his practice. It is because of this that we will unfailingly attain birth."

Of the many interpretations of Shàndǎo's words, however, Shinran's view is unique. First of all, *Namu*, namely, "to take refuge in Amida Buddha," means entrusting oneself absolutely to Amida Buddha. While it comprises a personal decision on our part, Shinran Shōnin nevertheless understands it as being engendered by a command or summons issued to us from Amida. "To take refuge in Amida Buddha" is Amida's command to us to come to him, that is, "Take refuge in me." In other words, through our encounter with the great compassion of Amida Buddha, we are impelled to take refuge in Amida Buddha. It is in a very deep dimension indeed that Shinran Shōnin reveals to us his unique understanding of faith (*shinjin*), firmly based on his own experience.

Secondly, when it is said that *Namu* also means "vow-making and virtue-transference," the phrase "vow-making and virtue-transference" is invariably understood in other traditions as a *devotee's* aspiration for the Pure Land and virtue-transference for that purpose. Shinran Shōnin, however, understood the phase as Amida "making his Vow and transferring his Virtue." In this respect our act of "taking refuge in Amida Buddha" is in its entirety a gift from the Buddha.

Thirdly, when it is said that *Amida-butsu* means "his practice," it does not mean the practice of a devotee but rather that undertaken by Amida for the purpose of saving all sentient beings whilst he himself was still at the Bodhisattva stage.

Thus, the devotee is absolutely assured of birth in the Pure Land, just as Shàndǎo says, "It is because of this that we will unfailingly attain birth."

Rennyo Shōnin then goes on to conclude in the letter, "In other words, this is Amida Tathāgata's transferring his virtue to all sentient beings. In *The Larger Sūtra*, it is described as 'enabling all sentient beings to reach the fulfilment of virtue.'" The Shin Buddhist faith is our awareness that *Namu Amida-butsu* in its entirety is Amida Buddha's great working of virtue-transference.

Regarding such an interpretation of *Namu Amida-butsu*, D. T. Suzuki writes,

> The interpretation the Shin people give to '*Namu Amida-butsu*' is more than literal though not at all mystical or esoteric. It is in fact philosophical. When Amida is regarded as the object of adoration, he is separated from the devotee standing all by himself. But when *Namu* is added to the Name the whole thing acquires a new meaning because it now symbolises the unification of Amida and the devotee, wherein the duality no longer exists. This, however, does not indicate that the devotee is lost or absorbed in Amida so that his individuality is no longer tenable as such. The unity is there as '*Namu*' plus '*Amida-butsu*,' but the '*Namu*' (*ki*) has not vanished. It is there as if it were not there.[408]

As explained by D. T. Suzuki, this oneness of *Namu* and *Amida-butsu* in *Namu Amida-butsu* is of vital importance. As everything is the great working of Amida Buddha, we become absolutely assured of our birth in the Pure Land.

The Shin Buddhist understanding of the phrase "attaining Nirvāṇa without destroying blind passions"[409] is a phrase found in *The Shōshinge*, with its textual origin in Tánluán's *Commentary on The Treatise on the Pure Land*. Let me cite a relevant passage from my own lectures on *The Shōshinge*. During a series of lectures on *The Shōshinge* I wrote that,

> When we examine more closely the precise meaning of these lines, however, we are faced with a rather delicate problem, namely how to interpret the final phrase: '*We attain Nirvāṇa without destroying blind passions*.' The question is, where exactly is it that we attain Nirvāṇa without destroying blind passions? Certainly it is in the here and now whilst still living in this world that we attain true faith by entrusting ourselves to Amida Buddha. Through this attainment of faith we become assured of our birth in the Pure Land. We have learned, however, that it is in the Pure Land that we attain Nirvāṇa. The question about locality

comes about because these two lines sound as though they mean it is when we are awakened to pure faith in this world that we attain Nirvāṇa without destroying blind passions. Shinran Shōnin's commentary on the two lines in question, as recorded in *Annotated Inscriptions on Sacred Scrolls*, states that, "*As the one thought-moment of joy and love arises within us*: Know that, when the true faith that brings us the one thought-moment of joy is awakened within us, so do we become definitely assured of our birth in the True Land of Enjoyment based on the Original Vow. *We attain Nirvāṇa without destroying blind passions*: Know that we, beings filled with blind passions, are assured of attaining the Supreme Nirvāṇa.["410]

From these comments it becomes abundantly clear that Shinran Shōnin himself thinks that the attainment of Nirvāṇa takes place only in the Pure Land. Whereas the right definite assurance of birth in the Pure Land is given in this world, Nirvāṇa is to be attained in the Pure Land after birth in the Pure Land.[411]

It is at the precise moment of "*Namu*" when we entrust ourselves absolutely to Amida Buddha that we become definitely assured of our birth in the Pure Land and attainment of Nirvāṇa there.

As seen above, even this taking refuge is in fact due to the great working of Amida Buddha. For this reason we enter the company of those absolutely assured of birth in the Pure Land without actually severing blind passions. We are impelled to take refuge in Amida Buddha through our encounter with the Buddha; our taking refuge in the Buddha is actually the working of the Buddha, our response to his command. We ourselves have nothing to add to it. We do not need to sever blind passions. Everything happens naturally through the power of the Original Vow. Filled with blind passions though we are, we are nevertheless to attain Supreme Nirvāṇa in the Pure Land. Though we certainly come in touch with the working of Nirvāṇa, it is not that we attain Nirvāṇa in this world. As regards this point, an intriguing conversation was recorded between Rennyo Shōnin and Junsei, one of his disciples. In Article 34 of *The Goichidai ki kikigaki* it is stated that,

Junsei questioned Rennyo Shōnin, "In *The Letters* you taught that as soon as an individual attains the one thought-moment of the awakening of faith, all his transgressions are eradicated and that person joins the nonretrogressive state of those who are rightly assured. On the other hand you have also stated that our transgressions exist as long as we live, which seems to contradict the *Letters*." Rennyo replied: "The eradication of all transgressions at the one thought-moment means that all past transgressions are no longer a hindrance, when our birth in the

Pure Land becomes assured with the power of the one thought-moment of faith. Therefore, this is the equivalent of the transgressions being erased. However, as long as we dwell in this world, we commit transgressions. Have you, Junsei, by any chance attained Enlightenment and are you free from all transgressions already? The Sacred Scriptures state that transgressions are eradicated as soon as the one thought-moment is awakened. Rather than debating the existence or nonexistence of our transgressions, it is better for us to consider repeatedly whether we have truly attained faith or not. It is completely within Amida's discretion to save us with or without our transgressions. It is not for us to argue the matter. What is of vital importance is faith alone," – thus did Rennyo Shōnin reiterate his point thoughtfully.[412]

In this context, the notion of "blind passions" covers a wide spectrum of meanings, including the consciousness in which, illumined by Amida's Light, Shin Buddhists become aware of their blind passions as "bad karma" or "transgressions".

CHAPTER SIXTY-FOUR

Attaining the Stage Proximate to Supreme Enlightenment

ON THE GREAT BENEFIT BESTOWED WITH THE AWAKENING OF THE ONE THOUGHT-MOMENT OF FAITH

FASCICLE V, LETTER SIX

Shōnin describes in a *wasan*[413] the way Amida imparts the great benefit of his unsurpassed virtue to devout followers who, in one thought-moment, entrust themselves to him,

> When sentient beings of this wicked world of the five defilements
> Entrust themselves to the selected Original Vow
> Incalculable, indescribable, and inconceivable virtue
> Fills the existence of these devotees."[414]

In this verse in Japanese, the expression *"sentient beings of this wicked world of the five defilements"* refers to all of us, women and wrongdoers included. Thus, though we ourselves are such wretched beings that we go on committing wrongdoings our whole lives through, nevertheless, as long as we entrust ourselves to Amida Tathāgata singleheartedly and steadfastly and entreat him to help us with Rebirth, there is no doubt at all but that Amida will save us all without fail. Amida bestows "incalculable, indescribable, and inconceivable great virtue" on us who entrust ourselves to the Buddha in this way.

"Incalculable, indescribable, and inconceivable virtue" means virtue so great there is no way to measure it. Because this great virtue is transferred to ourselves, sentient beings who in one thought-moment entrust themselves to Amida, karmic hindrances of the three periods, past, future and present, are instantly extinguished, and we find ourselves at the stage of those who are rightly assured, or those who have attained the stage proximate to Supreme Enlightenment. Once again, this is expressed in another verse from *The Shōzōmatsu Wasan*,

> Entrust yourselves to the Original Vow of Amida.
> All of you who entrust yourselves to the Original Vow,
> By virtue of the benefit of being embraced and never abandoned,
> Attain the stage proximate to Supreme Enlightenment.[415]

The phrase *"being embraced and never abandoned"* also means that those sentient beings who in one thought-moment entrust themselves to Amida are received within his Light and, as their own faith remains unchanging, will never be forsaken. Although other teachings exist besides this one, there should never be any doubt but that those sentient beings who simply entrust themselves to Amida in one thought-moment will, each and every one of them, be born in the Land of Enjoyment.

Most humbly and respectfully

COMMENTS

Although this particular letter bears no date like all the other letters of Fascicle Five, there can be little doubt according to several commentaries on the *Letters* that this letter must be one of those written by Rennyo during the last three years of his life, namely, between 1496 and 1499. As such, certain essential points of the Shin Buddhist teaching are expressed with particular clarity.

The words in the first paragraph, "Amida imparts the great benefit of his unsurpassed virtue to devout followers," are said to be based on an important passage from the concluding part of *The Larger Sūtra of Eternal Life*:

The Buddha said to Maitreya, "If there are people who hear the Name of the Buddha, are so happy they dance for joy, and think of him even once, then you know that they have gained a great benefit endowed with the unsurpassed virtue."[416]

The phrase, "to think of him even once" (乃至一念 jp. *naishi ichinen*), is understood in the Shin Buddhist tradition as representing the one thought-moment practice of *Nenbutsu* or the one thought-moment pronouncing of the Buddha's Name. It is in this sense that Shinran Shōnin interprets the phrase "thinking of him even once" in the second volume of his main writing, *The Kyōgyōshinshō*, the volume entitled "True Practice."

As frequently mentioned, the practice of saying the *Nenbutsu*, or of the pronouncing of the Buddha Name, is not separate from the faith-experience of entrusting oneself absolutely to Amida Buddha. In their source faith and practice are one and the same in Shin Buddhism, both originating in the great compassion of Amida Buddha. Both are gifts to us from Amida. On encountering the Name of Amida Buddha pronounced by all the Buddhas, a manifestation in itself of Amida's great compassion, we come to entrust ourselves absolutely to Amida Buddha. In Shin Buddhist teaching the *Nenbutsu* of our teacher or Dharma friends is referred to as "all Buddhas' pronouncing the Name of Amida Buddha." In other words, on becoming aware of the working of Amida's great compassion that manifests itself as the *Nenbutsu* of our good teacher or Dharma friends, we attain the pure faith of entrusting ourselves to Amida Buddha. We are impelled to do so by Other Power, issuing from the depths of our being. Our own *Nenbutsu* practice, or pronouncing of the Name, wells up spontaneously from our faith-experience. It is an expression of the greatest joy and the deepest gratitude we feel at the moment of attaining faith and finding ourselves in the embrace of the unconditional love of Amida Buddha. Our *Nenbutsu* practice springs from our faith-experience, not vice versa. Regarding this point Shinran Shōnin states in *The Kyōgyōshinshō*, "True faith is unfailingly accompanied by the Name. The Name is, however, not necessarily accompanied by the faith that is grounded on the Vow-power."[417]

With reference to this point, let us examine again the above quoted passage from *The Larger Sūtra of Eternal Life*. If you look closely at the flow of this passage, it is obvious that the one thought-moment of pronouncing the Name, expressed as "to think of him even once," follows the one thought-moment of faith, expressed as "we are so overjoyed that we feel like dancing." As discussed above, this one moment's thought of faith follows "hearing the

Name of Amida." This phrase "hearing the Name of Amida" refers of course to our encounter with the Buddha Name pronounced by all Buddhas or Dharma friends, not our own pronouncing of the Name. Our own individual one thought-moment practice of pronouncing the Name with joy and gratitude emerges at the very moment we attain the one thought-moment of faith. In essence the one thought-moment of practice and the one thought-moment of faith are one and the same, both having its original source in Amida Buddha.

Why, then, does Shinran Shōnin talk about those two things as though they are different? It is to clarify the meaning of the one thought-moment of *Nenbutsu* practice that issues from the experience of the one thought-moment of faith, and distinguish it from other forms of practice. The *Nenbutsu* practice after the attainment of faith is entirely an expression of our gratitude to Amida Buddha for all that he has done for us. It is not an attempt to gain anything. We do not pronounce the *Nenbutsu* in order to accrue virtue, or merit, that might help us reach the Pure Land. It is not a means to a goal, Nirvāṇa in this context, but a process in which the goal itself is made manifest. In other words, it is itself part of the working of that goal. The reason why Shinran Shōnin defines the words *naishi ichinen* "to think of him even once" in the concluding part of *The Larger Sūtra* as the one thought-moment of practice is to make clear that the true practice of *The Larger Sūtra* is the one thought-moment of practice, itself an expression of heartfelt gratitude to Amida Buddha, welling up from the one thought-moment of faith-experience.

In the second paragraph of the letter, Rennyo states with great kindness, "In this verse the expression 'sentient beings of this wicked world of the five defilements' refers to absolutely all of us, women and wrongdoers included." The Shin Buddhist faith has two important aspects: awakening to oneself or the irredeemable reality of one's karmic existence and awakening to Amida Buddha or his unconditional love. Both aspects are indispensable for the attaining of true faith. Unless we awaken to ourselves it is impossible for us to receive that universal love as a gift directed to us by Amida.

The original Japanese phrase for "*incalculable, indescribable and inconceivable virtue*" is *fukashō fukasetsu fukashigi no kudoku* 不可称不可説不可思議の功徳. Some commentators point out that *shō* 称 means both "to calculate" and "to praise," but in this context the proper meaning of the word is "to calculate," hence, *fukashō* means "incalculable." Thus Rennyo is perfectly right in saying "*incalculable, indescribable, and inconceivable virtue*" means virtue so great there is no way to measure it.

Another difficult term for us to understand in the third paragraph is "the stage proximate to Supreme Enlightenment" (*tōshōgaku* 等正覚). It is sometimes used in its shortened form "proximate Enlightenment" (*tōgaku* 等覚). Regarding this technical term and its two different meanings, I once stated in a talk on *The Shōshinge*, given at the Buddhist Society in London,

The way Sanskrit texts were translated into Chinese changed considerably around the time of Xuánzàng 玄奘 (600–664)[418] of the Táng Dynasty. Translations before Xuánzàng are referred to as 'old' and those after his time, including his own translations, are called 'new.' If you are not aware of the difference in the way of translation between 'new' and 'old' versions, you will be greatly confused and may even misunderstand the contents of the texts.

In this context we should pay particular attention to several Buddhist terms in order to understand the Eleventh Vow properly. One of these is the Buddhist term *tōshōgaku* 等正覚 (ch. *děngzhēngjué*). In 'old' translations this term meant Supreme Perfect Enlightenment (skt. *anuttarasamyaksambodhi*) or simply Supreme Enlightenment of the Buddha and therefore the phrase *tōshōgaku* 等正覚 was employed, for instance, as one of the ten epithets of the Buddha. In 'new' translations, however, the meaning of the term changed and the same term was now used to mean a Bodhisattva who would become a Buddha in his next life, or the spiritual stage reached by such a Bodhisattva. In this case the term *tōshōgaku* 等正覚 (or *tōgaku* 等覚) means a Bodhisattva stage proximate to the Supreme Enlightenment of the Buddha, with the word 等 clearly meaning 'proximate.' This is why, when translating the relevant part of *The Shōshinge*, I rendered the term as 'stage proximate to Enlightenment.'

Shinran Shōnin was definitely aware of the change in the meaning of the Buddhist term *tōshōgaku* 等正覚 or *tōgaku* 等覚 when it was used in 'new' translations. It goes without saying, therefore, that he understood what was meant by it when he saw it in the Eleventh Vow of the *Assembly of the Tathāgata of Eternal Life* and used the term 等覚 in *The Shōshinge*. The line in question from *The Shōshinge* reads: 'We attain the stage proximate to Enlightenment and will realise Great Nirvāṇa.'

The original Chinese for "Stage proximate to Enlightenment" in this line is 等覚, meaning a bodhisattva stage proximate to the Buddha's Supreme Enlightenment. What Shinran Shōnin clarifies in this line is that, through the attainment of true faith, you are led to a Bodhisattva stage that is proximate to the Buddha's Supreme Enlightenment. In his religious philosophy it is very important for us to understand that we attain 'the stage proximate to Enlightenment' in the here and now, while living in this world, and that then, after the moment of death, we will realise the 'Great Nirvāṇa.' The expression 'Great Nirvāṇa' (*Dànièpán* 大涅槃 in Chinese) in this line also comes from the Eleventh Vow of the *Assembly of the Tathāgata of Eternal Life*.

In Shinran Shōnin's own commentary, found in *Annotated Inscriptions on Sacred Scrolls*, he states that "*We attain the stage proximate to Enlightenment and will realise Great Nirvāṇa:* The stage proximate to Enlightenment is the stage of those definitely assured [of birth]. Nāgârjuna speaks of this stage as 'immediately entering the stage of the definite assurance [to attain Buddhahood]' and Master Tánluán as 'entering the company of those who have attained the right definite assurance.' All this means it is equal to the stage of Maitreya.'[419] [420]

Therefore, 'the stage proximate to Supreme Enlightenment' means a Bodhisattva stage that is proximate to the Supreme Enlightenment of the Buddha or the stage of those who are rightly assured of birth in the Pure Land. Rennyo himself states in this letter, "Because this great virtue is transferred to ourselves, sentient beings who singlemindedly entrust themselves to Amida, the karmic hindrances of the three periods, past, future and present, are instantly extinguished, and we find ourselves at the stage of those who are rightly assured or those who have attained the stage proximate to Supreme Enlightenment."

Another way that we are enabled to reach this stage is set out by Rennyo towards the end of this letter when he explains that those who entrust themselves to Amida Buddha find themselves at the stage proximate to Supreme Enlightenment by virtue of the benefit of "being embraced and never abandoned." He quotes another *wasan*,

> Entrust yourselves to the Original Vow of Amida.
> All of you who entrust yourselves to the Original Vow,
> By virtue of the benefit of being embraced and never abandoned,
> Attain the stage proximate to Supreme Enlightenment.

This is actually a combination of the first two lines of the very first *wasan* of the *Shōzōmatsu Wasan* and the last two lines of the twenty-fifth. These two *wasan* are,

> Entrust yourselves to the Original Vow of Amida!
> All of you who entrust yourselves to the Original Vow,
> Through the benefit of being embraced and never abandoned,
> Will attain Supreme Enlightenment.[421]

> Those who truly attain joyous faith,
> Transferred to them from Amida's Vow of Wisdom,
> By virtue of the benefit of being embraced and never abandoned,
> Attain the stage proximate to Supreme Enlightenment.[422]

The first *wasan* is very famous as being received by Shinran Shōnin in a dream when at the age of eighty-five he was confronting the very serious problem of his eldest son, Zenran (1212–1292). "Supreme Enlightenment" (*mujōkaku* 無上覚) refers to Buddhas' Enlightenment. It is after birth in the Pure Land that we will attain Supreme Enlightenment in this sense. This is different from "the stage proximate to Supreme Enlightenment," which is reached in the here and now whilst still remaining in this world.

I do not know why Rennyo should have chosen to devise such a *wasan* by combining two others. When I listen to the lines composed by him in this way, however, they sound to me like a direct call from Amida Buddha, and from Rennyo himself too, a call to us all from beyond time and space.

If we retain even the slightest element of pride on pronouncing the Buddha Name, it does not accord with Shin Buddhist teaching transmitted by its founder, Shinran Shōnin, or its restorer, Rennyo Shōnin. Although we are still at the stage proximate to Supreme Enlightenment, we can be absolutely confident of attaining Supreme Enlightenment in the Pure Land after death because our attainment of Buddhahood is entirely brought out by Amida's Original Vow, a manifestation of his unconditional Love based on Supreme Enlightenment.

CHAPTER SIXTY-FIVE

The Karmic Burden
Women Are Laden With

ON THE FIVE OBSTACLES
AND THREE SUBMISSIONS

FASCICLE V, LETTER SEVEN

Because a woman's life is encumbered with the so-called five obstacles and three submissions, women are weighed down by a burden of bad karma that is even more profound than that of men. For this reason, the Buddhas of the ten directions are unable, by their own power, to make any woman attain Buddhahood. It is Amida Tathāgata alone who saves women through the great Vow he made for their liberation. Unless women entrust themselves to this Buddha, it is impossible for them to become Buddhas.

If this is the case, what should be a woman's attitude of mind and how should women entrust themselves to Amida Buddha so that they themselves may become Buddhas?

Simply if they entrust themselves solely to Amida Buddha with steadfastness and an absence of double-mindedness, and with this singleness of heart and mind entreat his help with Rebirth, they will readily become Buddhas. Since their minds are free of the slightest doubt, they will be able to proceed unfailingly to the Land of Utmost Bliss and there become beautiful Buddhas.

What they also need to understand, however, is that, whenever they pronounce the *Nenbutsu*, they should bear in mind the following thought: "Our saying the *Nenbutsu* is solely in order to respond with joy and gratitude to all that Amida Tathāgata has done to save such wretched beings as ourselves."

Most humbly and respectfully

COMMENTS

Rennyo produced a great many letters on the subject of women's attainment of Buddhahood in the Pure Land. The letters of *Chapters 7, 10, 16, 25, 53, 61, 65, 72, 75* and *78* – that is, the seventh and tenth letter of Fascicle One, the first letter and tenth letter of Fascicle Two, the tenth letter of Fascicle Four, the third, seventh, fourteenth, seventeenth and twentieth letters of Fascicle Five, respectively – are all particularly addressed to women. In addition to these, numerous other letters exist, some included in the Five Fascicle version of *The Letters*, some not, that make explicit reference to women's attainment of Buddhahood.

In the Pure Land tradition as a whole there are many important documents on the attainment of Buddhahood by women, such as Shàndǎo's *Method of Contemplation on Amida* 觀念法門, Hōnen's *Commentary on The Larger Sūtra of Eternal Life* 大經釋 and Shinran's *Wasan* 和讚 (*Verses in Japanese*).[423] In the Shin Buddhist tradition, in addition to Shinran Shōnin's various writings, Venerable Zonkaku's writing, *Notes on the Birth of Women in the Pure Land* 女人往生聞書,[424] stands out. We can see that Rennyo's comments on women's birth in the Pure Land in his letters are based on those documents.

In comparison with other Pure Land teachers, Rennyo's writings concerning the birth of women in the Pure Land were prodigious, leading us to conclude that this was a subject that occupied him deeply. Why was this so, one wonders? Well, a woman's birth in the Pure Land signifies her attainment there of Buddhahood, so the problem, put another way, is whether women can in fact become Buddhas. If in Buddhism women are seen as inherently devoid of the possibility of attaining Buddhahood, however, that must surely amount to a most serious case of discrimination against them. Going back in time to the days of Śākyamuni Buddha, in fact, we can see that he himself allowed women to enter the Sangha, but with three refusals. Śākyamuni while at first reluctant in the light of his acute awareness of existing Hindu social structure and the need for the nascent Sangha to exist in harmony with the lay-community which supported it, was, to his great credit, persuaded to change his mind and permitted the creation of female monastic orders. Indeed we have records of their experiences of Enlightenment or Awakening. This means that the Buddha saw women as being perfectly capable of awakening to the ultimate truth of life and attaining a truly peaceful and happy state of mind.

All the sūtras of Early Buddhism do say, however, that it is relatively more difficult for women to attain Buddhahood than men. Nevertheless, according to these same early sūtras, Śākyamuni Buddha after a long period of consideration finally allowed women, including his mother-in-law, Mahāprajāpatī, and his wife, Yasodharā, to enter the Sangha. So, even at the beginning of Buddhism women were seen as able to attain Enlightenment. Even today awakened women often play a prominent part in Buddhist activities. My own first master, for example, the late Dharma-Mother Ekai, was a really awakened spiritual leader for innumerable followers at Shogyoji Temple, a Shin Buddhist Sangha.

In Buddhism the attainment of Buddhahood represents the highest stage of any human being. It is the source of all wisdom and love for others. In as much as women, just like men, have within themselves the same possibility of attaining this ideal, one feels there should be no discrimination against them. But this would be to disregard the nature of human society and the entire record of the human race. At no time in our history has there been a period entirely free of discrimination against women. Rennyo's time was no exception. The very reason he wrote a great number of letters specifically about the birth of women in the Pure Land was that he recognised the reality of the situation and wanted to free women from the unwarranted discrimination they faced.

As Buddhism developed it remained, unfortunately, far from free of the discriminatory tendencies of human karma. Almost all the various schools became tainted with discrimination against women, maintaining that women were incapable of becoming Buddhas or at the very least would find it next to impossible. As you know, Pure Land Buddhism, particularly Shin Buddhism, is a school for lay people that insists on the salvation of all human beings without any discrimination whatsoever. It was by returning to the original starting point of Śākyamuni Buddha that Shinran Shōnin, the founder of Shin Buddhism, and Rennyo Shōnin, the restorer of our tradition, were able to exort women to embrace the Pure Land faith, the faith of entrusting themselves solely to Amida Buddha and his promise to save women through his Original Vow.

Some people insist that Rennyo's letters display a discriminatory attitude towards women. It is not that there is no reason for this criticism. Such criticisms are understandable because, despite his ultimate concern about the salvation of women, when teaching them to attain the Shin Buddhist faith, he used a few discriminatory notions such as "five obstacles" and "three submissions" from the traditional vocabularies of Buddhism in general that were still predominant in society in his days. It is clear, however, that his ultimate concern was, after all, to liberate women from their karmic prison in which they were unduly discriminated against.

The first paragraph of this letter consists of three parts. If you look only at the first part, it certainly reflects a discriminatory view prevalent at the time. What Rennyo wanted to see, however, was not discrimination against women, but rather their attainment of Buddhahood through entrusting themselves to Amida Buddha. It was because he recognised all too well the reality of the discrimination shown towards women that he wanted to help them liberate themselves from the karmic reality of that discrimination.

Discrimination against women runs directly counter to the pure essence of Buddhism which is an absolute oneness beyond duality, into which different individuals can come together just as they are. If our understanding of different things remains purely centred on self and we continue to behave in a selfish way, we will bring about karmic discriminations that may hurt others. Discrimination against women is the karmic reality of the male-dominated world. It was with great sorrow that Rennyo was forced to confront this reality.

In the male-dominated society of those days the discriminatory view that women are burdened with the five obstacles and the three submissions was shared by almost all of the Buddhist schools. When Rennyo was forced to say "For this reason, the Buddhas of the ten directions are unable, by their own power, to make any woman attain Buddhahood," what was in his mind? He must have been speaking with extreme sadness at the discriminatory attitude of all the other schools. In this context "the Buddhas of the ten directions" stand for Buddhism in general or the teaching of all the Buddhist schools apart from that of Amida Buddha.

"The five obstacles" that beset women are mentioned in *The Lotus Sūtra* (法華經 *Hokke kyō*), in the Chapter Devadatta, and explained in detail in *The Chōnichimyō zanmai kyō* 超日明三昧經, *Sūtra of Samādhi of Light Surpassing Sunlight*.[425] These obstacles are that a woman cannot become a *brahmadeva, cakrodevānāmindraḥ*, demon king, *cakravartinrāja*, or Buddha. A commentary on *The Lotus Sūtra*, known as *The Hokke kyō yōge* 法華經要解 (ch. *Fǎhuá jīng yàojiě*), *Essentials of the Lotus Sūtra*, gives the following explanation.[426] Firstly women cannot become *brahmadeva* because to do so is the result of pure practice and women are full of impure attachments. Secondly they cannot become *cakrodevānāmindraḥ* because that is the result of a lack of greed and women are burdened with a great deal of greed. Thirdly they cannot become a demon king because to do so requires mental strength and power and women are feeble. Fourthly they cannot become *cakravartinrāja* because that can only be achieved through loving kindness towards others and women are full of jealousy and are harmful to others. Fifthly they cannot attain Buddhahood because a Buddha is endowed with myriad virtues whereas women are filled with blind passions.

The unfavourable attributes depicted here as characteristic of women are of course all found in men as well. Indeed, from a woman's point of view, it could be said that there are more men than women who are full of impure attachments, encumbered with greed, lacking mental strength, constantly jealous of others or burdened with selfish, blind passions. Analysing patterns of behaviour, you will find that often women only seem more attached to things because they feel responsible towards, and indeed take responsibility for, their immediate relatives, especially their children. They may exhibit selfish patterns of behaviour, even committing wrongdoing, but in most cases it will be in order to protect their children.

"The three submissions" that were seen to beset womankind are to be found in such documents as *The Gaṇḍavyūha, The Chōnichimyō zanmai kyō* and *The Sūtra of Sujātā* (玉耶經 *Gyokuya kyō*). These hindrances refer to three kinds of submission expected of a woman. Firstly when they were young women had to obey their parents. Secondly when they were married they were not free but had to obey their husbands. Thirdly when they were old they had to obey their children.

For instance, *The Gaṇḍavyūha* states that "when staying at home as a young woman she obeys her father and mother, when coming of age and getting married she serves her husband, and when losing her husband she follows her children to clear herself of suspicion."[427]

Although, as already mentioned, the five obstacles and three submissions said to beset women in those days were chiefly the reflections of the discriminatory views of a male-dominated society, awareness of their condition will also have helped women awaken to the karmic reality of their lives, entangled in petty discrimination, and helped them understand how important it was for them to free themselves from such karmic suffering. It will have been for this purpose that Rennyo made use in his letters of those descriptions of women's karma found in the documents of Buddhism in general at that time. His real intention, however, was to help women liberate themselves from their own karmic reality by entrusting themselves solely to Amida Buddha.

The statement found in the third paragraph, "they will be able to proceed unfailingly to the Land of Utmost Bliss and there become beautiful Buddhas," reveals in an elegant and appreciative way Rennyo Shōnin's true feelings of thoughtfulness towards women.

My own master, Ekai-sama, was an awakened lady of pure faith. I was extremely fortunate to have been able to meet her as a young man. Needless to say, when someone is truly awakened, their attitude towards those around them is full of love and compassion, but the kind words of such an enlightened woman were always sufficiently down to earth to be able to strip away any superficial understanding people might have of their personal situation. When I was eighteen years old, having passed the university entrance exams, I went to see Ekai-sama at Shogyoji Temple in order to say thank you. On catching sight of me at the morning assembly, she asked who it was sitting there so proudly. I immediately answered, "It is me, Taira, the third son of the Hōrenji Temple family," but as I spoke I became aware of the pride embedded in my voice and felt ashamed. "And for what purpose are you going to Kyoto?" she continued. "To study the teaching of Shinran Shōnin," I replied, "I want to look into myself in a far deeper dimension." To this she immediately responded, "Ah, so that's what you are doing. It is in order to dissect yourself."

Another story that demonstrates her unfathomable love and compassion took place when I brought one of my friends, Reverend Hōyu Takada, then aged nineteen, to the Summer Training Assembly at Shogyoji Temple. Having noticed his attainment of faith, I expressed my gratitude at one of the meetings, saying "Thank you very much. I now understand Mr Takada is a Bodhisattva for me." My words proceeded from some kind of inspired intuition. On hearing me make this pronouncement, Ekai-sama herself suddenly stood up and exclaimed, "Well said indeed! Mr Takada really is a Bodhisattva for you." The pleasure her words expressed was something quite indescribable and inexplicable. Her words emerged, I felt, from some unfathomable depths, entirely beyond my understanding. I felt embraced in the warmth of her great compassion. This revealed a spiritual dimension hitherto unknown to me: If you attain pure faith, all your Dharma friends are Bodhisattvas who protect and lead you to the Pure Land throughout your life.

For the liberation of women from the heavy burden of discrimination, Shinran Shōnin's decision of marriage seems to have played an incredibly important role in the history of Shin Buddhism. As described in *The Goden shō*, or *The Life of Shinran Shōnin*, by Kakunyo,[428] before his marriage Shinran had a dream towards the end of his one hundred day visit to Bodhisattva Avalokiteśvara of Rokkakudō in Kyoto. In this vision he received a message from the Bodhisattva, "When you find yourself bound by your past karma to come into contact with the female sex, I will incarnate myself as the most beautiful woman and become the object of your love. And throughout your life I will be your helpmate, adorning you with dignity and on your death I will lead you to be born in the Land of Bliss." It is doubtless that his marriage was based on his experience of this message that he had received in a vision. The crucial point of the account is that he not merely saw his wife as the object of his love but also respected her as the embodiment of Bodhisattva Avalokiteśvara, someone who would protect him throughout his life and eventually help him attain birth in the Pure Land. This story tells us that his wife was not a tool for his life but someone to respect with humility, certainly beyond all kinds of discrimination.[429]

CHAPTER SIXTY-SIX

Amida's Original Vow is for Me, Shinran, Alone

ON THE FIVE KALPAS OF MEDITATION

FASCICLE V, LETTER EIGHT

The five kalpas of meditation of the Original Vow and the countless kalpas or infinite period of practice are all manifestations of Amida Buddha's compassionate desire to save all sentient beings, each and every one of us, without exception. As a means of saving us, all sentient beings, Amida Tathāgata subjected himself to harsh, painstaking discipline and formulated the Original Vow that is *Namu Amida-butsu*. Amida himself became *Namu Amida-butsu*, for it was Amida Buddha's vow that he would not attain Supreme Enlightenment if he failed to save from the world of transmigration sentient beings who in one thought-moment abandoned all their miscellaneous practices and entrusted themselves to him steadfastly and singleheartedly. We should be aware that this is precisely why we can attain birth so readily in the Land of Utmost Bliss.

The six characters *Namu Amida-butsu* 南无阿彌陀佛 thus indicate how we, sentient beings, can attain birth in the Land of Enjoyment. When we take refuge by saying "*Namu*," Amida Buddha immediately saves us. The two characters *Namu* 南无 express the way sentient beings turn towards Amida

Tathāgata and entreat him to save them in the matter of Rebirth. It can then be seen that it is the meaning of the next four characters *Amida-butsu* 阿彌陀佛 that Amida Buddha saves without exception all those who entrust themselves to him.

Thus those who forsake all their miscellaneous practices and entrust themselves singlemindedly to Amida Buddha to save them in the matter of Rebirth will be saved without exception, ten out of every ten of them, one hundred out of every one hundred, even if they are people encumbered with the ten bad acts and the five grave offences, or even if, as in the case of women, they are encumbered with the five obstacles and the three submissions. Those who entrust themselves to Amida Buddha in this way, without harbouring any lingering doubts, will be born in his true Pure Land.

Most humbly and respectfully

COMMENTS

The opening sentence of the first paragraph of this letter brings to mind two passages in the *Kuden shō* by Kakunyo Shōnin, the third head priest of the Honganji Temple and grandson of Kakushin-ni, the daughter of Shinran Shōnin. The work, divided into twenty-one chapters, consists of doctrinal explanations by Kakunyo Shōnin based on sayings by Shinran Shōnin. The title of the book, *Kuden shō*, signifies a collection of teachings orally transmitted from person to person. One of the two passages comes from Chapter 7, entitled "On the Attainment by Ignorant Beings of Birth in the Pure Land",

> That is why Shinran Shōnin said, "The five kalpas of meditation and the billions of years of practice were all meant for me, Shinran, alone." Reflecting on this, what I would like to say to you is that the statement is not limited to our founder, Shinran Shōnin, alone, but applies to all of us. In so far as we are ignorant beings in this latter world, we are all to attain birth in the same way. Note this well.[430]

The other passage is from Chapter 19, "The Original Vow is for the Sake of Ignorant Beings",

> Nyoshin Shōnin (1239–1300), Shinran Shōnin's grandson, passed on to me words of wisdom that were transmitted to the Honganji Shōnin (Shinran) from his late teacher of Kurodani (Hōnen Shōnin): "People ordinarily think, *If a person burdened with bad karma may attain birth, how much more readily a good person.*" This view, in the distant

past, goes against Amida's Original Vow, and, in the more recent past, contradicts the golden words by Śākyamuni when he appeared in this world. For that reason, the five kalpas of labouring in contemplation and the six *pāramitāḥ* and other myriad practices that Amida Buddha endured were all for the sake of the liberation of the ignorant, and not at all for the sake of the sages.[431]

The Kuden shō by Kakunyo is very similar to *The Tanni shō* by Venerable Yuien (1222–1289), a direct disciple of Shinran Shōnin, in the sense that both are descriptions of the teaching of Shinran Shōnin firmly based on a record of his own words. An important passage bearing on the main subject of the two quotations from the *Kuden shō* is found in the postscript of *The Tanni shō*,

> "When I deeply reflect on the Vow of Amida, created through five kalpas of profound thought, I find the Vow is entirely meant for me, Shinran, alone. That is why I feel so grateful for the Original Vow in which Amida graciously resolved to save me, a person so heavily weighed down by karma."[432]

Both this utterance by Shinran Shōnin and the similar words attributed to him in Chapter 7 of the *Kuden shō* may share the same source, namely, his declaration at a meeting attended by both Venerable Yuien and Nyoshin Shōnin. Quite possibly Kakunyo heard the words from both of them, because, according to the *Boki eshi*, a biography of Kakunyo Shōnin by Jūkaku, Kakunyo met Nyoshin Shōnin in 1287 and Venerable Yuien in 1288.[433]

Both documents, *The Tanni shō* and *The Kuden shō*, record Shinran Shōnin's humble awareness that Amida Buddha's Original Vow was "entirely for me, Shinran, alone." This phrase reminds me of D. T. Suzuki's term "supra-individual individual," a unique concept he invented in his book *Japanese Spirituality*. Regarding this notion, let me quote from my commentary on *The Tanni shō*,

> D. T. Suzuki's term (supra-individual individual) was coined in connection with Shinran Shōnin's saying: "When I deeply reflect on the Vow of Amida, created through five kalpas of profound thought, I find the Vow is entirely meant for me, Shinran, alone. That is why I feel so grateful for the Original Vow in which Amida graciously resolved to save me, someone so heavily weighed down by karma." Commenting on Shinran Shōnin's statement, "I find the Vow is entirely meant for me, Shinran, alone" 親鸞一人がためなりけり, D. T. Suzuki says it shows Shinran Shōnin's 'supra-individual individuality.'
>
> The passage quoted above is a confession of faith. As I mentioned previously, Shin Buddhist faith has two aspects: 1. awakening to oneself

and 2. awakening to Amida. This confession of faith shows that Shinran Shōnin is fully awakened to himself and at the same time to Amida. He accepts Amida's Original Vow with gratitude, realising it is entirely for himself alone. These two aspects become one in his pure faith. In his faith he is united not only with Amida and but also with Hōnen Shōnin. For Shinran Shōnin, Hōnen Shōnin is the very embodiment of the Original Vow.

Furthermore, the expression, 'for me, Shinran, alone,' indicates the absolute passivity of the Shin Buddhist faith. In this absolute passivity one becomes a selfless recipient, through whom the great working of the Buddha can manifest itself freely. When one's individual self transcends the individual self, one becomes selfless and attains to the totality of oneness with others as a supra-individual individual. Although one is selfless and in a state of absolute passivity, one is clearly aware of the dynamics of one's karmic condition.

According to my understanding this awareness of one's unique exist-ence is the reality of one's individuality. This Shin Buddhist notion of individuality is different from the Western interpretation of the individual self. What I refer to by 'individuality' is not the notion of an inherently existing self but an awareness of oneself in light of one's interdependent karmic condition wherein one is linked karmically to all other things.[434]

Regarding the expression of his awareness that the Original Vow was "entirely for me, Shinran, alone," Venerable Yuien states in *The Tanni shō*, "It was the Master's merciful heart causing him to use himself as an example in an effort to awaken us to ourselves going astray without realising how deep is our karmic evil or how great is what has been done for us by [Amida] Tathāgata."[435] This means that Venerable Yuien understood Shinran Shōnin's words as being a way of teaching that Amida Buddha's Original Vow was for all of us, all sentient beings. Kakunyo, too, clarified this point in the *Kuden shō* when he wrote "Reflecting on this, what I would like to say to you is that the statement is not limited to our founder, Shinran Shōnin, alone, but applies to all of us."

Thus, when Rennyo says in the letter, "The five kalpas of meditation of the Original Vow and the countless kalpas or infinite period of practice are all manifestations of Amida Buddha's compassionate desire to save all sentient beings, each and every one of us, without exception," his statement is firmly based not only on *The Tanni shō* but also on *The Kuden shō*, Shin Buddhist documents chronicling person to person oral transmission.

Unless we become aware of the irredeemable reality of our karmic existence, we will never be able to entrust ourselves absolutely to Amida's unconditional love. On the other hand, without being awakened to Amida

Buddha's unconditional love, a love that discriminates against no one but calls upon all of us to come to him immediately without hesitation, we will never become aware of the irredeemable reality of our sad, selfish existence. At the very moment of awakening we entrust ourselves to Amida's Original Vow with no reservation at all and respond to his warm, loving words "Come to me immediately just as you are!" Shinran Shōnin's declaration that Amida's Original Vow was "entirely for me, Shinran, alone" was an expression of humility and gratitude, springing from just such an awakening of true faith. His words, as quoted above, are then followed in *The Tanni shō* text by the words "That is why I feel so grateful for the Original Vow in which Amida graciously resolved to save me, someone so heavily weighed down by karma."[436]

Unless we ourselves can attain "supra-individual individuality," as embodied in Shinran's Shonin's statement that Amida's Original Vow was entirely for him alone, we cannot have true confidence in the salvation of all sentient beings. Only the attainment of true individuality can inspire in us confidence of universal deliverance. The awakening of true or "supra-individual" individuality opens up the world of Amida's unconditional love where all sentient beings are saved without discrimination. Thus the awakening of true individuality is indispensable to the Shin Buddhist notion of true faith. It is an essential part, in other words, of the Shin Buddhist teaching. Not just Shinran Shōnin but all true Shin Buddhist followers are expected to realise this true individuality through their awakening of faith. It is in this way that I understand Kakunyo Shōnin's words, "The statement is not limited to our founder, Shinran Shōnin, alone, but applies to all of us. In as far as we are ignorant beings in this latter world, we are all to attain birth in the same way." What is most important is for us, followers of this tradition, is to internalise, through our own attainment of faith, the primordial experience of "supra-individual individuality" the Founder of the tradition expressed by the words "entirely for me, Shinran, alone."

Moving on to the second sentence of the first paragraph of the eighth letter of Fascicle Five, "As a means of saving us, all sentient beings, Amida Tathāgata subjected himself to harsh, painstaking discipline and formulated the Original Vow that is *Namu Amida-butsu*," this statement means that Amida Tathāgata revealed himself as "the *Dharma-kāya* in its manifested form,"[437] in other words as the Buddha of *Saṃbhoga-kāya* who made and fulfilled the Original Vow through long, hard discipline.

The essence of the Original Vow lies in encouraging all sentient beings to take refuge in Amida Buddha or to become *Namu Amida-butsu*. Rennyo Shōnin's words, "Amida himself became *Namu Amida-butsu*," refer to the fulfilment of the Original Vow that opened up the way for all sentient beings to become *Namu Amida-butsu*.

CHAPTER SIXTY-SEVEN

What is Meant by Anjin

ON THE PURPORT OF ALL

THE SCRIPTURES

FASCICLE V, LETTER NINE

The meaning of peaceful awareness in our tradition is fully expressed by means of the six characters *Namu Amida-butsu* 南无阿彌陀佛. That is to say, when we take refuge by saying "*Namu*," *Amida-butsu* immediately saves us. Thus the two characters *Namu* 南无 signify "taking refuge," the action of sentient beings who forsake all miscellaneous practices and entrust themselves steadfastly to Amida Buddha by entreating him to save them in the matter of Rebirth. Therefore Amida Tathāgata, that is, *Amida-butsu*, fully understands them and saves all of them without exception.

Accordingly, since Amida Buddha saves sentient beings who entrust themselves to him as they say "*Namu*," we can see that the six characters *Namu Amida-butsu* are a demonstration of the way we sentient beings have already been saved, each one of us without exception. Hence our attainment of Other Power faith is in itself a realisation of the meaning of the six characters *Namu Amida-butsu*. We should recognise, therefore, that the sole purpose of all the scriptures is to lead us to entrust ourselves to the six characters *Namu Amida-butsu*.

Most humbly and respectfully

COMMENTS

The expression "peaceful awareness" found in the first paragraph of this letter is my tentative translation of the original Japanese word *anjin* 安心.[438] Generally speaking, in the Shin Buddhist tradition, the word *anjin* is used synonymously with *shinjin* 信心, or faith.

The Chinese compound ānxīn 安心 (jp. *anjin*), as seen in Shàndǎo's *Liturgy on Birth*, can mean the act of "settling the mind," with the first character of the compound meaning "to quiet," "to settle," "to ease," "to establish," "to stabilise" or "make peaceful," and the latter signifying "mind." Or it can mean the resultant state of mind, of being "quieted" down and made "settled," or being made to be "at ease," or at "peace" with oneself. Nowadays the compound is seldom used in the sense of actively "settling the mind." Whenever it is used synonymously with *shinjin*, or faith, it refers to a peaceful state of mind and is usually translated as "settled mind," or sometimes as "peaceful mind."

It seems that Western Shin Buddhists are now used to using the expression "settled mind" as the standard translation of the word *anjin*. But I have noticed that some of my Western friends less familiar with Shin Buddhism are often quite troubled by the expression "settled mind." Once the term has been explained theoretically, however, they are able to understand it to some extent but only at an intellectual level. Ultimately, nevertheless, the phrase "settled mind" does not help them understand the profound meaning of the original word *anjin* (安心), a peaceful state of mind that can only be reached through the attainment of true faith, or *shinjin*. The true depths of meaning covered by the original word refer to the tranquility, peacefulness, stability, firmness, effortlessness and naturalness of true faith, or *shinjin*, attained by entrusting oneself absolutely to Amida Buddha. In an essay entitled *On the Way to the Land of Happiness*, my master, Dharma-Mother Ekai, after her attainment of faith, wrote,

> Later on in life, I damaged my stomach and bowels. Accompanied by my mother, I went to the Funagoya hot-springs to recuperate and stayed at an inn called Gyokusenkan. Unexpectedly this spa became an unforgettable place for me and one where I took my first step towards the attainment of faith. While there I fell into conversation with a certain Mr Zenjō Arita, a student who had also come to the hot springs to recuperate and was staying in the room next to mine. Mr Arita told me, "If you continue with this method of spiritual training of yours, you will have to spend the rest of your life seeking after truth and end up tracing only a very

gradual path of self-improvement. You may not reach the summit where lies a *peaceful mind* (安心 jp. *anjin*)." I was astonished at this simple statement and the student took on for me an air of great nobility. This was the first time I had ever been given such an intimation. Ever after I aspired with all my heart to the acquisition of the "peaceful mind" of Shinran Shōnin (親鸞聖人のご安心). Soon afterwards, my elder brother died from stomach cancer at the age of forty-eight. My longing for the "peaceful mind" became more intense, compelling me to seek the truth without delay.[439]

If my memory serves me well I was thirty-seven years old when I was allowed by my master, Dharma-Mother Ekai, to translate this essay with the kind help of Professor Taitetsu Unno, whom I happened to meet in Kyoto. At that time I translated *anjin* as "peaceful mind." In this special context the expression "peaceful mind" is passable, but it is still not adequate. If I were ever to retranslate this essay in the future I would prefer "peaceful awareness" to "peaceful mind." Reading the extract from my late master's essay hopefully helps you understand more clearly what is meant by the Japanese word *anjin*.

The Japanese word *shin* 心, which is usually translated into English as "mind," actually covers a wide range of meanings. In Buddhism, for instance, it can mean *Bodhicitta* 菩提心 Enlightenment mind, as well as its opposite, blind passions. What does it then mean in this special context of Shin Buddhism? The English word "mind" does not convey the special connotations of profundity and tranquility found in the Shin Buddhist use of the word. But one day a few years ago it occurred to me that the second character 心 of the compound 安心 could well be translated as "awareness."

As previously mentioned several times in my essays, the essence of the Shin Buddhist faith lies in simultaneous awakening firstly to oneself or the sad reality of one's karmic existence and secondly to the Buddha or his unconditional love that saves all beings with no discrimination. These are two aspects of the one and the same experience. Whoever has attained the awakening of faith always has this profound awareness, which consists of an awareness of oneself (*ki* 機) and that of Dharma (*Hō* 法) or Amida Buddha. When I translate *anjin* as "peaceful awareness," what I am referring to is this profound awareness consisting of these two aspects, an absolutely peaceful state of mind unshakable by anything else.

In the first paragraph of the letter Rennyo states that "The meaning of peaceful awareness (*anjin* 安心) in our tradition is fully expressed by means of the six characters *Namu Amida-butsu* 南无阿彌陀佛." The Name *Namu Amida-butsu* is made up of two parts, *Namu* and *Amida-butsu*. In turn they correspond to the two components of peaceful awareness (*anjin*): the awareness of *ki* 機, or self, and the awareness of *Hō* 法, or Dharma.

It should be noted that behind Rennyo Shōnin's teaching of *Namu Amida-butsu* there lies the notion of *Namu Amida-butsu* in which *ki and Hō* are one, a concept unique to Shin Buddhist philosophy. As stated in the latter part of the first paragraph, *Namu*, or "taking refuge," means not only forsaking all miscellaneous practices but also simultaneously entrusting oneself steadfastly to Amida Buddha. Without abandoning all miscellaneous practices there can be no true entrusting. The phrase "all miscellaneous practices" stands here for all types of ethical efforts undertaken out of self power. For as long as we remain attached to any kind of self power, we cannot entrust ourselves truly to Amida Buddha. The world of peaceful awareness instantaneously reached at the very moment of taking refuge in Amida Buddha lies far beyond the ethical realm of endless, gradual self-improvement.

CHAPTER SIXTY-EIGHT

The Essential Teaching of Shin Buddhism

WHAT IS TAUGHT BY SHŌNIN

IN THIS TRADITION

FASCICLE V, LETTER TEN

What is taught by Shōnin in this tradition is that faith is absolutely essential. This is because, when we throw away all the miscellaneous practices and singleheartedly take refuge in Amida Buddha, our birth is assured by the Buddha through the inconceivable working of his Original Vow. Attaining this state of mind is also explained as "entering the company of those whose birth is rightly assured, at the time the one thought-moment is awakened." Our *Nenbutsu*, or pronouncing the Buddha's Name, that follows should be understood as the *Nenbutsu* of gratitude for the fact that Tathāgata has assured our birth by virtue of all that he has done for us.

Most humbly and respectfully

COMMENTS

Brief as it is, amongst all the letters written by Rennyo Shōnin this is one of the most greatly appreciated. Nowadays, in actual fact, it is one of the two letters always read out at the monthly memorial service for Shinran Shōnin.

It is said that the two most important points of Shin Buddhist teaching are beautifully expressed in this short letter. These two points are: "Faith as the right cause" 信心正因 and "Pronouncing the Name in thankfulness for all that has been done for us" 称名報恩. Another important subject included in this letter is "Entering the company of those whose birth is rightly assured" 入正定聚. I myself think this point should be added to the two main ones, but it is usually explained as being an aspect of the first – "Faith as the right cause."

In the literature of Pure Land Buddhism there are to be found a great number of documents with passages that illustrate and support the vital importance of these three points: the Pure Land Sūtras, for example, the commentaries by the seven patriarchs or Shinran Shōnin's own writings. *The Shōshinge* by Shinran is a beautiful gāthā that well illustrates the essential ideas governing Shin Buddhist philosophy.

Regarding the first point, "Faith as the right cause," Shinran Shōnin says,

With the Vow of sincerity and joyous faith as its cause,
We attain the stage proximate to Enlightenment and will realise
　　Great Nirvāṇa.
This is due to the fulfilment of the Vow in which
He vowed to help us attain Nirvāṇa without fail.[440]

Actually these lines are based on *The Larger Sūtra of Eternal Life*, with special reference to Amida's Original Vow.

As regards the second point "Pronouncing the Name in thankfulness for all that has been done for us," Shinran Shōnin states,

He taught that, at the very moment we become mindful of Amida's
　　Original Vow,
We naturally enter the stage of the definitely assured,
And that, solely by always pronouncing the Name of the Tathāgata,
We respond with gratitude to his Great Compassion, to the
　　Vow of Universal Deliverance.[441]

The "He" in the above quotation refers to Nāgârjuna, author of such commentaries as *Daśabhūmika-vibhāśā Śastra* and *Mahāprajñāpāramitā Śastra* on which this part of *The Shōshinge* is based. It is clear, therefore, that the idea of "pronouncing the Name in thankfulness for all that has been done for us" originates with Nāgârjuna, the first patriarch of Pure Land Buddhism.

Concerning "Entering the company of those whose birth is rightly assured," this point has already been included in the two quotations. The phrase "We attain the stage proximate to Enlightenment" actually means our "entering that company." *The Shōshinge* states that,

> That which causes us to be rightly assured is faith alone.
> Once awakened to faith, ignorant beings of delusion and defilement
> Will realise that birth-and-death is Nirvāṇa itself.
> When they reach the Land of Infinite Light,
> They will unfailingly bring about the universal deliverance of all
>   beings in the various states of existence.[442]

These passages are based on Tánluán's *Commentary on The Treatise on the Pure Land*. Through faith alone we become absolutely assured of our birth in the Pure Land. This confidence of attaining Nirvāṇa in the Pure Land is extremely important and constitutes an essential part of the "peaceful awareness" with which we may proceed on the way to the Pure Land with complete certainty.

All these three points, being closely interrelated, are vitally important for the attainment of Shin Buddhist faith. They are each elegantly summarised in this short letter. Indeed the concluding passage always makes us feel certain of the embrace of Amida's unconditional love and encourages us to go forward in life with renewed confidence.

There are in existence a number of different versions of this letter from a highly similar short version to a much longer one. A few of the letters bear somewhat earlier dates. Although some people hold that this was Rennyo's first letter given to Dōsai (1399–1488), his closest disciple, I am not sure about this view. There is another letter dated March 1461, likewise believed to be the first given to Dōsai. The content of this letter includes the three points discussed above and is very similar to this one but is considerably longer. Taking all this into consideration it would seem that Rennyo had repeatedly been handing out different versions of the letter to his followers, polishing it over and over until it finally reached its final form. It is now confirmed at least that some of those letters were written in 1471 and in 1475.

CHAPTER SIXTY-NINE

The True Meaning of Shinran Shōnin's Memorial

ON THE ANNIVERSARY

OF SHINRAN SHŌNIN'S DEATH

FASCICLE V, LETTER ELEVEN

Amongst all those visiting with offerings and coming before Shōnin to respond to him and express, on this his anniversary, their gratitude for all that he has done for us, there may be alongside those who have attained faith some who have not. This is a matter of extreme concern, for, if we do not attain faith, it will not be possible for us to be born in the Land of Enjoyment at this time. Thus those who have not yet attained faith should try and acquire a decisive mind without delay.

The world of human beings is a place of uncertainty. The Land of Utmost Bliss, on the other hand, is a land of eternity. Accordingly, instead of being attached to the idea of remaining in the human world of uncertainty, we should aspire to be born in the eternal Land of Utmost Bliss. It follows too that, unless we appreciate the reason why faith is seen in our tradition as a matter of supreme importance, nothing has any meaning. We should make haste to attain peaceful awareness and aspire to be born in the Pure Land.

A popular misconception in this human world of ours is that if we simply recite the Name with our lips, without any understanding, we will be born in the Land of Utmost Bliss. That is not to be relied upon. What is actually meant by the attainment of Other Power faith is nothing less than a full understanding of the meaning of the six characters *Namu Amida-butsu* 南无阿彌陀佛. It is this that we call the decisive attainment of faith.

Concerning the essence of faith, the Sūtra states "we hear that Name and rejoice in the awakening of faith." Shàndǎo tells us: "*Namu* means 'to take refuge.' It also means the 'vow-making and virtue-transference.' *Amida-butsu* means 'his practice.'" The meaning of the two characters *Namu* is that we forsake the miscellaneous practices and, without doubting, entrust ourselves singleheartedly and steadfastly to Amida Buddha. The meaning of the four characters *Amida-butsu* is that without any difficulty at all Amida saves sentient beings who take refuge in him singleheartedly. This is what is meant by the four characters *Amida-butsu*. Accordingly, to understand the essence of *Namu Amida-butsu* in this way is to attain faith. This is, in other words, the *Nenbutsu* follower who has fully realised Other Power faith.

Most humbly and respectfully

COMMENTS

As previously mentioned, the twenty-two letters that make up Fascicle Five are all undated. At the time Venerable Ennyo was editing the Five Fascicle version of *The Letters* by Rennyo, he did not know their dates, but later research enables us to hazard a guess at when at least some of them were written. This eleventh letter is a case in point.

Amongst the various compilations of Rennyo's letters, there is one known as the Takada version. According to historical record it was known as the Ten Fascicle Version but we are only able to view a hundred and eleven letters of the seven fascicles still in existence. The other three fascicles are no longer extant. Takada is the name of one of the ten Shin Buddhist sects, but it was already independent of the Honganji Temple at the time of Rennyo Shōnin. Because this Ten Fascicle Version was edited and preserved in a different sect, the letters of the Takada version were unknown to Venerable Ennyo when he edited the Five Fascicle version of *The Letters*.

According to the date of the same letter found in the Takada version, the eleventh letter of Fascicle Five was written on 25th November in 1474, in fact, on the occasion of the seven day anniversary to commemorate the death of Shinran Shōnin.

The crucial point of the emphasis Rennyo placed on the memorial service for Shinran Shōnin is that we should attain true faith without delay and, once we have done so, recite the *Nenbutsu* with deepest gratitude to Shinran Shōnin for what he has done for us, because the world in which we live is one of impermanence, whilst the Pure Land is one of eternity.

Further to the subject of true faith, Rennyo criticised the popular teaching of that time which held that the important thing was simply to recite the *Nenbutsu* no matter whether one understood or not. As this distorted teaching was becoming very common in Hokuriku District, Rennyo wrote several similar letters in the same year, 1474. Those who held this erroneous belief maintained that, as ignorant beings, all we could do was simply recite the *Nenbutsu* and that would be enough for our salvation. Such a belief, however, allowed no room for deep awareness, sincere entrusting or sense of gratitude, hence his insistence on how vital it was we understood the meaning of *Namu Amida-butsu*.

This understanding is not so much intellectual as heartfelt, acquired through the faith of entrusting ourselves to Amida Buddha. Any real understanding of *Namu Amida-butsu* inevitably includes our taking refuge in Amida Buddha. In other words, only by taking refuge in Amida Buddha can the real understanding of *Namu Amida-butsu* fill our hearts. The instantaneous awakening of faith when taking refuge in Amida Buddha is at the core of the Shin Buddhist experience. Traditionally this is called "the one thought-moment of the awakening of faith" or "the faith of taking refuge in Amida Buddha in one thought-moment." *Namu* or "taking refuge" is certainly an instant leap of faith by entrusting oneself absolutely to Amida Buddha.

Quoting from Shàndǎo, however, Rennyo Shōnin goes on to clarify the Shin Buddhist understanding that this "taking refuge" is actually a manifestation of Amida's "vow-making" and "virtue-transference." The phrase "*Amida-butsu* means 'his practice'" actually signifies that all this is the great working of Amida Buddha.

Namu cannot be separated from *Amida-butsu* and *Amida-butsu* cannot be separated from *Namu*. When we take refuge Amida Buddha appears for us, and yet it is Amida Buddha's call that leads us to take refuge. Rennyo talks about this faith-experience in terms of "the oneness of *ki and Hō* in *Namu Amida-butsu*." The term *ki* means the "momentum" through which *Hō* or "Dharma" works, where *ki* actually refers to ourselves or to all sentient beings.

CHAPTER SEVENTY

Absolute Entrusting

AMIDA'S SLEEVE

FASCICLE V, LETTER TWELVE

There is no need for those who wish to know in detail the meaning of 'peaceful awareness' in our tradition to have any particular learning or wisdom. All that is needed is the realisation that we are but wretched beings, heavily weighed down by bad karma, and that it is Amida Tathāgata alone who saves even such beings as ourselves. When, without any effort on our part, but simply with the thought of holding fast to the sleeve of this Buddha, Amida, we entrust ourselves to the Buddha, entreating him to help us attain Rebirth, then Amida Tathāgata rejoices profoundly and, emitting from his body eighty-four thousand great beams of Light, embraces and holds us within that Light. This is clearly set out in *The [Meditation] Sūtra*: "Light shines forth throughout all the worlds of the ten directions, embracing and never abandoning those who practice the *Nenbutsu*." This should be known.

This being so, there is no need for us to worry about our attaining Buddhahood. How splendid is the Original Vow that transcends all the worlds! And how blissful is Amida Tathāgata's Light! Were we not conditioned to see this Light, our dreadful sickness of ignorance, burdened with karmic hindrances since the beginningless past, could never be cured.

Thanks to the working of this Light, however, those who have their past good matured have already attained Other Power faith, making it immediately clear that this is faith granted by Amida Tathāgata. Thus we now understand clearly that this faith is not something generated by us followers, but is in fact nothing less than Amida Tathāgata's great Other Power faith. Consequently all of us, once we have attained Other Power faith with the most generous help, should reflect deeply on Amida Tathāgata's benevolence and always recite the *Nenbutsu*, that is pronounce the Name, to respond to the Buddha with gratitude for what he has done for us.

Most humbly and respectfully

COMMENTS

Barring a few minor details, this letter consists of the latter part of the thirteenth letter of Fascicle Two, dated the 3rd July 1474, which circulated as a separate document. There is no need for me to repeat my commentary on this letter. When I discussed that letter, however, I left one important subject out: the working of the Light that I would like to consider in this context.

According to traditional understanding that the phrase "the sleeve of Amida Buddha" in the letter is a metaphor of the Original Vow, the entire phrase "with the thought of holding fast to the sleeve of this Buddha, Amida" stands for one's taking refuge in the Original Vow. In addition to this meaning this particular expression conveys to us another sense of the inclusion of some personal relationship. In the case of Shinran Shōnin, for example, it was through his encounter with Hōnen Shōnin that he took refuge in the Original Vow. His taking refuge in Amida Buddha overlapped with his encounter with his master, Hōnen Shōnin. In other words, to Shinran, Hōnen was an embodiment or manifestation of Amida Buddha. So, the sleeve of Amida Buddha was, applied to this case, at the same time, that of Hōnen Shōnin. Because it is through the encounter with a good teacher that we come to take refuge in Amida Buddha, the word "sleeve" not only stands for the "Original Vow" but also reminds us of our "good teacher."

"Then," Rennyo says, "Amida Tathāgata rejoices profoundly." This expression also conveys a sense of human warmth to the audience. Rennyo's words "Emitting from his body eighty-four thousand great beams of Light, embraces and holds us within that Light" refers to how Amida Buddha continues to help us, *Nenbutsu* followers, proceed on the path to the Pure Land throughout our lives.

As he himself states in the letter Rennyo's teaching is based on a passage found in *The Meditation Sūtra*.[443]

Amida's Light works upon us in two ways: form-light or physical light (*shikikō* 色光) and mind-light or spiritual light beyond form (*shinkō* 心光).

Amida's Light described in *The Meditation Sūtra* is Amida's form-light that illumines all the worlds and their inhabitants with absolute equality and universal love. But this is a sort of one-sided light (冥 jp. *myō* or *katahikari*) – that is, it is clear for Buddhas but we cannot see it, because of our ignorance heavily burdened with blind passions and karmic hindrances.

> Our sight being hindered by blind passions,
> We cannot see Amida's Light that embraces us;
> Yet his great compassion, without tiring,
> Illumines us all the time.[444]

How can we become aware of Amida's unconditional love that embraces us all always? It is through the awakening of faith alone that we really become aware of Amida's Light. Only when we are awakened to the sad reality of our karmic existence and entrust ourselves entirely to Amida Buddha, are we awakened to his Light of great compassion that has been embracing us all the time without any discrimination. Awakening to ourselves and awakening to Amida Buddha come about simultaneously. They are two aspects of the same reality. The Light of Amida Buddha, felt and received only through the attainment of faith, is called "mind-light." Once awakened to true faith, those who practice the *Nenbutsu* become aware of Amida's Light as the formless light of compassion that always embraces and protects us on the way to the Pure Land. When the "form-light" is received through the attainment of faith, the very source of the light that is formless is realised and called the "mind-light." *The Meditation Sūtra* states that the light embraces and never abandons those who recite the *Nenbutsu*.

The relevant passage in my translation of *The Shōshinge* reads,

> The mind-light that embraces us always illumines and protects us.
> Though the darkness of ignorance is already broken through,
> The clouds and mists of tenacious greed and repulsive hatred
> Still continue to cover the sky of true and real faith.
> It is as if, though the sun-light is veiled by clouds and mists,
> Below the clouds and mists brightness reigns and there is no darkness.[445]

We reach a peaceful inner awareness of the reality of our karmic existence and, at the same time, of the unconditional love that always protects us with no discrimination at all.

As mentioned in the letter, "this faith is not something generated by us followers, but is in fact nothing less than Amida Tathāgata's great Other Power faith."

CHAPTER SEVENTY-ONE

The Incomparably Profound Meaning of *Namu Amida-Butsu*

ON THE SUPREME AND MOST PROFOUND

FASCICLE V, LETTER THIRTEEN

First and foremost, because the phrase *Namu Amida-butsu* consists of only six characters 南无阿彌陀佛, we may not be fully aware of just how powerful it is, yet the immensity of the supreme, most profound virtues and benefits contained within this Name of six characters is immeasurable. It should be known, therefore, that these six characters in themselves already include the awakening of faith. There is no faith outside of these six characters.

Quite early on Shàndǎo gave the following explanation for these six characters of *Namu Amida-butsu*: "*Namu* means 'to take refuge.' It also means 'the vow-making and virtue-transference.' *Amida-butsu* means 'the practice.' For this reason we can be absolutely assured of birth."[446] How should we understand this commentary? Even if we are burdened, as indeed we are, with bad karma and blind passions, Amida Buddha, being fully aware of our existence, will not fail to save us, if we take refuge in him at this one thought-moment.

In other words, "to take refuge" means to entreat Amida Buddha to save us. Thus "the vow-making and virtue-transference" refer to Amida Buddha's transference of his own virtues with their profound and supreme benefits to those sentient beings who entrust themselves in one thought-moment. Since he imparts to us sentient beings great goodness and great virtue through "his vow-making and virtue-transference," the bad karma and blind passions we have accumulated over myriads of kalpas since the beginningless past are instantly extinguished. Thus all our blind passions and bad karma vanish and we find ourselves already at the stage of nonretrogression or in the company of those who are rightly assured of their birth in the Pure Land.

It should become increasingly clear to us, therefore, that the six characters *Namu Amida-butsu* by their very nature reveal the way we are to be born in the Land of Utmost Bliss. Thus, whether we call it "peaceful awareness" or "faith," those who fully understand the meaning of the six characters of the Name are said to be those who have attained Great Other Power faith. Since the Name has such an excellent meaning, we should entrust ourselves to it wholeheartedly.

Most humbly and respectfully

COMMENTS

In *The Collection of Rennyo's Letters Not Compiled in The Five Fascicle Letters*, edited by Venerable Daigyoin Reion Takehara, former Head Priest of Shogyoji Temple, there is another letter, *Teach Us Ignorant Beings*,[447] which is very similar in content to the present one, the only difference being that it is written in the form of a dialogue. Indeed it may well have come from an actual conversation between Rennyo and one of his followers. It is probable, in fact, that many of the letters addressed by him to his followers were written in response to their questions or requests. In this respect the letters can be said to mirror the lively relationship he enjoyed with his followers.

According to the letter written in the form of a dialogue, one of Rennyo's followers asked him to explain in more detail such teachings as "the immensity of the supreme and most profound virtues and benefits contained in *Namu Amida-butsu*" and "the awakening of faith already included in *Namu Amida-butsu*." He responded, as in the present letter, by commenting on Shàndǎo's interpretation of *Namu Amida-butsu* found in his main work, *Exposition of The Meditation Sūtra*.[448]

Concerning the first statement that *Namu* means "taking refuge" (帰命 *kimyō*), within other Pure Land traditions the act of taking refuge is understood as a personal decision on our part. Shinran Shōnin, however, sees "taking refuge in Amida Buddha" as Amida's command to us to come to him. In other words, on awakening to the great compassion of Amida Buddha, we are impelled to take refuge in Amida Buddha.

Secondly, when it says that *Namu* also means "vow-making and virtue-transference" (*hotsugan ekō* 発願廻向), the phrase "vow-making and virtue-transference" is understood in other traditions as a devotee's aspiration for birth in the Pure Land and his or her acquisition of virtue necessary for that purpose. Shinran Shōnin, however, understands the phrase *hotsugan ekō* as "Amida's making his Vow and transferring his Virtue." In this respect our act of "taking refuge in Amida Buddha" is in its entirety a gift from the Buddha.

Thirdly, when it is said that *Amida-butsu* means "the practice" (*gyō*), then that "practice," according to Shinran Shōnin, does not merely mean the practice engaged in by devotees but rather "his practice," that is, the practice undertaken by Amida himself, whilst still at the stage of a Bodhisattva, in order to save all sentient beings. From the viewpoint of those who have yet to attain faith, the word "*gyō*" is understood as a devotee's practice but in the light of the Buddha-dharma, "*gyō*" is entirely Amida Buddha's practice by which he saves all sentient beings without any discrimination. It includes all forms of goodness and virtue.

Thus, just as Shàndǎo says, "For this reason we can be absolutely assured of birth," it is through the power of the Original Vow that all this occurs.

Shinran Shōnin's reinterpretation of the Buddha Name, *Namu Amida-butsu*, clarifies the true meaning of Shàndǎo's commentary on the six-character Name and helps us understand how *Namu Amida-butsu* works for the salvation of all sentient beings. It is the shortest possible summarisation of Amida's way of saving all sentient beings. It is to stress Shinran Shōnin's reinterpretation that Rennyo Shōnin refers to Shàndǎo's commentary on the Name.

With reference to Rennyo's comments there are several important textual sources that support the notion that all forms of goodness and virtue are contained in the Buddha Name, *Namu Amida-butsu*. For instance, in *The Larger Sūtra of Eternal Life* we are told,

> The Buddha said to Maitreya, "If there are people who hear the Name of that Buddha, rejoice so greatly as to dance, and remember him (that is, pronounce the Name) even once, then you should know that they have gained great benefit by receiving unsurpassed virtue."[449]

Then, in the *Senjaku hongan nenbutsu shū* by Hōnen we read,

> Firstly, as regards superior versus inferior, the *Nenbutsu* is superior and the other practices are inferior. This is because the Name is the container into which all of Amida's uncountable virtues have flowed.[450]

And in *The Kyōgyōshinshō* by Shinran we find,

> The great practice is to pronounce the Name of the Tathāgata of Unimpeded Light. In this practice are embraced all good things and all the roots of virtue. They are instantly perfected as soon as the Name is pronounced. The Name is the treasure-ocean of the virtues accruing from the absolute reality of Suchness. Therefore it is called the great practice.[451]

Finally, in the *Verses on the Pure Land* by Shinran again we read,

> When a person hears the Name of Amida Buddha
> So great is their joy that they can only say the Buddha Name in praise.
> So perfect is the treasure of virtue they have come into
> Nothing exceeds the great benefit of that one thought-moment.[452]

Shinran Shōnin's own commentary on the last line of this wasan that "what can be called great benefit is reaching Nirvāṇa"[453] is also extremely important.

When he speaks of taking refuge, Rennyo Shōnin often says that our taking refuge in Amida comes about in one thought-moment, that is, not gradually but immediately or instantly. Our taking refuge is always accompanied by the awakening of the one thought-moment, or the instantaneous awakening of faith, an awakening to the irredeemable reality of our karmic existence and at the same time to the unconditional love of Amida Buddha. Since we are awakened to Amida's unconditional love, we are immediately impelled to entrust ourselves to Amida Buddha and abandon all forms of self-power practice. This notion of time, "the one thought-moment," is vital to any description of the experience of taking refuge in Amida Buddha. The awakening of faith is attained instantly by virtue of the power of the Original Vow.

I would also like to draw attention yet again to the crucial point that the four elements found in Shàndǎo's interpretation of *Namu Amida-butsu*, that is, "taking refuge," "vow-making," "virtue-transference" and "practice," are all activities of Amida himself that are made manifest and operate through individual sentient beings. The factual truth is paradoxical. Once awakened to the great compassion of Amida Buddha, you find yourself entirely encompassed by it. You shine radiantly with the Buddha's own light that embraces you. In other words the Buddha's light appears through your own individual existence. There is no hindrance on your way to the Pure Land.

As Rennyo states in this letter, even your bad karma and blind passions cannot be any hindrance to you in your attainment of birth in the Pure Land. As long as you live in this world, your blind passions and bad karma still remain with you. However, by virtue of the Original Vow, they exist as if they did not exist. The expression "instantly extinguished" means that, because of the great love and compassion you receive the instant you take refuge in Amida Buddha, they no longer hinder your birth in the Pure Land. This reminds me of Article 34 of *The Goichidai ki kikigaki* previously quoted in Chapter Thirty-one.

CHAPTER SEVENTY-TWO

The Salvation of Women without Discrimination

ON WOMEN OF NOBLE

AND HUMBLE BIRTH

FASCICLE V, LETTER FOURTEEN

Listen to me, all you ladies, though others may not be aware of it, you yourselves should be aware of how wretched you are, heavily burdened with bad karma, no matter whether you are of noble or humble birth.

This being the case, you may be asking how you can entrust yourselves to Amida Buddha. If you women entrust yourselves firmly and without any hesitation to Amida Tathāgata and entreat him to save you in the One Great Matter of Rebirth to come, he will definitely rescue you without fail. If you give over your whole existence, weighed down by bad karma, to Amida Buddha and ask Amida Tathāgata to save you in Rebirth just singleheartedly, there is no doubt that, knowing you through and through as he does, Amida will save you. All of you, whether you number ten or tens of ten, should harbour not the slightest doubt, be it as infinitesimal as a drop of dew, but that each and every one of you will without exception be born in the Land of Utmost Bliss.

Women awakened to faith in this way will attain birth in the Pure Land. You should go on ever more deeply entrusting yourselves to Amida Tathāgata, acknowledging how shameful it is that up until this moment you never followed such a simple path.

Most humbly and respectfully

COMMENTS

When Ennyo Shōnin (1491–1521) was compiling the Five Fascicle version of Rennyo Shōnin's *Letters*, the twenty-two letters brought together in Fascicle Five must have all been undated. Subsequently, however, a number of other letters, similar in content to those of Fascicle Five, have come to light and some of them are dated.

According to the *Rennyo Shōnin Ibun* edited by Professor Masamaru Inaba, such a letter similar to this one found in the Chōganji version of Rennyo's letters is dated March of the 7th year of Meiō (1498), just one year before his death, a time when he was still staying in Ōsaka.[454] A brief note attached to another very similar letter in the Najio version of his letters[455] reads "Sent to the Ōsaka Women's Association."

In Fascicle Five the third, seventh, fourteenth, seventeenth and twentieth letters are specifically addressed to women and are all said to have been sent to the Kanegamori Women's Association. In the case of the fourteenth letter, however, it would appear from the records to have been initially sent to the Ōsaka Women's Association, then later on to the Kanegamori Women's Association as well.

In the case of Fascicle Five, nearly a quarter of his letters are letters to women. This fact reminds us of how serious Rennyo was about the salvation of women. This concern of his springs from an abiding sense of sympathy and compassion he felt towards women, subjected in those days to a great deal of discrimination. Confronting to the best of his ability the social and religious prejudices of his day, he opened up a way for the spiritual liberation of women through his Pure Land teaching of salvation through faith alone.

Although the words found in the first paragraph of this letter may seem hard now for women to accept, Rennyo was making the assertion in order to lead women of the day to confront the reality of their existence in a social climate where they were beset by ill-conceived, petty discrimination.

In the case of this letter, those whom Rennyo urges particularly to entrust themselves to Amida Buddha are women. It is as a direct consequence of the compassion he feels for them that he talks to women about the importance of their awakening to the reality of their karmic existence.

Without awakening to oneself, one cannot entrust oneself to Amida Buddha. The pure faith of entrusting oneself to Amida is always accompanied by awakening to oneself and at the same time awakening to the great compassion of Amida Buddha. If you entrust yourself absolutely to Amida Buddha, there is no doubt but that his great compassion will save you without any discrimination at all.

This letter is very expressive not only of the awareness of the reality of one's existence "weighed down by bad karma," but also of the awareness of Amida's great compassion. With regard to Amida's love and compassion, Rennyo declares in the letter, "there is no doubt that, knowing you through and through as he does, Amida will save you." In particular the words "knowing you through and through as he does" generate deep reverberations in our hearts, reminding us as they do of the great wisdom of Amida Buddha. The Buddha's compassion wells up spontaneously out of his wisdom that knows everything and everyone just as they are. Through his unconditional love based on his great wisdom that "knows them through and through," Amida Buddha made the Original Vow to save all sentient beings just as they are, beyond all discrimination between good and bad, ignorant and wise, old and young, high-born and low-born, and, of course, men and women. If we go back to the very origin of Amida's Original Vow, we realise that it is through the spontaneous working of his great wisdom "knowing us through and through as he does" that we are awakened to ourselves and to the compassion of the Buddha.

Another point is that "you should go on ever more deeply entrusting yourselves to Amida Tathāgata, acknowledging how shameful it is that up until now you never followed such a simple path." The passage does not mean that we should repeat again and again our act of entrusting ourselves to Amida. Rather it means that, once we entrust ourselves absolutely to Amida Buddha, this faith-experience provides the foundation for the way we live in this world right up to the end of our lives. It continues to support us on the path to the Pure Land. Even if we are lost in the turmoil of our daily existence, the first faith-experience continues to sustain us every moment whether we are actually conscious of it or not. Whenever we become aware of our problems, we can go back to that first experience thanks to Amida's untiring love and compassion. This crucial point was expressed by Shinran Shōnin as being at "the stage of nonretrogression (skt. *avinivartanīya*, 不退転 jp. *futaiten*)" or as being in "the company of those who are rightly assured of birth in the Pure Land (正定聚 jp. *shōjōju*)" through the attainment of faith.

It is said in *The Shōshinge* that "we attain the stage proximate to Enlightenment and will realise Great Nirvāṇa." This phrase means that we attain the stage proximate to Enlightenment during our stay in this world and then reach Great Nirvāṇa in the Pure Land. It is through pure faith alone that we attain the stage proximate to Enlightenment. It is because we are all already in the embrace of Amida's great compassion that enfolds each of us and abandons none.

CHAPTER SEVENTY-THREE

Entrusting to the Original Vow

ON THE ORIGINAL VOW

OF AMIDA TATHĀGATA

FASCICLE V, LETTER FIFTEEN

Listen, what kind of sentient beings is it that Amida Tathāgata's Original Vow saves? Also, how should we entrust ourselves to Amida, and in what state of mind should we abide in order to be saved?

First of all, with regard to those who would be saved, even if they be people with bad karma who have committed the ten bad acts and the five grave offences, or even if they be women burdened with the five obstacles and three submissions, they should not worry about the depth and gravity of their bad karma. It is simply through great faith alone, coming from Other Power, that we truly attain birth in the Land of Utmost Bliss.

So, with regard to this faith, in what state of mind should we abide and how should we entrust ourselves to Amida?

In order to attain faith, we should simply discard the wrong-mindedness attached to miscellaneous practices, to mixed ways of practising and to self power, and instead take refuge in Amida singleheartedly and deeply with our whole being. Such faith of no doubt, we call true faith. Amida Tathāgata, with his profound understanding of those sentient beings who singleheartedly and steadfastly entrust themselves to him in this way, graciously emanates infinite light so that he may embrace them within that light and enable them to attain birth in the Land of Utmost Bliss. This is what is meant by "embraces all those who recite the *Nenbutsu*."

Once this is realised, we should understand that, though we recite the *Nenbutsu* throughout our lives, it is the *Nenbutsu* of gratitude that we are reciting, thanking the Buddha for all that he has done for us. Those who realise this can be called *Nenbutsu* followers who have fully acquired the heart of faith in our tradition.

Most humbly and respectfully

COMMENTS

The first paragraph of this letter raises three questions all relating to the Original Vow. Firstly, "What kind of sentient beings is it that Amida Tathāgata's Original Vow saves?" Secondly, "How should we entrust ourselves to Amida?" And thirdly, "In what state of mind should we abide in order to be saved?" Although the first two questions have often been discussed in his previous letters, the third is a new issue: With what state of mind we should entrust ourselves to Amida?

As the second paragraph shows, the last question is answered with the words "they should not worry about the depth and gravity of their bad karma." What is important when we entrust ourselves to Amida is to stop worrying about ourselves. When we worry about ourselves or the conditions of our karmic existence, there is a division of our being, a bifurcation of the self into observer and observed. Our minds still remain dualistic. When we encounter the great compassion of the Buddha, we entrust our whole being to him, including all such existential bifurcation of the self. Fully aware of this divided state of mind of ours illumined by the light of Amida Buddha, we entrust the entirety of our karmic existence to the Buddha's great compassion. Here in this context what Rennyo means is simply, "Do not worry. Go to Amida Buddha just as you are!"

There are those who regularly refer to themselves in negative terms and who assume that keeping such a humble attitude is important for maintaining their faith. They talk about themselves with considerable self-concern, but in many cases, although they may appear humble and honest with themselves, their self-concern is narcissistic and their humble attitude stems actually from an underlying pride. Buddhism speaks of this kind of pride as "pride cloaked in humility" (卑下慢 jp. *higeman*). In Shin Buddhism it is realised that this kind of pride is something dangerous that makes it difficult for us to awaken true faith. All that we really need to do is simply take refuge in Amida Buddha following his call – "Come to me just as you are!" This is the reason why Rennyo says people should not "worry about the depth and gravity of their bad karma."

He concludes the second paragraph with the brief but beautiful expression, "It is simply through great faith alone, coming from Other Power, that we truly attain birth in the Land of Utmost Bliss." Looking at the original, the Japanese phrase *tada tariki no daishinjin hitotsu nite* ただ他力の大信心 ひとつにて could be translated in many different ways: *tariki no daishinjin* 他力の大信心 signifying "great faith of Other Power," "great Other Power faith," "great faith in Other Power," "great faith, Other Power." After much thought and consideration, I decided at this point in time to translate it as "great faith alone, coming from Other Power," emphasising the fact that our faith is a gift from Other Power.

Towards the end of his letter he speaks of Amida's Light that embraces all and abandons none. Reading his remarks about Amida's Light, I get the feeling that Amida's light is not so much a notion or a symbol, but a living reality of his great all-encompassing compassion. As seen in Rennyo's comment Amida Buddha embraces us within his light and enables us to attain birth in the Pure Land.

As mentioned before, "Amida's light that embraces all and abandons none" is based on a description of Amida's light found in *The Meditation Sūtra*. Shinran Shōnin interprets this light as "mind-light" and declares in *The Shōshinge*, "The mind-light that embraces us always illumines and protects us."[456] From the practical and realistic view point of a Shin Buddhist Sangha, the word "protect" in this passage is extremely important on our journey to the Pure Land. For us Shin Buddhist followers, our temples, *taya* houses, gardens, Dharma friends, daily services and teachings, everything and everyone, are manifestations of Amida's light that always illumines and untiringly protects us on our path to the other shore of Enlightenment itself. Light is what shows us the direction we should take.

CHAPTER SEVENTY-FOUR

The Awareness
of Impermanence

WHITE BONES

FASCICLE V, LETTER SIXTEEN

As we quietly reflect on the transitory nature of the floating world, what is most unreliable is our own dreamlike life, ever ephemeral from start to finish. Thus one has never heard of a person who lived for ten thousand years. Our lives pass swiftly away. Who will now live for a hundred years? Who will die first, me or you? Today or tomorrow, we never know. People destined to die sooner or later are more numerous than the dewdrops running down stems and hanging on leaves. Thus, though we may be rosy-cheeked in the morning, we could be white bones by evening.

The wind of impermanence blows and in an instant the eyes close and the breath ceases forever. When cheeks lose their radiance and the rosy face is drained of life, even if relatives and family gather together and grieve bitterly, it will be of no avail. As the body cannot just be left like that, it is taken out into the fields to be cremated and at midnight turns to smoke. Nothing is left but white bones. There are no words to express how sad this is.

Thus, as the impermanence of human beings entails an uncertain lifespan for young and old alike, we should all immediately awaken to the Great

Matter of Rebirth and pronounce the *Nenbutsu* entrusting ourselves absolutely to Amida Buddha.

Most humbly and respectfully

COMMENTS

This is one of the most famous letters by Rennyo Shōnin. It is regularly read out not only at daily services but also at certain ceremonies related with funerals. Its poignancy lies in the way it appeals to our sense of the impermanence of this world and of human life.

As to the historical background of the letter, opinions differ, but the following account based on *The Ofumi raii shō* seems to me the most reliable.

In the first year of the Entoku (1489) there dwelt in a village near Yamashina-gobo, headquarters of the then Shin Buddhist Sangha, a *rōnin* or samurai who had no lord or master. His daughter, a beautiful girl of seventeen, was betrothed to a warrior from a rich samurai family. On 8th August, however, when the wedding ceremony was due to take place, this daughter passed away quite suddenly, despite all the preparations her father had made for her. So deep was the man's grief as he looked at the remains of his daughter that, after seeing her off to the other shore at the funeral ceremony, he himself took ill and passed away on the 12th of the same month at the age of fifty-one. The very next day the man's wife also died aged only thirty-seven from sheer emotional exhaustion. Rennyo was already well acquainted with the *rōnin* family and the relatives decided to donate the family's clothes to Yamashina-gobō. Just as Rennyo was preparing to write a letter on behalf of the *rōnin*'s relatives, however, Ebina Gorōzaemon, a steward on the estate, likewise lost his seventeen year old daughter. Thanking Rennyo Shōnin for conducting her funeral ceremony, he, too, donated his land to Yamashina-gobō and asked Rennyo Shōnin to write a letter on the impermanence of the world. Needless to say this letter was originally written for the *rōnin* family, but it is said that the letter was eventually given to Ebina Gorōzaemon.[457]

It is widely known that Rennyo based this letter directly on the *Zonkaku hōgo*, or "Dharma Words of Zonkaku" (1290–1373), which itself draws on the *Mujōkō shiki*,[458] or "Liturgy of Impermanence," composed by Ex-Emperor Gotoba (1180–1239) during his exile on the remote island of Oki. Almost all of the letter is taken from the *Zonkaku hōgo*, the relevant part of this document being itself a quotation from the *Mujōkō shiki*. Thus this special letter, apart from the concluding paragraph that encourages us to entrust ourselves to the *Nenbutsu* or Amida Buddha's name, can be said to be a modification of *The Mujōkō shiki*. Ex-Emperor Gotoba was someone whose life was always filled with drama, including the persecution of the *Nenbutsu* followers such as Hōnen Shōnin and Shinran Shōnin in 1207 and his own exile to Oki Island in 1221. *The Mujokō shiki* itself is an elegant liturgy filled with rhetorical flourishes that beautifully describes the transitory nature of this world. Rennyo adopted these impressive phrases in his own letter.

In the field of the philosophical study of Buddhist religious consciousness, I have noticed that there are a number of ongoing academic discussions that treat the contemplation of impermanence and the awareness of bad karma as if the two were totally separate and intrinsically different types of religious thought. In Shin Buddhism, for instance, scholars often argue that, whilst Shinran Shōnin was a person endowed with a deep sense of bad karma, Rennyo Shōnin was more given to profound contemplation of the impermanence of the world. If it were just a question of saying how much more emphasis which leader gave to which subject in their writings, there would be no problem, but scholars often seek to differentiate between the two types of religious leader as if one type were in opposition to the other. That, I feel, is quite wrong. In Buddhism both types of consciousness are closely related. In those who have attained true faith both are present, no matter which type is given greater expression in a leader's sayings or writings. Without a feeling for the impermanence of all things there could not be a true sense of bad karma, and the same the other way round.

Despite the fact that everything around us is in a constant state of flux, we tend to behave as though everything were permanent and insist on adhering rigidly to our own self-centred ways of understanding. But if we continue to cling on to our own self-centred views without sufficient awareness of the impermanence of things, this will result in damage both to ourselves and others. Those who have an acute sense of the impermanence of things are at the same time keenly aware of their undue attachment and understand how much the resultant bad karma harms both themselves and others. Conversely, those who in the light of the Buddha-dharma come to realise their bad karma are also found to be aware of the impermanence of their world in the deepest dimension of their consciousness.

When we look back to the starting point of Shinran Shōnin's spiritual development, we are immediately reminded that what prompted him to go and meet Hōnen Shōnin was, in fact, his urgent sense of impermanence of life. The three visions Shinran Shōnin experienced illustrate this. The first vision came to him at Shinaga when he was nineteen, the second at Daijōin when he was twenty-seven, and the third at Rokkakudō when he was twenty-nine.

Turning now to Rennyo, though some scholars highlight the emphasis he placed on impermanence, in almost all of his letters he also speaks of the consciousness of bad karma. In the Shin Buddhist experience of peaceful awareness, both types of consciousness are inextricably interrelated.

In accordance with the fundamental principles of Buddhism, impermanence (*anitya*), suffering (*duḥkha*), selflessness (*anātman*) and inner peace
(*Nirvāṇa*), the true faith of entrusting oneself to Amida Buddha, entailing
both an awareness of "the irredeemable reality of one's karmic existence" and
at the same time of "the unconditional love of Amida Buddha," is inseparably
fused, consciously or unconsciously, with the feeling of impermanence.

CHAPTER SEVENTY-FIVE

The Salvation
of All Women

ON ALL WOMEN

FASCICLE V, LETTER SEVENTEEN

Listen to me, all you womenfolk, if you are serious about the matter of Rebirth and if you deeply revere the Buddha-dharma, you should entrust yourselves wholeheartedly to Amida Tathāgata without any contriving, cast off all the miscellaneous practices, and singleheartedly and firmly entreat him to save you in Rebirth. There is no doubt that you will attain birth without fail in the Land of Utmost Bliss. Once you realise this, then, sleeping or waking, you should simply pronounce, "*Namu Amida-butsu, Namu Amida-butsu,*" understanding with deep faith how blissful and precious it is that without any difficulty you are saved by Amida Buddha. If you do this you can be called *Nenbutsu* followers who have attained faith.

Most humbly and respectfully

COMMENTS

This is another of the five letters from Fascicle Five especially addressed to the members of the Kanegamori Women's Association. Commentaries on Rennyo's *Letters* such as *Ofumi Ryakuge* by Enen (1693–1764), *Ofumi Kijishu* by Erin (1715–1789), *Ofumi raii shō* by Enin (written in 1689 and published in 1759) and *Ofumi Meitōshō* by Dōon (1741–1813) afford us a number of background accounts to each and every letter.

According to *The Ofumi raii shō*, Rennyo Shōnin wrote this letter to the wife of Katagiya Tōemon at the request of Tōemon's father, Dōken, on the 20th of September 1476. When Rennyo was staying in Sakai at a house donated by Dōken, Dōken visited Rennyo and asked him to write a letter to Otowa, his daughter-in-law. Dōken explained why he was making this request as follows: "Although my son Tōemon seems to have started listening to the Buddha-dharma, his wife Otowa shows no interest at all. Otowa's father, Mozuya Niuemon, who is actually my uncle, is a follower of Bhikkhu Shinryū of the Hossō school.[459] This monk taught Niuemon that, because almost all ordinary beings are included in those whose minds are not yet determined towards the fruit of Enlightenment, even if they believe in the sort of teaching which tells people that, by listening to the Buddha-dharma in daily life, they will eventually attain Nirvāṇa, they are actually quite unable to do so. Having accepted this monk's teaching as true, Niuemon never followed the *Nenbutsu* teaching that speaks of Rebirth in the Pure Land. My daughter-in-law being Niuemon's daughter, neither of them is ready to accept the Pure Land teaching. Please, impart your teaching to Otowa and it will surely influence my uncle as well."

Rennyo accepted Dōken's invitation to come to his home and conduct a memorial ceremony on the 20th of September for Dōken's mother. He profited from the occasion to speak with Otowa and gave her this letter. From that time Otowa joined the Sangha, later to be followed by her parents, and thus this letter is sometimes called "A Letter to Otowa."[460]

His other letters, too, were written in relation to particular circumstances in the Sangha in order to encourage people to attain pure faith in Amida Buddha. The fact that Rennyo wrote so many letters to female followers, certainly demonstrates his great concern for the salvation of those often neglected by other Buddhist schools. Although he is often inaccurately portrayed more as a politician than a man of spirituality, his letters reveal that in truth he was actually a person full of love towards all those around him.

CHAPTER SEVENTY-SIX

How to Attain
Peaceful Awareness

SHŌNIN OF OUR TRADITION

FASCICLE V, LETTER EIGHTEEN

To attain peaceful awareness as taught by Shōnin of our tradition, we should first of all, without any contrivance on our part, forsake our wretched existence, heavily burdened with bad karma, and set aside all our attachments to the miscellaneous practices and the mixed ways of practising. Then we should entrust ourselves to Amida Tathāgata in one thought-moment deeply with our whole being, entreating him singleheartedly to save us in Rebirth. If we do this, we will be saved without exception, ten out of ten, one hundred out of one hundred. We should not have the slightest doubt about this. Those who have got the heart of this point are called "followers of faith."

After this, whenever we think of the joy of being saved in the matter of Rebirth, whether sleeping or waking, we should pronounce "*Namu Amida-butsu, Namu Amida-butsu.*"

Most humbly and respectfully

COMMENTS

Obviously the content of this letter conveys the essentials of Shin Buddhism, as expressed repeatedly before. Rather than repeating my commentaries on previous letters, I would like to introduce some background information on the origin of this particular document. This is a not absolutely trustworthy but interesting account from a commentary on *The Letters* known as *The Ofumi raii shō*.[461]

In the seventh year of Bunmei (1475) Rennyo Shōnin gave this letter to his personal physician, Yoshimasu Hanshō. Some years previously he had become ill whilst visiting Kanegamori, a town in Gōshū Province, and Hanshō who happened to be there treated Rennyo by prescribing him certain medicines. Following this encounter Hanshō had often visited him in Kyoto and received his Dharma talks from time to time. But at this point Hanshō was not particularly interested in the Buddha-dharma. Following this series of encounters Rennyo was forced to leave for Yoshizaki in Hokuriku District, due to persecution from Tendai warrior-monks based on Mount Hiei. When he was finally able to return to the Kansai district, several years later, Yoshimasu Hanshō visited Rennyo Shōnin at his new temple at Deguchi in Kawachi Province in modern day Ōsaka Prefecture and their friendship was renewed. However Rennyo was sad to discover that Hanshō was struggling to deal with the recent loss of his parents and two children, one after another. Reflecting on these circumstances he wanted to help Hanshō find inner peace or peaceful awareness but he saw that it would be quite difficult to teach such a knowledgeable man.

"You are a good physician," Rennyo Shōnin said to Hanshō, "But let me ask you, would you be able to cure a patient who was reluctant to receive your treatment?" Rennyo Shōnin continued, "Although I have been trying to cure you, because you did not take the medicine I gave you, your illness remains."

To this Hanshō replied, "I have not been ill, nor received any medicine from you, and even if I were ill I do not think you could cure me."

But Rennyo Shōnin then said, "There are two kinds of illness, physical and spiritual. Physical diseases can be cured by a physician's medication but spiritual illnesses should be cured by the Right Dharma. I would like to cure your spiritual illness, of endless suffering, by giving you the medicine of Shōnin's teaching. Previously when I gave you this medicine you did not take it. You are my age, sixty-one years old, and so like me you may not have many more years of life ahead of you. Therefore take this medicine of Shōnin's teaching."

Hanshō was very moved to hear these words and asked Rennyo to teach him by composing the following *waka*,

To find the Dharma
there is no greater treasure

than this very life.
Live out your remaining time
in order to listen to the Dharma.

And he added, "Please give me the medicine that can cut out the roots of no-faith." In this way Rennyo came to compose this letter. Afterwards Hanshō received the *Gaikemon* or Repentance Document and continued to listen to Rennyo Shōnin's teaching. As a result he became a beautiful *Nenbutsu* follower.

CHAPTER SEVENTY-SEVEN

The Salvation of People with Bad Karma

ON PEOPLE WITH BAD KARMA

IN THE LAST DHARMA AGE

FASCICLE V, LETTER NINETEEN

Listen, men with bad karma and women in the Last Dharma Age, we should entrust ourselves singleheartedly and deeply with our whole being to Amida Buddha. Otherwise, no matter what teaching we believe in, we will never be saved in the matter of Rebirth.

How, then, should we entrust ourselves to Amida Tathāgata and how should we aspire to Rebirth? We should have not the slightest doubt but that all those who simply, without any misgivings, entrust themselves firmly and singleheartedly to Amida Tathāgata and entreat him deeply with their whole being to save them in Rebirth will be delivered without fail.

Most humbly and respectfully

CHAPTER 77

COMMENTS

It is said that the first passage of this brief letter is based on the two lines in *The Shōshinge* about Dàochuò's teaching,

> It is Dàochuò who has made indisputably clear the difficulty
>   of the Path of Sages in attaining Awakening.
> Our only access to Awakening is via the teaching of the Pure Land.[462]

The textual source of these lines by Shinran Shōnin can be traced back in turn to the *Passages on the Land of Happiness* (*Anraku shū* 安楽集, ch. Ānlè jí), a commentary on *The Meditation Sūtra* by Dàochuò 道綽 (562–645). Focusing on the difference between the Path of Pure Land followers and the Path of Sages, Dàochuò states, "*The Daijikkyō* states that in the Last Dharma Age, though billions of sentient beings decide to undertake practice and discipline themselves to attain Enlightenment, none in fact attains it.[463] In the current age of Last Dharma, the bad world polluted with the five defilements, the teaching of the Pure Land alone is the only access to Enlightenment."[464]

Based on the Pure Land tradition, and especially Dàochuò's teaching, Rennyo declares in the opening lines of the letter that, without entrusting ourselves absolutely to Amida Buddha, there would be no way for us in this, the age of Last Dharma, to attain Enlightenment. Therefore, he says in the last part of the letter, "We should have not the slightest doubt but that all those who simply, without any misgivings, entrust themselves firmly and singleheartedly to Amida Tathāgata and entreat him deeply with their whole being to save them in the matter of Rebirth will be delivered without fail."

CHAPTER SEVENTY-EIGHT

The Amida Buddha Who Vowed to Save All Women

WOMEN'S ATTAINMENT

OF BUDDHAHOOD

FASCICLE V, LETTER TWENTY

Listen! All women who entrust themselves steadfastly to Amida Tathāgata and entreat him to save them with regard to Rebirth will most assuredly be saved, for it was precisely for the sake of womenkind, abandoned as they had been by all the other Buddhas, that Amida Tathāgata made his Supreme Vow, telling himself "If I do not save women, what other Buddha will save them?" Having made up his mind to surpass all the other Buddhas in this respect, he meditated for five kalpas, underwent self-discipline for innumerable kalpas more and then produced his Great Vow, something beyond this world. Amida fulfilled this unsurpassable Vow, which promised the attainment of Buddhahood to women. For this reason all women who entrust themselves absolutely to Amida and entreat him to save them in respect to Rebirth will assuredly attain birth in the Land of Utmost Bliss.

Most humbly and respectfully

COMMENTS

This again is one of the five letters addressed to the Kanegamori Women's Association. It is worth noting that in this particular letter the salvation of women through faith is looked at in relation to Amida Buddha's Thirty-fifth Vow, which reads,

> If, upon my obtaining Buddhahood, women in all the innumerable and inconceivable Buddha-worlds throughout the ten quarters should not be filled with joy, faith and aspiration upon hearing my name and, abhorring their femininity, not awaken their thoughts to Enlightenment, and if after death they should yet again assume female form, may I not attain the Highest Enlightenment.[465]

The Thirty-fifth Vow was given different descriptive names by the various Pure Land masters. I would like now to consider just two of these titles: the one used by Hōnen Shōnin in his *Commentary on The Larger Sūtra*, namely, the "Vow to Make Women Attain Birth in the Pure Land,"[466] and the one chosen by Shinran Shōnin in his *Verses on the Pure Land*, the "Vow to Transform Women into Men."[467] Unless we take a brief look at the historical background that influenced the choice of such names, it will be very difficult to understand them, particularly the last one.

As discussed in *Chapter 7*, the formulation of the Thirty-fifth Vow reflects the underlying discriminatory attitude towards women prevalent in the androcentric society of that time. If viewed merely from the modern perspective of equality between men and women, it will certainly be extremely difficult for us to appreciate the true meaning of this vow, hidden behind the barrier of such discriminatory expressions. What is very important to understand is why such a vow was produced as one of Amida's forty-eight vows.

Needless to say, the essence of Amida's vows lies in universal deliverance of all sentient beings without any form of discrimination. For thousands of years, however, from ancient times right up to the present, the sorry course of human history has been marked by discrimination against women. According to my understanding of the vow, its purpose was solely to deliver women from the miserable reality of such unfair attitudes. Then why, one might wonder, were such discriminatory words employed?

With regard to the first title, "the Vow to Make Women Attain Birth," a somewhat strange title to modern ears, Professor Kōtatsu Fujita states in his main work, *Studies on Early Pure Land Thought*,

They are suddenly born amongst the lotus flowers in the Land of Utmost Bliss and those born there are all excellent and equal, women transformed into men. This idea of women being transformed into men is widely taught in Mahāyāna sūtras. It can be explained as representing the theoretical grounding that allows women to perform Mahayanistic Bodhisattva practices but it can equally be seen as symbolising a compromise between equality on the one hand and the Indian notion of sexism on the other.[468]

The idea of women being transformed into men is mentioned not only in Mahāyāna sūtras but also in a number of Pure Land sūtras, including *The Great Amida Sūtra* 大阿彌陀經,[469] the earliest version of the Chinese translations of *The Sukhāvātivyūha*. It is not anything added later but something that existed from the very start of Pure Land thought.

Why did Amida make a special vow for women when his Eighteenth, or Original Vow, already promised birth through the *Nenbutsu* for *all* sentient beings in the ten quarters? It was to secure women's deliverance from all the discrimination against them prevalent throughout human history. Sad to say, even in traditional Buddhism there was discrimination against women in those early days. This is the reason why the idea of transforming women into men made its appearance in the new Buddhist movements of Mahāyāna and Pure Land Buddhism. It was to allow women to practise the Buddhist way in the same way as men. Because Indian society in those days was so highly androcentric, women would have had to turn into men in order to be equal to them. Therefore to realise the equality of men and women within such a society, Mahayanists, including Pure Land Buddhists, resorted to the use of this discriminatory notion of women becoming men as a kind of compromise. In other words, they thought that in order to realise the equality of men and women, it was necessary to heighten the status of women to that of men. The Thirty-fifth Vow should be understood as a skillful way of enabling women to attain Buddhahood.

"The Vow to Transform Women into Men," was a name given to the vow by Shinran Shōnin himself. Shinran followed the Pure Land tradition but he did not categorise the Thirty-fifth Vow amongst "the true vows," such as the 11th, 12th, 13th, 17th, 18th, 22nd and 33rd vows, but counted it as one of the provisional vows. This name was solely an attempt, using the language and religious imagery of the time, to emphasise equality between men and women, both of whom are able, through faith alone, to attain birth in the Pure Land. In the olden days there was no concept of social equality between men and women. For Shin Buddhists, attaining faith, or attaining birth in the Pure Land, means transcending sexual distinction or, put another way, realising the equality of men and women in a purely spiritual sense. There is a verse in Japanese in which Shinran refers to this vow,

It is because Amida's great compassion commands such depth
That the inconceivable Buddha wisdom reveals itself as it does.
By making the Vow that allows women to change themselves into men
Amida gave all women the chance to attain Buddhahood.[470]

In Shin Buddhism, attaining birth in the Pure Land means attaining
Buddhahood soon afterwards. Shinran Shōnin thus refers to this vow, which
Hōnen Shōnin called "The Vow of Making Women Attain Birth," as "The Vow
of Enabling Women to Attain Buddhahood" by making them men on entry to
the Pure Land. In the ultimate spiritual dimension, no sexual distinction exists
and men are equal to women and vice versa. According to Buddhism, one's
innate quality as a human being culminates in the attainment of Buddhahood,
or becoming a Buddha. Accordingly Rennyo Shōnin, too, refers in this letter
to the Thirty-fifth Vow as "this unsurpassable Vow, which promised the
attainment of Buddhahood to women." Rennyo Shōnin's ultimate purport
in writing so many letters to women was to clarify the notion that female
followers who entrust themselves absolutely to Amida Buddha will surely
attain birth in the Pure Land.

Regarding the faith-experience of entrusting oneself absolutely to Amida
Buddha, Shinran states in *The Kyōgyōshinshō*, "Reaching the Pure Land of
Enjoyment in fulfillment of the Great Vow has nothing to do with gradua-
tion or classification. It leaps over and instantly ignores all differences of any
kind to attain incomparably perfect Enlightenment. Therefore, it is known
as 'leaping over crosswise.'"[471]

Thus women's attainment of faith defies all kinds of discrimination
against women. The faith-experience that leads us ultimately to attain
Buddhahood is something far beyond sexual distinction.

Although it is very sad to see such strongly discriminatory wording in
the Thirty-fifth Vow reflecting the Indian sexist attitude of the time, what
Shinran and Rennyo found lying behind such language was Amida's sincere
prayer that women should attain Buddhahood.

CHAPTER SEVENTY-NINE

Peaceful Awareness
and the *Nenbutsu*
of Gratitude

ON PASSAGES IN THE
SŪTRA AND COMMENTARIES

FASCICLE V, LETTER TWENTY-ONE

What is meant by 'peaceful awareness' in our tradition is that, no matter how heavily we may be burdened with bad karma, we just leave it all to the Buddha and, abandoning the inclination towards the miscellaneous practices and the mixed ways of practising, simply entrust ourselves to Amida Tathāgata in one thought-moment singleheartedly and deeply with our whole being. Those beings who entreat Amida to save them will all be delivered, ten out of every ten, one hundred out of every one hundred. Regarding this point there should not be the slightest doubt, even if it is as minute as a drop of dew. We speak of those who entrust themselves in this way as people who have fully attained 'peaceful awareness.'

Passages in *The Sūtra* and in commentaries[472] express this clearly, stating that "with the awakening of the one thought-moment of faith, followers dwell in the company of those who are rightly assured of their birth" and referring to them as "the followers who have completed the cause in daily life." We must bear in mind, therefore, that what is of vital importance is simply to entrust ourselves to Amida Buddha in one thought-moment deeply with our whole being. In addition to this, we should always say the *Nenbutsu*, whether walking or resting, sitting or lying down, with deep appreciation of all that Amida Tathāgata has done for us in order to save us so readily.

Most humbly and respectfully

COMMENTS

The passage in the letter, "with the awakening of the one moment's thought of faith, followers dwell in the company of those who are rightly assured of their birth," is not an exact quotation but a wonderful summarisation of the essence of the teaching of *The Larger Sūtra of Eternal Life* and commentaries on it by the Pure Land patriarchs. The other expression found in this letter, "the followers who have completed the cause in daily life," is another summarisation of the same content created by Kakunyo Shōnin (1270–1351), the third Head Priest of the Honganji, the word "cause" standing for faith. If you are really awakened to faith, this awakening of faith assures you of attaining birth and is called "the cause for birth in the Pure Land."

According to *The Ofumi raii shō*, written by Enin in 1689, this letter was given to Dōtoku on 1st January 1493, when he visited Rennyo at Yamashina and received the teaching of Other Power.[473] This famous account of Dōtoku's visit on New Year's Day appears as the first article of *The Goichidai ki kiki-gaki*.[474] However, there is no other historical evidence that supports the date of the letter set out in *The Ofumi raii shō*.

The first article of *The Goichidai ki kikigaki* is another beautiful story of encounter between master and disciple, in which Rennyo elucidates the essential aspects of the Shin Buddhist faith in such a lively way: "with the awakening of the one thought-moment of faith we immediately find ourselves in the embrace of Amida's great compassion and become assured of attaining birth in his Pure Land, so the *Nenbutsu* that wells up spontaneously after that attainment of faith is entirely an expression of our gratitude to Amida for all that he has done for us."

Although there is no historical evidence of the relationship between the two documents, I myself like to think it is possible that Rennyo wrote this letter after the conversation with Dōtoku in order to give textual and doctrinal grounds to their lively spiritual exchange.

CHAPTER EIGHTY

Other Power Faith in Shin Buddhism

ON THE TEACHING OF OUR TRADITION

FASCICLE V, LETTER TWENTY-TWO

Those who desire to realise fully the meaning of the teaching in our tradition and wish to be born in the Land of Utmost Bliss should first and foremost learn about Other Power faith. What is the main purpose of attaining Other Power faith?

It grants us, wretched ignorant beings, the provision by which we readily travel to the Pure Land.

What is Other Power faith like?

It is the kind of faith that moves us to entrust ourselves exclusively, singleheartedly and steadfastly to Amida Tathāgata with no contrivance on our own. When the one thought-moment in which we entreat Amida to save us is awakened, Amida Tathāgata unfailingly emits his all-encompassing light and continues to embrace us within this light for as long as we live in this world. It is in this way that our birth is assured.

Namu Amida-butsu is thus by its very nature the expression of our attainment of Other Power faith. We should understand that this faith is a realisation of the original purport of *Namu Amida-butsu*. It is because we attain this Other Power faith that there is no doubt at all that we will be born readily into the Land of Utmost Bliss.

How magnificent is the Original Vow of Amida Tathāgata! And how should we respond to Amida Buddha's gracious benevolence? Whether sleeping or waking, we should respond to Amida Tathāgata for what he has done for us simply by pronouncing *Namu Amida-butsu*. With what sort of understanding, then, should we pronounce *Namu Amida-butsu*? We should understand that we pronounce *Namu Amida-butsu* with a joyful mind, feeling very grateful and respectful to Amida Buddha for that great work of his through which we have been saved.

Most humbly and respectfully

COMMENTS

This is the last of the eighty letters compiled in the Five Fascicle version of *The Letters* by Rennyo. When I first set about studying it, I was fully expecting there to be something extra special about the letter to warrant its position in final place. In the course of my translation, however, I found the whole text to be just a repetition of the latter part of the fourteenth letter of Fascicle Two. What could this mean?

In the case of the fourteenth letter of Fascicle Two, entitled *On Secret Teachings,* the latter portion – that also takes up the entirety of the twenty-second letter of Fascicle Five – is a description of the right teaching, set forth in order to criticise the erroneous dogmas known as "secret teachings." In my own commentary on the fourteenth letter I barely touched on the latter part of the letter, concentrating instead on providing an explanation of those "secret teachings."

When this latter part of the fourteenth letter of Fascicle Two is isolated as an independent letter, however, it becomes crystal clear that of the whole eighty letters this twenty-second letter of Fascicle Five embodies the quintessence of the Shin Buddhist faith. It is for this reason that Rennyo reiterated the text in the form of a separate letter. On realising that there was in existence at least one other letter with the same content, Ennyo Shōnin, the editor of *The Five Fascicle Letters*, must have decided to use this shorter version as the concluding letter. We are not sure, however, whether this version was written as an independent letter before 5th July 1474, the date of the fourteenth letter of Fascicle Two, or only later. One thing we can be sure of, however, is that Ennyo Shōnin, given the talented and faithful editor he was, would never himself have dreamed of creating a separate letter out of the fourteenth letter of Fascicle Two. Be that as it may, the content of the letter is highly appropriate for compilation into *The Letters* right at the end, comprising as it does the essentials of Shin Buddhist faith, namely Other Power faith and its relationship to *Namu Amida-butsu*.

What is meant by the notion of Other Power faith in Shin Buddhism is a question which I considered at some length in a talk I gave in Cambridge at an Interfaith Dialogue between Christians and Buddhists, where the former Archbishop of Canterbury, Dr. Rowan Williams, was also a participant. It should be noted in advance of reading the following quotation that when Shin Buddhists speak of "salvation by faith alone" or Christians of "justification by faith," in each case faith is seen as a gift from the Absolute Other. Also bear in mind that, whenever I use the word "absolute" in my writing like this, I am referring to the transcendence of all conceptual opposition. Regarding the notion of Other Power faith, my talk goes as follows,

> What then is meant by 'justification by faith' or 'salvation through faith alone'? Let me quote from the New Testament: 'For by grace you have been saved through faith; and this is not your own doing, it is the gift of God – not because of works, lest any man should boast' (*Ephesians* 2:8,9). Brief as it is, this passage from *The Letter from St. Paul to the Ephesians* covers three essential aspects of the faith-experience.
>
> Firstly, justification through faith means that justification or salvation does not come from 'our own doing' or 'works of the law.' This point is further elaborated in the following passage: 'We ourselves, who are Jews by birth and not Gentile sinners, yet who know that a man is not justified by works of the law but through faith in Jesus Christ, even we have believed in Jesus Christ, in order to be justified by faith in Christ and not by works of the law, because by works of the law shall no one be justified' (*Galatians* 2:15,16).
>
> In Shin Buddhism we talk about the difference between self-power faith and Other Power faith. With self-power faith we retain our reliance on, and attachment to, self-power deeds. In as far as we rely on self-power deeds or 'our own doing,' even if such deeds are very worthy, there can be no pure faith of entrusting ourselves entirely to Other Power, be it God or Amida Buddha. Shin Buddhist followers become aware of the limitations of self power and entrust themselves absolutely to Amida Buddha, forsaking all attachment to self power.
>
> The law in the context of Christianity is something ethico-religious that belongs to the Holy One and encourages us to live in a better way, or the best possible way, during our time in this world. In our attempts to perform good deeds or 'works of the law,' we come to realise how self-centred, even sinful, if you like, we really are. The law brings about this consciousness of sin, or of 'bad karma' in Buddhism. After attaining faith, in as far as we live in this world, we continue to carry out good deeds, or 'works of the law', but in the full realisation of their limitations and entrusting our whole being singlemindedly to Other Power. In this

case, whilst still trying to do good in the world, we have no attachment to our own performance, we are like the wind sweeping across the sky. Everything is left to Other Power.

Secondly, the passage from *The Letter to the Ephesians* makes it clear that faith is a gift from God. Shin Buddhist faith is likewise understood as a gift from Amida Buddha. As we are all ignorant beings, heavily burdened with blind passions and karmic attachments, all we can do is simply respond to Amida's call to come to him just as we are, entrusting ourselves with pure faith to his unconditional love that knows no discrimination. It is through Amida's unconditional love that faith is awakened within us. In this sense the awakening of faith is entirely a gift from Other Power. Shinran Shōnin (1173–1262), the founder of Shin Buddhism, says in *The Tanni shō*, Chapter 6, 'It is all due to the karmic condition of things that some follow one master while others leave him. This being so, it would be absurd to say that one who turns from one master to another will not attain birth in the Pure Land. Do people mean to take back the faith given to each person by Amida as if it were something of theirs? Such views are most decidedly unreasonable.'

Thirdly, the passage from the New Testament quoted above also makes clear that faith is not something to boast about. Faith in its true sense is devoid of any kind of pride. In this world we usually tend to be proud of our own deeds or 'works of the law' in the case of Christianity and this pride causes attachment to our actions. Our minds are structured so self-centredly that it would be extremely difficult for us to do good just for the sake of it. Without the faith of entrusting ourselves to the unconditional love of Amida, pride and attachment to our own deeds, however laudable our efforts may seem, will end up causing conflict and damaging ourselves and others, in short, being 'sinful' in the Christian terminology. 'By works of the law shall no one be justified' (*Galatians* 2:16). Pure faith is free of any kind of self-justification and shows no attachment to one's own actions. We should understand that it is only from Higher Power, call it God or Buddha, that justification, or salvation, can come to us.

Pride is deeply embedded in the recesses of our consciousness and needs to be swept away. Even if our act is the *Nenbutsu*, that is, reciting *Namu Amida-butsu*, pride is a big obstacle in the attainment of pure faith. Shinran Shōnin states in his main writing, *The Kyōgyōshinshō*,

'As long as the sages of the Mahāyāna and Hīnayāna and all good followers everywhere take the recitation of the auspicious Name of the Original Vow to be their own good, they cannot attain faith nor realise the Buddha's wisdom. As they are unable to realise the establishment of the cause for birth, they cannot enter the Land of Enjoyment.'[475]

Even with the *Nenbutsu*, if we become proud of our practice and start looking on it as a virtue, we will be unable to attain pure faith in Amida Buddha and will fail to be born in the true Land of Enjoyment. For all of us the karmic burden of pride and selfish attachment is a stumbling block to the awakening of pure faith.

Despite the sad reality of our karmic existence, heavily burdened with blind passions, undue pride and tenacious attachment, we can still entrust ourselves absolutely to the all-embracing, unconditional love that manifests itself through the medium of a good teacher. After attaining faith we can then continue on the path of faith to the Pure Land, doing for the doing what seems good, with gratitude and repentance and no attachment to our own actions. In this respect, in Shin Buddhism, too, 'good works of the law' are restored after the awakening of faith."

In this context and with regard to the notion of Other Power, I would like to quote a poem that was a great favourite of the great Buddhist thinker, D. T. Suzuki, who often quoted it. The poem is by Saichi Asahara (1850–1932), a prolific Shin Buddhist poet who, in the course of the last eighteen years of his life, composed more than ten thousand poems whilst making a living as a *geta*-maker in a small town known as Yunotsu in Shimane Prefecture. Though only semi-literate, Saichi still managed to write down the poems, using his very limited knowledge of Japanese letters (*kana*) and characters (*kanji*) and his own unique phonetic spelling. Each poem is a perfect expression of Saichi's own faith-experience.

In Other Power
There is no self-power, no Other Power.
All around is Other Power.
Namu Amida-butsu, Namu Amida-butsu.[476]

The first two lines, 'In Other Power / There is no self-power, no Other Power', would seem to be a contradiction in terms. But in the first line 'Other Power' (*Tariki*) is used to refer to the absolute Other Power the poet now feels, whereas the 'self power' (*jiriki*)' and 'Other Power' that he negates in the second line are merely relative concepts, opposed to one another. Thus Other Power or *Tariki* in the first line is totally different from Other Power in the second line. The latter is only a concept of dualistic nature. The second line completely negates such a dualistic way of thinking, something that Saichi himself must have long been struggling with, right up until the moment he attained faith.

Regarding the third line, 'All around is Other Power,' it can be regarded as a spontaneous reflection on Saichi's part on his own firsthand experience of absolute Other Power. Such reflections can only be fleeting, however, for if our minds engage too long with them, then we will merely be introducing a new form of *Tariki*. Although religious philosophers can and do reach this point, if they remain attached to it, then it has to be seen as the last vestige of duality or mental bifurcation. What completely sweeps the notion of duality from our minds is Saichi's *Namu Amida-butsu* in the last line, the very essence of the poem. The quintessence of Shin Buddhism lies in *Namu Amida-butsu* itself, as Rennyo repeatedly states in his letter. Saichi's *Namu Amida-butsu* is actually Saichi himself becoming *Namu Amida-butsu*. The Name that Saichi chants is the Name chanting itself. This chanting of the Name is the absolute working of *Namu Amida-butsu*, a pure act of nonduality in which there is no one chanting and nothing being chanted, wherein neither subject nor object exists. With no distinction between them Saichi is one with the Name and the Name one with Saichi. Becoming *Namu Amida-butsu* itself, Saichi is going back to the Pure Land.

Another short poem by Saichi reads,

> Having gone through the moment of death and the funeral,
> Saichi lives in this world with *Namu Amida-butsu*.
> Saichi is Amida,
> Amida is Saichi.[477]

When you look closely at the origins of any great religion, you will find that what is fundamental, radical if you prefer, is the pure experience of the awakening of faith and its resultant immediate expression. If you yourself have undergone an experience equal in quality to that of acquiring pure faith, then you will have an insight into the purity of the awakening that lies behind such expressions of faith. Your faith-experience can be said to be equal to theirs, in that it is ultimately a gift from Other Power.

The awakening of faith is an instantaneous experience of leaping from the old world into the new. Buddhism speaks both of gradual and sudden awakening, but Shin Buddhism and Zen Buddhism are in principle religions of abrupt or sudden awakening.[478] In Christianity, too, St. Paul says in his *Letters to Galatians*, "I have been crucified with Christ; it is no longer I who live, but Christ who lives in me." What a wonderful way of verbalising the experience of regeneration through pure faith in the unconditional love of God! Saichi expresses almost the same idea in the phrase, "Having gone through the moment of death and the funeral." The old self dies and the new one is born. The life we live after such an ego death or experience of rebirth is a gift from the Buddha, to whose unconditional love we entrust ourselves with pure faith. But what makes us able to entrust ourselves to the love of the Holy One? It is because we feel, or are awakened to, his unconditional selfless love calling to us. It is extremely important for any great religion to be aware of the paradox that it is through conditioned individual existence that unconditional universal love manifests itself to us. It is because of our awareness of this unconditional love directed at ourselves, that we are impelled to entrust ourselves to that love absolutely.

Shin Buddhists are very much aware of the fact that, for as long as we live in this world, we are heavily burdened with blind bodily passions and for this reason cannot become Buddhas in the here and now. But Saichi is one with Amida Buddha in *Namu Amida-butsu*. Saichi says, "Saichi lives in this world with *Namu Amida-butsu*" – Amida Buddha's unconditional love now working in him.

In Buddhism, the original meaning of *Namu Amida-butsu* is "I take refuge in Amida Buddha." Understood in this way, *Namu Amida-butsu* is seen as the expression of our faith. Rennyo refers to this point in this letter by stating "*Namu Amida-butsu* is thus by its very nature the expression of our attainment of Other Power faith." At the same time it is the name of Amida Buddha, Amida Buddha having attained Buddhahood by fulfilling the loving prayer he made as a Bodhisattva that all sentient beings might take refuge in him simply by calling his Name – *Namu Amida-butsu*. In this sense *Namu Amida-butsu* is the great working of Amida's unconditional love. When Saichi writes, "Saichi lives in this world with *Namu Amida-butsu*," it means that he still lives in this world heavily burdened with blind passions, but does so in the embrace of the unconditional love of Amida Buddha.

Saichi then goes on to declare, "Saichi is Amida, Amida is Saichi." This does not mean that Saichi is perfectly enlightened like Amida Buddha, but simply that Saichi is one with Amida Buddha and Amida is one with Saichi, just as they are one in *Namu Amida-butsu*.

In Shin Buddhism, especially in Saichi's poems, the idea of the oneness of *Namu* and *Amida-butsu* is extremely important. *Namu* in this context stands for the person who takes refuge in Amida and *Amida-butsu* stands for the Buddha who saves that person. Through the *Nenbutsu* the complete oneness of that person and Amida Buddha is brought about. Saichi certainly enjoyed this mystical experience.

For Saichi the attainment of oneness with Amida came about after he had "gone through the moment of death and the funeral." What he was thinking of was not the actual physical death of the body, nor a so-called near-death experience, but something deeply spiritual, the death of the ego or selfish consciousness. After this kind of death Saichi says, "Saichi lives in this world with *Namu Amida-butsu*." *Namu Amida-butsu* is the vast activity of Amida Buddha where "Saichi is Amida and Amida is Saichi" in the great working of the Buddha's unconditional love.

At this deep level Saichi is experiencing eternal life way beyond the confines of birth and death. The life he now lives is an eternal life, newly bestowed through his pure faith in entrusting himself absolutely to Amida Buddha, the Buddha of Eternal Life. Another poem by Saichi reads, "If you like to die, do so, this body! Even if you die, I will not die. I go to the Pure Land living in *Namu Amida-butsu*."[479]

As Rennyo Shōnin concludes, the *Nenbutsu*, or *Namu Amida-butsu*, that we always pronounce, whether sleeping or waking, standing or lying, is a grateful expression of our Other Power faith and at the same time the great working of Amida's unconditional love, embodied as his Original Vow.

NOTES

1. Translation in this book is based on *The Five Fascicle Letters* of Rennyo, a text annotated by Masamaru Inaba (1865–1944) in his *Shohan-taikō gojō ofumi teihon* 諸版対校五帖御文定本, originally published in 1933 and republished in 1995, Hōzōkan, Kyoto. Inaba grounded his editorial work on *The Letters* handwritten and signed by Jitsunyo (1458–1525), the Ninth Head Priest of Honganji.

2. *Honganji sahō no shidai* 本願寺作法の次第 by Jitsugo (1492–1584), the tenth son of Rennyo.

3. *Honganji sahō no shidai*, Article 43, *Shinshū shiryō shūsei*真宗資料集成, Vol. 2, pp. 568–9.

4. *Daihasso onmonogatari Kūzen kikigaki* 第八祖御物語空善聞書 or *Kūzen's Record of the Eighth Patriarch's Words* by Kūzen (n.d.), one of Rennyo's disciples who attended him closely. Later this will also be referred to as *Kūzen kikigaki*, *Kūzen nikki* or *Kūzen ki*.

5. *Daihasso onmonogatari Kūzen kikigaki*, Article 34, *Shinshū shiryō shūsei*, Vol. 2, pp. 422–3.

6. The original Japanese title is *The Rennyo Shōnin goichidai ki kikigaki* 蓮如上人御一代記聞書, *The Record of Rennyo Shōnin's Words and Deeds throughout His Lifetime*. This document consists of 316 articles and was probably compiled by Jitsugo, Rennyo's tenth son, drawing from several different accounts of Rennyo's words and deeds such as *Daihasso onmonogatari Kūzen kikigaki* 第八祖御物語空善聞書 by Kūzen, known as *Kūzen ki* 空善記, *Rennyo Shōnin ichigoki* 蓮如上人一語記 by Jitsugo himself, known as *Jitsugo kyūki* 實悟旧記, and *Rennyo Shōnin onmonogatari shidai* 蓮如上人御物語次第 by an unknown author. In the annotation on each article quoted from *The Rennyo Shōnin goichidai ki kikigaki*, the author indicates the original text on which it depends with reference to the *Rennyo Shōnin zenshū* 蓮如上人全集, Vol. 4, Chōjun Ōtani ed., Chūō Kōronsha, Tokyo, 1998, and also to the *Shinshū shiryō shūsei* 真宗史料集成, Vol. 2, Dōbōsha Shuppan, Kyoto, 1983.

7. *Rennyo Shōnin zenshū*, Vol. 4, p. 30. *Jitsugo kyūki*, Article 19, *Shinshū shiryō shūsei*, Vol. 2, p. 445.

8. *Rennyo Shōnin zenshū*, Vol. 4, pp. 36–7. *Jitsugo kyūki*, Article 40, *Shinshū shiryō shūsei*, Vol. 2, p. 447.

9. *Rennyo Shōnin zenshū*, Vol. 4, p. 40. *Jitsugo kyūki*, Article 53, *Shinshū shiryō shūsei*, Vol. 2, p. 448.

10. *Rennyo Shōnin zenshū*, Vol. 4, p. 40. *Jitsugo kyūki*, Article 54, *Shinshū shiryō shūsei*, Vol. 2, p. 448.

11. *Rennyo Shōnin zenshū*, Vol. 4, p. 64. *Jitsugo kyūki*, Article 203, *Shinshū shiryō shūsei*, Vol. 2, pp. 456–7.

12. Hōonkō 報恩講, the most important Shin Buddhist annual ceremony for followers to commemorate the death of Founder Shinran Shōnin

and respond to him with gratitude for what he had done for them throughout his life. Traditionally this gathering is expected to continue for a week.

13 Higan'e 彼岸会, Buddhist services performed during the week of the equinox.

14 *Rennyo Shōnin zenshū,* Vol. 4, p. 37. *Jitsugo kyūki,* Article 40, *Shinshū shiryō shūsei,* Vol. 2, p. 447.

15 *Rennyo Shōnin zenshū,* Vol. 4, p. 30. *Jitsugo kyūki,* Article 19, *Shinshū shiryō shūsei,* Vol. 2, p. 445.

16 *Rennyo Shōnin zenshū,* Vol. 4, p. 40. *Jitsugo kyūki,* Article 54, *Shinshū shiryō shūsei,* Vol. 2, p. 448.

17 Kanoko no miei 鹿の子の御影, Rennyo's portrait at the age of six. See Illustration, Fig. 15.

18 *Shūjin ki* 拾塵記 by Jitsugo (1492–1584), tenth son of Rennyo.

19 *Shūjin ki, Shinshū shiryō shūsei,* Vol. 2, p. 599.

20 *Rennyo Shōnin goichigoki* 蓮如上人御一期記, or *The Record of Rennyo Shōnin's Life,* written by Jitsugo.

21 *Rennyo Shōnin zenshū,* Vol. 4, p. 193. *Rennyo Shōnin goichigoki,* Article 4, *Shinshū shiryō shūsei,* Vol. 2, p. 511.

22 Kakunyo 覚如 (1270-1351), Third Head Priest of Honganji, great grandson of Shinran. Rennyo copied Kakunyo's writings such as *Goden shō, Kuden shō, Hōonkō shiki* and *Saiyō shō.*

23 Zonkaku 存覚 (1290–1373), first son of Kakunyo. Rennyo copied Zonkaku's writings such as *Rokuyō shō, Nyonin ōjō kikigaki, Jimyō shō, Tandoku mon, Jōdo kenmon shū* and *Jōdo shinyō shō.*

24 Dōsai (1399–1488) is from Kanegamori, Ōmi Province.

25 Ōmi 近江 (present day Shiga Prefecture), a province next to Yamashiro (present day Kyoto) in the medieval time.

26 Based on *Honpukuji yurai ki* 本福寺由来記 by Myōshū (1469–1540), *Shinshū shiryō shūsei,* Vol. 2, p. 667.

27 *Rennyo Shōnin ibun* by Masamaru Inaba, 稲葉昌丸著『蓮如上人遺文, Hōzōkan, Kyoto, 1936.

28 *Kōchū Rennyo Shōnin ofumi zenshū* by Yūshō Tokushi (1879-1960), 禿氏祐祥著『校註蓮如上人御文全集, Bunkenshoin, Tokyo, 1922.

29 The first letter given to Dōsai. *Shinshū shiryō shūsei,* Vol. 2, p. 138. See Illustrations, Figs 8A & 8B, Rennō's handwritten copy stored in Gantokuji, Kadoma, Osaka.

30 *Tenshō sannen ki* 天正三年記 by Jitsugo.

31 Rensō 蓮崇 (–1499), a disciple who served Rennyo at Yoshizaki. Before leaving Yoshizaki, Rennyo excommunicated Rensō for being too politically involved and causing serious conflicts. Claiming to speak for Rennyo, Rensō had told followers they could rise and rebel against the local warlord. Towards the very end of his life, Rennyo met Rensō, however, and pardoned him.

32 *Rennyo Shōnin zenshū,* Vol. 4, p. 106. *Tenshō sannen ki, Shinshū shiryō shūsei,* Vol. 2, p. 412.

33 *Rennyo Shōnin zenshū,* Vol. 4, p. 148. *Daihasso onmonogatari Kūzen kikigaki,* Article 126, *Shinshū shiryō shūsei,* Vol. 2, p. 435.

34 *Rennyo Shōnin zenshū,* Vol. 4, p. 27. *Jitsugo kyūki,* Article 8, *Shinshū shiryō shūsei,* Vol. 2, p. 444.

35 *Rennyo Shōnin zenshū,* Vol. 4, p. 41. *Jitsugo kyūki,* Article 57, *Shinshū shiryō shūsei,* Vol. 2, p. 449.

36 *Rennyo Shōnin zenshū,* Vol. 4, p. 55. *Jitsugo kyūki,* Article 112, *Shinshū shiryō shūsei,* Vol. 2, p. 453.

37 *Rennyo Shōnin zenshū,* Vol. 4, p. 41. *Jitsugo kyūki,* Article 58, *Shinshū shiryō shūsei,* Vol. 2, p. 449.

38 *Daihasso onmonogatari Kūzen kikigaki,* Article 142, *Shinshū shiryō shūsei,* Vol. 2, p. 436.

39 See *Chapter 46.*

40 Rennō 蓮能, Jitsugo's mother. See Illustrations, Figs 8A & 8B, Rennyo's first letter to Dōsai that was later copied by Rennō.

41 Ishiyama-gobō 石山御坊, a temple at Ishiyama. After Honganji at Yamashina was attacked by Warlords, Hosokawa and Rokkaku, and Nichiren School followers, Shōnyo, the tenth Head Priest of Honganji, decided to make this temple their new Honganji, as it was a naturally fortified place. Later Osaka Castle was built on this site.

42 *The Letters,* Fascicle 4, Letter Fifteen, *Shohan taikō gojō ofumi teihon* by Masamaru Inaba, p. 98, or also *Shinshū shiryō shūsei,* Vol. 2, p. 286.

43 *Rennyo Shōnin itoku ki* 蓮如上人遺徳記, compiled by Rengo (1468–1543), Rennyo's seventh son, and completed by Jitsugo (1492–1584), Rennyo's tenth son.

44 *Shinshū shōgyō zensho,* Vol. III, 真宗聖教全書第三巻, Shinshū shōgyō zensho Hensansho, Kyoto: Ōyagi Kōbundō, 1964, p. 882.

45 *The Letters,* Fascicle 1, Letter One, *Shohan taikō gojō ofumi teihon,* p. 1, or also *Shinshū shōgyō zensho,* Vol. III, pp. 402–3.

46 The passages of conversation between Śākyamuni Buddha and Ānanda are from *The Larger Sūtra of Eternal Life* 大無量壽經, *Shinshū shōgyō zensho,* Vol. I, p.4.

47 "The Last Dharma Age", or "The Last Age," is based on the Buddhist eschatology that divides the time after the Buddha's decease into the three periods: the age of the Right Dharma in which Buddhist teaching, practice and Enlightenment all exist; the age of the Semblance Dharma in which teaching and practice exist without Enlightenment; and the age of the Last Dharma in which only teaching remains without practice and Enlightenment. "The Last Dharma Age" refers to the third and last period. It is said that after these three ages even the teaching or Dharma will fade away. Regarding the duration of those three periods there are a number of different views. For further explanation, see the author's commentary in *Chapter 32* on the second letter of Fascicle Three.

48 *The Letters,* Fascicle 5, Letter Nineteen, *Shohan taikō gojō ofumi teihon* by Masamaru Inaba, p. 113, or also *Shinshū shōgyō zensho,* Vol. III, p. 514.

49 "The five grave offences" and "slandering the Dharma" are the worst of the wrongdoings and are referred to in the exclusion clause of the Eighteenth Vow of *The Larger Sūtra of Eternal Life*. Despite this exclusion clause, Rennyo states that even those who commit those transgressions are saved through their pure faith. Regarding this point, see the author's commentary in *Chapter 62*. In some Mahāyāna texts such evildoers are called *icchantika* (ch. *yīchǎntí* 一闡提 jp. *ichisendai, issendai*), meaning "those who are devoid of the seed of Buddhahood."

50 In the Theravada tradition "five grave offences" consist of: killing one's father, killing one's mother, killing an arhat, destroying the harmony of the Sangha, and causing blood to flow from the body of a Buddha. In the Mahāyāna tradition the following five are listed: destroying temples or stūpas, burning sūtras or buddha images or stealing the belongings of the Three Treasures; slandering the Śrāvakayāna 声聞乗 (jp. *Shōmonjō*), the Pratyekabuddhayāna 縁覚 乗 (jp. *Engakujō*) and the Bodhisattvayāna 菩薩乗 (jp. *Bosatsujō*) and belittling their holy scriptures; obstructing the practice of a monk, by abusing, attacking, imprisoning or murdering; violation of the five grave offences mentioned above; and committing the ten bad acts denying the moral law of cause and effect.

51 The "ten bad acts" are: destroying life, theft, adultery, lying, talking nonsense, speaking evil of others, being double-tongued, greed, anger and ignorance.

52 Hōji san 法事讃 (ch. *Fashi zan*) by Shàndǎo, *Shinshū shōgyō zensho*, Vol. I, p. 567.

53 According to Sūtras such as *The Lotus Sūtra* (*Taishō daizōkyō*, Vol. 9, p. 35) and *The Chōnichimyō zanmai kyō* (*Taishō daizōkyō*, Vol. 15, p. 541), the "five obstacles" are explained as women's inability to become: Brahman, Indra, King of Demons, Cakravartin, or Buddha. For further explanation, see the author's commentary in *Chapter 65* on the second letter of Fascicle Five.

54 The three submissions are explained in Buddhist documents such as *Gaṇḍavyūha* (*Taishō daizōkyō*, Vol. 10, p. 790) and *Chōnichimyō zanmai kyō* (*Taishō daizōkyō*, Vol. 15, p. 541): Women had to obey their parents when young; they had to obey their husband and were not free when married; and they had to obey their children when becoming old. For further explanation, see the author's commentary in *Chapter 7* and *Chapter 65*.

55 A reference to Shinran Shōnin's words found in *The Tanni shō*, Chapter 6: "It is completely unreasonable for there to be quarrelling amongst our fellow followers reciting the *Nenbutsu* exclusively, with people saying that such and such are 'my disciples' whilst such and such are not. I, Shinran, have no disciples. The reason is this: if a man by his own efforts makes others recite the *Nenbutsu*, then he may call them his disciples. But it is most presumptuous to claim as 'my disciples' those who recite the *Nenbutsu* solely as a result of Amida's working within themselves. It is all due to the karmic condition of things that some follow one master whilst others leave him. This being so, it would be absurd to say that one who turns from one master to another will not attain birth in the Pure Land. Do people mean to take

back the faith given to each person by Amida as if it were something of theirs? Such views are most decidedly unreasonable. If one follows the truth of reality as it is, one will understand exactly how grateful to be to Amida, and how grateful to be to the master." *Shinshū shōgyō zensho*, Vol. II, pp. 776–7. Translation quoted here is from Kemmyo Taira Sato, *Great Living: In the Pure Encounter between Master and Disciple*, New York: The American Buddhist Study Center Press, 2010, p. 58.

56 Regarding this special concept, see the author's comments and notes to *Chapters 22, 28, 30, 57* and *67*, as well as *Appendix 4*.

57 "Most humbly and respectfully". The original Japanese wording for this phrase is *anakashiko anakashiko*, usually written towards the end of a letter in order to express the sender's humble respects to the receiver. Etymologically speaking, the word *ana* started out in life as an exclamation but, when used as an adverb, means "very", "most" or "extremely". *Kashiko*, the root of the adjective *kashikoshi* and the verb *kashikomu*, is a term that connotes the mental state of "being in awe" of someone or something. In the case of Rennyo's letters, the word *anakashiko* is used, not only to express sincere respect, but also to convey a deep sense of humility. Therefore, the author translated *anakashiko anakashiko* as "most humbly and respectfully." Respect and humility are both very important in the context of the Shin Buddhist experience of faith. In the Japanese language repetition of the same word is sometimes used to emphasise its meaning. Almost all of Rennyo's letters end with the phrase *anakashiko anakashiko*, "most humbly and respectfully."

58 See the author's book, *Great Living: In the Pure Encounter between Master and Disciple*, a volume of commentaries on the Shin Buddhist text *Tanni shō* in a new translation, New York: The American Buddhist Study Center, 2010.

59 *Shinshū shōgyō zensho*, Vol. II, p. 509. *Kōsō wasan,* verse 68.

60 "The *Sūtra*" in this translation of *The Letters* by Rennyo with no special reference means *The Larger Sūtra of Eternal Life* 佛説大無量壽經.

61 The phrase "immediately attaining birth and dwelling in [the stage of] nonretrogression" is from the passage on the fulfilment of the Eighteenth Vow in *The Larger Sūtra of Eternal Life. Shinshū shōgyō zensho*, Vol. I, p. 24.

62 "The commentary" here refers to *The Commentary on The Treatise on the Pure Land* by Tánluán. The quotation is, however, not the same as the original but an abridgement. Tánluán's original version reads, "It is only because we entrust ourselves to the Buddha that we wish to be born in the Pure Land and can attain birth by virtue of the power of the Buddha's Vow. Supported by the power of the Buddha we immediately enter the ranks of the Mahāyanists who are rightly assured [of birth]." *Shinshū shōgyō zensho*, Vol. I, p. 279.

63 *Shinshū shōgyō zensho*, Vol. II, p. 512. *Kōsō wasan,* verse 96.

64 The original Sanskrit for "nonretrogression" is *avinivartanīya* (ch. *bùtuìzhuǎn* 不退転 jp. *futaiten*), meaning not falling back into the realm of illusory attachment. In the context of Pure Land Buddhism this is identical to the state of definite assurance in which the believer

is absolutely assured of birth in the Pure Land through the attainment of true faith. It is also believed in Mahāyāna Buddhism to be equal to the first stage of joy, *shokangiji* 初歡喜地 (ch. *Chūhuānxǐdì*), one of the fifty-three stages for a Bodhisattva to go through.

65   "One thought-moment" is *ichinen* 一念 (ch. *Yīniàn*), originally from the Sanskrit word *ekakṣaṇa*. As seen in English expressions such as "quick as thought" or "quick as a flash" it represents one instant or the shortest possible duration of time. In his system of religious philosophy Shinran talks about "one thought-moment of faith" and "one thought-moment of practice." The former refers to the very moment of awakening of faith when one entrusts oneself absolutely to Amida Buddha whilst the latter stands for the very moment of pronouncing his Name as an expression of gratitude. These two are inseparably related.

66   *Rennyo Shōnin zenshū,* Vol. 4, p. 3. *Daihasso onmonogatari Kūzen kikigaki,* Article 57, *Shinshū shiryō shūsei,* Vol. 2, p. 426.

67   Nirvāṇa, *nehan* 涅槃 (ch. *Nièpán*), is the transliteration of the Sanskrit word *nirvāṇa*, originally meaning "blown out," "extinguished," "calmed," "disappeared," "deceased." Buddhists started to use the term to express the Buddha's Enlightenment, an absolutely quiet state of mind reached by extinguishing the fire of blind passions rooted in ignorance. In Buddhism it is synonymously used with Supreme Enlightenment, emancipation, true suchness, ultimate reality or the Pure Land. Nirvāṇa is sometimes referred to as *Parinirvāṇa,* Perfect Nirvāṇa, or *Mahāparinirvāṇa,* Great Perfect Nirvāṇa. In ordinary usage it can also mean death.

68   *Rennyo Shōnin zenshū,* Vol. 4, p. 14. *Daihasso onmonogatari Kūzen kikigaki,* Article 92, *Shinshū shiryō shūsei,* Vol. 2, p. 431.

69   *Shinshū shōgyō zensho,* Vol. I, p. 35.

70   The original Chinese phrase *wúshēng zhī shēng* 无生之生 (jp. *mushō no shō*) for "birth of no birth" is from *The Commentary on The Treatise of the Pure Land* by Tánluán. *Shinshū shōgyō zensho,* Vol. I, p. 327.

71   *Rennyo Shōnin zenshū,* Vol. 4, pp. 16–7. *Daihasso onmonogatari Kūzen kikigaki,* Article 99, *Shinshū shiryō shūsei,* Vol. 2, p. 432.

72   *Rennyo Shōnin zenshū,* Vol. 4, p. 76. *Jitsugo kyūki,* Article 174, *Shinshū shiryō shūsei,* Vol. 2, p. 461.

73   The Japanese phrase *nisōshijū* 二雙四重 literally means the 2x2=4 format. Because of its two "ways" times two "approaches" format, this classification comprises four groups of teachings. Shinran's references to the philosophical categorisation are found in two of his systematic writings, *The Kyōgyōshinshō* and *The Gutoku shō,* in *Shinshū shōgyō zensho,* Vol. II.

74   The details of Shinran's classification of Buddhist teachings are found at the beginning part of *The Gutoku shō* 愚秃鈔, *Shinshū shōgyō zensho,* Vol. II, pp. 455–6.

75   The Japanese word for "Buddha-nature" is *busshō* 佛性, which is sometimes translated as "Buddhahood," meaning the true nature of a Buddha. The term *busshō* not only means the Buddha's true nature or Buddhahood but also implies the potentiality for everyone to attain

it. Regarding the latter point there is a famous statement from *The Nirvāṇa Sūtra*, "All beings without exception are endowed with Buddha-nature." It is believed that the origin of the word *busshō* can be traced back to Sanskrit words such as *buddhatā*, *buddhatva* and *buddhadhātu*, a word synonymous with *Tathāgatagarbha* (*Nyoraizō* 如来蔵 ch. *Rúláicáng*).

76　*Shinshū shōgyō zensho*, Vol. 4, p. 683–4. A letter to his disciple Zenshō-bo 禅勝房 (1174–1258). It is in the *Wagotōroku* 和語燈録 or *wago* (Japanese language) section of the *Kurodani Shōnin gotōroku* 黒谷上人語燈, Vol. 5, compiled by Ryōe 了恵 (Dōkō 道光, 1243–1330). See *Jōdoshū zensho*, vol. 9, p. 609. Later it was compiled with some modifications into *Hōnen Shōnin gyōjō ezu* 法然上人行状絵図, Section 45. For another translation of the relevant part from the *Hōnen Shōnin gyōjō ezu*, see *Hōnen The Buddhist Saint: His Life and Teaching*, by R. Ishizuka and H. H. Coates, trans., The Society for the Publication of Sacred Books of the World, Kyoto, 1925, pp. 737–8.

77　The Japanese word *ekō* 廻向 originates from the Sanskrit *pariṇāma*, meaning the act of virtue-transference. This working of *ekō* or virtue-transference is in Shin Buddhism understood as coming from Amida Buddha, not from the devotee. According to Shinran's religious philosophy, it is through Amida's virtue-transference alone that one can go to the Pure Land for one's own salvation and come back to this world to save others. Whereas Amida's working of virtue-transference that enables one to go to the Pure Land is called 'outgoing *ekō*' (往相廻向 *ōsō ekō*), that which enables one to return to this world is called 'returning *ekō*' (還相廻向 *gensō ekō*).

78　*Nyorai* 如来 is a Japanese term for the Sanskrit *tathāgata*, one of the ten epithets of the Buddha, meaning one who has thus come or thus gone.

79　*The Kyōgyōshinshō* by Shinran, D. T. Suzuki, trans., Kyoto: Shinshū Ōtani-ha, 1973, p. 15, adapted. The word 'merit' in the translation has been replaced by 'virtue'.

80　The phrase "to complete the act in daily life" is a translation of the Shin Buddhist term *heizei gōjō* 平生業成, meaning the completion in daily life of the act that enables one to attain birth in the Pure Land.

81　The phrase "coming to meet us" is in Japanese *raikō* 来迎. It is unmistakably clear in the context of Japanese Pure Land Buddhism that this condensed Japanese expression actually means Amida's coming to meet us at the moment of death. For this reason the author rendered the phrase *raikō* according to its actual meaning for the English reader. Shin Buddhists do not anticipate Amida's coming. What is most important for them is the instantaneous awakening of faith in daily life.

82　This phrase "with the one thought-moment of awakening, joining the company of those who are rightly assured" is the literal translation of Rennyo's words *ichinen hokki jū shōjōju* 一念発起住正定聚. What the devotee is assured of at the very moment of awakening of faith is birth in the Pure Land.

83　The source of this phrase *sokutokuōjō jūfutaiten* 即得往生住不退転 is *The Larger Sūtra of Eternal Life*. *Shinshū shōgyō zensho*, Vol. I, p. 24.

84　This notion, "the benefit of the light that embraces all beings and never abandons them", originates from a relevant phrase 光明遍照十方世界念佛衆生摂取不捨 in *The Meditation Sūtra*: "Light illuminates all the worlds in the ten directions and embraces all who say the *Nenbutsu* never to abandon them." *Shinshū shōgyō zensho*, Vol. I, p. 57.

85 This is Rennyo's summary of the first letter of the letters by Shinran compiled into the *Mattōshō* (*Lamp for the Latter Ages*). *Shinshū shōgyō zensho*, Vol. II, pp. 656–8.

86 The Japanese phrase *jōjin-ichigyō geshi-ichinen* 上尽一形下至一念 "spending one's whole life at the upper limit, one thought-moment at the lower" originally comes from a passage in Shàndǎo's *Ōjō raisan ge* 往生禮讚偈 (ch. Wǎngshēng lǐzàn jì), "If one continues pronouncing the Name of Amida to the very end of one's life, or if one does so only ten times, or even once, one could readily be born in the Pure Land owing to the virtue of Amida's Vow." *Shinshū shōgyō zensho*, Vol. I, p. 651.

87 Kemmyo Taira Sato, *Great Living: In the Pure Encounter between Master and Disciple*, New York, American Buddhist Study Center, 2010.

88 *Shinshū shōgyō zensho*, Vol. I, p. 881.

89 K. T. Sato, *Great Living*, pp. 2–3.

90 The Shin Buddhist absolute confidence of ultimately attaining Nirvāṇa is based on Amida Buddha's Eleventh Vow: "If, upon my attaining Buddhahood, all humans and devas who are born in my country were not to abide in the company of those who have attained the right definite assurance and ultimately realise Nirvāṇa, may I not attain the Supreme Enlightenment."

Shinshū shōgyō zensho, Vol. I, p. 9, and translation from *The Kyōgyōshinshō* by Shinran, D. T. Suzuki, trans., p. 338.

91 Kashū is another name for Kaga Province. The three countries are Kaga Province, Noto Province and Etchū Province all in Hokuriku District.

92 *Rennyo Shōnin zenshū*, Vol. 4, p. 19. *Mukashi monogatari*, Article 1, *Shinshū shiryō shūsei*, Vol. 2, p. 611.

93 Gyōtokuji Temple is a Shin Buddhist temple built on the site where Dōshū lived.

94 *Rennyo Shōnin zenshū*, Vol. 4, p. 43. *Jitsugo kyūki*, Article 64, *Shinshū shiryō shūsei*, Vol. 2, p. 449.

95 *Rennyo Shōnin zenshū*, Vol. 4, pp. 42–3. *Jitsugo kyūki*, Article 63, *Shinshū shiryō shūsei*, Vol. 2, p. 449.

96 *Rennyo Shōnin zenshū*, Vol. 4, p. 60. *Jitsugo kyūki*, Article 127, *Shinshū shiryō shūsei*, Vol. 2, p. 455.

97 Rennyo called his letters *fumi* 文 or *ofumi* 御文. Nowadays, while the Ōtani-ha tradition still calls it *Ofumi*, the Hongwanji-ha calls it *Gobunshō*.

98 *Rennyo Shōnin zenshū*, Vol. 4, p. 89. *Jitsugo kyūki*, Article 250, *Shinshū shiryō shūsei*, Vol. 2, p. 468.

99 *Japanese Spirituality* by D. T. Suzuki, N. Waddell, trans., Japan Society for the Promotion of Science, Tokyo, 1972, pp. 170–1.

100 In this case, *dōjō* 道場 means a meeting place for Buddhist practice.

101 The original name for the document known as *Dōshū's Twenty-One Resolutions* is *The Resolutions Made on 24th December, 1st Year of Bunki*, a title given by Dōshū (ca. 1452–1516) himself at the age of fifty. See *Myōkōnin: Daijōbutten [The Mahāyāna Buddhist Literature], Japanese and Chinese Series, Vol. 28*, Tsutomu Mizukami and Taira Sato, eds, Chūō Kōronsha, Tokyo, 1987, pp. 18–22.

102 Kengyoku-ni 見玉尼 is the name of Rennyo's second daughter. The content of the letter entitled *Kengyoku-ni's Birth* is Rennyo's beautiful description of how she was awakened to faith and attained birth in the Pure Land at the age of twenty-five.

103 *Jōgai ofumi* 帖外御文 or *The Other Letters Not Compiled in The Five Fascicle Letters* is a common name for Rennyo's letters left out from *The Five Fascicle Letters*, the formal compilation of eighty letters by Ennyo. There are a number of different compilations or versions depending on who compiled them. *Rennyo Shōnin jōgai ofumi shō* 蓮如上人帖外御文鈔, or *The Collection of Rennyo's Letters Not Compiled in The Five Fascicle Letters*, Reion Takehara (1876–1951) ed., Gushikōsha, Fukuoka, 1932, is employed in this book.

104 Reion Takehara, ed., *Rennyo Shōnin jōgai ofumi shō*, pp. 40–1. *Shinshū shiryō shūsei*, Vol. 2, pp. 150–1.

105 Reion Takehara, ed., *Rennyo Shōnin jōgai ofumi shō*, p. 42. *Shinshū shiryō shūsei*, Vol. 2, p. 151.

106 *The Family Members from Kyoto* is *Kyoto no goichizoku bun* 京都の御一族分 in Japanese. Reion Takehara, ed., *Rennyo Shōnin*

jōgai ofumi shō, pp. 30–5. *Shinshū shiryō shūsei*, Vol. 2, pp. 157–8.

107 Ōshū is another name for Mutsu Province.

108 Its original source is a passage from *The Meditation Sūtra*, "Each light shines forth throughout all the worlds of the ten directions, embracing and never abandoning those who practice the *Nenbutsu*." *Shinshū shōgyō zensho*, Vol. I, p. 57.

109 *Ofumi kijishu* 御文記事珠 by Erin 慧琳 (1715–1789), woodblock print edition, Hōbunkan, Kyoto, 1841, Vol. II, pp. 1 right – 1 left.

110 Kūzen 空善, one of Rennyo's disciples who who tended Rennyo at his deathbed and left a record of Rennyo's words and deeds during his attendance, known as Kūzen kikigaki 空善聞書, full title *Daihasso onmonogatari Kūzen kikigaki* 第八祖御物語空善聞書. His birth year and death year are both unknown.

111 *Shinshū shōgyō zensho*, Vol. I, p. 12.

112 The phrase "to embrace and never to abandon" from *The Meditation Sūtra* is shèqǔbùshè 摂取不捨 *sesshufusha* in Japanese. *Shinshū shōgyō zensho*, Vol. I, p. 57.

113 Old Japanese lampstands are made of wood and their frameworks are covered by traditional Japanese paper.

114 From *The Record of Shōma's Words and Actions Just as They Are*, one of the Shin Buddhist documents compiled in *Myōkōnin: Daijōbutten [Mahāyāna Buddhist Literature], Japanese and Chinese Series, Vol. 28*, Tsutomu Mizukami and Taira Sato, eds, Tokyo, Chūō Kōronsha, 1987. The English

translation is from Kemmyo Taira Sato, *Great Living: In the Pure Encounter between Master and Disciple*, p. 61.

115 *Rennyo Shōnin zenshū*, Vol. 4, p. 653. *Jitsugo kyūki*, Article 140, *Shinshū shiryō shūsei*, Vol. 2, p. 457.

116 *Jishū* 時宗 is a unique Japanese Pure Land school founded by Ippen 一遍 (1239–1289). Scripturally it is based on *The Amida Sūtra* emphasising the importance of *The Avataṃsaka Sūtra* and *Lotus Sūtra*.

117 *Taya* 多屋 or 他屋 means a typically Shin Buddhist form of accommodation where Dharma friends are allowed to stay in order to listen to Dharma talks and discuss the matter of faith. Many *taya* houses were built at Yoshizaki for those who gathered to listen to Rennyo's teaching.

118 *Watakushi no Rennyo* 私の蓮如, *My Rennyo*, by Nobuhiko Matsugi 真継伸彦, Chikuma Shobo, 1981, pp. 88–9.

119 *Rennyo Shōnin zenshū*, Vol. 4, pp. 40–1. *Jitsugo kyūki*, Article 55, *Shinshū shiryō shūsei*, Vol. 2, p. 449.

120 From *The Great Nirvāṇa Sūtra*, *Taishō daizōkyō*, Vol. 12, p. 482. The original text is slightly different, having not "auspicious days and good stars" but "good days and auspicious stars."

121 This passage is found in *The Kyōgyōshinshō*, *Shinshū shōgyō zensho*, Vol. II, p. 175. Shinran quoted it from *The Sūtra of the Samādhi of All Buddhas' Presence*, *Taishō daizōkyō*, Vol. 13, p. 901.

122 The *Ofumi kōyō* 御文興要, or *Essentials of The Letters*, by Erin 慧林, five volume woodblock print edition, Ōsaka Shorin, 1768, Vol. 4, pp. 7 right – 7 left. The *Ofumi kōyō* says this story is based on the *Gōshōji ki* 豪攝寺記, an older commentary on *The Letters*, the original handwritten version of which is in the possession of the Library of Otani University. The relevant account is found in the *Gōshōji ki*, pp. 6 right – 6 left. As the *Gōshōji ki* is comprised of records of the original stories of almost all the important dated letters compiled in *The Letters*, it is often found quoted in various commentaries on *The Letters* written in the Edo period. Its full name is *Ofumi Gōshōji no ki* 御文豪攝寺之記, or *The Gōshōji Record of The Letters*, and the same document is also known as *Ofumi yuisho ki* 御文由緒記.

123 *Onomancy* is a sort of divination that tells a person's fortune from his name, popular in the East Asian countries where Chinese characters are used for their naming.

124 Kakuju Yoshitani 吉谷覺 (1842–1914), *Ofumi kōjutsu* 御文講述, Kyoto: Hōzōkan, 1910. The author is also called by his Dharma name, Ichijōin Kakuju.

125 *Haja kenshō shō* 破邪顕正鈔 by Zonkaku 存覺, eldest son of Kakunyo, third Head Priest of Honganji.

126 Zonkaku, *op. cit.*, *Shinshū shōgyo zensho*, Vol. III, pp. 171–2.

127 *Taishō daizōkyō*, Vol. 13, p. 901.

128 Regarding these two notions, "the five obstacles" and "three submissions," see *Notes 53 & 54* and *Chapter 7*. Rennyo actually employed those discriminatory notions, which were prevalent in those days, when teaching women the great love and compassion of

Amida Buddha, but his sincere intention throughout his life lay in guiding them, suffering from all kinds of discriminations, to the world of infinite light and unconditional love with no discrimination at all.

129 Regarding Japanese gods or *kami*, see *Appendix 1*.

130 *The Letters*, Fascicle 1, Letter Eight. *Shohan-taikō gojō ofumi teihon*, Masamaru Inaba (1867–1944), p. 23. *Shinshū shiryō shūsei*, Vol. 2, p. 173

131 Quotation from the author's unpublished talk.

132 *Rennyo Shōnin ibun* 蓮如上人遺文, "The Remaining Writings by Rennyo," Masamaru Inaba, ed., Hōzōkan, Kyoto, 1937, pp. 103–5. *Shinshū shiryō shūsei*, Vol. 2, p. 158.

133 *Gōshōji ki,* or *Ofumi Gōshōji no ki* 御文毫摂寺之記, a handwritten document in the possession of the Library of Otani University, pp. 6 left – 7 right.

134 Quotation from the author's unpublished talk.

135 The expression "human life as a flash of lightning or the morning dew" is found in the *Yuishin shō* by Seikaku (1167–1235), *Shinshū shōgyō zensho,* Vol. II, p. 744. The phrase "as a flash of lightning" is taken from the sentence "The pleasures of human and heavenly lives are like a flash of lightning", found in the *Exposition of The Meditation Sūtra* by Shàndǎo, *Shinshū shōgyō zensho,* Vol. I, p. 507, and the other phrase "as the morning dew" is originally found in the *Great Nirvāṇa Sūtra, Taishō daizōkyō,* Vol. 12, p. 873.

136 The original Japanese phrase for "the great river of three bad paths" is *sanzu no taiga* 三塗の大河, meaning an enormous violent river too difficult for those involved in the three bad paths to cross. There is another interpretation of the term, which can be translated as "the great river of three currents". The deceased are described in the *Ten Kings Sūtra*, an apocryphon made in the tenth century, to cross the three different currents according to their own past karma, whether good, bad or mixed.

137 This short description of next life is believed to be based on the relevant version found in the *Jōdo kenmon shū* by Zonkaku, *Shinshū shōgyō zensho,* Vol. III, p. 375–83. Zonkaku himself declares towards the end of the same writing that, in order to induce people to take this path to the Pure Land, he employed, just as a skillful means, such a description of the next life from the *Ten Kings Sūtra*, an East Asian apocryphon, never failing to emphasise that what is of vital importance in the Shin Buddhist tradition is the awakening of Other Power faith in daily life.

138 *Rennyo Shōnin ibun*, Masamaru Inaba, ed., pp. 94–5. The whole quotation is a part of the letter written by Rennyo on 1st February 1473 and constitutes a confession of repentance of one of his followers.

139 This is a brief note written by Rennyo himself. It's rare for him to have such an entry in front of the whole letter, but it happened not only in this letter but also in the following two letters, the thirteenth and fourteenth letters of Fascicle One. These three brief notes appear in the Jitsunyo version of *The Letters*, but not in the Shōnyo version. Note that, regarding the chronological order of those three letters, the author follows that

of the Shōnyo version as it seems properly organised in accordance with the dates when they were actually written. This, the twelfth letter of Fascicle One in the Shōnyo version is placed as the thirteenth one of the same fascicle in the Jitsunyo version and the thirteenth one of the Shōnyo version as the twelfth in the Jitsunyo version.

140 Chōshōji 超勝寺 is a Shin Buddhist temple in Echizen Province, with Rennyo's grand-uncle as first Head Priest. Regarding its details, see the author's commentary in *Chapter 12* on this, the twelfth letter of Fascicle One.

141 The three bad paths, or *sanzu* 三塗, are the realms of hell, hungry ghosts and animals.

142 *Hogo no uragaki* 反故の裏書, "Writings on the Back of Wastepaper," is a historical record by Kensei 顯誓(1499–1570), one of Rennyo's grandsons, about the Pure Land tradition from Hōnen to Kennyo, including the detailed descriptions of the last four generations, Rennyo, Jitsunyo, Shōnyo and Kennyo.

143 The three dangerous desires are *myōmon* 名聞 "desire for fame," *riyō* 利養 "desire for wealth," and *shōta* 勝他 "desire for domination."

144 *Kuden shō* 口伝鈔, "The Record of Oral Transmission," is a historical document of what Kakunyo directly received from Nyoshin (1235–1300), one of Shinran's grandsons, and dictated to his disciple Jōsen in 1331 and consists of 21 narratives. Unfortunately, the relevant story of this disciple of Hōnen Shōnin is not very trustworthy, containing some fatal chronological errors. This is why the author does not quote the monk's name in his commentary, only wishing to refer to the danger of those three desires.

145 A summary by the author of the relevant story related in *The Kuden shō, Shinshū shōgyō zensho*, Vol. III, pp. 14–7.

146 See *Note 139*.

147 The original full title of *The Treatise on the Pure Land*, or *Jodoron* 浄土論, by Vasubandhu is *The Treatise on The Larger Sūtra of Eternal Life*, or *Muryōjukyō ubadaisha ganshō ge* 無量壽經優婆提舍願生偈. Hōnen established the three Pure Land Sūtras – *The Sūtra of Eternal Life*, *The Meditation Sūtra* and *The Amida Sūtra* – and this article by Vasubandhu as the scriptural authority for his Pure Land teaching and Shinran followed Hōnen's view. The phrase "one mind of Other Power" in the text refers to Vasubandhu's expression of "one mind" in the beginning part of the treatise, "World-honoured One! I with one mind take refuge in the Tathagata of Unimpeded Light reaching the furthest ends of the ten quarters and aspire to be born in the Land of Peace and Happiness." *Shinshū shōgyō zensho*, Vol. I, p. 269.

148 See *Note 139*.

149 *The Commentary on the Mahāprajñāpāramitā Sūtra*, 大智度論 *Dai chido ron* (ch. *Dazhi du lun*), by Nāgârjuna. *Taishō daizōkyō*, Vol. 25, p. 63.

150 The original Japanese phrase for "think of the Buddha of Eternal Life steadfastly and exclusively," is *ikkō sennen muryōjubutsu* 一向専念無量壽佛. *Shinshū shōgyō zensho*, Vol. I, p. 24–5.

151 Ibid., p. 24.

152 *Shinshū shōgyō zensho*, Vol. II, p. 2. The English quotation is from *The Kyōgyōshinshō* by Shinran, D. T. Suzuki, trans., p. 9.

153 Rennyo expresses this view in one of his letters written in 1490 and collected outside of the five fascicle version. *Rennyo Shōnin ibun*, Masamaru Inaba, ed., pp. 372–3. *Shinshū shiryō shūsei*, Vol. 2, p. 262–3. In those days the followers of the Jishū branch known as "Ikkōshū" had their *dōjō* at Rengeji Temple located at Banba in Ōmi Province.

154 *Shinshū shōgyō zensho*, Vol. II, p. 33. The English quotation is from *The Kyōgyōshinshō* by Shinran, D. T. Suzuki, trans., pp. 58–9.

155 *Shinshū shōgyō zensho*, Vol. II, p. 24. The English quotation is from *The Kyōgyōshinshō* by Shinran, D. T. Suzuki, trans., p. 89.

156 *Shinshū shōgyō zensho*, Vol. I, p. 24.

157 *Shinshū shōgyō zensho*, Vol. I, p. 9.

158 "Eight difficulties," *hachinan* 八難 in Japanese, are eight kinds of calamities one can be born into: 1. to be born in hell, 2. to be born in the animal world, 3. to be born in the world of hungry ghosts, 4. to be born in the Heaven of Longevity, 5. to be born in the Uttarakuru (the northern country of longevity), 6. to be born blind, deaf and dumb, 7. to be born secularly wise, and 8. to be born before the birth or after the death of Śākyamuni Buddha. The calamity of being born in the Heaven of Longevity (4) and the Uttarakuru (5) is because they are so full of sensual pleasures that one born there has no chance to hear the Dharma.

159 *The Letters*, Fascicle 1, Letter Eight. *Shohan-taiko gojo ofumi teihon*, Masamaru Inaba (1867–1944), p. 11. *Shinshū shiryō shūsei*, Vol. 2, p. 160.

160 *Ōjō raisan shō* 往生禮讚鈔 by Gyōe 尭慧(–1395), Vol. 1, woodblock print edition, 1675, p. 23 right. In the possession of Otani University Library.

161 *Shinshū shōgyō zensho*, Vol. II, p. 44. *Shōshinge*, or *Gāthā of Right Faith in the Nenbutsu*, an important part of *The Kyōgyōshinshō* by Shinran, which is chanted by Shin Buddhists in their daily service.

162 *Ofumi raii shō* 御文来意鈔, *The Stories behind The Letters*, by E'nin 惠忍 (1693–1783). Its woodblock print editions on Fascicle 5 and on Fascicles 1 to 4 were published in 1759 and 1761 respectively. The author uses the modern edition published by Nishimura Kurōemon, Kyoto, in 1898. The story cited is a summary of the commentary on the first letter of Fascicle 2, pp. 63–6.

163 Regarding Dōshū 道宗, see the author's comments on the fifth letter of Fascicle One in *Chapter 5*.

164 The relevant passage quoted above is originally from *The Gaija shō* (*Passages to Correct the Erroneous Views*) by Kakunyo. *Shinshū shōgyō zensho*, Vol. III, p. 68.

165 The story of Revata from the *Zōhō zō kyō, Taishō daizōkyō*, Vol. 4, p. 457. The Sanskrit original of this Sūtra is no longer in existence.

166 The Japanese word *shinmei* 神明 is synonymous with *kami* 神 or gods, but carrying with it more feeling of respect for their divine virtues.

167 "That is the reason why", *gayuenari* がゆえなり in Japanese, is a concluding phrase to reconfirm that the whole paragraph is to show the reason why one should not belittle gods.

168 *Ofumi ryakuge* 御文略解, or *Short Commentaries on The Letters*, by Kōgon'in E'nen 香嚴院惠然 (1693– 1764), five volume woodblock print edition, Nishimura Kurōemon, Kyoto, 1888, Vol. 2, p. 5 left.

169 Concerning the three kinds of Buddha-body, see *Appendix 2*.

170 This statement is believed to be based on Bodhisattva Dharmākara's declaration, "I have made the Vow that is entirely beyond this world," the first phrase of "The Gāthā of Three Vows" found in *The Larger Sūtra of Eternal Life*. *Shinshū shōgyō zensho*, Vol. I, p. 13.

171 The original is 光明遍照十方世 界 念佛衆生摂取不捨 *kōmyōhenjō jippōsekai Nenbutsu shujō sesshufusha*. *Shinshū shōgyō zensho*, Vol. I, p. 57.

172 This is from *The Larger Sūtra of Eternal Life*. *Shinshū shōgyō zensho*, Vol. I, p. 31.

173 See the first paragraph of *Dai hatsunehan gyō* 大般涅槃經 (ch. *Dà pánnièpán jīng*), the Chinese version of *The Mahāparinirvāṇa-sūtra*. *The Great Nirvāṇa Sūtra* in English. *Taishō daizōkyō*, Vol. 12, p. 365.

174 The full name of *Yuikyō gyō* 遺 教經 is *Butsu sui hatsunehan ryakusetsu kyōkai kyō* 佛垂般涅槃 略説教誡經 (ch. *Fóchuí bānnièpán lüèshuō jiàojiè jīng*). *Taishō daizōkyō*, Vol. 12, p. 1110.

175 *Shinshū shōgyō zensho*, Vol. I, p. 57.

176 *Shinshū shōgyō zensho*, Vol. I, p. 31.

177 *Shinshū shōgyō zensho*, Vol. I, p. 272.

178 *Ōjō yōshū* 往生要集 by Genshin (源信 942–1017) was translated by August K. Reishauer, Edwin O. Reishauer's father, in 1930.

179 Reion Takehara 竹原嶺音 (1876– 1951), Former Head Priest of Shogyoji Temple.

180 Jōkan Chikazumi 近角常觀 (1870–1941), one of the greatest Shin Buddhist leaders of modern Japan.

181 *Shakaimondai kaiketsu* 社会問 題解決, or *How to Solve Social Problems*, is an article written by Reion Takehara in 1929 regarding this social movement to have abolished the introduction of "The Law of Religious Groups". *Gushikō* 遇斯光, or *Encounter with this Light*, by Reion Takehara, Vol. 2, Gushikōsha, 1963, pp. 75–130.

182 A detailed description of this faith movement is found in an article written by the Shōgyōji Archives Committee and entitled *How Faith Inspired the Save the Bell Movement*. Chan Jun Mun and Ronald S. Green, eds, *Buddhist Roles in Peacemaking: How Buddhism Can Contribute to Sustainable Peace*, Honolulu: Blue Pine, pp. 85–123.

183 Although the *Judaika kyō* 樹提伽經 itself is now lost, its *gāthā* quoted in the *Hōon jurin* 法苑珠林 (ch. *Fǎyuàn zhūlín*) by Dōse 道世 (ch. *Dàoshì*) includes the following two lines, "Regarding birth in heaven, the ten good deeds make one attain birth in heaven, regarding birth as a human being the five precepts enable one to be born as a human being." *Taishō daizōkyō*, Vol. 53, p. 680.

184 This Sūtra known as *Makebiku kyō* 魔化比丘經 is no longer extant, but its passage quoted in the *Benshō ron* 辯正論 (ch. *Biànzhèng lùn*) by Hōrin 法琳 (ch. *Fǎlín*) says, "The five precepts are the roots

of a human being and the ten good deeds are the seeds of a heavenly being." *Taishō daizōkyō,* Vol. 52, p. 495.

185 The phrase *jōja hissui* 盛者必衰, or "Those who prosper are sure to decline," from the *Heike Monogatari* is part of its most famous passage "The sound of the bell at Jetavana Vihāra conveys the truth that those who prosper are sure to decline." The second phrase from the *Taiheiki*, "those who meet are certain to part," is believed to have its origin in a phrase found in the *Yuikyō gyō* 遺教經: *ehitsu uri* 会必有離, "Meeting is always accompanied by parting." *Taishō daizōkyō,* Vol. 12, p. 389.

186 *Shinshū shōgyō zensho,* Vol. I, p. 35.

187 *Ōjō raisan ge* 往生禮讚偈 (ch. *Wǎngshēng lǐzàn jì*), or *Liturgy for Birth,* by Shàndǎo. *Shinshū shōgyō zensho,* Vol. I, p. 652.

188 *Iō ni munin* 易往而無人 in Japanese. *Shinshū shōgyō zensho,* Vol. I, p. 31.

189 *Shinshū shōgyō zensho,* Vol. II, p. 580. *Songō shinzō meimon* 尊号真像銘文, or *Annotated Inscriptions on Sacred Scrolls,* is a collection of Shinran's commentaries on sacred passages inscribed on calligraphic scrolls of the Buddha-Name or Pure Land masters' images. For another translation see *The Collected Works of Shinran,* Jōdo Shinshū Hongwanji-ha, Kyoto, 1997, p. 496.

190 *Shinshū shōgyō zensho,* Vol. II, p. 492. *The Jōdo wasan,* verse 55.

191 *Shinshū shōgyō zensho,* Vol. II, p. 496. *The Jōdo wasan,* verse 88.

192 *Shinshū shōgyō zensho,* Vol. II, p. 486. *The Jōdo wasan,* verse 3.

193 A brief explanation of the origin of the notion of *Dharma-kāya.* Although the Buddha's physical body (*rūpa-kāya*) had long since passed away, the truth (*Dharma*) he taught still remained, working within his indirect disciples. In Mahāyāna Buddhism people thought that the essence, or the true body, of the Buddha was the Dharma and called it *Dharma-kāya.* Even after Gautama Buddha's death, the *Dharmakāya,* in the eyes of Gautama's indirect disciples, is still constantly working with Wisdom and Love, two essential aspects of the Buddha. The *Dharma-kāya* in itself has no form and is beyond description. Because the *Dharma-kāya* is formless, it assumes every possible form. Therefore the *Dharma-kāya* provides itself with form. See *Appendix 2* and *Appendix 3.*

194 *Shinshū shōgyō zensho,* Vol. I, pp. 336–7. The English translation quoted is from *The Kyōgyōshinshō* by Shinran, D. T. Suzuki, trans., p. 189.

195 Regarding the relationship between *Dharma-kāya* as Dharma-in-itself, *hosshō hosshin* 法性法身, and *Dharma-kāya* in its manifested form, 方便法身 *hōbenhosshin,* see *Appendix 2* and *Appendix 3.*

196 *Shinshū shōgyō zensho,* Vol. III, pp. 24–5. See *Appendix 2.*

197 This phrase is originally from the *Shǐjì* 史記 by Sīmǎ Qiān 司馬遷, Chapter 82.

198 Refer to the author's previous commentary in *Chapter 23* on the eighth letter of Fascicle Two in which I discuss in more detail the reasons why Amida Buddha is regarded as the original teacher of all the other Buddhas.

199 *Shinshū shōgyō zensho*, Vol. II,
p. 5. The translation taken from
The Kyōgyōshinshō by Shinran,
D. T. Suzuki, trans., p. 15.

200 *Rennyo Shōnin zenshū,* Vol. 4,
p. 24. *Mukashi monogatari ki* 昔
物語記, Article 20, *Shinshū shiryō
shūsei*, Vol. 2, p. 612.

201 This phrase is from *The Meditation
Sūtra. Shinshū shōgyō zensho*,
Vol. I, pp. 55–6.

202 This is also from *The Meditation
Sūtra. Shinshū shōgyō zensho*,
Vol. I, p. 56.

203 Quoted from *The Commentary on
The Treatise* by Tánluán. *Shinshū
shōgyō zensho*, Vol. I, p. 301.

204 *Shinshū shōgyō zensho*, Vol. II,
p. 527.

205 Regarding the details of this false
teaching, see *Chapter 13*.

206 *Shinshū shōgyō zensho*, Vol. II,
pp. 773–4. The English translation
is from Kemmyo Taira Sato, *Great
Living: In the Pure Encounter
between Mater and Disciple*, p. 33.

207 *Shinshū shōgyō zensho*, Vol. II,
p. 774. The English translation is
from K. T. Sato, *Great Living*, p. 33.

208 *Shinshū shōgyō zensho*, Vol. II,
pp. 774–5. The English translation
is from K. T. Sato, *Great Living*,
p. 33.

209 The *Kuden shō* 口傳鈔 by Kakunyo
覚如, third Head Priest of Honganji,
Shinshū shōgyō zensho, Vol. III,
pp. 3–4.

210 The *Jōdo kenmon shū* 浄土見聞集
by Zonkaku 存覚, *Shinshū shōgyō
zensho*, Vol. III, pp. 378–9.

211 The names of the eight hells are
Saṃjīvaḥ (*Tōkatsu*), Kālasūtraḥ
(*Kokujō*), Saṃghātaḥ (*Shūgo*),

Rauravaḥ (*Kyōkan*), Mahārauravaḥ
(*Daikyōkan*), Tāpanaḥ (*Shōnetsu*),
Pratāpanaḥ (*Daishōnetsu*) and
Avīci (*Muken*).

212 The *Shōbōnen sho kyō* 正法念
處經 (skt. *Saddharma-smṛty-
upasthāna*, ch. *Zhèngfǎniàn chù
jīng*), *Taishō daizōkyō*, Vol. 17,
pp. 1–417.

213 "The Sūtra" refers to *The Kan
muryōju kyō* 觀無量壽經 (ch. *Guān
wúliángshòu jīng*), *The Meditation
Sūtra* or *The Contemplation Sūtra*
in English, *Shinshū shōgyō zensho*,
Vol. I, p. 57.

214 For more detailed explanations, see
the author's comments in *Chapters
22, 30, 67* and *Appendix 4*.

215 The original Japanese phrase
for this expression "Help me
attain Rebirth!" is *goshō tasuke
tamae* 後生助けたまへ, which
is characteristic of Rennyo and
frequently appears in his letters
and some records of his words.

216 The Japanese original for "secret
teachings," *hijibōmon* 秘事法
門, refers to heterodoxies that
diverged from Shinran's orthodox
teaching. At the early stage of Shin
Buddhist tradition they were called
"midnight teachings" or "hidden
doctrines" as they would often be
conveyed at night secretly. From
the traditional viewpoint based
on Shinran's religious philosophy,
"secret teachings" are misleading
and dangerous.

217 *The Letters*, Fascicle 3, Letter
Three. *Shohan-taikō gojō ofumi
teihon*, Masamaru Inaba, p. 52.
Shinshū shiryō shūsei, Vol. 2,
p. 200.

218 *Rennyo Shōnin ibun*, Masamaru
Inaba, ed., p. 488. *Shinshū shiryō
shūsei*, Vol. 2, p. 313.

219 *Rennyo Shōnin engi* 蓮如上人縁起, or *The Account of Rennyo Shōnin,* by Senkei 先啓 (1719–1797) is an historical record of Rennyo's words and deeds based on comparatively trustworthy resources.

220 *Rennyo Shōnin engi* by Senkei. *Shinshū zensho* 真宗全書, Vol. 69, Zōkyō Shoin, Kyoto, 1925, fascicle four, pp. 228–9.

221 *Shinshū shōgyō zensho*, Vol. II, pp. 776–7. Chapter 15 of *The Tanni shō* severely criticises the erroneous view that, through attaining faith, a Shin Buddhist follower can become a Buddha in this earthly body. See Kemmyo Taira Sato, *Great Living: In the Encounter between Master and Disciple*, pp. 120–7.

222 *The Gaija shō* 改邪鈔, or *The Passages to Correct the Erroneous Views*, by Kakunyo also criticises the aforementioned wrong view. *Shinshū shōgyō zensho*, Vol. III, pp. 84–6.

223 *Hogo no uragaki* 反故の裏書, or "Writings on the Back of Wastepaper," by Kensei 顯誓. In the *Hogo no uragaki* Kensei describes Nyodō as the originator of the secret teachings who continued to cause a lot of problems in the Shin Buddhist tradition. *Shinshū shōgyō zensho*, Vol. III, p. 984.

224 *Senshōji Ryakuengi* 専照寺略縁起, *The Abridged Story of Senshōji*. Senshōji is the Head Temple of the Sanmontoha school founded by Nyodō. The whole document is quoted in *The Shinshū Zenshi* 真宗全史 by Senshō Murakami (1851–1929), Heigo Shuppansha, Tokyo, 1916, pp. 340–1.

225 The original Japanese term for "ignorant being's body" is *bonjin* 凡身, meaning "the body of an ordinary ignorant person", whilst

that for "Buddha-body" is *busshin* 佛身, referring to "the Body of a Buddha, one who is enlightened." Of course, it is after birth in the Pure Land that "leaving our 'ignorant being's body' we will realise the 'Buddha-body'" by virtue of Amida's Original Vow.

226 *Shinshū shōgyō zensho*, Vol. III, pp. 645–6.

227 Ryūkan's three works, *Gose monogatari* 後世物語, *Ichinen tanen funbetsu ji* 一念多念分別事 and *Jiriki tariki ji* 自力他力事, are found in *Shinshū shōgyō zensho*, Vol. II, pp. 757–5, pp. 766–9 and pp. 770–2, respectively.

228 The Sanskrit term *icchantika*, *issendai* 一闡提 in Japanese (ch. *yīchǎntí*), originally means those who follow their cravings and desires. In Buddhism it refers to those who are destitute of Buddha-nature due to their selfish views and wrongdoings. There has been much discussion about whether they have any possibility to become a Buddha. Shinran states in *The Jōdo monrui jushō* 浄土文類聚鈔, "Those who slander the Dharma and those who are devoid of Buddha-nature, when they have spiritual reformation, all go to the Pure Land." *Shinshū shōgyō zensho*, Vol. II, p. 448.

229 See *Appendix 2*.

230 See *Appendix 4*.

231 Junsei 順誓 (1421–1510), one of Rennyo's disciples, who is well known by another name, Hōkyō 法敬.

232 *Rennyo Shōnin zenshū*, Vol. 4, pp. 15–6. *Daihasso onmonogatari Kūzen kikigaki*, Article 34, *Shinshū shiryō shūsei*, Vol. 2, pp. 431–2.

233 *Gengō kyō* 賢劫經 (ch. *Xiánjié jīng*), *Ninnō kyō* 仁王經 (ch. *Rénwáng jīng*), *and Nehan gyō* 涅槃經 (ch. *Nièpán jīng*), or *Nirvāṇa Sūtra*. All these sūtras follow the view that the age of the right Dharma lasted for 500 years. Shinran's calculation is based on this view.

234 *Shinshū shōgyō zensho*, Vol. II, p. 516. *The Shōzōmatsu wasan*, verse 2.

235 *Shinshū shōgyō zensho*, Vol. II, p. 516. *The Shōzōmatsu wasan*, verse 3.

236 *Shinshū shōgyō zensho*, Vol. II, p. 517. *The Shōzōmatsu wasan*, verse 8.

237 *Shinshū shōgyō zensho*, Vol. II, p. 517. *The Shōzōmatsu wasan*, verse 9.

238 The fifth five hundred year period since Śākyamuni's death. According to a doctrinal explanation of the Buddhist eschatology found in the *Daijikkyō* 大集經 (ch. *Dàjíjīng*, skt. *Mahasamnipata Sūtra*), *Taishō daizōkyō* Vol. 13 – No.397, there is a decline in the quality of Buddhist spirituality with the passage of time from the first five hundred years following the death of the Buddha to the fifth five hundred years.

239 *Shinshū shōgyō zensho*, Vol. II, p. 517. *The Shōzōmatsu wasan*, verse 11.

240 *Shinshū shōgyō zensho*, Vol. II, p. 519. *The Shōzōmatsu wasan*, verse 25.

241 *Shinshū shōgyō zensho*, Vol. II, p. 519. *The Shōzōmatsu wasan*, verse 28.

242 *Ofumi ryakuge* 御文略解 by E'nen 惠然 (1693–1764), five volume woodblock print edition, Nishimura Kurōemon, Kyoto, 1888, Vol. 3, pp. 5 left – 6 left. E'nen's description of Rennyo's stay for three days seems to be based on the *Ofumi Gōshōji no ki*, an older handwritten record on *The Letters*, kept in the Library of Otani University, pp. 16 right – 16 left.

243 Regarding a number of 'secret teachings' prevailing at that time in Echizen Province, refer to the author's translation of a paragraph from the *Rennyo Shōnin engi* 蓮如上人縁起, or *The Account of Rennyo Shōnin*, by Senkei, quoted in the author's commentary on the fourteenth letter of Fascicle Two, entitled *On Secret Teachings*.

244 *Rennyo Shōnin engi* 蓮如上人縁起 by Senkei. *Shinshū zensho* 真宗全書, Vol. 69, Zōkyō Shoin, Kyoto, 1925, fascicle four, p. 229.

245 Ibid., pp. 228–9.

246 Devadatta, Daibadatta 提婆達多 (ch. *Típódáduō*), is Śākyamuni Buddha's cousin and Ānanda's elder brother, who was originally Śākyamuni's disciple but later turned against him and tried to kill him. Amongst all kinds of vile acts he committed, the worst was the instigation he gave Prince Ajātaśatru to kill his father King Bimbisāra and rule the country together with him. Generally speaking, he is considered to be an *icchantika*, one who is devoid of the seed of Buddha-nature. In Shin Buddhism, however, the story is that, as he was falling into hell, his thoughts went out to the Buddha and, at that very last moment he cried, "Namu!" and found himself embraced in the Buddha's unconditional love. This sequel is understood to be very important. Thus Shinran states in the preface to his main writing *Kyōgyōshinshō*, "When the conditions were maturing for the Pure Land,

Devadatta succeeded in persuading King Ajātaśatru to commit a deadly crime. Thereupon, Śākyamuni came out into the world to make the mind of Vaidehī turn toward the Land of Peace and Happiness." *Shinshū shōgyō zensho*, Vol. II, p. 1. The translation quoted is from *The Kyōgyōshinshō* by Shinran, D. T. Suzuki, trans., p. 3.

247 The original Japanese term for "miscellaneous practices" is *zōgyō* 雑行 and that for "miscellaneous good acts" is *zōzen* 雑善, both referring to all kinds of practice and good unrelated to the teaching of birth in Amida's Pure Land.

248 *Rennyo Shōnin zenshū*, Vol. 4, p. 3. *Daihasso onmonogatari Kūzen kikigaki*, Article 57, *Shinshū shiryō shūsei*, Vol. 2, p. 426.

249 *Shinshū shōgyō zensho*, Vol. II, p. 103. The translation quoted is from *The Kyōgyōshinshō* by Shinran, D. T. Suzuki, trans., p. 175.

250 *Jōgai gobunshō* 帖外御文章, *The Letters Not Compiled in The Five Fascicle Version*, compiled in the *Shinshū shōgyō zensho*, Vol. V.

251 *Jōgai gobunshō*, *Shinshū shōgyō zensho*, Vol. V, pp. 335–6.

252 *Jōgai gobunshō*, *Shinshū shōgyō zensho*, Vol. V, p. 366. "Sūtras" in the quotation are said in the Shin Buddhist tradition to mean those such as *The Avataṃsaka Sūtra*, *The Laṅkāvatāra Sūtra*, and *The Pratyutpanna Samādhi Sūtra* (*The Hanju zanmai kyo*).

253 *Rennyo Shōnin zenshū*, Vol. 4, p. 54. *Jitsugo kyūki*, Article 108, *Shinshū shiryō shūsei*, Vol. 2, p. 453.

254 "The passage on the fulfilment of the Vow" refers to the passage on the fulfilment of the Eighteenth Vow in *The Larger Sūtra of Eternal Life*: "All beings, on hearing that Name, rejoice in the awakening of faith at least for one thought-moment. It is indeed from Amida's sincere mind that all this has been transferred to them. Desiring to be born in that land, they are immediately born there at that moment and abide in the stage of nonretrogression." *Shinshū shōgyō zensho*, Vol. I, p. 24.

255 *Shinshū shōgyō zensho*, Vol. II, p. 522. *Shōzōmatsu wasan*, verse 51.

256 *Shinshū shōgyō zensho*, Vol. II, p. 44. A phrase from *The Shōshinge*, a part of Shinran's main writing, *Kyōgyōshinshō*.

257 The Shèlùn School 摄論宗 (jp. Shōronshū), one of the thirteen Chinese Buddhist schools, founded by Paramārtha 真諦 (499–569), translator of *The Mahāyānasaṃgraha* (摄大乗論 Shèng dàchéng lùn) by Asaṅga 無着 (310–390). The School is based on this very famous Buddhist document that comprises the Consciousness Only philosophy.

258 *Shinshū shōgyō zensho*, Vol. II, p. 22.

259 *Shinshū shōgyō zensho*, Vol. II, p. 22.

260 *Shinshū shōgyō zensho*, Vol. II, p. 22.

261 *Shinshū shōgyō zensho*, Vol. II, p. 567. *Songō shinzō meimon*, or *Annotated Inscriptions on Sacred Scrolls*.

262 The translation in *Rennyo* by the authors Minor L. Rogers and Ann T. Rogers of *hotsugan ekō* as "to aspire to be born and direct virtue" cannot be considered entirely correct in this special context.

263 *Shinshū shōgyō zensho*, Vol. II, p. 522. *The Shōzōmatsu wasan,* verse 51.

264 *Shinshū shōgyō zensho*, Vol. II, p. 44.

265 *Shinshū shōgyō zensho*, Vol. I, p. 522. The quoted sentence is originally a part of the following passage, "Firstly 'close relationship' should be clarified. When sentient beings undertake practice, if they always recite the Buddha through their 'mouth', he hears them do so, if they always pay respect to him by their 'body', he sees them do so, and, if they always think of him with their 'mind', he knows them to do so. When they are mindful of him, he is also mindful of them. His three acts and their three acts are not separate from each other."

266 Regarding the *Anjin ketsujō shō* 安心決定鈔 or *The Decisive Attainment of Peaceful Awareness,* its author is unknown, but it is believed to be a work written by someone who belonged to the Seizan School, one of the Japanese Pure Land schools.

267 *Rennyo Shōnin zenshū,* Vol. 4, pp. 79–80. *Jitsugo kyūki, Article 186, Shinshū shiryō shūsei,* Vol. 2, p. 462.

268 *Gangan shō* 願々鈔, or *The Commentary on Vows,* by Kakunyo deals with the most important passages from *The Sūtra of Eternal Life* such as the 11th, 12th, 13th, 17th and 18th Vows and the Fulfilment of the 18th Vow. *Shinshū shōgyō zensho,* Vol. III, pp. 44–9.

269 *Shinshū shōgyō zensho*, Vol. III, pp. 45–6.

270 This unpublished passage is from one of the fragmentary notes D. T. Suzuki wrote down when he translated *The Kyōgyōshinshō* towards the end of his life.

271 The phrase "in his causal stage" refers to when Amida Buddha was still a Bodhisattva known as Bodhisattva Dharmākara.

272 *Shinshū shōgyō zensho,* Vol. II, p. 44. A phrase from *The Shōshinge,* a part of Shinran's main writing, *Kyōgyōshinshō.*

273 See also the author's commentary in *Chapter 29* on the 14th letter of Fascicle Two.

274 In *The Letters* (Five Fascicle Version) Rennyo broaches this same problem on three separate occasions: in the 13th letter of Fascicle One, in the 11th letter of Fascicle Two and again in this, the 8th letter of Fascicle Three.

275 See *Chapter 26*, the 11th letter of Fascicle Two.

276 From a series of lectures by Kemmyo Taira Sato on *The Shōshinge,* unpublished.

277 *Buddha of Infinite Light* by D. T. Suzuki, revised by Taitetsu Unno, Shambhala Publications, Boston, London, 1997, pp. 29–30.

278 The Japanese original for "our master" is わが聖人, literally, "our Shōnin."

279 From *Ōjō raisan ge* 往生禮讃偈 by Shàndǎo. *Shinshū shōgyō zensho,* Vol. I, p. 661.

280 *Hōonkō shiki* 報恩講式, a liturgy to praise the great work of Shinran, the founder of Shin Buddhism, written by Kakunyo, his great grandson, to read out at memorial services for Shinran such as Hōonkō, in which followers express their gratitude to Shinran

for what he has done for them. *Shinshū shōgyō zensho*, Vol. III, pp. 655–60.

281 According to the *Shinshū shiryō shūsei*, Vol. 2, forty out of the ninety-one dated letters written during his stay at Yoshizaki were compiled in *The Letters* (the Five Fascicle Version). The figure 'ninety-one' includes several slightly different versions.

282 A letter not compiled in the Five Fascicle Version. *Rennyo Shōnin ibun*, Masamaru Inaba ed., pp. 103–5. *Shinshū shiryō shūsei*, Vol. 2, p. 158.

283 The theory of *honji suijaku* 本地垂迹 (ch. *běndì chuíjī*) is the traditional Buddhist view of gods, including *kami*, or Japanese Shintō gods, as manifestations of Buddhas or Bodhisattvas. The origin of this kind of view can be traced back to the Nara Period and even further to early Chinese Buddhism.

284 *Maka shikan* 摩訶止觀 (ch. *Móhē zhǐguān*) by Chigi 智顗 (ch. Zhìyǐ, 538–97). *Taishō daizōkyō*, Vol. 46, p. 80. The original passage in the *Móhē zhǐguān* is "'Softening the light and conforming to the dust' is the first step in forming relationships; 'Attaining Enlightenment by going through the eight stages' refers to the completion of act for benefiting sentient beings." While the first phrase "Softening the light and conforming to the dust" is from Lǎozǐ's *Dàodéjīng*, the second phrase "Attaining Enlightenment by going through the eight stages" is a Buddhist statement that describes how Śākyamuni Buddha attained Enlightenment in this world. The eight stages he went through are said to be 'coming down from the *Tuṣita* Heaven, entering his mother's womb, coming out of it, leaving home, subjugating demons, attaining

enlightenment, teaching people and entering *parinirvāṇa*'.

285 Lǎozǐ's *Dàodéjīng* 道德經, Chapter 56.

286 *Shojin hongai shū* 諸神本懷集 by Zonkaku, *Shinshū kana shōgyō*, Hōzōkan, Kyoto, 1932, pp. 556–87. Also, *Shinshū shiryō shūsei*, Vol. 1, pp. 697–712.

287 Fifteen *Genze riyaku wasan* 現世利益和讃 or *Verses on Benefits in the Present Life* are found in the *Jōdo wasan* 浄土和讃, or *Verses of the Pure Land*, composed by Shinran. *Shinshū shōgyō zensho*, Vol. II, pp. 497–9.

288 *Shinshū shōgyō zensho*, Vol. II, p. 498. *The Jōdo wasan*, verse 106.

289 *Shinshū shōgyō zensho*, Vol. II, p. 499. *The Jōdo wasan*, verse 109.

290 *Shinshū shōgyō zensho*, Vol. II, p. 498. *The Jōdo wasan*, verse 107.

291 *Shinshū shōgyō zensho*, Vol. II, p. 165.

292 *Shōbō nen sho kyō* 正法念處經 (skt. *Saddharma-smṛty upasthāna*, ch. *Zhèngfǎniàn chù jīng*) or *Sūtra of Right Mindfulness*, *Taishō daizōkyō*, Vol. 17, p. 342.

293 In the commentary in *Chapter 17* on the second letter of Fascicle Two, the author likewise cited Shinran Shōnin's advice to his followers not to reveal their faith even if branded a 'cattle thief.' Regarding an interesting story of "a cattle thief" found in a Buddhist sūtra known as *The Zōho zō kyō*, see the author's comment on the same subject in *Chapter 17*.

294 These two quotations are from *The Larger Sūtra of Eternal Life*, *Shinshū shōgyō zensho*, Vol. I, pp. 27 and 46.

295 From Shàndǎo's *Exposition of The Meditation Sūtra, Shinshū shōgyō zensho*, Vol. I, p. 507.

296 From Shinran's *Kyōgyōshinshō, Shinshū shōgyō zensho*, Vol. II, p. 1.

297 *Shinshū shōgyō zensho*, Vol. I, p. 24.

298 In *The Kyōgyōshinshō* there is a special section where Shinran discusses the identity and difference between Vasubandhu's "One Mind" and the "triple mind" of the Original Vow, *Shinshū shōgyō zensho*, Vol. II, p. 59.

299 From Vasubandhu's *Treatise on The Pure Land. Shinshū shōgyō zensho*, Vol. I, p. 269.

300 *Shinshū shōgyō zensho*, Vol. II, p. 775. Quoted translation is from Kemmyo Taira Sato, *Great Living: In the Pure Encounter between Master and Disciple*, p. 39.

301 *Rennyo* by Minor L. Rogers and Ann T. Rogers, Asian Humanities Press, Berkeley, note 30 of Fascicle Two, pp. 187–8.

302 See *Appendix 2*.

303 The original Japanese for "the *Dharmatā* of eternal bliss" is *hosshō jōraku* 法性常楽, a description of the Pure Land. *Hosshō* or *Dharmatā* means Dharma itself or Dharma in itself and that is eternal and blissful.

304 Vaidehī, Idaike 韋提希 (ch. Wéitíxī), was the wife of King Bimbisāra of Magadha and mother of Prince Ajātaśatru. When her husband was imprisoned by Ajātaśatru, Queen Vaidehī asked Śākyamuni Buddha to teach her for her salvation. The Budda visited her and expounded *The Meditation Sūtra*. See *Note 246* on Devadatta in *Chapter 34*.

305 Devadatta, Daibadatta 提婆達多 (ch. Típódáduō) or Daiba 提婆 (ch. Típó). See *Note 246* on Devadatta in *Chapter 34*.

306 Ajātaśatru, Ajase 阿闍世 (ch. Āshéshì), was the son of King Bimbisāra and usurper of his throne. At the instigation of Devadatta he imprisoned his father to death, but later on the advice of his good friend, Jīvaka, he repented his trangressions and finally took refuge in the Buddha. Thus he became a great supporter of Buddhism. The details of the tragedy of Rājagṛha in which Bimbisāra, Vaidehī, Ajātaśatru and Devadatta were all deeply involved, are described in *The Nirvāṇa Sūtra* and *Meditation Sūtra*. What is of vital importance is the fact that through their encounter with the Buddha they were all saved. See *Note 246* on Devadatta in *Chapter 34*.

307 "Khitan" or Qìdān is the name of a race who established the Liao Dynasty in the northern part of modern-day China around the beginning of tenth century and continued to govern until 1125. After the fall of the Liao Dynasty, they moved to the central Asia and China. This Khitan visitor to Japan during the 15th century was a follower of the Tiāntāi school, a tradition based on *The Lotus Sūtra*, which was already popular in China around that time. It was the reason Rennyo referred to the relationship between the teaching of *Nenbutsu* and *The Lotus Sūtra*.

308 *Rennyo Shōnin Ōseno-jōjō, Article 199, Shinshū shiryō shūsei*, Vol. 2, p. 501.

309 All the details of the Indian tragedy that lies behind *The Meditation Sūtra*, Śākyamuni's teaching at Rājagṛha of Amida Buddha and his Pure Land, are related in *The Nirvāṇa Sūtra*. The figures

involved in the tragedy were all saved through their encounter with Śākyamuni Buddha. In the Shin Buddhist tradition the devotees' awakening of faith, that is the awakening to *ki,* or the sad reality of their karmic existence, and at the same time to *Hō,* or the unconditional love of Amida Buddha, is understood to be given through deep reflection on their family problems, as exemplified by the tragedy of the royal family at Rājagṛha. Regarding this essential point there is a Japanese book, entitled *The Great Rājagṛha* (王舎大城 *Ōshadaijō*), by Reion Takehara, one of the best friends of Jōkan Chikazumi. These two modern Shin Buddhist leaders have something common in emphasising the vital importance of the meaning of the tragedy of Rājagṛha to the awakening of Shin Buddhist faith.

310 *Shinshū shōgyō zensho*, Vol. III, p. 26.

311 *Waka* 和歌, literally meaning "Japanese poem," is the name for a special genre of literature, a 31-syllable Japanese poem.

312 The phrase "The benefit of entering the company of those who are truly assured" is from Shinran's *Kyōgyōshinshō*, *Shinshū shōgyō zensho*, Vol. II, p. 72, and it is originally based on Tánluán's *Commentary on The Treatise*, *Shinshū shōgyō zensho*, Vol. I, p. 324.

313 "Attaining Nirvāṇa without fail" is from *The Larger Sūtra of Eternal Life*, *Shinshū shōgyō zensho*, Vol. I, p. 9.

314 *Ofumi meitō shō* 御文明燈鈔 by Dōon 道隠 (1741–1813), *Shinshū Sōsho* 真宗叢書, Vol. 10, pp. 230–1, and *Ofumi kijishu* 御文記事珠 by Erin 慧琳, woodblock

print edition, pp. 33 left – 34 left, in the possession of Otani University Library.

315 *Ofumi kōjutsu* by Kakuju Yoshitani, Hōzōkan, Kyoto, 1910, pp. 764–5.

316 *Gobunshō kōwa* 御文章講話 by Shirō Sugi 杉紫朗 (1880–1947), Nagata Bunshōdō, Kyoto, p. 223 and *Ofumi kōjutsu* by Kakuju Yoshitani, pp. 766–7.

317 *Shinshū shōgyō zensho*, Vol. II, p. 44. The original Japanese is 憶念彌陀佛本願　自然即時入必定 唯能常稱如来號　應報大悲弘誓恩, a passage from *The Shōshinge*, part of Shinran's *Kyōgyōshinshō*.

318 *Rennyo* by Minor L. Rogers and Ann T. Rogers, p. 223.

319 *Shinshū shōgyō zensho*, Vol. I, p. 24.

320 The texual source of Rennyo's statement, "Indeed, they may serve as a condition leading to the praising of the Buddha Vehicle and as a cause leading to the turning of the Dharma Wheel." Bái Jūyì's original text is found in Erin's *Ofumi kijishu*. Vol. 9, pp. 31 left – 32 left.

321 *Rennyo Shōnin itoku ki* 蓮如上人遺 徳記. *Shinshū shōgyō zensho*, Vol. III, pp. 875–7.

322 *Honganji sahō no shidai* 本願寺 作法之次第, *The Ways of Practice at Honganji*, by Jitsugo. *Rennyo Shōnin zenshū*, Vol. 4, p. 260. Article 58, *Shinshū shiryō shūsei*, Vol. 2, p. 571.

323 *Ōgen nishu no ekō* 往還二種の 廻向. In Shin Buddhism *ekō* 廻 向, or "virtue-transference," is understood as coming from Amida Buddha himself to all sentient beings. Amida directs his great virtues to them for their going

to the Pure Land and for their returning to this world to help others. This is called "two forms of virtue-transference, outgoing and returning."

324 These seven letters read out during the Hōonkō Ceremony are called *Hōonkō Ofumi* 報恩講御文 in the Higashi Honganji tradition, whilst the eleventh letter of Fascicle Five read out twice during the Hōonkō Ceremony is called *Goshōki shō* in the Nishi Honganji tradition.

325 *Taishō daizōkyō,* Vol. 54, p. 307.

326 *Anraku shū* 安楽集 (ch. Ānlè jí), *Passages on the Land of Happiness,* is a commentary on *The Meditation Sūtra* by Dàochuò (jp. Dōshaku) of the Táng Dynasty, one of the seven patriarchs of the Shin Buddhist tradition. In this writing Dàochuò clarified the difference between the Holy Path and the Pure Land Path and exhorted people to practise the latter.

327 *Taishō daizōkyō,* Vol. 13, p. 363.

328 *Shinshū shōgyō zensho,* Vol. I, p. 378.

329 *The Letters,* Fascicle 1, Letter Nine, *Shohan taikō gojō ofumi teihon* by Masamaru Inaba, p. 12, or also *Shinshū shiryō shūsei,* Vol. 2, p. 160.

330 *The Letters,* Fascicle 2, Letter Thirteen, *Shohan taikō gojō ofumi teihon* by Masamaru Inaba, p. 42, or also *Shinshū shiryō shūsei,* Vol. 2, p. 195.

331 The Japanese word *ri* is the unit of distance, equivalent to 3.92 km.

332 *Shinshū shōgyō zensho,* Vol. II, p. 165.

333 *Sangan tennyū* 三願転入, or "Awakening of Faith through Three Vows," refers to the three-step process of development of religious consciousness in Shin Buddhism. Shinran describes his own experience of *sangan tennyū* in *The Kyōgyōshinshō,* Vol. 6. *Shinshū shōgyō zensho,* Vol. II, p. 166. *The Collected Works of Shinran,* p. 240. For more detailed explanation of *sangan tennyū,* see *Great Living: In the Pure Encounter between Master and Disciple* by K. T. Sato, pp. 132–6.

334 *Shinshū shōgyō zensho,* Vol. II, p. 776–7. For the English translation of Chapter 6 of *The Tanni shō,* see *Great Living: In the Pure Encounter between Master and Disciple* by K. T. Sato, p. 58.

335 *Shinshū shōgyō zensho,* Vol. I, p. 457.

336 In this special phrase, *kihō ittai Namu Amida-butsu* 機法一体 南无阿彌陀佛, or "The oneness in *Namu Amida-butsu* of *ki* and *Hō*," the character *ki* 機 means the 'momentum' through which *Hō* 法, or the 'Dharma', starts to work, actually referring to one who is saved by the Dharma. As said in the letter, whilst *ki* refers to "those who take refuge by saying *namu*," *Hō* means "Amida Buddha's Dharma that saves them." Those two, *ki* and *Hō*, become one in *Namu Amida-butsu.* This philosophical expression of the experience of the unity of *ki* and *Hō* in *Namu Amida-butsu* appears quite often in Rennyo's letters.

337 *Rennyo Shōnin zenshū,* Vol. 4, p. 30. *Jitsugo kyūki,* Article 19, *Shinshū shiryō shūsei,* Vol. 2, p. 445.

338 *Rennyo Shōnin zenshū,* Vol. 4, pp. 36–7. *Jitsugo kyūki,* Article 40, *Shinshū shiryō shūsei,* Vol. 2, p. 447.

339 Asahara Saichi (1851–1932) is one of the devout Shin Buddhists

known as *myokonin* 妙好人 and
a great poet who composed more
than ten thousand poems about
his religious experience for about
twenty years since the time of
attainment of faith until the very
end of his life. He loved *The Letters*
by Rennyo and used to read it out
one letter after another towards the
end of his daily service. His poems
show an incredible influence from
The Letters.

340 *Myōkōnin Asahara Saichi shū* 妙
好人浅原才市集, D. T. Suzuki, ed.,
Shunjūsha, Tokyo, 1967, p. 261.

341 *Rennyo Shōnin itoku ki* 蓮如上人遺
徳記, *Shinshū shōgyō zensho*, Vol.
III, pp. 875–6.

342 *Kūzen nikki* 空善日記, *Kūzen's
Diary*, an abbreviation of *Daihasso
onmonogatari Kūzen kikigaki*.
A short description of the epidemic
is found in the *Kūzen nikki*, Article
46, *Shinshū shiryō shūsei*, Vol. 2,
p. 424.

343 The English translation of the
parable used in this context is
from Keimei Takehara's M. A.
dissertation.

344 *Shinshū shōgyō zensho*, Vol. III,
p. 880. Sesshū is another name
for Settsu Province.

345 *Ofumi ryakuge* by E'nen, five
volume woodblock print edition,
Nishimura Kurōemon, Kyoto, 1888,
Vol. 4, p. 28 ,right.

346 *Ofumi raii shō* by E'nin 恵忍 (1693
–1783), Nishimura Kurōemon,
Kyoto, 1898, p. 190.

347 Hōkyō-bō is another name for
Junsei (1421–1510).

348 *Ofumi kōjutsu* by Kakuju Yoshitani,
pp. 835–6.

349 *Shinshū shōgyō zensho*, Vol. I,
p. 410.

350 *Shinshū shōgyō zensho*, Vol. II,
p. 45.

351 *Shinshū shōgyō zensho*, Vol. II,
p. 507. *The Kōsō wasan*, verse 55.
For another translation see *The
Collected Works of Shinran*, p. 375.

352 *Ofumi raii shō* by E'nin, Nishimura
Kurōemon, Kyoto, 1898,
pp. 195–7.

353 *Rennyo Shōnin ibun*, Masamaru
Inaba, ed., pp. 376–7. *Shinshū
shiryō shūsei*, Vol. 2, p. 264.

354 Both the *Honganji sahō no
shidai* 本願寺作法之次第 and the
*Yamashina gobō no koto narabini
sono jidai no koto* 山科御坊事
并其時代事 were recorded and
compiled by Jitsugo, Rennyo's
tenth son. Regarding those
relevant four articles, Articles
45, 49 and 53 of the former and
Article 7 of the latter, see *Shinshū
shiryō shūsei*, Vol. 2, p. 569, pp.
569–70, p. 570 and pp. 544–45,
respectively.

355 *Chionkō shiki* 知恩講私記, or
*The Liturgy to Remember What
Has Been Done [by Hōnen
Shōnin]*, is a biographical liturgy
to commemorate Hōnen Shōnin.
Shinshū shōgyō zensho, Vol. V,
pp. 715–19.

356 *Tandoku mon* 嘆徳文, *A Liturgy
to Praise the Virtues [of Shinran
Shōnin]*) by Zonkaku. *Shinshū
shōgyō zensho*, Vol. III,
pp. 661–3.

357 *Boki eshi* 慕帰絵詞 is a biography
of Kakunyo by Jūkaku (1295–
1360), the second son of Kakunyo.
Shinshū shōgyō zensho, Vol. III,
pp. 769–815.

358 *Ichinen tanen funbetsu ji* 一念
多念分別事, *On the Difference
between One Recitation and Many
Recitations*, is an important essay
written by Ryūkan that was highly

esteemed by Shinran. *Shinshū shōgyō zensho*, Vol. II, pp. 666–9.

359 *Jiriki tariki ji* 自力他力事, or *On Self-Power and Other Power*, is also another important document written by Ryūkan that was highly esteemed by Shinran. *Shinshū shōgyō zensho*, Vol. II, pp. 770–2.

360 Zenshin Mita, *Hōnen Shōnin shoden no kenkyū* 法然聖人諸傳の研究, or *A Study of the Various Biographies of Hōnen Shōnin*, Kyoto: Heirakuji Shoten, 1966, pp. 141–56.

361 Rensei 蓮誓 (1455–1521) was Rennyo's fourth son, Head Priest of Kōkyōji Temple at Yamada.

362 *Rennyo Shōnin zenshū*, Vol. 4, p. 255. *Honganji sahō no shidai*, Article 45, *Shinshū shiryō shūsei*, Vol. 2, p. 569.

363 Zenshin Mita, *Hōnen Shōnin shoden no kenkyū*, p. 142.

364 *Shinshū shōgyō zensho*, Vol. II, p. 513. *The Jōdo wasan*, verse 101.

365 *Shinshū shōgyō zensho*, Vol. I, p. 652.

366 *Shinshū shōgyō zensho*, Vol. I, p. 538.

367 *Tripitaka*, literally, "three baskets," means three divisions of Buddhist scriptures: 1. *sūtra*, the Buddha's teachings, 2. *vinaya*, his precepts and 3. *abhidharma*, the commentaries on those documents. Taken together the term refers to the entire corpus of Buddhist documents.

368 *Shinshū shōgyō zensho*, Vol. II, p. 202.

369 *Shinshū shōgyō zensho*, Vol. II, p. 769.

370 *Rennyo Shōnin zenshū*, Vol. 4,

p. 146. *Daihasso onmonogatari Kūzen kikigaki*, Article 117, *Shinshū shiryō shūsei*, Vol. 2, p. 434.

371 *Rennyo Shōnin zenshū*, Vol. 4, p. 146. *Daihasso onmonogatari Kūzen kikigaki*, Article 118, *Shinshū shiryō shūsei*, Vol. 2, p. 434.

372 *Rennyo Shōnin zenshū*, Vol. 4, p. 149. *Daihasso onmonogatari Kūzen kikigaki*, Article 130, *Shinshū shiryō shūsei*, Vol. 2, p. 435.

373 *Shinshū shōgyō zensho*, Vol. III, pp. 880–1.

374 *Shinshū shōgyō zensho*, Vol. III, pp. 881–2.

375 *Rennyo Shōnin zenshū*, Vol. 4, pp. 145–6. *Daihasso onmonogatari Kūzen kikigaki*, Article 116, *Shinshū shiryō shūsei*, Vol. 2, p. 434.

376 *Kanmuryōjukyō shijōsho dentsūki nyūshō* 觀無量壽經四帖疏傳通記糅鈔 by Shōgei 聖冏 (1341–1420), *Jōdoshū zensho* 浄土宗全書, Jōdoshū Shūten Kankōkai, Tokyo, 1908, Vol. 3, p. 935.

377 *Shinshū shōgyō zensho*, Vol. II, p. 778. Translation is from *Great Living: In the Pure Encounter between Master and Disciple* by K. T. Sato, p. 76.

378 One of them, in *The Compilation of Copies* [of Rennyo's letters] by Dōshū at Gyōtokuji Temple in Toyama Prefecture, states, "Written on the 10th of April in the seventh year of the Meiō period *inu-uma* (1498) at the age of eighty-four." Another, in the Najio version of *The Letters* by Rennyo stored at Kyōgyōji Temple in Ōsaka, says, "Written by an old man of eighty-four during the middle ten days of April of the seventh year of the Meiō period."

379 *Myōkōnin Asahara Saichi shū*,
D. T. Suzuki, ed., p. 447.

380 *Myōkōnin Asahara Saichi shū*,
p. 303.

381 *Asahara Saichi-ō o kataru* 浅原才
市翁を語る by Edatsu Teramoto,
Chiyoda Gakuen, Tokyo, 1952,
pp. 88–9.

382 *Shinshū shōgyō zensho*, Vol. I,
p. 457.

383 *Shinshū shōgyō zensho*, Vol. II,
p. 22.

384 *Shinshū shōgyō zensho*, Vol. I,
p. 588. *Songō shinzō meimon*,
or *Annotated Inscriptions on
Sacred Scrolls.*

385 D. T. Suzuki loves this poem.
Unfortunately, the original version
to this English translation cannot
be found anywhere amongst
the remaining scripts by Saichi
himself. Most probably it is now
lost. Fortunately, on the other
hand, we can find a very similar
version in the *Myōkōnin Asahara
Saichi shū*, D. T. Suzuki ed., p. 174.
This will be translated as follows:
"In Other Power / No self power, no
Other Power / All around is Other
Power / *Namu Amida-butsu.*"

386 When referred to as Ōsaka-dono
大坂殿, the suffix "dono" conveys
a sense of respect for the temple.
This honorific form applies to
buildings such as a temple as well
as their residents. Ōsaka-gobō 大坂
御坊 means the Ōsaka temple,
the word "*gobō*" being an honorific
for a Buddhist temple.

387 The ninth Head Priest of Honganji
is Jitsunyo Shōnin 實如上人
(1458–1525), Rennyo's fifth son,
and the tenth Head Priest is 證如上
人 Shōnyo Shōnin (1516–1554),
one of Jitsunyo's grandchildren.

388 Rokkaku Sadayori 六角定頼
(1495–1552), the fourth son of the
warrior lord Rokkaku Takayori 六
角高頼 (1462–1520).

389 *Shinshū shōgyō zensho*, Vol. III,
p. 880.

390 *Tennōji Shōtoku Taishi miraiki* 天
王寺聖徳太子未来記 or *The Tennōji
Record of the Predictions by Prince
Shōtoku.*

391 *Shinshū shōgyō zensho*, Vol. III,
pp. 972–3.

392 *Rennyo Shōnin zenshū*, Vol. 4,
p. 147. *Daihasso onmonogatari
Kūzen kikigaki*, Article 123,
Shinshū shiryō shūsei, Vol. 2,
p. 434.

393 *Rennyo Shōnin zenshū*, Vol. 4,
pp. 84–5. *Jitsugo kyūki*, Article
201, *Shinshū shiryō shūsei*, Vol. 2,
p. 464.

394 *Shinshū shōgyō zensho*, Vol. I,
p. 24.

395 Kōgatsuin Jinrei 香月院深
励 (1749–1817) explains in his
commentary on the first letter of
Fascicle One in the *Ofumi kōgi* 御
文講義 (*Shinshū zensho* 真宗全
書, Vol. 49, pp. 29–30) that in *The
Letters* by Rennyo the word *mōsu*
is used in the following four senses:
1. "To say or speak in words." For
example, "to say" the *Nenbutsu*.
2. "To be or to be defined as." For
example, Amida "is" or "is defined
as" the Buddha of Eternal Life. 3.
An auxiliary word added to a verb
to convey the sense of respect to
those spoken to. For example, I
have "humbly" brought this present
to you or we "respectfully" visit
the temple. 4. "To entreat" or "to
ask." For example, we "entreat"
the Buddha to save us. In classical
books the Chinese character 請

which means "entreat," "beg,"
or "implore" is actually read in
Japanese as *mōsu* and there
are a great many examples of the
use of this Japanese word in
the Shin Buddhist tradition in the
sense of "to entreat," "to ask"
or "request": *ofumimōsu* means
to ask for a letter (*ofumi*) and
mieimōsu means to request a
portrait (*miei*). *Mōshifumi* means
a letter (*fumi*) by which to make a
request (*mōshi*). *Moshigyo* means
asking for the chanting of Sūtras
(*gyo*). *Mōshimono nikki* means the
journal (*nikki*) [of the head temple]
in which requests (*mōshimono*) [by
the branch temples] are recorded.

396 *Ruizō shū* 類雑集, Vol. 5,
woodblock print edition, p. 59
right – p. 59 left.

397 Hakusan is a group of high
mountains in Hokuriku District,
extending over four prefectures,
Toyama, Ishikawa, Fukui and Gifu.

398 *Nanto* 南都 and *Hokurei* 北嶺
refer to "the Southern Capital,"
Nara, and "the Northern
Mountain," or Mount Hiei north
of Kyoto, respectively. These two
places were major academic
centres for Buddhist monks.

399 *Shinshū shōgyō zensho*, Vol. II,
pp. 773–4. Translation taken
from *Great Living: In the Pure
Encounter between Master and
Disciple* by K. T. Sato, p. 33.

400 K. T. Sato, *Great Living*, pp. 35–6.

401 *Shinshū shōgyō zensho*, Vol. I, p. 9.

402 *Shinshū shōgyō zensho*, Vol. I,
p. 65. In *The Meditation Sūtra*
aspirants for the Pure Land are
classified into the nine different
levels, namely the three grades
of the three ranks. "Those at
the lowest grade of the lowest
rank" means the vilest amongst

wrongdoers. Despite this
categorisation, according to
Shinran's profound interpretation,
Śākyamuni Buddha's emphasis on
the recitation of the Buddha-Name
towards the end of the *Sūtra* makes
it clear that these nine levels are
degrees in the process of deepening
awareness of a single person, in
which the sad reality of our karmic
existence becomes increasingly
revealed to us. The Shin Buddhist
tradition places great emphasis
on the universal deliverance of all
sentient beings through Amida's
unconditional love that has no
discrimination at all, even against
the vilest of wrongdoers.

403 This special formula, *Namu
Amida-butsu* 南无阿彌陀佛,
appears in *The Meditation Sūtra*
for the first time in the history of
Pure Land Buddhism.

404 *Shinshū shōgyō zensho*, Vol. I,
p. 65.

405 *Shinshū shōgyō zensho*, Vol. I,
p. 555. Translation is taken from
The Collected Works of Shinran,
p. 148.

406 *Shinshū shōgyō zensho*, Vol. I,
p. 567. Translation is taken from
The Collected Works of Shinran,
p. 149.

407 *Shinshū shōgyō zensho*,
Vol. II, p. 775. Translation is taken
from *Great Living: In the Pure
Encounter between Master and
Disciple* by K. T. Sato, p. 39.

408 D. T. Suzuki, *Mysticism: Christian
and Buddhist*, New York: Harper &
Brothers Publishers, 1957,
pp. 161–2.

409 The original Japanese phrase
for "attaining Nirvāṇa without
destroying blind passions" is
fudanbonnō tokunehan 不断
煩悩 得涅槃 found in a gāthā

known as *The Shōshinge* in *The Kyōgyōshinshō*. *Shinshū shōgyō zensho*, Vol. II, p. 44.

410 *Shinshū shōgyō zensho*, Vol. II, p. 575.

411 Quoted from the author's yet unpublished talk.

412 *Rennyo Shōnin zenshū*, Vol. 4, pp. 15–6. *Daihasso onmonogatari Kūzen kikigaki* Article 95, *Shinshū shiryō shūsei*, Vol. 2, pp. 431–2.

413 A *wasan* or "verse in Japanese," here the verse is from *The Shōzōmatsu wasan* 正像末和讃, *Verses on the Right, Semblance, and Last Dharma Age.*

414 *Shinshū shōgyō zensho*, Vol. II, p. 319. *The Shōzōmatsu wasan*, verse 31.

415 A combination of the first two lines of the very first *wasan* of *The Shōzōmatsu wasan, Shinshū shōgyō zensho*, Vol. II, p. 516, and the last two lines of the twenty-fifth *wasan*, p. 519.

416 *Shinshū shōgyō zensho*, Vol. I, p. 46.

417 *Shinshū shōgyō zensho*, Vol. II, p. 68.

418 Xuánzàng 玄奘 (jp. Genjō, 600–664), one of the greatest Chinese Buddhist translators, who left China for India in 629 to obtain Buddhist Sanskrit texts. He studied Buddhism, the Consciousness-Only school in particular, mainly in Nālandā in central India and made a pilgrimage around India. He returned via Central Asia in 645 with 657 Sanskrit texts and many Buddhist images and translated many of them into Chinese together with his disciples as a national enterprise of the Táng Dynasty. He carried out an epoch-making feat of translation and tried to translate the original texts with more accuracy. Compared to previous translations his translations came to be called "new translations." In addition to a huge number of translations, including that of *The Mahāprajñāpāramitā-sūtra* 大般若波羅蜜多經, he left an important historical record of his journey to India known as *The Dà Táng Xīyùjì* 大唐西域記.

419 *Shinshū shōgyō zensho*, Vol. II, p. 600. *Songō shinzō meimon*, or *Annotated Inscriptions on Sacred Scrolls.*

420 Quoted from the author's yet unpublished talk.

421 *Shinshū shōgyō zensho*, Vol. II, p. 516. *The Shōzōmatsu wasan*, verse 1.

422 *Shinshū shōgyō zensho*, Vol. II, p. 519. *The Shōzōmatsu wasan*, verse 25.

423 Shàndǎo states in his *Method of Contemplation on Amida* (*Guānniàn fǎmén* 觀念法門 jp. *Kannen bōmon*), "Whether ordained or lay, if there are people who say that women are unable to be born in the Pure Land, such a view is indeed fallacious. You should not follow it." *Shinshū shōgyō zensho*, Vol. I, p. 637. This absolute principle of women's attainment of birth was later confirmed by Hōnen in his discussion about the Thirty-fifth Vow in *The Commentary on The Larger Sūtra of Eternal Life* (*Daikyō shaku* 大經釋), *Shinshū shōgyō zensho*, Vol. IV, pp. 275–9 and followed by Shinran as seen in his *wasan*, "It is because Amida's great compassion commands such depth / That the inconceivable Buddha wisdom reveals itself as it does. / By making the Vow that allows women to change themselves into men / Amida gave all women the chance to attain

Buddhahood," *Jōdo wasan*, verse 60, *Shinshū shōgyō zensho*, Vol. II, p. 493. See also the author's commentary on the twentieth letter of Fascicle Five in *Chapter 78* where this *wasan* is cited. See *Appendix 5*.

424 *Nyonin ōjō kikigaki* 女人往生聞書 by Zonkaku, a detailed discussion on the significance of the Thirty-fifth Vow. *Shinshū shōgyō zensho*, Vol. III, pp. 109–18.

425 Regarding the sources, see the author's comments in *Chapter 10* on the tenth letter of Fascicle One.

426 *Hokekyō yōge* 法華經要解, or *The Essentials of the Lotus Sūtra*, *Dainihon zoku zōkyō*, Section 1, Volume 47, woodblock print edition, p. 316 right.

427 *Taishō daizōkyō*, Vol. 10, p. 790.

428 The full title of 御傳鈔 *Goden shō*, or *The Life of Shinran Shōnin*, is 本願寺聖人親鸞傳繪 *The Honganji Shōnin Shinran den'e*, which can be translated as *The Illustrated Biography of Honganji's Shōnin, Shinran*. Kakunyo (1270–1351), great grandson of Shinran, wrote this biography at the age of twenty-six, based on the documents he had collected from Shinran's relatives and disciples such as Nyoshin (1235–1300), Shinran's grandson, and Yuien (1222–1289), the author of *The Tanni shō*.

429 Regarding his marriage there are two more important stories, one preceding the vision mentioned in the *Goden shō* and the other following the vision, both of which came to be known to the public more widely than before through a recent publication by Tadashi Sasaki called *Shinran shiki* 親鸞始記, Chikuma Shobō, 1997. In the book Sasaki clarifies the importance of the *Shinran Shōnin shōmyō den* 親鸞聖人正明傳, 1352,

compiled by Zonkaku (1290–1373), the eldest son of Kakunyo, in which those two stories are recorded in detail. Unfortunately the *Shinran Shōnin shōmyō den* has long been ignored amongst Shin Buddhist scholars simply because, whilst almost all of them are from the biggest two Shin Buddhist denominations, the Higashi Honganji and the Nishi Honganji traditions, the document itself has been kept by the headquarters of the Takada tradition, another Shin Buddhist denomination. If we closely look at this biography of Shinran by Zonkaku, however, we would have to say that the authenticity of the document that describes the spiritual history of Shinran in detail is indisputable. See *Appendix 5*.

430 *Shinshū shōgyō zensho*, Vol. III, p. 11.

431 *Shinshū shōgyō zensho*, Vol. III, p. 31.

432 *Shinshū shōgyō zensho*, Vol. II, p. 792. Translation by K. T. Sato, *Great Living: In the Pure Encounter between Master and Disciple*, p. 140.

433 *Bokieshi* Vol. 3, *Shinshū shōgyō zensho*, Vol. III, pp. 779–800.

434 K. T. Sato, *Great Living: In the Pure Encounter between Master and Disciple*, p. 143.

435 K. T. Sato, *Great Living*, p. 140. *Shinshū shōgyō zensho*, Vol. IV, 792.

436 K. T. Sato, *Great Living*, p. 140. *Shinshū shōgyō zensho*, Vol. IV, 792.

437 Regarding the phrase "the *Dharmakāya* in its manifested form" which refers to *hobenhosshin* 方便法身, see *Appendix 3*.

438 Regarding the notion of *anjin*, see *Appendix 4*.

439 *Go-On*ごおん, Vol. 276, p. 1, K. T. Sato, trans., Shogyoji, 1978.

440 *Shinshū shōgyō zensho*, Vol. II, p. 43. Translation taken from a series of unpublished lectures on *The Shōshinge* by K. T. Sato.

441 *Shinshū shōgyō zensho*, Vol. II, p. 44. Translation taken from a series of unpublished lectures on *The Shōshinge* by K. T. Sato.

442 *Shinshū shōgyō zensho*, Vol. II, p. 45. Translation taken from a series of unpublished lectures on *The Shōshinge* by K. T. Sato.

443 See *Shinshū shōgyō zensho*, Vol. I, pp. 56–7. The most essential passage is, "The Buddha Amitayus possesses eighty-four thousand physical characteristics, each having eighty-four thousand secondary marks of excellence. Each secondary mark emits eighty-four thousand rays of light; each ray shines universally upon the lands of the ten directions, embracing, and not forsaking, those who are mindful of the Buddha. It is impossible to describe in detail these rays of light, physical characteristics and marks, transformed Buddhas, and so forth. But you can see them clearly with your mind's eye through contemplation." *The Three Pure Land Sūtras*, Hisao Inagaki, trans., BDK English Tripitaka, Vol. 12, 1995, p. 105.

444 *Shinshū shōgyō zensho*, Vol. II, p. 512. *The Kōsō wasan*, verse 95.

445 *Shinshū shōgyō zensho*, Vol. II, p. 44. Translation taken from a series of unpublished lectures on *The Shōshinge* by K. T. Sato.

446 From Shàndǎo's *Exposition of The Meditation Sūtra*. *Shinshū shōgyō zensho*, Vol. I, p. 457.

447 *The Collection of Rennyo's Letters Not Compiled in The Five Fascicle Letters*, Reion Takehara ed., pp. 164–7. *Shinshū shiryō shūsei*, Vol. 2, pp. 300–1.

448 Shàndǎo's *Exposition of The Meditation Sūtra*. *Shinshū shōgyō zensho*, Vol. I, p. 457.

449 *The Three Pure Land Sūtras*, Hisao Inagaki trans., BDK English Tripitaka, Vol. 12, 1995, pp. 87–8. *Shinshū shōgyō zensho*, Vol. I, p. 46.

450 *Senchaku Hongan Nenbutsu Shū*, M. J. Augustine and T. Kondō, trans., BDK English Tripitaka, Vol. 104-II, 1997, pp. 3–4.

451 *Shinshū shōgyō zensho*, Vol. II, p. 5.

452 *Shinshū shōgyō zensho*, Vol. II, p. 489. *The Jōdo wasan*, verse 30. For another translation, see *The Collected Works of Shinran*, p. 332.

453 This Shinran's own commentary is found in *Kokuhō-bon Sanjō Wasan Chūge* 國寶本三帖和讃註解, or *The Commentary on The National Treasure Version Three Fascicle Wasan*, Ranyū Tokiwai, ed., Kōdansha, Tokyo, 1972, p. 16.

454 *Rennyo Shōnin ibun*, Masamaru Inaba, ed., pp. 419–21.

455 The Najio version 名塩本 is the most important collection of letters by Rennyo amongst the many versions such as the Rensō collection, Dōshu collection, Rennō collection, Takada version, Sakai version, Chōganji version, and Honseiji version. According

to Dōon, the author of *The Ofumi meitō shō*, the Najio version is the original collection of Rennyo's letters from which Ennyo selected eighty letters to produce the formal edition, *The Five Fascicle Letters*. According to *The Rennyo Shōnin ibun* by Inaba, the number of the letters in the Najio version amounts to 245. Dōon states in his *Ofumi meitō shō* that this must certainly be the original collection of letters that Venerable Ennyo employed when he compiled *The Five Fascicle Letters*.

456 *Shinshū shōgyō zensho*, Vol. II, p. 44.

457 A summarisation of an account that relates to the letter appearing in the *Ofumi raii shō* 御文来意鈔 by E'nin 恵忍, Nishimura Kurōemon, Kyoto, 1898, pp. 349–54.

458 The relevant quotation from 無常 講式 *Mujōkō shiki* is found in the *Zonkaku hōgo, Shinshū shōgyō zensho*, Vol. III, p. 360.

459 The Hossō School 法相宗 is one of the eight Japanese Buddhist schools in the Heian Period, originating from the Făxiàng zōng, a Chinese Buddhist school founded by Kuīji 窺基 (632–682). The school is based on the Consciousness Only philosophy.

460 A summary of Dōken's request, the *Ofumi raii shō*, Nishimura Kurōemon, Kyoto, 1898, pp. 355–7.

461 The following is a summary of an account featured in the *Ofumi raii shō*, pp. 364–72.

462 *Shinshū shōgyō zensho*, Vol. II, p. 45.

463 This statement is not the exact quotation from the *Daijikkyo* but rather Dàochuò's summarisation of its content.

464 *Shinshū shōgyō zensho*, Vol. I, p. 410.

465 *Shinshū shōgyō zensho*, Vol. I, p. 12.

466 *Shinshū shōgyō zensho*, Vol. IV, p. 276.

467 *Shinshū shōgyō zensho*, Vol. II, p. 493.

468 Kōtatsu Fujita, *Genshi jōdokyō no kenkyū* 原始浄土思想の研究, or *Studies on Early Pure Land Thoughts*, Iwanami Shoten, Tokyo, 1970, p. 397.

469 Amida's second vow in *The Dai Amida kyo* 大阿彌陀經, or *Bussetsu Amida sanyasanbutsu sarubutsudan kadonindō kyō* 佛説阿彌陀三耶三佛薩樓佛檀過度人道經 in its full name, says, "Secondly, I vow that when I attain Buddhahood, there will be no women in my country, that women who want to come to my country will become men, that all those innumerable beings such as gods and human beings and insects wriggling and flying who come to my country will be born amongst lotus flowers in the pond of seven jewels, that when fully grown they will all become Bodhisattvas and that there will be innumerable arhats. When I have fulfilled this vow I will attain Buddhahood and unless this vow is fulfilled I may not attain Buddhahood." *Taishō daizōkyō*, Vol. 12, p. 301.

470 *Shinshū shōgyō zensho*, Vol. II, p. 493. *Jōdo wasan*, verse 60. For another translation of this *wasan*, see *The Collected Works f Shinran*, p. 341.

471 *Shinshū shōgyō zensho*, Vol. II, p. 73.

472 Regarding the phrase "passages in the Sūtra and in commentaries," "passages in the Sūtra" refers to

"the sentient beings who are born in that land all reside amongst those who are rightly assured" (*Shinshū shōgyō zensho*, Vol. I, p. 24) and "desiring to be born in that land, they are immediately born there at that moment and abide in the stage of nonretrogression" (*Shinshū shōgyō zensho*, Vol. I, p. 24) in *The Larger Sūtra of Eternal Life* and "passages in commentaries"refers to those such as "immediately entering the stage of the definite assurance" in Nāgārjuna's *Daśabhūmika-vibhāśā Śastra* (*Shinshū shōgyō zensho*, Vol. I, p. 259) and "entering the company of those who have attained the right definite assurance" in Tánluán's *Commentary on The Treatise of the Pure Land* (*Shinshū shōgyō zensho*, Vol. I, p. 324).

473 An account found in the *Ofumi raii shō*, Nishimura Kurōemon, Kyoto, 1898, pp. 379–80.

474 *Rennyo Shōnin zenshū*, Vol. 4, p. 3. *Daihasso onmonogatari Kūzen kikigaki*, Article 57, *Shinshū shiryō shūsei*, Vol. 2, p. 426.

475 *The Shinshū shōgyō zensho*, Vol. 2, pp. 165–6.

476 See the author's commentary on this poem in *Chapter 57*.

477 Edatsu Teramoto, *Asahara Saichi-ō o kataru*, or *Talks about Asahara Saichi*, Tokyo: Chiyoda Gakuen, 1952, pp. 60–1.

478 In Buddhism there are two streams of teaching, *tongyō* 頓教, or the teaching of sudden or abrupt awakening and *zengyō* 漸教, that of gradual awakening. Shinran describes the teaching of Other Power faith as *tonchū no ton* 頓中之頓, "the most sudden amongst the sudden" (*The Shinshū shōgyō zensho*, Vol. 2, p. 155). Regarding the Shin Buddhist method of dogmatic classification, see the author's commentary on the second letter of Fascicle One in *Chapter 2*.

479 *Myōkōnin Asahara Saichi shū*, D. T. Suzuki, ed., p. 403.

A CONCISE CHRONOLOGY
OF RENNYO'S LIFE

Date (Era Year)	[Age]	Event (Month and Day if known)
1415 (Ōei 22)	[1]	2.25. Born at Ōtani Honganji in Higashiyama, Kyoto, first child of his father, Zonnyo (1396-1457).
1420 (Ōei 27)	[6]	12.28. Mother leaves Ōtani Honganji with his portrait (*kanoko no miei*).
1422 (Ōei 29)	[8]	Stepsister Nyoyū born to stepmother Nyoen.
1429 (Eikyō 1)	[15]	Makes a resolution to restore Shinran Shōnin's tradition.
1431 (Eikyō 3)	[17]	Ordained at Shōren'in in the summer and given the Dharma name Kenju.
1433 (Eikyō 5)	[19]	Stepbrother Ōgen born.
1434 (Eikyō 6)	[20]	5.12. Copies *Jōdo monrui jushō*.
1436 (Eikyō 8)	[22]	3.28. Zonnyo succeeds Gyōnyo and becomes 7th Head Priest of Honganji.
		8. –. Copies *Sanjō wasan* by Shinran.
1438 (Eikyō 10)	[24]	8.15. Copies *Jōdo shinyō shō* compiled by Zonkaku.
		12.13. Copies *Kuden shō* by Kakunyo.
1439 (Eikyō 11)	[25]	5.10. Copies *Nenbutsu ōjō yōgi shō* by Hōnen.
		7.29. Copies *Gose monogatari* by Ryūkan.
		7. –. Copies *Tariki shinjin kikigaki* attributed to Ryōkai of Bukkōji.
1440 (Eikyō 12)	[26]	10.14. Grandfather, Gyōnyo dies.
1441 (Kakitsu 1)	[27]	9.7. Copies *Jōdo shinyō shō*.
1442 (Kakitsu 2)	[28]	Birth of first son, Junnyo, to first wife, Nyoryō.
1444 (Bun'an 1)	[30]	Birth of first daughter, Nyokei.
1446 (Bun'an 3)	[32]	1. –. Copies *Gutoku shō* by Shinran.
		Birth of second son, Renjō.
1447 (Bun'an 4)	[33]	1. –. Copies *Anjin ketsujō shō* by an unknown author.
		2. –. Copies *Rokuyō shō* by Zonkaku and also *Mattō shō* by Shinran.
		5. –. Travels to the eastern provinces.
1448 (Bun'an 5)	[34]	10.19. Copies *Gensō ekō kikigaki* attributed to Ryōkai of Bukkōji.
		Birth of second daughter, Kengyoku.
1449 (Hōtoku 1)	[35]	Spring. Travels to the Hokuriku district with Zonnyo and then the eastern provinces on his own.
		5.28. Copies *Sanjō wasan*.
		6.3. Copies *Anjin ketsujō shō*.
		7. –. Copies *Nyonin ōjō kikigaki* by Zonkaku.
		10.14. Copies *Goden shō* by Kakunyo.
1450 (Hōtoku 2)	[36]	8.11. Copies *Kyōgyōshinshō*.
		Birth of third son, Renkō.
1451 (Hōtoku 3)	[37]	8.16. Completes copying *Kyōgyōshinshō* with Zonnyo's postscript.

1453 (Kyōtoku 2)   [39]   11.22. Copies *Sanjō wasan*.

1454 (Kyōtoku 3)   [40]   4.17. Copies *Ōjō yōshū* by Genshin.
7.8. Copies *Kyōgyōshinshō*.
Birth of third daughter, Juson.

1455 (Kōshō 1)   [41]   7.19. Copies *Boki eshi* by Jūkaku.
Birth of fourth son, Rensei.
11.23 Death of first wife, Nyoryō.

1457 (Chōroku 1)   [43]   2.20. Copies *Saiyō shō* by Kakunyo.
4. –. Copies *Jimyō shō* by Zonkaku.
6.18. Death of his father, Zonnyo.
Becomes the eighth Head Priest of Honganji,
     with the great help and support from his uncle,
     Nyojō, Head Priest of Honsenji in Kaga Province.

1458 (Chōroku 2)   [44]   2.4. Copies *Sanjō wasan*.
6. –. Writes *Shōshinge taii* at the request
     of Dōsai of Kanegamori.
7. 28. Copies *Rokuyō shō* by Zonkaku.
8.10. Birth of fifth son, Jitsunyo, to second wife,
     Ren'yū, younger sister of Nyoryō.

1459 (Chōroku 3)   [45]   Birth of fourth daughter, Myōshū.

1460 (Kanshō 1)   [46]   1.26. Uncle, Nyojō, dies.
2.24. Presents a calligraphy of the ten character
     Buddha-Name (*jūji-myōgō*) to Hōjū of Katada.
10.4. Death of stepmother, Nyoen.
Birth of fifth daughter, Myōi.

1461 (Kanshō 2)   [47]   1. 6. Presents another calligraphy of the ten
     character Buddha-Name to Hōjū of Katada
     and followers over there.
3. –. Writes the first of his letters to his followers.
     (*Rennyo Shōnin Ibun* by Masamaru Inaba,
     abbrev. *RSI. RSI 1.*)
7. –. Copies *Kyōgyōshinshō* in Japanese style
     of writing (*nobegaki*).
10. –. Has Shinran's portrait (*anjō miei*) restored.
12.8. Copies *Tandoku mon* by Zonkaku.
12.23. Presents a dual seated portrait (*renza zō*)
     of Shinran and himself to Hōjū and followers
     at Katada.

1462 (Kanshō 3   [48]   Birth of sixth daughter, Nyokū.

1463 (Kanshō 4)   [49]   2.11. Visits Nara to see a firelight performance
     of *nō* drama (*takigi nō*) with family.
Birth of seventh daughter, Yūshin.

1464 (Kanshō 5)   [50]   Birth of sixth son, Renjun.
Conducts the twenty-fifth memorial service
     of his grandfather, Gyōnyo.

1465 (Kanshō 6)   [51]   1. 10. Ōtani Honganji attacked and partly
     demolished by warrior-monks from Enryakuji
     and local mercenaries.
. –. Escapes from Ōtani Honganji with Shinran's
     image and, after short says at Yamashiro, Settsu
     and Kawachi Provinces, eventually moves
     to Ōmi Province.
3. 21. Ōtani Honganji completely destroyed
     by Enryakuji warrior-monks.

3.23. Enryakuji warrior-monks attack Shin Buddhist
followers at Kanegamori, Ōmi Province.

3.24. Enryakuji warrior-monks attack Shin Buddhist
followers at Akanoi, Ōmi Province.

5.10. Bakufu government orders warrior-monks
not to attack Shin Buddhist followers in Ōmi.

12.9. Visits Kyōkaku at Daijōin in Nara, one of his
relatives, who taught him when young Buddhism
in general.

1466 (Bunshō 1)   [52]   7.8. Copies *Kyōgyōshinshō* in *nobegaki* style.

11.21. Conducts the Hōonkō ceremony at
Kanegamori, Ōmi Province.

Birth of eighth daughter, Ryōnin.

Writes the second dated letter. *(RSI 2)*

1467 (Ōnin 1)   [53]   from Kōshibō's *dōjō* at An'nyōji to Honpukuji
at Katada, both within Ōmi Province.

2.16. Copies *Kudenshō.*

3. –. Enryakuji decides to stop attacking Honganji
and Honganji agrees to become a branch of the
Tendai temple, Shōren'in.

11.21. Holds Hōonkō ceremony at Honpukuji,
Katada, Ōmi.

Birth of ninth daughter, Ryōnyo.

1468 (Ōnin 2)   [54]   1.9. Warrior-monks on Mt. Hi'ei plot to attack
Shin Buddhist followers at Katada.

3.12. Transfers Shinran's image from Honpukuji
to a small *dōjō* of Dōkaku, one of the followers
of Honpukuji, built at Ōtsuhama, Ōmi Province.

3.28. Signs a deed of transfer designating Jitsunyo
as his successor.

3.29. Warrior-monks from Enryakuji attack
Shin Buddhist followers at Katada and many of them
escape to Okinoshima, a small island in
Lake Biwa.

4.8. Visits Kyōkaku at Daijōin, Nara.

Travels to the eastern provinces for several months
and on his return builds Honshūji in Mikawa
Province.

10. –. Copies *Hōonkō shiki* by Kakunyo.

10. –. Travels to Mt. Kōya and Yoshino, Kii Province.

Birth of seventh son, Rengo.

Three dated letters during this year. *(RSI 3, 4, 5)*

1469 (Bunmei 1)   [55]   Builds a small temple at Chikamatsu in the southern
bessho (detached area) of Miidera, Ōtsu, Ōmi
Province, and enshrines Shinran's image in the
temple, later named as Kenshōji.

Birth of tenth daughter, Yūshin.

1470 (Bunmei 2)   [56]   11.9. Shin Buddhist followers of Katada return
home from Okinoshima.

12.5. Death of second wife, Ren'yū.

1471 (Bunmei 3)   [57]   4. –. Leaves Ōtsu and stays in Kyoto for a while.

5. –. Moves from Kyoto to Yoshizaki,
Echizen Province.

7.15. Writes *Letter I: 1* of *The Letters* (Five Fascicle Version).
7.18. *Letter I: 2.*
7.27. Builds a temple at Yoshizaki, Echizen.
12:18. *Letter I: 3.*
Four other dated letters. (*RSI 6, 7, 9, 11*)

1472 (Bunmei 4)   [58]   1. –. Prohibits people flocking together at Yoshizaki.
8.14. Second daughter, Kengyoku, dies at the age of 25.
9.10. Writes to Kyōkaku at Daijōin, Nara.
11.27. *Letter I: 4.*
Five other dated letters. (*RSI 13, 14, 15, 16, 17*)

1473 (Bunmei 5)   [59]   1. –. Moves from Yoshizaki to Fujishima, Echizen Province.
2.8. *Letter I: 5.*
4.25. *Letter I: 6.*
8.12. *Letter I: 7.*
9.11. *Letter I: 10.*
9.19. Kyōkaku at Daijōin dies.
9.22. *Letter I: 15*
9. –. *Letter I: 8, 9, 11, 12, 13, 14.*
10.3. Returns to Yoshizaki.
12.8. *Letter II: 1.*
12.12. *Letter II: 2.*
Seventeen other dated letters. (*RSI 19, 21, 23, 24, 29, 35, 36, 37, 38, 39, 42, 43, 44, 45, 46, 47, 48*)

1474 (Bunmei 6)   [60]   1.11. *Letter II: 3.*
2.15. *Letter II: 4.*
2.16. *Letter II: 5.*
2.17. *Letter II: 6.*
3.3. *Letter II: 7.*
3.17. *Letter II: 9.*
3. –. *Letter II: 8.*
3.28. The main temple and nine *taya* houses at Yoshizaki are destroyed by fire.
5.13. *Letter II: 10.*
5.20. *Letter II: 11.*
6.12. *Letter II: 12.*
7.3. *Letter II: 13.*
7.5. *Letter II: 14.*
7.9. *Letter II: 15.*
7.14. *Letter III: 1.*
7.26. Honganji followers in Kaga Province form an alliance with Governor Togashi Masachika to fight against Togashi Yukichiyo, Masachika's younger brother, who has allied with followers of Senjuji, another Shin Buddhist temple.
8.5. *Letter III: 2.*
8.6. *Letter III: 3.*
8.18. *Letter III: 4.*
9.6. *Letter III: 5.*
10.20. *Letter III: 6.*
11.1. Masachika-Honganji group defeats Yukichiyo-Takada alliance.

11.13. Jinson at Daijōin sends a letter to Rennyo.

11.25. *Letter V: 11. (RSI 75* note)

12. –. Writes back to Jinson.

Fifth son, Jitsunyo, ordained at Shōren'in.

Seven other dated letters. (*RSI 49, 51, 58, 62, 63, 70, 74*)

1475 (Bunmei 7)   [61]   2.23. *Letter III:7.*

2.25. *Letter III: 8.*

3. –. Honganji followers in Kaga Province beaten by Togashi Masachika.

5.7. Writes a letter of ten regulations. (*RSI 79*)

6.11. Jinson writes to Rennyo about their estate in Kaga Province.

5.28. *Letter III: 9.*

7.15. *Letter III:10,* a letter of six regulations.

8. –. Leaves Yoshizaki by ship and, travelling by land through Wakasa, Tanba and Settsu Provinces, arrives at Deguchi, Kawachi Province.

11.21. *Letter III:11,* a letter written for the Hōonkō ceremony held at the temple at Deguchi.

Four other dated letters. (*RSI 78, 80, 81, 85*).

1476 (Bunmei 8)   [62]   1.27. *Letter III: 12.*

7.18. *Letter III: 13.*

Builds a temple at Sakai and names it Shinshōin.

Plans to build a temple at Tonda in Settsu Province, later named Tonda-dono.

Two other dated letters. (*RSI 87, 89*)

1477 (Bunmei 9)   [63]   1.8. *Letter IV: 1.*

9.17. *Letter IV: 2.*

9.27. *Letter IV: 3.*

10. –. Dōsai of Kanegamori suggests building Honganji at Yamashina.

10.27. Copies *Kyōgyōshinshō taii.*

11. –. Writes a letter known as *Gozokushō.* (*RSI 96*)

12.2. *Letter IV: 4.*

12. –. Copies *Jōdo kenmon shū* by Zonkaku.

Birth of eleventh daughter, Myōshō, to third wife, Nyoshō.

Five other dated letters. (*RSI 91, 94, 95, 98, 99*)

1478 (Bunmei 10)   [64]   1. 29. Moves from Deguchi, Kawachi Province, to Yamashina, Yamashiro Province, in order to start rebuilding Honganji.

Begins construction of residential parts of the temple.

8.17. Death of third wife, Nyoshō.

Three dated letters. (*RSI 100, 101, 102*)

1479 (Bunmei 11)   [65]   Construction of Honganji at Yamashina is under way.

12.30. Ordination of sixth son, Renjun.

Two dated letters. (*RSI 103, 104*)

1480 (Bunmei 12)   [66]   1. –. Builds a small Buddha hall at Yamashina.

2.3. Starts building the Founder's Image Hall at Yamashina.

2.17. Restarts correspondence with Jinson about an estate at Kosaka in Kaga Province.

		8.28. Installs Shinran's portrait in Founder's Image Hall, almost completed by this day.

8.28. Installs Shinran's portrait in Founder's Image
Hall, almost completed by this day.

8.29. Receives an incense burner as a gift from
the Imperial Court for the construction
of Yamashina Honganji.

10.14. Hino Tomiko, wife of Shōgun Ashikaga
Yoshimasa, visits Yamashina Honganji.

10.15. Repairs Shinran's *Anjō* portrait and has two
copies newly made.

11.18. Moves Shinran's wooden image from
Chikamatsu, Ōmi Province, to Yamashina
Honganji, Yamashiro Province.

11.21. Holds the Hōonkō ceremony at Yamashina
Honganji.

Four dated letters. (*RSI 105, 106, 107 108*)

1481 (Bunmei 13)   [67]   2.4. Starts construction of the Hall of Amida
at Yamashina Honganji.

6.8. Enshrines Amida Buddha's wooden image
in a temporary altar in Amida Hall newly built
at Yamashina Honganji.

6.11. Conducts the twenty-fifth anniversary
of the death of his father, Zonnyo.

6. –. Kyōgō, fourteenth Head Priest of Bukkōji,
expresses his loyalty to Rennyo's Honganji.

12.4. The Shōgunate returns *Boki eshi* to Honganji.

Three dated letters. (*RSI 109, 110, 111*)

1482 (Bunmei 14)   [68]   6.15. Enshrines Amida's image in a completed altar
in Amida Hall at Yamashina Honganji.

11.21. *Letter IV: 5.*

Zenchin from Shōjōji at Yokogoe expresses his loyalty
to Rennyo's Honganji.

Birth of twelfth daughter, Renshū, to fourth
wife, Shūnyo.

1483 (Bunmei 15)   [69]   5.29. Death of first son, Junnyo.

8. –. Completion of the construction work
of Honganji at Yamashina.

8.29. Goes to recuperate at Arima hotsprings,
Settsu Province.

11.22. *Letter IV: 6.*

Three other dated letters. (*RSI 113, 114, 116*)

1484 (Bunmei 16)   [70]   9.16. Makes Prince Shōtoku's portrait.

11.21. *Letter IV: 7.*

Birth of eighth son, Rengei.

Another dated letter. (*RSI 118*)

1485 (Bunmei 17)   [71]   4.4. Restoration of the scroll of the ten character
Buddha-name (*jūji-myōgō*) written by Kakunyo.

11.23. *Letter IV: 8.*

Death of fourth wife, Shūnyo.

1486 (Bunmei 18)   [72]   Three dated letters. (*RSI 119, 120, 121*)

1487 (Chōkyō 1)   [73]   *Ikkō ikki* (Shin Buddhist followers' uprising)
escalates in Kaga Province.

Birth of thirteenth daughter, Myōyū, to fifth
wife, Ren'nō.

1488 (Chōkyō 2)   [74]   4.19. Shin Buddhist followers in Kaga Province attack Lord Togashi Masachika.

6.9. Togashi Masachika commits suicide
at Takao Castle.

8,25. Death of first disciple, Dōsai of Kanegamori.

1489 (Entoku 1)   [75]   4.28. Donation from the Imperial Court to Honganji.

8.28. Transfers the role of Honganji Head Priest
to Jitusnyo, fifth son, and retires to the
Southern Residence.

10.20. Makes corrections on a copy of
Kyōgyōshinshō taii.

10.28. Copies *Kyōgyōshinshō*.

1490 (Entoku 2)   [76]   7.24. Visits the Imperial Court.

10.28. Writes a second letter to confirm
the transference of the role of Head Priest
to Jitsunyo.

Death of seventh daughter, Yūshin.

Birth of ninth son, Jikken, to fifth wife, Ren'nō.

Two dated letters. (*RSI 122, 123*)

1492 (Entoku 4)   [78]   6. –. *Letter IV: 9.*

Birth of tenth son, Jitsugo.

Death of sixth daughter, Nyokū.

Sends Kūzen for Harima Province to seek
after his mother.

Another similar dated letter. (*RSI 124*)

1493 (Meiō 2)   [79]   1.1. Gives a Dharma talk on Other Power (*tariki*)
to Dōtoku of Kanshūji at Yamashina.

Shōe, Head Priest of Kinshokuji, expresses
his loyalty to Honganji.

One dated letter. (*RSI 125*)

1494 (Meiō 3)   [80]   11.28. Copies *Kyōgyōshinshō*.

Birth of eleventh son, Jitsujun.

One dated letter. (*RSI 126*)

1495 (Meiō 4)   [81]   Builds Gangyōji in spring and Honzenji
in autumn in Yamato Province.

Birth of twelfth son, Jikkō.

1496 (Meiō 5)   [82]   1.11. Copies *Hōnen Shōnin onkotoba*.

9.24 Decides to build a temple at Ishiyama
in Settsu Province.

9.29. Conducts a ground-breaking ceremony
in order to begin construction of the temple.

Four dated letters. (*RSI 127, 128, 129, 130*)

1497 (Meiō 6)   [83]   2.16. *Letter V: 8. (RSI 131)*

5.25. *Letter IV: 11.*

11. –. Construction of the temple at Ishiyama,
later known as Ōsaka-dono or Ishiyama-gobō,
is completed.

11. –. Attends the Hōonkō ceremonies at Tonda-dono
for the first three days and at
Ōsaka-dono for the last four days.

Letter IV: 10.

Letter V: 5. (RSI 139)

Letter V: 6. (RSI 140)

Letter V: 19. (RSI 138)

Birth of fourteenth daughter, Myōshū.

Six other dated letters. (*RSI 132, 133, 134, 135, 136, 137*)

1498 (Meiō 7)   [84]   2.25. *Letter IV : 12.*

3. –. *Letter V : 14. (RSI 143)*

4. –. Taken ill.

4.17. Examined by doctors.

4.11. *Letter IV : 13.*

4. –. *Letter IV : 14.*

5.7. Visits Yamashina Honganji to pay final respects to Shinran's image.

5.25. During his stay, despite his infirmity, goes to see Shinran's statue at Founder's Image Hall.

10.16. Asks Ryūgen to read out about ten of his letters.

11.19. *Letter V : 9. (RSI 155)*

11.21. *Letter IV : 15.*

Birth of thirteenth son, Jitsujū.

Thirteen other dated letters. (*RSI 141, 144, 146, 147, 148, 149, 150, 151, 152, 153, 154, 157, 158*)

1499 (Meiō 8)   [85]   2.16. Sends Kūzen to Yamashina Honganji to prepare for his funeral.

2.18. Leaves Ōsaka-dono for Yamashina Honganji.

2.20. Arrives in Yamashina.

2.21. Visits Founder's Image Hall to pay homage to Shinran's image.

2.25. Carried on a palanquin to examine the canal-embankment surrounding Yamashina Honganji.

2.27. Visits once again Founder's Image Hall and, on his return, is seated backwards as he departs in a palanquin, showing reluctance to part from his followers gathered there.

3.1. Visits Jitsugo at his Northern Residence (*Kita-dono*) and has a lovely chat with Jitsunyo and his other sons, referring to the importance of the awakening of faith.

3.7. Carried on a palanquin to see Founder's Image and makes his final farewells, "See you in the Land of Utmost Bliss!"

3.9. Meets and enjoys having Dharma talks with his discipes such as Kūzen, Junsei, Ryōchin and Ryūgen and at his request Ryūgen reads out three letters.

3.9. Cordially asks his five sons, Jitsunyo, Renkō, Rensei, Renjun and Rengo to cooperate with one another and with lay followers as well, in order to observe Founder Shinran's Dharma stream, which they promise to do.

3.19. Doesn't take any medicine, only saying the *Nenbutsu*.

3.20. Pardons Rensō.

3.22. Very moved to hear his letters read out by Hōkyō-bō (Junsei).

3.25. Dies at noon.

BIBLIOGRAPHY

Historical Sources

COLLECTIONS

***Dainihon zoku zōkyō*, Section 1, Vol. 47, 大日本續蔵經 第一經部 第四十七卷.
Kyoto: Zōkyōshoin.**

    Hokke kyō yōge 法華經要解 (ch. *Fǎhuá jīng yàojiě*), or *The Essentials of the
Lotus Sūtra*, by Kaikan 戒環 (ch. *Jièhuán*), woodblock print edition.

***Taishō (shinshū) daizōkyō* 大正新脩大蔵經 (TDK). Tokyo: Taishō Issaikyō
Kankō Kyōwai.**

    Zōhō zō kyō 雜寶蔵經 (ch. *Zábǎo zàng jīng*). TDK4-203.

    Ninnō kyō 仁王經 (ch. *Rénwáng jīng*). TDK8-834.

    Myōhō renge kyō 妙法蓮華經 (skt. *Saddharmapuṇḍarīka-sūtra*, ch. *Miàofǎ
liánhuá jīng*), generally known as *Lotus Sūtra* or *The Sūtra of the Lotus
of the Wonderful Dharma*. TDK9-262.

    Nyū hokkai bon 入法界品 (skt. *Gaṇḍavyūha*, Ch. Rù fǎjiè pǐn), the final chapter
of the immense *Avataṃsaka-sūtra* 華嚴經 (ch. *Huayan jing*). TDK10-293.

    Dai Amida kyo 大阿彌陀經 (ch. *Dà ēmítuó jīng*), or *Bussetsu Amida
sanyasanbutsu sarubutsudan kadonindō kyō* 佛説阿彌陀三耶三佛薩樓佛
檀過度人道經 (Ch. *Fóshuō ēmítuó sānyésānfó sàlóufótán guōdù réndào
jīng*) in its full name. TDK12-362.

    Dai hatsunehan gyō 大般涅槃經 (skt. *Mahāparinirvāṇa-sūtra*, ch. *Dà
bānnièpán jīng*), known as *Great Nirvāṇa Sūtra*. TDK12-374.

    Yuikyō gyō 遺教經 (ch. *Yíjiào jīng*), or *Butsu sui hatsunehan ryakusetsu
kyōkai kyō* 佛垂般涅槃略説教誡經 (ch. *Fóchuí bānnièpán lüèshuō jiàojiè
jīng*). TDK12-389.

    Daijikkyō 大集經 (ch. *Dàjí jīng*). TDK13-397.

    Hanjusanmai kyo 般舟三昧經 (Ch. *Bānzhōu sānmèi jīng*), or *Sūtra of the
Samādhi of All Buddhas' Presence*. TDK13-417.

    Gengō kyō 賢劫經 (ch. *Xiánjié jīng*). TDK14-425.

    Chō nichimyō zanmai kyō 超日明三昧經 (ch. *Chāo riming sānmèi jīng*).
TDK15-638.

    Shōbōnen sho kyō 正法念處經 (skt. *Saddharma-smṛty-upasthāna*,
ch. *Zhèngfǎniàn chù jīng*). TDK17-721.

    Daichi do ron 大智度論 (skt. *Mahāprajñā-pāramitôpadeśa*, ch. *Dazhi du lun*),

attributed to Nāgârjuna and translated into Chinese by Kumārajīva.
A one hundred fascicle commentary *on the Mahāprajñāpāramitā Sūtra*.
TDK25-1509.

Abitatsuma kusha ron 阿毘達磨倶舎論 (skt. *Abhidharmakośa-bhāṣya*,
ch. *Āpídámó jùshè lùn*) by Vasubabdhu. TDK29-1558.

Maka shikan 摩訶止觀 (ch. *Móhē zhǐguān*) by Chigi 智顗 (ch. Zhìyǐ, 538–597).
TDK46-1911.

Benshō ron 辯正論 (ch. *Biànzhèng lùn*) by Hōrin 法琳 (ch. Fǎlín, 572–640).
TDK 52-2110.

Hōon jurin 法苑珠林 (ch. *Fǎyuàn zhūlín*) by Dōsei 道世 (ch. Daoshi, –683).
TDK53-2122.

Shinshū shōgyō zensho, Vol. 1, 真宗聖教全書第一卷. Kyoto:
Ōyagikōbundō, 1957.

Dai muryōju kyō 大無量壽經 (skt. *Sukhāvatī-vyūha*, ch. *Dà wúliángshòu jīng*),
or *The Larger Sūtra of Eternal Life*.

Kan muryōju kyō 觀無量壽經 (ch. *Guān wúliángshòu jīng*) or *The Meditation
Sūtra*.

Amida kyō 阿彌陀經 (skt. [Smaller] *Sukhāvatī-vyūha*, ch. *Āmítuó jīng*)
or *Amida Sūtra*.

Muryōjukyō ubadaisha ganshō ge ganshō ge 無量壽經優婆提舎願生偈
(ch. *Wúliángshòujīng yōupótíshè yuànshēng jié*) by Vasubandhu,
usually abbreviated as *Jōdo ron* 浄土論 (ch. *Jìngtǔ lùn*) or *The Treatise
on the Pure Land*.

Jōdoron chū 浄土論註 (ch. *Jìngtǔlùn zhù*), or *The Commentary on The Treatise
on the Pure Land*, by Tánluán (476–542).

Anraku shū 安楽集 (ch. *Ānlè jí*), or *Passages on the Land of Happiness*,
by Dàochuò (562–645).

Kangyō sho 觀經疏 (ch. *Guānjīng shū*), or *The Exposition of The Meditation
Sūtra*, by Shàndǎo (613–681).

Hōji san 法事讚 (ch. *Fǎshì zàn*) by Shàndǎo.

Kannen bomon 觀念法門 (ch. *Guānniàn fǎmén*) by Shàndǎo.

Ōjō raisan ge 往生禮讚偈 (ch. *Wǎngshēng lǐzàn jì*) by Shàndǎo.

Ōjō yōshū 往生要集 by Genshin (942–1017).

Senjaku hongan nenbutsu shū 選擇本願念佛集 by Hōnen (1133–1212).

Shinshū shōgyō zensho, Vol. 2, 真宗聖教全書第二卷. Kyoto:
Ōyagikōbundō, 1964.

Ken jōdo shinjitsu kyōgyōshō monrui 顯浄土真實教行證文類, usually
abbreviated as *Kyōgyōshinshō* 教行信證, by Shinran (1173–1262).

Jōdo monrui jushō 浄土文類聚鈔 by Shinran.

Gutoku shō 愚禿鈔 by Shinran.

Jōdo wasan 浄土和讚 by Shinran.

Kōsō wasan 高僧和讚 by Shinran.

Shōzōmatsu wasan 正像末和讃 by Shinran.

Songō shinzō meimon 尊號眞像銘文 by Shinran.

Gose monogatari 後世物語 by Ryūkan (1148–1227).

Ichinen tanen funbetsu ji 一念多念分別事 by Ryūkan.

Jiriki tariki ji 自力他力事 by Ryūkan.

Tanni shō 歎異抄 by Yuien.

Shinshū shōgyō zensho, Vol. 3, 真宗聖教全書第三巻. **Kyoto: Ōyagikōbundō, 1964.**

Kuden shō 口傳鈔 by Kakunyo (1270–1351).

Gangan shō 願々鈔, or *Commentary on Vows,* by Kakunyo.

Gaija shō 改邪鈔, or *Passages to Correct the Erroneous Views,* by Kakunyo.

Nyonin ōjō kikigaki 女人往生聞書, or *Notes on the Birth of Women in the Pure Land,* by Zonkaku (1290–1373).

Haja kenshō shō 破邪顕正鈔 by Zonkaku 存覺.

Zonkaku hōgo 存覚法語 by Zonkaku.

Jōdo kenmon shū 浄土見聞集 by Zonkaku.

Anjin ketsujō shō 安心決定鈔, author unknown.

Honganji Shōnin Shinran den'e 本願寺聖人親鸞傳絵 by Kakunyo.

Hōonkō shiki 報恩講式 by Kakunyo.

Tandoku mon 嘆徳文 by Zonkaku.

Boki eshi 慕帰絵詞 by Jūkaku (1295–1360).

Rennyo Shōnin itoku ki 蓮如上人遺徳記, compiled by Rengo (1468–1543) and completed by Jitsugo (1492–1584).

Hogo no uragaki 反故の裏書 by Kensei (1499–1570).

Shinshū shōgyō zensho, Vol. 4, 真宗聖教全書第四巻. **Kyoto: Ōyagikōbundō, 1962.**

Kurodani Shōnin gotōroku 黒谷上人語燈, compiled by Ryōe 了惠 (1243–1330).

Shinshū shōgyō zensho, Vol. 5, 真宗聖教全書第五巻. **Kyoto: Ōyagikōbundō, 1963.**

Chionkō shiki 知恩講私記 by Ryūkan (1148–1227).

Jōgai gobunshō 帖外御文章.

Shinshū shiryō shūsei, Vol. 1, 真宗資料集成第一巻. **Kyoto: Dōbōsha, 1974.**

Shojin hongai shū 諸神本懐集 by Zonkaku.

Shinshū shiryō shūsei, Vol. 2, 真宗資料集成第二巻. **Kyoto: Dōbōsha, 1977.**

Tensho sannen ki 天正三年記 by Jitsugo.

Daihasso onmonogatari kūzen kikigaki 第八祖御物語空善聞書, or *Kūzen's Record of the Eighth Patriarch's Word,* by Kūzen 空善, also known as *Kūzen ki* 空善記 or *Kūzen nikki* 空善日記.

Rennyo Shōnin onmonogatari shidai 蓮如上人御物語次第, ed. unknown.

Rennyo Shōnin ichigo ki 蓮如上人一語記 by Jitsugo, known as *Jitsugo kyūki* 實悟旧記.

Rennyo Shōnin goichigo ki 蓮如上人御一期記, or *The Record of Rennyo Shōnin's Life*, edited by Jitsugo.

Yamashina gobō no Koto narabini sono jidai no koto 山科御坊事并其時代事 by Jitsugo.

Honganji sahō no shidai 本願寺作法之次第 by Jitsugo.

Shūjin ki 拾塵記 by Jitsugo.

Mukashi monogatari ki 昔物語記, ed. unknown.

Honpukuji yurai ki 本福寺由来記 by Myōshū (1469–1540).

Shinshū zensho Vol. 49, 真宗全書第四十九巻. Kyoto: Zōkyō Shoin, 1915.

Ofumi kōgi 御文講義, or *The Lectures on The Letters,* by Kōgatsuin Jinrei 香月院深励 (1749–1817).

Shinshū zensho Vol. 67, 真宗全書第六十七巻. Zōkyō Shoin, 1913.

Shinran Shōnin shōmyō den 親鸞聖人正明傳 by Zonkaku.

Shinshū zensho Vol. 69, 真宗全書第六十九巻. Zōkyō Shoin, 1915.

Rennyo Shōnin engi 蓮如上人縁起 by Senkei 先啓 (1719–1797).

Shinshū sōsho Vol. 10, 真宗叢書第十巻. Kyoto: Rinsenshoten, 1975.

Ofumi meitō shō 御文明燈鈔 by Dōon 道隠 (1741–1813).

Kana shōgyō Vol. 2, 仮名聖教第二, compiled by Ekū 惠空 (1644–1721), in the possession of the Library of Otani University.

Shojin hongai shū 諸神本懐集, or *Collection of Passages on the Original Intention of Gods,* written by Zonkaku in 1324.

Rennyo Shōnin zenshū Vol. 4 蓮如上人全集第四巻, Chōjun Ōtani ed. Tokyo: Chūō Kōronsha, 1998.

Rennyo Shōnin goichidaiki kikigaki 蓮如上人御一代記聞書, *The Record of Rennyo Shōnin's Words and Deeds throughout His Lifetime.*

Jōdoshū zensho Vol. 3, 浄土宗全書第三巻. Kyoto: Jōdoshū Shūten Kankōkai, 1908.

Kanmuryōjukyō shijōsho dentsūki nyūshō 觀無量壽經四帖疏傳通記糅鈔 by Shōgei 聖冏 (1341–1420).

Jōdoshū zensho Vol. 9, 浄土宗全書第九巻. Kyoto: Jōdoshū Shūten Kankōkai, 1908.

Kurodani Shōnin gotō roku 黑谷上人語燈, compiled by Ryōe 了惠 (1243–1330).

Ruizō shū Vol. 5, 類雑集第五巻, woodblock print edition, 1657. In the possession of Otani University Library.

Amaterasu-ōmikami's Divine Message.

INDIVIDUAL PUBLICATIONS

Kōchū Rennyo Shōnin ofumi zenshū 校註蓮如上人御文全集 by Yūshō Tokushi. Tokyo: Bunkenshoin, 1922.

Ofumi kijishu 御文記事珠 by Erin 慧琳 (1715–1789), woodblock print edition, Hōbunkan, Kyoto, 1841, in the possession of Otani University Library.

Ofumi kōyō 御文興要, or *The Essentials of The Letters*, by Erin 慧林 (1721–?), woodblock print edition. Osaka: Ōsaka Shorin, 1768.

Ofumi ryakuge 御文略解, or *Outlines of The Letters*, by Kōgatsuin Jinrei, woodblock print edition. Kyoto: Sawada Tomogorō, 1871. In the possession of Otani University Library.

Ofumi raii shō 御文来意鈔, *The Stories behind The Letters*, by E'nin 惠忍 (1693 –1783), woodblock print edition, Ōsaka Shinsaibashi, 1759 and 1761 in succession, and the modern edition published by Nishimura Kuroemon, Kyoto, in 1898. In the possession of Otani University Library.

Ofumi ryakuge 御文略解, or *Short Commentaries on The Letters*, by E'nen 惠然 (1693–1764), 1881.

Ōjō raisan ge shō 往生禮讃偈鈔 by Gyōe 尭慧(-1395), Vol. 1, woodblock print edition, 1675. In the possession of Otani University Library.

Rennyo Shōnin gyōjitsu 蓮如上人行實 by Masamaru Inaba, Kyoto: Hōzōkan, 1928.

Rennyo Shōnin ibun 蓮如上人遺文, or *The Remaining Writings by Rennyo*, by Masamaru Inaba (1865–1944). Kyoto: Hōzōkan, 1936.

Rennyo Shōnin jōgai ofumi shō 蓮如上人帖外御文鈔, or *The Collection of Rennyo's Letters Not Compiled in The Five Fascicle Letters*, Reion Takehara, ed. Fukuoka: Gushikōsha, 1932.

Senshōji ryakuengi 専照寺略縁起, *The Abridged Story of Senshōji*, quoted in *The Shinshū Zenshi* 真宗全史 by Senshō Murakami (1851–1929), Heigo Shuppansha, Tokyo, 1916.

Shohan-taikō gojō ofumi teihon 諸版対校五帖御文定本, *The Standard Edition of The Five Fascicle Version of The Letters through a Comparative Study of Various Versions*, by Masamaru Inaba (1865–1944). Kyoto: Hōzōkan, originally published in 1933 and republished in 1995.

Shōwa shinshū Hōnen Shōnin zenshū 昭和新修法然上人全集, Kyōdō Ishii, ed. Kyoto: Heirakuji Shoten, 1974. First published by Risōsha, Tokyo, in 1955.

Teihon gojō ofumi 定本五帖御文, Otani Chōjun and Nonaka Ekai, eds, Tokyo: Kawade Shobō Shinsha, 1995.

Modern Sources

WRITINGS IN ENGLISH

Amstutz, Galen, *Interpreting Amida: History and Orientalism in the Study of Pure Land Buddhism*. New York: State University of New York Press, 1997.

Arai, Toshikazu, *Grasped by the Buddha's Vow: A Translation of and Commentary on Tannishō*. California: Buddhist Churches of America Center for Buddhist Education, 2007.

Augustine, Morris J. and Kondo, Tesshō, trans. *Senchaku Hongan Nembutsu Shu*. BDK English Tripiṭaka, Vol. 104-II. Berkeley: Numata Center for Buddhist Translation and Research, 1997.

Bandō, Shōjun and Stewart, Harold, trans. *Tannishō: Passages Deploring Deviation of Faith*. Kyoto: The Eastern Buddhist Society, 1980.

Bloom, Alfred, *Strategies for Modern Living: a commentary with the text of the Tannishō*. Berkeley: Numata Center for Buddhist Translation and Research, 1992.

Bloom, Alfred, edit. *The Essential Shinran: A Buddhist Path of True Entrusting*. Bloomington: World Wisdom, 2007.

Bloom, Alfred, *The Life of Shinran: The Journey to Self-Acceptance*. Berkeley: Institute of Buddhist Studies, revised edition, 1994.

Blum, Mark L. and Yasutomi, Shinya, eds, *Rennyo and the Roots of Modern Japanese Buddhism*. New York: Oxford University Press, 2006.

Brazier, David, *The Feeling the Buddha*. London: Constable, 1997.

Dobbins, James G., *Jōdo Shinshū: Shin Buddhism in Medieval Japan*. Bloomington: Indiana University Press, 1989.

Fields, Rick, *How the Swans Came to the Lake: A Narrative History of Buddhism in America*. Colorado: Shambala, 1981.

Gomez, Luis O., trans. *Land of Bliss: The Paradise of the Buddha of Measureless Light – Sanskrit and Chinese Versions of the Sukhāvatīvyūha Sūtras –*. Honolulu: University of Hawaii Press, 1996.

Harvey, Peter, *An Introduction to Buddhist Ethics*. Cambridge: Cambridge University Press, 2000.

Heisig, James W., and Maraldo, John C., eds, *Rude Awakenings: Zen, the Kyoto School & the Question of Nationalism*. Honolulu: University of Hawaii Press, 1994.

Hongwanji International Center, trans.
Letters of Shinran: A Translation of Mattōshō. Kyoto: Jōdo Shinshū Hongwanji-ha, 1978.
Notes on Essentials of Faith Alone: A translation of Shinran's Yuishinsho mon'i. Kyoto: Jōdo Shinshū Hongwanji-ha, 1979.

*Notes on Once-calling and Many-calling: A Translation of Shinran's
Ichinen-tanen mon'i.* Kyoto: Jōdo Shinshū Hongwanji-ha, 1980.

*Notes on the Inscriptions on Sacred Scrolls: A Translation of Shinran's
Songō shinzō meimon.* Kyoto: Jōdo Shinshū Hongwanji-ha, 1981.

*Passages on the Pure Land Way: A Translation of Shinran's Jōdo monruij
jushō,* Jōdo Shinshū Hongwanji-ha. Kyoto, 1982.

A Record in Lament of Divergences: A translation of Tannishō. Kyoto:
Jōdo Shinshū Hongwanji-ha, 1995.

The Collected Works of Shinran, two volumes. Kyoto: Jōdo Shinshū
Hongwanji-ha, 1997.

Letters of Rennyo: A translation of Rennyo's Gobunshō. Jōdo Shinshū
Hongwanji-ha, Kyoto, 2000.

Inagaki, Hisao, trans., *Liturgy for Birth: Ōjōraisan compiled by Shan-tao.*
Singapore: Horai Association International, 2009.

Inagaki, Hisao, trans., *Nāgārjuna's Discourse on the Ten Stages: Daśabhūmika-
vibhāṣā.* Kyoto: Ryukoku University, 1998.

Inagaki, Hisao, trans., *Shan-tao's Kannenbōmon: The Method of Contemplation
on Amida.* Singapore: Horai Association International, 2010.

Inagaki, Hisao, trans., *T'an-luan's Commentary on Vasubadhu's Discourse
on the Pure Land.* Kyoto: Nagata Bushodo, 1998.

Inagaki, Hisao, trans. *The Three Pure Land Sūtras.* BDK English Tripiṭaka,
Vol. 12-II, III, IV. Berkeley: Numata Center for Buddhist Translation
and Research, 1995.

Inagaki, Hisao, trans. *Thus I have heard from Rennyo Shōnin (Rennyo
Shōnin Goihcidaiki Kikigaki).* Romania: Dharma Lion Publications, 2008.

Ishizuka, Ryūgaku, and Coates, Harper Harvelock, trans., *Hōnen The Buddhist
Saint: His Life and Teaching.* Kyoto: The Society for the Publication
of Sacred Books of the World, 1925.

Kakehashi, Jitsuken, *Hearing the Buddha's Call,* Toshikazu Arai, trans.
Hawaii: Buddhist Study Center, 2012.

Kanamatsu, Kenryō, *Naturalness: A Classic of Shin Buddhism.* Bloomington:
World Wisdom, 2002. Originally published in 1949.

Keel, Hee-Sung, *Understanding Shinran: A Dialogical Approach.* California:
Asian Humanities Press, 1995.

Kikumura, Nobuhiko, *Shinran: His Life and Thought.* Los Angeles: The Nembutsu
Press, 1972.

Kiyozawa, Manshi, *December Fan: The Buddhist Essays of Manshi Kiyozawa.*
Nobuo Haneda, trans. Kyoto: Higashi Honganji Publication Department, 1984.

Kobai, Eiken, *Misunderstandings of Rennyo.* Los Angeles: The Nembutsu
Press, undated.

Mizuno, Kogen, *Essentials of Buddhism: Basic Terminology and Concepts
of Buddhist Philosophy and Practice.* Tokyo: Kōsei Publishing Co., 1996.

Müller, Max, ed. *Sacred Books of the East*, Vol.49, including Max Müller trans. *The Larger Skhāvatī-vyūha* and *The Smaller Skhāvatī-vyūha* and Junjirō Takakusu trans. *The Amitāyur-Dhyāna-Sūtra*. Oxford: Oxford University Press, 1894.

Mun, Chanju & Green, Ronald S., eds, *Buddhist Roles in Peace-making: How Buddhism Can Contribute to Sustainable Peace*. Honolulu: Blue Pine, 2009.

Mun, Chanju & Green, Ronald S., eds, *Living in Peace: Insights from Buddhism*. Honolulu: Blue Pine, 2013.

Nagao, Gajin, *The Foundational Standpoint of Mādhyamika Philosophy*, John P. Keenan, trans. New York: State University of New York Press, 1989.

Nagao, Gajin, *Mādhyamika and Yogācāra: A Study of Mahāyāna Philosophies*, L. S. Kawamura, trans. New York: State University of New York Press, 1991.

Nishitani, Keiji, *Religion and Nothingness*, Jan Van Braft, trans. California: University of California Press, 1982.

Ohtani, Koshin, *The Buddha's Wish for the World*. New York: American Buddhist Center Press, 2009.

Ohtani, Yoshiko, *The Life of Eshinni: Wife of Shinran Shōnin*. Kyoto: Jōdo Shinshū Hogwanji-ha, 1990.

Otto, Rudolf, *India's Religion of Grace and Christianity Compared and Contrasted*, Frank Hugh Foster, trans. New York: Macmillan, 1930.

Paraskevopoulos, John, *Call of the Infinite: The Way of Shin Buddhism*. California: Sophia Perennis, 2009.

Pye, Michael, ed. *Listening to Shin Buddhism: Starting Points of Modern Dialogue*. Sheffield: Equinox, 2012.

Pye, Michael, ed., *Interactions with Japanese Buddhism*. Sheffield: Equinox, 2013.

Pye, Michael, ed., *Lay Buddhism and Spirituality*. Sheffield: Equinox, 2014.

Reischauer, August Karl, trans., *Genshin's Ōjō Yōshū: Collected Essays on Birth into Paradise*, in *The Transactions of the Asiatic Society of Japan*, 2nd series, 1930.

Rogers, Minor L. and Rogers, Ann T., *Rennyo: The Second Founder of Shin Buddhism*. Berkley: Asian Humanities Press, 1991.

Ryukoku Translation Center, trans.
The Shōshin Ge. Kyoto: Ryukoku University, 1961,
The Jōdo Wasan. Kyoto: Ryukoku University, 1965,
The Kōsō Wasan. Kyoto: Ryukoku University, 1974,
The Shōzōmatsu Wasan. Kyoto: Ryukoku University, 1980.
The Sūtra of Contemplation on the Buddha of Immeasurable Life. Kyoto: Ryukoku University, 1984.

Sato, Kemmyo Taira, *Great Living: In the Pure Encounter between Master and Disciple*. New York: American Buddhist Study Center, 2010.

Suzuki, Daisetz T., *An Introduction to Zen Buddhism*. New York: Grove Press, 1964.

Suzuki, Daisetz T., *Buddha of Infinite Light*, revised by Taitetsu Unno.
  Boston: Shambhala Publications, 1997.

Suzuki, Daisetz T., *Collected Writings on Shin Buddhism*, The Eastern
  Buddhist Society, ed. Kyoto: Shinshū Ōtani-ha, 1973.

Suzuki, Daisetz T., *Essays in Zen Buddhism*, First, Second and Third Series.
  London: Luzac and Company, 1926, 1933 and 1934.

Suzuki, Daisetz T., *Japanese Spirituality* 日本的霊性. N. Waddell, trans.,
  Tokyo: Japan Society for the Promotion of Science, 1972.

Suzuki, Daisetz T., *Mysticism: Christian and Buddhist*. New York:
  Harper & Brothers, 1957.

Suzuki, Daisetz T., *Outlines of Mahayana Buddhism*. London: Luzac
  and Company, 1907.

Suzuki, Daisetz T., *Selected Works of D. T. Suzuki Volume I: Zen*, Richard
  M. Jaffe, ed. California: University of California Press, 2014.

Suzuki, Daisetz T., *Selected Works of D. T. Suzuki Volume II: Pure Land*,
  James C. Dobbins, ed. California: University of California Press, 2015.

Suzuki, Daisetz T., *Shin Buddhism*. New York: Harper & Row, 1970.

Suzuki, Daisetz T., *Shinran's Kyōgyōshinshō: The Collection of Passages
  Expounding the True Teaching, Living, Faith, and Realizing of the Pure Land*.
  New York: Oxford University Press, 2012.

Suzuki, Daisetz T., *The Essence of Buddhism*. Kyoto: Hozokan, 1948.

Suzuki, Daisetz T., trans. *The Kyōgyōshinshō [by Shinran]: The Collection of
  Passages Expounding the True Teaching, Living, Faith, and Realizing
  of the Pure Land*. Kyoto: Shinshū Ōtani-ha, 1973.

Suzuki, Daisetz T., *Zen and Japanese Culture*. New York: Bollingen
  Foundation, 1959.

Tagawa, Shun'ei, *Living Yogācāra: An Introduction to Consciousness Only
  Buddhism*, Charles Muller, trans. Boston: Wisdom Publications, 2009.

Takakusu, Junjirō, *The Essentials of Buddhist Philosophy*, Wing Tsit Chan
  and Charles A. Moore, eds, Honolulu: University of Hawaii, 1947.

Takeuchi, Yoshinori, *The Heart of Buddhism*, James W. Heisig, trans. New York:
  Crossroad Publishing Company, 1983.

Tanaka, Kenneth K. and Nasu, Eisho, eds, *Engaged Pure Land Buddhism:
  Essays in Honor of Professor Alfred Bloom*. Berkley: Wisdom Ocean
  publications, 1998.

Ueda, Yoshifumi and Hirota, Dennis, *Shinran: An Introduction to His Thought*.
  Kyoto: Hogwanji International Center, 1989.

Unno, Taitetsu, trans. *Tannisho: A Shin Buddhist Classic*. Nonolulu:
  Buddhist Study Center, 1984.

Unno, Taitetsu, *River of Fire, River of Water*. New York: Doubleday, 1998.

Unno, Taitetsu, *Shin Buddhism: Bits of Rubble Turn into Gold*. New York:
  Doubleday, 2002.

Yamamoto, Kosho, trans., *Kyogyoshinsho or The Teaching, Practice, Faith and Attainment*. Tokyo: Karinbunko, 1958.

Yamamoto, Kosho, *An Introduction to Shin Buddhism*. Tokyo: Karinbunko, 1963.

Yanagi, Sōetsu, *The Unknown Craftsman: A Japanese Insight into Beauty*, trans. & ed., Bernard Leach, Mihoko Okamura, Hiroshi Mizuo and Sonoe Asakawa. Tokyo: Kodansha International, 1972.

WRITINGS IN JAPANESE

Aguru, Zuimu 騰瑞夢, *Shinshū busshōron kettaku* 真宗仏性論決擇. Kyoto: Nagata Bunshōdō, 2001.

Akamatsu, Toshihide 赤松俊秀, *Kamakura bukkyō no kenkyū* 鎌倉仏教の研究. Kyoto: Heirakujihsoten, 1957.

Asaeda, Zenshō 朝枝善照, *Myōkōninden kenkyū* 妙好人伝研究. Kyoto: Nagata Bunshōdō, 1987.

Bando, Shojun 坂東性純, ed. *Daijō butten: Japanese & Chinese Series, Vol. 29 (Kana hōgo)*, 大乗仏典中國・日本編 第29巻 (仮名法語). Tokyo: Chūō Kōronsha, 1991.

Chiba, Joryū 千葉乗隆, *Honpukuji shi* 本福寺史. Kyoto: Dōbōsha, 1980.

Fujita, Kōtatsu 藤田宏達, *Amidakyō kōkyū* 阿彌陀経講究. Kyoto: Higashi Honganji Shuppanbu, 2001.

Fujita, Kōtatsu 藤田宏達, *Genshi jōdo shisō no kenkyū* 原始浄土思想の研究, or *Studies on Early Pure Land Thoughts*. Tokyo: Iwanami Shoten, 1970.

Furuta, Takehiko 古田武彦, *Shinran shisō: Sono shiryō hihan* 親鸞思想: その史料批判, or *Shinran's Thoughts: A Critical Study of the Source Materials*. Tokyo: Toyama-bō, 1975.

Hachiya, Yoshikiyo 蜂屋賢喜代 *Rennyo Shōnin goichidaiki kikigaki kōwa* 蓮如上人御一代記聞書講話, Kyoto: Hōzōkan, 1936.

Hase, Shōtō 長谷正當, *Hongan toha nanika* 本願とは何か. Kyoto: Hōzōkan, 2015.

Hase, Shōtō 長谷正當, *Jōdo toha nanika* 浄土とは何か. Kyoto: Hōzōkan, 2010.

Hayashi, Chikō 林智康, *Rennyo kyōgaku no kenkyū* 蓮如教学の研究, Kyoto: Nagata Bunshōdō, 1998.

Higashi Honganji Kyōgaku Kenkyūsho 東本願寺教学研究所, ed. *Rennyo Shōnin gyōjitsu* 蓮如上人行実. Kyoto: Shinshū Ōtaniha Shūmusho Shuppanbu, 1994.

Honda Hiroyuki 本多弘之, *Jōdo: Sono kaitai to saikōchiku* 浄土−その解体と再構築. Tokyo: Jushinsha, 2007.

Honda Hiroyuki 本多弘之, *Jōdo: Sono hibiki to kotoba* 浄土−その響きと言葉. Tokyo: Jushinsha, 2007.

Honda Hiroyuki 本多弘之, *Jōdo: Ōinaru ba no hataraki* 浄土−大いなる場のはたらき. Tokyo: Jushinsha, 2007.

Hosokawa, Gyōshin 細川行信, Murakami, Munehiro 村上宗博 and Adachi, Yukiko 足立幸子, eds, *Rennyo gojō ofumi* 蓮如五帖御文. Kyoto: Hōzōkan, 1993.

Hosokawa, Gyōshin 細川行信, Murakami, Munehiro 村上宗博 and Adachi, Yukiko 足立幸子, eds, *Rennyo Shōnin goichidaiki kikigaki* 蓮如上人御一代記聞書. Kyoto: Hōzōkan, 1996.

Imai, Masaharu 今井雅晴, *Shinran to Rennyo no sekai* 親鸞と蓮如の世界. Ibaraki: Tsukuda Shoin, 2000.

Imai, Masaharu 今井雅晴, *Shiran to jōdo shinshū* 親鸞と浄土真宗. Tokyo: Yoshikawa Kōbunkan, 2003.

Inagi, Sen'e 稲城選恵, *Gobunshō gaiyō: Rennyo kyōgaku no chūshin mondai* 御文章概要—蓮如教学の中心問題. Kyoto: Hyakkaen, 1973.

Inagi, Sen'e 稲城選恵, *Rennyo kyōgaku no kenkyū* 蓮如教学の研究, Vol. 1, Vol. 2 and Vol. 3. Kyoto: Hōzōkan, 1993, 1994 and 1996.

Inagi, Sen'e 稲城選恵, *Tariki hongan ron* 他力本願論. Kyoto: Hyakkaen, 1970.

Ishida, Mitsuyuki 石田充之, *Senjakushū kenkyū josetsu* 選択集研究序説. Kyoto: Hyakkaen, 1976.

Ishida, Mitsuyuki 石田充之, *Rennyo* 蓮如. Kyoto: Nagata Bunshōdō, 1949.

Ishii, Kyodo 石井教道, *Senjakushū zenkō* 選擇集全講. Kyoto: Heirakuji S hoten, 1984.

Itō, Yuishin 伊藤唯信, *Jōdoshū no seiritsu to tenkai* 浄土宗の成立と展開. 1981.

Iwakura, Masaji 岩倉政治, *Gyōja Dōshū* 行者道宗. Kyoto: Hōzōkan, 1979.

Iwami, Mamoru 岩見護, *Rennyo Shōnin* 蓮如上人. Kyoto, Shōseien, 1949.

Iwami, Mamoru 岩見護, *Akao no Dōshū* 赤尾の道宗. Kyoto: Nagata Bunshōdō, 1956.

Kajiyama, Yūichi 梶山雄一, *Gōhō to rinne: Bukkyō to gendai no setten* 業報と輪廻—佛教と現代の接点. Kajiyama Yūichi Chosaku shū Vol. 8. Tokyo: Shunjūsha, 2011.

Kakehashi, Jitusen 梯實圓, *Rennyo: Sono shōgai no kiseki* 蓮如—その生涯の軌跡. Kyoto: Hyakkaen, 2002.

Kasahara, Kazuo 笠原一男, *Shinshū ni okeru itan no fukei* 真宗における異端の系譜. Tokyo: Tōkyō Daigaku Shuppankai, 1962.

Kasahara, Kazuo 笠原一男, *Shinran to Rennyo: Sono kōdō to shisō* 親鸞と蓮如—その行動と思想. Tokyo: Ronhyōsha, 1978.

Kashiwabara, Yūgi 柏原祐義, *Jōdo sanbukyō kōgi* 浄土三部經講義. Kyoto: Heirakuji Shoten, 1911.

Kashiwabara, Yūgi 柏原祐義, *Sanjō wasan kōgi* 三帖和讃講義. Kyoto: Heirakuji Shoten, 1917.

Kitanishi, Hiromu 北西弘, *Ikkōikki no kenkyū* 一向一揆の研究. Tokyo: Shunjūsha, 1981.

Kikufuji, Akimichi 菊藤明道, ed. *Myōkōnin kenkyū shusei* 妙好人研究集成, or *The Collection of the Articles on Myōkōnin*. Kyoto: Hōzōkan, 2016.

Kikufuji, Akimichi 菊藤明道, *Suzuki Daisetsu no Myōkōnin kenkyū* 鈴木大拙の妙好人研究, or *D. T. Suzuki's Study of Myōkōnin*. Kyoto: Hōzōkan, 2017.

Kusunoki, Kyō 楠恭, ed. *Teihon Myōkōnin Saichi no uta* 定本妙好人才市の歌. Kyoto: Hōzōkan, 1988.

Matsugi, Nobuhiko 真継伸彦, *Watakushi no Rennyo* 私の蓮如. Tokyo: Chikuma Shobō, 1981.

Mita, Zenshin 三田全信, *Hōnen Shōnin shoden no kenkyū* 法然聖人諸傳の研究. Kyoto: Heirakuji Shoten, 1966.

Miyazaki, Enjun 宮崎円遵, *Shoki shinshū no kenkyū* 初期真宗の研究. Kyoto: Nagata Bunshōdō, 1971.

Mizukami, Tsutomu 水上勉 and Sato, Taira 佐藤平, eds, *Daijō butten: Japanese & Chinese series, Vol. 28 (Myōkōnin)*, 大乘仏典 中國・日本編 第28巻 (妙好人). Tokyo: Chūō Kōronsha, 1987.

Mizukami, Tsutomu 水上勉, *Saichi* 才市. Tokyo: Kōdansha, 1989.

Nishitani, Keiji 西谷啓二, ed., *Kaisō Suzuki Daisetsu* 回想鈴木大拙. Tokyo: Shunjūsha, 1975.

Nishitani, Keiji 西谷啓二, *Kami to zettaimu* 神と絶対無. Tokyo: Sōbunsha, 1971.

Nishitani, Keiji 西谷啓二, *Shūkyō toha nanika* 宗教とは何か. Tokyo: Sōbunsha, 1961.

Oguri, Junko 小栗純子, *Nyonin ōjō* 女人往生. Kyoto: Jinbun Shoin, 1987.

Ōhashi, Shunnō, 大橋俊雄 *Jishū no seiritsu to tenkai* 時宗の成立と展開. Tokyo: Yoshikawa Kōbunkan, 1973.

Ōhara, Shōjitsu 大原性實, *Rennyo Shōnin kenkyū* 蓮如上人研究. Kyoto: Hyakkaen, 1948.

Ōmine, Ken 大峯顯, *Rennyo no radikarizumu* 蓮如のラディカリズム. Kyoto: Hōzōkan, 1998.

Odani, Nobuhciyo 小谷信千代, *Shinshū no ōjō ron* 真宗の往生論. Kyoto: Hōzōkan, 2015.

Sasaki, Tadashi 佐々木正, *Shinran shiki* 親鸞始記. Tokyo: Chikuma Shobō, 1997.

Sato, Taira 佐藤平 and Tokunaga, Michio 徳永道雄, eds, *Daijō butten: Japanese & Chinese series, Vol. 21 (Hōnen & Ippen)*, 大乘仏典中國・日本編第21巻 (法然・一遍). Tokyo: Chūō Kōronsha, 1995.

Satō, Taira Kemmyō 佐藤平顯明, *Suzuki Daisetsu no makoto: Sono ikkanshita sensō hinin wo tōshite* 鈴木大拙のまこと：その一貫した戦争否認を通して. Fukuoka: Shogyoji Kyōzō Shiryōshitsu, 2007.

Shimoda, Masahiro 下田正弘, *Nehangyō no kenkyū: Daijō butten no Kenkyū hōhō shiron* 涅槃経の研究－大乘教典の研究方法試論. Tokyo: Shunjūsha, 1997.

Soga, Ryōjin 曽我量深, *Tanni shō chōki* 歎異抄聽記. Kyoto: Higashi Honganji Shuppanbu, 1947.

Soga, Ryōjin 曽我量深, *Shōshin nenbutsu ge chōki* 正信念佛偈聽記. Kyoto: Higashi Honganji Shuppanbu, 1969.

Sugi, Shirō 杉紫朗, *Gobunshō kōwa* 御文章講話. Kyoto: Kōkyō Shoin, 1933.

Suzuki, Daisetz T. 鈴木大拙, *Bukkyō no taii* 仏教の大意. Kyoto: Hōzōkan, 1947.

Suzuki, Daisetz T. 鈴木大拙, *Daisetsu tsurezuregusa* 大拙徒然草. Tokyo: Yomiuri Shinbunsha 1966.

Suzuki, Daisetz T. 鈴木大拙, *Mushin to yū koto* 無心ということ. Tokyo: Daitō Shuppansha, 1939.

Suzuki, Daisetz T. 鈴木大拙, *Myōkōnin* 妙好人. Kyoto: Ōtani Shuppansha, 1948.

Suzuki, Daisetz T. 鈴木大拙, ed. *Myōkōnin Asahara Saichi shū* 妙好人浅原才市集. Tokyo: Shunjūsha, 1967.

Suzuki, Daisetz T. 鈴木大拙, *Nihonteki reisei* 日本的霊性. Tokyo: Daitō Shuppansha, 1944.

Suzuki, Daisetz T. 鈴木大拙, *Shūkyō keiken no jijitsu* 宗教經驗の事實. Tokyo: Daitō Shuppansha, 1943.

Suzuki, Daisetz T. 鈴木大拙, *Shinran no sekai* 親鸞の世界, or *The World of Shinran*, Higashi Hoingannji Shuppanbu, ed. Daisetz T. Suzuki's dialogue with Soga Ryōjin, Kaneko Daiei and Nishitani Keiji. Kyoto: Higashi Honganji Shuppanbu, 1964.

Suzuki, Daisetz T. 鈴木大拙, *Suzuki Daisetsu shinshū nyūmon* 鈴木大拙真宗入門. Sato Taira, trans. Tokyo: Shunjūsha, 1983.

Suzuki, Daisetz T. 鈴木大拙, *Suzuku Daisetsu zenshū Vol. 6* 鈴木大拙全集第六巻. Tokyo: Iwanami Shoten, 1968,
> *Jōdokei shisō ron* 浄土系思想論,
> *Waga jōdo kan* わが浄土觀,
> *Waga shinshū kan* わが真宗觀,
> *Shinshū gairon* 真宗概論.

Suzuki, Daisetz T. 鈴木大拙, *Tōkō no kokoro* 東洋の心. Tokyo: Shunjūsha, 1965.

Takasaki, Jikidō 高崎直道, *Hōshō ron* 宝性論. Tokyo: Kōdansha, 1989.

Takehara, Chimyō 竹原智明, *Shōshinge eza* 正信偈会座. Fukuoka: Shōgyōji, 2005.

Takehara, Chimyō 竹原智明, *Shōzōmatsu wasan eza* 正像末和讚会座. Fukuoka: Chōkaisha, 2012.

Takehara, Reion 竹原嶺音 (Daigyōin, 1876–1951), *Gushikō* 遇斯光, two volumes. Fukuoka: Shōgyōji, 1963. Originally published from 1953 on.

Teramoto, Edatsu 寺本慧達, *Asahara Saichi-ō o kataru* 浅原才市翁を語る. Tokyo: Chiyoda Gakuen, 1952.

Takemura, Makio 竹村牧男, *Shinran to Ippen* 親鸞と一遍. Kyoto: Hōzōkan, 1999.

Taya, Raishun 多屋頼俊, *Tannishō shinchū* 歎異抄新註. Kyoto: Hōzōkan, 1973.

Tamura, Encho 田村圓澄, *Hōnen Shonin den no kenkyū* 法然上人傳の研究. Kyoto: Hōzōkan, 1956.

Tokiwai, Ranyū 常盤井鸞猷, ed. *Kokuhō-bon Sanjō wasan chūge* 國寶本三帖和讚註解, or *The Commentary on The National Treasure Version Three Fascicle Wasan*. Tokyo: Kōdansha, 1972.

Tsujikawa, Tatsuo 辻川達雄, *Rennyo: Yoshizaki fukyō* 蓮如–吉崎布教. Tokyo: Seibundō Shinkōsha, 1984.

Ueda, Yoshifumi 上田義文, *Daijō bukkyō shisō no Konpon kōzō* 大乘仏教思想の根本構造. Kyoto: Hyakkaen, 1957.

Ueda, Yoshifumi 上田義文, *Yuishiki shisō nyūmon* 唯識思想入門. Kyoto, Asoka Shorin, 1964.

Umehara, Shinryū, 梅原真隆, *Rennyo Shōnin kikigaki shinshaku* 蓮如上人聞書新釋. Kyoto: Nishi Hongwanji Shuppanbu, 1982.

Umehara, Takeshi 梅原猛, *Shinran yottsu no nazo o toku* 親鸞「四つの謎」を解く. Tokyo: Shinchōsha, 2014.

Uno, Enkū 宇野圓空, ed. *Rennyo Shōnin* 蓮如上人. Tokyo: Kokusho Kankō Kai, 1976.

Uryūzu, Ryūshin 瓜生津隆真, *Gendaigoyaku Rennyo Shōnin goichidaiki kikigaki,* 現代語訳蓮如上人御一代記聞書. Kyoto: Daizō Shuppan, 1998.

Yamaguchi, Susumu 山口益, *Hannya shisō shi* 般若思想史. Kyoto: Hōzōkan, 1951.

Yamaguchi, Susumu 山口益, *Bukkyōgaku josetsu* 仏教学序説. Kyoto: Heirakuji Shoten, 1981.

Yamaori, Tetsuo 山折哲男, *Ningen Rennyo* 人間蓮如, Tokyo: Shunjūsha, 1970.

Yoshitani, Kakuju 吉谷覺壽, *Ofumi kōjutsu* 御文講述. Kyoto: Hōzōkan, 1910.

GLOSSARY

Ajātaśatru 阿闍世 ch. Āshéshì, jp. Ajase. The son of King Bimbisāra and usurper of his throne. At the instigation of Devadatta he imprisoned and starved his father to death, but later through an encounter with his good friend, Jīvaka, he repented his transgressions and finally took refuge in the Buddha. As a result he spent the rest of his life as a great supporter of Buddhism.

Amida Buddha 阿弥陀佛 skt. Amitâbha Buddha, Amitâyus Buddha, ch. Ēmítuó Fó, jp. Amida Butsu. Amida Buddha is the Buddha of Infinite Light and Eternal Life. These epithets represent the activity of his great wisdom illumining all of the worlds and his great compassion extending throughout the three times of the past, present and future. According to the Pure Land sūtras, "Any being or person qualified to inhabit his land naturally partakes of the same qualifications as those of the creator himself" (D. T. Suzuki's *Preface to The Kyōgyōshinshō*).

Ānanda 阿難 ch. Ānán, jp. Anan. One of the ten great disciples of Śākyamuni Buddha and his constant attendant throughout his life. It was Ānanda, who, through his prodigious memory, narrated the teachings given by Śākyamuni Buddha to his disciples, which were transmitted to later generations as the Buddhist sutras.

awakening of faith The essence of Shin Buddhist faith (jp. *shinjin*) lies in an instantaneous awakening with two aspects: awakening to one's own karmic reality as an unenlightened being and awakening to Amida Buddha's unconditional love.

bad karma 悪業 jp. *akugō*, 罪業 jp. *zaigo* or 罪 jp. *tsumi*. The negative karma that burdens living beings and forces them to remain in their unenlightened state of birth-and-death (skt. *saṃsāra*). Shinran Shōnin regarded all our self-powered actions, even ostensibly 'good' ones, as still being not free from blind passions such as greed, anger, and ignorance, and indeed saw them as rooted in our selfish karmic experience whose origins stretched so far back into the past as to defy comprehension. At the same time, when we entrust ourselves to Amida Buddha, such karma forms no hindrance to the inconceivable working of the great love and compassion of Amida Buddha who has vowed to deliver all beings to the Pure Land.

birth in the Pure Land 往生 jp. ōjō. In Shin Buddhism there are two kinds of 'birth in the Pure Land'. One meaning is to go beyond transmigration (birth-and-death) and is synonymous with the attainment of Nirvāṇa or Enlightenment in the Pure Land. The second meaning is that if a person attains pure faith in the Buddha their new life is embraced by, and to some extent participates in, the Light of the Pure Land whilst remaining within the limitations of this world. The attainment of faith in this world, that is, birth in the Pure Land in the latter sense, assures the ultimate attainment of Nirvāṇa, birth in the Pure Land in the former sense.

blind passions 煩悩 skt. *kleśa*, ch. *fánnǎo*, jp. *bonnō*. Illusions, delusions, attachments, afflictions, defilements, etc. Amongst innumerable blind passions, greed (skt. *rāga*), anger (skt. *pratigha*) and ignorance (skt. *avidyā*) are the most basic ones known as 'three poisons,' working together with pride (skt. *māna*), false views (skt. *dṛṣṭi*) and doubts (skt. *vicikitsā*). As human beings we reconstruct our experience of this world through our intellect (mind) and our five senses (body). The world-view we thus form is entirely self-centred because we are not fully aware of the limitations of our intellect and sense organs. Usually we consider that our views represent the truth and that this truth is absolute and eternal and we remain strongly and selfishly attached to our views. Yet such an attitude, unless we become aware of it, leads to untold suffering and affliction in our lives.

Bodhisattva 菩薩 ch. púsà, jp. bosatsu. A person who has vowed to attain Buddhahood and works for the salvation of all beings.

Buddha-nature 佛性 skt. *buddhatā, buddha-dhātu*, ch. *fóxìng*, jp. *busshō*. The true nature of a Buddha or the absolute potential for all beings to become a Buddha. In Shin Buddhism, Buddha-nature is synonymous with faith or *shinjin*, a gift from Amida Buddha freely given to all sentient beings when they entrust themselves to the Buddha through the working of his Original Vow.

Devadatta 提婆達多 ch. Dīpódáduō, jp. Daibadatta. Śākyamuni Buddha's cousin and Ānanda's elder brother, who was originally Śākyamuni's disciple but later turned against him and tried to kill him. Amongst all kinds of vile acts he committed, the worst was the instigation he gave Prince Ajātaśatru to kill his father King Bimbisāra and rule the country together with him.

Dharma 法 ch. *fǎ*, jp. *hō*. In Buddhism, Dharma means the teaching given by the Buddha or the formless absolute truth of life he was awakened to. The original Sanskrit term also refers to all existing things and their true nature.

Dharma-kāya Dharma-body, 法身 ch. *fǎshēn*, jp. *hosshin*. The formless, ultimate truth of the Buddha-dharma or the absolute nature of the Buddha's Enlightenment which no words can express. The Buddha's Dharmakāya exists beyond his rūpakāya (色身 ch. *sè shēn*, jp. *shikishin*) or corruptible physical form.

Dharmatā 法性 ch. *fǎxìng*, jp. *hosshō*. The pure nature of Dharma or its reality-in-itself that is eternal and blissful.

Enjoyment Body Synonymous with Reward or Response Body. Their original Sanskrit term is *saṃbhoga-kāya* (報身 ch. *bàoshēn*, jp. *hōjin*).

faith 信 ch. *xìn*, jp. *shin*, 信心 ch. *xìnxīn*, jp. *shinjin*. The meaning of faith in Shin Buddhism is a twofold and simultaneous awakening both to one's own karmic reality and the unconditional love of Amida Buddha, which leads one to entrusting oneself to the Buddha. The essential teaching of Shin Buddhism is salvation through faith alone.

five grave offences 五逆 ch. *wǔnì*, jp. *gogyaku*. In the Theravada tradition "five grave offences" consist of: killing one's father, killing one's mother, killing an arhat, destroying the harmony of the Sangha, and causing blood to flow from the body of a Buddha. In the Mahāyāna tradition the following five are listed: destroying temples or stūpas, burning sūtras or Buddha images or stealing the belongings of the Three Treasures; slandering the Śrāvakayāna 声聞乘 (jp. *shōmonjō*), the Pratyekabuddhayāna 縁覚乘 (jp. *engakujō*) and the Bodhisattvayāna 菩薩乘 (jp. *bosatsujō*) and belittling their holy scriptures; obstructing the practice of a monk, by abusing, attacking, imprisoning or murdering; violation of one or more of the five grave offences of the Theravada tradition mentioned above; and committing the ten bad acts denying the moral law of cause and effect.

five right practices 五正行 ch. *wǔ zhèngxíng*, jp. *go shōgyō*. The teaching of Five Right Practices is found in *The Exposition of The Meditation Sūtra* by Shàndǎo. They are: Reciting the Pure Land Sūtras, Contemplating Amida Buddha and his Pure Land, Bowing to Amida Buddha, Pronouncing Amida's Name, Praising and making offerings to Amida. These are further sub-divided into 'Right Practice' which is 'Pronouncing Amida's Name' (*Namu Amida-butsu*) and the other four practices which are known as 'Supportive Practices'.

gāthā 偈 ch. *jì*, jp. *ge*. Buddhist verse or hymn. The verse portion of sutras or commentaries.

goshō 後生 ch. *hòushēng*, jp. *goshō*. The origin of the Japanese word *goshō* 後生 can be traced back to a statement found in *The Larger Sūtra of Eternal Life*, 後生無量 寿佛国, "You will next be born in the country of the Buddha of Eternal Life." Thus it means next birth or Rebirth in the Pure Land, not as sometimes translated next life or afterlife. Rebirth in the Pure Land is also known as the 'birth of no birth', meaning the complete transcendence of the world of transmigration through birth-and-death. In Shin Buddhism *goshō* or Rebirth in the Pure Land is only assured through the attainment of faith in the here and now. Therefore, when the Great Matter of *goshō* (Rebirth in the Pure Land) is mentioned, it also indicates the absolute importance of the awakening of faith in everyday life. Because the attainment of faith means entering a new life in which *goshō* or Rebirth in the Pure Land is definitely assured, not only birth in the Pure Land at the moment of death but also the attainment of faith in this life is likewise called 'birth in the Pure Land'.

gratitude Gratitude for "what has been done for us". Once we become aware of Amida Buddha's unconditional love through the acquisition of true faith (the state of mind which has no doubt), the *Nenbutsu* that issues from our mouths is an expression of our supreme gratitude. On attaining pure faith we become grateful not only to Amida Buddha but also to everyone and everything that has helped us encounter the Buddha.

hearing that Name The literal translation of the phrase 聞其名号 (jp. *mon go myōgō*), from the passage on the fulfilment of the Eighteenth Vow in *The Larger Sūtra of Eternal Life*. Here, the Name that is being heard refers to Amida Buddha's statement in the Seventeenth Vow: that, unless all Buddhas pronounce his Name in universal praise, he would not attain the Supreme Enlightenment. The great working of the *Nenbutsu* from the world of Enlightenment is here being described in terms of the Name that is being pronounced by all Buddhas and the same Name that is being heard by all sentient beings. In short, on hearing the Name pronounced by another, one attains the awakening of pure faith in the *Nenbutsu*.

Higan'e 彼岸会. Buddhist services performed during the week of the equinox.

hiraza 平座. Manner in meetings propagated by Rennyo, meaning "sitting as equals on the same floor level".

Honganji 本願寺. In the days of Rennyo there were several schools of the Jōdo Shinshū tradition and Honganji was the Head Temple of one of them prior to its further separation into its Eastern and Western branches.

Hōnen 法然. (1133–1212) Master of Shinran and the first founder in Japan of an independent Pure Land tradition.

Hōonkō 報恩講. The most important Shin Buddhist annual ceremony held for followers to commemorate the death of its Founder Shinran Shōnin and respond to him with gratitude for what he has done for them throughout his life.

icchantika 一闡提 ch. *yīchǎntí*, jp. *issendai*. Sanskrit term that originally means those who follow their cravings and desires. In Buddhism it refers to those who are destitute of Buddha-nature due to their selfish views and wrongdoings.

ignorant being 凡夫 ch. *fánfū*, jp. *bonbu*. An ordinary, unenlightened person.

Jōdo Shinshū 浄土真宗. Originally meaning the 'True Pure Land Teaching' that Shinran Shōnin received from Hōnen Shōnin, it became later the name of the Buddhist tradition which has Shinran Shōnin as its founder. Often abbreviated to "Shin Buddhism".

karma 業 ch. *yè*, jp. *gō*. Literally means 'action' and also refers to the causality of our actions, the way that each and every action has an effect on our subsequent deeds. According to the teaching of the Buddha each person is responsible for each action he or she takes. When the notion of "wrongdoing" or "bad karma" (*zaigō* or *akugō*) is referred to, it is always with this principle in mind. Because one is responsible for everything one does, one becomes aware in the light of the Buddha that such actions, carried out selfishly, constitute "wrong-doing" or "bad karma" and should be viewed as such. When those dark, negative aspects are vanquished, illuminated by the instantaneous awakening of faith, there opens up for us that deepest spiritual dimension where we can live our lives positively, always hoping to benefit ourselves and others at the same time.

karmic existence One's karmically conditioned existence in the world of birth-and-death.

Kyōgyōshinshō 『教行信証』 The popular, abbreviated title of Shinran Shonin's major work which is formally called the *Ken jōdo shinjitsu kyōgyōshō monrui* (*The Collection of Passages Expounding the True Teaching, Practice, and Realizing of the Pure Land*). Completed in 1224 it consists of a systematic presentation of the Jōdo Shinshū teaching through the use of carefully selected quotations from the Buddhist Canon set alongside Shinran's own comments.

Land of Enjoyment 報土 jp. *hōdo*. See 'Pure Land'.

Land of Happiness 安楽国 jp. *anraku-koku*. See 'Pure Land'.

Land of Utmost Bliss 極楽 jp. *gokuraku*. See 'Pure Land'.

Larger Sūtra of Eternal Life The most important sūtra in Pure Land Buddhism which relates Amida Buddha's original vows by which he created his Pure Land for the salvation of all sentient beings without any form of discrimination between them.

miscellaneous practices 雑行 jp. *zōgyō*. All religious practices other than 'Five Right Practices', i.e. practices unrelated to Amida Buddha. Also known as Sundry Practices in other translations.

Name 名號 ch. *mínghào*, jp *myōgō*, or 佛號 ch. *fóhào*, jp. *butsugo*. In Pure Land Buddhism this refers to the Name of Amida Buddha, *Namu Amida-butsu*, literally meaning 'I take refuge in Amida Buddha.' The Name expressed in this act of taking refuge in Amida Buddha is understood to be due entirely to the working of Amida

Buddha. The moment we entrust ourselves to Amida Buddha we find the Name wells up from within. The Name is the activity of the Buddha-kāya that carries us to Amida's Pure Land for our ultimate attainment of Enlightenment. As a formula expressed in words, the Name works for our salvation through our senses and intellect; at the same time, the Name goes beyond the limits of senses and intellect, as the inconceivable working of Amida Buddha. In daily usage the Name also means the calligraphy of *Namu Amida-butsu* 南无阿弥陀佛.

Nenbutsu To pronounce the Name of Amida Buddha or to be mindful of Amida Buddha. The *Nenbutsu* in Shin Buddhism is to call the Name (jp. *myōgō*) of Amida Buddha with joy and gratitude having awakened to both the Unconditional Love of Amida Buddha and the reality of one's own karmic existence. It is pronounced thereafter as an expression of our gratitude, not as a meritorious act or as a form of religious practice by which to gain some good result.

Nirvāṇa 涅槃 jp. *nehan*. The Sanskrit word Nirvāṇa means 'to be extinguished', 'to be calmed', 'to disappear', or 'to be deceased.' In Buddhism it refers to 'tranquillity as the fruit of Enlightenment,' the state of mind in which all blind passions binding one to transmigration through birth-and-death have been extinguished. It includes characteristics such as the extinction of suffering, awakening to the truth of life, formless wisdom, utter tranquillity, inner peace and, ultimately, universal love or sympathy for all beings. In ordinary usage it can also mean death.

One Mind Mind of pure Other Power faith.

one thought-moment 一念 jp. *ichinen*. ch. *yīniàn*, skt. *eka-kṣaṇa*. One thought-moment stands for the very shortest moment or instant of time. Faith is attained instantly at the very moment one takes refuge in Amida Buddha.

oneness of *ki* and *Hō* 機法一体 jp. *kiho ittai*. The character *ki* 機 means the 'momentum' through which *Hō* 法, or the 'Dharma', starts to work, actually referring to one who is saved by the Dharma. *Ki* refers to "those who take refuge by saying *namu*," *Hō* means "Amida Buddha's Dharma that saves them." Those two, *ki* and *Hō*, are one in *Namu Amida-butsu*. This oneness of *ki* and *Hō* in *Namu Amida-butsu* represents Rennyo's realisation of faith.

Original Vow 本願 jp. *hongan*, ch. *běnyuàn*, skt. *pūrva-praṇidhāna*. Amida Buddha's Eighteenth Vow from *The Larger Sūtra of Eternal Life* to save all sentient beings universally without any form of discrimination.

Other Power 他力 ch. *tālì*, jp *tariki*. The power of Amida Buddha's Original Vow that works to save all sentient beings, delivering them from the karma of transmigrating endlessly through birth-and-death. Through Other Power we are awakened to the ultimate truth of interdependent origination, the very source of Amida's Original Vow. Historical research shows that the Chinese term 他力 *tālì* also refers to the notion of interdependency.

past good conditions 宿善 jp. *shukuzen*. A term often used by Rennyo Shōnin to describe all the factors and conditions that have led to our encounter with the Buddha-dharma. Amongst these factors some originally consist of 'bad' or 'evil' karma. Such karma is transformed through our encounter with the working of the Buddha-dharma. On attaining the true faith of entrusting ourselves to the Original Vow, we rediscover with gratitude that everyone and everything has helped us reach this point. Once we awaken to Other Power faith, in the new light of awareness that comes about through our involvement in the Buddha-dharma, everything in our life is affirmed in its totality and found to be 'good'.

pāramitā 波羅蜜 jp. *haramitsu*, ch. *bōluómì*. The Sanskrit term *pāramitā* (lit., 'perfection') has been translated into Chinese as 'crossing over', 'reaching the infinite', or 'reaching the other shore.' It is by means of *pāramitā* practice that one leaves this shore of birth-and-death and reaches the other shore of Nirvāṇa. The original six *pāramitā* practices of Early Buddhism were the perfections of donation, observance of precepts, patience, endeavour, meditation and wisdom. Because of their altruistic concerns the Mahayanists added to the original six a further four: the perfections of skilful means, vows, strength, and transcendental knowledge. In Mahāyāna Buddhism *pāramitā* practice is understood as the practice of bodhisattvas in general, and in Shin Buddhism as that of Bodhisattva Dharmākara (Amida Buddha) in particular.

peaceful awareness 安心 jp. *anjin*. Refers to 'the awareness attained through the awakening of faith'. "Peaceful awareness" or *anjin* means 1) the awareness of the sad reality of one's existence, filled with blind passions and karmic hindrances, and 2) the awareness at the same time of the Buddha's unconditional love that saves all beings just as they are without any discrimination at all. Such peaceful awareness of salvation through the Buddha's great compassion is gained through the experience of having the pure faith to entrust oneself absolutely to the Buddha just as one is. In other words "peaceful awareness" is the absolutely stable state of mind in which one is fully aware of oneself and of the Buddha, both at the same time.

Pure Land 浄土 jp. *jōdo*, ch. *jìngtǔ*. In Pure Land Buddhism it refers to the realm brought into being by Amida Buddha where all its inhabitants can attain Nirvāṇa. In the original Sanskrit the Pure Land is *sukhāvatī* which means 'Land of Utmost Bliss'. The Pure Land is the world of Enlightenment where there is no birth and no death. Thus the Pure Land is also said to be the equivalent of Nirvāṇa. By virtue of Amida's Original Vow, birth in the Pure Land means ultimately attaining Buddhahood. Because every inhabitant therein can enjoy attaining Buddhahood, the Pure Land is also called the Land of Enjoyment.

right practice 正行 jp. *shōgyō*, ch. *zhèngxíng* or 正定業 jp *shōjōgō*, ch. *zhèngdìng yè*. Amongst the five right practices, 'pronouncing the Name of Amida Buddha' is called the right practice that rightly assures our birth in the Pure Land, distinguished from the other four supportive right practices. Right practice as pronouncing the Name is synonymous with saying the *Nenbutsu*, an invocation of *Namu Amida-butsu*.

salvation Salvation in Buddhism means to become free from the transmigration of birth-and-death through being awakened to the truth of life or, in other words, attaining Enlightenment.

Sangha 僧伽 skt. *saṃgha*, ch. *sēngqié*, jp. *sōgya*. Originally being the title of the monastic order founded by Śākyamuni Buddha, the term nowadays describes any community or grouping of Buddhist followers. The Sangha is one of the 'Triple Treasures' (Buddha, Dharma, Sangha) and responsible for the preservation and transmission of the teachings.

secret teachings 秘事法門 jp. *hijibōmon*, refers to a group of heterodoxies that diverged from Shinran's teaching and were often transmitted through esoteric forms. At the early stage of Shin Buddhist tradition they were called "midnight teachings" or "hidden doctrines" as they would often be conveyed at night secretly. From the traditional viewpoint based on Shinran's religious philosophy, "secret teachings" are biased, misleading and dangerous.

self power 自力 jp *jiriki*, ch. *zìlì*. Refers to the use of or attachment to one's self-centred efforts in order to obtain enlightenment. In Shin Buddhism the essence of faith-experience lies in awakening and entrusting oneself to Other Power or the power of Amida's Original Vow.

Shin Buddhism Term coined by D.T. Suzuki as an abbreviation of Jōdo Shinshū.

Shinran Shinran 親鸞 (1173–1262) was a Tendai monk and later became a disciple of the famous Pure Land teacher Hōnen. Although Shinran never attempted to found his own sect, his innovative and unique approach to the Pure Land teaching became known as the Jōdo Shinshū or Shin Buddhism. He left a great many of his own writings such as his main work *Kyōgyōshinshō, Gotoku shō* and the *Wasan* or *Japanese Hymns*.

supportive practices 助業 jp. *jogō*. See 'Five Right Practices' above.

Tathāgata 如来 jp. *nyorai*, ch. *rúlái*. One of the ten epithets of a Buddha; lit., 'one who has thus come' or 'one who has thus gone'.

taya 多屋 or 他屋 in Japanese. A residence, usually in or near a temple or *dōjō*, built to accommodate Shin Buddhist followers so that they can stay there to listen to the Buddha-dharma and discuss the matter of faith. The *taya* system originated in Rennyo Shōnin's day but has now almost died out in Japan, with the notable exception of Shogyoji, a Jōdo Shinshū temple in Fukuoka, Japan, which revived the tradition in the mid-twentieth century.

ten bad acts 十悪 jp. *jūaku*, ch. *shíè*. Destroying life, theft, adultery, lying, talking nonsense, speaking evil of others, being double-tongued, greed, anger and ignorance.

Tendai 天台 ch. Tiāntái. A major Buddhist tradition originally founded in China by 智顗 Zhìyǐ (538–597) and transferred to Japan by 最澄 Saichō (767–822).

three bad paths 三塗 jp. *sanzu*, ch. *sāntú*, skt. *apāya*. The realms of hell, hungry ghosts and animals.

three dangerous desires 名聞 jp. *myōmon* is "desire for fame," 利養 jp. *riyō*, "desire for wealth," and 勝他 jp. *shōta*, "desire for domination."

three submissions 三従 jp. *sanshō*, ch. *sāncóng*. The three kinds of hindrances said to encumber women: Women had to obey their parents when young; they had to obey their husband and were not free when they married; and they had to obey their children when becoming old.

three minds 三心 jp. *sanjin*, ch. *sānxīn*. This is a term found in *The Meditation Sūtra* and refers to the "the mind that is true and sincere," "the deep mind" and "the mind desiring to be born in the Pure Land." These three minds are taught to lead people to the triple mind of Other Power faith in *The Larger Sūtra of Eternal Life*.

triple mind 三信 jp. *sanshin*, ch. *sānxìn*. The "triple mind" is a term found in *The Larger Sūtra of Eternal Life* and refers to the threefold mind of "sincerity," "faith" and "aspiration for birth in the Pure Land." These three are considered to be the three aspects of the "One Mind of Other Power faith."

virtue-transference 廻向 jp. *ekō,* ch. *huíxiàng,* skt. *pariṇāma.* The original meaning of the term *pariṇāma* or "virtue-transference" is to transfer one's virtue to people to benefit oneself and others. It is understood in Shin Buddhism, however, that "virtue-transference" only comes from Amida Buddha himself to all sentient beings. Amida directs his great virtues to them for their going to the Pure Land to attain Enlightenment themselves and for their returning to this world to help others to do so. This is called "two forms of virtue-transference, outgoing and returning."

wasan 和讚 jp. *wasan.* Buddhist hymns written in Japanese. Regarding the *wasan* composed by Shinran, there are three main collections: *Jōdo Wasan* – Japanese Hymns on the Pure Land, *Kōsō Wasan* – Hymns on the Patriarchs of the Pure Land Tradition and *Shōzōmatsu Wasan* – Hymns on the Periods of Right Dharma, Semblance Dharma and Last Dharma. Rennyo Shōnin established the liturgical use of the *wasan* and published an edition of the three collections for chanting. Since that time six of these *wasan* are chanted each day during the main daily services in Shin Buddhist temples.

what has been done for us 恩 jp. *on,* ch. ēn, skt. upakāra. Translation of the Chinese character '*on*'. It is said in Buddhism in general that there are four kinds of '*on*': 1) that of one's parents, i.e. what has been done for us by our parents, 2) that of the ruler, i.e. what has been done by the ruler in his or her role as a symbol of state, 3) that of all sentient beings, meaning what has been done for us by other people or other living beings, and 4) that of the Triple Treasure (Buddha, Dharma and Sangha), signifying what has been done for a seeker after truth by the Triple Treasure. The word *on* has also been rendered as benevolence, grace, favour, benefit, kindness, gift, indebtedness etc. The reason that it is rendered as "what has been done for us" is because it is extremely important in the context of Buddhism for us to know or become aware of all that has been done for us by others.

APPENDICES

Appendix 1

The notion of gods in Japanese Buddhism.

The concept of gods or *devas* in Buddhism is different from the notion of God found in theistic religions. These gods are unenlightened beings who reside within the world of illusion. The gods or *kami* of indigenous Japanese religions also differ from the Western, theistic notion of 'gods' and include a vast and diverse range of phenomena. As the late 18th century scholar Moto'ori Norinaga (1730–1801) in the field of Japanese literature states in his main writing, *Kojiki den*, "Among various things such as human beings of course, birds and animals, trees and grasses, mountains and oceans, whatever seems extraordinary, possessed of excellent virtues, and inspiring a feeling of awe is called *kami*."

According to Mahāyāna cosmology the whole universe consists of ten realms, namely those of buddhas, bodhisattvas, *śrāvakas*, *pratyekabuddhas*, gods (*devas*), human beings, *asuras*, hungry ghosts, animals and hellish beings. Those ten realms are classified into two groups; the first four are called the realms of enlightenment and the second are known as the six realms of illusion. Each one of these realms is said to mutually interpenetrate and include all of the others.

The realm of gods (*devas*) is part of the world of illusion that is known as the Triple World or the Six Realms. This Triple World is made up of the World of Desire, the World of Form and the World of Formlessness. Gods exist in all three of these Worlds and are classified into three groups, gods (*devas*) of the World of Desire, gods of the World of Form and gods of the World of Formlessness.

The World of Desire consists of the Six Paths or Forms of Existence, namely those of devas (gods), human beings, *asuras*, hungry ghosts, animals and hellish beings. The beings who reside in these forms of existence are all deeply attached to carnal desires. There are six kinds of gods inhabiting the World of Desire within six different heavens. Unlike the gods who live in the World of Form and the World of Formlessness, the gods who live in this world are unable to free themselves from their desires.

Within the World of Form there are eighteen kinds of gods and their heavens. These are grouped within four main heavens containing the gods belonging to the first, second, third and fourth stages of meditation (*dhyāna-bhūmi*). The gods who live in this world are much less attached to the strong desires which exist in the World of Desire but are not free from their attachment to form.

The World of Formlessness contains four kinds of gods and their heavens. This is the realm where the gods who are free from desire and the attachment to form reside. It is made up of four stages: the stage of spatial infinity, the stage of the infinity of consciousness, the stage of nothingness and the stage of neither consciousness nor unconsciousness.

After the transmission to Japan of this profound Buddhist philosophy, traditional Japanese gods (*kami*) were merged into the Buddhist cosmology. According to the Buddhist theory known as *honji suijaku setsu* (本地垂迹説) that originally started in China and prevailed in Japan after the import of Esoteric Buddhism within schools such as the Tendai and Shingon traditions, Japanese gods are explained as being manifestations of Buddhas or Bodhisattvas. In other words, Japanese gods in their original state are held to have been Buddhas and Bodhisattvas.

See *Chapter 40* and *Appendix 2*.

Appendix 2

The Mahāyānist notion of Buddha's "triple body" (skt. *trikāya*, 三身 ch. *sānshēn*, jp. *sanjin*).
Whilst, according to Tánluán's Buddhist philosophy found in his *Commentary on the Treatise on the Pure Land*, the *Buddha-kāya* is seen as having two modes: the *Dharma-kāya* as Dharma-in-itself and the *Dharma-kāya* in its manifest form, in the Mahāyāna tradition there is another famous theory of the *Buddha-kaya*, known as the Buddha's *trikāya* (triple body) doctrine: '*Dharma-kāya, Saṃbhoga-kāya* and *Nirmāṇa-kāya*.' According to this teaching, when the *Dharma-kāya* works for all beings in its manifest form it is seen as '*Saṃbhoga-kāya*.' Amida Buddha is such a Buddha of *Saṃbhoga-kāya*. '*Saṃbhoga-kāya*' is a term sometimes translated as 'Body of Recompense' and sometimes as 'Enjoyment-body.' In the sense that Amida is a Buddha who attained Buddhahood as a result of a long period of self-discipline based on his Original Vows when still a bodhisattva, the term can be translated as 'Body of recompense'. As such Amida is also a Buddha of Enjoyment-body, because he is now enjoying receiving the fruit of his own Enlightenment and at the same time making others receive it in his Pure Land. Amida as the Buddha of *Dharma-kāya* in its manifest form in the framework of Tánluán's Pure Land philosophy stands for the *Saṃbhoga-kāya* (Enjoyment-body or Body of Recompense) in the three *Buddha-kāya* doctrine, both the *Dharma-kāya* in its manifested form and the *Saṃbhoga-kāya* coming originally from formless truth or Dharma-in-itself. *Nirmāṇa-kāya* stands for Śākyamuni Buddha, a Buddha who appears as a human being in this world.The very foundation of *Nirmāṇa-kāya* is again the *Dharma-kāya* as Dharma-in-itself. *Dharma-kāya* is also believed to appear as "various body-forms," including bodhisattvas and gods. According to the philosophy of Mahāyāna Buddhism, all the phenomena of the universe are viewed as manifestations of Dharma-kāya, formless truth or Emptiness. Therefore the *Buddha-kāya*, or *Dharma-kāya*, seen as a whole, is not form nor is it no-form. Tánluán states in *The Commentary on the Treatise on the Pure Land*, "The reason why the '*Dharma-kāya*' is described as 'unconditioned' is in order to show that the *Dharma-kāya* is neither form nor no-form. A double 'No' does not mean 'Yes' as opposed to 'No.' Rather it is an absolute 'Yes' with no 'No' standing against it. It is 'Yes' all by itself. It is not waiting for any 'No' to come up and negate it. This kind of 'Yes' is, therefore, neither 'Yes' nor 'No.' It is something beyond description even by 'one hundred negations'."

In the Shin Buddhist tradition, how to understand Amida's *Buddha-kāya* is discussed in Chapter 15 of *The Kudenshō* (*What Shinran Taught*) by Kakunyo (1270–1351). This text has recently been translated into English by Wayne Yokoyama. The beginning of Chapter 15 is as follows:

Defining Amida Nyorai as a reward-body Nyorai [*Saṃbhoga-kāya Tathāgata*] is not a question of our sect versus other sects, but is an ancient concept that has been with us for a long time. Thus, Keikei (荊溪 ch. *Jīngxī*, 711–782) also says that, "The various teachings' praise is mostly directed towards Amida," and Kakuun Kashō (覺運和尚 935–1007) of Danna-in (Tendai) comments that, "The fact that Amida attained Buddhahood in the ancient past is a point that has long been explained in different sutras" (*Nenbutsu hōgo*). Not only that, this was also pointed out by the predecessors to the teachers in our land. The commentary of one of our school's masters (*Hōjisan* by Zendō 善導, ch. *Shàndǎo*) says, "Ever since the time of Kaitoku, the very first Nyorai, down to the present one of Śākyamuni, there have been many Buddhas; all of them rode on the Universal Vow and practiced both compassion and wisdom." Therefore, all the Buddhas who appeared in the world one after another from the time of Kaitoku Buddha down to the present teacher Śākyamuni, rode on Amida's Universal Vow and manifested in themselves the mind to benefit self and benefit others. If we place Kakuun Kashō's comment that "Shakyamuni is also the Amida who attained the highest enlightenment in the ancient past" next to the interpretation of Kashō (Zendō) mentioned above, this amounts to logical proof that all the Buddhas from the very first one, Kaitoku, on down are necessarily the transformation bodies of Amida who achieved perfect enlightenment in the ancient [timeless] past.

In the Shin Buddhist tradition, the last phrase of this quotation "Amida who achieved perfect enlightenment in the ancient past" stands for the *Dharma-kāya* as Dharma-in-itself and is not something separate from the *Dharma-kāya* in its manifested form or Amida as the *Saṃbhoga-kāya*. In the Shin Buddhist tradition Amida as the *Saṃbhoga-kāya* is understood in its interdependent relationship with the very foundation of the Buddha, the *Dharma-kāya* as Dharma-in-itself.

See *Chapter 18, Chapter 23* and *Appendix 3*.

Appendix 3

Amida Buddha as *hōben hosshin* 方便法身 or "the Dharma-kāya in its manifested form".

Although the original Japanese word *hōben* 方便 (*upāya* in Sanskrit, meaning "means") has various meanings such as "the means of leading sentient beings to the truth," "the provisional teachings to lead sentient beings to the final doctrine," "relative wisdom appearing from the absolute wisdom of *prajñā*" and "unselfish service to sentient beings with relative and absolute wisdom," the word "means" in this special context signifies "manifestation of the truth", particularly "the *Dharma-kāya* in its manifested form." This particular phrase is the translation of the Chinese phrase 方便法身 (ch. *fāngbiàn fǎshēn*, jp. *hōben hosshin*). As a systematic way of understanding the *Buddha-kāya*, the phrase 方便法身 *hōben hosshin* is paired with the other phrase 法性法身 *hosshō hosshin*, "the *Dharma-kāya* as Dharma-in-itself." Tánluán (476–542) states in his *Commentary on the Treatise on the Pure Land*, "The two modes are distinguishable in the *Dharma-kāya*, whose manifestations are Buddhas and bodhisattvas. One mode is the *Dharma-kāya* as Dharma-in-itself; the other is the *Dharma-kāya* in its manifested form. The manifested form exists depending on the Dharma-in-itself, and the Dharma-in-itself is known by expressing itself in its manifestations. These two modes are distinguishable but are not to be regarded as two independent existences. They are one and yet not to be identified. Therefore, they are to be understood as the interfusion of the general and the particular under the one word, Dharma."

All this is an ontological interpretation of Amida Buddha. The *Buddha-kāya* known as *hōben hosshin* or "the *Dharma-kāya* in its manifested form" stands for Amida Buddha. *Hosshō hosshin*, or "the *Dharma-kāya* as Dharma-in-itself," is formless truth and when this formless truth takes form, it is "the *Dharma-kāya* in its manifested form," that is Amida Buddha. "The *Dharma-kāya* in its manifested form" issues from "the *Dharma-kāya* as Dharma-in-itself" and it is through "the *Dharma-kāya* in its manifested form" that "the *Dharma-kāya* as Dharma-in-itself" comes to be realised.

According to another doctrinal explanation of the *Buddha-kāya*, the "Triple-body (*tri-kāya*) Theory," Amida Buddha pertains to the *Saṃbhoga-kāya*, or the body of enjoyment, that, having fulfilled the Original Vow, enjoys the fruit of Supreme Enlightenment and helps visitors to his Pure Land enjoy the same fruit.

Thus Amida Buddha as the *hōben hosshin*, "the *Dharma-kāya* in its manifested form," can also be seen as the *Saṃbhoga-kāya*, the enjoyment-body.

See *Chapter 18, Chapter 23, Chapter 31, Chapter 66* and *Appendix 2*.

Appendix 4

The textual sources of the word *anjin* 安心 (ch. *ānxin*) in Pure Land Buddhism.

Amongst the Pure Land texts written by the seven patriarchs of the Shin Buddhist tradition, *The Commentary on (Vasubandhu's) Treatise on the Pure Land*, a work by a Chinese Pure Land monk, Tánluán (476–542), provides the first appearance of the word 安心: "Having entered the company [of the Tathāgata's great assembly] (the second gate of virtue amongst the five gates of virtue), [the bodhisattva] can enter the residence (the third gate of virtue) where he can practise [*śamatha*] and quiet the mind (安心)." (*Shinshū shōgyō zensho*, Vol. I, p. 344). It seems that this compound 安心 refers to the act of quieting the mind or the state of quieted peaceful mind by which the bodhisattva can concentrate on the [*śamatha*] practice.

When Shàndǎo (613–681) used the same word in his *Liturgy for Birth*, it was to ask how "to quiet the mind (安心 jp. *anjin*)," a question he raised simply to develop his argument. (*Shinshū shōgyō zensho*, Vol. I, p. 648). His answer to his own question was that *anjin*, or faith, could be attained through the realisation of the "three minds" expounded in *The Sūtra of Meditation*: 1) the mind that is true and sincere, 2) the deep mind and 3) the mind desiring to be born in the Pure Land by means of virtue-transference. According to Shin Buddhist philosophy, these three minds expounded in *The Meditation Sūtra* are provisionally differentiated from the triple mind found in *The Larger Sūtra of Eternal Life* (sincerity, faith and aspiration for birth in the Pure Land); in this context the three minds are taught as a way of bringing about awakening to Amida's true mind and the triple mind is to be understood as three aspects of the true mind itself. From the fundamental view-point of Shinran Shōnin's religious philosophy, however, both are expressions of Amida's true mind and the true, hidden meaning of the three minds intrinsically accord with the triple mind, Amida's true mind realised in ourselves as true faith, or *shinjin*. When we consider Shàndǎo's use of the word *anjin*, we have to realise that it is from this fundamental view-point of Shinran Shōnin's religious philosophy that the word *anjin*, the realisation of the three minds, is understood as being synonymous with *shinjin*, or true faith.

Another passage where Shàndǎo used the word *anjin* is found in his *Bānzhōuzàn* 般舟讚 (jp. *Hanjusan*) : "By quieting the heart (安心) and settling the mind (定意), you will be born in the Land of Peace and Happiness." (*Shinshū shōgyō zensho*, Vol. I, p. 696).

Regarding the further development of the notion *anjin* in Japanese Pure Land Buddhism, see *Chapter 22, Chapter 28, Chapter 30, Chapter 57* and *Chapter 67*.

Appendix 5

Two accounts from *The Shinran Shōnin shōmyō den* 親鸞聖人正明傳, or *The Authentic Biography of Shinran Shōnin*, by Zonkaku.

With regard to Shinran's marriage there are two further important stories that exist, one predating the vision the *Godenshō* mentions him having and the other postdating it. Both stories have been brought to the attention of a wider public through a recent work, the *Shinran shiki* 親鸞始記 by Tadashi Sasaki. In his book Sasaki emphasises the importance of the *Shinran Shōnin shōmyō den* 親鸞正明傳 written by Kakunyo's oldest son, Zonkaku (1290–1373), which records both stories in considerable detail. Unfortunately little attention has hitherto been paid by Shin Buddhist scholars to the *Shinran Shōnin shōmyō den*. Many Shin Buddhist academics from the two biggest Shin Buddhist denominations, the Higashi Honganji and the Nishi Honganji traditions, have been ignoring this document that had been kept at the headquarters of the Takada tradition, another important Shin Buddhist denomination, despite the fact that it was published as woodprint in 1733 and 1738 and also as a part of *Shinshū Zensho* Vol. 34 in 1914. A closer and more careful examination of this biography by Zonkaku, however, in addition to providing sufficient evidence as to the document's authenticity, will offer a far clearer explanation of Shinran's marriage from the viewpoint of his spiritual development.

One of the two stories concerns Shinran's encounter at the age of twenty-six with a young noblewoman whilst on his way back to Mt. Hiei from Kyoto. As he was quietly performing a service of sutra-chanting at a Shinto shrine, a beautiful lady, apparently from the Imperial Court, appeared from behind the hedge shielding the shrine. Very unusually for that time, she approached Hannen (Shinran's name when young) and quietly besought him to take her to Mt. Hiei. But Hannen refused her request and bid her return home, saying that Mt. Hiei was a holy mountain reserved for the training of monks. Women burdened with the five obstacles and the three submissions would never be allowed to enter. At this she began to lament with tears in her eyes, saying "What unhelpful words I hear from you! As a wise monk who praises Great Master Dengyo, haven't you ever heard of a sacred piece of text that tells us that all sentient beings possess Buddha-Nature without exception? There is a distinction between male and female, whether we are talking about humans or animals. Are you telling me that, when we take into account both birds and animals, there is no female of any description living on that mountain? If you exclude women from Perfect and Immediate Enlightenment, then yours cannot be the real teaching. If Perfect and Immediate Enlightenment is confined to men, then contemplation of the Ten Realms' Interfusion into Oneness cannot fulfil the promise of all beings attaining Buddhahood. Although the Lotus Sutra teaches that women cannot be recipients of the Dharma, the dragon (*nāga*) girl still succeeded in attaining Buddhahood..." Finally the lady left Shinran with a beautiful stone that reflected the rays of the sun, telling him "The sun is the highest of all things and the stones and soil are the lowest. Yet without some sort of medium it is impossible for the sun to become a light that descends on its own. It can only become a treasure to illumine a dark night through its reflection in a polished stone. What sort of virtuous effects can the water of the Buddha-dharma produce high up in the mountains? Only by descending to the valley below will it be able to benefit all sentient beings. You must be a wise monk in this age of the Last Dharma. Never stray from this truth."

If this intriguing story from the *Shinran Shōnin shōmyō den,* told here in summary, is genuine, it must have been recounted in the first place by Shinran himself. In that case the problem the young noblewoman spoke about must have been weighing on Shinran's mind and preoccupying his thoughts for a long time as he sought a solution, before it finally led to his receiving this vision from Avalokitêśvara at Rokkakudō three years later in April, 1201. According to the biography, the lady was herself a manifestation of Bodhisattva Avalokitêśvara.

An event relating to the other story is said in the *Shinran Shōnin shōmyō den* to have taken place in October of the same year, when Kujō Kanezane, the nation's former regent, visited Hōnen Shōnin and asked him a very important question, "Amongst your many disciples, the others are all monks of pure practice and virtuous wisdom. Only I, Kanezane, am a lay follower. Is there any difference in the virtue of the *Nenbutsu* of a holy monk and the *Nenbutsu* of a lay follower such as myself?" To this Hōnen Shōnin replied, "Whether one is a monk or lay follower, the virtue of a person's *Nenbutsu* is the same, neither superior nor inferior." The lord then said, "I am extremely dubious about this point. Surely the *Nenbutsu* practised by holy monks who have no contact with women and who partake only of vegetarian food must be full of high virtues? Why is the *Nenbutsu* of those who have contact with women morning, evening and night and who consume both meat and alcohol not considered inferior?" Hōnen Shōnin answered, "In the case of the Path of Sages such is indeed the teaching.

In the teaching of the Path of the Pure Land, however, as Amida vowed to save all sentient beings in the ten quarters, there is no selection between those who observe the precepts and those of no precepts, no difference between monks and lay followers. Shàndǎo made it very clear that all ordinary beings, whether good or bad, can attain birth in the Pure Land without exception and this is all due to the power of Amida Buddha's Great Vow that works as the efficient cause. You should have no doubt about it." Thereupon the lord said, "If, as you tell me, there should be no discrimination of any kind, would you give me one of your disciples, someone who has had no sexual commitment throughout his life, in order to provide a good example of equal attainment of birth in the Pure Land by men and women lay followers in the age of the Last Dharma?" Unabashed by the request, Hōnen Shōnin answered, "No problem at all. Shakkū (the name Hōnen had given to Shinran), you should obey the lord's request." Bowing low but with tears in his eyes, Shakkū was too overcome to reply. After a short while he said, "Since I left my parents of noble lineage to be ordained under Bishop Jien, I have been a disciple of Śākyamuni. I also left the Tendai school to become a steadfast follower of the *Nenbutsu*, as you know. Why out of your several hundred followers have you chosen me, Shakkū, for such a purpose? Have all the Buddhas and devas forsaken me? What a disgrace!" So saying he wept such copious tears he almost seemed to have to wring out his sleeve.

According to the *Shinran Shōnin shōmyō den*, referring to the message Shakkū had received from Bodhisattva Avalokitêśvara at Rokkakudō in April of the same year, Hōnen Shōnin himself told Shakkū to marry one of the daughters of Kujō Kanezane, and Hōnen's senior disciples, Shinkū and Seikaku, also encouraged Shakkū to do so. As a result Kujō Kanezane took Shakkū home in the same carriage and had him marry his daughter and live a new life at his palace at Gojō Nishi-no-tōin.

As seen from this account, Shinran was encouraged to marry by his master Hōnen in order to provide a good example of equality between men and women in the matter of birth in the Pure Land through pure faith.

INDEX

ACKNOWLEDGEMENTS

It was at the request of my dearest friend, Professor John White, that in 2001 I first embarked on delivering a series of talks on *The Letters* by Rennyo Shōnin, based on a new translation together with commentaries on each and every one of the eighty letters read out day by day during the morning and evening services. It was again at Professor White's recommendation that I decided to publish those talks in the form of the current book. I am very grateful not only to Professor White but also to all the Dharma fri ends who attended our meetings on *The Letters*, held both at The Buddhist Society and at Three Wheels. Their continuous participation was a great source of encouragement for me.

I would also like to express my deepest gratitude to Venerable Chimyō Takehara, Head Priest of Shogyoji Temple, and to all the Dharma friends over in Japan for the help and encouragement, both practical and spiritual, they showed me in support of this publication. Had it not been for the Shogyoji Sangha, this project would never have seen the light of day.

This book is thus the product of our Sangha rather than being my own personal work. As English is my second language, some of my English Dharma friends helped in the writing process to improve my English in various ways. First of all, Mrs. Dilly Suzuma, my English teacher, kindly went through the entire manuscript. I also received a great deal of good advice from my Dharma friends, Mr. Andrew Webb, Mr. Andy Barritt and Mr Christopher Duxbury. I owe a lot to Andrew for all the work he put into making the glossary.

At the stage of compiling the manuscript into book form, Professor John White was once again kind enough to go through the whole script twice in fine detail and raised some very important questions, which I have endeavoured to address. His participation has contributed much to improving this publication, I hope and feel, in the sense that the quintessence of Shin Buddhism is all the more clearly presented when Shin Buddhism is viewed through the prism of the Western critical mind.

I am very grateful to Mr Wayne Yokoyama for giving me a lot of good advice. I am also very grateful to Otani University Library and SOAS Library for allowing me to view all the documents I needed for this publication.

Regarding the illustrations, I would like to express my heartfelt thanks to those who allowed me to use the pictures, especially to Venerable Satoru Kiyosawa, Head priest of Gantokuji Temple, originally founded by Jitsugo, Rennyo's tenth son.

Last but not least I would like to thank Doctor Desmond Biddulph, President of the Buddhist Society, for publishing this book via the Society's publication section, and also his editorial staff, Mr Jonathan Earl, Ms Sarah Auld and Ms Avni Patel, for their excellent work and very kind help in the process of making this publication.

Kemmyo Taira Sato